PRAISE FOR
The Two Koreas:

"A well-reported if unfinished story, well told by someone who has been a Korea-watcher for almost four decades. . . . Probing behind events to reveal the machinations of key politicians, generals, and bureaucrats, often re-creating the dynamics shaping their behavior, is the strength of this book. . . . Oberdorfer chronicles with impressive detail the pathos of the nuclear crisis and the freezing of North-South relations it precipitated. What emerges from *The Two Koreas* is a portrait of precisely why the peninsula is so volatile: two rivals competing for national legitimacy in a culture where compromise is tantamount to defeat. . . . Oberdorfer refrains from punditry and predictions, letting his powerful material tell the story."—*The Boston Globe*

"[A] fine book. . . . [Oberdorfer's] gripping narrative should chasten our leaders and inform our citizenry about the continuing perils and costs of America's involvement with Korea. At a time when frivolous sensationalism dominates the media, [*The Two Koreas*] illustrates the virtues of a life given to honest, independent, inquiring journalism. . . . [It is] a detailed insider's account of the period since President Nixon opened China. . . . Oberdorfer excels at weaving together the characters and events of the period (often ones that he covered as a reporter) with more recent interviews with major participants in Washington, Seoul, Pyongyang, Beijing and Tokyo. He also pays more attention than usual to the work of scholars on Korea. What results is not really the history of the two Koreas but of American relations with Korea in the last 25 years. Oberdorfer is often definitive on that subject, deploying information that even specialists do not know."—Bruce Cumings, *The Los Angeles Times*

"Oberdorfer is one of America's keenest analysts of the international scene." —James A. Baker III, former U.S. Secretary of State

"An authoritative and readable work of history that will inform [Oberdorfer's] colleagues and the public at large as they watch the future of the Cold War's last remaining division unfold. . . . Even for those who know a lot about recent diplomacy, Oberdorfer fills in gaps, having interviewed many key participants." —*USA Today*

"Though he is an old Asia hand who has made many visits to the Korean peninsula—including two to North Korea—he deliberately keeps himself out of this book. Mistrusting his impressions, Oberdorfer, a retired diplomatic correspondent for *The Washington Post*, researched exhaustively, conducting more than 450 interviews. The result is a comprehensive and informative . . . account of postwar Korean history, from the Korean War to the rise of democracy in the South to the nuclear-weapons crisis in the North."—*The Globe and Mail*

"A most timely book to understand what could happen if North Korea implodes or attacks South Korea."—*St. Louis Post-Dispatch*

"[A] fine new book. . . . Oberdorfer is the sort of well-informed and conscientious journalist with a lifetime of experience that academic specialists can learn a lot from, and general readers will find this a lively, interesting, accessible, and satisfying book. It is not quite a contemporary history of the two Koreas (there are only a few Korean voices, and large swaths of domestic Korean history are left out), but it is the best history of the past 30 years of American-Korean relations. . . . Oberdorfer pens remarkably accurate portraits of a string of South Korean presidents. . . . *The Two Koreas* should give pause to those who think we should fight wars to keep the instruments of war out of the wrong hands." —*Bulletin of the Atomic Scientists*

"Oberdorfer, veteran *Washington Post* diplomatic correspondent who has met every South Korean president on their home ground and every North Korean foreign minister during their annual trips to the United States, does an excellent job of filling in the blanks in our knowledge of events from 1953 until today. . . . The picture Oberdorfer presents is by no means a clear view of sweetness and light and democracy on our side, and communist tyranny and terror on their side."—*Florida Times-Union*

"A fine overview of Korea's recent past."—*Kirkus Reviews*

"Combining the depth and authority of a first-rate textbook with the readability of a good novel, [*The Two Koreas*] has proven to be a wonderful teaching tool for instructors and students alike."—Carter J. Eckert, Professor of Korean History, Harvard University

"A useful primer on policy."—*The Weekend Australian*

"Packed with great details and anecdotes which bring the whole extraordinary saga [of the two Koreas] to life . . . [Oberdorfer] is particularly good at detailing how the South gained the military and economic upper hand from the 1980s onwards as the North's communist backers deserted it. He sheds much light on how the Soviet Union stepped in to bankroll Kim Il-sung after China reduced its support under new leader Deng Xiaoping. And how with the Soviet Union's collapse seven years ago, North Korea, refusing to contemplate reforms, went into economic free-fall. . . . Oberdorfer's description of the friendship forged between [Carter and Il-sung] . . . is worth the price of the book alone. . . . [A] skillful mixture of reportage and history which opens the door to understanding what will happen next."—*South China Morning Post* (Hong Kong)

"Engrossing, informative, wise. A rare achievement, the best account yet of a tragically divided country."—Ezra Vogel, Director, Asia Center, Harvard University

"Award-winning contemporary history from a veteran correspondent whose contacts book is as fat as the Old Testament. Here he traces the last 50 years of divided Korea, a tragic situation that we have all too readily learned to live with. With expert knowledge of both sides of the DMZ, Oberdorfer is able to trace common currents of Koreanness that unite the two halves. The real strength of the book is in its meticulous research about how other countries have treated Korea, a natural emphasis in the case of a country crucial to the security interests of Japan, China, Russia and the United States. . . . Oberdorfer . . . stitch[es] together a wonderful tapestry of fact and anecdote, all impeccably sourced to firsthand information from key players like Gorbachev and George Schultz. Journalism is known as the first draft of history, but this will probably stand unchallenged."—*The Daily Yomiuri* (Tokyo)

THE TWO
KOREAS

THE TWO KOREAS

A CONTEMPORARY HISTORY
REVISED AND UPDATED
Third Edition

DON OBERDORFER
AND ROBERT CARLIN

BASIC BOOKS
A MEMBER OF THE PERSEUS BOOKS GROUP
NEW YORK

Published by Basic Books,
A Member of the Perseus Books Group

Books published by Basic Books are available at special discounts
for bulk purchases in the United States by corporations,
institutions, and other organizations. For more information,
please contact the Special Markets Department at the Perseus
Books Group, 2300 Chestnut Street, Suite 200, Philadelphia, PA
19103, or call (800) 810-4145, ext. 5000, or e-mail
special.markets@perseusbooks.com.

Designed by Pauline Brown

Library of Congress Cataloging-in-Publication Data

Oberdorfer, Don.

  The two Koreas : a contemporary history / Don Oberdorfer,
Robert Carlin. — Revised and updated third edition.

      pages cm

Includes bibliographical references and index.

  ISBN 978-0-465-03123-8 (pbk.) — ISBN 978-0-465-05088-8
(e-book) 1. Korea (South)—History. 2. Korea (North)—
History. I. Carlin, Robert, 1947– II. Title.

  DS922.2.O25 2013

  951.904—dc23

                              2013030124

  10 9 8 7 6 5 4 3 2

For the people of the two Koreas
May they be one again, and soon.

CONTENTS

Photographs follow page 264.

CHINA

RUSSIA

MONGOLIA

CHINA

JAPAN

KOREA

Tumen River

Najin

Chongjin

CHINA
NORTH KOREA

NORTH KOREA

Yalu River

Yongbyon

EAST SEA
(SEA OF JAPAN)

Wonsan

Pyongyang

NORTH KOREA
SOUTH KOREA

Kaesong

Panmunjom

Kangnung

3

Inchon

Seoul

SOUTH KOREA

YELLOW SEA

Taegu

Pusan

Kwangju

Cheju Island

SCALE IN MILES

0   50   100

PREFACE TO THE
NEW EDITION

In the twelve years since Don Oberdorfer finished updating his well-respected account of the events and personalities that shaped Korean history after the Korean War, much has happened on the divided peninsula, yet the situation remains frozen in many ways. The South is richer than ever, but is facing the same serious demographic problems that plague much of the industrialized world—low birthrates, wrenching changes in the traditional family structure, underutilization of its educated younger generations, and the need to develop social safety nets to deal with an aging population. All of these challenges have been compounded by the South's ongoing confrontation with North Korea—a confrontation that, in some ways, has become more dangerous than at any time in the past thirty years.

North Korea is today no closer to achieving its economic goals than it has ever been and is falling further and further behind the rest of the countries in Northeast Asia. Internal pressures are growing from a population no longer as docile as it once was, nor as willing to accept the promises of a better tomorrow from a state that the people now realize cannot provide even for their basic needs. Meanwhile, development of nuclear weapons, a goal of North Korea's for the past three decades, has not brought it security.

The one new element in the North is the advent of a young leader educated, for at least a few years, in the West. Kim Jong Un is an unknown quantity to the outside world, but in his first eighteen months in power he has demonstrated that he is prepared to lead the country in new directions. At times he is more confrontational than his father, Kim Jong Il, but he is no less capable of keeping his neighbors on edge.

Over the past decade, China has emerged as a player in Korea as it has not been for well over a hundred years. How far Beijing is willing to assert itself on the Korean peninsula is not yet clear, though everyone in Asia knows that they are watching an emerging China replace the influence of what appears to be, by contrast, a diminished United States.

When Don Oberdorfer asked if I would help revise and update *The Two Koreas*, it was a simple decision to make. After forty years in Washington, all of them focused on Asia (indeed, virtually all of them focused on Korea), it was an offer I could not refuse. I knew that to match Don's experience was impossible, though his name ended up opening many doors for me as I conducted interviews. Matching the rhythm and richness of the previous editions' prose was a goal I set early, because the impact of the story of *The Two Koreas* is not just in the content but in the telling. Throughout the first sixteen chapters, Don frequently referred to his own experience and observations of people and events, using the first-person pronoun. For the sake of consistency, we decided to continue that practice in the three new chapters, that is, the first-person pronoun refers to Don. Again, for the sake of consistency, in the new chapters my own involvement in events is handled in the third person.

Like Don, I am not a historian, though I lived some of the history in this book and saw firsthand at least some of what unfolded in the years covered in the three new chapters. Many people helped me learn what I did not know, and I hope I have done a decent job of telling the story as they saw it. Part of the task before me was updating the earlier sixteen chapters, if there was anything left to add. I knew if anyone would have a grasp of new information on old events, it would be the scholars at the Wilson Center's Cold War History Project. They did, and their work deserves great respect.

Johns Hopkins University and the Pacific Century Institute supported this project; it would not have been possible without them. I am especially grateful to Spencer Kim for his backing and encouragement in this endeavor. Stanford University's Center of International Security and Cooperation has given me an academic home for many years, and my ongoing contact with CISAC's experts and scholars has been invaluable.

My greatest disappointment is that the North Koreans, despite repeated requests, would not take the opportunity Don and I offered them to contribute their perspective to this new edition. Someday, officials in Pyongyang will understand that a history of their country written without them does them no favors. Apparently, that day has not yet come.

It soon becomes obvious to anyone who deals with Korea for more than a few years that it is a drama on many levels, with great historical forces grinding at a people who for more than a hundred years have not been left in the peace and quiet that their country, with its rows of hills shrouded in morning mist, might offer in abundance. Perhaps the next edition of this book can end on a happy note. But as Don observed in his preface to the second edition, "The outcome of the drama on the Korean peninsula is still beyond our reach." For this third edition, the story remains unfinished, and, sadly, the dangers remain profound.

—*Robert Carlin, Washington, May 2013*

PREFACE TO THE
SECOND EDITION

We are now traveling the length of free Korea by troop train, from the southern tip, the port of Pusan, to almost the farthest point therefrom, Inchon on the northwest coast.... Our first impressions, at Pusan, were miserable and pathetic. The dirtiest children I have ever seen anywhere evaded MPs around the train to beg from GIs. One boy crawled around the train on his only leg; what had been his left one was off at the thigh. When our train pulled out, several boys threw rocks at the train.... Out of Pusan, however, the picture is better. The Korean countryside is quite mountainous, with villages in the little stretches of valleys between the rugged, unadorned crags. The people in the villages till the soil and wash in the muddy water holes, and the children do God-knows-what. They line the sides of the railroad and shout, "hello, hello" at the troop train, hoping to be thrown cigarettes or candy or something of value.
—FROM MY DIARY, *August 11, 1953*

This was my introduction to Korea as a US Army lieutenant weeks after the armistice that ended the bloody three-year war on the peninsula and the beginning of a lifelong interest in an embattled and amazing country. In my field artillery unit just south of the cease-fire line, we were dug in and ready to renew the battle against heavily armed North Korean units stationed across the hills only a mile or two away. We did not know how fragile or hardy the armistice would be or how long the truce would hold, but none of us would have believed that the state of no-war, no-peace would persist into the twenty-first century.

The massively fortified strip bisecting the Korean peninsula was one of the world's most dangerous potential flash points throughout the Cold War. Although the barriers have come down nearly everywhere else, at this writing Korea remains—as President Bill Clinton said in his 1997 State of the Union address—"the Cold War's last divide." The misnamed "demilitarized zone" (DMZ), a verdant but heavily mined sanctuary for wild birds and animals, continues to be the focal point of the most powerful concentrations of opposing military forces of the post–Cold War world despite both secret and open attempts at reconciliation. Close to 2 million troops, including 37,000 from the United States who would be instantly involved in new hostilities, are on duty in North or South Korea, with many on hair-trigger alert wielding powerful weapons of war. Today, despite dramatic and hopeful recent developments, American overseas commitments and military forces are at greater risk at the Korean DMZ than anywhere else on earth.

While the confrontation across the DMZ continues, almost everything else has changed dramatically. South of the dividing line, the Republic of Korea (ROK) has developed since the 1970s into an economic powerhouse. By 1997 it was the world's eleventh largest economy and one of the foremost producers of ships, automobiles, electronics, steel, and a host of other goods, with a per capita income of more than ten thousand dollars per year. By that time, its feisty democracy had thrown off all vestiges of military rule and imprisoned the two generals who had led the country in the 1980s. Late in 1997, it was suddenly beset by a massive financial crisis that began in Southeast Asia. In this atmosphere, it elected longtime opposition leader Kim Dae Jung as its president for the next five years. He immediately set about to stabilize and reform the economy and undertake new and positive engagement toward the North. Although economic reform is still incomplete, his determined and persistent policy toward the North paid off in an unprecedented summit meeting in June 2000 and the promise of extensive North-South interaction in economic, political, and even military fields.

North of the dividing line, the Democratic People's Republic of Korea (DPRK), which developed its own unique brand of communist Confucianism, remains militarily powerful but has lost the race in every other way. Early in the 1990s, North Korea was abandoned by its former sponsor and ally, the Soviet Union, which established close relations with South Korea and then collapsed, and was devalued by its other major sponsor and ally, China, which became more interested in markets than in Marxism. Following the death of its founding leader in 1994, North Korea suffered a sharp economic decline, which was a central factor in a famine in outlying areas that led to massive loss of life.

Under the successor leadership of the enigmatic Kim Jong Il, the eldest son of the founder, Pyongyang was forced to turn to the outside world for humanitarian assistance in the mid-1990s. Late in the decade, North Korea undertook new policies of engagement with South Korea, the United States, and a variety of other Asian and European countries. At this writing, it is yet uncertain whether Kim Jong Il's limited opening and cautious domestic reforms will continue and, if so, whether these actions will bring about a revival of the North Korean economy and secure the survival of the regime. In the preface to the first edition of this book, I wrote that it seemed unlikely that the DPRK could survive in its existing form without such major changes. As risky as they may be, the North's new policies, I believe, have improved its odds.

I have sought to record here the ways in which the two halves of this ancient and homogeneous people, thoughtlessly divided at the end of World War II by the great powers, have grappled with each other for advantage and supremacy in the past three decades and how they have dealt with the powerful forces all around them. The course of their struggle, like those that enveloped the Korean peninsula for many centuries past, has been deeply affected by the actions of the surrounding powers—China, Japan, and Russia. Since World War II and especially since the Korean War, in which nearly 1.5 million Americans served and 36,000 Americans were killed, the United States has played a major role. Korea is the only country in the world where the interests and security concerns of these four powers directly intersect. Although the major powers have had a large impact on Korea's fate, the hardy, gutsy, independent-minded Koreans on both sides of the DMZ have demanded and won for themselves important roles. Beginning with the North-South summit meeting of June 2000, they have begun to take their future into their own hands as never before.

Because of its turbulent history, its strategic location, and its enduring state of tension, Korea has often flitted across the world's newspaper headlines and television screens in the past thirty years, only to disappear from view when the immediate dangers seemed to pass. The episodic nature of the world's attention means that most people in most countries have little idea how the recurrent Korea crises developed or what their significance has been. Whether acts of war, terrorism or heroism, showdowns over nuclear weapons, the sudden deaths of Korean leaders, the starvation of the people of the North, or the turn toward peaceful engagement, the news from and about Korea has been marked by a remarkable absence of historical context, background, or basis for understanding.

Upon retiring from daily journalism in 1993, I set out to remedy this omission by producing a history of the North-South conflict and conciliation in contemporary Korea, with special attention to the roles of the outside powers. It seemed presumptuous for an American to undertake this task, but I realized I had advantages not available to most others. I was a witness to some of the events described here during my 1972–1975 tenure as Northeast Asia correspondent for the *Washington Post* and lived through other major events in Washington or in nearly yearly trips to Korea as the newspaper's diplomatic correspondent in the seventeen years thereafter. I have met all of South Korea's presidents, except its founding president, Syngman Rhee, and most of the other senior political leaders of that country. Starting in the mid-1980s, I met North Korea's foreign minister or his senior deputy almost every year during their annual trips to the

United Nations General Assembly in New York. These and other contacts led to my visits to North Korea in 1991 and 1995. I have been fortunate to have had many associations with present and former officials of the governments in Washington, Beijing, Moscow, and Tokyo, who provided unusual access to international aspects of the story.

The original edition of this book was four years in the making, nearly equally divided between research and writing, during which I examined the past while keeping up with fast-paced current events. The sponsorship of Johns Hopkins University's Nitze School of Advanced International Studies, which appointed me journalist-in-residence upon my retirement from the *Washington Post,* and grants from the Rockefeller Brothers Fund and the Korea Foundation made it possible for me to concentrate almost full-time on this effort in 1993–1997 and to travel extensively to interview hundreds of participants in the events described here. After the dramatic events of 1998–2000, I decided to add a new chapter to bring the story up to date.

Despite all efforts, I continue to be impressed with what I do not know, especially about North Korea. Despite the limited opening, the decision-making and moving forces behind the scenes in Pyongyang remain obscured in a secrecy that is unique in the world for its thoroughness and pervasiveness. Unlike the former Soviet Union and even China, North Korea has revealed virtually none of the documentation of discussions and decisions, even from its earliest era. Using sources available to me elsewhere, including archival materials from the Soviet Union and the (East) German Democratic Republic (GDR) as well as former diplomats and experts from those countries, I have done my best to discover and understand what underlay thought and action in North Korea in earlier times.

This is my third book of what has been called "contemporary history," which seeks to transcend journalism but is written only a few years after the events it describes. Like my first book, *Tet!,* on the crucial battle of the Vietnam War, and *The Turn* (more recently republished as *From the Cold War to a New Era*), on the diplomacy of the United States and the Soviet Union between 1983 and 1991, this volume goes to press while the outcome of the drama on the Korean peninsula is still beyond our reach. As in my earlier works, I was inspired by a quotation from British historian Dame C. Veronica Wedgwood: "History is written backward but lived forward. Those who know the end of the story can never know what it was like at the time." What follows is intended to convey what it was like at the time, before the end of the story is known.[1]

—*Don Oberdorfer, Washington, March 2001*

A NOTE
ON KOREAN NAMES

The remarkable thing about Korean names is that so many of them are almost the same. The three most common surnames, Kim, Lee, and Park, account for more than 40 percent of the entire population of South Korea, according to a recent census. The surname Kim is associated with the mythical founder of the Silla dynasty. Lee (or Yi, in Korean) is the name of the dynasty that ruled Korea from 1392 to the annexation of Korea by Japan in 1910. Park also has an ancient origin. Only about 250 different surnames are known to exist among South Korea's 44 million people.

As is the case with most other East Asian names, the surname is usually written first, as in Kim Il Sung or Kim Young Sam. I have followed this practice throughout the book, except for a few figures whose names are widely known in reverse order, such as South Korea's first president, Syngman Rhee.

A list and brief identification of the principal characters whose activities are described in this book can be found starting on page 465.

1

WHERE THE
WILD BIRDS SING

ALOFT ON DAZZLING white wings, the great cranes wheel in the sky and float down for a landing in a richly forested, unspoiled two-and-a-half-mile strip of land that stretches like a ribbon for 150 miles across the waist of the Korean peninsula. Here several hundred rare white-naped cranes stop over each spring and autumn in migration between their breeding grounds in northeastern China and Russia and their winter home in Japan. Amid a profusion of wildflowers, the birds join even rarer endangered red-crowned Manchurian cranes, the most elegant and highly prized member of the crane family and a symbol of good luck, fidelity, and long life in Asia for more than a thousand years. Ornithologists have recorded 150 species of cranes, buntings, shrikes, swans, geese, kittiwakes, goosanders, eagles, and other birds passing through or living in the verdant strip each year, joining other year-round residents such as pheasant, wild pigs, black bears, and small Korean deer.

Under the terms of the armistice that ended the Korean War in 1953, all civilian activity is banned in the zone except for one tightly controlled farming village on each side. Due to a densely planted underground garden of deadly land mines, which the birds and animals somehow use a sixth sense to avoid, military patrols stick closely to well-worn paths. For the most part, it is a unique and leafy sanctuary in the midst of a crowded, increasingly urbanized peninsula.

The serenity is deceptive. The demilitarized zone, or DMZ, between North and South Korea is bordered by high fences of barbed and razor wire on the north and south and guarded on the two sides by more than a thousand guard posts, watch towers, and reinforced bunkers across the width of the peninsula. On hair-trigger alert behind the fortifications are two of the world's largest aggregations of military force—1.1 million North Koreans facing 660,000 South Koreans and 28,000 Americans, the latter backed by the full military power of the world's most powerful nation. All sides are heavily armed and ready at a moment's notice to fight another bloody and devastating war. This pristine nature preserve marks the most dangerous and heavily fortified border in the world.

Across these fortified lines have flowed the passion and invective of an ancient nation that was suddenly and cruelly divided in the twentieth century by the great powers. The DMZ has been violated by tunnels, defiled by infiltrators, and scarred by armed skirmishes. The melodic call of its birds has been marred by harsh propaganda from giant loudspeakers erected on both sides to harass or entice the troops on the opposite lines. At the Joint Security Area (JSA) in the clearing at Panmunjom, the only place along the course of the buffer zone where the barbed wire and mines are absent, low-slung conference buildings have been placed squarely atop the line of demarcation, and the negotiating tables within them are so arranged that the dividing line extends precisely down the middle. Here for decades the hostility was palpable and open. Northern and southern troops would scowl, spit, and shout obscenities at each other outside the conference buildings, and there were shoving matches, injuries, and even deaths.

Panmunjom has also seen hopeful moments: meetings of special emissaries and political leaders, both publicized and secret; the transit of official delegations from one side to the other; the passage of relief supplies to ameliorate the effects of floods and famines; the return of prisoners and detainees from both sides; and the arrival and departure of would-be peacemakers and political leaders from the United States and other countries. If the hostility and tension on the Korean peninsula are ever to be alleviated through negotiation, the clearing at Panmunjom is likely to play a major role.

THE EMERGENCE OF TWO KOREAS

Korea is a peninsula of approximately eighty-five thousand square miles, roughly the size of New York and Pennsylvania combined, that juts down from the northeastern part of the vast mainland of Asia. It is well defined, with seas on the east, west, and south and two large rivers, the Yalu and the Tumen, providing a natural boundary with the landmass on the north. Archaeological exploration has confirmed that it was inhabited at least twenty thousand years ago, and some sites suggest that its human habitation began much earlier. By the fourth century BC the antecedents of the Korean state, a tribal kingdom called Choson, had emerged near the Chinese border in northern Korea. By AD 300 the Koreans had thrown off Chinese rule and developed three separate kingdoms in the north, southeast, and southwest of the peninsula. In AD 668 the Silla kingdom, with Chinese help, overwhelmed the other two and unified nearly all of Korea.

From that early time on, for nearly thirteen hundred years until the mid-twentieth century, Korea developed as a unified country under a single administration with a distinctive language and strong traditions. It invented its own ingenious writing system and the first known movable metal type a century before Gutenberg's invention in Europe.

Geography dealt Korea a particularly difficult role. Located in a strategic but dangerous neighborhood between the greater powers of China, Japan, and Russia, Korea has suffered nine hundred invasions, great and small, in its two thousand years of recorded history. It has experienced five major periods of foreign occupation—by China, the Mongols, Japan, and, after World War II, the United States and the Soviet Union.

Of the major powers, China had by far the greatest influence and was the most acceptable to Koreans. Like many others on the rim of the Middle Kingdom, the Korean kings embraced Chinese culture, paid tribute to the Chinese emperor, and received recognition and a degree of protection in return. When unified Japan began its major expansion in the sixteenth century, its leader, Hideyoshi Toyotomi, attacked Korea as the first phase of an invasion of the Chinese mainland. The Korean navy under Admiral Yi Sun Sin fought back with an early class of ironclad warships, known as turtle ships, which inflicted severe losses on the Japanese. Eventually, the Japanese were driven out, but only after laying waste to the land, thus setting a lasting pattern of enmity.

In the wake of the Japanese invasion and a subsequent invasion by the Manchus, who were soon to take power in China, Korea established a rigid policy of excluding foreigners, except for the Chinese and a small Japanese enclave that had been established at the southern port of Pusan. The imperial rulers of the Hermit Kingdom, as it was often called, created a governmental and social system modeled on Chinese Confucianism, with strictly regulated relations between ruler and subject, father and son, and husband and wife.

Korea's isolation ended in the mid-nineteenth-century age of imperialism, when major powers, including the United States, European countries, and Japan, sent warships forcibly to open the country to trade. In 1882, as a defensive measure against its neighbors, Korea signed a "Treaty of Amity and Commerce" with the United States, its first with a Western power, in which the United States promised to provide "good offices" in the event of external threat. It was reported that the Korean king danced with joy when the first American minister to Korea arrived. Among the treaties that followed shortly was one with czarist Russia, which had recognized the importance of the strategic peninsula and would soon begin building the Trans-Siberian Railway. The Russian foreign minister Count Vladimir Lamsdorff would later write, "Korea's destiny as a component part of the Russian empire, on geographical and political grounds, had been foreordained for us to fulfill."

In 1902 Japan carved out a strong position for itself by entering into an alliance with Britain, the most important European power in the area. Japan recognized British interests in China in return for British recognition of Japanese special interests in Korea. Sensing the weakness along the rim of the Chinese mainland, Russia began moving forces into Korea and immediately came into conflict with Japan. In an attempt to head off a clash, Japan proposed that the two countries carve up Korea into spheres of influence, with the dividing line at the thirty-eighth parallel—the same line chosen by the United States for the division of Korea after World War II. Russia's refusal to accept this and other proposed compromises led eventually to the Russo-Japanese War of 1904. Japan's surprise victory, its first over a Western power, put the Japanese in a powerful position to dominate Korea.

In 1905, in what many Koreans consider their first betrayal by the United States, Secretary of War (later president) William Howard Taft approved Japan's domination of Korea in a secret agreement with the Japanese foreign minister, in return for assurances that Tokyo would not challenge US colonial domination of the Philippines. Later the same year, Japan's paramount political, military, and economic interests in Korea were codified in the Treaty of Portsmouth (New Hampshire), in which President Theodore Roosevelt played peacemaker and deal maker between Japan and Russia, and for which he was awarded the Nobel Peace Prize. With no opposition in sight, Japan occupied Korea in 1905 and annexed it outright as a Japanese possession in 1910. Japan then ruled as the harsh colonial master of the peninsula until its defeat in World War II.

What many Koreans consider the second American betrayal—the division of Korea—occurred in the final days of World War II. The United States, Britain, and China had declared in the Cairo Declaration in 1943 that "in due course, Korea shall become free and independent," and at the 1945 Yalta Conference President Franklin D. Roosevelt proposed a US-Soviet-Chinese trusteeship over Korea. Beyond these few words, there was no agreement among the wartime allies and no practical planning in Washington about the postwar future of the peninsula. It was reported that in 1945, Secretary of State Edward Stettinius asked a subordinate in a State Department meeting to please tell him where Korea was.

Only in the last week of the war, when the Soviet Union finally declared war on Japan and sent its troops into Manchuria and northern Korea, did the United States give serious consideration to its postwar policy in the peninsula. Suddenly, Washington realized that Russian occupation of Korea would have important military implications for the future of Japan and East Asia.

At this point, according to Yale University historian Richard Whelan, "the U.S. government would probably have been happiest if Korea simply had not existed." About two thousand civil affairs officers had been trained for military government duty in Japan, and elaborate plans had been drawn up for that country, but no one had been trained and no plans had been made for Korea. Despite Korea's well-known antipathy to its Japanese overlords, Washington had rebuffed efforts by Korean exile groups for recognition during the war. Thus, as World War II drew to a close, there had been no consultation with Koreans about the future of their country.

On the evening of August 10, 1945, with Tokyo suing for peace and Soviet troops on the move, an all-night meeting was convened in the Executive Office Building next to the White House to decide what to do about accepting the impending Japanese surrender in Korea and elsewhere in Asia. Around midnight two young officers were sent into an adjoining room to carve out a US occupation zone in Korea, lest the Soviets occupy the entire peninsula and move quickly toward Japan. Lieutenant Colonels Dean Rusk, who was later to be secretary of state under Presidents Kennedy and Johnson, and Charles Bonesteel, later US military commander in Korea, had little preparation for the task. Working in haste and under great pressure, and using a *National Geographic* map for reference, they proposed that US troops occupy the area south of the thirty-eighth parallel, which was approximately halfway up the peninsula and north of the capital city of Seoul, and that Soviet troops occupy the area north of the parallel.

No Korea experts were involved in the decision. Rusk later confessed that neither he nor any of the others involved were aware that at the turn of the century, the Russians and Japanese had discussed dividing Korea into spheres of influence at the thirty-eighth parallel, a historical fact that might have suggested to Moscow that Washington had finally recognized this old claim. "Had we known that, we almost surely would have chosen another line of demarcation," Rusk wrote many years later.

The thirty-eighth-parallel line was hastily incorporated into General Order Number One for the occupation of Japanese-held territory. Despite the fact that US forces were far away and would not arrive on the scene for several weeks, the Soviets carefully stopped their southward advance at the parallel. Thus, Korea came to be divided into two "temporary" zones of occupation that, as the Cold War deepened, became the sites of two antagonistic Korean regimes based on diametrically opposed principles and sponsors.

US forces were eventually sent from Japan for occupation duty, an assignment that was not popular with the troops. Colonel Harry Summers, who later became a prominent military strategist, recalls arriving for duty as a US Army private and being lectured by the occupation commander, General John R. Hodge, that "there are three things American troops in Japan are afraid of: diarrhea, gonorrhea, and Ko-rea." Under Hodge's guidance, the US-backed Republic of Korea was officially proclaimed on August 15, 1948. The Soviet-backed Democratic People's Republic of Korea in the North, was proclaimed on September 9, 1948. The South inherited a larger population and more of the agriculture and light industry, while the North obtained most of the heavy industry, electric power, and mineral resources. Each regime claimed sway over the entire peninsula; these claims persist today.

Summing up, Gregory Henderson, a former US Foreign Service officer and noted Korea scholar, wrote in 1974, "No division of a nation in the present world is so astonishing in its origin as the division of Korea; none is so unrelated to conditions or sentiment within the nation itself at the time the division was effected; none is to this day so unexplained; in none does blunder and planning oversight appear to have played so large a role. Finally, there is no division for which the U.S. government bears so heavy a share of the responsibility as it bears for the division of Korea."

As these events and those of its more distant past illustrate, Korea has been a country of the wrong size in the wrong place: large and well located enough to be of substantial value to those around it and thus worth fighting and scheming over, yet too small to merit priority attention by more powerful nations on all but a few occasions. Korea's fate was often to be an afterthought, subordinated to more immediate or compelling requirements of larger powers, rather than a subject of full consideration in its own right.

Yet Koreans are neither meek nor passive, but a tough, combative, and independent-minded people with a tradition of strong centralized authority. They are characteristically about as subtle as *kimchi,* the fiery pepper-and-garlic concoction that is their national dish, and as timid as a *tae kwon do* (Korean karate) chop. Confronted with the reality of their bitter division, North and South Korea have grappled unceasingly for advantage and supremacy over each other—and with the greater powers outside. How they have done so in the past forty years, and with what risks and results, is recounted in these pages.

WAR AND ITS AFTERMATH

To head its regime in the North, the Soviet Union chose a thirty-three-year-old Korean guerrilla commander who had initially fought the Japanese in China but had spent the last years of World War II in Manchurian training camps commanded by the Soviet army. Kim Il Sung, as he called himself (his birth name was Kim Song Ju), had a burning ambition to reunite his country. In the South the United States gave the nod to seventy-year-old Syngman Rhee, who had degrees from George

Washington University, Harvard, and Princeton and had lived in exile throughout most of the Japanese occupation. Rhee had a messianic belief that he was destined to reunite Korea under an anticommunist banner.

Late in 1948 the Soviet army went home, turning North Korea over to the regime it had created. The following June, US troops followed suit. Before the summer was over, civil war broke out in clashes of battalion size along the thirty-eighth parallel. Each side was building its forces with an eye to gaining military supremacy.

On June 25, 1950, North Korea, with Soviet and Chinese backing, invaded the South in an effort to reunify the country by force of arms. The invasion was contested and ultimately repulsed by the forces of the United States, South Korea, and fifteen other nations under the flag of the United Nations (UN). The Chinese intervened massively on the other side to save North Koreans from defeat. Internationally, the bloody three-year Korean War was a historic turning point. It led the United States to shift decisively from post–World War II disarmament to rearmament to stop Soviet expansionism, tripling US military outlays and doubling its troop presence in Europe to bolster the newly formed North Atlantic Treaty Organization (NATO). The war cemented the alliance between the Soviet Union and China for most of a decade and made the United States and China bitter enemies for more than twenty years. The battle for Korea firmly established the Cold War and brought the Korean peninsula to the center of global attention.

Until recently, the origins of the war have been a matter of intense dispute. As late as 1993, North Korea republished its version in a paperback volume titled *The US Imperialists Started the Korean War.* However, documents from the Soviet archives show clearly that in March, August, and September 1949 and January 1950, Kim implored Stalin and his diplomats repeatedly to authorize an invasion of the South, at one point telling Soviet Embassy officers, "Lately I do not sleep at night, thinking about how to resolve the question of the unification of the whole country. If the matter of the liberation of the people of the southern portion of Korea and the unification of the country is drawn out, then I can lose the trust of the people of Korea."

On at least two occasions in 1949, Stalin turned down Kim's requests, but the documents establish that in early 1950, he approved the war plan due to the "changed international situation." At this writing, scholars are still unsure what led to Stalin's reversal. Was it the victory of Mao's Communist Party in China, the development of the Soviet Union's atomic bomb, the withdrawal of US forces from South Korea, or Secretary of State Dean Acheson's famous statement excluding South Korea from the US defense perimeter—all of which took place in 1949 or early 1950—or a combination of these and other causes? We still do not know.

The Korean conflict was considered the prototype of a limited war in that neither of the big powers used the nuclear weapons available to them, and the United States refrained from attacking Soviet or Chinese territory. On the peninsula, however, the war was savage in its destructiveness. Although the figures are uncertain, a widely accepted estimate is that 900,000 Chinese and 520,000 North Korean soldiers were killed or wounded, as were about 400,000 UN Command troops, nearly two-thirds of them South Koreans. US casualties were 36,000 dead.

In Korea the war devastated both halves of a country that had only just begun to recover from four decades of Japanese occupation and the sudden shock of division. Around 3 million people, roughly a tenth of the entire population of both sides at the time, were killed, wounded, or missing as a result of the war. Another 5 million became refugees. South Korea's property losses were put at $2 billion, the equivalent of its gross national product (GNP) for 1949; North Korean losses were estimated at only slightly less.

When the fighting finally stopped in July 1953, the front line was an irregular tangent slanting across the thirty-eighth parallel very close to where it had all begun. In keeping with the Armistice Agreement, the forces on each side pulled back two thousand meters from the cease-fire lines to create the demilitarized zone. Although both sides were exhausted by three years of combat, there were fears—which have never died—that the battle might be resumed at any moment.

One of the most important consequences of the war was the hardening of ideological and political lines between North and South. The antipathy that had developed between the opposing regimes was deepened into a blood feud among family members, extending from political leaders to the bulk of the ordinary people who had suffered at the hands of the other side. The thirteen-hundred-year-old unity of the Korean people was shattered.

In the aftermath of the war, the Rhee regime in the South became increasingly dictatorial and corrupt until it was forced out of office in 1960 by a student-led revolt. After a year the moderate successor government was ousted by a military junta headed by Major General Park Chung Hee, a Japanese-trained officer who had flirted with communism immediately after the Japanese surrender. Park's background created concern in Washington and initial hope in Pyongyang. Early on, Kim Il Sung dispatched a trusted aide to the South to make secret contact with Park. But instead of exploring a deal, Park had the emissary arrested and executed.

In the North, Kim Il Sung systematically purged his political opponents, creating a highly centralized system that accorded him unlimited power and generated a formidable cult of personality. As the great communist divide between the Soviet Union and China emerged in the mid-1950s, Kim, though profoundly disturbed by it, learned to play off his communist sponsors against each other to his own advantage. In July 1961 he went to Moscow and finally persuaded Nikita Khrushchev to sign a treaty of "friendship, cooperation and mutual assistance," pledging to come to Pyongyang's aid in case of a new war on the divided peninsula. Moscow had been resisting the North's requests for such a formal alliance since 1958, but now Khrushchev wanted to recruit Kim as an ally against China. With the new agreement in hand, Kim proceeded to Beijing and asked Chinese leaders to match the Moscow treaty, which they did by signing their own nearly identical accord.

While both North and South Korea gave lip service to eventual re-unification, there was little but hostility between them in the 1950s and 1960s. In the most notable incident, in January 1968, a thirty-one-man North Korean commando team attempted to assassinate the South Korean president. The team penetrated to within a thousand yards of the Blue House, the South Korean equivalent of the White House, before being repulsed by police and security forces. The prospects for any sort of reconciliation on the divided peninsula appeared slim indeed.

THE ORIGINS OF NEGOTIATION

On July 9, 1971, Henry Kissinger landed secretly in Beijing on a Pakistani airliner to begin the historic Sino-American rapprochement that openly split the communist world and changed global politics. Access to documents from the time and new scholarship are advancing, and to some extent altering, understanding of Pyongyang's response to this geostrategic earthquake, but the full story undoubtedly remains to be told. Some earlier accounts had suggested that Kim Il Sung was secretly in Beijing during the Kissinger visit, but that does not seem to have been the case. Nevertheless, within days of Kissinger's departure, Zhou Enlai was in Pyongyang for two long meetings with Kim. Two weeks later, Kim sent a senior official–Kim Il—to Beijing for more discussions. In the summer of 1971, it had been only a year since Sino–North Korean relations had emerged from a serious downturn during China's Cultural Revolution. Kim was probably not inclined to see ties fray again so soon, his relations at that point with Moscow were not very good, and, in any case, Zhou was apparently persuasive that Sino-US rapprochement represented an opportunity rather than a threat to North Korea. Kim would have perked up his ears if Zhou recited to him what Kissinger had said during the discussions in Beijing—that under certain circumstances it was "conceivable" that by the end of President Nixon's second term, "most, if not all," American troops would be withdrawn from Korea. Given Pyongyang's enduring suspicions of the Chinese, Kim may not have completely bought

Zhou's arguments. The sudden shift in Beijing's approach effectively left Pyongyang exposed in its confrontation with the United States. But the North Korean leader was very much a pragmatist, and if anyone could make a silk purse from a sow's ear, he could. After a few weeks' reflection, he decided to try.

So far as can be determined, it was Vietnam rather than Korea that figured in Nixon's desire to end the decades of hostility with China, which had begun with Chinese intervention in the Korean War. By simultaneously improving ties with both Moscow and Beijing, Nixon hoped to demonstrate that North Vietnam was vulnerable in a larger game being played by major powers. Though probably unintended, the vulnerability was felt by North Korea and, to Washington's dismay, by South Korea as well. Both Korean regimes felt more insecure than ever before. Both, for the first time, decided to try to take the settlement of their conflict into their own hands.

Later in the year, the Chinese approved new economic aid and signed the first agreement on military aid to North Korea in fifteen years. The results began to appear the following April, when newly arrived Chinese tanks clanked through Pyongyang's Kim Il Sung Square in the parade for the North Korean leader's birthday. At the same time, China began supplying North Korea with its models of Russia's MiG-19 supersonic fighter planes.

Kim broke his public silence on Sino-American developments on August 6, 1971, at a mass rally in Pyongyang honoring his closest foreign friend, Cambodian head of state Prince Norodom Sihanouk. In a surprise move, Kim announced that "we are ready to establish contact at any time with all political parties, including the [ruling] Democratic Republican Party, and all social organizations and individual personages in South Korea." This was an abrupt reversal of the long-standing position, reiterated by North Korea's foreign minister only four months earlier, that the ouster of the ruling party was an essential condition for negotiations with the South.

In Seoul President Park Chung Hee was also shaken by the news of Nixon's opening to China. Like the rest of America's allies, Park had had no advance notice from Washington, and he too found it shocking because it raised new doubts about the constancy and reliability of his great power sponsor. To Park, the rapprochement implied US acceptance of a hostile, powerful, and revolutionary country in South Korea's immediate neighborhood, tied by a military alliance to North Korea. Since the announcement of the "Nixon Doctrine" in mid-1969—that Asians should provide the manpower for their own wars—the United States had appeared to be moving steadily toward disengagement. Early in 1971, over Park's vehement objections, Washington had withdrawn twenty thousand of the sixty-two thousand American troops stationed in South Korea, at the same time that it was pulling back American forces from South Vietnam. Despite the reassuring words of US political leaders and diplomats, Park took these developments as "a message to the Korean people that we won't rescue you if North Korea invades again," according to his longtime aide, Kim Seong Jin. Now on top of everything else, the White House was suddenly, and without notice to him, consorting with Beijing.

Meeting privately with reporters at the Blue House on the day Kissinger's secret trip to China was announced, the South Korean president was gloomy. "The United States has long been trying to reach a rapprochement with Red China, but China has not changed," Park complained, suggesting that Washington had made all the concessions. In a subsequent off-the-record dinner with Blue House correspondents, Park declared that 90 percent of the Nixon visit to China was a domestic maneuver intended to aid the president's reelection. In view of Nixon's "low-posture diplomacy" toward Beijing, Park told reporters, the pressing question for South Korea was, "How long can we trust the United States?"

Weeks later, Park addressed his concerns directly to Nixon in a letter that was delivered to Secretary of State William Rogers by Foreign Minister Kim Yong Shik. The South Korean president was particularly worried that deals might be made about the Koreas during Nixon's forthcoming trip to Beijing, and he wanted to discuss it with Nixon at a meeting. But in Washington Park's concern was such a low-priority question that it took three months for the State Department and Nixon's National Security Council (NSC) staff to frame and present a presidential reply. When it finally came, it was a ritual declaration from Nixon that during his Beijing trip, he would not seek accommodation with China at the expense of South Korea's national interest. Park was told that a summit meeting was out of the question. Recalling his feelings about the maneuvering surrounding the US rapprochement with China years later, Park wrote that "this series of developments contained an unprecedented peril to our people's survival. . . . [The situation] almost reminded one of the last days of the Korean Empire a century earlier, when European Powers were similarly agitating in rivalry over Korea."

Even before Kissinger's secret trip to Beijing, North Korea had been putting forth discreet feelers for direct talks with the South, and Park's government had been quietly discussing how to respond. After Kim Il Sung's August 6 announcement, the South moved quickly by proposing a meeting in the context of Red Cross societies. The North immediately accepted.

On August 20, 1971, eighteen years after the armistice ended the Korean War, representatives of the two Red Cross societies met in Panmunjom for the first exploratory discussions between the two halves of the divided peninsula. To no one's surprise, the talks did not go smoothly.

On November 20, after three months and nine rounds of fruitless sparring, South Korean "Red Cross delegate" Chong Hong Jin, who actually was deputy director of the international affairs bureau of the South Korean Central Intelligence Agency (KCIA), handed a note proposing private and separate meetings at Panmunjom to his counterpart, North Korean "Red Cross delegate" Kim Duk Hyun, actually a senior official of the Workers Party Organization and Guidance Department, the party's most important department. Like these two, many of the participants in the Red Cross exchanges actually were intelligence or party officials. In the decades to come, because these agencies were powerful, discreet, and tightly controlled by their respective leaders, they would become frequently used channels for the many secret communications between North and South.

The South's bid for higher-level talks was promptly accepted. North Korean leaders were ready and very willing. Gathering in secret as the contacts were beginning, a plenary meeting of the Central Committee of the Workers Party approved a large-scale peace offensive toward the South in response to "the changing domestic and foreign political situation." The Central Committee was composed of the top-ranking members of the party in all fields, and its plenary meetings often marked key decision points in the regime's domestic and foreign policy. This was definitely such a moment.

On March 28, 1972, following eleven rounds of secret contacts with his counterpart, South Korea's Chong slipped out the northern door of the North Korean pavilion of Panmunjom instead of returning to the southern side. He was taken by car to the nearby North Korean city of Kaesong and then by helicopter to Pyongyang—the first of many South Korean officials to go to that capital for talks. There it was arranged for the secret contacts to go to a higher level: the chief of South Korea's intelligence agency would come to Pyongyang for talks, and a senior North Korean would reciprocate by making a trip to the South. In late April a direct telephone line linking the offices of the KCIA and the Workers Party was secretly installed between Seoul and Pyongyang.

The man in charge in the South was Lee Hu Rak, a former noncommissioned officer in the Japanese army and former chief of staff to President Park before being named to head the KCIA. Although it took its name and some of the functions from its US model, in many respects the KCIA was more like the prewar Japanese *kempeitai* or the Soviet KGB in its unbridled power in the domestic as well as the foreign arena. The former US diplomat and Korea scholar Gregory Henderson called the KCIA "a state within a state, a vast shadowy world of . . . bureaucrats, intellectuals, agents and thugs." By the early 1970s, the director of the KCIA was more powerful and more feared at home than the prime minister or any other governmental figure except the president himself.

After receiving written instructions from the president about visiting the "special zone," Lee traveled secretly through Panmunjom to Pyongyang in early May. Looking back on it, Lee recalled that "I felt the kind of anxiety that is quite indescribable" because "we simply had no ghost of a precedent to guide me as to how to open up some sort of mutually acceptable communication." He was also mindful that, as the chief of intelligence for the Republic of Korea, he was the person the northern communists would like most to get their hands on, after Park himself.

His hosts took him to see the sights of Pyongyang and to a revolutionary opera extolling Kim's anti-Japanese exploits. Then on his second night in Pyongyang, Lee was awakened and driven through a rainstorm to a well-guarded building in the hills around the North Korean capital. He was not told where he was being taken. At fifteen minutes after midnight, at the end of the harrowing ride, the thoroughly shaken KCIA director, who thought he might never live to see the dawn, found himself face-to-face with Kim Il Sung.

KIM IL SUNG

The Great Leader, as he was known to his subjects, is among the most fascinating figures of the twentieth century, dominating his country during his lifetime as few individuals are ever able to do. From the late 1950s his power was virtually unlimited within the borders of North Korea, and his decisions often had repercussions involving life and death in South Korea and beyond. As a national leader, Kim surpassed all others of his time in longevity. When he died in July 1994 at age eighty-two, he had outlived Joseph Stalin by four decades and Mao Tse-tung by almost two decades, and he had remained in power throughout the terms of office of six South Korean presidents, nine US presidents, and twenty-one Japanese prime ministers.

The future founder and leader of North Korea was born in Pyongyang on April 15, 1912, the day the *Titanic* sank. His parents were both Christians. His mother was the devout, churchgoing daughter of a Presbyterian elder, and his father had attended a missionary school.

Kim had only eight years of formal education, the last two in Chinese schools in Manchuria, where his father moved to operate an herb pharmacy. When he was seventeen years old, he was expelled from school for revolutionary activities and never returned to the classroom. After being jailed briefly, in the early 1930s he joined guerrilla bands fighting the Japanese who, after turning Korea into a Japanese colony in 1910, had invaded and occupied Manchuria. The Korean guerrillas were organized by and attached to an army led by the Chinese Communist Party.

Although Kim's activities fell short of the brilliant, war-winning exploits later concocted by North Korean propagandists, he was successful enough that the Japanese put a price on his head. By 1941 Kim's unit and other parts of the Chinese guerrilla army were forced to retreat across the Manchurian border to Soviet army training camps, where they spent the next four years. During these years Kim married a Korean partisan and fathered two sons, the elder of whom was Kim Jong Il, his eventual political heir and successor.

It is still unclear how Kim was selected to lead North Korea. Having spent years in a Soviet training camp, Kim was well known to the Soviet officers who occupied the area north of the thirty-eighth parallel in 1945, and he had a reputation for being reliable and courageous. He appeared in Pyongyang immediately after the war in the uniform of a Soviet army captain, according to a Soviet general who served in the occupation force. Some accounts suggest that Joseph Stalin himself made the final choice of Kim from several candidates. Stalin is reported to have said, "Korea is a young country, and it needs a young leader."

As a leader, Kim was cordial to and comfortable with ordinary people. He emerged from a family of hardworking ordinary people and described himself in his memoirs as "an ordinary man." Vadim Medvedev, a Gorbachev aide who was Kim's escort for several days in Moscow in 1986, wrote later that he was "greatly surprised" to find in him "an absolutely normal person, with whom you could talk not only about politics but also weather, exchange opinions on events happening around and impressions on what we saw."

Yet at the same time, Kim came to live in luxury and exclusiveness beyond the dreams of kings. He inhabited at least five sumptuous palaces in North Korea and innumerable guesthouses built for his comfort and amusement, all completely cut off from anyone except servants, bodyguards, and carefully screened guests. Uninvited people were barred from even setting foot on the wide and well-tended road leading to his Pyongyang residence. Like Stalin and Mao, whose cults of personality he emulated but far outdistanced, his automobile used special lanes, and other traffic was banished when he moved through the streets of his capital. When he went to the Soviet Union by train in 1984, all rail traffic was stopped along his route at the demand of the North Koreans, so that his luxurious special train could travel unimpeded by any competing or oncoming trains. (This caused massive tie-ups in the Soviet rail system.) When his train stopped to take on supplies or to give Kim a breath of air along the way, the station platforms were cleared of their normal throngs, left vacant except for specially authorized people, some of whom had been recruited to applaud and cheer him.

In deference to his health, a special institute was established in Pyongyang to concentrate on the aging process of this one man, with doctors and medical specialists monitoring his every move and special fruits and vegetables produced solely for his consumption. When Kim traveled to Berlin on his 1984 European trip, according to a former East German diplomat who helped arrange the visit, Kim's aides arranged for a special bed to be flown ahead for his sleeping comfort (as was often the case with Ronald Reagan as US president). In addition, they brought a special toilet with built-in monitoring equipment that instantly analyzed whatever the Great Leader eliminated for any sign of health problems. The former German diplomat said that medical specialists from different friendly countries were assigned primary responsibility for consultation on different parts of the leader's body, with East German doctors being given responsibility for Kim's head and neck, including the large but benign tumor on the back of his neck that had been visible since the early 1970s.

From his education in Chinese schools and his four years in a Soviet military camp, Kim was fluent in Chinese and conversant in Russian. His complex relationship with the two giants of communism—his neighbors, sponsors, and, for most of his life, his allies—was central to nearly all that he did or said. To a large extent, he owed his career as well as his country's well-being to China and Russia, yet he was always wary of their dominant power. In a tradition practiced by Koreans throughout their history, Kim went to extraordinary lengths to gain and maintain as much independence as possible.

Oleg Rakhmanin, a former Soviet official who had extensive meetings with Kim over a twenty-five-year period, said that when Kim was being actively wooed to take Moscow's side against Beijing, he was "careful and prudent, weighing his every word. He was afraid the Chinese would learn what he said to us. . . . [Kim was] a calculating character—a chess player who calculates his every move." Another former Soviet official, who had been posted in the Soviet Embassy in Pyongyang, described Kim as "a flexible and pragmatic politician, an Oriental Talleyrand. He would agree with our leaders and give a lot of promises, but afterward he would pursue the same line, his own line."

Due perhaps to his limited formal education, Kim was not a book reader and could not be fairly described as an intellectual. In deference to the intellect, he added a pen to the traditional communist hammer-and-sickle as North Korea's official emblem, but in personal conversations he rarely referred to world history or to any work of serious literature. "He knows a lot of Confucianism and a smattering of Marx, Lenin, Hegel, and such," said a former communist diplomat who dealt with Kim extensively.

Most of his government's philosophical utterances dealt with "the *juche* idea," which was hailed in North Korea as Kim's original, brilliant, and revolutionary contribution to national and international thought. But Kim acknowledged on occasion that *juche* was not original with him. Although the fact was rarely mentioned in the North, the term and concept go back at least to Korean scholars in the early years of the twentieth century. Kim explained that "I have just laid special emphasis on it."

Kim's version of *juche,* emanating from North Korea's militant nationalism, is usually described in shorthand as "self-reliance," but there is much more to it. According to Han S. Park of the University of Georgia, a leading American expert on *juche* as a philosophical system and state religion, "*Juche* views Korea as a chosen land, as people are told consistently that world civilization originated from the Korean peninsula."

Beyond its sanctification of Kim's decisions, *juche* was a declaration of political independence from his two communist sponsors. Although it was originally called "a creative application of Marxism-Leninism," eventually all reference to Marxist connections was abandoned. The *juche* philosophy has deep traditionalist roots and great appeal to the Korean antipathy for external domination. In practice, it became synonymous with North Korea's famous autarky.

For a visitor from afar, the most extraordinary thing about the Kim Il Sung era was the unrestrained adoration, bordering on idolatry, built up around the Great Leader, which seemed to reflect a craving for adulation that could never be sated. Kim's photograph, later joined by a separate picture of his son Kim Jong Il, was on the wall in every home as well as every shop and office. Starting in the 1960s, at the son's order, every North Korean adult wore a badge bearing the senior Kim's likeness on his or her suit, tunic, or dress.

Within his country Kim was nearly always referred to as *suryong,* or Great Leader, a term referring to the greatest of the great that Kim reserved for Lenin, Stalin, and Mao before he began applying it to himself in the 1960s.

In the late 1980s, according to one count, there were at least thirty-four thousand monuments to Kim in North Korea, not including benches where he once sat, which were protected with glass coverings, and other memorabilia of his many visits throughout the country. The main square in the capital, the leading university, the highest party school, and many other places and institutions were named for him. During Kim's travels as well as his everyday meetings, an aide followed behind him, writing down his every observation, many of which were published in several languages and considered holy writ by North Koreans. In the 1960s, near the beginning of the buildup, a Soviet party official who had experienced the deification and later downfall of Stalin had the temerity to ask Kim directly, "How is it possible there is this cult of personality in your country?" Kim's answer was, "You don't know our country. Our country is used to paying respect to elders—like China and Japan, we live by Confucian culture." It is unlikely that anyone was bold enough to ask this question of him in later years.

Kim created an impermeable and absolutist state that many have compared to a religious cult. No dissent from or criticism of Kim Il Sung, his tenets, or his decisions was permitted. Citizens were arrested, and some even sent off to one of the country's extensive gulags, for inadvertently defacing or sitting on a newspaper photograph of the Great Leader or his son and chosen successor. Reports of inhuman treatment, torture, and public execution for failure to conform with Kimism were rife. Prison camps were established in remote areas containing as many as 150,000 people, many of whom were held in ghastly, inhuman conditions with little chance of ever being released.

Kim's biographer Dae-Sook Suh of the University of Hawaii wrote that Kim became "a ruler who wields more power than the notorious monarchs of the old Korean kingdom," building a state that practices "a peculiar brand of oriental despotism" rather than communism. "There was no such thing as a conversation with Kim Il Sung," said a prominent South Korean who was Kim's guest on numerous occasions. "If he spoke to a North Korean, that person stood up, in effect at attention, to receive instructions or orders." With his personal guests who were important to him or his state, Kim was a stickler for detail. While in Pyongyang, "he would call me every day," said this South Korean, always asking, "How are you feeling? Is everything all right?"

In a revealing speech in the 1970s, Kim told government officials that "whatever I am doing, I cannot rest easy unless I have the whole situation at my fingertips." As the restless and energetic leader of a small country, Kim telephoned the chief of the general staff every night for a report on the military situation and the foreign minister for a report on diplomatic developments. Based on the reports, he said he issued immediate instructions.

During most of his years in power, Kim traveled incessantly within the country on personal inspection tours, giving "on-the-spot guidance." As late as 1980, Kim told Representative Stephen Solarz (D-NY), the first US political figure to visit Pyongyang, that each year he spent ten to fifteen days on such tours in each of the ten provinces and three special cities. Kim boasted to Solarz that as a result of his conversations with farmers in their fields, he had personally countermanded government instructions about the planting time for rice—and claimed that the amended policy produced a bumper crop.

Because his many directives took on the aura of holy writ, they proved difficult to change if they became outdated or were mistaken from the start. Even Politburo members and government ministers were forced to undergo "self-criticism," and some were ousted from their jobs, for making proposals that inadvertently breached policy lines previously laid down by

the Great Leader. "Once said by Kim, it is said forever," according to a diplomat who spent four years in Pyongyang. "Nobody is allowed to change
anything; the smallest sign of deviation means the system has developed
a dangerous crack."

In the spring of 1972, Kim had just celebrated his sixtieth birthday
with great fanfare, a traditional milestone for Korean elders, after which
they are greatly venerated. Kim's *hwangop* birthday was the occasion for
the opening of the ninety-two-room Museum of the Revolution, devoted to
glorifying him, and the unveiling of his sixty-six-foot-high bronze likeness, painted in gold, on a scenic spot overlooking Pyongyang, where a
shrine had been erected for worship of the Japanese emperors during the
Japanese occupation. It was the largest statue ever built by Koreans for any
leader in their long history. Still in his physical prime, Kim was a burly
man with a rolling walk and heavy-rimmed glasses. *New York Times* correspondent Harrison Salisbury, the first American correspondent granted
an interview with the Great Leader, called him "a big, impressive man
with a mobile face and a quick chuckle" and nearly constant gestures to
emphasize his words. At this point in his long career, Kim turned his attention and his considerable charisma to creating his first political opening
to South Korea.

CONVERSATIONS WITH THE SOUTH

The historic initial secret meeting between Kim Il Sung and the second
most powerful figure in the South began with an exchange of pleasantries
and assurances of trust. In the early-morning hours of May 4, 1972, Lee
Hu Rak, director of the ROK intelligence agency, broke the ice by praising
the achievements of construction he had been shown on his first day in
Pyongyang. Kim Il Sung responded by praising the South Korean president for sending Lee as "an expression of his trust," and he commended
Lee as "a very bold person" and "a hero" for making the journey to the
opposite camp.

The meeting, whose record was kept by Lee's aide and not disclosed
until seventeen years later, was remarkable for the shared antipathy to the
major powers and the heavy emphasis by both sides on reaching accords
and eventual reunification.

LEE: President Park Chung Hee and I believe unification should be
achieved by ourselves without interference of the four powers
[the United States, China, Japan, and the Soviet Union]. . . .
We are never front men of the United States or Japan. We
believe we should resolve our issues by ourselves. . . .

KIM: Our position is to oppose reliance on external forces on the issue of unification. This is where I agree with Park Chung Hee. . . .

LEE: I'd like to tell you that President Park is a person who detests foreign interference most.

KIM: That being so, we are already making progress to solve the issue. Let us exclude foreign forces. Let's not fight. Let's unite as a nation. Let's not take issue with communism or capitalism. . . .

LEE: A nation with 40–50 million people is a powerful country. [The population of the South in 1972 was 32 million, that of the North 14 million.] One hundred years ago we yielded to big powers because we were weak. In the future the big powers will yield to us. I'd like to make it clear to you, the big powers only provide lip service to our hope for unification. But in their hearts, they don't want our unification.

KIM: Big powers and imperialism prefer to divide a nation into several nations.

In a further attempt to clear the air, Kim apologized for the actions of the North Korean commando team that had attempted to assassinate Park in 1968. Kim suggested, improbably, that he did not know of the famous Blue House raid in advance, blaming it on "leftist chauvinists within our structure" and saying that when he had learned of it, he fired his chiefs of espionage and security. (In fact, there was a purge of military and paramilitary officials afterward.) "Tell President Park I feel very sorry," said Kim.

After the secret return visit to Seoul by DPRK deputy premier Park Sung Chul, who conferred with President Park, North and South Korea surprised the outside world by publicly issuing a joint statement on July 4, 1972, a date that seemed to have been chosen to illustrate their independence from the nation that celebrates its own independence then.* The statement declared that the two sides had reached full agreement on three principles:

First, unification shall be achieved through independent efforts without being subject to external imposition or interference.

Second, unification shall be achieved through peaceful means, and not through use of force against one another.

---

* The ROK government notified the US Embassy in Seoul several days in advance of the announcement and gave American diplomats an advance look at the text. Although supposedly a state secret, news of the statement circulated freely in Seoul. The twenty-one-year-old son of Francis Underhill, the deputy US ambassador, shocked his father the night before the announcement by telling him he had heard about the secret diplomacy and the impending joint statement from Koreans at a tea shop along the main street in Seoul.

Third, a great national unity, as a homogeneous people, shall
be sought first, transcending differences in ideas, ideologies, and
systems.

As part of the joint statement, the two sides agreed "not to defame and
slander one another" and to take positive measures to prevent inadvertent
military incidents. In order to avoid officially granting recognition to each
other, however, the statement was not signed by the two governments but
simply by KCIA director Lee Hu Rak and Director of Organization and
Guidance Kim Young Joo, Kim Il Sung's brother, "upholding the desires
of their respective superiors."

In a press conference, Pyongyang's emissary to the South, Deputy
Premier Park, announced the North's interpretation of these accords. He
declared, "Now that there exists no threat of aggression in South Korea
from the North, nor . . . any need of protection and [because] our nation
is settling its internal problems according to its own faith, the U.S. imperialists must no longer meddle in the domestic affairs of our country; they
must withdraw at once, taking with them all their forces of aggression."

Kim Il Sung saw the North-South dialogue as a way to wean the
South Korean regime away from the United States and Japan and to bring
about the withdrawal of US troops. Shortly after the July 4, 1972, joint
statement, Kim's ambassador in Berlin, Lee Chang Su, in a confidential
presentation to the East German Politburo, explained Pyongyang's engagement of its longtime enemies in Seoul this way: "The [communist]
party and government of North Korea will concentrate on forcing South
Korean leaders into agreement, to free them from U.S. and Japanese influence and to allow no U.S. intervention." He revealed that a North Korean
peace offensive had been authorized in meetings of the Workers Party in
November 1971 and July 1972, and he said the effort had "undermined
the attempts of the U.S. imperialism to retain its troops in Korea, as well
as the attempts of the Japanese imperialists to invade Korea again. . . .
The Park Chung Hee clique will capitulate to this peace offensive. The
tactical measures we adopted proved successful with the holding of talks
with the enemy."

President Park, according to his longtime aide, Kim Seong Jin, saw the
dialogue as a helpful tactic in a harsh environment in which North Korean
military power was a serious threat. "As long as you can touch an opponent
with at least one hand," said Park, "you can tell whether he will attack."
Park had no belief or interest in unification in his lifetime, his aide said,
and little interest in making compromises to bring fruits from the North-
South contacts. Unlike his successors, Park also expressed no interest in
meeting Kim Il Sung. "He told me directly, I have no intention at all [to
meet Kim Il Sung]," said his aide. "Why should I meet that fellow?"

Most of the world, however, greeted the surprising news of the conciliatory joint statement with soaring optimism about the chances for a rapprochement between the two bitter enemies. Among those most fascinated were the veteran correspondents who had covered the Korean War and were still following events on the divided peninsula. Keyes Beech, Tokyo correspondent of the *Chicago Daily News*, was among the most eminent of these. At the outset of the war in 1950, Beech had telephoned NBC correspondent John Rich in the Japanese capital to tell him that hostilities had broken out at the thirty-eighth parallel. "We'd better get over to Korea, there's a war on," said Beech. Twenty-two years later, after hearing the dramatic news of the North-South joint statement, Beech again telephoned Rich and reminded him of their 1950 discussion. This time it had a different twist. "We'd better get over to Korea," said Beech, "there's a peace on." Both men were in Seoul within days.

2

THE END OF
THE BEGINNING

THE FIFTY-FOUR MEMBERS OF the North Korean Red Cross delegation, each wearing a Kim Il Sung badge and some dressed in the
high-necked cadre suits typical of the Chinese communists, walked across
the dividing line at Panmunjom a few minutes before 10:00 A.M. on September 13, 1972. As they stepped into the South for the first time since
the bloody war that had left millions dead, the northerners were greeted
with embraces, handshakes, and laughter from their southern counterparts
and bouquets of flowers from pigtailed schoolgirls. For one emotional moment, the two delegations seemed to transcend the bitter ideological and
political conflict that had plagued the peninsula for decades. Suddenly,
they showed themselves to be brothers, sisters, and cousins—all Koreans.

The first visit of North Koreans to the South, openly and in peace,
since the Korean War came two months after the July 4 joint statement,
which had surprised Koreans on both sides and the rest of the world. Although their leaders were privately cynical, for the ordinary people of the
two Koreas, this was among the most hopeful moments in the second half
of the twentieth century. There was widespread popular anticipation that
the beginning of the North-South dialogue could mean the dawning of an
era of peace and the reuniting of divided families and the nation.

On the roadsides leading to the center of Seoul, hundreds of thousands,
perhaps a million, people turned out to stare and wave at the visitors from
across the lines. Streets and roadways along the route had been washed
and swept, new shrubs planted, and anticommunist signs taken down or
painted over. Very few of the forty-three thousand American troops who
were then in Korea were in evidence; only ten, many fewer than usual,
were on duty at Panmunjom, and the rest had been instructed to stay out
of sight.

The first exchange of North-South Red Cross delegations had taken
place two weeks earlier in the North. There everything had been meticulously

prepared: people along the route to Pyongyang had lined up to greet the visitors dressed in their Sunday best, shops in the capital had been specially stocked for the occasion, and public buildings illuminated. It was all too perfect for Chung Hee Kyung, the principal of Ehwa Girls High School in Seoul, and the only woman among the southern delegates. The North Koreans she saw and met seemed to her dolls who had been programmed to say and do as they were told. When she returned to a large, loud, and unruly welcome in the South, to her own surprise she began weeping uncontrollably with relief and joy to be among familiar human beings with human reactions. "It was my most genuine experience of patriotism," Chung recalled.

The North Koreans who came to Seoul, following an afternoon of leisure, were taken to an elaborate reception at historic Kyongbok Palace, the seat of the Choson dynasty, the country's long-lasting and final royal kingdom. With an eye to history, the ROK government staged the reception in the Pavilion of Joyous Meeting, first built in 1412 as a greeting place for diplomatic delegations and royal visitors to the Korean court.

Inside the historic two-story pavilion, which is anchored in a pond near the former quarters of the Korean queens, were banks of colorful flowers, a sumptuous buffet, and several dozen gorgeous young women, many wearing filmy dresses, miniskirts, or other alluring modern garb. I walked up to one of the beautiful hostesses and asked who she was and why she was there. "I'm a Red Cross volunteer," she replied firmly, refusing to answer further questions. After receiving the same answer from another hostess of stunning beauty, I turned to a South Korean journalist familiar with the preparations. From him I learned that the KCIA, which had devised the program of the North Koreans, had asked for and received the services of some of the country's most beautiful young women from the national airline, modeling firms, and television companies and provided each one with a substantial sum of money to buy whatever dress she thought showed off her features best. In return, she was to show up as a hostess for the North Korean visitors, without revealing how this had come about.

The communist visitors professed to be unimpressed by the glamour of the hostesses or the symbolism of the reception in the historical surroundings. An austere man wearing a Mao jacket and a Lenin cap to complement his Kim Il Sung button, Yun Ki Bok, who was the chief political adviser of the North Korean delegation, observed sourly that the palace buildings were "outright testimony that the ruling class in the past exploited the people." The following night, the visitors were guests at a risqué display of bikini-clad, high-kicking South Korean dancers at Walker Hill, which had been built as a rest-and-recreation center for American troops. Some of the North Koreans, whose society was officially prudish, covered their faces or averted their eyes. They complained that the show was "the result of American imperialism" and lodged an official protest about the sexy display.

The visitors were lodged in the Tower Hotel, located on a mountain overlooking the capital city. Businesses in the city's tall buildings were asked to leave their lights on all night to present a more impressive view and, not incidentally, to prove that Seoul had electricity to spare. At the time of the division of the country, North Korea had inherited the main municipal power plant, which had been located well north of the city. Until the South built a new power plant, the North had caused privation and consternation by shutting off the electricity whenever it chose.

In yet another effort to impress, the government took the visitors for a drive on the recently opened expressway that ran from Seoul down the length of the peninsula to the southern city of Pusan. To create more traffic, Seoulites were asked to drive their cars on the highway even if they had no place to go, and a transport firm was asked to drive its big trailers along the nearby parts of the road. A northern visitor, perhaps getting wind of this exercise in mobilization (the kind of thing that was commonplace in Pyongyang), congratulated one of the heads of the southern delegation for his success in "bringing all the vehicles in the country to Seoul" to buttress its claims to prosperity. "That was difficult, but not nearly as hard as bringing all the tall buildings here for you to look at" was the reply.

The opening ceremony in a hotel ballroom dramatized the political character of the meeting. Believing that the highly ideological northerners would overreach and offend the broad mass of the generally conservative South Korean public, which was passionately in favor of unification but also fearful of communism and imbued with the memory of the 1950–1953 war, the Seoul government had decided to televise the speeches live. The North Korean political adviser, Yun Ki Bok, attacked the United States, referred to "the nation's glorious capital, Pyongyang," and praised "the Great Leader," whereupon hundreds of telephone calls of protest, some stimulated by Seoul's ubiquitous intelligence agency, flooded the switchboards of the television station and local police. Responding in part to signals from the top, the country's mood shifted abruptly, from hope to anger. When the North Koreans left the hotel after the opening ceremony, for the first time they encountered silence rather than applause. A North Korean delegate waved to a crowd outside, but this time nobody waved back.

As a spectacle and a roller-coaster ride of deeply felt emotions, the first open diplomatic foray by northerners to the South was impressive. As a negotiating forum, however, it was a flop. It quickly became apparent that the North had little interest in the limited accommodations for divided families that were proposed by the South, demanding instead such moves as repeal of the South's Anti-Communist Law and extensive exchange of political cadres down to the lowest governmental levels.

Rather than have the talks fall apart in Seoul, however, President Park ordered his delegation to sign a meaningless joint agreement extolling the spirit of "brotherly love" and "Red Cross humanitarianism" and postponing serious negotiation for a future meeting in the North Korean capital. Park decided it would not be in keeping with Korean courtesy to clash sharply with the visitors and have the talks collapse at such an early point while he was the official host.

PARK CHUNG HEE

The dominant figure in South Korea was in many respects almost the opposite of his North Korean counterpart. Whereas Kim Il Sung had been an anti-Japanese guerrilla fighter, Park Chung Hee had attended the Japanese military academy, had become an officer in the Japanese army, and, as required at the time, had even temporarily taken a Japanese name, Masao Takagi. And whereas Kim was a big man, who tended to dominate with his presence and his outgoing, confident personality, Park Chung Hee was small and wiry, seemingly self-contained and often aloof. During my one personal interview with Park, in June 1975, this powerful and greatly feared political leader seemed reticent and shy, almost smaller than life, as he sat in a big chair in his Blue House office. As we talked, he toyed with a tiny chihuahua dog in his lap and rarely looked me in the eye.

Responding to different sets of external relationships and espousing different ideologies, Park and Kim had one thing in common: each had come to dominate his respective section of the Korean landmass. In his eighteen-year reign, from the military coup he led in 1961 to his assassination in 1979, Park left his mark on South Korea to a greater extent than any other person in modern times; his tenure and his impact were equaled only by Kim's extraordinary run of nearly a half century in the North. Both men were strong rulers who owed much to the Confucian tradition of deference to authority that long predated twentieth-century Korea.

Park was born in a village near Taegu on September 30, 1917, the son of a small farmer who had been a minor county official. At age twenty, he graduated from a teachers' college and taught primary school for three years before volunteering for the Japanese army. Soon his record was so outstanding that he was sent to the Japanese military academy in Manchuria and was commissioned a lieutenant. His orderly mind and neat handwriting from his teaching days proved to be lifelong attributes, as did the sense of organization and use of power that he learned in military training. When his private safe was opened after his death, aides discovered files of handwritten personal notes on individuals, meticulously arranged in Park's own indexing system.

After the Japanese surrender and the division of the country in 1945, Park joined the newly established South Korean military academy and graduated as an officer the following year. In a much-disputed episode of his life, Park was arrested as leader of a communist cell at the Korean Military Academy following the 1948 Yosu rebellion, in which army troops under communist leadership refused to follow orders and proclaimed a short-lived "people's republic." Park was sentenced to death by a military court, but his sentence was commuted by President Syngman Rhee at the urging of several Korean officers and on the recommendation of Rhee's American military adviser, James Hausman, who knew him "as a damned good soldier." Park then switched sides, turning over a list of communists in the armed forces and becoming an intelligence official at army headquarters whose job it was to hunt them down.

This bizarre history caused worry in Washington when then major general Park suddenly emerged as leader of the 1961 military coup. At Park's request, Hausman flew to Washington and told high officials that despite his early history, Park was no communist and "there is nothing to worry about." The US Embassy, in a cable to the State Department, rejected the possibility that Park could be a secret communist, "mainly because his defection from communists and turnover apparatus would make him victim no. 1 if communists ever took power." Park's political opponents sought to use his early leftist activities against him, but when he was strong enough he prohibited further public mention of it. In the early 1970s, an American correspondent, Elizabeth Pond of the *Christian Science Monitor,* was barred from the country for writing an article discussing Park's past.

Given his prewar Japanese education, his Confucian heritage, and his military background, there was nothing in Park's previous life to suggest fealty to democracy American style, which he considered an inconvenient and unproductive practice. After he led the 1961 coup, it took heavy pressure from the Kennedy administration to persuade him to return the country to nominal civilian rule and to run for election as president. He successfully did so in 1963 and 1967, then insisted on a change in the constitution permitting him a third term. He narrowly won that third election in 1971 against opposition leader Kim Dae Jung after pledging never to ask the people to vote for him again. In 1972 he redeemed that pledge literally, though certainly not in spirit, by abolishing direct presidential elections and creating a method of indirect election, under which he could be (and was) reelected by an easily controlled national convention for the rest of his life.

An assessment by the US military command in Korea in 1975 noted, "From the time he led the 1961 coup, it has been evident that President Park had little admiration for or interest in the craft of politics. His approach to his stewardship as ROK head of state has remained that of a general who desires that his orders be carried out without being subjected to the process of political debate."

South Korea under Park was dependent militarily and to a large degree economically on the United States. This dependence grated on Park, who worked steadfastly to increase his independence from Washington, much as Kim Il Sung struggled to gain independence from his Soviet and Chinese sponsors. Park's relationship with his principal foreign backer was fundamentally lacking in trust. The extent of American confidence in Park in the 1960s is suggested by the later disclosure of former ambassador William J. Porter that US intelligence had installed listening devices in Park's Blue House office, though he said they had been removed by the time of his arrival in 1967. Following disclosure of the bugging, Park had the Blue House swept by his own surveillance experts and installed special multilayered glass windows with static between the panes to foil electronic eavesdropping from outside, activated by a switch near his desk. "Whenever he'd call me to his office, he'd turn on the switch and lower his voice," one of Park's ministers recalled.

Fifteen years after his death, however, Park was remembered less for his conflicts with Washington and successive waves of political repression than as the father of his country's remarkable economic progress. More than two-thirds of South Koreans polled by a Seoul daily in March 1995 said Park was the country's greatest president, more than five times the number that gave that honor to any other chief executive. The overwhelming reasons cited were the economic progress and development under his regime and its relative stability. (Park's standing went down again during liberal President Roh Moo-hyun's rule [2003–2008], when focus was again put on his repression.)

South Korea's economic rise under Park started from a low point. Looking back after a decade in power, Park wrote that when he took over the country as leader of the 1961 coup, "I honestly felt as if I had been given a pilfered household or a bankrupt firm to manage. Around me I could find little hope. . . . I had to destroy, once and for all, the vicious circle of poverty and economic stagnation. Only by reforming the economic structure could we lay a foundation for decent living standards." For Park, rapid economic growth was essential not only as the source of prosperity but also for two other goals, which he held even higher: enhancing national security, in an era when US willingness to protect the country against the North was waning, and winning political legitimacy for his regime, which had taken power by force of arms against a legitimately elected government.

Only a month after seizing power, Park established the Economic Planning Council, which later became the Economic Planning Board, to provide central governmental direction for the economy. The first five-year development plan, produced shortly thereafter, declared that "the economic system will be a form of 'guided capitalism,' in which the principle of free enterprise and respect for freedom and initiative of free enterprise will be observed, but in which the government will either directly participate in or indirectly render guidance to the basic industries and other important fields."

As that passage suggests, Park's model for economic development was the highly successful postwar Japanese system. In 1965, in a very unpopular personal decision that nonetheless gave a powerful boost to the Korean economy, Park normalized relations with Japan. Despite fierce domestic opposition based on antipathy to the former colonial masters, the Seoul-Tokyo normalization, which was strongly encouraged by Washington, brought an immediate Japanese assistance package of $800 million and led to many more millions in Japanese investments and valuable economic tie-ups with Japanese firms. In another far-reaching decision of the mid-1960s, Park sent two divisions of Korean troops to fight alongside American forces in South Vietnam, for which he received Washington's gratitude and Korean firms received a major share of war production and construction contracts. In 1966 revenues from the war made up 40 percent of South Korea's foreign exchange earnings, making Vietnam the country's first overseas profit center.

Park took personal charge of the economy, bringing highly professional economists, many of them American educated, into the planning agencies. He established an economics situation room next to his office in the Blue House to monitor the implementation of the plans, and he frequently met with economic officials and businessmen who were developing projects with government support. Much like the "on-the-spot guidance" practiced by Kim Il Sung in the North, Park incessantly visited government offices in the economic area and construction sites in the field to check up on what was happening.

Park refused to be guided by economists when he was determined to move ahead with one of his visionary projects. When American and World Bank economists said that South Korea could not successfully build, operate, or support an integrated steel mill and refused to approve financing, Park remained determined to build it. Declaring that "steel is national power," he obtained Japanese loans and personally pushed through construction of a massive mill at Pohang, on the southeast coast, which became the world's largest steel-production site and a foundation of Korea's heavy industry. Park was the driving force behind the ambitious Seoul-to-Pusan expressway, which experts had also said was impractical. An engineer on the project recalled that "after a while, I found myself thinking of him, of all things, as a sort of conductor of an orchestra—with his helicopter as his baton. Up and down he would go, this time with a team of geologists to figure out what was wrong with some mountainside that had crumbled on our tunnel-makers, the next time with a couple of United Nations hydrologists to figure out how our own surveyors had got some water table wrong. If he didn't know the answer on Tuesday, Mr. Park was back with it on Thursday or Saturday."

"President Park monitored the progress of every single project, both public and private, and closely governed the industrialists by the stick-and-carrot method," according to Kim Chung Yum, who was a senior economic aide to Park and eventually his chief of staff. Park chose the firms that would be awarded contracts on large government-backed projects and provided or withheld credit through government banks, depending on their performance. The growth sectors of the national economy came to be dominated by a few highly organized, diversified industrial-business conglomerates known as *chaebols,* loosely modeled on the Japanese prewar *zaibatsu* or its postwar *zaikai.* Although this facilitated Korea's dramatic economic rise in the 1970s and beyond, the intimate relations between government and business also set the mold for the corruption charges that later were to plague the retirement years of Park's successors.

Although he wielded enormous economic power, Park never became a rich man and was not personally corrupt. He usually had a simple bowl of Korean noodles for lunch and ate rice mixed with barley, to save on rice. He had bricks placed in his Blue House toilet to conserve water. Setting a modest style, he wore open-collar shirts without neckties in the summer months and encouraged civil servants to do the same.

Park's personal hold over the economy was embodied by his ambitious Heavy and Chemical Industries Promotion Plan, a massive program to build up six strategic industries—iron and steel, shipbuilding, chemicals, electronics, nonferrous metals, and machinery. Initiated in late 1971 and formally announced in January 1973, the plan was designed by Park to enhance his political legitimacy and to respond to what he saw as a perilous security combination: the North Korean military buildup, which became intensive as Pyongyang asserted greater independence from the Soviet Union and China in the mid-1960s, and his decreasing confidence in American security assurances, as the United States disengaged from the Vietnam War and sought to reduce its commitments elsewhere in East Asia.

The Heavy and Chemical Plan, which Park conceived and rammed through despite the misgivings of the Economic Planning Board and other economists, was the foundation of Korea's later success in automobiles, shipbuilding, and electronics, but it was also very costly and eventually was scaled back considerably. Cho Soon, a prominent economist and scholar who later became mayor of Seoul, wrote in a retrospective analysis that the scale of Park's projects "exceeded by far what the country could accommodate" and substituted government decision making for private initiative in the economy. Accordingly, Cho wrote, "The results were waste and distortions in resource use, inflationary pressure, the emergence of immense conglomerates, and widening inequality in the distribution of income and wealth."

Nevertheless, the overall results of the development program that Park put in place between 1961 and 1979 were spectacular. In broad terms, according to the World Bank, South Korea's inflation-adjusted GNP tripled in each decade after Park's first year in office, thereby condensing a century of growth into three decades. At the same time, the country dramatically reduced the incidence of poverty, from more than 40 percent of all households living below the poverty line in 1965 to fewer than 10 percent in 1980. Per capita income shot up from less than one hundred dollars annually when Park took power to more than one thousand dollars at the time of his death and more than ten thousand dollars today. In view of these achievements, it is small wonder that he is viewed by most South Koreans in retrospect as a leader of unparalleled greatness.

WASHINGTON BLINKS AT PARK'S COUP

At 6:00 P.M. on October 16, 1972, Park's prime minister, Kim Jong Pil, notified US ambassador Philip Habib of a sweeping change in the country's political direction, requesting that it be kept secret until made public twenty-five hours later. The surprise announcement by Park, a copy of which was handed to Habib, declared martial law, junked the existing constitution, disbanded the National Assembly, and prepared a plan for indirect election of the president. At the same time, to silence opposition, Park arrested most of the senior political leaders of the country.

Park called his new system *yushin*, which his spokesmen translated as "revitalizing reforms," and justified his actions on the grounds that the nation must be strong and united to deal with the North and maintain its independence in a changing international environment. The proposed announcement laid heavy stress on perils beyond Korea's shores, as "the interests of the third or smaller countries might be sacrificed for the relaxation of tension between big powers."

Despite the emphasis on external threats, Habib had no illusions about the real purpose of Park's dramatic moves. He cabled Washington within a few hours to say that "the measures proposed are designed to insure that President Park will stay in office for at least twelve years with even less opposition and dissent and with increased executive powers" and that "if these proposals are carried out Korea will indeed have, for all practical purposes, a completely authoritarian government." While the ambassador conceded that Park might believe that he must strengthen his domestic position to deal with the North, Habib informed Washington that "there is little doubt that these measures are unnecessary given any objective view of the situation."

The pressing question was what the United States should do in view of its extensive interests and its historic leverage in South Korean politics. In the aftermath of World War II and the division of the peninsula, Washington had played the central role in anointing Syngman Rhee as the country's first president, and in 1960, in the face of a student-led popular uprising, it had also played a major role in forcing him to leave power. In 1961 the US Embassy and the US Command had spoken out publicly but ineffectually against General Park's military coup against the constitutionally elected post-Rhee government, but it had then successfully applied steady and persistent pressure to force Park to reestablish civilian government. Now the United States was confronted with what amounted to a coup in place, a power grab by Park to eliminate all legal opposition and retain power for as long as he wished.

Habib, a tough-talking, politically astute Foreign Service veteran from Brooklyn with extensive previous experience in Korea, was furious that his embassy had obtained no early warning of Park's surprise from its own sources. As he was well aware, the timing for the move had been chosen with care. Only three weeks earlier, Washington had done nothing when Philippine president Ferdinand Marcos, in a very similar maneuver that had been closely watched by Park, declared martial law and jettisoned his country's existing political institutions. Both Marcos and Park had sprung their power grabs during the campaign period of a US presidential election, when American presidents are more reluctant than usual to make controversial decisions in foreign affairs. The Nixon-Kissinger White House, which prided itself on realpolitik in diplomacy, was fixated on the politically difficult situation in Vietnam, according to then Assistant Secretary of State Marshall Green, at the time the State Department's senior Asia expert. "They didn't have time to be bothered" by Korea developments, he recalled.

With the plans drawn up and already in motion, Habib reported to Washington that "only the most drastic, positive and immediate actions by the U.S. might turn Park from the course on which he has embarked." In a pivotal judgment that established the limits of American engagement, Habib declared that "it is not incumbent upon the U.S. to take on the responsibility of getting Park to reverse his course within the next few hours. Nevertheless, we believe that in the long run, Park is creating major problems for himself and for his relationship with us and with others." Habib recommended that "we should be extremely circumspect in our public comments while making it clear that we are not in any way associated with the government's internal actions."

Washington accepted the advice of its ambassador and decided not to oppose Park's actions. The State Department cabled Habib, "We agree that [Park's] contemplated measures are unnecessary, and have grave reservations about the course he has embarked upon." Habib was instructed to tell Park that taking such a far-reaching decision without a serious exchange of views with the United States was "incomprehensible in light of the past sacrifices and present support which we have given to the Republic of Korea and specifically to the present government." Nevertheless, no action was recommended to change Park's mind. If he were asked whether the United States would recommend against imposing martial law, Habib was instructed to answer that "this is an internal matter. . . . It is up to him to decide."

Washington's main concern seemed to be the proposed public statement accompanying the announcement, citing the American rapprochement with China and the resulting international fluidity as among the new perils to the Republic of Korea that justified drastic action. Habib was instructed to protest these statements, and in Washington Secretary of State William Rogers took them up personally with Korean ambassador Kim Dong Jo—all before the bombshell declaration was made public in Seoul. The references to US policy in the prepared announcement were dropped, although to Washington's displeasure some references to maneuvering by "big powers" were retained. The Korean foreign minister solemnly told Habib that the phrase "big powers" was not intended to include the United States.

After Park's announcement had been made and tanks and troops had been put into the streets to implement martial law, after political figures had been arrested or silenced and the sometimes-feisty Korean press had been placed under heavy censorship, Habib took a more careful look at the implications of what was being done. In an October 23 cable to Washington, the ambassador reported:

> It is clear that Park has turned away from the political philosophy which we have been advocating and supporting in Korea for 27 years. The characteristics of the discarded system which he regarded as weaknesses—the limitations on executive powers, the dissent and inherent uncertainties which arise in direct presidential elections—we regard as strengths. Because of our historic relationship with Korea, our security commitments, and the presence

of a substantial number of American troops, we are confronted with the problem of our reaction to these developments.

Habib reported that attempting to dissuade Park from the course of action he had chosen would be "impractical," but that seeking to soften the repressive aspects of new policies would be seen as giving tacit US endorsement to the *yushin* plan as a whole. What remained, Habib concluded, was "a policy of disassociation," in which the United States would say it had not been consulted or involved in Park's actions and would stay clear of involvement in the reorganization of the Korean political system. In his cable, the ambassador faced squarely the consequences of the hands-off policy he recommended:

> In following such a course we would be accepting the fact that the U.S. cannot and should no longer try to determine the course of internal political development in Korea. We have already begun a process of progressively lower levels of U.S. engagement with Korea. The process of disengagement should be accelerated. The policy we propose would be consistent with the disengagement trend, and Park's actions will contribute to the process.

Three days later Washington responded: "We agree with the Embassy's preference for a posture of disassociation. . . . In furtherance of this policy, we intend to refrain from arguing with the ROK in public, and seek to advance our counsel privately only where necessary and appropriate." When Prime Minister Kim Jong Pil visited the US capital three months later, President Nixon told him privately that "unlike other presidents, it is not my intention to interfere in the internal affairs of your country." With these decisions, most of which were never announced, the United States acquiesced in a diminished role in South Korea's political future.

North Korea did not seem to mind Park's shift to a more authoritarian system that was more like its own arrangements, possibly believing that this would make it easier to negotiate accords with him. On October 21, in the immediate aftermath of martial law, the two Koreas jointly announced that KCIA chief Lee Hu Rak would travel to Pyongyang on November 2 for another meeting with Kim Il Sung and that North Korea would send a top-level negotiator to Seoul shortly thereafter. The joint announcement was taken as a sign that the North-South dialogue remained on track.

THE IMPACT OF *YUSHIN*

Within the South Korean body politic, the imposition of Park's *yushin* system provoked intense opposition from many quarters. Acting through the KCIA, the Army Security Command, and his increasingly powerful personal bodyguards, Park sought to silence all those who interfered or disagreed with his policies by temporary detention, arrest, or imprisonment. In a brutal procedure known as the Korean barbecue, some opponents were strung up by their wrists and ankles and spread-eagled over a flame in KCIA torture chambers; others were subjected to water torture by repeated dunking or the forcing of water down their throats.

Chang Chun Ha, a distinguished Korean nationalist, told me how he had been seized on his way downtown and taken to a KCIA jail for a week of nearly continuous interrogation, in an unsuccessful effort to persuade him to endorse Park's martial-law "reforms." Meanwhile, his distraught family, as his captors repeatedly pointed out to him, did not know what had happened to him or if he would ever return. Three years later, Chang, an independent-minded man who had fought for Korean independence while Park was in the Japanese army, was killed under mysterious circumstances that the government attributed to a mountain-climbing mishap but that his family and friends believed was political assassination. A doctor who examined Chang's body was beaten and intimidated by the secret police, but he broke his silence many years later to declare that Chang's wounds were inconsistent with a fall from a cliff and to suggest that he had been murdered. (The case was back in the news again in 2012, an old wound reopened, when the body was exhumed and his remains relocated.)

Security organs worked hard to stifle the Korean press. For more than a year following the *yushin* decree, KCIA operatives came daily to major Korean newspapers and broadcast stations to tell them what news they could or could not report, at times specifying the size of the headlines and the prominence of the display to be given to particular items. Due to this system, Park's picture and activities dominated the news. If Korean editors or reporters resisted, they were called in for grilling and often beaten.

Not all dissent was silenced. The most articulate, authoritative, and unbridled voice of opposition was Kim Dae Jung, Park's opponent in the hotly contested 1971 presidential race and a favorite son of the rebellious southwestern provinces of Cholla, where long ago an independent Korean kingdom had existed. Before the voting, Kim accurately predicted that if Park won, he would become a "generalissimo" and arrange to be in office forever. Kim escaped being silenced with other political leaders in October 1972 because he happened to be in Japan when martial law was imposed. He immediately condemned the action as dictatorial, unconstitutional, and unjustified. Rather than return home to be arrested, Kim kept up his caustic criticism from abroad.

On August 8, 1973, Kim was lured to a luncheon meeting with two visiting Korean parliamentarians in a suite at a Tokyo hotel. As he said good-bye in the corridor, he was shoved into a nearby room by three men in dark suits, then punched, kicked, and anesthetized. He was taken by car down an expressway to a port and placed aboard a motorboat and then a large ship, where he was tightly trussed and weights placed on his hands and legs.

Kim's abduction was sensational news in Japan, where externally directed political violence was rare and, coming from Korea, a particularly painful affront to Japanese sovereignty. In Seoul, Ambassador Habib decided that strong and immediate action was necessary to save Kim's life and avert a serious crisis within South Korea and between South Korea and Japan. Calling in senior embassy officials, Habib instructed them to find out within twenty-four hours who had kidnapped Kim. US intelligence officers quickly identified the KCIA as the culprit, whereupon the ambassador, in his characteristically blunt and salty language, laid down the law to the high command of Park's government, declaring that there would be grave consequences for relations with the United States if Kim did not turn up alive.

Habib's quick action probably saved Kim's life. After a few hours at sea, the weights were suddenly taken off Kim's body, and his bonds were loosened. Five days after his abduction, he was released, battered and dazed, a few blocks from his residence in Seoul. After thirty-six hours during which Kim was permitted to speak publicly of his ordeal, he was placed under house arrest. Park's government made no effort to identify or penalize his abductors.

Three weeks after Kim's kidnapping, North Korea suspended both the North-South political-level talks and the Red Cross talks, invoking the kidnapping of the popular opposition politician as the reason for its action. However, Pyongyang had been losing interest in the dialogue even in the months before the kidnapping. It was increasingly clear that the inter-Korean talks were not leading to the withdrawal of US military forces. Moreover, the exposure of North Korean delegates to the more prosperous South was making Pyongyang's leaders uncomfortable. According to a report from the Hungarian Embassy in Pyongyang, opposition from the North Korean military to the shift toward a "peaceful unification" line had been so strong that Kim Il Sung had to convene a special meeting of the army in the autumn of 1972 in order to explain and justify the change in approach.

Park's regime, which had used the North-South talks to justify its brutal political coup, now sought to salvage the talks. Late in the year, the South proposed a series of meetings of the vice chairmen of the political-level North-South Coordinating Committee. The first meeting coincided with a major event in the South—the ouster of the powerful

KCIA director, Lee Hu Rak, who had negotiated with Kim Il Sung but had also engineered the kidnapping of Kim Dae Jung.

After a prominent Seoul National University law professor was tortured to death in October 1973, CIA station chief Donald Gregg protested the killing and told the Blue House he found it personally difficult to work further with Lee. A week later, Lee was fired by President Park and replaced with a former justice minister, who initiated reforms in KCIA operations. With Lee out of the picture as chief contact with the North, the prospects seemed better to revive the discussions with Pyongyang. From December 1973 to March 1975, ten North-South vice-chairmen meetings were held under the aegis of the North-South Coordinating Committee, at Panmunjom, but they accomplished little.

Why did the initial attempt at North-South dialogue flower and then wither? How sincere were Park Chung Hee and Kim Il Sung? What did their initial contacts suggest for the future?

From a historical perspective, it seems clear that both Korean leaders had been jarred out of their previous patterns of inflexibility by fast-moving international developments. Whether through hope or fear, each had decided he had more to gain than to lose by dealing directly with the opposing state, something that had never been done before. As it turned out, both benefited in important ways from the experiment in coexistence, even though the practical results were nil.

The dialogue proved extremely useful to Park. It was helpful to his regime internationally, especially in the United States, whose previous ambassador, William J. Porter, had been promoting the case for dialogue for several years. Domestically, the opening to the North was broadly popular with the South Korean public, raising hopes for family reunions, a lowering of tension, and eventual unification, all of which were held out as potential benefits by Park's government. Most important, Park used the requirement for national strength and unity in dealing with the North to justify his *yushin* regime, which gave him the upper hand against the civilian politicians whom he despised and guaranteed him an unlimited tenure in the presidency.

Kim Il Sung also found the dialogue with the South to be beneficial, especially in breaking out of his diplomatic isolation. At the end of 1970, before the move toward talks began, North Korea had diplomatic relations with only thirty-five countries, nearly all of them socialist regimes, while South Korea had diplomatic relations with eighty-one countries. Immediately following the start of North-South dialogue, Pyongyang gained recognition from five Western European nations and many more neutral countries. Within four years, North Korea was recognized by ninety-three countries, on a par with South Korea's relations with ninety-six. The North also gained entry for the first time to the UN's World Health Organization and, as a result, sent its first permanent UN observer missions to New York and Geneva.

Also for the first time, as part of its peace offensive, North Korea communicated directly with the United States, initially by inviting journalists from the *New York Times* and the *Washington Post* to Pyongyang for extensive interviews and then by addressing a diplomatic message directly to Washington. In April 1973, North Korea's legislature, the Supreme People's Assembly (SPA), sent a telegram to the US Congress referring to the developments on the divided peninsula and asking the American lawmakers for help in removing US troops from South Korea, as they had just been removed from South Vietnam. Congress did not reply, but this letter set the stage for a succession of direct and indirect communications to Washington in the years to come.

Near the end of 1972, both Park and Kim reaped some personal rewards from their headline-making interaction. In November, using the dialogue with the North as his justification, Park won approval, through a nationwide referendum, of the new constitution, granting him virtually unchecked and unlimited power. The charter was approved after an extensive sales campaign that took place under martial law, with newspapers censored and the opposition unable to be heard. In December Park was elected unanimously, with no debate permitted, to a new six-year term as president by the handpicked National Conference for Unification.

Not to be outdone, Kim put through a new constitution in the North, also without objection or dissent. Under the new charter, the nation was to be guided by the *juche* idea "as a creative application of Marxism-Leninism." Kim, who had held the title of prime minister as well as general secretary of the ruling Workers Party, promoted himself to president. Although this did not increase his already all-encompassing power, the new title put him on a semantic par with the leader of the South.

Neither Kim Il Sung nor Park Chung Hee harbored the belief that his indirect dialogue would lead to unification of the divided peninsula, although this hopeful prospect was, at least briefly, widespread among the respective publics of both men. Neither leader was willing to seriously compromise the policies and interest groups on which their respective regimes were based to pursue the long-term goal of national unity. To a great degree, the military-backed governments of both the North and the South had been shaped by the rivalry between them. Although both Kim and Park were in favor of unification, each was fiercely opposed to a merger on the other leader's terms. Without a strong push from the outside powers, who had conflicting interests and were paying little attention to the Korean peninsula, the two rival states were incapable of sustaining their dialogue.

Nonetheless, the exchanges of the early 1970s were a turning point in the Cold War on the Korean peninsula, holding out the possibility, for the first time, of mutual cooperation and eventual peaceful reunification. An aspiration of immense appeal on both sides had flickered into life in tangible and tantalizing fashion. It would never be entirely extinguished, despite the many trials to come.

3

THE TROUBLE
DEEPENS

PRESIDENT PARK CHUNG HEE was droning on, reading his prepared speech in Korean without flourishes or gestures, rarely pausing to look up from his papers at the audience of distinguished citizens and foreign diplomats. I was nodding off from boredom. The scene was the National Theater in Seoul, on a national holiday, August 15, 1974—the twenty-ninth anniversary of the country's liberation from Japan. Suddenly, a loud *pop* from the back of the hall broke the monotony, and I turned to see a figure in a dark suit running down the center aisle of the theater, firing a weapon as he ran. More shots rang out, and presidential security guards raced onto the stage from the wings, guns drawn, some blazing. Amid the pandemonium in the hall, Korea's first lady slumped to the floor from her seat on the stage and was carried out by attendants, her bright-orange *hanbok,* the traditional flowing Korean gown, stained with blood. She would die within hours from a bullet wound to her head.

As the final shots were heard, the assassin was lost from view in a pileup of security men, then hustled from the hall. A high school girl, who was part of the chorus singing for this state occasion, was also carried out. She later died of her wounds, apparently from a presidential bodyguard's wild shot.

Startled by the eruption of violence, I had lost sight of Park during the melee. But now, as it subsided, he reappeared from behind the bulky—and bulletproof—lectern, where he had taken refuge when the shooting began. As he rose, he waved his hand to the stunned crowd, which broke into loud applause. Park told an aide later that he never saw the assassin's face.

Order was restored in surprisingly few minutes. Then to my astonishment, Park resumed the reading of his prepared speech. At the end, he sat patiently while the high school chorus—minus the unfortunate sixteen-year-old victim—calmly sang a musical selection as planned. On his way out, Park noticed his wife's shoes and handbag under the chair where she had been sitting, and he picked them up as he left. Explaining Park's impassive behavior at a moment of supreme stress, his longtime aide Kim Seong Jin described the president as "a man of responsibility, who has got to finish what he set out."

The gunshots in the National Theater marked the start of a period of intensified tension on the Korean peninsula, during which earlier moves toward North-South rapprochement were replaced with undisguised hostility. The impetus for the deepening struggle came in part from the failure of the decade-long US military effort in Indochina. While Saigon was falling, Kim Il Sung made a bid to renew his open warfare against the South, but China refused to go along, and the Soviet Union avoided even inviting Kim to visit Moscow to make his case. By the mid-1970s, both the giants of international communism had much too great a stake in their own relations with the United States to risk another war on the Korean peninsula. At the same time, US diplomats intervened with secret persuasion and powerful threats to stop Park Chung Hee from proceeding with a South Korean nuclear weapons program that could bring new dangers of escalation that nobody, including the great powers, would be able to control. Washington's veto of Seoul's nuclear ambitions proved that the United States could still wield impressive clout on security issues when convinced that its most vital interests were at stake.

TENSIONS INCREASE

For months before the Independence Day shooting, tension in Seoul had been building toward a crisis as Park and his domestic opponents engaged in an escalating political struggle. As the shock of martial law had worn off, protests had grown—especially after the kidnapping of opposition leader Kim Dae Jung from Tokyo, which galvanized anti-Park forces. Pyongyang's subsequent suspension of the North-South dialogue robbed the government of its strategic justification for the internal crackdown.

Two of the most important groups in the growing democratic opposition were students and the Christian community, both traditional foes of tyranny in Korea. The unusual stature of students in Korean society and especially in political activism is the product of a tradition stretching back over many centuries. Undergirded by the Confucian emphasis on scholarship, students had spearheaded nationalistic movements against Japanese colonial rule. They saw themselves, and were seen by others, as guardians of state virtue and purity, and they were expected to demonstrate opposition to any compromise with those ideals.

The practice of student political activism had been powerfully reinforced in the early 1960s. Massive student protests in 1960 against Syngman Rhee's increasingly authoritarian government were halted by police gunfire that killed 130 students and wounded another 1,000 in Seoul alone. The government's brutality robbed it of legitimacy in the eyes of the public and led to its replacement. The military coup led by General Park that took over the government by force in 1961 was never accepted as legitimate by many activist students, who passionately opposed the existence of military-dominated regimes.

After liberation from Japan, the thirst for education had led to rapid growth in the South Korean student population, from fewer than 8,000 college and university students in 1945 to 223,000 by 1973. Although only a small percentage of Korean students were politically active, this vanguard was intensely engaged, prone to rigid, often radical political and social theories, and ready to do battle with government authority by employing their bodies as well as their voices.

Christianity, too, was strongly associated with Korea's resistance to Japan's colonial rule. As advocates and symbols of Western-oriented modernization, Christians have had high prestige in Korean society. From an estimated 300,000 in North and South Korea in 1945, the number of Christians had grown rapidly by 1974 to an estimated 4.3 million in South Korea (3.5 million Protestants and 800,000 Roman Catholics). Except for the largely Catholic Philippines, South Korea is the most Christianized country in Asia.

As the dissident movement grew, the government periodically cracked down with detentions and arrests. Virtually no news of this confrontation appeared in the tightly controlled Korean press, though due to the international press and the many outside connections of regime opponents, the struggle was well publicized outside Korea. The governments of the United States, Japan, and a number of European countries were uncomfortable and made their views known in official démarches and unofficial statements, urging Seoul to take a path of caution and moderation.

In Washington, congressional criticism of Park's human rights policies and the activities of the KCIA in intimidating Korean Americans led to Capitol Hill hearings and congressionally mandated cuts in US military aid to South Korea. Seoul's response to these political pressures was to try, in time-honored Korean fashion, to purchase favor in ways that presaged scandals in the 1990s over Asian efforts to influence US politics. This included sealed envelopes with thousands of dollars in hundred-dollar bills handed to a White House aide. The US Embassy strongly objected, to little avail.

Early in 1974, Park used his martial-law powers to issue emergency decrees criminalizing criticism of the constitution and outlawing a student federation as subversive. Violators faced trial by closed military courts. A confidential US military assessment quoted intelligence sources as saying that "there was little or no validity to the charge of communist activity by the students" but that the accusation appeared designed "to tarnish opposition to the government with a communist image and to justify the repressive measures."

By the time of the August 15 Independence Day celebration, nearly two hundred people had been sentenced to death or long prison terms under the emergency decrees. Among those found guilty were a prominent Roman Catholic bishop, a popular dissident poet, and the only living former president of South Korea, Yun Po Sun. The struggle within the South, added to the permanent conflict with the North, made Seoul as tense as a war zone. When Park moved from room to room in his presidential mansion, the corridors were cleared of all but essential people because of what a senior US Embassy official called his "morbid fear of assassination" by North Koreans.

All this was in the background when the gunshots rang out in the National Theater. In view of the intensity of the internal struggle, there had been a growing sense that Seoul's crisis was reaching an explosive point. A sudden act of violence was not so surprising. But from what direction had the gunshots come? Political dissidents? A rival military group? And what would happen next, now that Park had survived the attack?

THE STRUGGLE WITH JAPAN

The man who tried to change Korean history with a .38 caliber pistol was a twenty-two-year-old Korean resident of Osaka, Japan, who confessed to being instructed and assisted by an official of a North Korea–oriented residents association in Japan. The identity of the would-be assassin and the fact that his attack had been launched from Japan led to a serious crisis between the two US allies in Northeast Asia, which were closely intertwined economically but had never come to terms politically with their unhappy history.

Mun Se Kwang had flown from Japan to South Korea on August 6, bringing a handgun stolen from a Japanese police station and concealed in a radio. He checked in to Korea's best hotel and on the morning of the Independence Day ceremony hired a limousine and driver from the hotel, paying him extra to perform obsequious bows at the entrance to the National Theater. Mun then strode past dozens of security officers as if he were an important guest.

The assassin had planned to shoot Park in the lobby, but failed to get an unobstructed view. As the ceremony began, he was swept inside and was only able to find a seat close to the back of the large hall. Near the middle of Park's address, he rose from his seat, intending to stride quickly down the center aisle, pause, and take careful aim as he had been trained to do. But as Mun moved into position, he accidentally squeezed the trigger of his pistol, and the gun went off, grazing his left thigh. At that point, the gunman made a run for it down the aisle, firing rapidly—but not accurately—as he ran.

Taken to KCIA headquarters and treated for his superficial wound, the gunman initially insisted he was "a revolutionary warrior" who should be treated as a prisoner of war. For a full day, he refused to say anything more than his name, Mun Se Kwang, and his address in Osaka. On the second day, one of the Korean prosecutors said to Mun, "You are a jackal, aren't you?" With this reference to the Frederick Forsythe novel *The Day of the Jackal,* about a plot to assassinate French president Charles de Gaulle, Mun for the first time looked startled and showed emotion. He answered, "Yes." Assured that he would be treated not as a common criminal but as a man who was "looking for something big," Mun began to confess.

Korea and Japan, which are separated only by a narrow body of water, have a complex and tangled history, with more periods of conflict than friendly relations. Continental Asian culture originally made its way to Japan via the Korean peninsula. The two countries share an overlapping cultural heritage, yet in many ways the tension between them is more impressive. For all their recorded history, Japan has been more populous and militarily stronger. In modern times, imperial Japan's occupation of Korea from 1905 until its downfall in 1945 left bitter resentment on the part of Koreans. The Japanese, for their part, mixed feelings of superiority with trepidation about the Koreans in their midst and abroad.

During the Japanese occupation and especially during World War II, more than 2 million Koreans were forcibly brought to Japan, mainly as laborers. Although most were repatriated after Japan's defeat, about 600,000 remained, largely in the lowest-paying and least-skilled jobs. By 1974 they constituted the main exception to Japan's famed homogeneity, making up nearly nine-tenths of the entire "alien" population amid 108 million Japanese. Although Mun Se Kwang, like many others, was born and raised in Japan, and could not even speak Korean, his birth certificate and alien registration papers described him as a South Korean whose permanent home was near Pusan. Under law and practice in Japan, he and others like him had little hope of ever becoming Japanese citizens and were relegated to secondary jobs and status.

One year earlier, Japan had been furious at the violation of its sovereignty in the Tokyo kidnapping of South Korean opposition leader Kim Dae Jung. Now, after Mun Se Kwang's deadly run down the aisle of the National Theater on the day commemorating Korean liberation from Japan, it was Seoul's turn to be furious. Mun was a resident of Japan, had used a Japanese police pistol, and had entered Korea on a Japanese passport obtained under false pretenses. Citing these facts, the South Korean president demanded an apology from Japan, punishment of all those in

Japan who were connected with the case, and disbandment of the pro–North Korean residents association, Chosen Soren. Japan balked at such strong measures, and to make matters worse, the Japanese Foreign Ministry issued a statement refusing to accept any Japanese responsibility for the assassination attempt.

Park and others were outraged. The speaker of the ROK National Assembly, Chung Il Kwon, said Japan's reaction "shows how much they despise and look down on Koreans. . . . If [Chinese leader] Mao's wife had been killed by a Chinese raised in Japan, the Japanese prime minister would crawl on his hands and knees from Tsingtao to Beijing to apologize for Japan's responsibility, but they sneer at us because we're Korean." Because of Japanese mishandling and latent anti-Japanese sentiments, South Korea seemed more furious about the involvement of Japan than about that of the North Koreans who hatched the assassination plot.

Park personally summoned the Japanese ambassador and threatened dire consequences if Japan did not cooperate. To emphasize his anger, Park refused to speak to the ambassador in Japanese—though, having been a lieutenant in the Japanese army, he knew the language perfectly—insisting that his foreign minister interpret his words instead. As added pressure, Park instigated and orchestrated daily anti-Japanese demonstrations in the capital, during one of which protesters chopped off their fingers in ritual sacrifice against Japan and marched on to storm the Japanese Embassy and smear its walls with blood. Most important, Park made serious preparations to break off diplomatic relations with Japan and nationalize all Japanese assets in Korea if satisfaction was not forthcoming.

At that moment, the United States was transfixed with its own domestic crisis. Just six days before the assassination attempt in Seoul, Richard Nixon resigned the presidency as a result of the Watergate scandal, and Gerald Ford became president. Although Asia experts in Washington were aghast at the dangerous breach between the two US allies, the orders to American diplomats were to stay out of the dispute.

Disregarding the instructions, Deputy Chief of Mission Richard Ericson, in charge of the embassy in Seoul after the departure of Philip Habib to be assistant secretary of state, placed his career on the line to work out a face-saving accommodation. In secret meetings with Japanese Embassy officials and ROK prime minister Kim Jong Pil, Ericson arranged a carefully phrased Japanese letter of regret, pledges of a limited crackdown on "criminal acts" of pro–North Korean elements in Japan, and a peacemaking visit to Seoul by a respected Japanese elder statesman.

The showdown with the mistrusted Japanese and the venting of national emotion over the killing of Park's wife temporarily unified the South Korean body politic behind Park. He took advantage of the changed political climate to repeal the most draconian of the emergency decrees, for the moment easing the confrontation with his domestic opponents.

The most profound impact of the shooting, however, was to remove the influence of the first lady, who had been highly popular among even those who feared or disliked her husband. Yook Young Soo (Korean women keep their maiden names after marriage) had been Park's second wife, or third if one counts a common-law liaison in the late 1940s. She had come from a prominent family and was graceful, physically attractive, and articulate—all the things he was not. She had been a check and balance for her husband, a sounding board and humanizing influence. Following her death, Park became even more isolated, withdrawn, and remote.

Ten weeks after his wife's death, Park wrote in the diary that he kept, "Already into the last week of October! The dying fall holds only loneliness. In the garden the chrysanthemums bloom, beautiful, peaceful, as they did a year ago, but the autumn leaves, falling one by one, only make me sad."

Mun Se Kwang was convicted of attacking the president and killing his wife and on December 20, 1974, was hanged in a Seoul prison.

THE UNDERGROUND WAR

In November, three months after the assassination attempt on Park, a South Korean army squad on routine patrol discovered steam rising from high grass in the southern part of the demilitarized zone, about two-thirds of a mile south of the military demarcation line that marks the border. Hoping to find a hot spring, a soldier poked his bayonet into the ground, which gave way to a widening hole, revealing the top of a reinforced tunnel about eighteen inches below the surface. As the soldiers probed further, they were interrupted by automatic weapons fire from a North Korean guard post. They returned fire before breaking off the engagement, the first clash of arms between the two opposing armies in twenty months.

Further exploration revealed a sophisticated underground construction about four feet high and three feet wide, with walls of reinforced concrete, electric lines and lighting, areas for sleeping and weapons storage, and a narrow-gauge railway for excavating soil. The US Command calculated that about two thousand troops could be squeezed into the tunnel from its source, about two miles away in North Korea, to its planned exit south of the DMZ, and that additional troops could be put through at a rate of five to seven hundred men per hour. Suddenly, American and South Korean forces faced a threat of surprise attack behind their forward defense lines.

North Koreans are masters of tunneling, a practice they developed as protection against American air power during the Korean War. Late in

1970 and early in 1971, five attempts by North Korean forces to tunnel under the south fence of the DMZ had been detected. These were small tunnels, which military experts concluded had been dug by reconnaissance personnel in an effort to observe southern positions.

In November 1973, a sentry in the southern part of the DMZ heard a faint tapping beneath his feet in the early morning, as if someone were knocking softly at a door. Although listening devices and seismic instruments were brought in, efforts to pinpoint the source of the noise were unsuccessful.

An important break came in September 1974, when a North Korean Workers Party functionary from the city of Kaesong, just north of the DMZ, defected, bringing with him knowledge and diagrams of some tunnel locations beneath the southern lines. The defector, Kim Pu Song, said that extensive digging had been ordered from the highest echelons of the party in late 1972, not long after the North-South joint statement in which the two sides agreed "not to undertake armed provocations against one another, whether on a large or small scale."

According to the defector, the tunnel digging was highly organized, with North Korean army teams working in shifts around the clock, augmented by supervisors, engineers, technicians, and guards. The defector said that the wartime purpose of the tunnels was to infiltrate light infantry and special forces personnel into the South as part of a lightning attack; in peacetime the tunnels could facilitate infiltration of North Korean agents.

Based on Kim's information as well as its own estimates, the South Korean Command projected the existence of fifteen tunnels under the DMZ. Later the US Command increased the number of actual or suspected tunnel locations to twenty-two.

Even with the defector's information, it took the accident of the steam rising in tall grass to locate the precise location of the first tunnel. In February 1975, a second tunnel was pinpointed after extensive drilling and lowering a specially developed camera into a tiny borehole. At the time of its discovery, the tunnel ran three-fourths of a mile into the South Korean side of the DMZ. Aerial photography eventually identified its starting point at the base of a mountain more than a half mile into North Korean territory.

Tunnel number two, as it was called, was an extraordinary engineering feat, bigger and longer than the first one, constructed through solid granite more than fifty yards belowground using modern drilling machinery imported from abroad. Several months after it was found, I made my way down the steep-sloped intercept passage to inspect this impressive construction, accompanied by an American explosive ordnance team and South Korean troops. The floor and ceiling were uneven, but my six-foot frame was able to stand erect at most points along the two hundred yards where I was permitted to go. I could stretch both arms toward the sides of the chamber without touching them. The US Command estimated that the dark, dank chamber could accommodate about eight thousand troops and put through another ten thousand men per hour with light artillery and other supporting weapons. Its intended discharge point would have been well behind South Korean forward defense lines.

Outside the tunnel, I saw South Korean soldiers digging new lines of trenches and bunkers at the approaches to the DMZ to protect themselves against North Korean troops who might pour out of underground structures. Most surprising was that, despite the discovery of two tunnels, formal US and ROK protests, and much publicity, sounds of digging continued to be detected under the surface of the DMZ. All indications were that Kim Il Sung had authorized the digging, and nobody else could give an order to stop.

The US Command and the ROK military responded to the underground challenge with increasingly sophisticated and largely secret efforts to locate more tunnels. Eventually, a total of 245 standard and experimental seismic listening devices were placed along the DMZ to record underground activity at suspect sites. The Pentagon tried everything—even hiring psychics to find more tunnels. Without their help, eventually two more fully developed tunnels were discovered, in 1978 and 1990.

How much danger the tunnels posed to South Korea, once the first ones were detected, is questionable. US and ROK forces quickly adjusted their defense lines to take into account possible incursions from underground. There is no doubt, though, that the intercepted tunnels served Seoul and Washington as tangible evidence of North Korea's aggressive intentions. According to Nathanial Thayer, the CIA national intelligence officer for East Asia in the mid-1970s, "Anytime anyone wanted more money for CIA, I would go up to see [House Speaker] Tip O'Neill. The argument was, if [North Koreans] are not aggressive, why are they building these tunnels?" The money was always forthcoming.

CHALLENGE FROM THE NORTH

As the underground war suggests, the struggle for military supremacy did not stop or even slow because of the North-South contacts of 1971–1972; on the contrary, the fluidity and uncertainty that gave rise to the dialogue also gave rise to an intensified arms race on the divided peninsula. Instead of a turn toward peace, the two Koreas were competing to build and import more and deadlier weapons of war. A retrospective US military analysis of North Korea's development identified 1972–1977 as a time of "remarkable North Korean Army growth," surpassing any other period since the Korean War. In parallel fashion, it was also a period of remarkable growth in South Korean military power.

Divided against each other at the DMZ and backed by rival world powers, both Korean states had become heavily militarized following the mutual devastation of the 1950–1953 war. In May 1961, Major General Park Chung Hee seized power in Seoul at the head of a military group. Four months later, Kim Il Sung finally cemented his undisputed authority over rival factions at the Fourth Workers Party Congress, buttressed by his military comrades-in-arms from his years as a guerrilla fighter. The militarized ruling group in the North promulgated the slogan "Arms on the one hand and hammer and sickle on the other." Kim also formulated a policy known as the Four Great Military Lines: to arm the entire populace, to fortify the entire country, to train each soldier to become cadre, and to modernize military weapons and equipment.

Tracking North Korean military activity is immensely difficult for any outsider, as virtually all aspects have been and remain closely guarded secrets in Pyongyang. North Korea has never published realistic information on its military forces, procurement, or operations. Fiercely independent and worried about the intentions of its communist allies, North Korea shared remarkably little information even with Moscow and Beijing after the 1950s. A retired Chinese officer who served twelve years as a Chinese military attaché in Pyongyang told me that North Korean officials would not disclose even to their close allies the size or organizational structure of their army. On infrequent visits to North Korea units in the field, he said, "we were just like sightseers" and were given no detailed information.

For all these reasons, former CIA director Robert Gates described North Korea as "without parallel the toughest intelligence target in the world." Donald Gregg, a career intelligence officer who served as CIA station chief in South Korea in the early 1970s and as US ambassador to Seoul in 1989–1993, said, "North Korea is the longest-running intelligence failure in the world."

Aside from the rare defector with operational details, the best source of information about the North Korean military has been aerial photographs and electronic intercepts provided by US reconnaissance satellites. However, in these expensive operations, Korea only intermittently had a high priority. As US forces withdrew from Vietnam in 1972 and détente seemed to be breaking out between Seoul and Pyongyang, the Joint Chiefs of Staff (JCS) reduced American military intelligence resources devoted to the Korean peninsula by more than 50 percent. Given all this, estimates of North Korea's military buildup at the time—and especially of the motivations behind it—must be treated with caution.

What is clear from a variety of sources is that in the 1970s, Pyongyang was very active militarily. In May 1972, Kim Il Sung himself told Harrison Salisbury and John Lee of the *New York Times* that due to the hostile attitude of the United States, "we frankly tell you, we are always making preparations for war. We do not conceal this matter." In the early 1970s, as it sought to restore relations with Pyongyang, Beijing renewed military assistance to North Korea even as China moved toward rapprochement with the United States. Military supplies from the Soviet Union were still at a high level, although beginning a slow decline, as Pyongyang found it harder to pay and as US-Soviet détente flourished. In addition to the supplies from its allies, the North by the end of the decade was producing large quantities of its own field artillery pieces, rocket launchers, armored personnel carriers, main battle tanks, and surface-to-air missiles.

By 1974, according to the US Command's intelligence estimate at that time, the North Korean army had grown to 408,000 troops, the fourth largest among the world's communist armies, and was "an efficient, well trained, highly disciplined force which is undergoing continual modernization." Of its twenty-three infantry divisions, fourteen were lined up from east to west, close to the DMZ. Moreover, North Korea was developing a formidable air force of Chinese and Soviet bombers and fighters and a small but highly versatile navy.

In mid-1973, concerned by the buildup in the North, the US Army assigned to Korea one of its ablest and most flamboyant combat leaders, Lieutenant General James F. Hollingsworth, who had extensive battle experience in World War II and Vietnam. Given command of the ROK–US I Corps forces charged with defense of Seoul, Hollingsworth was visited at his new command post one night by a worried President Park, who asked, "Are you going to do the same thing here you did in Vietnam?" Hollingsworth's response: "I'm here to fight and die to save your country. That's what I'm going to do."

The existing war plan was an essentially defensive document calling for American and South Korean forces, in case of attack, to pull back in phases to the Han River, which bisects the capital city. But in 1974 Hollingsworth, telling his ROK subordinate commanders, "I'm going to turn you into an offensive army," began moving the bulk of his artillery as far forward as possible, near the southern edge of the DMZ, where it was in position to strike well into North Korean territory. Two brigades of the US Second Division were targeted to seize Kaesong, the most important city in the southern part of North Korea, in case of attack from the North. Hollingsworth's forward-defense concept envisioned a massive use of US and ROK firepower, including around-the-clock B-52 strikes, to stop a North Korean advance north of Seoul and deliver a powerful offensive punch to win the war within nine days.

Donald Gregg, CIA station chief in Seoul at the time, recalls Hollingsworth standing on the southern shore of the Imjin River, just a mile south of the DMZ, and declaring with bravado, "We'll kill every son of a bitch north of the forward edge of the battle area, and we won't retreat one inch." Privately, said Gregg, Hollingsworth wasn't sure he had enough firepower to do the job, but his offense-minded battle plan helped to calm the jittery South Koreans, as it was intended to do. Park, an enthusiastic supporter, supplied millions of dollars in construction funds for new roads, ammunition bunkers, and other facilities near the DMZ.

North Korea did not have to learn about Hollingsworth's new strategy from spies. In a press conference widely reported in Seoul, the colorful general announced his "violent, short war concept" before the plan had the approval of the Joint Chiefs of Staff or other military elements in Washington. There were unpublicized objections from the staff of the White House National Security Council on the grounds that the nine-day war plan involved "almost immediate U.S. air interdiction, and possible use of nuclear weapons," for which there was no prior authorization. Hollingsworth got away with it because of the strong backing of the South Koreans and Secretary of Defense James Schlesinger.

North Korea responded in kind to the augmentation and repositioning of US and ROK forces and Hollingsworth's aggressive plans to use them in case of war. Just as the growth spurt in North Korean forces stimulated the United States and South Korea to increased efforts, so the changes in firepower and strategy south of the DMZ helped stimulate large increases in North Korean forces and their repositioning closer to the dividing line with the South. With the failure of the initial efforts at productive North-South dialogue, the arms race could not be restrained by the two regimes themselves, nor did the outside powers have sufficient will or consensus to call a halt. The buildups, therefore, continued strongly.

The crucial military question in the mid-1970s was whether North Korea's allies in Beijing and Moscow would give military backing to a new attempt to unite the peninsula by force. The US Command's 1974 intelligence estimate pointed out that although Pyongyang was "capable of initiating offensive action," it was unlikely to do so in the short run without Chinese and Soviet assistance. In the view of the US Command, "these countries would not likely support adventurism on the part of NK's leader, Kim Il Sung. They probably would, however, assist NK against any invasion mounted by the ROK."

These assumptions were tested in the spring of 1975 as the massive US effort in Indochina was collapsing in the face of communist guns. On April 18, the day after the Chinese-backed Khmer Rouge took over the Cambodian capital and as the final battle for Saigon was getting under way, Kim Il Sung was received in Beijing with elaborate ceremony at the start of an eight-day state visit. Speaking at a welcoming banquet, the North Korean leader celebrated the communist victories in Indochina and forecast the collapse of the US-backed regime in Seoul and the worldwide victory of Marxism-Leninism.

"If revolution takes place in South Korea we, as one and the same nation, will not just look at it with folded arms but will strongly support the South Korean people," Kim declared. Then, in a takeoff on Karl Marx's famous dictum that in revolution, the working class has nothing to lose but its chains, Kim added, "If the enemy ignites war recklessly, we shall resolutely answer it with war and completely destroy the aggressors. In this war we will only lose the Military Demarcation Line and will gain the country's unification."

Untangling what Kim said from what he meant and what he expected in terms of support from the Chinese is still not at all clear. Kim arrived in Beijing just as China's leader, Mao Tse-tung, was about to begin an internal political struggle with a group who opposed the newly rehabilitated Deng Xiaoping. For this, among other reasons, Mao would not have been interested in the situation flaring up in Korea, and Kim would almost certainly have been astute enough to realize that this was not a good time to expect support. Moreover, North Korean officials reportedly told East European diplomats around that time that Pyongyang was not happy with Vietnam's victory because it meant the US military would be free to shift its focus and resources back to Korea.

By contrast, another view is that Kim took heart from events in Vietnam and sought to capitalize on the moment to press his own priorities but was rebuffed by Beijing. According to a Chinese source with intimate knowledge of Korean affairs, Kim told Chinese leaders it would be "no problem" to liberate South Korea, but Premier Zhou Enlai and his colleagues opposed any such idea. Without addressing Kim's ideas specifically, according to this source, Chinese leaders stressed the need for stability on the Korean peninsula, and "Kim was clever enough to understand" without having to lose face. About the same time, according to a former Soviet diplomat who was working on Korean issues at the time, Moscow made it explicitly clear to Kim that "we only support peaceful means for solution of the [South Korean] problem." Significantly, Kim did not stop in Moscow during an extensive trip to Eastern Europe and North Africa immediately following his Beijing visit. In a sign of discord between Kim and his senior communist sponsor, the North Korean leader even flew many hundreds of miles out of his way to avoid passing through Soviet airspace.[*]

---

[*] On this point, as with the other aspects of Kim's travels in the spring of 1975, the evidence is contradictory. According to a Hungarian Embassy cable to Budapest in July 1975, Kim had wanted to visit Moscow after his trip to Beijing, but "the date he proposed did not suit the Soviet leaders." Of course, the explanation that the dates were inconvenient might simply have been Moscow's way of telling Kim not to come. "North Korea's Efforts to Acquire Nuclear Technology and Nuclear Weapons: Evidence from Russian and Hungarian Archives," Wilson Center Working Paper 53, Document no. 26, 52.

ECHOES OF SAIGON

Even more than flirtation with China, Park was shocked and alarmed by
the US failure in Vietnam. The prospects and plight of South Vietnam,
the US-backed anticommunist half of another divided country, bore an
uncomfortable resemblance to the situation in South Korea. At the American behest, Park's government sent two divisions of Korean troops to fight
in Vietnam, and they had remained until 1973, when the slow withdrawal
of American forces was nearly complete. Although Korea was well paid for
its efforts through procurement and construction contracts, to the point
that revenues from the Vietnam War made up as much as 40 percent of its
foreign exchange earnings, Park considered his troop commitment to be
a self-sacrificing contribution to the anticommunist cause and a payback
to Washington for saving the South in the Korean War. In Park's view,
the American pullout from Vietnam and especially the betrayal of South
Vietnam in the Paris negotiations with communist North Vietnam raised
agonizing doubts about the reliability of the United States.

As South Vietnam was collapsing that April, Ambassador Richard
Sneider in Seoul appealed to Washington for an urgent review of American policies in view of "declining ROK confidence in [the] U.S. commitment," accompanied by a "risk of North Korean provocation to test both
U.S. intentions and ROK capabilities." Sneider, a cerebral State Department officer who had studied communist political operations during the
Korean War, wrote in a secret cable that "Korea is not repeat not yet in
a crisis era" but that this could come. To head it off, he recommended a
long list of potential confidence-building measures, ranging from more
weapons and economic support for the Seoul government to contingency
planning for special US air and naval deployments to Korea in case of a
serious threat of a North Korean attack.

The broader and longer-term problem, Sneider wrote, was the need
for a fundamental shift in the US relationship with a Korea that, "while
still dependent on us, is no longer [a] client state." Sneider recommended
immediate initiation of a major review of Korea policy in Washington.

Two months later, in June 1975, Sneider fired off a more extensive
rendition of his views to a US capital that was still preoccupied with the
aftermath of the failure in Vietnam. Sneider wrote in a remarkable twelve-
page cable:

> Our present policy toward Korea is ill-defined and based on an
> outdated view of Korea as a client state. It does not provide a
> long-term conceptual approach to Korea, geared to its prospec-
> tive middle power status. It leaves the ROKG [ROK government]
> uncertain what to expect from us and forces us to react to ROKG

on an ad hoc basis. We have not for example made clear to the Koreans what the prospects are for a continued, long-term U.S. military presence. Nor have we clarified what the ROKG can expect from us in the way of military technology, although we discourage President Park's efforts to develop his own sophisticated weapons. These uncertainties lead President Park into preparations for what he sees as our eventual withdrawal, preparations which include internal repression and plans for the development of nuclear weapons. They also induce optimism on the part of North Korea about our withdrawal and doubts in Japan about our credibility and about the future of Korea.

Sneider saw two main alternatives to the existing policy: disengagement or the establishment of a new basis for durable partnership.

Back in Washington, now assistant secretary for East Asian and Pacific Affairs, Philip Habib was on the receiving end of Sneider's cables. Habib had observed at the time of Park's martial-law takeover in October 1972 that the process of US disengagement from Korea had "already begun" and "should be accelerated." However, in the wake of the debacle in Vietnam, Sneider made the case that "disengagement, whether gradual or otherwise, is now far too risky as long as the North Korean posture remains militant; it would escalate the possibility of conflict and risks a breakdown of Japanese confidence in our treaty commitment." Perhaps as a gesture to Habib's views, Sneider added, "Under different circumstances, a gradual disengagement could be worth serious consideration."

Sneider called his preferred alternative "durable partnership" with long-term guarantees for Korea, along the lines of the NATO and Japanese partnerships. He wrote, "The longer we stave off the inevitable decision as to whether our relationship, including our military presence, is temporary or durable, the more President Park and Kim Il Sung will pursue their premises that it is in fact temporary, adding further to the instability on the Korean peninsula."

As he saw it, an improved relationship would involve such things as greater Washington-Seoul consultation, a transition from economic aid to private investment (which was already happening), and a higher priority for Korea on the US negotiating agenda with China and the Soviet Union. However, the most important element he recommended was "a significant U.S. force presence with indefinite tenure . . . publicly projected with major reductions linked to changes in the security situation in Northeast Asia and arrangements between North and South reducing tensions on the Korean peninsula."

In the aftermath of Vietnam, Washington was wary of open-ended commitments. President Gerald Ford had told Park during a brief visit to Seoul in November 1974 that "we have no intention of withdrawing U.S. personnel from Korea." However, this statement was interpreted by Ford's National Security Council staff as applying only to total, not to partial, withdrawals. Responding to the South Korean fears of a US pull-out during a visit to Seoul in August 1975, Secretary of Defense James Schlesinger privately reassured Park that he foresaw "no basic changes over the next five years" in the level of US forces. But when this comment got back to the White House via a memorandum of the conversation, a National Security Council staff aide objected that Schlesinger had gone beyond administration policy.

In any case, it was obvious that Ford would face serious Democratic opposition the following year, which could change the situation. Schlesinger told Park that "he expects President Ford to be reelected, but if not the Democrats are not likely to eliminate U.S. support for South Korea." Schlesinger may not have known or cared that Democrat Jimmy Carter, then considered a long-shot contender for his party's presidential nomination, was already advocating the complete withdrawal of American ground troops from Korea.

With the election looming, no new American relationship along the lines of Sneider's recommendation was instituted. Despite US attempts at reassurance, Park continued to feel a deep sense of vulnerability. In mid-1975 he put three laws through the National Assembly to set the nation on a wartime footing: a tightened public security law, coming on top of the issuance of Emergency Decree Nine, which in effect banned all political criticism of the government; a civil defense law creating a paramilitary corps of all males between the ages of seventeen and fifty; and a broad new defense tax.

The government doubled defense expenditures in the 1976 budget and continued to increase them sharply for the next three years. In 1979 they doubled again, bringing them to four times the expenditure level of 1975. Although the South was devoting a far smaller percentage of its economic output to the military than the North, in absolute terms ROK military spending began outpacing that of the North in the mid-1970s, according to estimates of the International Institute of Strategic Studies. Although military spending on both sides was rising, the South's by the end of the decade was more than double that of the North's.

Following the fall of Saigon, Park gave high priority to his Heavy and Chemical Industries Promotion Plan, which had been initiated earlier to provide the sinews of enhanced military power. Between 1975 and 1980, more than 75 percent of all manufacturing investment in South Korea was committed to this industrial base. With these resources, Park created a mechanized army division and five special forces brigades for mobile warfare, doubled the size of his navy, and modernized his air force with faster, deadlier US jets and missiles.

North Korea could not keep up with the South's rapidly rising military expenditures or its increasing lead in military technology. On the other hand, North Korea continued to increase the numbers of its troops and to move more forces closer to the DMZ and therefore closer to Seoul, the fast-growing South Korean capital only thirty miles south of the dividing line. Increasingly, parts of Seoul were within range of North Korean heavy artillery and rockets. The upshot of all this was to heighten the military tension on the divided peninsula.

THE SOUTH KOREAN NUCLEAR WEAPONS PROGRAM

Park's ultimate effort to secure the country's future was to launch a secret and serious effort to develop a South Korean nuclear bomb. According to Oh Won Chol, a senior adviser to Park on nuclear and military production programs, Park created an Agency for Defense Development, which included a clandestine Weapons Exploitation Committee, answerable only to the Blue House, after faster and better-armed North Korean speedboats overwhelmed a South Korean patrol boat in June 1970 and forced it to the North. Only weeks later, Park was shocked by the decision of the Nixon administration to withdraw the US Seventh Division from Korea, despite his vehement protests. Park believed that the South Korean army was simply incapable of defending the country by itself with its outmoded arms and equipment, according to Oh. His nuclear adviser said that Park had not decided actually to produce a South Korean bomb, but that he was determined to acquire the technology and capability to do so on a few months' notice, as he and many others believed the Japanese could do. "Park wished to have the [nuclear] card to deal with other governments," Oh told me in 1996. In this field, the capability to produce nuclear weapons is almost as potent as possession of the bomb itself.

A major element in Park's effort was to acquire a reprocessing facility to extract plutonium from the irradiated uranium fuel produced in civilian power plants. Although most of South Korea's ambitious civil nuclear power program was based on American equipment and technology, Park steered clear of Washington in seeking reprocessing equipment and technology, and in 1972 he began working with France in this high-priority effort. By 1974 the Korean-French collaboration produced the technical design of a plant to manufacture about twenty kilograms of plutonium per year, enough for two nuclear weapons with the explosive power of the atomic bomb that the United States dropped on Hiroshima.

Work on an independent South Korean nuclear program and the rest of Park's defense development was centered in Taeduk, a science center south of Seoul. In 1973 South Korea began a quiet drive to recruit ethnic Korean nuclear, chemical, and engineering specialists from the United States and Canada. It also began shopping abroad for exotic materials and equipment useful for nuclear weapons.

India's nuclear test in 1974, the first by a developing nonaligned country, jolted the world awake to the dangers of the spread of nuclear weapons. Suddenly, nuclear proliferation became a high-priority concern in Washington. US intelligence officials began giving renewed scrutiny to import data on sensitive materials, and "when they got to Korea, everything snapped into place," an American analyst recalled years later. Based on these telltale hints, according to Paul Cleveland, who was a political counselor of the US Embassy in Seoul, "people were sent to work, and in a relatively short period of time developed absolute confirmation from clandestine sources" that South Korea was secretly embarked on a program to build the bomb.

In November 1974, the embassy sent to Washington a highly classified intelligence assessment that South Korea "is proceeding with initial phases of a nuclear weapons development program." This kicked off an interagency intelligence study in Washington that concluded that the ROK could develop a limited nuclear weapon and delivery capability within ten years, but that its efforts to build a bomb would become known well before that time, with significant political impact on neighboring countries. A secret cable to the embassy in Seoul from Secretary of State Henry Kissinger, with the concurrence of the Ford White House, emphasized the gravity of the issue:

> In the case of Korea our general [proliferation] concerns are intensified by its strategic location and by the impact which any Korean effort to establish nuclear capability would have on its neighbors, particularly North Korea and Japan. ROK possession of nuclear weapons would have major destabilizing effect in an area which not only Japan but USSR [Soviet Union], PRC [People's Republic of China] and ourselves are directly involved. It could lead to Soviet or Chinese assurances of nuclear weapons support to North Korea in event of conflict. . . . This impact will be complicated by fact that ROK nuclear weapon effort has been in part reflection of lessened ROKG confidence in U.S. security commitment, and consequent desire on Park's part to reduce his military dependence on U.S.

American policy as set forth in the secret instructions was "to discourage ROK effort in this area and to inhibit to the fullest possible extent any ROK development of a nuclear explosive capability or delivery system."

The administration decided on a multifaceted approach, using both direct US pressure and the development of common policies with other nuclear supplier nations to inhibit South Korean access to nuclear weapons technology. The tough issue was how to accomplish this without a serious rift in the US-ROK alliance, especially at a time when Korean confidence in the United States was plummeting due to the developments in Vietnam.

Initially, the emphasis was on persuading France to revoke its offers of nuclear cooperation. US ambassador Sneider cautioned the French ambassador in Seoul, Pierre Landy, that "the United States has no doubts that the Koreans have in mind putting to ulterior military ends what they can make use of such as plutonium." The French refused to give up potential sales to Seoul, saying they would cancel their plans only if the Koreans asked them to do so.

South Korean officials denied they were embarked on a nuclear weapons program. Many of those who denied it probably didn't know the carefully hidden truth. "We have the capability," Park told columnist Robert Novak in early June 1975, but he denied that his government was using it. He added, in a plea for continuing US support, "If the U.S. nuclear umbrella were to be removed, we have to start developing our nuclear capability to save ourselves."

US officials decided at the outset not to reveal to South Korea their certain knowledge of its clandestine program, but instead centered their attack on its openly acknowledged plans to import a reprocessing plant. In July 1975, Ambassador Sneider was authorized to begin taking the American objections about reprocessing directly to ROK officials. A National Security Council memorandum recognized that the campaign to persuade Seoul to forgo the planned reprocessing plant would approach the limit of what the South Korean government would accept from the United States. In order not to confront Park and to allow him to save face, Sneider took the case against the reprocessing plant methodically up the chain of command, first to the minister of science and technology, then to the foreign minister, and eventually to the secretary general of the Blue House. The US ambassador never made direct allegations that Seoul was embarked on a weapons program, recalled Cleveland, who accompanied him on the visits, but emphasized "how important it was that Korea not buy this because of the appearances of things and the kinds of suggestions this would make back in the United States and the difficulties that it would cause."

Sneider's efforts were closely coordinated with those in Washington. On his morale-boosting visit to South Korea in August 1975, Secretary of Defense Schlesinger personally told Park that a South Korean nuclear weapons program was the one thing that could endanger US-ROK relations. In what he later called "an elliptical conversation," Schlesinger did not refer to the US intelligence findings, and Park did not admit to a secret weapons program. The US defense secretary got the feeling, though, that "he knew that I knew."

In Washington that fall and winter, Assistant Secretary of State Philip Habib held increasingly intense conversations with South Korean ambassador Hahm Pyong Choon. By this time, the French contract had been signed; Habib demanded the Koreans cancel it. Through his ambassador, Park refused, declaring that this could not be done "as a matter of honor."

Washington concocted a number of incentives in return for cancellation of the French plant, including guaranteed access to reprocessing under US auspices when it was needed by the ROK civilian nuclear industry and access to additional American technology under a formal science and technology agreement. On the disincentive side, the administration, with congressional help, threatened to block Export-Import Bank financing of the next steps in Seoul's ambitious civil nuclear power program if the proliferation concerns were not resolved. Finally, both Sneider and Habib were authorized to employ the heaviest threat ever wielded by the United States against South Korea: that the entire US security relationship would be put in doubt if Seoul went through with the plan.

At the height of the campaign in December 1975, Sneider pointedly informed a senior ROK official that the "real consideration" for Koreans was "whether Korea [is] prepared [to] jeopardize availability of best technology and largest financing capacity which only U.S. could offer, as well as vital partnership with U.S., not only in nuclear and scientific areas but in broad political and security areas." In deciding what to do, said Sneider, the ROK government "had to weigh the advantages of this kind of support and cooperation which USG [US government] could provide against the French option." According to an ROK participant, Donald Rumsfeld, who succeeded Schlesinger as secretary of defense, bluntly told his ROK counterpart in May 1976 that the United States "will review the entire spectrum of its relations with the ROK," including security and economic arrangements, if Seoul insisted on developing nuclear weapons.

Faced with such adamant US opposition—all done in secret—Park reluctantly canceled the contract. The episode demonstrated that when the United States was determined—and when it believed its security interests on the peninsula were at stake—it retained the clout in the mid-1970s to overwhelm even the most determined intentions of the Seoul government.

In the aftermath, Sneider worried that this was not the end of the affair. What concerned him most about Korea's future, he told National Security Adviser Brent Scowcroft in a White House meeting, was "Park's emotionally charged drive to seek self-sufficiency and self-reliance through a program of nuclear weapons and missile development." He recommended that after a decent interval, the United States begin confronting Park anew on the issue, lest the program be revived, resulting in the temptation for North Korea "to go the same route." Sneider observed that "Park was guilty of sloppy thinking in believing he could somehow obtain greater security by these policies; yet, given U.S. attitudes, one had to admit that South Koreans had some reason for their concern over their future security."

Although Park was forced to give up the French reprocessing plant and later to forgo purchasing a new Canadian heavy-water reactor, the program refused to die. Rather than disband his clandestine nuclear team, Park gave it a new organizational parent, the Korean Nuclear Fuels Development Corporation, and a new objective, the manufacture of nuclear fuel rods for the country's reactors. In 1978 South Korea once again began discussions with France about reprocessing facilities. Again Washington blocked the deal, this time with the personal intervention of President Carter with French prime minister Valéry Giscard d'Estaing.

Nonetheless, Son U Ryun, one of Park's former press secretaries, later wrote that during a walk on a beach in January 1979, the president confided that "we can complete development of a nuclear bomb by the first half of 1981." When this happens, Park went on, "Kim Il Sung won't be able to dare to invade the south." Son claimed Park said he planned to show the bomb to the world in the Armed Forces Day parade in 1981 and then announce his resignation as president. Son's account is widely disputed by former officials who were close to Park. However, it is consistent with the testimony of Kang Chang Sung, chief of the powerful Defense Security Command under Park. Kang said Park told him personally in September 1978 that 95 percent of the nuclear weapons development had been completed by the Agency for Defense Development and that atomic bombs would be produced by South Korea in the first half of 1981.

MURDER IN THE DEMILITARIZED ZONE

On the morning of August 18, 1976, five South Korean workmen, accompanied by a ten-man American and South Korean security detail, gathered around a prominent poplar tree near the western edge of the Joint Security Area at Panmunjom. The JSA, roughly circular and about eight hundred yards in diameter, was for decades the only part of the demilitarized zone without fortifications, barbed-wire fences, and land mines marking the division between the North and South. On that day, tension was unusually high due to recent frequent threats, obscenities, and shoving matches.

The purpose of the work detail on that steamy August day was to trim a forty-foot tree that, in its summer foliage, obstructed the view between two guard posts manned by US and ROK forces within the Joint Security Area. As the work got under way, two North Korean officers and nine

enlisted men appeared and asked what was going on. After first seeming to approve, the Korean People's Army (KPA) commander, Lieutenant
Pak Chul, a combative eight-year veteran of the JSA, demanded that the
trimming stop, warning that "if you cut more branches, there will be a big
problem." The senior American officer, Captain Arthur Bonifas, a West
Point graduate who was within three days of ending his one-year tour in
Korea, ignored the protest. Lieutenant Pak then sent for reinforcements,
who arrived by truck carrying metal pipes and ax handles, raising the KPA
total on the scene to about thirty men. They surrounded the tree trimmers.
The North Korean officer again demanded that the work stop, saying to
the South Korean officer who served as the interpreter, "The branches that
are cut will be of no use, just as you will be after you die." Captain Bonifas
told the interpreter that he believed the North Koreans were bluffing. He
ordered the work to proceed.

Bonifas turned away from the North Korean officers, and Pak removed
his watch, wrapped it in a handkerchief, and put it in his pocket. The other
KPA officer rolled up his sleeves. Pak then shouted, *"Chookyo!"* (Kill!), and
smashed Bonifas from behind with a karate chop, knocking him to the
ground. This signaled a general KPA attack. Bonifas was beaten to death
by five or six North Koreans wielding clubs and with the blunt edge of an
ax. Lieutenant Mark Barrett, the other American officer present, was also
knocked down and beaten to death. The South Korean interpreter was
injured, along with four of the US and ROK enlisted men. A US Quick
Reaction Force, stationed nearby as a precaution, arrived after the fight
had ended and the North Koreans had regrouped on their side of the lines.

The deaths of the two American officers were the first fatalities in the
Joint Security Area since it had been established at the end of the Korean
War. Within days the killings would result in the gravest threat of all-
out war from the 1953 armistice to the nuclear crisis of the 1990s. As in
the nuclear crisis, Kim Il Sung showed his pragmatic side at the crucial
moment, narrowly averting a widening clash. But the fact that the United
States and North Korea were the principal actors left the leadership of
South Korea on the sidelines and far from satisfied with the outcome.

When news of the fatal skirmish reached Washington, President Ford
was at the Republican National Convention in Kansas City, where he was
competing for his party's presidential nomination against Ronald Reagan, who accused him of being too conciliatory to communists. In Ford's
absence, Secretary of State Henry Kissinger chaired the meeting of the
Washington Special Actions Group (WASAG), the top-level crisis committee of the Ford administration, in the secure basement-level White
House Situation Room.

A CIA briefer, making the initial presentation, noted there was no
indication of North Korean troop movements or other preparations for a

general attack. But he also expressed the view that the killings were not spontaneous. The agency submitted a written report, saying, "We are virtually certain that this incident was a deliberate provocation. We believe it was intended to support North Korea's diplomatic offensive against the US and South Korea . . . and also to arouse US public opinion about the American troop presence in Korea during the presidential election campaign."

The chief of naval operations, Admiral James L. Holloway, representing the uniformed Joint Chiefs of Staff, said that given "a military stand-off" on the peninsula, a North Korean attack could be successful only if it was a surprise, and because the killings had put everyone on alert, "we therefore do not believe that the North had a major attack in mind."

As in many such emergencies, the policy makers had only a dim idea about how the clash had arisen. Neither the CIA nor other agencies at the table seemed to know that this was not the first encounter over the poplar tree, until a cable was handed to Kissinger while the meeting was already under way. It revealed that twelve days earlier, a South Korean work party had approached the big poplar tree with saws and axes, intending to cut it down, but had withdrawn after a North Korean guard ordered them to leave it alone. This incident, however, had not been reported to military headquarters in Seoul. "They told us not to do it," commented William Hyland, the deputy national security adviser, when the cable was handed around the White House meeting.

The US policy makers did not discuss the broader background of sharply rising tension on the peninsula, which in retrospect was a crucial factor in the clash. Within a little more than a year, Secretary of Defense Schlesinger had threatened North Korea with nuclear attack in response to ROK concern following the fall of Saigon, nuclear-capable F-111 swing-wing fighter-bombers had landed in South Korea for military exercises amid great publicity, and the United States and South Korea had staged Team Spirit 76, the first of a long-running series of large-scale joint maneuvers. The parachute drops, amphibious landings, and other maneuvers provoked a near-hysterical reaction from the North, which saw Team Spirit as a dress rehearsal for an invasion from the South.

On August 5, the day before the initial tree-cutting incident, North Korea had issued a lengthy government statement charging that the United States and South Korea were stepping up plans to invade the North. Pyongyang claimed they "have now finished war preparations and are going over to the adventurous machination to directly ignite the fuse of war." The declaration was highly unusual, being only the third official government statement on a Korea peninsular issue since the armistice. Puzzled, several American intelligence analysts attempted to have a warning sent to US forces in Korea. However, this was not done.

For the policy makers in the White House meeting following the killings, the central topic was retaliation against North Korea. Kissinger, who had spoken with Ford by telephone, was in a brutal mood. "The important thing is that they beat two Americans to death and must pay the price," the secretary of state announced. One participant in the meeting came out of it quoting Kissinger as saying, "North Korean blood must be spilled."

According to the minutes of the meeting, the discussion was remarkably free from many of the restraints that complicated US policy making in other circumstances during the Cold War. There was no expression of concern about the potential for touching off a wider war, nor was there discussion of the likely reaction of China or the Soviet Union to American action. There was no discussion of the probable views of Japan or the ROK, or the repercussions for them. As for Pyongyang's reaction, Kissinger observed that "it will be useful for us to generate enough activity so that the North Koreans begin to wonder what those crazy American bastards are doing or are capable of doing in this election year."

Even before the meeting was convened, General Richard Stilwell, the US commander in Korea, had recommended one potential response: to return to the JSA and cut down "the damned tree," as it was referred to during nearly all the governmental deliberations. This quickly won approval of the WASAG, but Kissinger wanted to do much more. After some discussion, the group set in motion—and Ford subsequently ordered—the raising of the American (and South Korean) alert status to greater readiness for war, deployment of a squadron of F-4 fighters from Okinawa and F-111 fighter-bombers from Idaho to Korea, preparations for "exercise" flights of B-52 heavy bombers from Guam to make practice bombing runs close to North Korea, and preparations for redeploying the aircraft carrier USS *Midway* from Japan to the Korean straits.

While deciding on this massive show of American force in the area— and the felling of the tree—the WASAG meeting left undecided the punitive military action that Kissinger favored and that he told the meeting Ford wished to explore. During the meeting Admiral Holloway suggested US forces could lay mines or seize a North Korean ship. Another participant, according to Hyland, suggested that a nuclear weapon be exploded at sea near the North Korean coast as a warning. In discussion with Kissinger following the meeting, Hyland suggested an air strike in the eastern end of the DMZ, "where it would be unexpected and where it would not necessarily touch off something we couldn't handle." Kissinger seemed interested.

At Kissinger's request, the US military explored two other options for punitive American actions to be taken at the time of the tree cutting. One was to destroy the nearby Bridge of No Return, across which prisoners of war had moved at end of the Korean War, by artillery fire, demolition charges, or precision-guided missiles. The other option was an artillery attack against the DMZ barracks of the North Korean border guards. Both were strongly opposed by the Joint Chiefs of Staff as putting UN and ROK forces at the DMZ at great risk.

The JCS, however, told Kissinger it was exploring other punitive options to use "precision guided air munitions, surface-to-surface missiles, and unconventional warfare (SEAL) teams to destroy North Korean installations of military or infrastructure significance" after the tree felling was complete. "Henry thought we were being wimpish" by simply cutting down the tree, recalled National Security Adviser Scowcroft, who was with Ford in Kansas City but in constant touch with Kissinger. After a second WASAG meeting to discuss US responses, Deputy Secretary of Defense William Clements and Admiral Holloway called at the White House to see Hyland, who recalled them "wringing their hands that we may be headed into another Korean War" by taking strong action. In a sentiment characteristic of many near the top of the government, they told Hyland, "These [North] Koreans are wild people."

In the end, Ford decided against any military reprisals because of their potential for escalation into a general war on the Korean peninsula. He explained later, "In the case of Korea to gamble with an overkill might broaden very quickly into a full military conflict, but responding with an appropriate amount of force would be effective in demonstrating U.S. resolve."

While the United States was pondering its course, the rival Korean states were reacting in very different ways. In response to the upgrading of American and South Korean alert status, North Korean radio broke into regular programming to announce that the entire army and reserve force was being placed into "full combat readiness." A strict blackout was imposed in Pyongyang, and the populace was crowded into underground shelters as air raid sirens wailed. Front-line troops were prepared for battle. Senior North Korean officials were evacuated into previously prepared and fortified tunnels.

Immediately after the incident, North Korea publicly began describing the clash as a "melee," giving itself room to step back from a larger confrontation. Also, the North quickly agreed to a meeting of the Military Armistice Commission to discuss the clash. This suggested to Stilwell, he told the Pentagon privately, that the killings might well have been "a spontaneous, low-level overreaction" by North Korean guards. Interestingly, the GDR Embassy in Pyongyang had reached much the same conclusion.[*]

---

[*] In a long cable to Berlin at the end of August, the GDR Embassy in Pyongyang concluded that the clash was not calculated but an "over-reaction' by the DPRK personnel involved in the incident, whose background probably lies in fanatical feelings of hate." See http://digitalarchive.wilsoncenter .org/document/114291 (quotations in the original).

In Seoul President Park was privately furious at the killings, writing in his diary that "I cannot tolerate this barbaric act by crazy Kim Il Sung's gangs. . . . You stupid, cruel, violent gangs—you should know there is a limit to our patience. Mad dogs deserve clubs." In an initial meeting to discuss the military response, however, Park impressed General Stilwell as "calm, deliberate and positive throughout." Park advocated both "the strongest possible protest" to Pyongyang, including demands for an apology, reparations, and guarantees against repetition, all of which he admitted were not likely to be forthcoming, and "appropriate counteraction" by military force to teach North Korea a lesson, but without the use of firearms. Stilwell believed Park did not wish to break the long-standing ban on using firearms in the Joint Security Area.

To improve the balance of forces there without introducing heavy arms barred by agreement from the DMZ, Park offered—and Stilwell accepted—the services of ROK unarmed special forces troops with multiple black-belt honors in *tae kwon do* as reinforcements in case of trouble. (As it turned out, the "unarmed" ROK troops were carrying grenades and had M16 rifles, antitank weapons, grenade launchers, and light machine guns hidden as they moved into action. The Americans only found out by accident when they came upon the troops trashing an empty North Korean guardhouse on the way to the jumping-off point.) In a second meeting to go over Stilwell's plans, Park expressed a firm belief that the military response should be limited to removal of the poplar tree and that "escalation should only evolve if the North escalates." Otherwise, he added, "the matter drops."

At 7:00 A.M. August 21, three days after the killings, a convoy of twenty-three American and South Korean vehicles rolled into the JSA to begin what was named Operation Paul Bunyan. Aboard was a sixteen-member US engineering team with chain saws and axes, who immediately began working on the massive trunk of the poplar and also removing two unauthorized barriers the North had erected in the JSA. Accompanying the US team was a thirty-man security platoon armed with pistols and ax handles and sixty-four ROK special forces troops.

This little band, with its narrowly limited mission, was backed up by a mighty array of forces appropriate to the initiation of World War III. Hovering overhead was a US infantry company in twenty utility helicopters, accompanied by seven Cobra attack helicopters. Behind them on the horizon were the B-52 bombers, escorted by the US F-4 fighters and ROK F-5 fighters. Waiting on the runway at Osan Air Base, armed and fueled, were F-111 fighter-bombers. The *Midway* aircraft-carrier task force was stationed offshore. On the ground at the approaches to the DMZ waited heavily armed US and ROK infantry, armor, and artillery forces.

Stilwell's battle plan, approved by Washington, called for mortar and artillery fire to cover the withdrawal of the tree-cutting force in case KPA guards resisted the operation with small arms. Under a last-minute White House order, American artillery were to open fire on the North Korean guard barracks in the DMZ in case of armed resistance. In the event of a KPA ground attack, the backup forces were to assist the withdrawal of all UN elements from the JSA while hundreds of rounds of heavy artillery rained down on nearby North Korean targets. That would have been the opening round of a wider war.

Five minutes into the operation, North Korean officials of the Military Armistice Commission were formally notified that a UN work party would enter the JSA "in order to peacefully finish the work left unfinished" on August 18. If not molested, the notification said, the UN force would take no further action. Within a few minutes, five North Korean trucks and about 150 troops armed with automatic weapons gathered on the far end of the Bridge of No Return, looking across at the poplar. The troops watched in silence as the big tree was felled in forty-two minutes, three minutes fewer than Stilwell had estimated.

"We know it was very scary to the North Koreans, because we were listening," said an American official in Washington with access to North Korean front-line communications. A US intelligence analyst monitoring the radio net said that "it blew their fucking minds."

The North Korean leadership quickly recognized that the killings at the DMZ were a dangerous mistake and moved to reduce the danger. Kim Il Sung claimed later that the Americans had started the fighting to help Ford win the US presidential election but that the incident "no sooner happened than we realized that our soldiers had been taken in by the enemy's political scheme. So, we decided not to aggravate the incident any further."

Within an hour after the operation, the senior North Korean representative to the armistice commission requested a private meeting with the chief American representative, Rear Admiral Mark Frudden, to convey a message from Kim Il Sung. The personal message was Kim's first to the UN Command in the twenty-three-year history of the armistice. Kim declared it "regretful" that an incident had occurred in the JSA and proposed that "both sides should make efforts" to avoid future clashes. The State Department initially rejected the message as unacceptable because it did not forthrightly admit guilt, but then reversed itself after Habib and other Korea experts said that it was as close to an apology from Kim that anyone would get.

On August 25, in another surprise, North Korea proposed that to prevent future incidents, the Joint Security Area be divided at the military demarcation line, and that thenceforth KPA guards stay north of the line and UN guards should stay south. The UN Command had made similar proposals in the past, but North Korea had not agreed. This time the concept was approved and details worked out with a minimum of controversy.

In the aftermath, some in the South harshly criticized the United States for not taking stronger action. As his fears subsided in the face of the US buildup and North Korea's soft reaction, Park's belligerence toward North Korea seemed to grow. Questioned about Park's attitude at a White House meeting in mid-September, Sneider said that Park has "a parochial, Israeli complex stemming in part from the protection we have accorded to Korea for so long—Park tends to ignore or discount the costs we have to calculate in deciding how to react to North Korean provocations." The ambassador added, "Park may also have been influenced by his generals who were egging him on."

With different decisions in Washington on punitive actions or Kim Il Sung's statement of regret, the killings in the DMZ might have led to a wider conflict on the peninsula with unknown results. A different set of decisions by Kim or a subordinate commander—especially an attempt to contest Operation Paul Bunyan with force of arms—would almost certainly have led to a sharp escalation.

As it was, the assertions of US power and authority—secretly against South Korea's nuclear weapons program, and very openly against North Korea's barbaric actions in the Joint Security Area—demonstrated that despite its failure in Indochina, the United States continued to be a potent force on the Korean peninsula. Washington did not, however, heed Ambassador Sneider's call to establish a more durable partnership with the ROK. Instead, US policy in the period to come intensified the discord between Washington and Seoul.

4

THE CARTER CHILL

A MERICA'S REACTION AGAINST MILITARY commitments abroad in the wake of the Vietnam disaster found its voice in its first post-Vietnam president, Jimmy Carter. As early as January 1975, in the first days of his candidacy for president, Carter advocated the withdrawal of US troops from South Korea, which after the pullout from Vietnam were the only remaining US military deployment on the mainland of Asia and a trip wire that guaranteed immediate US involvement in case of a North Korean attack. After the little-known former governor of Georgia surprisingly won the nomination of his party and then the presidential election, he ordered that his idea be put into practice, despite the absence of serious consideration within the government and despite the opposition of South Korea, which was alarmed, and Japan, which was gravely concerned. He also made little effort to negotiate with China and the Soviet Union, the other major powers involved, or with North Korea, to facilitate the American withdrawal.

For two and a half years, as opposition mounted inside and outside his administration, Carter stubbornly fought to sustain his plan with the same dogged persistence he deployed in successfully pursuing the Camp David agreements on the Middle East and the Panama Canal Treaty. In the end, he was forced to give it up, even though in theory he had the power to order the troops home from Korea with the stroke of his pen as commander in chief.

Carter's ill-fated withdrawal effort is a case study in the hidden limitations on presidential power in the American system. It is also a study in unintended consequences, which in this case included the fatal weakening of a South Korean president and the inoculation of the US body politic for years to come against further attempts to withdraw forces from Korea.

Nobody, including Carter himself, seems to know precisely how and when he developed his unyielding determination that American forces should be withdrawn from Korea. "The origin of my position is not clear to me," the former president wrote me while I was preparing this book.

Zbigniew Brzezinski, Carter's White House national security adviser and his closest collaborator on the withdrawal plan, called its origin "a mystery not yet unraveled." Cyrus Vance and Harold Brown, who grappled with the proposal and its author as secretary of state and secretary of defense, respectively, were equally uninformed about the roots of Carter's resolve, as were many others I interviewed from the Carter campaign staff and administration. Apparently, nobody had the temerity to ask Carter at the time why he had concluded that US troops were no longer needed.

Even before his policy ran into trouble, Carter was reluctant to discuss its substance or consider alternatives; he knew what he wanted to do, and his mind was made up. During the transition between his election and his inauguration, he turned down an offer of a CIA briefing on Korea, and he rarely attended any of the National Security Council discussions of Korea in the course of his administration. In *Keeping Faith*, Carter's memoir of his presidency, he devoted much space to foreign affairs but never mentioned the Korean withdrawal issue.

CARTER'S WITHDRAWAL: ORIGINS AND IMPLEMENTATION

As it happened, I was among the earliest to learn firsthand of Carter's determination. In late-May 1975, Carter visited Tokyo while I was serving as the *Washington Post* correspondent for Northeast Asia, based in the Japanese capital. Over drinks with me and *New York Times* correspondent Richard Halloran and in a speech the following day, Carter said he favored withdrawing all US troops, both ground and air forces, from Korea over a period of perhaps five years. To accomplish this, he advocated a major buildup of South Korea's own air force. When Halloran observed that the ROK air force had deliberately been kept weak so that it would not be used to attack North Korea and start another war, Carter began having second thoughts. Within days he limited his withdrawal proposal to ground troops only, proposing to leave the US Air Force in place or even build it up.

My story on Carter's statements in Tokyo was reduced by *Post* editors from eight paragraphs to two sentences. This was typical of the short shrift that would be given his views on Korea during the campaign, during which it never became a high-profile issue.

In itself, the idea of reducing or even completely withdrawing US ground troops from Korea was hardly novel. In 1971 President Nixon had withdrawn the Seventh Infantry Division, which constituted roughly one-third of the sixty thousand US troops then in Korea, despite passionate opposition from the Seoul government. Later Nixon's secretary of defense from 1969 to 1972, Melvin R. Laird, signed off on a plan within the Pentagon to reduce the remaining US ground combat unit, the Second Infantry Division, to a single brigade, but implementation was blocked by Alexander Haig and Henry Kissinger, who feared the political effects in Asia after the American opening to China. By coincidence, the very day I met Carter in Tokyo, May 27, 1975, the Ford White House launched a secret study of American policy toward Korea, specifically including the question of reducing the American military presence. No decisions were reached.

In 1977 Carter's White House press secretary, Jody Powell, in seeking to explain the roots of the policy, told me that Carter had been familiar with the discussions in Washington surrounding Laird's withdrawal plan. Powell added that Carter's views arose from "his basic inclination to question the stationing of American troops overseas." Carter, in his 1994 letter to me, said, "Contrary to the opinion of many U.S. leaders, then and now, it was not a goal of mine just to deploy as many of our forces around the globe as host countries would accommodate."

While Carter was running for the presidency, the post-Vietnam aversion to military involvement abroad was at a high point. In the month that Saigon fell, April 1975, only 14 percent of Americans responding to a Louis Harris public opinion poll favored US involvement if North Korea attacked the South, while 65 percent said they would oppose it. This made a strong impression on Carter, who still recalled these results in his letter to me two decades later.

Two weeks before Inauguration Day, in the first informal meeting of the Carter administration's National Security Council team, policy toward Korea was one of fifteen items Carter selected for priority review and decision making. Presidential Review Memorandum/NSC 13 (PRM-13)—issued January 26, 1977, six days after the inauguration, and sent to the heads of key national security departments and agencies—ordered "a broad review of our policies toward the Korean peninsula," including "reductions in U.S. conventional force levels." Despite the neutral-sounding words, officials of the new administration were shocked to discover that the basic decision had already been cast in concrete. The new secretary of state, Cyrus Vance, returned from the White House with instructions that the review should not consider *whether* to withdraw American ground troops from Korea, but only *how*.

The "review" was hardly under way before Carter sent Vice President Walter Mondale to Tokyo, at the end of January, to inform the Japanese of his determination to withdraw American ground troops from Korea over a period of years. Publicly the Japanese were understanding, but privately they were deeply worried how a general American pullback might affect their own security. Deputy Assistant Secretary of Defense Morton Abramowitz, a career holdover from previous administrations who accompanied Mondale on the trip, argued it was a serious mistake to move so quickly and especially not to fly on to Seoul to inform South Korean leaders in person of the decision, which was bound to be deeply upsetting. Summing up his strong belief, Abramowitz, who later loyally defended in public the policy he opposed in private, told Mondale, "We *can't* withdraw." The new vice president retorted breezily, "Hey, Mort, there's been an election."

On February 15, Carter sent a letter to South Korean president Park Chung Hee affirming the US commitment to ROK security but broaching the issue of troop withdrawals and urging him to take steps to improve his human rights posture. The letter was presented to Park by Ambassador Richard Sneider and General John Vessey, the US military commander in Seoul. Vessey, who had met Carter in the White House a few days before, said no decision had been made about withdrawing troops. Moreover, Vessey said Carter asked him to convey that he "would make no changes in the troop deployments until after careful consultations with President Park." Park, citing many press stories about withdrawal plans, asked that quiet consultations begin very soon.

In early March, when ROK foreign minister Park Tong Chin came to Washington to begin the consultations, however, he found a US president whose mind was made up. In a handwritten memo to Brzezinski and Vance on March 5, shortly before meeting the Korean minister, Carter said bluntly that Park must understand:

A) American forces will be withdrawn. Air cover will be continued.
B) US-Korean relations as determined by Congress and American people are at an all time low ebb.
c) Present military aid support and my reticence on human rights issue will be temporary unless Park voluntarily adopts some open change re political prisoners.

Talking points for the meeting Brzezinski sent to Carter suggested that Carter justify his decision by saying, "In view of the expansion in South Korea's economy and military strength as well as the apparent desire of all the great powers to avoid war on the peninsula, our ground forces will be withdrawn." Minister Park, however, recalled that Carter's main justification was that "troop withdrawal is my campaign pledge." The meeting made it crystal clear that Carter was determined to go ahead with the withdrawal, though the president also said that the withdrawal would be gradual and that Washington would support the strengthening of South Korean defense capabilities to compensate for the American troop cutbacks.

Before he took office, Carter said he would seek guarantees of South Korea's security from China and the Soviet Union before making a decision to withdraw troops. In fact, he did not. As late as mid-June 1977, well after the withdrawal plan had been announced, the administration still had not provided even an authoritative briefing for the Chinese and Soviets on what the United States had in mind.

In July 1977, Vance wrote in a memorandum to Carter that a diplomatic initiative involving the two Koreas with possible Chinese participation was "the missing dimension in our troop withdrawal policy." Carter responded favorably, and the State Department was authorized to begin consultations initially with Seoul and then with Beijing on a possible four-power conference to seek a political settlement on the peninsula. Vance took up the proposal with Foreign Minister Huang Hua on a trip to Beijing in late August, but the Chinese were unenthusiastic. There the idea seems to have been dropped for nearly two years.

Carter had declared during the presidential campaign, "We've got 700 atomic weapons in Korea. I see no reason for a single one." (According to government documents, there were actually 683 warheads in South Korea at the time, remarkably close to Carter's statement.) His plan had been to order their removal as the first order of business. Secretary of Defense Harold Brown, a physicist and nuclear expert, spearheaded a successful drive to persuade Carter to consider the removal of nuclear weapons along with, rather than ahead of, withdrawal of US troops, lest sudden action in this sensitive area destabilize the situation on the Korean peninsula.

Carter's iron-willed resolve to move ahead posed a professional dilemma for many officials of his government, who believed in loyalty to presidential decisions yet who increasingly believed Carter's policy courted unnecessary and possibly unacceptable political and military risks. Unlike the classic Washington struggle of contending forces within the executive branch engaged in "a battle for the president's mind," this came to be "a battle against the president's mind." There were increasingly explicit private conversations among the conspirators, who might have been fired if their conniving had come to light. According to Richard Holbrooke, who was assistant secretary of state for East Asian and Pacific affairs and in the middle of the battle, it was "a full-scale rebellion against the president." Somehow, news correspondents covering the administration, including me, never grasped the full extent of the guerrilla war within the administration, or how high it reached.

Facing fundamental questions of loyalty and responsibility, Brown's guideline was to "obey direct orders, but otherwise try to turn the president around." The most difficult thing for Brown was defending a policy in public that he opposed in private. Vance, who resigned on principle in 1980 in opposition to the hostage-rescue mission in Iran, was able to maneuver within the limits of his conscience on the Korea withdrawal, keeping his misgivings to himself while vowing that he had to "find a way to change the president's mind." Brzezinski, who knew better than anyone else that Carter's view on the Korean issue was "strongly held, almost emotional," stuck with the president in high-level meetings until the bitter end, although he did nothing to stop the maneuvering of others to thwart Carter's idea.

On the military side, the politically appointed Joint Chiefs of Staff accepted the withdrawal policy on the condition that American support elements remain and that South Korea receive adequate compensation for the reduction in American strength. Officers in the field, however, did not disguise their opposition. Major General John Singlaub, chief of staff of the US Command in Korea, told *Washington Post* correspondent John Saar that "if U.S. ground troops are withdrawn on the schedule suggested, it will lead to war." Stung by what he considered military insubordination, Carter summoned Singlaub to the White House, reprimanded him, and summarily removed him from Korea, reassigning him to a domestic post. The episode created a political storm, deepening the controversy over the withdrawal plan.

The opposition's initial tactic was to seek to delay, modify, and water down the pullout plan so that the first withdrawals would be minor, leaving room for reflection and reversal. Carter, however, insisted on pushing ahead. In early May, he signed a top-secret order containing a clear timetable: one brigade of the Second Division (at least six thousand troops) to be withdrawn by the end of 1978 and a second brigade and its support elements (at least nine thousand troops) withdrawn by the end of June 1980. American nuclear weapons in Korea were to be reduced and eventually removed along with the troops. Undersecretary of State Philip Habib, formerly US ambassador to Korea, and General George Brown, chairman of the Joint Chiefs of Staff, were sent to brief the South Korean and Japanese governments.

In Seoul President Park had not taken the withdrawal idea seriously at first, telling Korean reporters in an off-the-record luncheon that "I don't think it's going to happen soon." When Carter announced his decision publicly, Park summoned his national security advisers to the Blue House. Doing his best to control his emotions, the ROK president surprised his aides by saying he would not openly oppose the proposed withdrawal but would ask for compensation to maintain the North-South military balance. Park's attitude arose from his searing personal experience in 1970, when he had passionately opposed withdrawal of the Seventh Division, only to have all his objections overridden by Vice President Spiro Agnew, who had been sent to deliver the news. Agnew had emphasized that a US president could assign his forces wherever and whenever he wished. In the face of this White House trump card, Park decided it would be unavailing and demeaning to mount a frontal attack on Carter's program.

Spurred on by doubts or outright opposition in the executive branch and the military, American domestic opponents of the withdrawal became more numerous and more vocal. To compensate for the withdrawal of American forces, Carter promised that $1.9 billion in military aid would be provided "in advance of or parallel to the withdrawals." This required congressional approval, but in July 1977, when Defense Secretary Brown briefed lawmakers at the White House, not a single senator or representative spoke up in support of the withdrawal, and many expressed their opposition. "It is clear that we face an uphill battle on this issue with Congress," Brzezinski reported to Carter.

Congressional support for South Korea had become a contentious topic independent of the troop-withdrawal issue. Human rights abuses, especially the arrest and conviction of eighteen prominent Christian leaders for issuing a manifesto complaining of the lack of freedom, provoked strong reactions from American churches and the public. In April 1976, shortly after the arrest of the Christian leaders, 119 senators and representatives had signed a letter to President Ford condemning "continuing suppression" in Korea and warning that ongoing US military support could make the United States "an accomplice to repression." Six months later, after conviction of the Christians, 154 members of Congress wrote Park Chung Hee to protest "disrespect for human rights," which they said was undermining American–South Korean relations. Carter, who sought to make human rights and morality central tenets of his foreign policy, found the Park regime's abuses particularly offensive.

Another intense controversy had erupted on October 24, 1976, when the *Washington Post* reported that a Korean agent, Park Tong Sun, had distributed $500,000 to $1 million a year to bribe as many as 90 members of Congress and other officials and that US eavesdropping devices had recorded the planning for the bribery scheme. The *Post* story was based on leaks from a secret grand-jury investigation initiated by the Justice Department. Coming on the heels of the Watergate scandal, which had driven President Nixon from office, the bribery saga quickly became known as Koreagate. Carter took a posture of full cooperation with congressional probes, writing in a confidential memo to his staff that "we should move without reticence to provide all possible informations re: violations of U.S. law."

By the end of 1977, Carter's first year in office, four full-scale congressional investigations of Korean activities were under way, and the Federal Bureau of Investigation (FBI) and Internal Revenue Service had launched additional investigations. Eventually, only one member of Congress, Representative Richard Hanna (D-CA), was convicted of being bribed. But with charges of bribery and an avalanche of investigations filling the news, nobody wanted to vote for compensatory aid for the South Korean military. "By the spring of 1978," noted Robert Rich, the State Department country director for Korea, "Congress probably could not have passed a bill stating that Korea was a peninsula in Northeast Asia."

The showdown on the withdrawal issue came on April 11, when Brzezinski met with the secretaries of state and defense and the administration's senior Asia experts. Brzezinski informed Carter in advance that based on his soundings, "everybody, even Vance, is against you" on the troop withdrawal. Carter pleaded with his subordinate, "Zbig, you've got to protect me. This is my last foreign policy proposal from the campaign I haven't walked away from."

Although most of the policy advisers privately had grave doubts about the US troop withdrawal, none was so bold as to say so in the White House Situation Room. They believed, as Brown acknowledged later, that officials "had either to support [Carter's] decision or resign." Instead, the officials made a case for delaying the withdrawal because of the unwillingness of Congress to approve funds to compensate South Korea as promised. "The issue is not the withdrawal but the Park Tong Sun affair," Assistant Secretary of State Richard Holbrooke told the meeting. "Because of 'Koreagate,' congressmen fear political retribution at the polls if they vote for any sort of aid to Korea this year." Moreover, Holbrooke said, to proceed with withdrawal without the aid package would be seen "as part of a retreat from East Asia" and could torpedo the administration's plans to normalize American relations with China. Michael Armacost, then a National Security Council staff member and later US ambassador to Tokyo, warned of "extraordinarily adverse consequences in Japan" if troops were withdrawn without providing compensating aid as promised. The Defense Department's Morton Abramowitz said that proceeding without the compensation package would likely bring about the resignation of General Vessey, the US military commander in Korea. He added that such a move "will lose the Joint Chiefs of Staff," which had reluctantly accepted the withdrawal policy.

With Brown, Vance, and most of the others counseling delay or cancellation of the next withdrawal element, only Brzezinski addressed the real but unspoken issue. "This [withdrawal policy] may have been the wrong decision, but now it has been made. We cannot afford to go back on it," the NSC adviser said. In the end, Brzezinski devised and sold Carter on a plan to water down rather than delay the first pullout of combat troops, limiting the immediate withdrawal to only one battalion of troops, about eight hundred men, plus about twenty-six hundred noncombat personnel, instead of the planned six thousand combat troops, with the rest theoretically to come out later. As many in the meeting hoped and assumed, the administration's rollback signaled that further withdrawals were much less likely.

Carter reluctantly accepted the face-saving maneuver. In private he bitterly upbraided Brown for seeking to stymie his program. He expected more loyalty, he told his defense secretary heatedly. Brown was surprised at Carter's outburst but stood his ground, saying he felt obligated to give his best advice and judgment in private, especially since he had been the administration's point man in defending the withdrawal in congressional testimony. Having found himself earlier in his long governmental career intimidated by the powerful opinions of Presidents John Kennedy and Lyndon Johnson, Brown was determined to tell Carter what he really thought despite potential damage to their relationship. "Carter felt he was up against the establishment" on the touchy withdrawal issue, said Brown, "whereas we felt we were trying to save him from doing things that would cause big trouble with allies."

THE VIEW FROM PYONGYANG

In Pyongyang Kim Il Sung was keenly aware of Carter's proposal to withdraw American troops from South Korea. Such a move had long been one of Kim's central goals, in the belief that this would lead inevitably to reuniting the peninsula under his leadership, whether by peaceful or violent means. In public and in private, Kim had made Washington enemy number one, harshly condemning the United States for a variety of real or imagined sins, from dividing the peninsula in 1945 to sustaining Park Chung Hee as a military dictator. On the eve of Carter's inauguration, however, the harsh rhetoric softened, and the "American imperialist aggressor army" became simply "American forces" in Pyongyang's statements. The Panmunjom incident was blamed specifically on the outgoing Ford administration rather than on the US generally, giving the incoming president a clean slate in Pyongyang.

Behind the scenes, Kim made energetic efforts to engage Carter directly. In November 1976, immediately after Carter's election, Kim sent a personal letter through the president of Pakistan to the US president-elect at Plains, Georgia, asking for direct contact. This was followed in February 1977 by a message to Secretary of State Vance from North Korean foreign minister Ho Dam, through the US Embassy in Pakistan, expressing Pyongyang's desire to avoid confrontation with the United States, to pursue reunification peacefully, and to open direct US-DPRK peace talks, which at least initially would exclude South Korea. The American reply expressed interest in discussions with the North, including discussions of "more permanent Armistice arrangements," but only if Seoul was permitted to participate fully.* At the time, this was a nonstarter in Pyongyang. In gestures to Pyongyang, Carter lifted the ban on travel to North Korea by US citizens in March and for the first time invited North Korea's UN representative to an official US reception.

In July 1977, in this era of high expectations, a US Army helicopter strayed over the northern side of the DMZ and was shot down, killing three crewmen and leaving the fourth a captive. In a remarkably mild reaction, Carter described the flight as a mistake and played down the conflict. In response, North Korea returned the bodies and the captured American within three days, an unprecedentedly short time for such a move.

Yet as Carter was forced to modify and stretch out his program of American withdrawal, Kim became increasingly critical. "Carter has not kept his election pledges," Kim told visitors, charging that the withdrawal pledges were "aimed at deceiving the world." In a talk with a Japanese editor, Kim bitterly called the US president "a con man" because of his changing stance on Korean issues.

In early-December 1977, Kim received a visit from Erich Honecker, the general secretary of the East German Socialist Unity (Communist) Party, who came to be one of Kim's closest and most useful overseas friends. Both were lifelong revolutionaries who had advanced to high places with Soviet backing. Like Korea, Germany had been divided as a result of World War II. East Germany, like North Korea, was struggling to survive against a more populous and more prosperous capitalistic regime across a heavily militarized dividing line. Encouraged by the Soviet Union and recognizing the similarities, East Germany had been an important source of economic aid during all of North Korea's existence. The major difference, and one that apparently worried Kim, was that East Germany was half of a divided country but did not pursue unification—the USSR's view was that a unified Germany was a threat to the peace—whereas Pyongyang's strongly held position was that Korea had offended no one and had been divided arbitrarily and unjustly after the war.

Kim prepared meticulously to receive Honecker, whom he had never met. To flatter his guest, he staged a mass rally of close to a half-million people, including North Korean musicians performing revolutionary German songs from Honecker's glory days as a youth leader. "It was the biggest reception of his lifetime. This old man was in tears," said an East German diplomat who was present.

---

* Over the succeeding months, Kim Il Sung sent messages to Carter through President Omar Bongo of Gabon in May 1977, Yugoslav president Marshal Tito in October 1977, and President Nicolae Ceaușescu of Romania in April 1978. In each case, Kim declined to deal with the ROK government while it was under Park's leadership; in each case, Carter replied that he would negotiate with the North only with South Korean participation.

The transcript of the confidential discussions with Honecker on December 10 provides a window into Kim's private views in the late 1970s. While acknowledging that his country faced problems, many of which he attributed to "American imperialism," Kim was supremely confident of his position and the ascendancy of his self-reliant *juche* ideology. Kim declared that his number-one priority was unification of the country, and he outlined three strategic directions that he had set forth in the early 1960s and adhered to for the rest of his life: "first, to successfully carry out the organization of socialism in the northern part of the country; second, to support the revolutionary struggle in South Korea; third, to develop solidarity and unity with the international revolutionary forces."

Kim first described for his guest the extraordinary mobilization of the population, something he justified as necessary to create a powerful revolutionary base for the Korean peninsula and beyond. He told Honecker without overstatement that "everyone, apart from infants, is included in the organizational life" of the nation. Of North Korea's 17 million people, at that time 2.2 million were in the Workers Party (a relatively high percentage compared with other communist countries),[*] and except for infants all the others belonged to various organizations of children, youths, women, farmers, or workers.

Kim also described the social engineering that was so much a part of North Korea. To "revolutionize and reform women, according to the example of the working class," according to Kim, they were being "freed from heavy domestic work" and placed in jobs outside the home. About 80 percent of farmworkers were women, he said, and over 90 percent of workers in light industry. Without giving numbers, he explained that this was necessary because "many young people in our country are in the army." To compensate for the absence of mothers and to start inculcating its ideology early, North Korea had built nurseries and kindergartens for 3.5 million children so they could be "taken care of and educated by society."

Absent from Kim's briefing was mention of the fact that despite North Korea's strenuous efforts, by 1977 the balance of economic power on the peninsula was shifting decisively in favor of the South. In the first decades after the Korean War, the North's centrally directed economy had recovered from the destruction and grown faster than the South's. But in the early 1960s, the two economies took decisive turns: the North opted for an inner-directed one, centered on building heavy industry at home

---

[*] In June 1971, according to an official Romanian document, Kim told Romanian party head Ceaușescu that the Workers Party had 1.6 million members as of its Fifth Party Congress in October 1970. If that figure was right, it means the party grew by more than a half-million members in seven years. Woodrow Wilson International Center for Scholars, North Korea International Documentation Project, *New Evidence of Inter-Korean Relations, 1971–1972,* Document Reader 3, September 2009, Document no. 1.

and shying away from integration with the outside; the South, guided by American-trained Korean economists and the promise of a share in the American and Japanese markets, turned toward an externally directed economy centered on exports and initially on light industry. These fateful turns eventually determined the outcome of the economic race on the peninsula, and they deeply affected the political and diplomatic spheres as well.

By the mid-1970s, by most outside estimates, the North's *juche* economy was falling behind. The North's GNP, adjusted for inflation, doubled between 1965 and 1976, a highly creditable performance for a developing economy. But at the same time, South Korea's real GNP more than tripled. In the mid-1970s, as poverty was reduced below the thirty-eighth parallel, South Korea passed the North in per capita GNP for the first time since the division of the country.

Part of North Korea's economic problem was its heavy spending for military purposes. From the mid-1960s to the mid-1970s, the North devoted an estimated 15 to 20 percent of its economy to its military. The South spent an average of 5 percent on its military, though due to Park's massive armament program the proportion briefly jumped to near 10 percent in the mid-1970s.

In the early 1970s, with the bad timing that has often plagued its decisions, Pyongyang abruptly shifted its autarkic policies to a "great leap outward," purchasing entire factories from Western Europe and Japan, in a burst of economic activity that matched its sudden outwardly directed drive for negotiations with the South. One Japanese-Danish venture, for example, was to provide North Korea with the largest cement factory in the world. But in the worldwide economic dislocation following the 1973 Middle East war and oil embargo, North Korea found itself unable to meet the fast-rising payments on its external debts. As a result, its access to international credit was severely restricted, whereas South Korea's growing international trade made it a major player on the global scene.

Soft-pedaling these troubling trends, Kim reiterated his belief in the superiority of the North, notably in regard to the revolutionary struggle in the South. Referring to the fight that he and his guerrilla band had waged against the Japanese, while Park Chung Hee and others were serving in the Japanese army, Kim expressed confidence in his superiority because "the leading circles of South Korea are traitors, whereas we here are patriots." Contrary to existing evidence and belief in the South, Kim claimed that North Korean communists had been behind the student revolution that overthrew the regime of Syngman Rhee in 1960 and that the United States had organized the military junta headed by General Park Chung Hee that took power in 1961. In all these years, said Kim, the South

Korean students had supported North Korea and "have not demonstrated against us even a single time," although they had demonstrated repeatedly against "the puppet regime."

Kim expressed to Honecker a hoary tenet of North Korean policy, that after the withdrawal of US troops, when the South Korean people chose their own way, "then they would choose the way of socialism." In the meantime, he said, the crucial objective for the North was to isolate Park and his government rather than return to the 1972–1973 era of North-South dialogue. The Americans hoped to see dialogue restarted, he said, but "if we get together with Park Chung Hee and hold negotiations, there is the danger of weakening the South Korean political forces who are opposing Park Chung Hee." This belief that their own policies had a significant impact on the possibility of revolution in the South was more central to Pyongyang's calculations than most outsiders realized.

On the first day of his visit, Honecker committed East Germany to having "no relations" with South Korea, but Kim continued to stress the need to isolate the South, perhaps in hopes that his visitor would pass along his views to Moscow, which Pyongyang always watched nervously for signs of apostasy on the Korean question. Honecker's pledge would prove to be costly to East Germany; over the years that followed, each time the GDR was tempted to trade with the South, a sharp protest from Pyongyang reminded Honecker of his commitment, and the proposed deal was squelched.

Honecker at the time was considered a slavish follower of Soviet leadership, and thus Kim made special efforts to persuade him that he was not leaning to the Chinese side in the decades-long Sino-Soviet split. The North Korean leader emphasized his troubles with Beijing during the Cultural Revolution, complaining that the Chinese had set up giant loudspeakers at the Sino-Korean border and delivered deafening attacks on "Korean revisionists" from 5:00 A.M. to midnight every day. Since those days, relations had been repaired, but "we do not follow China blindly," Kim emphasized. On the other hand, he added, "We also do not participate in the Soviet Union's polemics against China." Opting out of the Sino–Soviet conflict "does not mean that we are opportunists, but that the situation does not allow us anything else."

Finally, talks dealt with Kim's views of Japan and the United States. Although he was concerned about the danger of a revival of Japanese militarism, Kim conceded that "the Japanese nation is not as it was before" due to the lessons learned from World War II and the US atomic bomb attacks. Looking to the future, he declared that a triumph of communism on the Korean peninsula would be "beneficial for stimulating the revolution in Japan."

As for the United States, after nearly a year of trying to make contact with the new American president, Kim was scornful about Carter. The decision to stretch out the US troop withdrawal from South Korea was "a deceitful maneuver against the people" and an attempt to manipulate public opinion, Kim told Honecker.

Kim confided that his military reconnaissance teams constantly observed US maneuvers in South Korea. American officers were uncomfortably aware of this aspect of the secret war on the divided peninsula. In 1975 a North Korean reconnaissance team was discovered while photographing and sketching the US air base at Kwangju and a nearby ROK missile site, and in 1976 a North Korean team wearing ROK-style uniforms covered sixty to seventy miles on foot south of the DMZ before being caught. By the time of the Kim-Honecker meeting, the US Command in Seoul had acknowledged in a confidential report that "the North can infiltrate or exfiltrate its agents or special warfare units by land, sea or air to virtually any location within the ROK." On the other hand, American and South Korean operations inside North Korea were extremely limited. US knowledge of North Korean military affairs, however, was beginning to receive much higher priority.

END OF THE CARTER WITHDRAWAL

An important assumption underlying Carter's plan was that during and after the departure of American ground troops, the military balance on the peninsula would remain favorable to the South. Even before Carter came to office, however, this assumption was being thrown into doubt by new US intelligence estimates that depicted the North's military forces as much more numerous and better armed than previously believed. The new estimates proved to be a fatal blow to Carter's already embattled withdrawal plan.

The beginning of the end started with a twenty-nine-year-old intelligence analyst named John Armstrong, who in May 1975 was bent over a light table at Fort Meade, Maryland, scrutinizing aerial photographs of North Korean tanks. Armstrong, a West Point graduate who had served in Vietnam before becoming a civilian analyst for the army, had been laboriously counting the tanks when he reached a surprising conclusion: there were many more than expected on the basis of earlier reports. Within a few weeks, Armstrong identified an entirely new tank division (about 270 tanks and 100 armored personnel carriers) in a valley about fifty miles north of the DMZ.

For many years, the principal source of intelligence on North Korea had been aerial photography from American spy planes and reconnaissance satellites, augmented by electronic eavesdropping. Because the central US military concern was a surprise attack, the photographs were carefully examined for evidence of southward movement or other signs of impending assault, then filed away. Until Armstrong came along, there was little effort to compare the overall strength of North Korean units in the latest pictures with those of previous months or years.

Armstrong's first intensive study, completed in December 1975, reported North Korean tank forces to be about 80 percent larger than had been previously estimated. Armed with this alarming finding, he persuaded the army to assign six more full-time analysts to his project. Over the next two years, his team documented the development of North Korean special forces units and a major increase in the number and forward deployment of North Korean artillery.

When Armstrong finally took his findings to the US Command in Seoul in December 1977, he found a receptive audience in General Vessey, the US commander, and others who were fighting the Carter withdrawal program. The following month, Vessey requested a complete intelligence reassessment of North Korea's strength, complaining to the Pentagon of the adverse effects "on overall U.S. military policy and decision-making" of overly conservative estimates of the enemy. In response, the army initiated a much more extensive study in Washington, with a reinforced team of thirty-five analysts summoned from all over the world. They went to work reexamining all the intelligence reports on North Korean forces since the armistice and scrutinizing every frame of overhead photography and all the signal intelligence obtained since 1969. The results, officially reported in classified briefings beginning in mid-1978, were startling.

Due to a strong and steady buildup since 1971–1972, North Korea was credited in the new estimate with about seven hundred maneuver battalions, nearly twice the number carried on the books a decade earlier and nearly double the size of the South Korean force structure. Moreover, the North was estimated to have many more tanks and artillery pieces than previously known, giving it a more than two-to-one advantage over the South in terms of the numbers of those weapons. The study, which eventually identified every North Korean unit down to the infantry company and artillery battery level, found the bulk of the forces positioned closer to the DMZ than had been expected. The overall size of the North Korean ground forces, previously estimated at 485,000, was now put at 680,000, an increase of about 40 percent. For the first time, the North was estimated to have more men under arms than the South, whose population was twice as large. In North Korea, according to the new data, one out of every twenty-six persons was on active duty in the army, the highest proportion of any major nation. This was the basis of Kim Il Sung's explanation to Honecker about a labor shortage because so many "young people are in the army."

Senior officials were quick to recognize that the new findings had tremendous implications for the withdrawal program. Nathanial Thayer, who was national intelligence officer at the CIA, recalled that "everyone was thinking the same thing—this is a good way for Carter to get off this issue." In early-January 1979, results of the new estimate leaked to the *Army Times* and became front-page news in other papers, including my report in the *Washington Post*.

The findings intensified congressional pressure to halt the withdrawal program. Carter was skeptical of the validity of the intelligence reassessment, and decades later he remained so. Recalling the leaks and political impact of the report, Carter wrote me while I was preparing this book, "I have always suspected that the facts were doctored by DIA [Defense Intelligence Agency] and others, but it was beyond the capability even of a president to prove this."

By late-January 1979, Carter himself was just about the only person in the administration who favored continuing with the troop withdrawal, and even he was aware that support for his views on Korea—and nearly everything else—was eroding drastically. He was being battered from every side following the forced departure of the shah from Iran and the triumph of the Iranian revolution earlier in the month, which led to a redoubling of world oil prices, intensified inflation, and other economic dislocations worldwide.

On January 22, he was persuaded to authorize a new review of Korea policy, chaired by the State Department, "in the light of recent developments affecting the Korean peninsula," including the "new judgments on North Korean order of battle." This artful piece of bureaucratic prose never explicitly mentioned the US withdrawal as a matter for review, but everyone except Carter knew that was its central topic. Unlike most other such studies, which aimed at bringing the bureaucracy into line behind new policies, Presidential Review Memorandum/NSC-45 was aimed by the bureaucracy at persuading the president to abandon an old policy he continued to cherish.

In order to avoid disclosing their real intent or backing Carter into a corner, his senior lieutenants conducted the "review" in extraordinary secrecy worthy of the most sensitive covert operation. Usual interagency channels of communication for classified information were bypassed in favor of hand-carried memoranda between the offices of the top national security officials of government. For once, news of a major policy-making enterprise did not leak.

In the spring, aides recommended an idea that had been under discussion for many months: Carter should visit Korea, following his trip to Tokyo for the June summit meeting of the Group of Seven (G-7) industrialized nations. The advisers saw the trip as an integral part of a scenario leading inexorably to further adjustment of the withdrawal plans: first absorb the new intelligence, then discuss it with leaders in Tokyo and

Seoul, and then report back to the US congressional leadership on changes required by the altered circumstances. Carter reluctantly agreed to the visit, realizing it would probably be the occasion for reconsideration of his plan. He made it clear, however, that he did not wish to discuss the withdrawal issue with President Park, whom he had never met but whose record and regime were distasteful to him.

As the trip preparations were under way, Carter arrived at the Oval Office one morning with a novel—and startling—idea. Following the precedent of the Camp David accords the previous September between the leaders of Egypt and Israel, the president proposed to invite Park and Kim Il Sung to meet him in the demilitarized zone during his forthcoming trip, to establish a path toward peace. The Asia experts among the aides were horrified. They thought Park and Kim would not agree to meet, and the proposal would be seen as a "flaky" stunt. The plan also met massive resistance from the US ambassador in Seoul, William Gleysteen. A career Foreign Service expert on Asia who had grown up in China, the son of missionary parents, Gleysteen "just fell out of my chair" when informed of it. The experts persuaded Brzezinski and, through him, Carter to abandon the scheme. The idea was quietly dropped, without the South Korean leadership or anyone else getting wind of it.

As this incident suggests, Carter had been turning over in his mind the possibility that US diplomacy could encourage a North-South settlement that would make long-term presence of American troops unnecessary. The four-power talks involving China, the United States, and the two Koreas that Vance had suggested early in the administration had gone nowhere. However, the establishment of full US diplomatic relations with China on January 1, 1979—a major accomplishment of the Carter administration—revived the possibility that Beijing might help to defuse the conflict on the divided peninsula. At the end of January, when Chinese leader Deng Xiaoping visited Washington, Carter asked him to help arrange North-South talks. Deng responded that the North was ready to talk to Americans, the Park government, and others in the South on the terms that it had previously proposed (which were unacceptable in Seoul and Washington). Deng said China would not pressure North Korea, lest it lose its influence there, but he assured Carter there was absolutely no danger of a North Korean attack.

Rebuffed in his plan for a grand three-way summit meeting in the DMZ, Carter settled for proposing tripartite talks of lesser diplomats. The South Koreans had strongly resisted such an idea for many months, fearing a sellout by the United States in the pattern of Vietnam diplomacy. Ambassador Gleysteen, directed by Washington to obtain agreement in Seoul, found that the entire South Korean government was adamantly opposed to three-way talks except for Park himself, who was persuaded

to consider it in the context of ending the US withdrawal program. In
the end, Park ordered his government to accept the proposal, possibly believing that he would win points with Carter and that Pyongyang would
reject it anyway. The proposal, which was announced during Carter's trip
to Seoul, appeared to be stillborn when North Korea lodged the expected
objections. But as Korean diplomacy developed later on, the idea of three-
way talks came back to life in a variety of circumstances.

On the evening of June 29, Carter arrived in Seoul aboard Air Force
One from the G-7 summit meeting in Tokyo and immediately helicoptered to Camp Casey, the headquarters of the Second Infantry Division, to
spend the night. After jogging with and addressing the troops, he traveled
back to Seoul for a rousing official welcome by an estimated half-million
people and bands playing such Carter favorites as "Onward, Christian Soldiers," lining the route to the Blue House.

Inside the presidential palace, the meeting between the two delegations quickly went off track. The South Korean president had been asked
in advance by American officials to say little or nothing about the withdrawal issue so as not to upset the delicate minuet they had devised for
Carter, but Park had his own ideas. The former schoolteacher had written
out in his neat hand a lengthy presentation of the strategic reasons why
withdrawing American troops would be a cataclysmic mistake in view of
the North's growing strength, and he boldly delivered it to the increasingly
furious American president.

Nicholas Platt, the National Security Council expert on Asia, could
see Carter silently working his jaw muscles, as he tended to do under great
tension, and on the other side of the table he observed Park snapping his
fingers to make his points, as he did unconsciously under extraordinary
stress. Vance could feel the temperature in the room drop with Carter's
cold fury. As Park continued his forty-five-minute oration, the president
passed a note to Vance and Defense Secretary Brown: "If he goes on like
this much longer I'm going to pull every troop out of the country." Instead
of responding at once, Carter adjourned with Park to the next room for a
private talk where he brought up human rights issues and demanded to
know why the ROK, with a far bigger economy, did not match the North
militarily. It was, Assistant Secretary of State Richard Holbrooke later observed, "as terrible a bilateral meeting between treaty allies as you can have."

When the meeting was over, Carter, Vance, Brown, and Brzezinski
climbed into the presidential limousine for the short ride to the US ambassador's residence. Gleysteen, summoned by Carter to join them, sat
on a jump seat facing the president. Berating Park, Carter threatened to
continue the withdrawal despite all opposition and accused his aides of
conspiring against him. Gleysteen, who barely knew the president and had
never had a serious discussion with him before, took the brunt of Carter's

anger, responding in strong terms about the vast difficulties of continuing the pullout and the benefits that might be gained by calling it off. After what seemed to Gleysteen an eternity, with the angry president wagging his finger in his face, Vance and Brown joined the argument on his side. Brzezinski remained silent. For more than ten minutes, the top policy makers of the Carter administration continued their heated debate in the closed car, sitting under the front portico at the ambassador's residence, with a long motorcade of puzzled officials stalled and stretched out behind them. In the second car, which could see but not hear the animated argument, Holbrooke turned to Platt and said, "I guess the meeting on Korea that we've been trying to arrange all this time is finally taking place."

When he cooled off, Carter agreed to return to the previously suggested scenario for reconsidering the withdrawal program, on two conditions: first, that Park order a substantial increase in ROK military expenditures along the lines the two presidents had discussed in their contentious private meeting and, second, that Park make a significant move in the human rights field, such as release of a large number of jailed dissidents. That afternoon, Vance wrote later, "our Korean policy hung in the balance," while the US team sought and won agreement to Carter's demands from Park's government. Ironically in view of later events, the aide designated by Park to negotiate with the Americans on the prisoner release, which ultimately involved eighty-seven dissidents, was KCIA director Kim Jae Kyu.

By the time Carter left Seoul, his demands had been agreed to, a Korean band had serenaded the first family with "Sweet Georgia Brown," and the withdrawal minuet was back on track. In the limousine en route to the airport, Carter tried in a most unusual way to reach out to Park. The devout US president asked his counterpart about his religious beliefs. When Park replied that he had none, Carter said, "I would like you to know about Christ." He proposed to send Chang Hwan (Billy) Kim, an American-educated Baptist evangelist who fashioned himself as the Korean Billy Graham, "to explain our faith." The Korean president agreed to receive him and did so shortly thereafter.

On July 20, three weeks later, Brzezinski announced at the White House that further withdrawal of US combat elements was being suspended until 1981, which would have been the start of Carter's second presidential term, to "await credible indications that a satisfactory military balance has been restored and a reduction in tension is under way." Carter had no second term. In 1981, having been defeated for reelection, he was on his way home.

In the two and a half years of the withdrawal program, only one combat battalion of 674 ground troops actually left Korea, while twelve more air force F-4 fighters and their crews, totaling 900 troops, had been sent to augment those already in Korea. Including various noncombat units and some that had previously been scheduled for reduction, Carter reduced the total US military strength in Korea by only about 3,000 troops, leaving nearly 37,000 in place. Although he did not achieve his fervent aim of eliminating all US nuclear weapons from Korean soil, Carter did reduce their number from nearly 700 to around 250 and consolidated them all at a single site, Kunsan Air Base, rather than having them spread around several locations.

In his haste and lack of finesse, an inexperienced president had transformed a general impulse to reduce US military forces in South Korea into a highly controversial policy with which he was personally, and negatively, identified. Many of the American diplomatic and military officials dealing with the issue were not opposed to substantial reductions if pursued in well-planned fashion, but they were horrified by the peremptory and damaging way the issue was pursued by the Carter White House. By refusing to heed or even hear the objections until he had backed himself against the wall, Carter undermined his own position.

Even a determined president proved unable to decouple the United States from the high-stakes military standoff on the Korean peninsula. The major impact of Carter's unsuccessful effort was to intensify among his Asian allies concerns that had been generated by the American withdrawal from Vietnam. In Seoul Carter's conflict with Park inadvertently diminished the standing of the South Korean president. The consequences were soon to come.

5

ASSASSINATION AND AFTERMATH

O N THE EVENING OF October 26, 1979, President Park Chung Hee dined with KCIA director Kim Jae Kyu, with whom he was increasingly at odds, in a new KCIA operations building on the grounds of the Blue House. The president was accompanied by the powerful chief of presidential security, Cha Chi Chol, and the chief of the Blue House secretariat, Kim Kye Won. Sitting on the floor on either side of Park at a traditional Korean low dining table and pouring liberally from a bottle of Chivas Regal were two young women—a university student and a well-known singer.

As the dinner proceeded, Park criticized KCIA director Kim for failing to keep abreast of the massive domestic disorders that had erupted over political and economic issues. Security chief Cha, who was advocating a harsher crackdown on students and strikers, also berated the KCIA director for contributing to the unrest by espousing policies that were too conciliatory. After a few minutes of abuse, the intelligence chief left the dining room. He returned with a .38 Smith & Wesson pistol hidden in his pocket, pausing to instruct his own guards to shoot the presidential bodyguards, who were waiting outside the dining room, if shots were fired inside.

After checking to make sure his aides were ready, Kim pulled out his pistol and demanded of Park, "How can you have such a miserable worm as your adviser?" Then he fired at point-blank range, first at Cha, then at Park, severely wounding them both. When the gun jammed, he borrowed another from a KCIA guard and finished the two men off. KCIA aides took the shooting as their signal to attack, killing several presidential bodyguards. Within minutes, the turbulent and historic eighteen-year reign of Park Chung Hee ended in a blaze of gunfire.

The assassination of Park opened a new era of uncertainty, during which the United States sought unsuccessfully to nudge South Korean leaders toward a more democratic and participatory system to replace the authoritarianism of the past. US influence had some small successes, but as American officials had already learned, their power to affect Korean politics was limited when the stakes were high for the domestic actors involved.

Moreover, by the end of the 1970s, the balance of power between the two countries had shifted dramatically. No longer an economic-aid client of the United States, South Korea had emerged as a rising middle power with a large and complex economy. The United States was still expected to deter the North by stationing troops that would guarantee automatic US involvement in case of war, but nearly all the Americans had been pulled back to reserve positions, leaving South Korean troops to defend most of the DMZ front line. Reflecting these changes, Ambassador Gleysteen reported to Washington in one of his first dispatches after the killing, "We should keep in mind that the Korea of 1979 is not the Korea of the early '60s when we were able to bully the early Park regime into constitutional reforms."

One of the first things Korean authorities did on the night of October 26 was to notify Gleysteen. General Lew Byong Hyon, the senior Korean officer in the recently established Combined Forces Command, came to the ambassador's residence around midnight and reported that "there's been an accident" involving Park. Lew didn't know how much to say and, at that point, didn't know all the facts himself. Gleysteen went to the embassy to use his secure line to alert Washington (where it was early afternoon).

About two hours later, when it was clear that Park was dead and that Prime Minister Choi Kyu Ha would take over, at least temporarily, as mandated by Park's 1972 constitution, the US National Security Council convened at the White House. The president had already left for a previously planned weekend at Camp David.

As always in moments of crisis on the peninsula, Washington's foremost concern was for the security of South Korea and the US troops stationed there to defend it. American forces and South Korean forces under US operational control were put on a higher degree of alert, and an aircraft-carrier task force was ordered to Korean waters as a show of force to deter the North. Two Airborne Warning and Surveillance (AWACS) planes were placed on station to monitor North Korean military movements. The State Department quickly announced that the United States would "react strongly in accordance with its treaty obligations to the Republic of Korea to any external attempt to exploit the situation." Washington privately passed the same message, intended for North Korea, to China and the Soviet Union. Unannounced, the United States also stepped up spy-plane surveillance of North Korea and closely monitored electronic intercepts. For the moment, Pyongyang remained quiet, apparently unclear about events and not wanting to be accused of having a hand in the assassination.

GROWING DOMESTIC TENSIONS

In the months preceding the assassination, Park's regime was under great strain. After a long period of rapid growth, South Korea had been afflicted by the worldwide inflation and recession that arose from the redoubling of oil prices after the Iranian revolution early in 1979. An unprecedented wave of bankruptcies and strikes swept the country. The large-scale release of dissidents under the unannounced agreement with Carter during his visit in early July had emboldened Park's critics, especially opposition New Democratic Party (NDP) leader Kim Young Sam, who began denouncing the government in scathing terms.

On August 11, the government outraged Kim and exacerbated its problems when steel-helmeted riot policemen invaded NDP headquarters and dragged out 190 female employees of the bankrupt Y. H. Industrial Company, who had staged a sit-in to enlist public sympathy. A month later, Kim publicly appealed to the United States in a *New York Times* interview to end its support of Park's "minority dictatorial regime." In response, on Park's instructions, Kim was expelled from the Korean National Assembly, precipitating the mass resignation of opposition-party deputies and plunging the country into a political crisis.

In mid-October antigovernment demonstrations in Kim's home area of Pusan spread from campuses to the rest of the city, prompting the imposition of martial law in Pusan for the first time since Park's muscular imposition of his unchallenged rule in 1972. The Pusan protests, the US Embassy reported to Washington, "probably resulted from a combination of political and economic frustrations including considerable weariness with the Park government and widespread objection to the government's recent heavy-handedness." Massive protests also erupted in the nearby industrial city of Masan.

As a show of American disapproval of Kim Young Sam's ouster from the National Assembly, Ambassador Gleysteen was briefly but publicly recalled to Washington. But on October 18, Gleysteen was back in Korea to accompany Secretary of Defense Harold Brown, who was in Seoul for annual high-level military consultations, to an intimate meeting with Park. There they presented a personal letter from Carter expressing concern about the political developments. Brown warned Park that security ties with Seoul could be affected if he did not return to a more liberal path. In this period, Gleysteen reported to Washington, "I was struck by the pervasiveness within the establishment of worry about where the government's hardline policies were leading Korea. People in almost all sectors and all levels told us of their anxiety and were becoming increasingly bold in identifying President Park as the man making the wrong decisions, listening to advisors who were telling him what they thought he wanted to hear."

In the last years of his life, especially after the assassin's bullets in 1974 that narrowly missed him and killed his wife, Park was the subject of extraordinary security measures imposed to protect him from outside threats. A half mile from the presidential mansion, windows in hotels were taped or shaded to obstruct outsiders from getting a view of the Blue House. When Park appeared in public, guests were required to be in their places an hour before he appeared. Because of these draconian measures, Park was increasingly cut off from normal human contact. But as it turned out, not even these measures could provide absolute security for a chief executive who had outlived his welcome.

By the time of his death, Park's regime was held together by fear and force. With his popularity waning and the economy faltering, Park was in trouble even in his own entourage. Seemingly immune to all external pressures to step aside, Park was removed by a privileged insider across the dinner table in his own presidential compound. When American officials, headed by Vance, flew into Seoul for Park's funeral, which was attended by huge crowds, they initially found surprisingly little sincere grief in the general public or among the officials who had served the late president. "His time had come," a senior ROK official told Assistant Secretary of State Holbrooke privately. "There wasn't a wet eye in Seoul," Holbrooke observed.

The motives of Kim Jae Kyu, Park's assassin, have never been fully established. Kim had been considered a close friend of the president. His selection in 1976 to head the KCIA, the most sensitive instrument of Park's personal control, testifies to their intimate relationship. Like a number of other senior officers and officials, however, Kim felt increasingly alienated from Park's policies. At his trial, he told the court he had decided to kill Park years earlier in order to end the dictatorial *yushin* system, and claimed that his objective was "a revolution for the restoration of democracy." On the basis of conversations with Kim, his lawyer, Kang Sin Ok, told me that Kim had decided a few weeks earlier to kill Park at his first opportunity.

On the other hand, there were signs that Kim's plot was hastily improvised. The first pistol had not been used for a long time and misfired. More telling, Kim had not devised a serious plan for taking over the government. There had been rumors that Kim would soon be ousted from his job by the dissatisfied president, giving rise to the theory that he had acted in part from fear of dismissal or worse. Along with several other officials, Kim had clashed bitterly with chief bodyguard Cha in the past, adding a personal factor to their policy dispute.

Given Washington's well-known unhappiness with Park's policies, there was immediate speculation among conspiracy-minded Koreans and some Americans that the United States had had a hand in the assassination, especially when the news of Park's death was reported by American news agencies from Washington before it was officially announced in Seoul, where it was still in the middle of the night. Nearly a month after the assassination, Gleysteen reported in a cable to Washington that suspicion of US complicity persisted in Korea, but that "I have checked with Dick Sneider [his predecessor] and can state flatly that neither of us ever signaled to Kim Jae Kyu or any other Korean that we thought the Park government's days were numbered or that we would condone Park's removal from office."

A more difficult question is whether the American clashes with Park over the withdrawal of American troops, the Koreagate scandal, and human rights abuses had weakened the Korean president and contributed to his demise. Kim Kyung Won, who was special assistant to Park for international affairs, noted that the KCIA had full access to the barrage of negative comment about Park in the US administration, Congress, the press, and elsewhere. "It is not implausible to me that [KCIA director Kim] may have convinced himself that if he got rid of this Park Chung Hee, then his action would be welcome," the former aide said. Gleysteen, while convinced that the KCIA director's violent act resulted from madness of some kind, also believed that American behavior inadvertently fed it and that Kim Jae Kyu, who had been the interlocutor with Americans on human rights issues during the Carter visit and at other times, had "misread us."

Immediately after the killings, Kim Jae Kyu met Army Chief of Staff Chung Seung Hwa and tried to persuade him to go to KCIA headquarters and declare martial law, although the assassin did not disclose that he had killed the president. Instead, Chung convened a meeting at Korean military headquarters, in which Kim participated—again without disclosing his role in the president's death. The truth came out several hours later when the other surviving principal from the fatal dinner, the chief of the Blue House secretariat, Kim Kye Won, finally turned up. At that point, the KCIA chief–turned-assassin was arrested. He was later found guilty of murder and executed, along with his aides who had killed the president's bodyguards.

An emergency cabinet meeting named Prime Minister Choi Kyu Ha, a soft-spoken former diplomat, acting president, as specified in Park's *yushin* law constitution. With American concurrence, martial law was declared over most of the country, and Army Chief of Staff Chung was named martial-law commander.

In Pyongyang, two days after Park's assassination, Kim Il Sung addressed a military meeting, drawing a stark contrast between South Korea, "one half of our territory . . . under the occupation of the U.S. imperialists and reactionaries, landlords and capitalists," and the DPRK, where "our people are enjoying a happy life to the full, without any worries about food, clothing, medical treatment and education." While approving the elimination of "traitor" Park Chung Hee, the North Korean leader cautiously told the military assembly, "We must wait and see what change this will bring about in the revolutionary situation in South Korea." Other than this, North Korea said and did very little, except to heighten the readiness posture of its armed forces, probably in response to similar actions south of the DMZ. The US Command in Seoul and officials in Washington, however, remained concerned that the North might seek to take advantage of turmoil in the South.

With the demise of Park and the nominal passage of power to a civilian authority, South Korea entered a delicate transitional period. Acting president Choi, taking US advice, repealed Park's emergency decree forbidding criticism of the constitution and released the most prominent opposition leaders and dissidents from house arrest or prison. An outpouring of ideas and emotions came from an uncertain yet excited populace. Apparently becoming ambitious in his own right, Choi spurned US advice that he announce he would serve as interim president for only a year—which American officials had hoped would buttress his standing and encourage a peaceful transition.

Although both Washington and a Korean consensus favored changes in the constitution, the government and military leaders insisted that Park's discredited *yushin* charter remain in effect through the selection of Park's successor rather than open the process to the popular political contenders. Using *yushin*'s easily controlled procedures, Choi was elected to the presidency on December 6. Choi, who had no independent political backing, was not a forceful leader. It seemed likely that the military leadership was the real power. The question was, which military leaders?

THE COMING OF CHUN DOO HWAN

The answer came suddenly on the night of December 12, when a group of generals headed by Chun Doo Hwan shifted troops into key positions and used force to depose the existing military authorities. Moving without warning, they arrested the martial-law commander and army chief of staff, General Chung Seung Hwa, and commanders loyal to him and occupied army headquarters, the Defense Ministry, media outlets, and key bridges and road junctions. The takeover was so swift and decisive that there were few firefights or casualties.

The justification for the mutinous action was suspicion that General Chung had had a hand in Park's assassination, which Chun Doo Hwan, as defense security commander, was charged with investigating. Another reason, more cogent to US military officers, was that the established army leaders were making plans to rid themselves of the ambitious and troublesome Chun Doo Hwan by reassigning him to a distant command. Chun and his coconspirators moved first.

Ambassador Gleysteen and the senior US commander in Korea, General John Wickham, spent a tense and surreal night in the fortified command bunker at Yongsan, headquarters of the joint US-ROK Combined Forces Command headed by Wickham and created a year earlier to provide continued American military leadership even if US ground troops were withdrawn. In theory, the underground bunker was the most important control center for military forces in South Korea. The bunker had been built by the Japanese army during its long occupation of Korea and was inherited, along with the base where it sat, by the US Army after World War II. Nearly thirty-five years later, the Americans still commanded both base and bunker, but on this night their influence did not go much further. The US ambassador and senior commander were onlookers as power was wrested from one Korean group by another almost before their eyes, with massive implications for the future of the country.

Gleysteen and Wickham, sitting at the worn wooden table in the VIP section of the bunker, received fragmentary reports of ROK troops moving in and around Seoul and of a shoot-out at the residence of General Chung. American and South Korean officers were unable to contact some major units, which did not answer telephones or radios, but Washington came through loud and clear on a secure telephone line from half a world away, demanding to know what was happening and offering advice. From time to time, the occupants of the bunker could hear shooting nearby. Out of growing concern for the security of the ambassador and the US commander, a detail of American troops was summoned for guard duty around the underground facility.

Powerless to command a halt to the action, Gleysteen and Wickham drafted a statement in the name of the US government, warning "any forces within the ROK" that disruption of progress toward a broadly based government would have a "seriously adverse impact" on US-ROK relations. The statement was conveyed to the Blue House and both factions of the Korean military and was broadcast by Voice of America and other official American media, but it had no effect. Most Koreans were not aware of it because all Korean news outlets had been seized by the insurgents. Ignoring calls from the US commander, the CIA station chief, and others, the coup leaders refused direct contact with the Americans until they had established effective control.

In midevening South Korean defense minister Ro Jae Hyun and chairman of the Joint Chiefs of Staff General Kim Chong Hwan, both looking pale and nervous, arrived at the bunker. Using US communications, they tried to establish the loyalty of their subordinates, with mixed results. Wickham urged them not to order an attack on the insurgents at least until daybreak, fearing a nighttime battle with bloody and even more divisive results. Later Ro left for his headquarters nearby, where he was seized by plotters and compelled to assist in obtaining ex post facto authorization from President Choi for the arrest of the martial-law commander.

The nighttime takeover was in part a generational battle within the military. The deposed army chief of staff and many other occupants of top military posts were members of the eighth class of the Korean Military Academy; Chun Doo Hwan and his coconspirators were largely members of the younger eleventh class. To the shock and dismay of Wickham, who was charged with operational control of US and ROK forces defending South Korea, part of a front-line division headed by Chun's classmate and close friend General Roh Tae Woo had left its positions near the DMZ without authorization to take part in the showdown in Seoul.

"We have been through a coup in all but name," Gleysteen reported to Washington when the morning dawned. "The flabby facade of civilian constitutional government remains but almost all signs point to a carefully planned takeover of the military power positions by a group of 'Young Turk' officers," the ambassador cabled Washington. As to his first "groggy conclusions," Gleysteen wrote:

> The December 12 incident is bad news from our point of view. The military of Korea who have remained remarkably united for 18 years under the firm, authoritarian hand of Park Chung Hee have now engaged in actions of insubordination which have not only generated animosities that may take years to work their way out but have also set a precedent for others to follow. In doing so, they totally ignored the Combined Forces Command's responsibilities, either ignoring the impact on the U.S. or coolly calculating that it would not make a difference. By their actions they have also run a serious risk vis-à-vis North Korea without giving it much thought.

The events of 12/12, as the night of the generals came to be called in Korean lore, cut short the reemergence of democratic and civilian rule, to which South Korea aspired after nearly two decades of domination by Park and his uniformed friends. Over the coming months, as the military again took power, many Koreans felt that, once more, the government had been hijacked by a new and unknown ruling group using force rather than the mandate of heaven or the consent of the governed. The showdown between opposing forces illuminated the real political landscape of South Korea as in a flash of lightning: US control of the ROK military was purely nominal in a domestic struggle for power, civilian control over the military under President Choi was nonexistent, and a little-known figure named Chun was now the man to see in South Korea.

Chun Doo Hwan was born on January 18, 1931, in a village near Taegu, a major city in southeastern Korea, the home region of Park Chung Hee and many other political leaders of modern Korea. Chun's father, a Confucian scholar, was forced to flee with his family to Manchuria in 1939 because of a violent feud with a Japanese policeman. After returning to Korea, Chun's family was poor but proud. Chun graduated from Taegu Technical High School in 1951, in the midst of the Korean War, and joined the Korean Military Academy. He graduated in 1955 in the academy's eleventh class—the first class to receive a full four-year military education and the first to have its curriculum based on an American rather than a Japanese model.

As a junior officer in 1959–1960, Chun spent a year in American military schools at bases in North Carolina and Georgia, which left him with a tenuous command of English and a sense of easy familiarity with the United States. Unlike Park Chung Hee, who was Japanese educated and never entirely comfortable with Americans, Chun felt he knew Americans and could deal with them without complexes. As a foreign military student, he bought a used car, obtained a US driver's license, and often traveled on weekends. He was fond of telling aides his surprise one night in seeing a car ahead of him stop for a traffic light, even though no police or anybody else could be seen for miles. This impressed Chun with the law-abiding spirit of the American people, a trait he proclaimed was "essential for freedom and democracy."

After Park's military coup in 1961, Chun served for a year as a secretary for civil affairs at the Supreme Council for National Reconstruction, the official name of the ruling junta. Turning down Park's suggestion that he embark on a political career, Chun returned to army duty. Nonetheless, his military duties were often entwined with politics. In 1964 he, Roh Tae Woo, and a handful of other Korean Military Academy graduates formed a secret club within the military that they named Hana-hoe, or "One Group," devoted to solidarity and patriotism and, as it turned out, self-advancement. Park gave the members of the club, which was headed by Chun, fast promotions and special perks. Hana-hoe members made up the core of the group that took power by force after Park's death.

As a battalion commander of the politically sensitive Capital Security Command in 1968, Chun led the chase against North Korean commandos who had attempted to attack Park's Blue House. After a tour as regimental commander of ROK forces fighting in Vietnam, he moved to the presidential security force at the Blue House, where he had frequent personal contact with Park. In February 1979, eight months before Park's assassination, he became commanding general of the Defense Security

Command, which Park used for political control and as a check on his politically active bodyguard force and the KCIA.

On December 14, two days after his midnight takeover of the military, Chun engineered sweeping changes in the ROK army, moving the old guard aside and placing his classmates and close friends in sensitive posts. Roh became commanding general of the Capital Security Command; others of the Taegu Seven Stars, as the innermost group of insurgent generals were called, became commanders of the Special Warfare Command, the ROK Third Army, and other key units.

The same day, Chun held his first meeting with Gleysteen, coming at the ambassador's invitation to the US Embassy. In response to Gleysteen's plea for a return to constitutional order, Chun insisted that he supported President Choi, that the events of December 12 were an accidental outgrowth of his investigation of Park's assassination, and that he harbored no personal ambition. The purge of the army, which resulted in Chun's unchallenged control of the most important levers of power, was a glaring contradiction of this claim. While recognizing his intelligence and drive, Gleysteen came to distrust Chun and eventually consider him "almost the definition of unreliability . . . unscrupulous . . . ruthless . . . a liar."

The events of December brought American officials face-to-face with the limited extent of their leverage on South Korean political developments. As in the 1961 military coup that brought Park to power, the military showdown of December 1979 was an accomplished fact before the United States could react. The US Embassy had sought briefly but unsuccessfully to reverse the 1961 coup by announcing its continuing support of the elected government, but the effort was an embarrassing failure, a cautionary reminder to officials who came later. When a Korean academic urged Gleysteen to "nullify what General Chun did and kick him out . . . teach Koreans a lesson that the United States does not support just anyone," the ambassador rejected the idea out of hand. "Cannot act as a colonial governor," Gleysteen responded.

American officials, realizing it would be fruitless, made no effort to undo what Gleysteen privately called Chun's "power grab." Gleysteen explicitly told Chun's military colleagues that "we are not trying to reverse the events of December 12." Instead, the United States pressed Chun to refrain from interfering with the Korean political process or taking political power in his own right, which he soon did anyway.

No one could deny that the United States had important stakes in the future of South Korea, but by 1979 it was unclear how far Washington could go in shaping that future. American diplomats relied mainly on persuasion, telling Chun and his colleagues that their takeover threatened national security and economic growth, in which the United States had major interests. In arguments often repeated later, Gleysteen told Chun in their initial meeting that "the [December 12] actions had set a dangerous precedent within the ROK military, run great risks in light of the North Korean threat, and raised further questions internally about the ability of the Choi government to sustain progress toward orderly political liberalization, and externally about the prospects for stability." Gleysteen stressed that "the ROK had to maintain a civilian government and could not afford to lose the support of the U.S. military and businessmen who were deeply disturbed by what had happened."

Chun received these arguments politely, but was not swayed. He and his fellow generals believed they knew more about the North Korean threat than the Americans did, and they did not consider it an imminent danger. Indeed, in view of the recently proposed US pullout, it was arguable how much danger the United States actually perceived from the North. As for economic issues, the economy was still in trouble, but it was questionable whether US business leaders seeking profits had clear-cut views on who should lead the country. The generals also sensed correctly that Washington, obsessed by the plight of American diplomats held hostage in Tehran since November 4, felt under great pressure not to push so hard in Seoul that they created "another Iran."

In an effort to press Chun and deny him full legitimacy, Gleysteen and Wickham, with Washington's approval, avoided meeting with him on a regular basis and sought to do as much business as possible through the official channels of the Choi government. The embassy and the State Department pressed Choi to take bolder steps to assert his authority, without success. He was increasingly a figurehead. Nonetheless, Carter sent a personal letter to Choi in early January saying he was "deeply distressed" by the events of December 12 and that any similar actions "would have serious consequences for our close cooperation." In an unusual gesture, the embassy distributed the letter widely throughout the ROK government and military establishment.

In a message to Washington at the end of January, Gleysteen summed up the dilemma he felt in accepting "an unprecedentedly activist role" in Korean domestic affairs. "If we don't do enough, dangerous events could occur; if we try to do too much, we may provoke strong, chauvinist reactions." This is particularly difficult, he observed, because "most Koreans sense a reduction in the real power of the U.S. and are increasingly concerned over what they perceive as our unwillingness to face up to the Soviet challenge, and they are also somewhat skeptical of our ability to handle Beijing." Apparently referring to the Iran hostage crisis, Gleysteen added that Koreans "suspect that we may be too preoccupied elsewhere to respond resolutely to difficulties on the peninsula."

Nevertheless, he concluded, "All significant political elements seek the image of U.S. support and many seek rather crude U.S. intervention to

shore up their weaknesses; ultimately we will therefore be criticized for undue interference in domestic affairs by those who see our support for them
as less helpful than desired. Few of them realize that our influence is limited in large part by the fact that we could not pull our powerful security
and economic levers without risk of destroying the ROK's stability."

THE KWANGJU UPRISING

In early 1980, with the economy sagging and the country still under partial martial law, the South Korean government modestly began to relax
the repression. Opposition politicians began to speak up, and student
demonstrations, traditional in the spring, began on an increasingly large
scale to demand that martial law be lifted and an early date be established
for a presidential election. Well-known political figures began maneuvering publicly with an election in mind. Chun, operating with the immense
power of martial law, was at the same time extending his personal network
throughout the armed forces from his post as chief of the Defense Security
Command. In mid-April he had Choi name him acting KCIA director, an
act that provided him immense new authority and that convinced the US
Embassy that he was bent on taking over the presidency. In a gesture of
disapproval of Chun's move, Washington "indefinitely postponed" the
annual Security Consultative Meeting (SCM) between the top defense
officials of the two countries and informed ROK officers of its reasons for
doing so.

As the number of student demonstrators demanding elections grew
to the tens of thousands and spilled off the campuses into the streets, both
the civilian and the military sides of the South Korean government raised
with American officials the possibility of using military forces to back up
the hard-pressed police. On May 8, Gleysteen reported that he would
try to defuse "this uncomfortable situation" the following day in separate
meetings with Chun and with Choi Kwang Soo, the civilian chief of staff
at the Blue House. "In none of our discussions," he told Washington, "will
we in any way suggest that the USG opposes ROKG contingency plans
to maintain law and order, if absolutely necessary by reinforcing the police
with the army. If I were to suggest any complaint on this score, I believe we
would lose all our friends within the civilian and military leadership." The
State Department responded, "We agree that we should not oppose ROK
contingency plans to maintain law and order, but you should remind Chun
and Choi of the danger of escalation if law enforcement responsibilities
are not carried out with care and restraint."

In conversation with Gleysteen, Chun blamed the unrest on "a small
number" of student radicals, professors, and ambitious politicians. He described the situation as not critical and said military force would be used

only as a last resort. Wickham, meeting with the ROK defense minister and chairman of the Joint Chiefs of Staff the same day, emphasized the dangers of escalation if troops were used against civilians. The exchanges left Gleysteen with the impression that the student demonstrations might be handled with moderation, although they were reaching massive proportions and becoming larger by the day.

On May 13, however, Chun suddenly played the North Korean card, telling Wickham that Pyongyang was the "hidden hand" behind the students and that the decisive moment for a North Korean attack on the South might have arrived. Wickham reported to Washington that Chun's stress on danger from the North appeared to be a pretext for a move into the Blue House. American scrutiny of its intelligence turned up no sign of preparations for attack, and the State Department, concerned about rumors in Seoul, made a public statement to that effect. Years later a Korean military intelligence officer said he had been ordered by officials close to Chun to fabricate the supposed threat.

On the night of May 17 and the early-morning hours of May 18, military authorities began widespread arrests of student leaders and senior political figures, including the three most likely candidates for president, the "three Kims"—opposition leaders Kim Dae Jung and Kim Young Sam and former prime minister Kim Jong Pil. All political activity was banned under a declaration of full martial law, a step beyond the partial martial law previously in effect. The National Assembly was closed at bayonet point and heavy censorship reimposed on the Korean press. The army seized control, occupied many campuses, and closed all universities.

Gleysteen reported to Washington that the actions meant that "the military [has] all but formally taken over the country." In a "flash" cable, reserved for communications of the highest urgency, he declared that "the military leaders have shown disregard for constituted authority in the ROK—and for us. We have been presented with a *fait accompli* suggesting that the military leaders either do not know or care about the consequences of treating us in this manner." The ambassador, presenting sharp protests to President Choi and to the army chief of staff, said the United States found the actions "shocking and astounding." The CIA station chief in Seoul, Bob Brewster, made a similar protest to Chun. The State Department issued an unusually strong statement about an American ally, saying the United States was "deeply disturbed" and concerned that the use of military force would "exacerbate problems" in Korea.

One of the most serious issues was the fate of late President Park's old rival, Kim Dae Jung. Because of his spectacular kidnapping from Tokyo by KCIA agents in 1973 and subsequent persecution by the Park government, the opposition figure and former presidential candidate was better known abroad than any other living South Korean. At home he inspired passionate loyalty, especially in his native Cholla provinces, but also fierce antipathy among conservatives, especially in the military. His release from house arrest and reemergence to prominence after Park's assassination was considered particularly threatening by those who had been close to Park.

As the country moved toward elections, it seemed distinctly possible, perhaps likely, that Kim could win a free and fair presidential balloting in light of his popularity, the widespread respect for what he had suffered at the hands of Park, and the strong popular reaction against military rule. As early as mid-March, Gleysteen had observed the inherent contradiction in the emergence of Chun and the reemergence of Kim, and he reported to Washington that this ultimately would have to be resolved, "yet no one knows exactly how and when."

As martial law was declared, a large number of soldiers invaded Kim's house, searched it thoroughly, and took Kim away. Soldiers also arrested several of his secretaries, bodyguards, and close political associates. Just a few hours earlier, as rumors circulated that Kim would be arrested on charges of inciting student demonstrations, Gleysteen had warned Blue House chief of staff Choi that arrests of any politicians amid the growing tension was "ill advised" and that the arrest of Kim Dae Jung could be "incendiary."

The ambassador's prediction proved to be accurate. While troops quickly imposed a sullen order on Seoul, the declaration of martial law and especially the arrest of Kim touched off passionate protests in Kwangju, the capital of Kim's home region of southwestern Korea. After relatively routine clashes between students and combat police early that Sunday, aggressive black-beret special forces troops arrived to quell the demonstrations. Tim Warnberg, a Peace Corps volunteer, recounted what he saw next:

> The soldiers charged and began swinging their clubs. We ran along with the panicked crowd and I ended up in a small store along with about 15 other people, including one other PCV [Peace Corps volunteer]. A soldier came into the store and proceeded to club everyone over the head with his truncheon until he came to the other volunteer and me. He stopped, startled, hesitated a moment, and then ran out. We went out into the side street and found that the troops had retreated to the main street, leaving behind wounded people everywhere. Most of the injured had suffered serious blows to the head, arms or legs. . . . One young boy, bleeding from a gash on his forehead, told us he had been playing billiards when the paratroopers burst in and beat each person sharply on the head and then withdrew. The others

had similar stories—though some were actively demonstrating, many were simply attending to their business when the troops indiscriminately began to beat them.

Martha Huntley, a missionary who had lived in Kwangju for nearly fifteen years, reported:

> One man we knew, a businessman about thirty, was pulled off the bus he was riding (along with other youngish-looking people), and was kicked about the head so bad he lost an eye. Another young mother about the same age, thirty or early thirties, was taking her two children to Sunday school, was beaten and left unconscious on the sidewalk—she had to have stitches in her scalp and was incoherent for four months—her husband joined the students Sunday afternoon when they fought with the soldiers. No one knew what was happening or why.

Early on May 21, after three days of indiscriminate attacks by special forces and increasingly large, passionate, and violent opposition from Kwangju residents, townspeople commandeered military vehicles and raided weapons dumps to seize pistols, rifles, and thousands of rounds of ammunition. After a pitched battle with the soldiers, a group of students set up a machine gun on the roof of a local hospital. When it became clear that their brutal tactics were not succeeding, the troops were withdrawn to the outskirts and sealed off the city.

The following day, more than thirty thousand Kwangju people gathered in front of the provincial administration building, now controlled by protesters, to cheer demands that the troops stay out of town and that the government release all those in detention and pay compensation for the dead and wounded. Based on information supplied by the government, Gleysteen, in a cable to Washington, called the Kwangju events "a massive insurrection" that is "out of control and poses an alarming situation for the ROK military."

As the standoff continued, the lull in the crisis provided the opportunity for a negotiated settlement, which Washington strongly favored. On May 22, the State Department and the US Embassy issued a statement calling for maximum restraint on both sides and a peaceful settlement and also warning North Korea against attempting to exploit the situation. The South Korean news media, now under heavy censorship, did not report the statement. Seoul's military authorities agreed to airdrop leaflets containing the statement into Kwangju, but never did so. On the contrary, the government-controlled radio station heard in Kwangju reported that the United States had approved the dispatch of the hated special forces troops into Kwangju. Gleysteen protested and demanded a retraction. It was never given.

At the White House on May 22, a National Security Council meeting considered the crisis. According to the highly classified report on the meeting, "There was general agreement that the first priority is the restoration of order in Kwangju by the Korean authorities with the minimum use of force necessary without laying the seeds for wide disorders later. Once order is restored, it was agreed that we must press the Korean Government, and the military in particular, to allow a greater degree of political freedom to evolve." Regarding the immediate next steps, "We have counseled moderation, but have not ruled out the use of force, should the Koreans need to employ it to restore order," the meeting agreed. National Security Adviser Brzezinski summed up the approach: "In the short term support, in the longer term pressure for political evolution."

The final military assault on Kwangju, using the ROK Twentieth Division and some special forces troops wearing regular army uniforms to disguise their identity, began at 3:00 A.M. on May 27. Compared with the earlier brutal and bloody encounters, the military action was relatively swift and effective. According to official government figures, by the time the city was retaken, 170 people had been killed, most of them in the first few days. The official toll was raised to 240 in 1995 as a result of a reinvestigation, but Kwangju people claim that the real number was far higher. The outcome fueled a long-lasting and intense opposition to Chun, Roh, and the other generals and fervent anti-Americanism among citizens of the Cholla provinces and many Korean students.

Charges of American acquiescence or even approval of the Kwangju events reverberated in Korea. On May 16, before martial law was declared, the Korean military had made the required notification to remove two elements of the ROK Twentieth Infantry Division from operational control of the US-ROK Combined Forces Command. Before the division was sent to Kwangju to retake the city in the second week of conflict there, Wickham was asked to approve its redeployment to Kwangju, even though such an approval was not required once the division was out from US operational control. After checking with Washington, Wickham and Gleysteen agreed it would be preferable to deploy the Twentieth Division rather than the hated special forces units, which had never been under US command. These facts were used by Chun's propaganda organs to suggest US sponsorship of the crackdown in Kwangju.

The "Kwangju massacre," as it was called, remained a central issue in Korean life for many years thereafter. The United States, which was held responsible by many Koreans, for a long time spoke only sparingly and ineffectively about its role, evidently out of consideration for Chun. In

1985, after the US Information Agency library was occupied by students protesting Kwangju, the embassy recommended that it be permitted to make an extensive statement of the facts about American involvement. Washington said no. It was not until June 1989, nine years after the fact and with Kwangju still a traumatic issue, that the United States responded to questions from a special committee of the ROK National Assembly by making public an extensive account of its involvement in the Kwangju events.

In the immediate wake of the violent denouement, the United States adopted a "cool and aloof" public stand toward Chun and the other generals in order to signal disapproval and in hopes of affecting their future behavior. Washington indefinitely postponed a planned US economic mission to Seoul and asked the Asian Development Bank to delay action on two pending loans to South Korea. In Seoul Gleysteen met Chun twice in June, the month after the Kwangju uprising, and again in early July to advocate political liberalization and, on the last occasion, to emphasize the US view that Chun had "abused" the US-ROK security relationship. Nonetheless, US intelligence reported, "Chun feels that he can more or less do as he pleases, irrespective of U.S. warnings." Donald Gregg, now an NSC official, commented, "We do have limited leverage, and Chun knows this." He thought Gleysteen's strong words might strengthen the US hand. But Deputy National Security Adviser David Aaron argued that these are "all empty words . . . the only way to get leverage on this guy is to start a dialogue with the North." That course was rejected.

It was in this chilly diplomatic climate, on a weeklong visit in mid-July 1980, that I first met Chun and Roh Tae Woo. My meetings with them were arranged by Sohn Jang Nae, the KCIA minister in the ROK Embassy in Washington, a retired major general who had been Chun's and Roh's English teacher at the Korean Military Academy. To my surprise, I found two very different personalities: one decisive, strong, and ambitious; the other conciliatory, flexible, and much less openly ambitious.

Roh, whom I met at his Seoul Security Command headquarters, was so eager to explain himself that a conversation of several hours in length was continued at his request over lunch at his home the following day. I had never met a senior ROK general on active duty before—they had usually stayed away from American correspondents—and was impressed by Roh's openness, intelligence, and supple mind. I was also surprised that Roh said emphatically that he did not believe any military man was ready to become Korea's political leader. "We are not expert in economics or politics," he insisted, and should leave those issues to people who are. The crucial thing for the next leadership is a strong national consensus, Roh told me. "Our intention is very sound: defending the nation and not becoming involved in politics."

The conversation with Chun was very different. He saw me at the headquarters of the recently formed standing committee of the Special Committee for National Security Measures, of which he was chairman and chief executive. Situated in a small building across from the historic Kyongbok Palace, where North Korean delegates had been welcomed to Seoul in 1972, the standing committee was a shadow government with far more clout than the official one in the nearby Blue House, as it demonstrated nearly every day with arrests, edicts, and press attention. Rather than wearing a uniform like Roh, Chun was dressed in a blue suit with a light-blue shirt and sat in a wicker chair simpler than the others in the room, occasionally smoking a cigarette. He impressed me as a physically powerful man operating for the moment under great restraint. As a symbol of his unlimited ambition, there was a large globe in the office, which was unusual even for civilian officials of the South Korean government.

Chun began by saying, with a grin, that he felt like a schoolboy undergoing examination in being interviewed by me. If so, he had done his lessons well. He proceeded to answer my questions with an impressive directness and self-assurance that contrasted with my memory of interviewing Park Chung Hee and other Koreans of an earlier generation. Chun was coy only about his ambition for the presidency, and then only to preserve the formalities. Asked point-blank if he would seek the office, he said he was unable to foresee the future or answer with confidence but quickly added, "I've never run away from problems since the sudden death of the president." He had not planned or scheduled what had happened to him since October, he said, but attributed it largely to "divine Providence," which had given him few choices about his course of action. He spoke of the importance of a strong presidency, given the external and internal challenges before the country. As a former political reporter, I had little doubt that he was preparing to move to the Blue House.

On August 7, Chun had himself promoted to four-star general in preparation for retiring from the army. The next day, he received a political boost from an unexpected source: General Wickham told Sam Jameson of the *Los Angeles Times* and Terry Anderson of the Associated Press in an interview that Chun might soon become president and that "lemming-like, the people are kind of lining up behind him in all walks of life." Speaking with astonishing frankness on background as a "highly placed U.S. military official," but one whose identity became quickly known, Wickham said the United States would support Chun's move into the Blue House if he came to power legitimately, demonstrated a broad base of support over time, and did not jeopardize the security situation on the peninsula. Declaring that "national security and internal stability surely come before political liberalization," the US general declared, "I'm not sure democracy the way we understand it is ready for Korea, or the Koreans ready for it." The State Department disavowed Wickham's remarks, but to little effect.

Shortly thereafter Choi resigned the presidency, publicly claiming he was doing so to set a precedent for the peaceful transfer of power. Privately, he told a military-led committee that he was resigning to take responsibility for the Kwangju events, which he called "a grave mistake" by the armed forces. On August 27, after receiving the endorsement of the ranking commanders of the armed forces, Chun Doo Hwan was elected president without opposition by the rubber-stamp National Conference for Unification. Carter sent him a private message that pointedly did not include congratulations but that urged early elections under a new constitution and "greater personal freedom" to enhance stability. Holding the new regime at arm's length, Washington banned cabinet-level visits to Seoul and postponed the annual US-Korea security conference. Chun's main bid for popularity was his "purification" drive, in which close to ten thousand people were dismissed from government or arrested on corruption charges. The embassy learned to its dismay, however, that the new president and his aides were handing out cash to their followers on an even bigger scale than their predecessors had. "We had to deal with these guys. We had no choice," explained Gleysteen. "At the same time, we couldn't go along and get in bed with them."

THE FIGHT TO SAVE KIM DAE JUNG

Chun's trump card with the United States was the nemesis of the ROK military, Kim Dae Jung. Formally accused of plotting the insurrection in Kwangju that was touched off by his arrest on May 18, Kim was put on trial by court-martial, found guilty, and sentenced to death on September 17. The US Embassy protested every step of the way, beginning with a strong démarche the day after Kim's arrest. Under heavy pressure from the embassy, the Martial Law Command permitted an American diplomat to attend the trial. When it was over, the State Department publicly described the charges against Kim as "far-fetched."

Several senior military figures insisted, in talks with me in 1980, that Kim, whom most of them had never met, was or had been a communist working for North Korea. I had had numerous interviews with Kim over the years and never believed the accusations. Although he was a man of immense ambition, he was also the political figure with more innovative ideas about his country's present and future than anyone else on the scene.

In a midsummer meeting presided over by Deputy Secretary of State Warren Christopher, the Carter administration decided to make a high-priority effort to free Kim and later to save his life. This decision played into the hands of Chun, whose pride and political position were suffering from the undisguised US disapproval of his regime. As the year wore on, the Chun government linked Kim's fate to normalization of the chilly relations between Washington and Seoul. In the final months of the Carter administration, the fate of Kim Dae Jung dominated American–South Korean relations, despite the wide variety of other issues at stake. It was also a major issue between South Korea and Japan, largely due to the residue of Japanese anger over Kim's abduction from Tokyo in 1973.

In mid-December, in an exception to its ban on cabinet-level visits to Seoul, the outgoing Carter administration sent Defense Secretary Harold Brown to see Chun with an appeal for clemency toward Kim Dae Jung. According to Donald Gregg, who accompanied the defense secretary, Chun told him that he was "under terrific pressure from the military" to execute Kim. Chun insisted that despite the intense feelings abroad, "I can't possibly succumb to foreign pressure."

After the American election on November 4, 1980, the defeated Carter team rapidly lost even the minimal clout it had with Chun, who eagerly awaited the new, more conservative Reagan administration. Reagan had made it clear from the start that he wanted no part of withdrawing US troops, an initiative thoroughly associated with Carter and, by now, thoroughly discredited. However, his views on the Kim Dae Jung case were unknown. Carter administration officials were alarmed to learn of a preelection remark to a Korean official in Washington by Alexander Haig, soon to become Reagan's first secretary of state, that the Seoul government should consider itself free to make any decision it chose about Kim Dae Jung. The Carter team feared that the remark and the attitude it conveyed would be an open invitation to execute Kim.

Reagan's incoming national security adviser, Richard Allen, was more sympathetic and more concerned about the international repercussions of Kim's fate. At the end of November, Allen met General Lew Byong Hyon, chairman of the ROK Joint Chiefs of Staff, who had been sent from Seoul to discuss the case. Without being explicit, Lew spoke of the serious insurrection that had been put down and said that "as long as the source of the trouble remains, we strongly feel that we should deal with it appropriately." Allen concluded that Lew was telling him that Kim Dae Jung would be executed. Not knowing what to do or say, Allen stalled for time.

There followed a series of confidential meetings between Allen and Korean officials on December 9, December 18, and January 2, orchestrated and led by Sohn Jang Nae, the KCIA minister in the ROK Embassy. The key South Korean participant in the most important meeting was Lieutenant General Chung Ho Yong, a member of Chun Doo Hwan's inner circle and commander of ROK special forces who had been so abusive in

Kwangju. According to Korean notes of the meeting, Chung bluntly said that Kim Dae Jung was "the most dangerous person" to Korean national security and "must be executed in accordance with law." Allen responded that the execution of Kim would jeopardize the otherwise excellent chance for a major improvement in American–South Korean relations. In an interview in 1994, the former lieutenant general told me that he personally opposed executing Kim and believed that Chun was using threats about Kim's fate as "a card" to obtain what he badly wanted—an early official visit to Reagan in the White House.

By the end of the third meeting, Allen, with encouragement from the outgoing administration, had arranged a deal to save the condemned dissident in return for a Chun visit to the White House and normalization of Chun's relationship with Washington. On January 21, 1981, the day after Reagan's inauguration, the White House announced Chun's impending visit. Three days later, Chun announced the lifting of martial law and commutation of Kim's death sentence to life imprisonment.[*]

On February 2, less than two weeks after taking the oath of office, Reagan welcomed a broadly smiling Chun and his party at the diplomatic entrance of the White House with a trumpet fanfare. The controversial Korean was received at the White House even before the leaders of such important American allies as Britain or France. In a cable from Seoul in preparation for the visit, Gleysteen reported that "to a considerable extent Chun will see the visit as made possible by his decision in the Kim Dae Jung case, but he will not wish to have it characterized as a crude tradeoff."

Discarding the restrained remarks drafted for him by the State Department, Reagan delivered a wholehearted embrace of the leader whom the previous administration had held at arm's length. In his toast at a glittering East Room luncheon, Reagan reminisced about General Douglas MacArthur's handing back the battered city of Seoul to President Syngman Rhee after liberating the capital from North Korean occupation in 1950. With his accustomed oratorical skill, Reagan declared, "We share your commitment to freedom. If there's one message that I have for the Korean people today, it is this: Our special bond of freedom and friendship is as strong today as it was in that meeting thirty years ago."

The Americans had no misconceptions about what the reversal of the chilly Carter-era relationship meant for Chun. A memorandum from Haig to Reagan in advance of the meeting pointed out that the first visit by a Korean president to the United States in twelve years would "symbolize the normalization of US-ROK relations after a period of prolonged strain"

---

[*] In December 1982, Kim was released from confinement and permitted to fly to exile in the United States.

and "consolidate [Chun's] position within South Korea and legitimatize his new government in the eyes of the world." Haig pointed out in that although Chun "has preserved democratic forms, like his predecessor, his style is Confucian and authoritarian," backed by the army. "Chun expects us to be concerned with Korean internal developments and is prepared to consider our advice when it is offered privately and in the context of basic cooperation. His ability and willingness to accommodate foreign concerns over the Kim Dae Jung issue is a measure of how much he has matured."

In a complete reversal of what was viewed as Carter's wimpish attitude toward Korea, Reagan assured Chun that the new administration had no plans to withdraw American troops—in fact, Reagan eventually increased the forces to forty-three thousand Americans, the largest number on duty in Korea since 1972 and three thousand more than when Carter had begun his withdrawal program. The two presidents announced they would immediately resume previously postponed military and economic consultations. Not publicly announced was that Reagan informed Chun that the United States was prepared to sell Korea F-16 warplanes, the most modern in the US inventory, an arrangement that had been agreed to in principle during the Carter administration, but which Carter had personally prevented from coming to fruition.

Reagan's warm White House reception was a major turning point for Chun, convincing most South Koreans that his takeover was a fait accompli. By his actions, Reagan built a store of obligation and goodwill with Chun that he drew upon later in connection with other issues. He also left a store of bitter antagonism and a sense of betrayal among Koreans who had previously admired the United States but now held it responsible for Chun's military coup, the bloody suppression of opposition in Kwangju, and the high-profile endorsement of Chun's rule.

How much Reagan understood—or cared—about the political situation in Seoul is doubtful. At the November 20 meeting of the outgoing and incoming American presidents, their only meeting during the post-election transition period, Carter thanked Reagan for sending a message to Chun urging that Kim Dae Jung's life be spared. Up to that point in the briefing, the newly elected US president had had nothing to say, even as Carter discussed such issues as control of nuclear weapons in times of crisis and a long list of foreign-policy challenges from the Soviet Union and the Middle East to China. However, when Carter touched on Korea and the Kim case, Reagan suddenly exclaimed, "Mr. President, I'd like to have the power that Korean presidents have to draft dissenters." The outgoing chief executive, who had championed human rights in quarrels with South Korean presidents, was startled.

6

TERROR AND TALK

FAMILIES AND FRIENDS OF the passengers of Korean Air Lines flight 007 waited with growing apprehension at Seoul's Kimpo airport on the morning of September 1, 1983. The flight, which originated in New York and refueled in Alaska, had mysteriously disappeared from the skies overnight en route to Seoul. Within a few hours, American intelligence agencies pieced together radio intercepts that revealed a story of the discovery, tracking, pursuit, and destruction of the civilian airliner by Soviet air defense forces as it strayed over Soviet territory north of Japan. Playing back the tapes of transmissions recorded during the night, officials at an American-Japanese listening post heard the chilling report of a Russian fighter pilot to his headquarters: "The target is destroyed."

The first public revelation of the fate of KAL 007 came when Secretary of State George Shultz grimly announced that a Soviet fighter plane had shot down the airliner. Shultz called this "an appalling act" for which there was no excuse. President Reagan in subsequent statements called the action a "massacre," an "atrocity," and a "crime against humanity." The Soviet Union initially denied destroying the plane but later admitted it and justified the action on grounds that the airliner had violated its "sacred" borders on an espionage mission concocted by the United States and its South Korean ally.*

---

* Due to the "spy plane" charges and the failure to locate the airplane's black box, or inflight data recorder, the circumstances of the tragedy would be controversial for nearly a decade. It was only in January 1993, a year after the Soviet Union had collapsed, that the long-hidden black box and recordings of air-defense conversations were unveiled by the Russian government that had succeeded to power in the Kremlin. These records conclusively established that the airliner had strayed 360 miles off its scheduled course due to a series of innocent navigational errors and that a trigger-happy Soviet air-defense commander had ordered the plane shot down by air-to-air missiles on the mistaken assumption it was on an espionage mission. The tapes also disclosed that the KAL cockpit crew members were unaware that they had strayed off course, oblivious to the danger they were in, and never knew what hit them when they and their passengers tumbled uncontrollably for twelve minutes to a watery grave.

The KAL 007 shoot-down soon became a white-hot issue in international politics. It drove US-Soviet relations to new depths at a moment when relations were already extremely tense due to the imminent deployment of American missiles in Europe. For a time, it also slowed progress toward healing the breach between the Soviet Union and South Korea. Prior to the shoot-down, the Soviet government, over the passionate objections of the North Koreans, had for the first time quietly decided to permit Soviet trading companies to deal with South Korean firms through third parties. In a bolder move, a delegation of Soviet parliamentarians had been preparing to travel to Seoul to participate in the International Parliamentary Union convention when KAL 007 was shot down. Due to the international furor, and the bitterness in South Korea, the trip was canceled. For the time being, improvement in Soviet–South Korean ties was put on the back burner.

A second severe shock to South Korea came only a few weeks later, October 9, 1983, during the state visit of President Chun Doo Hwan to Rangoon, Burma. At the ceremonial beginning of the visit, the best and the brightest of the South Korean government stood side by side in the Martyr's Mausoleum at the National Cemetery, awaiting Chun's arrival for a wreath-laying in honor of Burma's founder. Some of the Korean officials were chatting, and a few were standing with their hands by their sides, looking off in the distance. The Korean ambassador arrived ahead of the president in his official car, with its ROK flag flapping in the breeze, and an anxious Burmese trumpeter decided to practice his part in the ceremony to follow.

At that moment, North Korean army major Zin Mo, mistaking the beflagged car for the South Korean president's and the bugler's call as the start of the ceremony, detonated a powerful bomb that he and two other North Korean operatives had planted two days previously in the roof of the mausoleum. In the thunderous explosion, four members of the South Korean cabinet, two senior presidential advisers, and the ambassador to Burma were blown to bits by shrapnel and deadly steel pellets. Among those killed were Foreign Minister Lee Bum Suk, who as chief of the South Korean Red Cross delegation had welcomed and hosted the North Koreans in Seoul in September 1972; Presidential Secretary-General Hahm Pyong Choon, former ROK ambassador to Washington and a leading foreign-policy intellectual; and Presidential Secretary Kim Jae Ik, an architect of South Korea's economic development. President Chun, still on his way to the site, escaped injury.

Before the explosion, reclusive Burma and reclusive North Korea, each pursuing a distinctive brand of Asian socialism, had been the best of friends. This collegiality vanished as the truth of what happened emerged. Burmese police quickly apprehended the North Korean agents responsible.

One of them, Captain Kang Min Chul, confessed, exposing the elaborate planning in Pyongyang that had gone into the attack. In response, the Burmese, furious and embarrassed over the deaths of seventeen visiting South Koreans and four Burmese at the nation's most revered ceremonial site, derecognized North Korea—a decisive step beyond simply breaking diplomatic relations.* Pyongyang denied all complicity, but its denials were unconvincing in view of physical evidence linking it to the bombing and Captain Kang's confession.

This was not the first North Korean attempt on Chun's life. In 1982 plans had been made to kill Chun in Gabon while he was on a state visit to Africa. According to Koh Yong Hwan, a North Korean diplomat who took part in the plot but later defected to the South, the operation was called off at the last minute on the personal instructions of Kim Jong Il, who had recently been given control of the North's clandestine operations.

A sophisticated man who later became Kim Il Sung's French-language interpreter, Koh said he believed the cancellation was ordered because the assassination of the South Korean president in an African country could have devastated North Korea's important African support in the UN General Assembly.

South Korea did not know of the Gabon plot at the time, but concerns about Chun's safety in his overseas travels may have saved his life in Rangoon in 1983. Asked to provide surveillance of Chun's plane by airborne-radar aircraft during his trip, US experts suggested that the route be moved farther away from the Vietnamese and Chinese coastlines, causing a change in the ROK president's planned schedule. Instead of arriving at 4:00 P.M. and going by motorcade directly to the ceremony at the Martyr's Mausoleum, where a mix-up like the one the next day might not have occurred, Chun arrived in Rangoon after 6:00 P.M., putting off the wreath-laying ceremony to the following morning.

The sudden deaths of South Korea's leading high officials caused a new outpouring of anger and grief in Seoul, and much of the same in official Washington, where the Rangoon victims were all well known. As a show of resolve and warning to North Korea, the aircraft carrier USS *Carl Vinson* and its battle group were kept in Korean waters beyond their scheduled departure date, and heightened security measures were taken along the DMZ. No unusual North Korean troop movements were observed, but a few weeks later South Korean officials charged that Pyongyang had planned to launch commando raids after what they thought would be Chun's assassination.

---

* By the early 1990s, the two had resumed contacts and trade but did not establish formal diplomatic relations again until April 2007.

A shaken Chun flew home with what was left of the elite governmental team he had taken to Rangoon. He traveled directly from the airport to a meeting of the surviving members of his cabinet and security team at the Blue House. At the meeting, Minister of Defense Yun Song Min proposed that the South Korean air force bomb the North in retaliation, but Chun rejected the proposal. US intelligence learned that a senior South Korean commander at the DMZ was also advocating a punitive response. Chun said later he met with commanders who were eager to attack the North and declared that only he would decide whether to take military action—and that anyone who jumped the gun would be guilty of disloyalty. In a visit to Chun, Ambassador Richard Walker prepared to make a strong argument against retaliation, even though he said the United States had no doubt that North Korea was behind the attack. Chun responded, "I want to assure your president that I'm in full control of this government and military officers, who report to me. I have no intention of doing anything foolish or anything without full consultation with your government." When President Reagan visited Seoul the following month, he made a point of telling Chun in a private meeting that "we and the whole world admired your restraint in the face of the provocations in Rangoon and over Sakhalin Island [referring to the downing of KAL 007]."

THE NEGOTIATING TRACK

Oddly enough, as the Rangoon bombing plot developed, North Korea was simultaneously pursuing its most important diplomatic initiative toward the South in more than a decade. On October 8, 1983, the day before the bombing, Chinese diplomats passed a message to Washington from North Korea saying for the first time that it would take part in three-way talks with the United States and South Korea to bring peace to the peninsula, accepting Seoul as a full participant. For Pyongyang, this was a major departure from long-standing policies, and it established the basis for much of its diplomacy for the rest of the decade.

It was hardly surprising that Kim Il Sung decided to use the Beijing channel for his initiative toward the United States and South Korea. Since the initial breakthrough between the United States and China in 1971, Beijing had consistently played the role of diplomatic messenger between Washington and Pyongyang. Henry Kissinger had discussed Korea with Chinese premier Zhou Enlai or other officials on at least eleven occasions during the Nixon and Ford administrations. In the mid-1970s, Kissinger sought secretly but unsuccessfully to use the Chinese contacts to persuade North Korea to accept the continued presence of American troops in the South "for at least the short term," in return for a commitment "to reduce and ultimately withdraw U.S. forces as the security situation on the peninsula is stabilized."

In September 1983, Kim paved the way for his diplomatic bid with a speech in which he dropped his previously standard condition that the Chun regime be replaced before talks begin. Later that month, in a conversation with US secretary of defense Caspar Weinberger, Chinese leader Deng Xiaoping proposed that the United States and China work together to reduce tension and promote peaceful reunification on the Korean peninsula. Deng said that North Korea had "neither the intention nor the capability" to attack the South but that if the South attacked the North, "China will not be able to stay out." American policy makers may have been mindful of this warning when they insisted that Chun not permit military retaliation for the Rangoon bombing.

In the aftermath of Rangoon, Deng was furious at Pyongyang for staging the bombing immediately after he had passed along Pyongyang's conciliatory initiative to the Americans. For weeks afterward, Deng refused to see any North Koreans. He was especially angry at Kim Jong Il, whom he apparently thought was behind the bombing, and refused to meet with the younger Kim for the rest of his life.

The overlapping of Pyongyang's peace initiative and act of bloody terrorism is a puzzle that has never been conclusively solved. If the North Korean military had, indeed, been making preparations months in advance, the peace proposal would seem to be an elaborate smoke screen. On the other hand, the key element of the proposal—accepting Chun as an interlocutor—was in a very authoritative article in an important North Korean party journal in early October, suggesting Kim's subtle signal on the possibility of meeting with Chun was serious. It was not the first time the North acted in contradictory ways, nor the last.

The idea of three-way peace talks involving the United States and the two Koreas had been discussed in Washington in the spring of 1978 by two maverick communists close to Kim Il Sung, Yugoslavia's president, Marshal Josip Broz Tito, and Romanian president Nicolae Ceauşescu, in separate conversations with President Carter. The idea had received a big boost during Carter's 1979 trip to Seoul, when President Park Chung Hee agreed to back the proposal despite the misgivings of nearly everyone else in his government. The fear of a repetition of the Paris talks on Vietnam, where the South Vietnamese had been overshadowed by Hanoi and Washington and relegated to a devastating secondary role, was still strong in Seoul and lingered for years after.

At the beginning of the Reagan administration in 1981, Secretary of State Alexander Haig had rejected the idea of three-way talks and instructed the State Department to oppose them. However, a number of

American diplomats did not agree, and the American Embassy in Beijing continued to promote the plan in discussions with the Chinese. Moreover, a US démarche to North Korea through Beijing in September 1983, not long before Deng Xiaoping passed Kim Il Sung's message to Washington, mentioned trilateral talks among a list of items that could improve relations with the United States.

The Rangoon bombing would have seemed to kill the North's proposal for three-way talks. Pyongyang must have been astonished when the following month, Reagan, addressing the South Korean National Assembly during a visit to Seoul, declared that "we would, as we've often stressed, be willing to participate in discussions with North Korea in any forum in which the Republic of Korea is equally represented." The phrase was boilerplate, and certainly was not in the speech as a signal to the North. But it was too good for the North Koreans to pass up, and they jumped on the president's words as their ticket out of their Rangoon problem.

In December the North picked up where it had left off on October 8, and in January 1984 it put forth a proposal for tripartite talks in very high-level and high-profile fashion: during an official visit to Washington, Chinese premier Zhao Ziyang brought it in writing to Reagan and Shultz at the White House. Hours after Zhao's presentation, North Korea broadcast the full text.

Once Pyongyang endorsed three-way talks, however, Washington rejected the very idea it had previously espoused. Reagan counterproposed, in discussions with Zhao, that peace talks on the peninsula should begin with North-South bilateral negotiations, and if that did not suffice, four-way talks that also involved China should begin. South Korea took the same position and also declared that Pyongyang must apologize for the Rangoon bombing before talks could begin. China seemed to be interested in participation in four-way talks, but the North strongly opposed China's entry.

It is questionable how much sincerity was behind this maze of proposals and counterproposals in any of the capitals. Both the Reagan administration in Washington and Chun Doo Hwan's government in Seoul were leery of becoming involved in formal talks with Pyongyang. In May 1984, during a visit to Berlin, Kim Il Sung told Erich Honecker that a major aim of his tripartite-talks proposal had been to make it more difficult for Reagan to increase US troop strength in South Korea. Besides, he told Honecker, "with these talks [proposals] we want to expose the United States excuses" for staying in Korea. "To show the world that the United States does not want reunification, it is necessary to keep making new peace proposals." And again reflecting the North's misperceptions of the situation south of the thirty-eighth parallel, he stated, "This is also necessary to encourage the South Korean population in their struggle."

FLOODS AND FACE-TO-FACE TALKS

The leaderships and publics of both North and South Korea saw the struggle for influence and supremacy on the peninsula as a zero-sum game,
in which any gain for the South was a loss for the North and vice versa.
Moreover, for both regimes, considerations of "face" or prestige were often
more important than issues of substance. Thus, North-South discussions
in the public arena tended to bear fruit only when both countries could
credibly claim victory, which was uncommon. A parallel secret dialogue
between Pyongyang and Seoul, only hints of which were made public
when they occurred, was less constrained but often even more difficult,
because the issues involved were more important.

In early-September 1984, discussions between North and South were
given sudden and unexpected momentum by an act of nature—torrential
rains and landslides in the region near Seoul that killed 190 people and
left 200,000 homeless. North Korea, in a gesture implying superiority,
grandly offered to send relief supplies to its better-heeled cousins in the
South. To everyone's surprise, Chun's government did not spurn the offer
but prepared to receive rice, cement, textiles, and medical supplies. "Along
a worn concrete road gone to weeds, hundreds of North Korean trucks
entered South Korean territory today carrying the first supplies to pass
between the two countries since the Korean war ended 31 years ago,"
wrote the *New York Times*'s Clyde Haberman, who was on the scene at the
DMZ. Some of the rice turned out to be wormy and the cement nearly
unusable, but the South did not highlight the deficiencies or complain,
even as Pyongyang hailed the flood relief in *Rodong Sinmun* headlines as
a "Great Event, the First in the History of Nearly 40 Years of Division."

As the relief goods were delivered, the chairman of the North Korean
Red Cross Society urged that success in this venture be used to launch
"multisided collaboration and exchange." Capitalizing on the moment, the
South proposed, and the North accepted, the opening of North-South
economic talks and the resumption of the Red Cross talks.

With this surprising beginning, the North and South in a period of
a little more than a year held thirteen public discussions, including five
economic meetings, three Red Cross meetings, three working-level Red
Cross contacts, and two preliminary contacts for a North-South parliamentary exchange proposed by Pyongyang. In September 1985, thirty-five
South Koreans crossed the DMZ to visit family members in Pyongyang,
and thirty North Koreans crossed in the other direction to meet family
members in Seoul. After years of formal meetings, most of them sterile
recitations of fixed positions, the emotional reunions of even a few divided
families seemed at last to be a tangible payoff for the inter-Korean talks
and a promise of better times to come.

Unknown to all but a few on each side, the progress was facilitated by secret talks at a high level, which had also resumed late in 1984 and reached a peak in the fall of 1985 as the family reunions were taking place. One of the lessons of the quarter century of North-South dialogue is that it rarely made progress unless the top leaders were involved. In the early 1970s and mid-1980s, most of the involvement of the heads of state was in secret; exchanges involving top leaders would emerge in the public arena only in the early 1990s.

The mid-1980s secret diplomacy began on the day after Christmas 1984, when a tall, urbane Korean who had lived in the United States for many years sat down to a four-hour meeting and luncheon with Kim Il Sung in Pyongyang. Channing Liem, who at seventy-four was two years older than the Great Leader, had been the South Korean delegate to the United Nations under the short-lived reform government that was toppled by the 1961 military coup. After the coup, he became a political science professor at the State University of New York at New Paltz and a vocal critic of the Park regime. Liem had previously visited Pyongyang in 1977 as a private citizen. This time, however, he came as an emissary of South Korean president Chun Doo Hwan, recruited for the task by Sohn Jang Nae, the activist intelligence chief in the ROK Embassy in Washington who had played a key role in negotiating Chun's triumphal visit to Reagan.

In his discussion with Liem, Kim Il Sung agreed to explore a North-South summit. The following week, Kim used his annual New Year's message to the Korean people to make a pointed endorsement of North-South dialogue, saying that success in the ongoing rounds of lower-level public talks could lead gradually to higher-level talks and "culminate in high-level political negotiations between North and South."

The meeting with Liem was unpublicized and known only to senior echelons in North and South. But the very next day, in one of those incidents that suggest pulling and hauling in influential circles in Pyongyang, *Rodong Sinmun* carried an oblique and, at the time, puzzling attack on accommodation with the South. "Sacrifice" and "struggle" are the keys to the victory of the revolution, said the paper, arguing that those who retreat from this road "in fear of being sacrificed" will inevitably "surrender" or become "turncoats."

In Seoul the secret meeting with Kim whetted the appetite of those few who were aware of it. This was especially true of Chang Se Dong, another former general and chief presidential bodyguard who became chief of the Agency for National Security Planning (NSP), the renamed South Korean intelligence agency, in February 1985. With the confidential contacts with the North beginning to show promise, he took them under his direct control.

To aid him in this delicate work, Chang in March 1985 brought in a rising young star from the Blue House staff, the forty-two-year-old presidential secretary for political affairs, Park Chul Un. Park soon became the South's most energetic practitioner of secret diplomacy, not only in North Korea but in Hungary, the Soviet Union, and other countries as well, eventually earning acclaim in the Seoul newspapers as "the Korean Henry Kissinger." Park was bright, having graduated from Seoul National University Law School at the top of his class, and also well connected, being a cousin of the wife of General Roh Tae Woo, Chun's classmate, comrade, and eventual successor. Bold and ambitious—traits in short supply among South Korea's cautious senior bureaucrats—Park quickly made contact with senior figures in the North.

Within a short time, Park was authorized by Chun, and later by Roh, to be the South Korean secret channel to the North. His counterpart in Pyongyang was Han Se Hae, a fifty-year-old graduate of Kim Il Sung University who had taken part in the Red Cross talks in 1972 under an assumed name and subsequently was vice minister of foreign affairs and DPRK ambassador at the United Nations. A fluent English speaker who was considered one of the North's most urbane and accomplished diplomats, Han became attached to the staff of the Central Committee of the Workers Party to pursue his contacts with the South.

Park and Han established a direct telephone connection between their desks in Seoul and Pyongyang, on which they had frequent conversations. The two met face-to-face a total of forty-two times between May 1985 and November 1991 in a wide variety of places, including Pyongyang, Seoul, Panmunjom, Paektu Mountain in North Korea, Cheju Island in South Korea, Singapore, and elsewhere. Some of the meetings lasted as long as five days, but except for a few sightings, most of this diplomacy remained secret.

Chun had repeatedly proposed a summit meeting with Kim Il Sung and recently had said he was willing to meet Kim anywhere in the North, South, or a third country, except for Panmunjom. To advance the summit diplomacy, a five-member North Korean delegation headed by Ho Dam, who had been put in charge of the Workers Party department handling South Korean affairs in a shakeup following the Rangoon debacle, and special envoy Han Se Hae secretly visited the South on September 4–6, 1985, and met Chun Doo Hwan at the private mansion of a Korean industrialist on the outskirts of Seoul. Chun had heard that Kim had seven presidential mansions in the North and wanted to show that luxurious accommodations outside the Blue House were available to him as well. The North Korean emissaries brought a letter from Kim Il Sung to Chun sending "warm regards" and saying, "I sincerely hope to see you in Pyongyang." The letter from Kim to the man who had narrowly missed assassination by a North Korean bomb two years earlier ended, "Be well." In the secret talks, Ho Dam insisted that the Rangoon killings "had nothing to do with us" and warned that if Pyongyang were required to apologize, it would mean the end of the talks.

The South Korean president spoke at length in the secret discussions about the military situation on the peninsula, including its nuclear dimensions. After taking power in 1980, Chun had decisively—some say harshly—shut down the clandestine South Korean nuclear program, dispersing its scientists and engineers, in response to intense American concern about the project. However, he told Ho it would not be technically difficult for either the North or the South to produce nuclear weapons, should it decide to do so. The restraining factor, he declared, was the strong desire of both the Soviet Union and the United States to prevent nuclear wars involving small countries, which inevitably would spread to the great powers. Chun urged that Kim Il Sung, then seventy-three years old, turn away from conflict so that North-South issues could be resolved while he was still alive.

In a return visit the following month, Chang Se Dong, senior emissary Park Chul Un, and three others secretly visited the North Korean president. The southerners brought a letter from Chun calling for an early summit meeting "as a shortcut to peace where both of us meet face to face and open hearts to exchange conversation, build up trust and prevent a war." Kim appeared appreciative and friendly, but on the final day of talks, his aides presented their draft of a North-South nonaggression pact, which the southerners considered full of unacceptable rhetoric. The North also demanded, as it had the previous month, that the coming US-ROK military exercise, Team Spirit '86, be called off. The South rejected both proposals.

After the October meeting, the prospects of an early summit meeting between Kim Il Sung and Chun Doo Hwan rapidly diminished. According to Sohn Jang Nae, who had returned to Seoul as a deputy director of South Korean intelligence, the summit negotiations failed because Chun lacked the will to proceed in the face of North Korean demands and bureaucratic rivalries in the South. "The talks bogged down in arguments over details," Sohn said in an interview for this book. An American intelligence official, who was given full access to the transcripts of the talks by Chun's government around the time that they took place, said that the two sides "got tied up in all sorts of linguistic tangles" such as what words to use to describe the level and nature of the proposed summit meeting. It seemed from the transcripts, the US official said, that "the North was not very interested in making progress, and the South was also bringing up things that would irritate the North."

The final blow was the approach of the Team Spirit exercise, which under Chun had been built up to a powerful array of about two hundred thousand US and ROK troops in increasingly realistic—and threatening—

military maneuvers south of the DMZ, involving ground, sea, and air forces. Chun's intention in working with the Americans to enlarge Team Spirit, according to a former aide, was to scare the North Koreans. If so, he succeeded. Pyongyang in most years put its own forces on full alert during the maneuvers, which lasted up to two months, and acted as if it feared a real attack. "Every time the opponent carries out such a maneuver we must take counteractions," Kim Il Sung told Erich Honecker. Citing the need to mobilize large numbers of reservists to supplement regular troops on guard against attack, Kim estimated that these annual mobilization exercises cost the country "one and a half months of working shifts . . . a great loss." Beyond the practical considerations, the North Korean leader considered the US-ROK exercises an effort to intimidate him, and he reacted bitterly.

On January 20, Pyongyang issued a joint statement in the name of all its public negotiating teams—economic, Red Cross, and parliamentary exchange—denouncing this "nuclear war maneuver intended against North Korea" and indefinitely postponing all further discussions. With that, talk of an early summit meeting faded from view.

KIM IL SUNG AND THE SOVIET CONNECTION

When Kim Il Sung boarded his special train on May 16, 1984, for an eight-day ride to Moscow, it was his first official trip to the Soviet Union since 1961. The Great Leader traveled in imperial fashion, leading a huge entourage of 250 members, including bodyguards, interpreters, pretty young female aides, and even a masseuse, as well as his prime minister, foreign minister, defense minister, and other officials. His train resembled those of American tycoons earlier in the twentieth century—one railroad car was set aside for Kim's meetings, another for his dinners, still another as his bedroom. Internal security troops were posted at frequent intervals along the route of thousands of miles in the Soviet Union, after which Kim went on by rail to Poland, East Germany, Czechoslovakia, Hungary, Yugoslavia, Bulgaria, and Romania.

Kim's trip to the Soviet Union marked a major effort to restore relations with Moscow after two decades of cool ties. The Soviet Union had played a powerful role in North Korea, in its creation, in the selection of Kim Il Sung as its leader, and in the conduct of the disastrous 1950–1953 war. Materials from Soviet archives depict a central role for Stalin in the war, suggesting that he personally insisted on continuing the conflict for well over a year after Kim was ready to seek a negotiated way out. Then, two weeks after Stalin's death, the Soviet leadership reversed his position and issued secret orders to communist negotiators to end the fighting.

Following the Korean War armistice in 1953, Kim remained heavily dependent on the Soviet Union economically and militarily, and he visited Moscow often before the full onslaught, in the early 1960s, of the great schism between the Soviet Union and China. The split between the two giants of international communism, which were also his most important patrons, created enormous problems for Kim, who struggled to keep on good terms with both of them even while being denounced for his internal policies and independent stance. Kim reacted bitterly to Nikita Khrushchev's reformist policies and his denunciations of Stalin's "cult of personality" that Kim emulated. He was even more offended when the Chinese attacked him as a counterrevolutionary revisionist, aristocrat, and capitalist during the radical phase of the Cultural Revolution. Eventually, Kim found the silver lining, that the Sino-Soviet dispute gave him space to maneuver between the two great powers of communism, each of which was forced to tolerate his independence for fear of pushing him decisively to the opposite camp.

Vadim Tkachenko, a leading Korea expert on the staff of the Central Committee of the Soviet Communist Party from 1962 to 1991, said Moscow was concerned about Pyongyang's often surprising and uncontrollable policies: "North Korea was an independent country which took the kind of actions that were difficult to explain. They would down a plane, capture a ship, join the nonaligned countries, and we would only learn of it from the newspapers." According to Tkachenko, "We didn't know [KCIA director] Lee Hu Rak was in Pyongyang in 1972; the Americans told us. We didn't know about the negotiations when the [US spy ship] *Pueblo*[*] was seized [in 1968]; the Americans told us. You'd make a mistake to think that Kim Il Sung was Moscow's man."

However much the Russians privately distrusted Kim and his regime, they saw North Korea as a strategic ally in Asia. A Central Committee official put it well at a closed conference in Moscow in 1984: "North Korea, for all the peculiarities of Kim Il Sung, is the most important bastion in the Far East in our struggle against American and Japanese imperialism and Chinese revisionism." For this reason, the Soviet Union continued to fuel North Korea's economy and military machine throughout the Cold War, although the nature and extent of the support varied over time.

---

[*] The USS *Pueblo*, an electronic surveillance ship on a mission off the east coast of North Korea, was seized by the North Korean navy on January 23, 1968. The North claimed the ship was in its waters; the United States said the vessel was in international waters. The crew was held until December 1968, when the United States offered an apology that was immediately rescinded once the men were safe in American hands. The *Pueblo* was docked for many years in the east coast port of Wonsan. It was moved in 1999 to the Taedong River in Pyongyang, where it was turned into a museum. The ship is slated to be moved again to become part of the exhibit of the newly built Fatherland Liberation War Museum in 2013.

In early 1984, China's relations with the United States were improving rapidly, with President Reagan planning a trip to Beijing in late April, and Kim was once again worried about the direction of Chinese policy. As soon as Leonid Brezhnev died in November 1982, the North had begun signaling interest in improving ties with Moscow. Brezhnev's successor, Yuri Andropov, died in February 1984, before much could be accomplished, and so Kim moved quickly to get an invitation to pay an official visit in May to meet Konstantin Chernenko, Andropov's successor.

When the Chinese learned of Kim's planned trip, they hurried to pay court to him. In their Beijing talks with Reagan, Chinese leaders stressed their backing for the North's recent three-way-talks proposal, and Communist Party general secretary Hu Yaobang urged Reagan to withdraw US troops from Korea, saying "they could return in a day" if hostilities should start again. On May 4, three days after Reagan flew home, Hu arrived in Pyongyang for an eight-day official visit. Two million people turned out to greet him in what North Korea called "the greatest welcome in Korean history." For Kim, Hu's visit was an important part of his delicate balancing act between his two communist sponsors and a useful prelude to his Moscow trip.

In the Kremlin talks with Chernenko and other officials, Kim's central purpose was to reconnoiter the likely course of Soviet politics, according to Oleg Rakhmanin, longtime Asia expert of the Communist Party Central Committee, who took part in the talks. "Kim understood the position of Chernenko perfectly" as a transitional leader, Rakhmanin recalled. Among those on hand for the talks and related social occasions was Politburo member Mikhail Gorbachev, who received his first personal exposure to this "socialist monarchy" in Asia, as he later referred to North Korea. Kim told his Soviet interlocutors, according to a confidential report on the talks furnished to Eastern European communist officials, that he expected this to be his last foreign journey—that thenceforth his son and heir, Kim Jong Il, who this time remained behind to run the country, or Prime Minister Kang Song San would visit foreign countries on his behalf.

Sitting with Soviet leaders in the Kremlin, Kim volunteered to discuss his relations with China and declared them to be good. Yes, it was true that China was flirting with the Americans and Japanese, but Kim declared that this was because "China is a poor country with a population of one billion people and its leadership is seeking help with modernization from the United States and Japan." At another point in his tour, Kim said that despite his confrontation with the United States and Japan, his greatest fear was "of socialism not being maintained in China." With Deng Xiaoping moving rapidly into market economics and hosting Reagan, "we must all insure that they follow a socialist way and none other," Kim told an Eastern European communist leader.

In the Kremlin, Kim told Chernenko that North Korea had no intention of attacking the South and spoke of his recent proposal for three-way talks with the United States and South Korea. While Washington was insisting on bringing in the Chinese to make a four-party negotiation, Kim said that "China is against such an arrangement." Kremlin officials responded that "the Americans are urging the Chinese toward a solution that suits them and their allies, but which creates the danger of the Korean problem being solved behind the backs of the Koreans themselves." Not surprisingly in view of the acute Korean sensitivity to outside interference, "we got the impression that the approach of China to solving the Korea problem was also causing some anxiety in Pyongyang," wrote a Soviet official who made notes on the Kremlin talks.

Kim assured Chernenko that in the future, North Korea would give closer study to "the experience of the construction of socialism in the Soviet Union." Then, having refurbished high-level Communist Party and government ties between the two countries, Kim asked for more Soviet economic and military assistance. He was remarkably successful.

The Soviet Union had been North Korea's main source of external economic support since the creation of the DPRK, regardless of the ups and downs of political relations. By 1983, however, Soviet trade had fallen to less than 40 percent of Pyongyang's exports to all countries and about 25 percent of its imports. After Kim's 1984 visit, the flow of goods to and especially from the Soviet Union increased rapidly. Due initially to an extensive aid package approved as a result of Kim's visit, imports from the USSR jumped from $471 million in 1984 to $1,186 million in 1986 and $1,909 million in 1988, when they accounted for roughly two-thirds of North Korea's imports from all countries. Moscow not only financed a growing trade deficit with Pyongyang but also provided Soviet coal and oil at cut-rate prices, well below those of the world market. Kim also achieved a long-term North Korean goal, an agreement from Moscow to supply light-water nuclear power reactors.

On the military side, Chernenko was equally forthcoming. Since the early 1970s, Moscow had refused to provide sophisticated warplanes to North Korea despite supplying them to such nations as Egypt, Libya, and Syria, because of a Soviet fear that Kim might use the planes rashly. However, on the basis of the newly improved USSR-DPRK relationship and because the Reagan administration was supplying the South with high-performance F-16s, Chernenko promised to supply North Korea with sixty MiG-25 fighters—probably no match for the F-16s but a quantum jump beyond the DPRK's previous weapons. The planes began showing up in North Korean skies the following spring. The Kremlin's military aid package also included SAM-3 surface-to-air missiles and Soviet surface-to-surface SCUD missiles with a fifty-mile range.

In return, in a remarkable breach of its neutral stance in the Sino-Soviet split, the North permitted Soviet military aircraft to begin regular overflights of its airspace. By the end of 1985, they had flown twenty-one missions over North Korea. Soviet warships also began making port calls in North Korea. Even before this flowering of Moscow-Pyongyang military cooperation, the US Command in South Korea was sufficiently concerned that it notified American forces whenever Soviet satellites were expected overhead, in order to implement "avoidance techniques" to mask American activities from overhead spying.

Besides obtaining military and economic assistance, another top-priority aim of Kim Il Sung's 1984 trip was to persuade the Soviet Union to forswear relations or even contacts with the South. Having failed to unify the country through military means in the Korean War, Kim was passionately opposed to the development of "two Koreas," which implied a long-lasting division of the country. He was particularly allergic to any dealings with or recognition of South Korea by the Soviet Union or China—but his own dealings with the South sapped the force of his argument. If he could deal with Seoul, his allies reasoned, why couldn't they? Moreover, the South's rapid economic strides and growing international stature made contacts with Seoul increasingly attractive to members of the communist bloc. South Korea fought hard to undertake and improve these relationships, step by step. And in zero-sum fashion, North Korea fought hard against them, each step of the way.

For a long time, the Soviet Union rejected all relations with South Korea. But in 1973, following the North-South joint statement and President Park's drive for normal relations with communist countries, the Soviet Union began to permit South Korean citizens to participate in international conferences and sports events in the USSR. Pyongyang immediately protested, but Moscow responded that if it barred South Koreans from legitimate international activities, its own participants could be barred, and "there is even a danger that the Soviet Union would be expelled from important organizations."

Around the same time, North Koreans protested sharply after spotting a Soviet correspondent dining in a fashionable Paris café with two South Korean diplomats. The Soviet Foreign Ministry denied any wrongdoing but cabled its overseas posts that "unauthorized, reckless encounters with South Koreans harm our national interests and undermine trust in the integrity of Soviet foreign policy by the DPRK leadership." On another occasion, eagle-eyed North Korean diplomats detected a few South Korean stamps in an international postal exhibition in Moscow, prompting a high-level complaint and hurried removal of the offensive stamps from the display cases.

With South Korea's growing stature and strength in the 1980s, however, a more realistic assessment was beginning to permeate academic and governmental ranks in Moscow. Following Kim Il Sung's 1984 trip, the Korean-born deputy director of the Institute of Oriental Studies, Georgi Kim, said at a closed meeting of the Communist Party Central Committee that the Soviet Union should stop looking at Seoul through Pyongyang's biased eyes. He declared, "It is obvious that South Korea is a successful and respected country which is genuinely interested in being our friend. To respond positively to Seoul's overtures correlates with the U.S.S.R. national interest." This viewpoint was becoming increasingly influential in Moscow.

The emerging Soviet relationship with South Korea was one of the principal issues on Kim Il Sung's mind in October 1986, when he flew to Moscow to meet Mikhail Gorbachev, who had taken power the previous year after the death of Chernenko.* Kim also sought to persuade the new Soviet leader to press the United States to remove its nuclear weapons and troops from South Korea, suggesting that the Seoul regime would be in trouble if its US props were removed. Kim told Gorbachev with considerable exaggeration, "There is a big movement in favor of socialism in the South, and work is underway to create a national front. One third of South Korean parliamentarians support the North. Unlike the recent past when Americans were perceived as liberators and supporters, now many, not to mention the students, speak against the American presence." According to Vadim Medvedev, a senior aide to Gorbachev who participated in the talks, Kim was openly concerned that the interests of North Korea might be ignored in the heightened Soviet-American dialogue, just as he believed was happening in the Sino-American dialogue.

Several months before Kim Il Sung arrived, the Soviet Politburo had decided to shift to a more conciliatory economic and political posture toward South Korea that, a May 1986 Politburo document acknowledged, "was becoming a factor [in the] global, military-strategic balance." Trade with South Korean firms through third countries was encouraged and began to increase rapidly. Exchanges were permitted with South Korea in art, sports, and culture. Nevertheless, in his meeting with Kim in the Kremlin, Gorbachev unexpectedly excoriated China for doing business with South Koreans and declared flatly, "The Soviet Union won't engage with them." Vadim Tkachenko, the Korea expert on the Central Committee, was thunderstruck by Gorbachev's declaration, which contradicted the policy decisions that had been recently made with Gorbachev's participation. When Tkachenko asked higher-ups the next day what policy to follow, he was told to ignore Gorbachev's surprising declaration and "work as before."

---

* In explaining Kim's decision to make an imperial-style rail trip across the Soviet Union in 1984, North Koreans had told Soviet officials that Kim's doctors recommended that he not fly, due to back trouble. In 1986 they said the doctors no longer objected to his flying.

When Kim and Gorbachev met, the Soviet leader had been in power nineteen months, but, as Gorbachev told me in a 1994 interview, "We ourselves by that time had not yet moved very far in developing and shaping the new Soviet line" in foreign and domestic affairs. Earlier in the month, Gorbachev had met Reagan in a high-stakes bargaining match over nuclear weapons at the Icelandic capital of Reykjavik and had returned to Moscow without an agreement. The Soviet leader was coming under fire for the first time from conservatives and some of the military for giving away too much to the West; this criticism may have accounted for his surprising declaration of solidarity in the meeting with Kim. In private, "Gorbachev had an ironical attitude to the claims of the Great Leader and considered him as a burden he had from the past," recalled Anatoly Chernyayev, Gorbachev's national security assistant. As Gorbachev would write in his memoirs, despite his misgivings about Kim's unusual ideology and a personality cult unique in the world, "North Korea was seen as a privileged ally, close to us through the socialist family group and the treaties of mutual friendship and protection. For this reason, we fulfilled virtually all of Pyongyang's wishes for weapons deliveries and economic help."

During the talks with Gorbachev, Kim was able to reconfirm the pledges of economic and military aid that had been offered by Chernenko two years earlier. Specifically, he obtained promises of thirty MiG-29 fighters, supersonic warplanes more advanced than those he had received from Chernenko, plus SU-25 fighters, SAM-5 missiles, and an advanced radar system for early warning and control of ground forces. As the pledges became realities, Soviet military aid to North Korea reached its post–Korean War peak levels, even while Gorbachev was reducing tensions on other fronts and dissolving conflicts with the West.

As a result of Kim Il Sung's diplomacy and the intensification of the Cold War in the early years of the Reagan presidency, cooperation between Moscow and Pyongyang flourished in many fields in the mid-1980s. In 1987, the year following Kim's meeting with Gorbachev, the Soviet Union sent forty-five delegations to North Korea, while North Korea sent sixty-two delegations to Moscow. Nonetheless, there is considerable evidence that Kim Il Sung did not trust the new Soviet leader, especially as his liberalizing reforms, glasnost and perestroika, began to take hold and his relations with the capitalist world improved. Word was circulating among Pyongyang's diplomatic elite that Kim considered Gorbachev even more of a revisionist than the dreaded Nikita Khrushchev had been. Pyongyang increasingly feared a turn for the worse in relations with Moscow.

7

THE BATTLE FOR
DEMOCRACY IN SEOUL

FOR NEARLY ALL ITS existence since the liberation from Japan and the division of the country in 1945, South Korea had been dominated by strong rulers exercising virtually unchecked powers. As in the Kim regime in the North, this was in part a legacy of the leadership style of the Japanese colonial rulers, validated and justified by the national security requirements of the life-or-death struggle on the divided peninsula. During General Park Chung Hee's lengthy reign and the successor rule of General Chun Doo Hwan, the South experienced dramatic economic gains, but its political arrangements seemed frozen in time. This discrepancy gave rise to growing public discontent, expressed passionately by potent antigovernment political and social forces that even the strongest rulers had never been able to stifle. As the end of Chun's regime approached, the sense of imminent danger from North Korea diminished and South Koreans demanded an end to military rule enforced by the heavy-handed activities of secret police agencies.

"The June Resistance," as the political crisis of mid-1987 is sometimes known, was the turning point for South Korea in its shift from authoritarianism toward democratic practice, from strong-arm politics to civil society and the rule of law. Although many trials and controversies still lay ahead, by the end of 1987 South Korea had taken a new road from which there was no turning back. At a crucial moment, the United States played an important supporting role.

CHUN'S SUCCESSION STRUGGLE

The opportunity for peaceful transition emerged in the first instance from Chun's pledge, soon after taking office, to serve only a single presidential term. Chun made his pledge, according to a close associate, because he drew a profound lesson from watching the regime of his mentor, President

Park, decline, decay, and collapse in a hail of gunfire when its leader stayed on too long. In June 1980, while dominating the political scene as the top-ranking general before assuming the presidency, Chun told Richard Walker, a conservative professor with extensive Asian experience who would shortly be US ambassador to Korea, "If I were to become president, I would like the history books to say that I was the first one in Korea to turn over power in a legitimate and constitutional manner."

The fears and wishes of his family also had a major impact on Chun. In 1981 Lee Soon Ja (Mrs. Chun) told me that when her husband was inaugurated on September 1, 1980, their children asked that he finish his presidency properly and hand over the office to his successor. On Chun's first day in office, in a small meeting with her husband and his top aides, the first lady repeated this advice, according to a participant. She added that George Washington was eternally revered in the United States because he refused to be installed permanently in office but insisted on leaving the presidency. "Please help my husband act like that," she implored the officials present. Two days later, while presenting letters of appointment to the members of his initial cabinet, Chun publicly declared, "More than anything else, I am fully determined to establish a tradition of peaceful transfer of power." Subsequently, he announced at a press conference that he would serve a single term—which was set by his new constitution at seven years—and then return to private life.

Chun's declarations were greeted with great skepticism. Having seized power through military means and cemented his power in the Kwangju bloodbath—and having subsequently been elected president by a rubber-stamp college of electors—in the eyes of his people Chun lacked legitimacy. It seemed unlikely that this stern, aloof, highly unpopular general would be the person to inaugurate a democratic tradition. Chun, however, took his one-term pledge seriously. He made plans to center his postpresidential life in a one-story marble office building constructed for this purpose in a parklike setting, replete with fruit trees, behind high steel gates, south of Seoul. "Chun's fortress," as it was dubbed by Seoulites, was the headquarters of the Ilhae Foundation, a think tank named for Chun's honorific pseudonym and financed with $90 million in forced contributions from South Korea's big businessmen. Showing a keen interest in his life after stepping down from power, Chun quizzed FBI director William Webster, on a visit to Seoul, about the US system for protecting former presidents.

President Reagan and other senior American officials repeatedly and publicly praised Chun's "farsighted" commitment to turn over power through constitutional processes, statements intended to lay down markers so that the pledge could not be ignored. "Chun Doo Hwan had made a commitment, and we wanted him to realize that the United States expected him to keep it," according to Secretary of State Shultz, who suspected that

Chun would abandon the commitment if he could devise a way to do so. Yet Chun insisted he was sincere, volunteering to Reagan in a meeting at the Blue House in November 1983 that because of the precedents of Presidents Rhee and Park, who unilaterally extended their terms of office and were finally ousted by force, "the people believe that a change of presidents is possible only through violence. This is a very dangerous way of thinking. . . . My term is scheduled to end in 1988, and it will."

Nevertheless, Chun found it more difficult than he expected to keep his promise. "In a country like ours, it requires a lot more courage to give up power than to grab it," he confided at a dinner for Blue House reporters. He was well aware of the immense personal risks of dismounting from the tiger he had been riding since December 1979, including political and legal retribution from those who had suffered under his rule.

An important factor in the Korean political transition was the worldwide trend in the mid-1980s toward democratization of authoritarian, military-backed regimes. The most dramatic case in Asia was the Philippines. Ferdinand Marcos's 1972 power grab, in which Washington had acquiesced, had encouraged Park Chung Hee to impose his *yushin* system in Korea months later. But in 1986, Washington approved the "people power" revolution that ousted Marcos, and it prodded the falling dictator to leave for exile in Hawaii aboard a US Air Force plane. These spectacular events emboldened the Korean opposition and focused an international spotlight on South Korea as the next potential flash point.

The opposition was also emboldened by the approach of the 1988 Summer Olympics to be held in Seoul, an event that promised to enhance the country's international prestige and was thus of towering importance to all Koreans. The president of the International Olympic Committee, Juan Antonio Samaranch, had made it known that the Games might be moved elsewhere in case of massive disorders in Seoul. This added substantially to the government's reluctance to use lethal force to put down protest demonstrations.

By the start of 1986, Korean public life was focused on post-Chun political arrangements. In April the president returned from a European trip convinced that moving to a parliamentary system would best suit South Korea; many suspected it might also permit him to retain power as prime minister or power broker after his presidency ended. The opposition, seeing such a change as a threat, demanded a return to the earlier practice of direct election of the president rather than through the easily controlled college of electors, established in President Park's martial-law "reforms." With the press still muzzled and the National Assembly a toothless body, the political contest moved to the streets, with the opposition seeking to demonstrate insurmountable national support.

In keeping with tradition, politically active elements of the 1 million students from Korea's 104 higher education institutions constituted the bulk of participants in public demonstrations, joined sometimes by industrial workers. I watched the students in action on a May 1986 visit to the port city of Inchon. The occasion was an opposition-party rally to protest Chun's policies, but nearly an hour before the rally was to begin, the students precipitated a battle with police. First I heard the pop of tear-gas canisters, and then, rounding the corner of a central plaza, I saw students charging the police lines, hurling Molotov cocktails, bricks, and rocks. Soon they were pushed back by a phalanx of law officers—many about the same age as the students. The rout became complete when police brought up a big tanklike vehicle spewing great clouds of tear gas, to which generous amounts of noxious pepper had been added to make it more unbearable. I watched in fascination—until my burning eyes and throat forced me to retreat inside Citizens' Hall, where opposition-party leaders were placing wet compresses over their faces and expressing dismay.

The following day, I met with three student leaders who were on the run from the police. The students, one of whom was an elderly twenty-eight years old, said they had deliberately disrupted the rally out of anger at the opposition's alleged willingness to compromise with the "fascist" regime. These young insurgents were virulently anti-Chun and anti-American, insisting that the United States was responsible for Chun's rule and that Washington was manipulating Korea for its own Cold War purposes. The killings at Kwangju in 1980 were cited as the moment when "imperialism [the United States] and fascism [Chun] got together" in Korea. I found the students wildly unrealistic, but polls suggested that their ideas were not atypical of campus thinking.

With Chun relying on Washington for political and military backing, US policy makers were in a delicate position. It was clear that a large proportion of Koreans strongly favored a transition to a more democratic regime, but American officials were leery of undermining Chun and thereby destabilizing the country with unpredictable results. With North Korea still a threat and more than forty thousand American troops at risk, stability in Seoul was a central—at times an overriding—U.S. objective. Adding to the reluctance to intervene was the recognition that Koreans were highly sensitive about the American role in their political affairs.

In February 1987, the State Department put its toe in the water with a New York speech by Assistant Secretary of State Gaston Sigur. In a calculated attempt to affect the political transition in Seoul, Sigur announced US backing for creation of "a new political framework" through constitutional and legislative reform. He specifically advocated the "civilizing" of the country's military-dominated politics. Sigur, considered a conservative in the Washington political spectrum, was also a committed advocate of democratic reforms in Asia. Surprisingly, he made this important policy speech without prior clearance from his superiors. Shultz initially termed the speech "outrageous" when he learned of its clear-cut prescriptions, but later backed it strongly, telling Chun in Seoul that spring that "every sentence, every word, every comma is the policy of our government."

In mid-April, despite Sigur's call for "accommodation, compromise and consensus," Chun suddenly banned all further consideration of constitutional revision until after the 1988 Olympics. If permitted to stand, this ban meant that the next president, to be chosen before the end of the year, would be elected by an electoral college that Chun could easily control. In practical terms: Chun could dictate selection of his successor. Washington had only brief advance notice of Chun's decision, but did not object forcefully. Opposition protest, however, was immediate and vociferous.

On June 2, Chun summoned the Central Executive Committee of the ruling Democratic Justice Party to dinner at the Blue House and announced that he had chosen his longtime associate and friend Roh Tae Woo as the party's presidential candidate. Roh had retired from the army as a four-star general when Chun became president and then held a succession of civilian jobs, including minister of home affairs, president of the Seoul Olympics Organizing Committee, and ruling-party chairman. Civilian or not, he was seen by much of the public as "the bald man with a wig," meaning Chun in disguise—just another general who would continue dictatorial rule with support of the army.

Within hours of Roh's formal nomination on June 10 by the ruling-party convention, massive, violent protests erupted across the country, spreading to more than thirty cities. Pitched battles, the largest since the 1960 student revolution that had toppled President Syngman Rhee, broke out between demonstrators and police, more than seven hundred of whom were injured in the first two days. Tens of thousands of protesters were arrested. Citizens suffered in clouds of tear gas as the demonstrations paralyzed the central districts of Seoul as well as other cities that had rarely experienced such mayhem. Yet usually conservative, middle-class Koreans displayed widespread sympathy and support for the protests as never before.

Coming on the heels of the Philippine revolution and before the Seoul Olympics, the Korean crisis attracted extensive international attention. In the last two weeks of June, it was the single largest story in the American press, even surpassing the ongoing hearings on the Iran-Contra political scandal. An outpouring of resolutions, bills, hearings, speeches, and press conferences about the Korean crisis came to the fore in Congress. The Reagan administration, already under siege due to the Iran-Contra scandal, was under heavy domestic pressure to take a stand.

A principal concern in Washington was that Chun might use military force to suppress the demonstrations. Another concern was the possibility of a coup imposing a new era of military rule, although this was considered less likely in view of Chun's control of his former army colleagues and Roh's standing with them. Even before the eruption of the extensive protests on June 10, administration officials were considering how American influence might head off a potential disaster.

As in earlier crises, Washington saw its central role as protecting the South from external threat. A message sent via Beijing warned North Korea not to take advantage of the trouble in the South. Fortunately, Pyongyang limited itself to rhetoric about events, and was cautious even in that.

One idea discussed at high levels in Washington was to send a presidential emissary to take the administration's views directly to Chun, much as Reagan's friend Senator Paul Laxalt had gone to see Marcos at a crucial point in the Manila developments. ROK ambassador in Washington Kim Kyung Won strongly advised against this plan on the grounds that it would put Chun on the defensive publicly and complicate the situation.

Officials then developed the idea of a personal letter from Reagan to Chun calling for restraint—but how to do this without seeming to interfere in Korea's domestic affairs was a problem. Ambassador Kim recalled that in April, during an official visit to Washington, the ROK defense minister had carried a letter from Chun to Reagan. It was decided that Reagan's intervention in the turbulent Korean scene would take the form of a belated reply to the forgotten letter.

Composed in Washington and sent to California for the president's signature, the missive was couched in sympathetic, gentle, and inoffensive language, which Reagan preferred when dealing with allies. Saying that he was writing "as a friend," the letter seemed to endorse ideas that Chun had already expressed. Yet it was unmistakably a call for political rather than military solutions:

> I believe that political stability based on sound democratic institutions is critical to insuring the long-term security of your country, and you have often expressed the same sentiments. . . . Therefore, I applaud your commitment to a peaceful transfer of Presidential power next year as a crucial—and, as you say, unprecedented and historic—step in strengthening that institution of democratic government. . . .
>
> The release of political prisoners, and further steps along the lines you have recently taken toward effectively dealing with police officials who abuse their authority, would send to the world a dramatic signal of your intent to break free of what you correctly

term "the old politics." A free press and balanced coverage by television and radio are essential to realizing your commitment to fair elections. Dialogue, compromise, and negotiation are effective ways to solve problems and maintain national unity. Let me assure you that we will support all significant steps in these directions.

Finally, Reagan held out a personal sweetener—the promise of a visit to the United States by Chun after leaving office peacefully in 1988.[*]

The US Embassy in Seoul received word on Wednesday night, June 17, that a letter from Reagan calling for restraint would soon be on its way and asked for an appointment with Chun for Ambassador James Lilley to present it in person. The Korean government stalled—or in the word of the American political counselor Harry Dunlop "stonewalled"—on making an appointment as dozens of Korean cities became war zones. In the capital, thousands of protesters virtually took over many central streets. They overran a unit of eighty policemen, beat some of them badly, and burned their shields, masks, and tear-gas rifles in bonfires. In Pusan hundreds of police officers were injured as fifteen thousand protesters battled with rocks and firebombs against tear-gas assaults. Protesters in Taegu, the hometown of Chun and Roh, set several police posts on fire, overturned a fire truck, and turned its water cannon on riot police.

The usually decisive Chun was worried and frustrated. He had been telling aides for days that putting down the protests under the guns and bullets of martial law would damage the nation domestically and internationally and would constitute "a sad chapter in history," yet if the police lost control, he would be forced to take that step. By Friday morning, Chun seemed to have made up his mind to use the army. Meeting at 10:00 A.M. with his defense minister, uniformed service chiefs, and the director of the intelligence agency, he ordered deployment, by 4:00 A.M. the next day, of battle-ready troops on a variety of campuses and cities. The US Command was to be notified, as required, about those forces that would be withdrawn from the front lines. Student demonstrators were to be arrested. Under the emergency decree he was preparing, Chun told the meeting, he could dissolve political parties and open military courts to deal with dissenters. Another meeting with the military leaders was scheduled for 5:00 P.M.

The Blue House, meanwhile, finally acceded to the insistent American demands that Lilley deliver Reagan's letter. At 2:00 P.M. Lilley, an Asia

---

[*] In fact, Chun did come in April 1988, two months after leaving office, and was welcomed as an elder statesman.

expert who had been born in China and spent a career in the CIA before becoming an ambassador, presented Chun with the letter. Aware that the situation was extremely serious, Lilley had met beforehand with the US military commander in Korea, General William J. Livesey, and obtained his verbal agreement that use of military force was undesirable in the political crisis. Armed with this assurance, Lilley went beyond the gentle language of the Reagan letter to warn that intervention by the military would stretch the alliance in dangerous fashion and court a repeat of the damaging events of the 1980 Kwangju uprising. "This is the American position. The [US military] command is with me. I speak for all of the United States," Lilley declared. Chun, who by that stage of his presidency often monopolized meetings with visitors, listened intently. He did not say what he would do, but he left Lilley with the belief that the presentation had made a serious impression. About an hour after Lilley left the Blue House, aides to Chun were told that the mobilization order had been suspended. Chun had put his sword back into the scabbard and turned to a political solution.

How much of a role the United States played in staying Chun's hand is difficult to determine. At the time and in retrospect, while acknowledging Washington's supporting role, American officials gave principal credit to Koreans. This view was given considerable credence by former general Chung Ho Yong, one of the inner circle of the Chun-Roh group of military leaders and commander of the special forces at the time of the Kwangju incident. Chung had resigned as minister of home affairs the month before the June crisis. According to Chung, he was visited by younger generals and colonels alarmed by the extensive preparations that had been made to use force against the demonstrations. These military men—like the rest of society—thought the demonstrators had a just cause and that a crackdown would be a disaster. Chung took their concerns to Roh, telling him that the use of the military would have grave consequences for society and Roh's own political future. According to Chung, Roh saw the president within hours and strongly recommended against using military force. Roh recalled in an interview for this book that at that "very difficult moment," he had taken his opposition directly to the president. Of crucial importance, he said, was that "the military themselves felt the army should not be mobilized," which was a significant sign of the growing maturity of the ROK armed forces. Another Korean official close to the situation said Reagan's letter added to the impact of advice from a senior aide to Chun that if he put tanks and troops into the streets, the military commanders might develop a mind of their own about using their power, much as Chun had challenged his own seniors and gained control of Seoul in December 1979.

After June 19, emphasis shifted from the streets to a negotiating track. On June 21, the National Assembly members of the ruling party held an unusual daylong caucus, at which the issue of compliance with the opposition demand for direct presidential elections was seriously discussed for the first time. On June 22, Chun announced a plan to meet opposition leader Kim Young Sam to seek a political solution to the crisis. Surprisingly, the two men had never met. The meeting took place on June 24, but ended without agreement.

On June 25, Assistant Secretary of State Gaston Sigur, who had peeled off from a Shultz trip in Australia shortly after the presentation of the Reagan letter, met Chun to observe the political situation firsthand and to reiterate that military force should not be used. Sigur found a distraught and nervous Chun. Though not confiding his views about settlement of the crisis, Chun made it clear he would not seek to stay in office. "Don't you think I know what my people think about me? They don't want me in here anymore. And I don't want to stay under those circumstances," Chun said. "Tell the president, don't worry about that. I'm getting out. I'm not going to stay." At a private dinner arranged by the foreign minister, a cabinet member who had been counted among the most militant Chun loyalists told Sigur, "There's a fever going on and that fever is democracy. And we cannot turn it back."

On June 29, Roh stunned Koreans by accepting the central opposition demand for direct election of the next president—a daring move in view of the unpopularity of the ruling party. In an eight-point program, Roh also advocated complete amnesty for Kim Dae Jung, freedom of expression for the tightly controlled press, and autonomy for the nation's closely monitored colleges and universities. According to a key adviser, Roh came close to advocating an official apology for the Kwangju massacre but backed away at the last minute due to concern about the military reaction. Roh made his startling announcement in the form of recommendations to Chun, whose views were not immediately known but who endorsed Roh's program two days later.

In the national jubilation that followed, Roh was acclaimed a hero by many Koreans, especially as there was widespread speculation that he had taken the bold steps with only grudging assent from Chun. The president said nothing to refute this belief and steadfastly refused to discuss his role in Roh's decisions. In early 1992, more than four years later, Chun's former press secretary published detailed notes of presidential conversations from June 1987, indicating that Chun had originated the decision to accept direct elections and arranged for Roh to take the credit in order to enhance his candidacy. Whatever the true origin of Roh's dramatic reversal, it ended the crisis of June 1987 and put South Korea decisively on the path to political reform.

THE ELECTION OF 1987

The South Korean election of December 1987 was the first popular balloting for president since President Park Chung Hee's narrow victory in 1971. Roh Tae Woo was praised for his summertime role in agreeing to a direct presidential election, but it was widely assumed that he could not win in December because of his military background. Chun Du Hwan thought otherwise. Even before Roh's dramatic June 29 declaration, Chun told aides he had no worry that the ruling party would lose a popular vote "because the government has made numerous accomplishments and the economy is doing well." He also believed that clashes between the two most important opposition figures would sap their strength.

Indeed, a central problem for the opposition was the presence of two powerful leaders, more rivals than colleagues, each with a different geographical and political base. Both Kim Young Sam and Kim Dae Jung were civilian leaders who had long been persecuted. Together they represented a formidable force, but the big question was whether they could work together.

I was in Seoul that August and took the opportunity to meet separately with Roh and the two Kims, all of whom I had known for years.

The meeting with Roh took place amid the trappings of his political power in the spacious corner office he occupied in the National Assembly building as leader of the ruling party. Since our first meeting in 1980, I had seen him several times in Washington and Seoul, and it seemed to me this time he was more articulate as well as a bit grayer. Wearing a conservative business suit, he nevertheless hooked his thumbs into his belt as we talked, as if he missed his uniform. When I reminded him of his statement at our first meeting that soldiers should not become involved in politics, he responded that he had not changed his mind. He went on to say, in the whispery voice he used to discuss sensitive topics, "I found myself in this situation. It may be the will of heaven—this is my destiny. That's my best answer."

The contrast with the hard-edged Chun could not have been greater. I noticed that in an hour's conversation, Roh never mentioned Chun except when I brought up his name, although the office contained a framed photograph of the two men in their shirtsleeves, in addition to the obligatory official presidential portrait. When I asked about Chun, Roh said that their friendship and loyalty to each other had "not changed," though their relationship was somewhat different since the announcement of direct popular balloting. Although it was not generally known at the time, Chun privately agonized about whether he could really trust Roh as his successor, according to Kim Yoon Hwan, who had known both men since high school days and held senior Blue House positions under both of them.

Roh Tae Woo was born on December 4, 1932, in a farming village near Taegu. His father, who worked in the village office, was killed in an automobile accident when Roh was seven, and he was raised by his mother. After brief military service at the start of the Korean War, Roh joined the Korean Military Academy in its first four-year class, the famous eleventh class, which included Chun and many others who later came to power as political and military leaders.

Chun and Roh became close friends. Chun, two years older, was almost always in the leadership role, with Roh a supportive follower. Before becoming president, Roh had been the successor to Chun in at least five key military or security posts. When Chun led the December 1979 military coup, Roh played an essential supporting role, bringing troops from his Ninth Infantry Division from the front lines.

A person who knew both men well since their military academy days described Chun as "a very simple man who sees pictures in black and white" and Roh as "a man of environment and situation." Another Korean, who had watched both men as political leaders at close range, said that "the secret of Chun's leadership was his assertiveness," whereas Roh was "calculating and cautious" as well as surprisingly artistic, interested in music, poetry, and novels.

My interview with opposition leader Kim Young Sam took place over breakfast at the Japanese restaurant of the modern Lotte Hotel. A man at ease with himself, he quickly discarded his suit jacket and rolled up his sleeves as we ate fish, rice, miso soup, and pickles. Kim had met the rival opposition leader, Kim Dae Jung, ten times in the previous six weeks and said he planned to continue meeting at least weekly until they reached a decision about which of them would run for president. "The public expectation is for the nomination of one [opposition] candidate as soon as possible," he said. In the meetings, "we promised each other we would have a united front to achieve democracy."

The personal rivalry between the two Kims went back to 1970, when they had contended for the nomination of the major opposition party to run against President Park. Kim Dae Jung had been the victor in the nominating convention due to deft maneuvering. Although the two Kims and their respective factions sometimes worked together, they were never comfortable with each other.

Kim Young Sam was born on December 20, 1928, on Koje Island near Pusan, at the southeastern tip of the Korean peninsula. His father, a successful island businessman, sent him to the elite high school in Pusan and to Seoul National University, the nation's most prestigious university. Kim was elected to the National Assembly on the government ticket at age twenty-five, the youngest national legislator on record. He soon rebelled against the Syngman Rhee government's dictatorial tactics and was an original member of the opposition Democratic Party, embarking on a lifelong advocacy of democracy.

In 1960 the Koje Island home of Kim's parents was invaded by two men demanding money. As Kim's mother grappled with one of the men, she was fatally wounded by a gunshot to the abdomen. A year later, one of the robbers was caught and confessed to being a North Korean agent seeking money to buy a boat. The family tragedy, which was well known in Korea, colored Kim's attitude toward the North and shielded him from the red-baiting that was common against opposition politicians. His elite schooling and establishment roots made him unusually acceptable to the middle and upper ranks of Korean society. Of the three leading presidential contenders in 1987, he was the closest to a normal politician.

As an opposition leader, Kim had long been outspoken and undaunted by oppression. During the Park era, he was jailed for opposing military rule and in 1969 was the victim of an acid attack while opposing Park's drive to amend the constitution to allow him a third term. A decade later he was expelled from the National Assembly for publicly calling Park a dictator and asking the United States to intervene. After Chun took power, Kim was placed under house arrest for two years for demanding democratic reforms and went on a twenty-three-day hunger strike. In our conversations while he was in opposition, I found Kim Young Sam a steadfast advocate of reform and democracy but vague on other issues.

The setting for my meeting with Kim Dae Jung was very different—his house in central Seoul, a walled compound I had visited many times while he was under various forms of house arrest. This time his front parlor was crowded with a claque of supporters, many of them from his home region of southwestern Korea. That area, the current North and South Cholla Provinces, has had a distinctive history, going back at least thirteen hundred years to the time when it was the site of a separate Korean dynasty. Disadvantaged under President Park, who like both Chun and Roh was a native of a rival political center around Taegu, in the mid-1980s Cholla had notably fewer government ministers, generals, and heads of large conglomerates and a lower average income than most other regions. Kim Dae Jung was the hero and standard-bearer of Cholla and other downtrodden people in Korea, but at the same time he was distrusted and even feared by many people from other regions.

Kim Dae Jung was born on January 6, 1924, on a small island off the southwest Korean coast. Unlike his long-standing rival, however, he was not born to wealth or privilege and was an outsider to the mainstream of Korean elite society. Despite his fame and his important role in so many historic political developments, many leading Koreans had never met him in person.

After his victory over Kim Young Sam for the opposition-party nomination in the 1971 presidential election, he vaulted to the top rank of political leadership by winning 46 percent of the vote against President Park in an election that was heavily rigged for the incumbent. Park hated and feared Kim Dae Jung and had tried to do away with him permanently. Chun Du Hwan continued the vendetta, if a bit less fiercely than had his predecessor.

Shortly before I saw him in 1987, Kim had finally been cleared of all outstanding charges and had his full political rights restored. Until then, he told me, there had been only two months since his kidnapping from Japan fourteen years earlier when he had been free of house arrest, prison, exile, or some other serious official restriction. The years in isolation and adversity had deepened his self-knowledge and political awareness. He had worked out his answers to major questions facing the country and could articulate them clearly.

In the weeks before our meeting, the army chief of staff, General Park Hee Do, had publicly expressed military opposition to Kim Dae Jung's potential candidacy. There was very serious doubt that military leaders would permit Kim to take office if he should be elected, and many supposed they would kill him. As we sat in the family dining room of his house, eating a Western breakfast of eggs and bacon from atop a red-checkered tablecloth covered by plastic, Kim declared his refusal to give in to such threats. In contrast to 1979–1980, when Chun seized power, he was sure the Korean people would fight this time rather than submit to continued military rule. "Democratization means neutralization of the military," he said.

Several weeks after I saw them, the two leading opposition figures pledged publicly that they would not oppose each other, in order not to betray the people's wishes for political change. Nevertheless, a few days after that, Kim Dae Jung appeared at a huge public rally in his home region of Cholla and began touring the country like a candidate. Later Kim Young Sam did the same, starting with his hometown of Pusan. Each claimed the right to be the opposition's choice on the basis of a long history of standing up for democracy, and each became convinced he would win the election. Heedless of their pledges, both ran for president.

Roh Tae Woo, meanwhile, enjoyed the advantages of the leader of the incumbent party, including massive funding and extensive coverage in the media, which was heavily, if not totally, controlled by the government. At the same time, he sought to separate himself from Chun in the public mind. Although the US Embassy was under orders to remain strictly neutral, Roh managed to meet President Reagan at the White House in a mid-September trip to Washington to burnish his image as an internationally respected figure. This seemed to many Koreans a virtual US endorsement. Neither of the opposition competitors sought a trip to Washington to test that idea.

On December 16, election day, Roh won the presidency with 36 percent of the popular vote, as Kim Young Sam and Kim Dae Jung split the opposition majority between them. Manwoo Lee, a Korean American professor who made an intensive study of the election, wrote that "each candidate was like a Chinese warlord occupying his own solid territory" based on his region of origin.

Roh's victory in a hotly contested direct election gave him the political legitimacy that Chun had lacked. It made it possible for him to permit a greater degree of free speech and free press than his predecessors had and to reduce government control of business. Roh's victory also permitted him to ease South Korea's hard anticommunist stance and to bid successfully for amicable ties and eventual diplomatic relations with Eastern European communist countries, the Soviet Union, and China, thereby undercutting North Korea's alliances and drastically changing the strategic situation in Northeast Asia.

8

THE GREAT OLYMPIC
COMING-OUT PARTY

FOR MOST OF THE world, the 1988 Olympic games at Seoul were a great sporting festival. Global television brought the opening ceremonies to the eyes of more than a billion people, the largest television audience in history for any event until that time. But for Koreans, the games were much more. As the government and people in the South saw it, the Twenty-fourth Olympiad was their international coming-out party, an opportunity to show the world that South Korea was no longer a poverty-stricken Asian war victim but a strong, modern, increasingly prosperous country with a vibrant society. The South hoped the 1988 Olympics would enhance its economic growth and global stature as the 1964 Tokyo Olympics had famously done for Japan. Moreover, the universality of the games provided a golden opportunity for South Korea to play host to the Soviet Union, China, and the communist-led countries of Central and Eastern Europe, which were North Korea's allies and which, at the North's insistence, had shunned the South. For much the same reasons, North Korea loathed and feared the coming of the Seoul Olympics, seeing the Games as an essentially political enterprise that would permit the South to improve its image in the world arena and move toward relations with Pyongyang's communist allies. North Korea waged a strenuous battle, month by month, to halt or downgrade the Games. But its effort failed. The Olympics marked major strides in South Korea's drive to win recognition and accommodation from the communist world.

THE COMING OF THE OLYMPICS

From the very first, South Korea recognized the political possibilities of hosting the Olympics. President Park Chung Hee, who had approved the plan to bid for the 1988 Games shortly before his death in 1979, specified that one of the major objectives would be "to demonstrate Korea's economic growth and national power," and another would be "to create favorable conditions for establishing diplomatic relations with both communist and non-aligned nations." The potential diplomatic payoff added a unique and powerful incentive to South Korea's drive.

After nearly a quarter century on other continents, it was generally accepted that an Asian city would have first claim as host in 1988. For this reason, Seoul's most important competitor was Japan's entry, the city of Nagoya. Seoul had several advantages. Japan, a developed country, had already hosted one Olympics. Because of the intense diplomatic rivalry between the two Koreas, South Korea had embassies and consulates in nearly all third-world countries, which made up the bulk of the Olympics participants, while Japan had substantially fewer. Furthermore, many developing countries were sympathetic to one of their own.

In the end, Seoul simply worked harder. Chung Ju Yung, chairman of the giant Hyundai group, was named chairman of the committee to bring the Olympics to Seoul. As the vote approached, he and other Korean industrialists traveled widely, wining and dining Olympic committee delegates of other countries. South Korean prime minister Lho Shin Yong led an intense lobbying campaign with foreign diplomats in the corridors of the annual UN General Assembly session in New York.

In September 1981, when the Olympic delegates arrived at Baden Baden, West Germany, for the voting, they found impressive scale models of the Olympic Village that Seoul pledged to construct for the Games. They were also greeted by dazzling smiles from dozens of Korea's most beautiful young women, including five former Miss Koreas and ten beautiful Korean Air Lines hostesses. According to a member of the victorious Korean delegation, Chung spent several million dollars in obtaining goodwill the same way he won construction contracts for Hyundai in the Middle East, with offers of airplane tickets, women, and money to any wavering delegates. Korea won over Japan by a resounding two-to-one margin.

North Korea was slow to react publicly to these developments. It took more than two months after Seoul was awarded the Games for *Rodong Sinmun* to acknowledge the South's victory, and then it zeroed in on the political ramifications: "Recently South Korean military fascists have been mobilizing high-ranking officials and related staff of the puppet government as well as pro-government trumpeters to raise a ridiculous hullabaloo every day about the Olympics, which are said to be going to be held in Seoul in 1988. Now the puppets of South Korea are approaching socialist nations and nonaligned countries in the hope of establishing diplomatic and official relations in order to have their 'state' recognized as a legitimate one."

As the time for the Games approached, Pyongyang increasingly portrayed the issue to its communist allies in momentous terms. In June 1985,

Hwang Jang Yop, then secretary for international affairs of the Workers Party, wrote the East German communist party that the Seoul Games were not merely an athletic issue but "an important political question touching on the basic interests of world revolution, of whether the attraction of socialism or capitalism will be strengthened on the Korean peninsula." Two years later, the North was still on that wicket. In a May 1987 cable to Berlin, East German ambassador Hans Maretzki reported Pyongyang viewed the issue as "a strategic political fight against the Seoul regime and its imperialistic supporters." With its stubborn approach, he observed, the North was "once again putting itself in self-imposed isolation."

Following a suggestion from Cuba's Fidel Castro, North Korea proposed that the Seoul Olympics be recast as the "Chosun Games" or the "Pyongyang-Seoul Games," with North Korea as cohost, sharing equally in the sports events as well as the television revenues. North Korea insisted to its allies that "if the U.S.A. and the South Korean puppets do not accept our justified suggestions, then the socialist countries—as in the case of the [1984] Olympic games in Los Angeles—should collectively carry out a mighty strike and stand up against holding the games in South Korea."

Another boycott of the Games by the Soviet Union and its Eastern European allies, which had boycotted the LA Olympics, was never a serious possibility. Soviet foreign minister Eduard Shevardnadze made it clear on a visit to Pyongyang in January 1986 that Soviet-bloc athletes were not prepared to sit out another Olympics, no matter what Pyongyang's problems might be. In a confidential report on his visit, Shevardnadze wrote, "We have the impression that internally [North Koreans] have already come to terms with the unavoidable participation of the USSR and the other brother countries in the games." He added that North Korea had asked him emphatically to delay announcing Soviet participation for as long as possible and to support the cohosting proposal. Moscow agreed to keep its planned participation in Seoul a secret and gave lip service to the cohosting idea. Nonetheless, Soviet Olympics officials took an active part in preparations for the Games, attending the convention of national Olympic committees in Seoul in April 1986, although they requested that their presence be given as little publicity as possible.

Meanwhile, negotiations were under way between the two Koreas, under the auspices of the International Olympic Committee (IOC), on possible North Korean participation. Full cohosting of the Games awarded to Seoul was out of the question, something Pyongyang presumably understood from the start; nevertheless, it went ahead building major facilities and churning out T-shirts, banners, and pins for the Games. According to Park Seh Jik, president of the Seoul Olympics Organizing Committee, he and IOC president Juan Antonio Samaranch agreed to try to keep North Korea under control by dragging out the bargaining for as long as possible, even though they saw little hope for final agreement. In the end, they believed, North Korea would never agree to grant full access to tens of thousands of athletes, officials, and accompanying journalists from the West. But while the negotiations continued, it was difficult for North Korea to exert its maximum pressure against the participation of its communist allies in the Games.

The negotiations came to a head in August 1987, when Pyongyang refused to accept a final IOC compromise proposal. On September 24, South Korea rejected a North Korean proposal for another direct North-South meeting on the issue. With this, in the view of the ROK Olympics chief, "North Korea was completely cornered. . . . Patience, mutual cooperation and careful planning by the IOC and South Korea for three years had finally succeeded in isolating North Korea. By the demonstration that the IOC and South Korea were doing their best to appease North Korea, the USSR and Eastern European countries were granted the option to participate freely in the Seoul Olympics."

The North Korean version seems to confirm that the South and the IOC worked to stretch out the talks but were never serious about the discussions. In the summer of 1987, just before a crucial meeting with the IOC (July 14–15), the secretary-general of the DPRK Olympic Committee told a visiting American that the issue of cohosting the Games was discussed at Olympic Committee–related meetings in late 1984 and early 1985. In October 1985, at the first joint meeting of the IOC and the two Korean committees in Lausanne, the North put forward a proposal for free travel between Olympic sites in the two Koreas, including opening ports and airports. In that meeting, it also proposed cohosting, first calling for a fifty-fifty split of the Games (i.e., eleven events), but eventually reducing its request to eight. In June 1986, the IOC offered the North two full games (table tennis and archery) and two partial cycling events, as well as one of the preliminary soccer competitions. According to the North's account, Samaranch presented this as a take-it-or-leave-it offer. The North's reply was, "You shouldn't back us into a corner." With barely eighteen months left until the Games, Samaranch proposed another meeting in February 1987. At that meeting, a bilateral one, Samaranch told the North Koreans that if they took the offer, then there could be further talks concerning such things as the name of the Olympics, television rights, and the locale of opening and closing events. The North Koreans replied that things should proceed without conditions, so Samaranch agreed to another meeting a few months later. To the American visitor, the North Korean official said that the North could be flexible on which specific games it got, but that getting one-third of the events was "a matter of principle." On soccer, he said, the North was inflexible—it was already building the world's biggest soccer stadium to host the matches.

THE BOMBING OF KAL FLIGHT 858

North Korea did not take South's September checkmate lightly. Two weeks later, on October 7, 1987, two highly trained espionage agents were summoned to their headquarters in Pyongyang and assigned to destroy a South Korean airliner. They were told that the order came directly from Kim Jong Il, son of the North Korean president, and that its aim was to dissuade the nations of the world from participating in the Seoul Olympics. On November 29, a bomb planted by the two operatives destroyed Korean Air Lines flight 858, on its way from Abu Dhabi to Seoul. All 115 persons onboard, mostly young South Korean men on their way home from engineering projects in the Middle East, were killed.

Kim Seung Il, a seventy-year-old veteran North Korean espionage agent posing as a Japanese tourist, and Kim Hyon Hui, a twenty-five-year-old agent on her first espionage operation, had boarded the flight in Baghdad and disembarked at the next stop, Abu Dhabi. They left behind, tucked away in an overhead luggage rack, a time bomb concealed in the hollowed-out innards of a portable radio. The original plan called for the two to immediately board a flight from Abu Dhabi back to Rome and then Vienna, where they would meet North Korean diplomats who would arrange their trip home. However, unexpected airport procedures in Abu Dhabi forced them to fly to Bahrain instead. There they languished for two days waiting for seats on a Rome-bound flight while the world absorbed the news of the mysterious airline explosion and intelligence agencies gradually zeroed in on the father-and-daughter "Japanese tourists" who had briefly traveled on the ill-fated plane.

Japanese police determined that the young woman's passport was a forgery. She and her companion were arrested at the airport in Bahrain while preparing to board their Rome-bound plane. As they were seized, both of them bit into poison ampules hidden in the filter tips of cigarettes they carried. The veteran agent died instantly, but Kim Hyun Hui survived, due to the quick reaction of a Bahraini policewoman who snatched the cigarette from her mouth. After Bahrain was convinced she was a North Korean, she was transported under heavy guard to Seoul, where for eight days she steadfastly held to a prepared cover story before finally confessing to her true identity and details of her act. Kim was tried and sentenced to death for the bombing but eventually received a presidential pardon on grounds that she was merely a brainwashed tool of the North Korean leadership.

Years later I sat in a downtown Seoul office with Kim, who told me the story of her life as a diplomat's daughter, a trained terrorist, and, lately, a devout Christian who had substituted Jesus for Kim Il Sung as her savior. Although I had interviewed many defectors in the course of decades of reporting, this interview was uniquely unnerving. I found Kim to be very beautiful, elegant, demure, and calm, tastefully dressed. I did not know then that she had been trained in North Korea to run ten miles in a single stretch, to bench-press 150 pounds, to shoot a silenced pistol with great accuracy, and to deliver karate chops that would swiftly kill. It was chilling to connect this attractive and intelligent young woman to the murder of 115 innocent people traveling home to their families.

As she had flown amid the passengers soon to be killed by the bomb in the luggage rack above her head, she did not dwell on their fate but on her challenging mission. She had been told and believed that her act "was for national unification, which was a great purpose and aspiration of the nation" and therefore justified the human sacrifices. "People in democratic countries find it hard to believe, but I thought about it as a military order, to be accepted without question," she said.

From her youngest days, Kim had been a star. She was selected as a small child to be a leading actress in the country's first Technicolor film. At age ten, she was chosen to present a bouquet of flowers to the senior South Korean delegate to North-South talks in Pyongyang. At age eighteen, while attending Pyongyang Foreign Language College, she was selected for espionage work, given an assumed name, and sent to a military camp for rigorous ideological and physical training. Other training in the arts of espionage followed. She was carefully molded for seven years before being assigned in October 1987 to bomb the South Korean airliner.

When she was brought to Seoul, her initial resolve was to maintain her cover story. Kim told me, "I had heard so many things about the torture and cruelty of the South Korean CIA that I was full of uneasiness and fear. I made up my mind I would have to face the worst part of this to keep my secret." Rather than torture, however, skillful South Korean treatment had a profound effect. South Korean television and walking tours of Seoul contradicted North Korean depictions of a corrupt, poverty-stricken American colony. "I began to doubt that the order [to bomb the airliner] was for unification of the country. I discovered I had just committed the crime of killing compatriots." After eight days of insisting she was a Chinese native residing in Japan, she spoke to her interrogators for the first time in her native Korean, "Forgive me. I am sorry. I will tell you everything."

In the wake of Kim's confession, Washington assigned a senior diplomat to make sure her story was true and had not been coerced. Once satisfied, the United States placed North Korea on its list of countries practicing state terrorism, triggering new economic and political sanctions, and it instituted an interagency drive to assist the South in sophisticated security arrangements for the upcoming Olympics. President Reagan and Secretary of State Shultz personally took up the threat of North Korean efforts to disrupt the Games with Soviet foreign minister Shevardnadze in March 1988. "Do not worry," Shevardnadze told Reagan and Shultz. "We [the Soviet Union] will be in Seoul to compete. There will not be any terrorism." He proved to be right.

THE RISE OF *NORDPOLITIK*

The Twenty-fourth Olympiad, September 17–October 2, 1988, provided the pivot for South Korea's foreign policy at the end of the 1980s. Roh's "northern politics" shifted South Korea's declared policy toward Pyongyang and eventually launched new rounds of public and secret negotiations with North Korea's leaders. More immediate, dramatic, and lasting were the fruits of Roh's drive to establish relations with the allies of North Korea, as a new pragmatism and efforts at reform swept over communist regimes in the Soviet Union, China, and Eastern Europe. In time, these changes would alter the strategic alignments around the Korean peninsula in historic fashion.

Washington Post Tokyo correspondent Fred Hiatt and I interviewed Roh on July 1, 1988, midway between his February inauguration and the opening of the Olympic Games in September. In this first meeting with Roh as president, I found him more relaxed and confident than he had been before, even though the government party had surprisingly lost its parliamentary majority in April elections and he was undergoing a rough political shakedown. Roh described to us a fundamental change in policy toward North Korea. In the past, Roh noted, Seoul and Pyongyang had tried hard to isolate each other, each doing all in its power to interfere with the adversary's relations with outside powers. "We have changed this," he said. "We will ask our allies, our friends, to induce North Korea to come out into international society as a regular member of the international community."

Roh's effort to establish relations with North Korea's allies followed a previously established path. Contacts with the Soviet Union and China had long been a goal of Seoul governments, in the belief that such relationships would enhance the South's security and potentially undercut the North. In June 1983, Foreign Minister Lee Bum Suk declared the effort to normalize relations with the Soviet Union and China to be a formal objective of South Korean diplomacy. Lee, who was killed in the Rangoon bombing four months later, called the policy *Nordpolitik,* after the West German *Ostpolitik* policy with East Germany. In early 1985, specialists from several ROK ministries systematically studying the issue concluded that for the *Nordpolitik* policy to succeed, it was necessary to synchronize it with a more positive effort to negotiate with North Korea, lest it merely alarm Pyongyang as well as its allies. The task of implementing a more assertive negotiating strategy toward both North Korea and its allies was placed in the hands of Park Chul Un, the ambitious relative-by-marriage of Roh Tae Woo, who was made a special assistant to the chief of the ROK intelligence agency.

During his campaign for the presidency in 1987, Roh pledged to pursue a northern policy vigorously, declaring in a speech at Inchon that "we will cross the Yellow Sea" to China in order to resume a historic relationship with Korea's neighbor and promising new prosperity to the country's west coast areas. Whereas on the surface China was cool to Roh's entreaties, Deng Xiaoping's market-oriented reforms in China augured well for eventual success, as did Mikhail Gorbachev's reformist "new thinking" in foreign policy that was sweeping the Soviet Union and Eastern Europe.

To implement his policies, Roh recruited as his special assistant for foreign affairs Kim Chong Whi, a fifty-two-year-old US-educated defense intellectual who had strong ideas about both the conception and the execution of South Korea's external affairs. With Roh's consistent backing, Kim steadily increased the authority of his office to hold sway over diplomacy, defense issues, and eventually North-South relations as well. During five years at Roh's side, Kim energized previously reactive South Korean policy, seizing the initiative on a variety of issues regarding North Korea and its communist allies, while taking advantage of Seoul's swiftly growing economic strength and the approaching end of the Cold War.

The first high-profile public initiative was Roh's *Nordpolitik* speech on July 7, 1988, announcing a new policy toward the North and an intensified effort to establish relations with North Korea's communist allies. Addressing himself to "my sixty million compatriots," a figure that included the people of both North and South, Roh unveiled a six-point program, including promotion of trade, exchanges of visits at all levels, and humanitarian contacts between the two Koreas. He also announced that Seoul would no longer oppose its allies engaging in nonmilitary trade with North Korea and that Seoul would cooperate with the North in its efforts to improve relations with the United States and Japan. In parallel, he announced, "We will continue to seek improved relations with the Soviet Union, China and other socialist countries." Although he made no mention of the Olympics in his announcement, Roh's aides said at the time that the northern policy was explicitly designed, in part, to smooth the way politically for communist nations to participate in the Seoul Games.

North Korea's first reaction to the new policy directions was negative, though with signs that Pyongyang was not closing the door to dealing with Roh. When the South Korean president in an October 4 speech proposed an inter-Korean summit, the North "welcomed" his offer to travel to Pyongyang, though laid down its own conditions.

The first benefits of South Korea's intensified effort to establish relations with North Korea's allies came in Hungary, whose pragmatic "goulash communism" made it the least ideological of the Eastern European countries. A pathfinder for this breakthrough was a businessman, Chairman Kim Woo Choong of the giant Daewoo group, an energetic and successful salesman who became increasingly close to Roh during his presidency. Always looking for new fields to conquer, Kim had pioneered the establishment of business deals and official ties with several countries who previously had relations with Pyongyang but not with Seoul. In the early 1980s, he began knocking on the door of China but concluded that an early breakthrough was too difficult, whereupon he turned his attention to Eastern Europe and the Soviet Union.

In December 1984, the Daewoo chairman flew to Budapest aboard his private jet for conversations that broke the ice between the two countries. With Hungarian government and party acquiescence, a series of business exchanges took place, culminating in an agreement between the two chambers of commerce and the opening of trade promotion offices in each other's capitals in late 1987 and early 1988.

As Roh's *Nordpolitik* drive gathered force, Seoul pressed for full diplomatic relations with Hungary. Its timing was fortunate. In May 1988, a new and more Western-oriented team of officials took office. The following month, word came to Seoul from the chairman of the newly organized Hungarian Credit Bank, Sandor Demjan, that Hungary would be willing to establish diplomatic relations before, during, or after the Olympics on the condition that Korea provide $1 billion in economic aid. The Hungarians were also very interested in increased trade with Korean firms.

Demjan's proposition touched off a series of secret negotiations between the two governments, in which financial aid was a key element. From July 5 to 14, a Korean team headed by Park Chul Un, Seoul's special negotiator with communist countries, visited Budapest, staying in a guarded villa on the outskirts of the capital. In the talks, the Koreans offered $400 million in loans, while Hungary reduced its asking price to $800 million. Then Hungary agreed to establish an official mission in Seoul short of full relations in return for $400 million in loans, and to go all the way to diplomatic relations in return for an additional $400 million.

A second round of secret talks in Seoul, August 8–12, produced a tentative agreement to establish consular-level missions before the Olympics and full diplomatic relations within six months. An announcement of a breakthrough with at least one communist country before the Olympics was important to Seoul, which believed this would improve the political atmosphere for the Games and lead to progress with other nations afterward.

To finalize the deal, a third round of secret diplomacy in Budapest, August 22–27, with meetings sometimes lasting long past midnight, was necessary. In the end, Hungary settled for $625 million in loans, mostly on a commercial basis, to take the first dramatic step. The exchange of ambassadorial-level missions was announced by the two nations on September 13, just four days before the opening ceremonies for the Seoul Olympics. Full diplomatic relations were established less than five months later, on February 1, 1989.

The reaction from North Korea was vehement and bitter. Pyongyang recognized that Hungary's act would have important significance for other East-bloc countries. Natalia Bazhanova, a Russian researcher who has studied the record of secret policy making in Moscow regarding Korea, reported that as North Korea suspected at the time, Hungary did consult the Soviet Union before establishing relations with Seoul and obtained approval. After the September announcement, an authoritative "Commentator" article in *Rodong Sinmun* accused Hungary of committing "a treacherous grave act against the principles of Marxism-Leninism and the revolutionary cause of the working class." The lengthy denunciation asked, "Is Hungary so strapped that it has no choice but to beg for a few dollars even from the South Korean puppets, breaching faith with a friend to survive?"

Only two weeks before the announcement of ties with the South, Kim Pyong Il, the younger half-brother of Kim Jong Il, had arrived in Budapest as North Korean ambassador, whether sent into the looming disaster by Kim Jong Il to embarrass him or to get last-minute traction with the Hungarians is an interesting question. North Korea downgraded its relations after the establishment of full Seoul-Budapest diplomatic relations but did not break them off. Moreover, barter trade between the two countries continued to flourish. "North Korea is very pragmatic" when its economic interests are concerned, commented a Soviet bloc diplomat from Pyongyang.

Not surprisingly, as athletes of 160 nations marched into Olympic Stadium in Seoul for the opening ceremonies of the games on September 17, Hungary's Olympic team was deliriously cheered by the predominantly Korean audience. Cheers were also notably enthusiastic for the groundbreaking appearance by athletes of the Soviet Union. Korean spectators cheered wildly for the Soviet basketball team as it vanquished the American team, to the shock and dismay of many American viewers.

In the new era of Soviet public diplomacy under Gorbachev, Moscow's athletes had been preceded in Seoul by an impressive procession of cultural and political emissaries, including the Bolshoi Ballet, the Moscow Philharmonic Orchestra, and the Moscow State Radio and TV Choir, the latter group including two Soviet-Korean vocalists.

Korean Air Lines, the national flag carrier whose Boeing 747 airliner had been shot down by a Soviet fighter plane five years earlier, was given special permission to fly over Soviet territory in connection with the Olympics. The Seoul government, in return, played host in Inchon

Harbor to the 12,800-ton *Mikhail Sholokov,* a floating hotel for nearly two hundred Soviet athletes and officials. With ROK blessing, the Russians took home with them the computers they were given in Seoul to record the Games and the cars and buses that were used to transport the Soviet delegation.

Of the 160 nations participating in the Games, 24 had no diplomatic relations with South Korea. Nevertheless, global television via satellite leaped across nearly all political boundaries. The nations of the world broadcast an average of ten to twelve hours of the Olympics per day to a huge audience, ranging from the modern cities of Europe, Asia, and North America to tiny villages in remote parts of the third world. The one political boundary that proved to be impervious was on the Korean peninsula. The Olympics were not broadcast in North Korea, and its athletes did not participate.

WASHINGTON LAUNCHES
A MODEST INITIATIVE

On July 5, 1988, Vice Minister of Foreign Affairs Shin Dong Won traveled from the Foreign Ministry, just across a broad boulevard in downtown Seoul, to the American Embassy on the opposite side. Calling on Ambassador James Lilley, Shin brought a copy of the special six-point declaration on North Korea that President Roh planned to make public two days later, which had been developed within the Blue House independently of the United States. Because South Korea lacked direct communication with the Soviet and Chinese governments, however, Washington loomed large as a transmission belt and potential influence on Moscow and Beijing. Shin asked for US support and requested that the United States pass advance copies to the two big communist powers.

Lilley pointed out that the planned ROK declaration "implies changes in U.S. policy toward North Korea," which previously had required that Pyongyang take specific steps to improve relations with the South before any improvement in American–North Korean relations could be made. The South Koreans fully understood that their shift would have consequences for US policy and were cautious about what this would mean in practice. When I had asked Roh in the July 1 interview if South Korea would stop objecting to North Korean applications for visas to visit the United States, he replied, "The change of government policy cannot be too drastic. There is a risk involved in changing everything too quickly." Nonetheless, he added, the basic policy would be to ask the United States and others "to help us draw [North Koreans] out to the international community."

US diplomats passed advance copies of Roh's announcement to the Soviets and Chinese as requested, and publicly praised the South Korean initiative as "positive and constructive." (In private, the State Department was more effusive, calling the move in an internal document "a major— indeed historic—reversal of traditional ROKG policy.") At the same time, however, Washington announced that no immediate US action toward North Korea was required, though it would keep the issue under review. The United States passed word to Pyongyang that it would consider taking positive steps if North Korea did not attempt to disrupt the Olympic Games and if North-South dialogue were resumed.

The principal leverage for Washington and the main issue under review was the touchy question of direct talks between the United States and North Korea. Kim Il Sung's regime had been appealing for such discussions since 1974, in hopes of persuading the Americans to withdraw from the divided peninsula. Washington consistently refused even to talk without South Korean participation.

For many years, the "contact guidance" for American diplomats permitted them to speak to North Korean officials only about "nonsubstantive" matters if they happened to meet in social situations; even then discussions were to be terminated as quickly as common courtesy allowed. Twice before, in September 1983 and March 1987, the State Department had issued new guidance permitting substantive discussions with North Koreans in neutral settings. Nothing much came of this except for a few "getting to know you" chats at foreign embassies because both times, the more flexible rules were soon canceled due to North Korean acts of terrorism: the Rangoon bombing in October 1983 and the bombing of Korean Air Lines flight 858 in November 1987. Following Roh's declaration, Assistant Secretary of State Gaston Sigur and his senior deputy, William Clark, who had served earlier as political counselor in Seoul, became convinced it was time to move again with Pyongyang—this time more seriously.

"We came to the conclusion that if you're really going to achieve some sort of a semblance of peace on the Korea peninsula, the only way to do that is to take some steps to try to open the place," recalled Sigur. The Soviets and Chinese, he pointed out, had forever been pushing Washington to deal with Pyongyang. A central barrier had been Seoul's objections, and now those seemed to have lessened. The main issue at hand, therefore, was one of tactics. Here Clark suggested a "modest initiative" that would be unilateral rather than conditional on North Korea's response.

In October 1988, following the successful completion of the Seoul Olympics, the State Department drew up and won White House approval for its plan, consisting of four points:

- Encouraging unofficial, nongovernmental visits by North Koreans to the United States. Since the beginning of 1988, only eight visas had been requested by North Koreans, of which four—to attend a speed-skating event in St. Louis—had been denied.
- Easing stringent financial regulations that impeded travel to North Korea by American citizens.
- Permission for limited commercial export of humanitarian goods to North Korea.
- Renewed permission for substantive discussions with North Koreans in neutral settings, with the expectation that this time serious communication might take place.

Although no North Korean steps would be required to trigger these limited US moves, Pyongyang would be asked for a "positive, constructive response." In private and public statements, Washington listed five items that could be considered encouraging symbols of a more constructive policy. These were progress in the North-South dialogue, return of the remains of Americans missing in action from the Korean War, elimination of anti-American propaganda, implementation of confidence-building measures along the DMZ, and credible assurances that North Korea had abandoned terrorism as an instrument of state policy.

The American steps were discussed with Roh at the White House on October 20, when he met Reagan and Shultz during a four-day US visit to address the UN General Assembly. Roh, who had been publicly appealing for a summit with Kim Il Sung and whose UN address was unusually conciliatory, approved the American initiative but asked that it not be made public until a few days after he returned to Seoul, which was done. In the meantime, US diplomats briefed foreign governments on the initiative. In an October 25 cable to its embassies, the State Department emphasized that "these proposed measures are being taken both to stay in step with (but not in advance of) the ROKG in this matter, but also because we have substantial interests of our own in seeking to reduce tensions on the Korean peninsula and in promoting dialogue between the North and the South."

On October 28, three days before the public announcement, the State Department sent out instructions for special presentations of the new policies to the Soviet and Chinese governments, with the Chinese explicitly asked to pass the briefing to Pyongyang. "The door is open for the DPRK to pursue an improvement of relations with the United States, if the DPRK abandons belligerence, confrontation and terrorism in favor of dialogue," Moscow and Beijing were told. The American briefers added that Washington hoped for a "constructive response."

It did not take long for North Korea to ask for a bilateral meeting with US diplomats in Beijing. Although Washington did not consider this a truly "neutral setting," it approved the meeting between a North Korean diplomat and the political counselor of the US Embassy in Beijing, Raymond Burkhardt, to take place at the Chinese Foreign Ministry's International Club. There in a small second-floor room, which Americans assumed was bugged by the Chinese, the US–North Korean talks began on December 5, 1988. Burkhardt, who had never dealt with North Koreans before, was surprised that they turned out to be serious and businesslike diplomats who wasted no time with bluster or the usual obligatory praise of Kim Il Sung. The discussions were centered squarely on the main issues of the day as seen in the two capitals.

Thus, in late 1988 for the first time, North Korea achieved the mutually authorized, direct channel for diplomatic business with the United States that it had long been seeking. This, however, was fundamentally the result of Seoul's policy reversal rather than a reflection of new thinking in Washington. US diplomats made it clear from the beginning that the Beijing talks were for communications but not for negotiations. The United States continued to insist that any deal making regarding the divided peninsula would have to involve Seoul.

As it turned out, the meeting between American and North Korean diplomats in the International Club in Beijing was the first in a series of thirty-four such sessions, in which messages were passed but little progress was made, between December 1988 and September 1993.

9

MOSCOW SWITCHES SIDES

A MONTH AFTER THE successful conclusion of the Seoul Olympics, the Soviet Union's ruling Politburo took up for the first time the question of relations with South Korea. This unheralded Politburo meeting on November 10, 1988, whose decisions as usual were made in secret, marked the start of a historic Soviet drive toward friendly accommodation with a long-standing antagonist on the Korean peninsula. As was often the case in major power deliberations regarding Korea, the Politburo decisions that day were based almost entirely on considerations of Russian national interest, with their impact in the peninsula given secondary consideration. Nonetheless, the reversal that was set in motion reverberated powerfully on both sides of the thirty-eighth parallel. Prodded and induced by the ROK, the Soviet Union was transformed over the next two years from godfather, superpower guarantor, and economic benefactor of North Korea to partner and, in some respects, client of South Korea. This was of monumental importance.

By the time of the Politburo meeting, the Cold War ice was breaking up between the Soviet Union and the United States, and Mikhail Gorbachev was at the height of his powers. The previous month, Gorbachev had ousted from the Politburo Yegor Ligachev, the most influential critic of the shift away from the traditional Soviet foreign policy support for "class struggle" and ideological allies, and he had placed foreign affairs under the supervision of Alexander Yakovlev, a leading exponent of a foreign policy based on "new thinking" and accord with the West. Gorbachev had been to Washington to sign a nuclear-weapons reduction treaty with the United States, and Ronald Reagan had been to Moscow to celebrate their new relationship and walk in Red Square with Gorbachev. Just two days earlier, on November 8, Vice President George Bush had been elected US president to succeed Reagan, prompting Gorbachev to plan a December visit to New York to meet the president-elect and proclaim from the rostrum of the United Nations a new Soviet foreign policy based on "universal human values." In describing his new foreign policy, Gorbachev declared at the UN, "Today, the preservation of any kind of 'closed' society is hardly possible"—words that must have chilled Pyongyang. To confirm the seriousness of his policy, he took the occasion to announce a massive unilateral reduction of Soviet military forces and conventional armaments and a large-scale military pullout from Eastern Europe, Mongolia, and the Asian part of the Soviet Union.

In the case of Korea, the fundamental reason for the Soviet policy shift was economic. The Soviet treasury needed money, a lot of it. Among the documents considered in the Politburo meeting of November 10 was a glowing memorandum from Vladimir Kamentsev, deputy prime minister in charge of foreign economic ties, who shared the view earlier endorsed by the ministers of foreign trade, finance, and oil and gas industries that the dynamic economy of South Korea was "the most promising partner in the Far East." Trade with Seoul, which was still being conducted in cumbersome fashion through unofficial contacts and third countries, was climbing steadily, and eager South Korean businessmen were knocking on Moscow's doors with attractive offers of more lucrative trade and potentially even subsidies and outright aid, on condition that state-to-state relations be established. The conclusion of Kamentsev's memorandum, according to the notes of a participant in the meeting, was that "unless we undertake to normalize our relations with South Korea, we may be late."

Gorbachev announced that he agreed with Kamentsev's recommendation to move toward South Korea. There was no dissent. At the same time, the Soviet leader expressed the need for caution in implementing the shift, saying that the Korean issue "should be approached in the context of our broad international interests, as well as our domestic interests." In this respect, he said it was too early to establish political relations with the South before discussing the matter with other members of the Soviet bloc. In the meantime, he decided, cultural, sports, and other ties should be opened wider. "This will come as a signal to Kim Il Sung and to the United States," Gorbachev commented.

Having decided to move in a decisive although evolutionary way, Gorbachev sought to rationalize the action by suggesting it could add to a strong wave of nationalism in South Korea and thereby provide impetus for the withdrawal of US military forces there. This proved to be wildly unrealistic.

Ruling out "shock methods" with respect to Moscow's old dependency on the Korean peninsula, Gorbachev suggested that Foreign Minister Eduard Shevardnadze stop in Pyongyang during the course of a forthcoming trip to Japan to explain to the North Koreans the evolution of Soviet relations with South Korea. When Prime Minister Nikolai Ryzhkov remarked that Kim Il Sung might refuse to see Shevardnadze to receive such a message, Gorbachev acknowledged this could happen—but in any case, "we will make this gesture, and give North Korea a notice."

Nobody had any illusion that the explanation would be easily accepted. The Politburo had before it classified reports from the Soviet Embassy in Pyongyang reporting that Gorbachev's perestroika reform was already coming under sharp criticism from Kim Il Sung's regime, which increasingly considered Gorbachev a "revisionist" departing from the true faith of Marxism-Leninism. Gorbachev reacted calmly to these reports, noting that he had already experienced similar opposition in several other fraternal countries. Whatever the repercussions in North Korea, the Soviet leader was determined to change Moscow's long-standing Korea policies. He summed up the discussion by announcing, "We will firmly proceed on the way to rapprochement and establishing relations with South Korea. We are now taking this necessary decision."

THE ROOTS OF CHANGE

The ground had been prepared for Moscow's shift in policy several months earlier, by Soviet participation in the Seoul Olympics, which had dramatically altered official, journalistic, and popular attitudes toward South Korea.

Until the Gorbachev era, very little information about South Korea had appeared in the Soviet press, and nearly all of that negative. However, in the Olympic year of 1988, there were 195 stories in leading Soviet newspapers and magazines, most of them firsthand accounts by Soviet correspondents. In addition to sports news, the correspondents covered Korean economic achievements, culture, and lifestyle, with authentic impressions of Korean reality.

Remarks by Soviet reporters illustrate the overnight change in attitudes toward South Korea. Vitaly Ignatenko, who served as leader of the Soviet press at the Seoul Games and later became Gorbachev's press secretary and director general of Tass, the Soviet news agency, said his first visit to Seoul was "a shock" to him. "Everything I had read before turned out to be outdated; I arrived into the 21st century." Correspondent Vitaly Umashev of the influential weekly *Ogonyok* said, "My vision of South Korea as a Third World country disappeared." The Communist Party newspaper *Pravda*, which had previously depicted South Korea mainly as a bastion of American militarism, summed up its impression after the close of the Games: "The sports facilities in Seoul are the best in the world, and the values of the Korean traditional smile and etiquette have been greatly underestimated."

Even more powerful was the impact of television. Almost 200 million Soviet viewers watched the ceremonial opening of the Games, with attention also directed outside the stadium to scenes of Seoul. Many Russians were stunned and delighted to see Korean spectators rooting for Soviet teams in the Games, even against American competitors. An aide to Gorbachev told the Soviet leader, "There is definitely no other place on earth where people so heartily welcome Soviets."

Even before the Games, South Korea had engaged in a series of probes with Moscow. In the summer of 1988, Park Chul Un, the Blue House point man for northern politics, traveled to Moscow with a letter from President Roh to Gorbachev. The letter praised the very perestroika policies being damned in Pyongyang and called for establishing Soviet–South Korean diplomatic relations as a step toward peace and stability in Asia. A few weeks later, Gorbachev sent a return letter.

As Park prepared to leave Moscow, he was informed that the Soviet Union intended to improve its unofficial ties with Seoul and was advised pay attention to a speech to be delivered by Gorbachev in Krasnoyarsk in Siberia on September 16, the day before the opening of the Olympics. In that speech, Gorbachev addressed himself for the first time in public to the potential thaw, declaring that "within the context of a general improvement in the situation on the Korean peninsula, opportunities can open up for forging economic ties with South Korea." He also proposed a multinational initiative to limit and reduce military forces and activities "in the areas where the coasts of the USSR, PRC, Japan, DPRK and South Korea merge close." Roh responded in his October address to the UN General Assembly, calling for "a consultative conference for peace" involving the five powers mentioned by Gorbachev plus the United States. The Soviet UN ambassador and other officials noted the resemblance between the two proposals.

Quite apart from politics, the South's growing economic dominance on the peninsula made the country difficult to ignore. Although in the first decades after the Korean War the economy of the North was considerably ahead, by 1988 South Korea's GNP was at least seven times larger than the North's, and the gap was growing rapidly.

Up to 1984, the Soviet Union had provided more than $2 billion in foreign aid and credits to North Korea, much of it in the form of whole factories financed by soft loans that were never repaid. Following the trips to Moscow by Kim Il Sung in 1984 and 1986, the Soviet Union had provided increasing quantities of oil and gas, weapons, and a variety of other goods on easy credit and concessional terms. In 1984, however, Pyongyang stopped paying even interest on its smaller debt to Western creditors, and three years later it was officially declared in default, making it ineligible for further commercial loans. By 1988 Moscow was shipping $1.9 billion in goods to North Korea while receiving less than $0.9 billion in return. This heavily subsidized Moscow-Pyongyang trade made up nearly three-fifths of North Korea's total trade turnover.

The vibrant economy of South Korea, on the other hand, was booming, with economic growth rates over 10 percent annually and a large
global trade surplus, as its automobiles, ships, television sets, and computer chips made their mark on the international economy. No longer the
recipient of foreign aid, Seoul in mid-1987 had become an aid-dispens-
ing nation by establishing an Economic Development Cooperation Fund
to assist developing countries. In their contacts with Moscow, leaders of
South Korea's highly successful *chaebols* were expressing intense interest
in investment and trade in Siberia, a high priority in Soviet economic
plans for which massive foreign investment was needed. Moscow initially
had hoped for major Japanese funds, but the unresolved dispute over the
Soviet-held Northern Islands interfered with this prospect. The ROK was
the logical substitute.

Even before the Politburo decision to move toward ties with the
South, North Korea demanded an explanation from its Soviet ally for its
growing trade relations with Seoul. In a memorandum in late-Septem-
ber 1988, the International Department of the Soviet Communist Party's
Central Committee responded in astonishingly frank terms:

> The USSR, to solve its economic problems, is interested in new
> partners. South Korea possesses technology and products that can
> be of use, especially in the Far Eastern regions of our state. As is
> well known, South Korea maintains commercial links with almost
> all countries in the world, including such socialist states as the
> People's Republic of China. The opening up of direct economic
> contacts between the Soviet Union and South Korea will also
> benefit peace and stability in the Asia-Pacific region. We don't
> want to rush developing these ties. We'll move gradually, mea-
> suring progress in the economic field with the political trend in
> the region.

The memo added, "At the same time the USSR remains loyal to obligations to the DPRK. We don't intend to start political relations with South
Korea."

In December 1988, a month after the Politburo decision on improving
ties with South Korea, Seoul passed word that it would favorably consider
Moscow's request for a $300 million commercial loan and also study a
possible $40 million project to build a trade center in the Soviet Far East.

As Gorbachev had directed in the Politburo meeting, Shevardnadze
traveled to Pyongyang that month to inform the North Korean leadership
directly of Moscow's decision. The North Korean capital struck members
of the Soviet traveling party as depressingly cold and gray with unsmiling
people and little clouds of dust in the streets. Kim Il Sung, however, did

his best to stay on the good side of his visitors, and in an internal report the Soviet foreign minister described the discussions as "especially cordial."

It was left to Foreign Minister Kim Yong Nam, the official who often performed the job of presenting Pyongyang's most intractable positions, to fiercely attack Moscow's shift in policy. According to Shevardnadze's report, his counterpart "rather sharply accused the socialist countries of not evaluating the situation in South Korea correctly, of deepening the division of the country and hindering inter-Korean dialogue and [charged that] some socialist countries are betraying socialism for the sake of money." Shevardnadze reported that "these fabricated accusations were firmly rejected by us." The Soviet foreign minister assured the North Koreans that Moscow's relations with Seoul would continue to be unofficial, and he included this commitment in the formal communiqué issued at the end of the talks.

Shevardnadze did not repeat in public or in his internal report his most emphatic statement in Pyongyang. At the height of the argument with his North Korean counterpart, he declared heatedly that "I am a communist, and I give you my word as a party member: the USSR leadership does not have any intention and will not establish diplomatic relations with South Korea." This would be thrown back in his face later by North Korea—and sooner than anyone guessed.

GORBACHEV MEETS ROH

In 1989, a year of dramatic change in the external relations of the Soviet Union, ideology gave way to pragmatism and internationally accepted standards. The last Soviet troops left Afghanistan in February, ending an occupation that had severely damaged Moscow's standing abroad. In May Mikhail Gorbachev traveled to Beijing to terminate once and for all the decades-long dispute between the two giants of communism. In August, with Gorbachev's approval, the Polish Communist Party gave up power to a coalition headed by the noncommunist trade-union movement Solidarity. This spelled the end of the Brezhnev doctrine, under which Soviet military power enforced the loyalty of its peripheral satellite states. A series of spectacular events in Eastern Europe followed, in which the communist governments of Hungary, Czechoslovakia, Bulgaria, and Romania were ousted or their leaders forced to reverse their political direction. In November the crossing points in the Berlin Wall were flung open, bringing the symbolic end of the Iron Curtain that had divided Europe since World War II and leading in time to the absorption of communist East Germany by the West. At a windblown, sea-tossed summit meeting with President George Bush in Malta in December 1989, Gorbachev gratefully accepted American economic aid and declared that the United States and the Soviet Union were no longer enemies.

While his foreign policy was winning praise abroad, Gorbachev was under growing criticism at home. The Soviet Union was in the first stages of a painful economic transition, with consumer-goods shortages causing longer and longer lines and the budgetary deficit soaring to 12 percent of GNP, at that point considered abnormally high. Public confidence in the Soviet leadership was sharply declining, just when loosening controls on expression made it possible for the public to declare its views.

In these circumstances, Gorbachev saw better relations with Seoul as a promising new source of economic help for the embattled Soviet leadership. Moreover, by forging visibly close ties with South Korea, Moscow was poking a finger in the eye of the standoffish Japanese, who were refusing to provide economic assistance because of the Northern Islands issue. Gorbachev had diminished concern about North Korea, which was seen as a holdover from the Stalinist era and the epitome of the Cold War states that were rapidly passing from the scene in Europe.

Looking back on the Korean developments, Gorbachev wrote in his memoirs, "Our interest in South Korea, one of the East Asian dragons which had succeeded in creating an economic miracle, grew in relation to the worsening of the economic situation in the USSR." In an interview for this book, the former Soviet leader also pointed out other factors, noting that he took up relations with Seoul "after a serious change in US-Soviet relations and after the concept of New Thinking began to materialize, after the important process of change got under way in Eastern Europe, and after we abandoned the so-called Brezhnev doctrine."

In Seoul President Roh watched the signs of a developing Soviet shift, particularly Gorbachev's two policy speeches on Asian affairs in July 1986 in Vladivostok and September 1988 in Krasnoyarsk. "I took this as an indication that the time was right, the opportunity had come to make ourselves available" for realizing the goal of establishing relations, Roh told me in 1993. "I would say I started smelling their real intention."

At the end of 1988, Moscow lifted entry restrictions to the USSR by South Koreans, giving them for the first time the same treatment as citizens of other capitalist and developing countries. Shortly thereafter, the two nations opened postal, telegraph, telephone, and telex links. In January 1989, Korea's most senior business figure, Chung Ju Yung of Hyundai, Korea's largest conglomerate, visited Moscow and reached an agreement on business cooperation with the Soviet Chamber of Commerce. Soon after, the deputy chairman of the Soviet chamber traveled to Seoul and agreed on the exchange of unofficial trade offices in the two capitals. When the South Korean office in Moscow opened, it was immediately mobbed by hundreds of Soviet entrepreneurs and government officers proposing deals.

Korean industrialists flocked to Moscow, where they were feted by Soviet officials and presented with requests to help in a wide variety of enterprises, ranging from building consumer-goods factories to converting Soviet military industries to civilian uses. Trade between the two nations increased rapidly.

Trying to respond, in early 1989 North Korea launched a spirited campaign to persuade Gorbachev to visit Pyongyang, hoping that this could reverse or at least halt the drift toward Seoul. It was widely known that Gorbachev planned to visit China in the spring, which would provide a convenient occasion for a stopover in Pyongyang. High-ranking North Korean leaders and their ambassador in Moscow used every possible tactic to get Gorbachev to add Pyongyang to his itinerary, including begging, demanding, and threatening. "It was very hard for us to invent new reasons all the time why he couldn't come," said a Gorbachev aide who prepared his trip to Beijing. Gorbachev's national security assistant, Anatoly Chernyayev, said Gorbachev feared his reformist reputation would suffer in Pyongyang because "he realized that once he went [there] and they staged a performance of hugging and kissing, everyone would accept it as a double standard."

Gorbachev's refusal to visit was difficult for Pyongyang to swallow. This was especially so because the resolution of the Sino-Soviet dispute— which the Gorbachev journey to Beijing symbolized—created a new situation in which neither major communist power would be fearful about pushing Kim Il Sung's regime into the arms of the other. Kim was worried about losing leverage with them both, and worse, the potential threat to the North either might pose.

In Beijing Gorbachev spoke of his fast-developing friendship with South Korea in terms that would have been impossible during the Sino-Soviet split. Briefing materials prepared for him in Moscow noted that "Beijing energetically promotes unofficial ties with Seoul. The PRC's volume of trade with South Korea is $3 billion, ours is less than $200 million. This connection with Seoul does not harm China's relations with Pyongyang and at the same time helps the peace process on the Korean peninsula." Gorbachev told Chinese premier Li Peng, "We think that the USSR is behind China in developing ties with South Korea. Very far behind." Li responded, "If you mean trade volume, you are right."

On the political side, Moscow was reaching out to Seoul through its party-dominated think tanks. In February 1989, the Institute of the U.S.A. and Canada, headed by the influential Georgi Arbatov, hosted Kim Dae Jung, the most internationally prominent opposition leader. The Institute of World Economic and International Relations, headed by the redoubtable Yevgeni Primakov, invited Kim Young Sam, his political rival.

Kim Young Sam's visit in June 1989 coincided with a trip to Moscow by North Korean Politburo member Ho Dam. Soviet authorities arranged for the two to meet. Acting on the basis of an understanding reached with the Blue House before his trip, Kim declined Ho's invitation to visit Pyongyang, insisting that a North-South summit meeting come first. Had Kim accepted and traveled to Pyongyang, the contacts and understandings with the North that resulted might have changed Korean history. As it turned out, Kim's careful handling of the Moscow visit and the invitation from Pyongyang won acclaim from the government in Seoul and paved the way for his political alliance with Roh Tae Woo in January 1990— an alliance that eventually resulted in Kim becoming Roh's successor as president.

Throughout this period, a struggle over Korea policy was taking place in Moscow. On one side were most Foreign Ministry officials, the Soviet military, and the Korea experts in the Central Committee, who favored caution because of the long-standing ties to North Korea; on the other side were members of the Soviet political and economic leadership, who considered the North Korean tie an anachronism and were eager to move ahead quickly with the South to obtain economic assistance. The central issues concerned pace and procedure rather than direction. "We understood the inevitability of future recognition of South Korea, but we were calling for going to this aim step by step," said a senior Foreign Ministry official. However, he said, some departments in the Central Committee and some personal aides to Gorbachev insisted on taking dramatic steps at once, due to their urgent desire for financial aid. Vadim Tkachenko, the veteran Korea expert on the Central Committee staff, who favored a measured approach, said the top decision makers "from the beginning converted the issue into trade [where] the most important thing was money. . . . [They were] doing everything on the spot, without thinking."

The moment of truth arrived in May 1990, when Gorbachev met privately in his office with former Soviet ambassador to the United States Anatoly Dobrynin, who had returned to Moscow to become a senior foreign policy adviser to the Soviet leader. Dobrynin had been invited to visit Seoul for a conference of the InterAction Council, an unofficial group of former heads of state and senior diplomats organized by former West German chancellor Helmut Schmidt. In view of the sensitivity of this trip to Seoul by a high-ranking Soviet official, Dobrynin was required to obtain Gorbachev's permission.

The day they met, Gorbachev had just received a report from his finance minister on the dire state of the Soviet Union's coffers. Foreign goods were urgently needed in an effort to keep living standards from sinking while reforms were under way, but financial markets were refusing to supply further credit because of Moscow's inability to pay its debts. Searching for money wherever he could, Gorbachev was in the process of authorizing a series of secret financial appeals to the West German government as part of the intense negotiations on the future of Germany.

Dobrynin recalled that Gorbachev's words to him were "we need some money." With that practical preamble, Gorbachev proposed that Dobrynin use the trip to Seoul to explore the possibility of a major loan from the South Korean government. At this stage, Gorbachev was not ready to go to Seoul himself, but he told Dobrynin that he would be willing to meet Roh somewhere else, perhaps in the United States, where he was scheduled to have a summit meeting with Bush in late May or early June.

Dobrynin arrived in Seoul on May 22 and the following day was taken to a secluded Korean-style building on the grounds of the Blue House. There he met secretly with Roh and his security adviser, Kim Chong Whi, the architect of the *Nordpolitik* maneuvers. Dobrynin relayed the news that Gorbachev was willing to meet the South Korean leader, a powerful symbolic step tantamount to official recognition and certain to lead rapidly to full diplomatic relations. "You are the third to know," Dobrynin told the Korean president, "and you are the fourth," he said to Roh's aide. Emphasizing the need for secrecy, the Soviet emissary obtained a commitment that the Korean Foreign Ministry would not be informed until the last minute, because the Soviet Foreign Ministry had also been kept in the dark. It was agreed that the meeting would take place two weeks later in San Francisco, which Gorbachev planned to visit after the completion of his Washington summit. Dobrynin did not inform Foreign Minister Shevardnadze of the meeting until shortly before it was publicly announced, and the Soviet Foreign Ministry took no part in the session—extraordinary given the event's importance.

According to Dobrynin, he discussed with Roh a loan of some billions of dollars, though without being specific on figures. In a 1993 interview for this book, Roh quoted Dobrynin as telling him that Soviet leaders "were in a desperate situation for their economic development." Having seen what Korea had done economically, Roh recalled, "they expected that South Korea could somehow play a role in the success of *perestroika*. As a model, they were attracted by the Korean economic development. That was their top priority at the time, and they naturally expected that South Korea could contribute to this." Roh told Dobrynin that Korea would make a major contribution to the Soviet Union, but only if and when full diplomatic relations were established.

From the Korean perspective, a full breakthrough with the Soviet Union would be of immense importance. It would deprive North Korea of the undivided support of its original sponsor, its most important source of economic and military assistance, and an important military guarantor against American power. Moreover, the spectacle of the general secretary of the Communist Party of the Soviet Union meeting with the president of South Korea meant the legitimization of the Seoul government virtually everywhere and the final collapse of North Korea's long-standing effort to wall off the southern regime from communist nations. There was little doubt that eventually China would follow Moscow's example.

Although the meeting of Gorbachev and Roh took place on American soil, the United States played only a minimal role in bringing it about. Secretary of State James Baker had discussed Korea with Shevardnadze in several meetings early that year, but these talks centered on the North Korean nuclear problem, and, in any case, Shevardnadze was not involved in setting up the breakthrough with South Korea. The subject of a possible South Korean connection with the Soviet Union had been discussed in the spring by Roh's foreign policy aide, Kim Chong Whi, with Assistant Secretary of State Richard Solomon and US ambassador to Korea Donald Gregg. Solomon agreed to help but felt that a breakthrough was unlikely during 1990.

Once the Gorbachev-Roh meeting was arranged, the United States worked to facilitate it. At the urging of the Blue House, which considered a signal of continued US alliance to be vital, President Bush agreed to receive Roh at the White House following the California event. The visible show of American support for the breakthrough, Gregg reported to Washington, "may finally drive a stake through the heart" of a widespread South Korean belief that the United States was opposed to direct contacts between Seoul and Moscow.

Selecting the site for the meeting in San Francisco turned out to be tricky. For security, convenience, and possibly symbolic reasons, the Soviet side proposed the Soviet Consulate General in the Northern California city, but the Koreans adamantly resisted this because of historical overtones they considered shameful. In 1896 King Kojong had taken refuge in the Russian legation in Seoul for a year to escape assassination by the Japanese, with the result that Russia won special rights and benefits in a weakened Korea. This humiliation had never been forgotten in Korea, where historians coined a special word, *akwanpachon,* for "kings taking refuge in the Russian legation." After much discussion, the Soviets agreed to hold the meeting in Gorbachev's suite at the Fairmont Hotel.

Although the meeting itself was an unremarkable exchange of generalities, the event marked "a radical change" in Soviet policy from exclusive alliance with North Korea, as Gorbachev acknowledged later in an internal Kremlin report. There was no explicit decision to move to full diplomatic relations, though this was clearly implied and rapidly accomplished after Gorbachev and Roh shook hands. According to Kim Jong In, who was then Roh's senior economic aide, Roh stated near the end of the meeting that the Korean government was prepared to offer "several billion dollars" in economic support. Soviet notes of the meeting said Roh "announced a readiness to grant considerable credit" for the purchase of South Korean consumer goods and also pledged cooperation in creation of joint enterprises and in the opening of Soviet Asia. Others who were interviewed for this book insisted that money was not discussed, though everyone knew the issue was an important one.

When Gorbachev asked if Roh had a message for Kim Il Sung, Roh replied that he would welcome Soviet efforts to bring about a North-South rapprochement. Specifically, he asked Gorbachev to do three things: tell Pyongyang that Seoul was ready to meet officially for the discussion of any outstanding question, use Soviet influence to place the North on the path of external opening and internal reform, and convey ROK willingness to discuss and take steps to reduce military confrontation on the peninsula. When Soviet diplomats tried to pass on Roh's message, Pyongyang refused to accept it, calling it "an unbelievable concentration of lies and slander."

At the end of the brief meeting, Roh eagerly asked for a photograph of the two men together, knowing its political impact on both sides of the thirty-eighth parallel. Gorbachev was reluctant but was finally persuaded by Dobrynin, who argued that "it won't get published in Russia." The official Korean photographer recorded a broadly beaming Roh with his left arm in friendly fashion on the elbow of Gorbachev, who managed only a wisp of a smile.

Roh's press conference immediately afterward was broadcast live to South Korea. With the fall of the Berlin Wall and the prospect of German unification, Roh noted, Korea remained in June 1990 the only nation still divided by Cold War politics. "As a result of today's meeting, the cold war ice on the Korean peninsula has now begun to crack. We expect that this will be the first major step toward a peaceful and unified Korea," he declared. Roh repeated that Seoul did not wish to isolate the North Korean regime but that the ultimate objective of his *Nordpolitik* policy was to induce North Korea to open up. "The road between Seoul and Pyongyang is now totally blocked," he said. "Accordingly, we have to choose an alternative route to the North Korean capital by way of Moscow and Beijing. This may not be the most direct route but we certainly hope it will be an effective one."

THE SHEVARDNADZE MISSION

In September 1990, three months after the Gorbachev-Roh meeting and less than two years after swearing "on my word as a party member" that the Soviet Union would not grant diplomatic recognition to South Korea, Soviet foreign minister Shevardnadze returned to Pyongyang to break the news that Moscow had decided to do just that. Shevardnadze's special Aeroflot plane arrived in a gusty wind so strong there was doubt whether it could land, and his awkward mission met turbulence throughout. When he flew out of Pyongyang two days later, an angry Shevardnadze was smarting from accusations and threats, including a threat of accelerated nuclear weapons development, hurled at him by his North Korean counterpart, Kim Yong Nam. The Soviet foreign minister told his party, as his plane took off, that the experience had been "the most difficult, most unpleasant talk of my life."

Eduard Shevardnadze, a white-maned politician who had succeeded the long-serving Andrei Gromyko as foreign minister in 1985, was a remarkable figure. A native of the southern republic of Georgia, Shevardnadze had no diplomatic experience before being chosen by Gorbachev, an old friend. Perhaps because of his minority-group status as a Georgian in the Russian-dominated Soviet Union, Shevardnadze proved to be sensitive to the concerns of smaller nations and troubled peoples. Among the strongest advocates of democratic policies in domestic affairs and of the New Thinking in relations with the West, Shevardnadze was notably cautious about a rapid policy change on Korea. Alexander Bessmertnykh, who was a senior deputy to Shevardnadze, said that "he reasoned we have an ally, not an attractive one but a powerful one. He didn't want to give this up by forcing the pace." Another senior Foreign Ministry official, who worked closely with him on Asian matters, called Shevardnadze a very wise man. "He said it is very easy to worsen our relations with North Korea, but it would be extremely difficult to restore them."

How strongly Shevardnadze argued these points within the Kremlin inner circle during the consideration of Korea policy is uncertain. Gorbachev's aide Anatoly Chernyayev, who sat in on Politburo meetings, recalled that "Shevardnadze more than once reminded the Politburo that certain things might evoke irritation on the part of North Korea." According to his account, however, Shevardnadze did not throw the full weight of his influence against the rapid improvement of relations with the South in 1990 but instead told Gorbachev, "You do whatever you want but without me."

Following Gorbachev's meeting with Roh, the decision was made in Moscow to establish full diplomatic relations with South Korea as of January 1, 1991. In discussing how to inform Pyongyang, it was suggested that Shevardnadze send his Asia chief, Deputy Foreign Minister Igor Rogachev, to do the distasteful job. However, Shevardnadze, a man of courage and honor, felt obligated to go himself, knowing that convincing North Korea to accept the change would be formidable.

On his plane en route to Pyongyang, Shevardnadze worked hard on his brief and his tactics. He decided to tell North Korean foreign minister Kim Yong Nam in a one-on-one meeting at the start of his talks, then to try to persuade Kim Il Sung, later in the visit, to accept the Soviet reversal calmly.

In the one-on-one meeting, Shevardnadze gave the bad news to Kim. He argued that North Korea would benefit from Moscow's diplomatic relations with Seoul because Soviet officials would be able to talk directly with the South on North-South issues, the problem of US troops and nuclear weapons, and other topics of importance to Pyongyang. Kim responded with passion against recognition of the South, saying it would reinforce the division of the country and severely aggravate relations between Moscow and Pyongyang. He asked that it be reconsidered.

After more than an hour of private discussion, the two ministers invited the other members of their delegations into the large, high-ceilinged conference room. Shevardnadze repeated the decision he had brought from Moscow and elaborated the reasons for it. He said the Soviet Union could not ignore such an important country as South Korea, which had become a major economic and political factor in the region and the world. He insisted that recognition of the South would not change the nature of Soviet relations with the North or Moscow's views on Korean unification. Specifically, he declared, all Soviet obligations toward North Korea, including the 1961 treaty of alliance, would remain in force.

There were three microphones on each side of the long conference table, and the Soviet officials noticed that the Korean foreign minister spoke into his as if addressing an unseen audience of greater importance than the delegation in front of him. At first he said he was not ready to reply to Shevardnadze's presentation but would do so later. Then, after being handed a note by an aide who entered the room from outside, he pulled out a prepared document and launched into a lengthy and bitter response, which featured the following points:

- Establishment of ties between the Soviet Union and South Korea would give international legitimacy to the permanent division of Korea. Formal recognition by Moscow would be fundamentally different from and more serious than that by other nations because the Soviet Union, along with the United States, had been responsible for the division of the country in 1945, and because the Soviet Union had been the first to recognize the DPRK as the sole legitimate state in Korea.
- Recognition would embolden South Korea to try harder to destroy socialism in the North and swallow it up, along the lines of the East German scenario. It would lead to deepening confrontation in the peninsula.
- If Moscow recognized another part of Korea as legitimate, Pyongyang would be free to recognize other parts of the Soviet

Union, which would create trouble for Moscow. (According to one participant, Kim named several places where Pyongyang might establish diplomatic relations, including Khazhakstan and other Central Asian republics of the USSR and the Baltics, which were straining to obtain independence.)

- Soviet recognition of the South would destroy the basis of the 1961 security treaty. Then the North would feel free to take its own actions in the Asia-Pacific region and not be obligated to consult the USSR in considering its policy.
- With the alliance a dead letter, North Korea would consider itself no longer bound by pledges not to create any weapons it desired. (On this point, some Soviet participants recall Kim specifically threatened to create nuclear weapons, but in any case the meaning of his words was clear.)

At the end of the meeting, Shevardnadze asked for time to consider what Kim had said, and he promised to reply the following morning. When he did so, he reiterated that the Soviet Union intended its relationship with North Korea to remain unchanged despite impending recognition of South Korea. As to the threat to take up relations with Soviet republics, Shevardnadze was unconcerned, saying that such contacts could be in the mutual interest of everyone.

Shevardnadze bore down hardest on the threat to create nuclear weapons. As a friend, he said, he would advise against this. Production of nuclear weapons would severely harm the DPRK's relations with the West and the international community, and the Soviet Union would have to react as well. He added, in an echo of Kim Il Sung's official line for years, that there was no possibility of using nuclear weapons on the Korean peninsula, because they would devastate not only the South but the North as well, and also damage China.

In reply, Kim Yong Nam repeated, in even harsher terms, his statements from the previous day. In response to a direct question, he said it would be "very difficult" for the Soviet foreign minister to see President Kim Il Sung, who—he said—was out of Pyongyang.

Shevardnadze took this news in good grace at the meeting, but privately he was angry and upset, inasmuch as trying to explain the Soviet policy to Kim Il Sung had been his principal purpose in coming to Pyongyang. Back at his guesthouse—a notably smaller and less well-appointed one than that he had occupied two years earlier—Shevardnadze decided to leave at once, abruptly gathering his staff and departing several hours earlier than scheduled.

The Soviet foreign minister was still smarting from his treatment in Pyongyang when he went to New York for the UN General Assembly meetings later in September. While there, he planned to make a joint announcement with South Korea to establish Soviet-ROK diplomatic relations as of January 1. At a diplomatic reception several days before the planned announcement, South Korean foreign minister Choi Ho Joong, under instructions from Seoul, buttonholed Shevardnadze and pleaded with him to move up the date, arguing that "this is a good and right thing, so why not do it immediately?" To Choi's surprise, at their meeting on September 30, Shevardnadze readily agreed. With a flourish, the Soviet foreign minister took out his pen and struck through "January 1, 1991" on the prepared announcement, substituting "September 30, 1990" as the date for inaugurating the new relationship. As Shevardnadze crossed off one date and entered the other, he said under his breath in Russian, loud enough for his party to hear, "That will take care of our friends."

Pyongyang responded bitterly in *Rodong Sinmun* under the headline, "Diplomatic Relations Sold and Bought with Dollars." Citing past promises from Gorbachev and Shevardnadze not to recognize South Korea, the article declared that "the Soviet Union today is not the Soviet Union of past days when it adhered to socialist internationalism but it has degenerated into a state of a certain other character. . . . The Soviet Union sold off the dignity and honor of a socialist power and the interests and faith of an ally for $2.3 billion" (the amount of a reported South Korean economic cooperation fund for Moscow). The article appeared under the byline "Commentator," a designation meant to signal a highly authoritative statement from North Korea's leadership.

North Korea's relations with Moscow were headed into a deep freeze, with immense practical as well as political consequences. The Soviet Union was by far Pyongyang's most important trading partner, providing North Korea with most of its imports of weapons and weapons technology and large amounts of machinery and equipment. Moscow was also an important supplier of petroleum, though not as large as China. Soviet exports to North Korea were supplied on a highly concessional basis that most other nations would not have accepted. Even so, North Korea had failed to pay for much of what it bought, leaving huge overdue bills to the Soviet Union. Now that trading relationship, and more, was in doubt.

"HOW LONG WILL THE RED FLAG FLY?"

The Soviet Union's rapid movement to diplomatic relations with Seoul was only the latest in a string of developments that were making Kim Il Sung's globe spin out of control. Within little more than a year, the South had established full diplomatic and important economic ties with Hungary, Poland, Yugoslavia, Czechoslovakia, Bulgaria, and Romania, all of them Kim's former allies, all of which had previously shunned the Seoul regime. The maverick Romanian communist leader Nicolae Ceauşescu, who had been Kim's special friend, had been overthrown and executed. Kim's other special European friend, East German leader Erich Honecker, had been deposed, and the East German regime was in the process of being taken over by the capitalistic West. As a result of the fall of communism in Europe, there was intense speculation that Kim Il Sung and his regime would be the next to go.

In advance of the sensational Gorbachev-Roh meeting in San Francisco, it had been highly uncertain how North Korea would react. Three days before the meeting, the State Department's Korea desk had speculated in a confidential briefing paper that "the shock of Gorbachev's meeting with Roh—especially when he has avoided visiting North Korea—could spark a major leadership crisis in Pyongyang, which could heighten military tensions on the peninsula. It will be hard for the North to let an insult of this magnitude pass. In their rage and frustration, Kim Il Sung and Kim Jong Il might lash out at the USSR, the ROK, or us." The department's Bureau of Intelligence and Research (INR), in a separate confidential memorandum, speculated that in the aftermath of the San Francisco meeting, a "firestorm" was likely in Pyongyang. In talking points submitted by the State Department to the White House in preparation for President Bush's conversation with Roh following the meeting, a central question on the minds of American officials was, "Could Pyongyang strike out irrationally?"

In fact, rather than turn inward or "lash out," Pyongyang sharply intensified a flurry of diplomatic activism with China, Japan, and South Korea that it had started several months earlier. Overtures were also being made to the United States, but Washington wasn't listening. In sum, North Korea sought to match the diplomatic accomplishments of its rival below the thirty-eighth parallel. However, it was less prepared and less well equipped to make serious gains.

Only a week after Shevardnadze's abrupt departure from Pyongyang, Kim Il Sung traveled to Shenyang, in northeast China, for unannounced meetings with Jiang Zemin, general secretary of the Chinese Communist Party, on September 11 and Deng Xiaoping, the senior Chinese leader, on September 12. Among old friends, Kim did not disguise the fact that he had been severely shaken by the loss of his friends and allies in Europe and even more by the Soviet Union's decisions. According to a former Chinese diplomat who had access to the details, Kim Il Sung's central question for Deng was, "How long will the red flag fly?" In other words, how long will communism last, in view of the European and Soviet developments? Deng responded optimistically that the outlook was still bright. Although the Soviet Union was faltering, Deng insisted that Asian countries were defending the faith and that Marxism-Leninism was still strong in China, Vietnam, and Cuba as well as in North Korea.

Kim also raised the question of North Korean economic reforms. Deng, who had been urging Kim for years to follow his reformist example, encouraged him anew. The North Korean leader also made a subtle plea that China not follow the Soviet lead in recognizing the South, or at least slow down its moves in this direction. Beijing's trade with Seoul was rapidly growing, sea and air routes were opening, and informal contacts initiated among business and government leaders. Despite Kim's plea, China agreed with South Korea a month after the Shenyang meeting to exchange trade offices equipped with quasi-diplomatic consular functions, an important step but not a dramatic one. China was willing to go slow but not to stop the advance toward Seoul.

Kim Il Sung's interaction with the other great Asian power, Japan, was more dramatic. On September 24, as a result of contacts that had begun in the spring, a chartered Japan Air Line plane landed in Pyongyang bearing forty-four Japanese Diet members with accompanying Foreign Ministry officials, aides, and journalists—by far the most important Japanese official mission to that point to visit the North. Over the next four days, Kim deployed all his personal charm and diplomatic skill to negotiate an unexpected breakthrough.

Japan had normalized its relations with South Korea in 1965, expressing deep regret for the "unfortunate period" of Japanese occupation from 1910 to 1945 and providing $800 million in grants and credits as compensation. In the years that followed, Japanese trade, investment, and technology had been powerful forces behind the South's rapid economic development. Allied with both countries, the United States strongly supported the South Korean rapprochement with Japan.

North Korea's relations with Japan had been more tenuous. Kim Il Sung had made overtures in the early 1970s, at the time of the US-China opening, and then-Japanese prime minister Tanaka had been interested, but such a Pyongyang-Tokyo rapprochement was vehemently opposed by Seoul and given no encouragement from Washington. Unofficial contacts between the Japanese government and North Korea were carried on mainly through parliamentarians of the Japan Socialist Party. The relationship between the two countries was dramatically illustrated by the legend printed on Japanese passports, "This passport is valid for all countries and areas except North Korea (Democratic People's Republic of Korea)."

Late in 1988, Pyongyang began making cautious overtures to Tokyo. Shevardnadze carried a message from Tokyo expressing interest, and the following month, in January 1989, a Japanese Foreign Ministry statement declared that "Japan does not maintain a hostile policy toward North Korea" and that it would be appropriate "to move positively toward improved relations" if Pyongyang so desired. The statement also expressed hope for the release of two Japanese fishermen held on espionage charges by North Korea since 1983 for permitting a stowaway to leave aboard their ship.

The Diet delegation that flew into Pyongyang was unique in containing leaders of Japan's ruling Liberal Democratic Party as well as those of the Socialist Party, and especially because it was headed by the most powerful figure in Japanese politics, Shin Kanemaru. The gruff seventy-five-year-old LDP kingmaker held no formal government post but was widely considered the power behind several prime ministers.* Kanemaru, who had no foreign policy experience, overrode objections from the Foreign Ministry in accepting the North Korean invitation at the time he did.

On the second day of the visit, the Japanese delegation was taken to the Myohyang Mountains (literally, Mountains of Delicate Fragrance), one of North Korea's great scenic spots and the site of Kim Il Sung's favorite villa. That afternoon, the delegation returned to Pyongyang—minus Kanemaru and a few aides, who remained behind at Kim's insistence. In the evening and the following morning, Kim and Kanemaru had two lengthy, intimate meetings in which Kim won Kanemaru's confidence and trust. There were no Japanese witnesses and no notes taken, but a Japanese official who spoke to Kanemaru soon after the meetings said Kim was furious at the Soviet Union and spoke of the necessity for "yellow skins" to stick together against "white skins." The official said it was clear to him that Kim was worried about the Russians most of all, even more than the Americans. Kanemaru came out of his talks with Kim with tears in his eyes and praise for the sincerity of the Great Leader.

During these and parallel meetings among the officials who had returned to Pyongyang, North Korea proposed immediate normalization of relations with Japan, surprising not least because it implied Japanese acceptance of two Koreas, which North Korea had always opposed. The payoff would be a large sum of Japanese reparations, in keeping with the precedent of the 1965 Japan–South Korea accord. Taking a page from the Hungarian and Soviet playbooks with the ROK, Pyongyang proposed that some of the money, which it reckoned in the billions of dollars, be paid even before diplomatic relations were established.

After a marathon negotiating session from which the accompanying Foreign Ministry representatives were excluded, the Japanese delegation issued a joint statement with the North Korean Workers Party. Among other things, the statement declared that Japan should "fully and formally apologize and compensate the DPRK" for the thirty-six years of Japanese

---

* Two years later, when Kanemaru fell from power and was jailed for tax evasion after $51 million in gold bars, cash, and other assets were found in his home, the scandal helped drive the LDP from power for the first time in thirty-eight years.

occupation of Korea and also for the forty-five years of abnormal relations after World War II. This created a furor in Tokyo and Seoul because it was issued without coordination with South Korea, because its went well beyond the 1965 Tokyo-Seoul accord, and because of fear that some of Japan's funds could be used to support North Korea's military and nuclear weapons program.

After the delegation returned home, negotiations with North Korea for the normalization of relations were turned over to the Foreign Ministry, which stiffened the Japanese position on the nuclear question and other issues. Not surprisingly, the talks got nowhere. The only tangible and lasting result of Kim Il Sung's initiative with Kanemaru was release of the two Japanese fishermen.

Perhaps the most significant North Korean initiative in this period was to move ahead with high-level public—and also secret—talks with South Korea. On May 31, just days before the Gorbachev-Roh meeting, the Supreme People's Assembly, the North's legislature, called for the North-South dialogue to resume immediately across the board.

Three weeks later, the North sent a telephone message to the South denouncing its "flunkyist and divisive antinational acts" with the Soviet Union but, more important, proposing to restart preparations for high-level North-South talks. Preliminary meetings continued over the summer, resulting in an agreement that a delegation headed by the North Korean prime minister would visit Seoul on September 4–7, and that the South Korean prime minister would then lead a delegation to Pyongyang on October 16–19. These meetings, at the level of heads of government from each side, marked a significant step, at least symbolically, in the long and winding road of inter-Korean relations.

In early October, between the first and second rounds of the prime ministerial talks, a three-man delegation headed by NSP (formerly KCIA) director Suh Dong Kwon met secretly in a Pyongyang villa with Kim Il Sung and Kim Jong Il. A month later, the North sent Yun Ki Bok, a Workers Party secretary who had been the political commissar for the 1972 Red Cross talks, and two other officials to meet Roh secretly in Seoul.

Suh told me in an interview for this book that these meetings came close to agreement on a North-South summit conference, to be held in North Korea early in 1991, but failed due to disagreement on a proposed joint declaration dealing with unification. Another senior ROK official familiar with the meetings, however, scoffed at this idea, saying that the two sides were never close to bridging fundamental disagreements.

The Pyongyang meeting with Suh was the only time during his father's lifetime that Kim Jong Il met with senior representatives of the South. While his father did most of the talking, the younger Kim occasionally interjected an opinion in a seemingly insecure way that did not

impress the Seoul officials. When asked at the meeting, Kim Jong Il readily agreed to a separate meeting with Suh, but later the visitors were told
he was unable to keep this promise because he was "too busy." Kim Il
Sung pointedly told the South Koreans, "As long as I'm alive, I will rule
the country."

Leaving no stone unturned, Kim Il Sung also made efforts to achieve
a breakthrough in ties with the United States. On May 24, 1990, the day
after Dobrynin's secret meeting with Roh in Seoul, Kim delivered an important policy speech to a formal meeting of the North's legislature. Departing from his unyielding stand against the acceptance of US military
forces on the peninsula, Kim declared, "If the United States cannot withdraw all her troops from South Korea at once, she will be able to do so
by stages." In case Washington was not paying attention, Pyongyang used
the tenth meeting of American and North Korean political counselors in
Beijing on May 30 to pass along the text of Kim's speech. In the meantime,
on May 28, North Korea made its first positive response to US requests
for the return of Korean War remains, transferring five sets of remains.
On May 31, the day that the Gorbachev-Roh meeting was publicly announced, North Korea made public a new disarmament proposal that was
notably free of anti-US or anti–South Korean rhetoric and that appeared
to be more realistic than earlier proposals.

At this point, the United States, increasingly alarmed at the progress
of North Korea's nuclear program, was in no mood for conciliatory responses. State Department talking points drafted for Bush's June 6 meeting with Roh, following the San Francisco meeting with Gorbachev, did
not reflect any of Pyongyang's moves except for a brief mention of the return of the US remains. Nevertheless, White House press secretary Mar-
lin Fitzwater made an unusual unsolicited announcement following the
Bush-Roh meeting: "The United States reaffirms that it is not a threat to
North Korean security, and we seek to improve relations with that country." He added that "the pace and scope of any improvement will depend
importantly on North Korea's actions," mentioning specifically North Korea's willingness to permit international nuclear inspections. Beyond the
press secretary's remarks, however, Washington made no effort to engage
the unpopular—and stricken—North Koreans.

In retrospect, Washington's failure to explore improvement in relations
with Pyongyang in the last half of 1990, when North Korea was still reeling
from the blow inflicted by the Soviet Union, was an opportunity missed.
The chances seem strong that Kim Il Sung would have responded eagerly
to a US initiative at a time when his traditional alliance with Moscow was
in shambles and his alliance with Beijing was under growing stress. But
while the United States continued to pressure North Korea on the nuclear
issue in public and private, it offered no incentives to Pyongyang to take the

actions it sought, even "modest initiatives" of the kind that had been taken near the end of the Reagan administration. This was due in part to the Bush administration's preoccupation with the Persian Gulf following the Iraqi invasion of Kuwait on August 2, 1990, but it was also due to the inability of Washington policy makers to agree on any actions regarding North Korea. The gridlock would continue until Bush's nuclear initiatives in September 1991, which were prompted by developments in the Soviet Union rather than Korea-related considerations.

SOVIET–SOUTH KOREAN
ECONOMIC NEGOTIATIONS

The months following the Gorbachev-Roh meeting in San Francisco were busy ones for Soviet–South Korean negotiations, most of which centered on the Soviet requests for aid. Two weeks after meeting Roh, Gorbachev wrote to him inviting a Korean economic delegation to Moscow to work on the issue. Headed by Roh's senior economic and foreign policy advisers at the Blue House, the delegation went to the Soviet capital in early August. It discussed forty potential projects in the Soviet Union but insisted that no economic aid programs could be made final until after the establishment of official diplomatic relations. Shevardnadze's impromptu action at the United Nations on September 30, recognizing South Korea, took care of that problem and cleared the way for further economic negotiations.

After correspondence in October between the two heads of state, in which Roh expressed his desire to meet Gorbachev in Moscow, Gorbachev aide Vadim Medvedev, a member of the newly empowered Presidential Council, traveled to Seoul in November with an invitation to Roh to make a state visit before the end of the year. Medvedev also brought a request from Gorbachev for $4 billion in credits, some to finance purchases of Korean goods and some in untied loans. The visitor suggested that this be announced by Roh during his forthcoming meetings in Moscow.

In the Kremlin on December 13–16, Roh met Gorbachev and with him issued a Declaration of General Principles of Relations. In deference to North Korea, the declaration was careful to state that "the development of links and contacts between the ROK and the USSR must not in any way affect their relations with third countries or undermine obligations they assume under multilateral or bilateral treaties and agreements." Even though by that time he already had his own secret channels to the North, Roh asked Gorbachev to "exert an appropriate influence" on North Korea to develop a more cooperative relationship. The Soviet leader said he was doing what he could—which wasn't much, in view of Pyongyang's angry reaction to his new friendship with Seoul.

Roh brought with him to Moscow twenty Korean business leaders as a sign of interest in the Soviet economy, but he declined to discuss aid projects or figures in detail. According to a former Soviet official, Roh told Gorbachev, "Don't worry about the aid; just take my word for it."

The two sides did agree that an aid program would be negotiated in Seoul in mid-January by Deputy Prime Minister Yuri Maslyukov, who had handled the Soviet side of the preliminary discussions. Before this could happen, however, Gorbachev on December 31 suddenly decided to send Deputy Foreign Minister Igor Rogachev to Seoul as a special envoy, seeking a major infusion of cash to help see the Soviet Union through the winter. This was dismaying to Gorbachev's professional Korea watchers and much of his economic team, who feared that cash aid from Seoul would be wasted on short-term spending rather than applied to productive long-term projects. But Gorbachev was desperate. That fall he had even made a private and personal appeal for immediate financial help to Secretary of State James Baker, who then solicited a $4 billion line of credit for Moscow from traditionally anticommunist Saudi Arabia.

On January 6, Rogachev flew into Seoul with a team of economic and diplomatic officials, carrying a letter from Gorbachev asking for $5 billion in aid, including $2 billion in an immediate untied bank loan—in effect, ready cash. The Koreans were shocked by the size and nature of the request. Roh had said publicly on his trip to Moscow that cash grants were "out of the question" because such a big country as the Soviet Union "would not accept grants from a small country like ours even if we offered them."

To Rogachev's unexpected request, the Koreans initially offered $350 million in ready cash. Rogachev declared the offer "unacceptable" in view of his long journey and the many statements of support that had been made by Koreans during earlier discussions. After intense bargaining and a threat to break off the talks and return home preemptorily, Rogachev managed to raise the offer to $500 million. Suddenly, the tables had been turned on the Moscow-Seoul relationship; the supposed superpower was the supplicant, and the Korean side was deciding what it could provide. On the third day of negotiations, the Koreans agreed to supply $1 billion in cash and to negotiate later with Maslyukov on the rest of the aid program.

Maslyukov's mission three weeks later resulted in an agreement to supply $1.5 billion more in loans to finance Soviet imports of Korean consumer goods and industrial raw materials, and $500 million for the financing of plants and other capital goods. Together with the $1 billion bank loan obtained by Rogachev, the total was $3 billion, all of which was to be repaid at prevailing interest rates after a three-year grace period.

The deal was controversial in Seoul, especially because Korea had to borrow the money to lend to the Soviet Union. Korean officials justified the arrangement by arguing that the relationship with Moscow was a valuable asset to national security. According to a senior Korean official, Kim Chong Whi told Maslyukov during the negotiations that it would be politically impossible to aid the Soviet Union while Moscow continued to supply arms to North Korea. Maslyukov responded that he had personally rejected a recent North Korean request to Moscow for a new tank factory and would take similar action on future requests. Soviet exports of military equipment to North Korea dropped sharply in 1991, but it is unclear whether this was due to changed political decisions or simply to the economic straits of both Moscow and Pyongyang.

The last official meeting of Gorbachev and Roh, when the Soviet leader stopped at Korea's Cheju Island after a state visit to Japan in April 1991, included a financial transaction of a different sort. Gorbachev returned to Moscow with an unannounced gift from Roh of $100,000 in US currency. An aide to Roh told me later that the money was at least nominally intended for "victims of Chernobyl," the Soviet civil nuclear disaster that had taken place five years earlier. Gorbachev's chief of staff, Valéry Boldin, said the Soviet leader eventually had papers drawn up contributing the money to a children's hospital.

Slightly less than half ($1.47 billion) of the ROK aid for the Soviet Union was actually paid out before the collapse of the USSR in December 1991. As the successor state, Russia assumed the debts but lacked the money to make more than token repayments. Eventually, Russia began providing tanks, helicopters, missiles, and spare parts to Seoul in partial repayment of the loans. By then Russia had again become an arms exporter to the world, but this time to nations that could pay with hard cash rather than to those with which it shared ideological solidarity. In supplying South Korea with arms, Moscow reversed its historic role as an armorer and ally of the state it had created north of the thirty-eighth parallel.

The Soviet reversal and later the Soviet collapse would have a powerful impact on North Korea. Strategically, it left Pyongyang more vulnerable and more isolated than before. Economically, the loss of North Korea's most generous and most important trading partner began a steady decline that would increasingly sap the strength of the Kim regime.

10

CHINA SHIFTS ITS GROUND

IN MID-JUNE 1991, a Chinese civil airliner bringing Foreign Minister Qian Qichen, and his official party from Beijing floated down slowly over a flat green landscape toward a landing on the outskirts of Pyongyang. Making its gradual approach to the capital's airport, the plane passed over a seemingly deserted country, with ribbons of roadways nearly empty of traffic and hardly any people visible in the neatly divided plots of farmland or around big apartment houses and other buildings. Seated in the tourist section of the plane, behind the foreign minister's first-class compartment, I peered down for the first time at the territory of North Korea and wrote in my journal that it looked to be a strange land "left deserted by some invisible plague."

Then as the plane roared down the runway, hundreds of people came into view: a colorful crowd lined up in well-ordered rows on the tarmac, enthusiastically waving pink plastic boughs. As we taxied up and the motors were turned off, we could hear martial music from a khaki-clad military band. From the roof of the terminal building, a giant portrait of Kim Il Sung looked down on the scene.

Waiting near the foot of the steps to welcome the Chinese guest and his party was North Korean foreign minister Kim Yong Nam, the man who was also instrumental in my own invitation to visit. It was pure coincidence that I arrived on the same plane and was in Pyongyang at the same time as the Chinese foreign minister. Although the North Koreans told me nothing of the discussions between the two neighbors, I realized later that I had witnessed the launching of an episode of diplomatic theater that had led to a major readjustment of the relations between Beijing and Pyongyang.

From its short-lived conquest of ancient Choson before the time of Christ until the twentieth century, China had been the foreign nation with the greatest importance in the Korean world. For more than a thousand years, until Korea's invention of its *hangul* alphabet in the fifteenth century, Chinese characters formed the basis of the Korean written language, and they remained important in classical writing into the modern era. Korea adopted not only Buddhism from China but also Confucianism, which remains at the heart of many Korean relationships, public and private. Throughout most of its history, Korea paid tribute to its giant neighbor at the court of the Middle Kingdom. Koreans called China *daeguk,* "big state" or "elder state."

China's intimate alliance with North Korea dates back to the Chinese communist sponsorship of Kim Il Sung's rebel bands against the Japanese in World War II and the participation of Koreans on the side of the communists in Manchuria during the Chinese civil war. A few years later, the newly established People's Republic of China saved the North Korean regime from defeat—and possibly extinction—in the Korean War by sending its "volunteer" troops across the Yalu River, at the cost of close to a million of its own soldiers killed or wounded.

Even more than the Soviet Union, China maintained a warm official friendship with the North Korean state through most of its existence, relations seriously marred only by the revolutionary tumult of the Cultural Revolution. Even after the 1971–1972 shift in Beijing's foreign policy, Chinese leaders were careful to maintain close ties with North Korea, which was seen as an important ideological client and ally on China's border. Despite subsequent ups and downs in relations, both sides knew that the undeniable realities of geography meant they could never afford to drift too far apart.

Until recent years, Beijing had kept aloof from anticommunist South Korea, which was the only Asian nation to continue to recognize the Nationalist regime on Taiwan as the legitimate government of China into the 1990s. Although Sino–South Korean trade had grown steadily after China opened up to market economics, Beijing was more cautious than Moscow in moving toward normalization of political relations with the South.

Nonetheless, by mid-1991 Beijing was following Moscow's lead in moving toward a much closer relationship with Seoul. The previous year, according to Beijing's figures, Chinese trade with South Korea had been seven times larger than its trade with the North and was increasing rapidly, bringing with it a greater need for multifaceted relations. Moreover, the termination of the Sino-Soviet dispute and Moscow's sharply diminished ties with North Korea made Chinese leaders less concerned with the possibility that adjusting their policy toward South Korea could push Kim Il Sung into the arms of the Soviet Union. In addition, China could see a potential domestic political gain in establishing diplomatic relations with South Korea, because it would force Seoul to terminate its long-standing official relationship with Taiwan, thus giving a sharp blow to the island state.

The seriousness of its new situation with China had been brought home dramatically to North Korea during the four-day visit of Chinese premier Li Peng in May, the month before Foreign Minister Qian's trip to Pyongyang. According to a variety of reports, Li broke the unwelcome news that China did not oppose admission of both North and South Korea to the United Nations and would not veto South Korea's application, despite the opposition of Pyongyang to dual admission. China's refusal to veto would ensure Seoul's entry because the only other obstacle—a possible veto by the Soviet Union—had been eliminated in April when Gorbachev, during his visit to South Korea's Cheju Island, had promised that Moscow would support Seoul's application for UN membership.

On May 27, after some in the Pyongyang leadership—apparently including Kim Jong Il—worked for months to overcome Kim Il Sung's deep aversion to dual entry,* North Korea announced it had "no choice" but to apply for UN membership because otherwise the South would join the United Nations alone. This forced reversal at the hands of Moscow and Beijing was a symbol of North Korea's diminished clout with its former communist sponsors. It also may have been the underlying reason for Foreign Minister Qian's visit three weeks later, which was long on ceremony and short on substance. For years Qian had blocked efforts within the Chinese leadership to move faster toward normalizing ties with the ROK. Sending him to Pyongyang appeared to be China's way of mending relations after forcing the North Koreans to swallow the bitter pill of dual North-South admission to the UN.

A VISIT TO NORTH KOREA

Although it was a coincidence that I arrived with the Chinese minister, given the limited air traffic into the North, it was hardly surprising that someone of diplomatic importance shared my commercial airline flight. The Chinese civil aviation jet was the only plane to arrive from the outside world that day in the entire country of more than 20 million people. In 1991 only eight scheduled airplane flights and seven trains a week entered North Korea, making it one of the most reclusive—and mysterious— nations on earth.

---

* This was a point on which Kim had long been adamant. In November 1972, Kim told South Korean delegates to high-level talks taking place in Pyongyang, "Why should we, a homogeneous nation, enter the international arena as two states? I will not agree to the separate entry of north and south into the UN as long as our country remains divided." See CWIHP, Document 35, "Conversations with the South Korean Delegates to the High-Level Political Talks Between North and South Korea," November 3, 1972. When in a speech on June 23, 1973, South Korean president Park Chung Hee advocated such a course, Kim responded within hours with a five-point reunification proposal that marked the beginning of the end of the dialogue.

My traveling companion, *Washington Post* Tokyo correspondent T. R. Reid, and I were greeted in the airport terminal by our official hosts and transported to our hotel in two chauffeured red Mercedes sedans. So few other vehicles were visible in either direction on the twelve-mile road into town that I could easily count them: twenty-three cars, six buses, three minivans, three trucks, and two jeeps. Hundreds of people could be seen walking along the roadside or waiting patiently for the few overcrowded buses. More than just transportation, the energy shortage seemed to have idled much of North Korea's industry as well. I saw a number of overhead construction cranes during my week of travels, but not one that was in operation.

For North Korea, 1991 was a terrible year economically. Beginning in January, the Soviet Union demanded hard currency for its exports to Pyongyang rather than continue the traditional concessional arrangements of the past. As a result, North Korean imports from its most important trading partner declined precipitously. The drop was particularly sharp in energy imports, which fell by an astonishing 75 percent from the 1990 level, suddenly making the North dependent on China for more than two-thirds of its imported energy. China, however, was unwilling or unable to make up for the Soviet losses, and in May notified Pyongyang that it would soon discontinue its concessional sales. The dire result was that in 1991–1992, North Korea was forced to abruptly reduce its total petroleum consumption by between one-fourth and one-third, resulting in the deserted roadways and idle construction projects that I observed.

One might expect from all this to find a regime in a deep funk, fearful of the future and uncertain about which way to go. The greatest surprise to me was that Pyongyang's officialdom was, outwardly at least, undaunted by the revolutionary reversals in their alliances. In the North Korean worldview, the faltering of communism in the Soviet Union and its collapse in Eastern Europe proved the correctness of Kim Il Sung's independent policy of *juche* and his consistent refusal to formally join the Soviet bloc. Foreign Minister Kim Yong Nam spoke optimistically to me of "our people advancing along the road of the socialism they have chosen—socialism of their own style." This phrase, reminiscent of China's "socialism with Chinese characteristics," which justified Beijing's swing toward market economics, had first appeared the previous December in a Workers Party organ. In this case, "our own style" justified the absence of change rather than a deviation from the previous well-worn path.

To the evidence before my eyes in 1991, North Korea was unique, a land unlike any other I had seen in my extensive travels as a correspondent. The capital, Pyongyang, had been so leveled by American bombing in the Korean War that the head of the US bomber command had halted further air strikes, saying that "there is nothing standing worthy of the name." Kim Il Sung had rebuilt it from the ashes to a meticulously planned urban center of broad boulevards, monumental structures, and square-cut apartment buildings that resembled a stage set more than a working capital. Indeed, it was a synthetic city in many respects: according to foreign diplomats, the population was periodically screened, and the sick, elderly, or disabled, along with anyone deemed politically unreliable, were evicted from the capital.

Pyongyang was dominated by homage to Kim Il Sung. Among its most imposing features was the Tower of the *Juche* Idea, an obelisk almost as high as the Washington Monument, which was erected for the Great Leader's seventieth birthday to celebrate his self-reliance dogma; an Arch of Triumph larger than the one in Paris, celebrating Kim's return from victory over Japan in 1945; and Kim Il Sung Stadium, seating one hundred thousand people for mass demonstrations of loyalty to the ruler and the regime. Less celebrated but equally prominent was a mammoth 105-story hotel, built to be the tallest in Asia, but now standing unfinished and abandoned. Rumor had it that the structure had fatal architectural flaws and could never be finished.* Pyongyang struck me as well suited for gigantic displays but not very convenient for people, who had few cars and buses and, unlike Beijing, no bicycles to help them traverse the capital's massive spaces.

On a guided tour of the city, we encountered several hundred fourth-grade boys, led by an adult instructor, doing mass exercises with wooden swords or, lacking these, pieces of flat wood cut to the length of swords. The boys slashed, jumped, and shouted with enthusiasm and on cue. This was only one of many manifestations of the collective activities that were being emphasized. On the other hand, there were signs that behind the public facade, North Koreans had not lost their individuality and humanity. During a performance at the Pyongyang Circus, a spectacular display of acrobatic talent, children squealed with laughter and uninhibited delight at an act featuring trained dogs. Another evening at the apartment of the sister of one of our guides, we experienced the warmth of Korean family life as a seven-year-old in pigtails played a small piano and her reluctant five-year-old sister was coaxed into doing a little dance. The apartment, while modest by Western standards, was doubtless better than most, and a special allocation of food had apparently been granted to provide the guests with an abundant home-cooked dinner. Although hardly typical, it was the closest to everyday life that we were permitted to come.

---

* The rumors of construction flaws were apparently unfounded. Construction resumed in 2009, and the building was being made ready for at least partial occupancy by 2012. In April 2013, however, in the middle of unusually high tensions on the peninsula, the company involved—Kempinski Hotels—backed away, artfully explaining it was "simply not possible at this time to enter the market and allow us to operate a hotel according to our standards."

Outside the capital and away from the country's few highways, the landscape reminded me of what I had seen in the South in the 1950s and 1960s. An overnight train to Kaesong, just north of the demilitarized zone, took six hours to go about 120 miles, with antiquated equipment over a rough roadbed. Along the way, I saw a steam locomotive still in use, no doubt burning coal from North Korean mines. I awoke early in the morning to look out at hills and rice paddies shrouded with the familiar heavy morning mist and small houses with chimney pipes on the side arising from traditional under-the-floor heating. Here and there, the landscape was broken by dreary gray buildings that had been thrown up to house members of collective farms.

All this was in startling contrast to the traffic-choked, neon-lit modernity of Seoul and the dramatically improved living conditions of the South Korean countryside I had seen in recent years. Although poverty had not been abolished, the wealth and health of most South Korean citizens had undergone revolutionary change for the better since I first observed them in the immediate aftermath of the Korean War and immense change from the early 1970s when I spent so much time in South Korea as a correspondent. In the 1970s, the South had the look and feel of a rawboned, gutsy frontier country with garlic on its breath, where its cities gave rise to a hundred pungent odors and even the newsprint had a peculiar musky smell. By 1991 South Korea had arrived, with high-rise buildings crowding out most of the slanting roofs of traditional houses in Seoul and other cities and good roads and modern conveniences in the countryside. Nearly 10 million people, close to one in four of South Korea's 43 million citizens, were licensed drivers of the country's 4.2 million motor vehicles, making it increasingly difficult to get from here to there, at least in Seoul. More than 3 million foreign tourists visited the South, and close to 2 million ROK citizens traveled abroad during the year. From rock music to high fashion, South Korea was connected to the world.

The nexus between North and South was the Joint Security Area at Panmunjom, the principal destination on our trip from Pyongyang. Approaching from the North through the DPRK's hilltop pavilion, the JSA appeared benign and ordinary. Compared with the heavily manned southern side, we saw remarkably few troops. As our small party of myself, fellow correspondent Tom Reid, and North Korean escorts approached the military demarcation line, an American sailor and two American MPs stood just across the line, assiduously taking our pictures. I felt little of the atmosphere of menace that I recall from visits to Checkpoint Charlie in Berlin before the wall came down, or even from my earlier visits to Panmunjom from the southern side. Perhaps it was because I was inside the enemy tent, having just been briefed by a North Korean major who was accompanying us, and for once I was not concerned about an imminent breach of the peace from the North, or from the South either.

Earlier in Pyongyang, Foreign Minister Kim Yong Nam had emphasized the high priority his government placed on negotiations to reduce tension at the DMZ and on the peninsula generally, because "we still have heavy danger of war." Kim painstakingly recounted North Korea's efforts to begin direct talks with the United States or three-way talks that would also include South Korea. "We have the intention and willingness to improve relations with the United States, but we cannot accept all the unjust demands of the U.S. side," he said. Recognizing that the issues are deeply rooted in history, he said, "the two countries must first of all officially make public their will to improve bilateral relations and start negotiations." Knowing the apprehension about North Korea in Washington and the deep reluctance to engage its diplomats, I had great doubt this would happen anytime soon.

Kim Yong Nam, born on February 24, 1928, had risen step by step, by diligence and loyalty, through the ranks of the Workers Party to become party secretary for international affairs and, two months after the Rangoon bombing of October 1983, vice premier and foreign minister. The disaster in Rangoon had touched off an extensive reorganization of the bureaucracy dealing with North-South and international affairs. As the new foreign minister, Kim had set about restructuring DPRK diplomacy along more professional lines, in the process becoming the sponsor of many of the country's career diplomats.

A Chinese official who had known Kim for many years said that he has extremely good literary skills and that he drafted many speeches for Kim Il Sung. This may have been the source of his unusually close relationship to the Great Leader, who elevated him to full membership in the Politburo in 1980, while he was still party secretary for international affairs—a job that did not usually carry such weight. Kim's younger brother, Kim Du Nam, was also close to Kim Il Sung, being a four-star general and military secretary to the Great Leader.

I had met Kim Yong Nam during his first trip to the United Nations as foreign minister in 1984—at the time, a rare visit to New York by a high-ranking North Korean. My persistent requests for an interview finally won out over the extreme caution of Pyongyang's UN observer mission. A lengthy first meeting in a cavernous Manhattan hotel suite was notable for Kim's prepared declaration, which he read from a cloth-covered notebook he took from his pocket, that North Korea was interested in talks with the United States on the "confidence building measures" mentioned by President Reagan in his UN address several weeks earlier. This was a reversal of the previous North Korean dismissal of confidence-building proposals and was clearly intended to be an important signal to Washington.

The Reagan administration, which at this point was contemptuous of North Korea and busily preparing for the US presidential election in November, did not respond. But when the *Washington Post* placed my account of the interview on page 1, the North Korean diplomatic hesitation about me vanished, at least temporarily. After that I saw Kim or his senior deputy, Kang Sok Ju, nearly every time they came for their annual UN visits, even though their interview pronouncements never made the front page again.

In my 1991 meeting in Pyongyang, as in other meetings with him over the years, I found Kim Yong Nam a puzzling figure. In greetings before business began, he was cordial and relaxed, but once at work, he relentlessly followed his script in a way that reminded me of former Soviet foreign minister Andrei Gromyko. Koh Yong Hwan, a former North Korean diplomat and high-level interpreter who defected to the South, called Kim a "model" for North Korean officialdom: "If Kim Il Sung was pointing to a wall and said there is a door, Kim Yong Nam would believe that and try to go through it." Yet by all accounts, he is highly intelligent and, due to his high position and prestige within the system, an important behind-the-scenes figure in Pyongyang.

The foreign minister's polar opposite in demeanor was the colorful and flamboyant Kim Yong Sun, another important figure in Pyongyang's diplomacy, whom I met for the first time on my 1991 trip. Born in 1934, his career path was notable for its craggy leaps and reverses. Originally a politically minded provincial official in the southeastern part of the country, he served in political posts in other areas before joining the International Department of the Workers Party. In the mid-1980s, he was demoted and reportedly sent to work in a coal mine as punishment for decadent behavior in organizing Western-style dancing at party headquarters. According to North Korean lore, he was rescued from oblivion by his friendship with Kim Kyong Hui, the younger sister of Kim Jong Il. In contrast to the austere foreign minister, Kim Yong Sun was reputed to be a hard-drinking, partying buddy of Kim Jong Il, a ladies' man and devotee of high living.

Unlike all others whom I interviewed in Pyongyang in 1991, Kim Yong Sun did not wear a Western coat and tie but a zippered olive-drab short jacket similar to the US Army's "Ike jacket." Sitting across a conference table at Workers Party headquarters, he apologized for his casual dress, saying that he had come straight from a meeting with workers and peasants in the countryside, who had encouraged him to return quickly to the capital when he told them he had an appointment with *Washington Post* reporters. It was a somewhat flattering touch, until I learned from a delegation of American Quakers months later that he had told them the same story, wearing the same jacket, at the start of their meeting.

Kim Yong Sun had more self-confidence and flair than anyone else I met in North Korea. His authoritative yet freewheeling style appeared to be grounded in intimacy with the Dear Leader, as Kim Jong Il was then known. It was notable that of a half-dozen senior officials I saw, only Kim Yong Sun volunteered to discuss the role of the Dear Leader, whom he described as "giving guidance in all fields: politics, economics, national defense, and diplomacy." The party secretary said he received frequent personal instructions, including telephone calls, from Kim Jong Il.

While Kim Yong Sun's fundamental positions did not deviate from the policy line of the party he served, he managed to present them in more accessible and impressive ways. At the end of our long conversation, which contained a plea for dialogue and cooperation with the United States, Kim said to me, "I understand you know Baker," referring to the US secretary of state. "Please tell him I want to meet him." Although he and other officials were highly critical of American policy, the fact of my presence and the messages they gave me suggested eagerness for a direct relationship with the United States. North Korea, it seemed, was seeking in its "own style" to compensate for its losses in the communist world. What wasn't known at the time was that Kim Il Sung had already decided that normalizing relations with the United States was a strategic imperative to counter potential threats to the DPRK from China and Russia and that this goal would be the engine of North Korean foreign policy for years to come.

CHINA CHANGES COURSE

The Chinese foreign minister left Pyongyang several days before the end of my own weeklong trip, but the change in the relationship of the two Koreas to its giant neighbor continued to be a subject of immense importance on both sides of the thirty-eighth parallel. And in the early 1990s, those relationships, like others involving the outside powers, were in flux. For China, the challenge was to adjust its relations from one-sided support of the North Korean ally to productive ties with both South and North. It was of great importance to Beijing to do so without suffering a precipitous loss of influence with Pyongyang, as had been the case with the Soviet Union.

As late as January 1979, senior leader Deng Xiaoping told President Carter that North Korea "trusts China" and that "we cannot have contact with the South, or it will weaken that trust." Ironically, Deng's own reformist policies of pragmatism and emphasis on market economic forces made it imperative for China to amend its one-sided policy of ignoring the South.

China and South Korea, situated across the Yellow Sea from one another and with complementary and increasingly vibrant economies, proved to be natural trading partners. Beginning with indirect commerce through

Hong Kong and other places, Sino-ROK trade leaped from $19 million in 1979 to $188 million in 1980, $462 million in 1984, $1.3 billion in 1986, and $3.1 billion in 1988. Chinese trade with North Korea was left far behind, stagnating at about $0.5 billion in the late 1980s, much of it heavily subsidized by China. Although other aspects played their roles, this natural economic affinity with South Korea was of fundamental importance in overcoming Beijing's inhibitions about dealings with Seoul. Party elders and aged former generals could reminisce about their exploits with North Korea in bygone times, but South Korea loomed much larger for officials dealing with the economy.

In 1985 a small Chinese delegation visited Seoul, ostensibly for an academic exchange. On its return, it produced a report for Deng Xiaoping about South Korea and the possibilities for improving PRC-ROK relations. After reading the report, Deng reportedly wrote in the margin, "We need to expedite development of China–South Korea relations." Quiet meetings between Chinese delegations led by China International Trust and Investment Company chairman Rong Yi-ren and South Korean business leaders followed in Seoul and Beijing. Anxious to move as quickly as possible, the next year the South Koreans offered China a five-year, $2.5 billion interest-free loan if Beijing would establish ties. Many on the Chinese side were in favor of accepting, but Foreign Minister Qian rejected the idea, arguing that China could not afford to alienate North Korea. Over the next several years, Qian vetoed a number of proposals for establishing relations, much to the annoyance of those Chinese officials who wanted to move ahead. Even Vice Premier Tian Ji-yun, the head of the special "South Korean Affairs Office" established for dealing with Seoul, fumed at Qian's obduracy but was unable to overrule him. One member of the Chinese group went back and forth so often that at one point, the South Koreans went to a Seoul tailor to buy him a new suit, hoping to make him less conspicuous. "The American and the Taiwan embassies are watching you," his Korean contacts told him.

Like so much else that happens on the Korean peninsula, the first crack in the political firewall between Beijing and Seoul had emerged from a violent incident—the hijacking in May 1983 of a Chinese airliner by six Chinese, who shot and wounded two crew members and forced the pilot to fly to South Korea. China sent a thirty-three-member official delegation to Seoul, where the two nations smoothly negotiated a deal for the return of the plane, its passengers, and its crew.

North Korea was quick to protest to China about this first official contact between Beijing and the Seoul government. Chinese officials responded that this was a special case and renewed the pledge that they would not depart from "China's firm stance" against ties with the South.

In March 1985, in another violent incident, two mutinous seamen opened fire with AK-47s aboard a Chinese navy torpedo boat in the Yellow

Sea, killing the captain and five other crewmen. As the vessel ran out of fuel and drifted helplessly at sea, a South Korean fishing boat towed it to a nearby South Korean port. China sent three warships steaming into Korean territorial waters in search of the missing torpedo boat, and ROK air, naval, and coast guard forces were mobilized. In an atmosphere of impending crisis, Seoul CIA station chief James Delaney and Ambassador Richard Walker urgently communicated with Beijing to urge caution. The Chinese warships backed off, and the United States helped arrange the Sino-ROK negotiations that returned the ship and its crew to China in exchange for Beijing's apology for "inadvertently" entering Korean waters.

The amicable settlement of these emergencies coincided with one of the dips in Sino–North Korean relations as Kim Il Sung's trips to Moscow in 1984 and 1986 led to warming Soviet security ties and large new shipments of Soviet weapons. Chinese military officials were unhappy with Kim's agreeing to Soviet air force overflights of North Korean territory and Soviet navy visits to North Korean ports, all on the rim of China.

According to the account of a former Chinese official, a very senior North Korean military official, probably Defense Minister O Jin U, sought to match the Soviet weaponry with Chinese weaponry in the mid-1980s, making extensive requests for ships, planes, and other major weapons during an unpublicized trip to Beijing. After a study by the Defense Ministry of the requirements and costs, Deng rejected the entire request and directed his aides to supply nothing. The North Korean minister left for home, furious about the denial of military aid.

While unofficial contacts with South Korea continued to develop—most prominently, the participation of several hundred Chinese athletes in the 1986 Asian Games in Seoul—the greatest shifts developed after the advent of President Roh Tae Woo. As noted previously, during his campaign for the presidency in 1987, Roh had pledged to "cross the Yellow Sea" to China during his term, and he began working on China relations immediately on taking office. Only eight days after his inauguration, he invited to the Blue House an old friend, a Chinese-born medical doctor who had lived three decades in Korea, and authorized him to go to China as an unofficial emissary to pave the way for diplomatic relations. This was the first of a large number of unofficial approaches by Korean businessmen and others authorized by Roh to make the case for full-scale ties. A number of influential Chinese, including Deng's daughter and his handicapped son, visited Seoul as guests of Korean industrialists. "We were sure they would send back their impressions to Deng and higher-ups without any filter," said a senior aide to Roh. To keep his hand in developments, Roh had his brother-in-law play an active role in the behind-the-scenes contacts.

While the Soviet Union and Eastern European countries were moving toward political ties with South Korea in the wake of the Seoul Olympics,

China held back, insisting on the clear-cut separation of politics from economics. Roh, however, continued to signal his interest to Beijing in every way possible. When the Chinese government's June 1989 suppression of prodemocracy demonstrators in Tiananmen Square created widespread revulsion and endangered China's hosting of the 1990 Asian Games, Roh lobbied Asian sports leaders not to penalize China. He also urged President George Bush and British prime minister Margaret Thatcher, among other world leaders, to restrain their reactions to the Tiananmen crackdown, and he made sure that Beijing leaders knew of his efforts.

In the spring of 1990, China finally activated a channel for unofficial contacts aimed at eventual diplomatic relations with Seoul. The initial discussions, resembling the meetings of go-betweens exploring a marriage to unite two Asian families, involved Lee Sun Sok, president of the Sunkyung corporation in Seoul, whose board chairman's son had married Roh Tae Woo's daughter, and a Chinese Army colonel who was the son-in-law of Li Xiannian, a prominent member of the Chinese leadership. A subsequent series of meetings between the Korean businessman and high-ranking Chinese trade officials led to the establishment of semiofficial trade offices with consular functions in the two capitals at the end of 1990. The South Korean "trade representative" in the Chinese capital was not a businessman or economic official but in fact a veteran and senior diplomat, Ambassador Roh Jae Won (no relation to the president), who assumed a key role in the quasi-diplomatic negotiations with China.

The year 1991 was crucial in the revision of Chinese policy. Beginning with Deng Xiaoping's travels in southern China, the Beijing regime regained the confidence and momentum it had briefly lost in the bloody tumult of Tiananmen Square two years earlier. Once more it attuned its diplomacy to the external sources of capital, markets, and technology for rapid economic growth, which meant the capitalistic nations of North America, Western Europe—and South Korea, just across the Yellow Sea. Unproductive ideological commitments, such as that to North Korea, slipped down on the priority list.

In May 1991, during Premier Li Peng's official visit to Pyongyang, China changed its basic trade policy with Pyongyang from concessional and barter exchanges to trade based on convertible currency at international prices, change implemented over a two-year period. Later that year, Seoul's new status as a full member of the world body provided a venue and a rationale for upgrading Sino–South Korean ties. Immediately after the South's UN entry in September 1991, Chinese foreign minister Qian Qichen met for the first time with his South Korean counterpart, in a UN conference room in New York. Although Qian was noncommittal about early normalization of bilateral relations, the meeting itself was unprecedented, and a landmark.

On November 21, when he traveled in Seoul on the occasion of the third general meeting of the Asia Pacific Economic Coordination organization, Foreign Minister Qian became the first Chinese official to meet Roh Tae Woo. Roh, who had prepared extensively for the session, observed that the Korean relationship with China "had a 5,000 year history, going back to ancient days, of good neighbors closer to each other than any other country," and that the period of severed relations since World War II was without precedent and cause for shame. He reminded Qian that in the sixteenth century Korea refused to permit the Japan warlord Hideyoshi Toyotomi to use Korean territory to stage an attack on the Chinese Ming dynasty—after which the Japanese invaded Korea and laid waste to the peninsula.

Roh assured his visitor that "we fully understand China's loyal relationship with North Korea that was forged through the Korean War." Nonetheless, he went on, "I believe that China, [South] Korea and North Korea can build a relationship without betraying that loyalty. As I have stated several times, we are not thinking, not even in dreams, of a German style unification by absorption, which North Korea is worried about. What we want to do with North Koreans, who are of the same nation, is to abandon hostility and restore confidence and to establish a cooperative relationship. It is not our position to dominate them based on our economic power."

Qian responded by addressing the long historical relationship of Korea and China and, invoking a common enemy, spoke of their "similar experiences of historic sufferings, which were caused by Japan." As for the unnatural absence of relations with South Korea, Qian blamed this on the outcome of World War II. He added that as North-South relations, Japanese–North Korean relations, and American–North Korean relations improved, normalization between China and South Korea would be easy. "I would like to tell you that China encourages North Korea to have a dialogue with South Korea. We believe the United States and Japan can be helpful in improving the position of North Korea."

Roh was ecstatic about the results of the meeting. He reminded his aides that during their interaction over many centuries past, the Korean kings always sent their emissaries to pay court to China, "but this time I received a kowtow" from the Chinese foreign minister.

In January 1992, in the wake of the Roh-Qian meeting and of a formal Sino–South Korean trade agreement signed in December, the Chinese Foreign Ministry held a series of strategic planning meetings that ended with a recommendation for full normalization with Seoul. A Chinese source said that, as a result, the Foreign Ministry listed normalization as one of its priority diplomatic objectives for 1992.

The timing of China's move was unclear to Seoul until Qian confidentially informed the South Korean foreign minister, Lee Sang Ok, on the morning of April 13, 1992, that China was ready to open negotiations leading to full-scale relations. The revelation was made in a conference between the two ministers at the State Guest House in Beijing, where Lee was staying as a participant in a meeting of a UN regional agency. The Chinese foreign minister, delivering the news in a matter-of-fact and soft-spoken way, emphasized that secrecy was essential.

Qian's declaration caused great excitement in Seoul among the handful of officials who were told of it. The ensuing secret negotiations, including a monthlong pause while the Chinese prepared North Korea to absorb this new blow, took only four months. Together with the Korea policy reversal and subsequent collapse of the Soviet Union, the establishment of diplomatic relations between China and South Korea on August 24, 1992, and the state visit of Roh Tae Woo to Beijing two months later created a dramatically changed geopolitical situation around the divided peninsula.

What brought about the Chinese resolve to move so quickly, according to sources on both sides, had less to do with the Korean peninsula than with China's sensitivity to developments on Taiwan, where a campaign for greater international recognition had been intensifying. The worldwide flowering of Taiwan's informal and paradiplomatic contacts and visits was disturbing to Beijing, and its few breakthroughs were maddening. In January 1992, the Baltic nation of Latvia, newly freed to seek its own destiny by the collapse of the Soviet Union, established official relations with Taiwan, despite intense protests from China. Shortly before the April decision to begin negotiations with South Korea, Beijing learned that the West African nation of Niger had decided to establish full diplomatic relations with Taiwan. The way to retaliate, Chinese leaders reasoned, was to move quickly to establish diplomatic relations with Seoul, thus forcing South Korea to drop its diplomatic ties with Taiwan and depriving Taiwan of its last remaining official toehold in Asia.

When Taiwanese authorities got wind of the secret PRC-ROK negotiations, they sent a high-ranking envoy, the secretary-general of the presidential office, to remind Seoul that the Nationalist governments of China, the lineal ancestors of the current Taiwan regime, had supported the Korean nationalists in exile during the Japanese occupation, given strong support to the independence of South Korea in UN politics in 1948, and been close comrades-in-arms in anticommunist struggles after Chiang Kai-shek had been forced into exile.

If Seoul snubbed Taiwan in the face of this long relationship, its representatives implied, Taiwan would retaliate by opening official relations and expanding its trade with North Korea. But if, on the other hand, Seoul managed to continue its diplomatic relations with Taiwan, South Korean firms would receive top priority in construction contracts and special trade benefits for five years. No such deal was in the cards, however. Taiwan had little bargaining power, since for strategic as well as economic reasons, fully normalized relations with China were far more important to South Korea than its ties with Taiwan.

For China, the delicate question was how to manage the establishment of diplomatic relations with the South in a way that did not alienate the North, as the Soviet Union had done with Gorbachev's abrupt maneuvers. This Beijing accomplished with accustomed political and diplomatic finesse. While carefully moving toward Seoul in October 1991, Chinese leaders hosted Kim Il Sung with elaborate ceremony in what they announced was his thirty-ninth visit since the founding of the DPRK, a ten-day tour in which he was accompanied for several days by Communist Party general secretary Jiang Zemin. In April 1992, as Seoul was being secretly informed of China's willingness to initiate negotiations, Yang Shangkun, the president of the People's Republic, traveled to Pyongyang and personally intimated to Kim Il Sung that the change was coming. In the midst of negotiations with Seoul, China sent its president's brother, Yang Baibing, another powerful figure who was secretary-general of the Communist Party's Central Military Commission, on an eight-day "goodwill visit" to North Korea.

After July 29, when the substance of the Sino–South Korean arrangements was fully agreed and secretly initialed by both sides, the Chinese insisted on delaying the announcement for nearly a month until August 24, evidently for the sole purpose of further preparing the way in Pyongyang. During this time Foreign Minister Qian took the news to Pyongyang in an unannounced trip that met with much greater understanding than had Shevardnadze's tumultuous mission of the same sort two years earlier. Qian maintained that the normalization of relations with Seoul had been undertaken at the order of senior leader Deng Xiaoping, which left the North Koreans little room for argument.

Chinese officials later claimed that flattery and saving face had been keys to obtaining North Korea's acceptance of the change. According to this self-serving account, Beijing told the North Koreans that "we need your help, because China has to respond to Taiwan's gaining recognition abroad." The Chinese called on North Korea as old friends to magnanimously assist by permitting Beijing to recognize South Korea, thereby penalizing Taiwan for its actions. This account has elements of a put-down, underestimating the North's ability to recognize its own predicament and to hold in their anger, especially after public venting in a similar situation with the Soviets had gained them nothing.

When the Beijing-Seoul rapprochement was announced, North Korea accepted the blow with official silence. A month later, at the United Nations, I asked North Korean foreign minister Kim Yong Nam about the switch; he replied that China's new relationship with Seoul was "nothing special . . . nothing [that] matters to us." This posture of public nonchalance was belied by signals the North sent in September and October on the occasion of PRC National Day (October 1) and the anniversary of the Chinese People's Volunteers into the Korea War (October 25), registering in subtle but clear ways Beijing would not miss that Pyongyang was furious. In North Korean eyes, the Chinese had again proved themselves unreliable and all too willing to sell out the North.

The newest change in the great power alignments around the peninsula mattered greatly to Pyongyang, which was seeking to establish relations with the United States and Japan and hoped that China would withhold its official ties with South Korea until a package deal could be arranged. Pyongyang had elaborate warning that the Chinese shift was coming, but the timing of it must have been galling, because it arose from Beijing's desire to slap back at Taiwan rather than from any consideration of its impact on the Korean peninsula. North Korea's realization of its true standing in the priorities of its giant neighbor, along with sharply rising international pressures to curb its nuclear program, contributed to its growing troubles. This realization may have contributed to Pyongyang's decision in the summer of 1992 to explore steps in the nuclear arena that would result in an escalation of tensions early the following year.

11

JOINING THE
NUCLEAR ISSUE

IN THE EARLY 1990S, North Korea's program to develop nuclear weapons concentrated the minds of many of the world's political and military leaders and held their attention to an unprecedented degree. This frightening development was a potential threat not only to South Korea, the American troops on guard there, and the immediate Asian neighborhood; it was a threat as well to international stability and world order. A North Korean bomb, it seemed, could touch off a dangerous nuclear arms competition involving South Korea, Japan, and perhaps other industrialized nations and spread nuclear weapons materials to pariah nations in the Middle East through North Korean sales. More than that, an atomic weapon in the hands of an isolated and seemingly unpredictable regime with a record of terrorism would be a nightmare. It was, as South Korea's presidential national security adviser, Kim Chong Whi, told me while he was in office, not an issue of normal politics but "a question of civilization."

The more the outside world feared it, the more its nuclear program was a valuable asset to North Korea, which had few other resources of external worth after the decline of its alliances with the Soviet Union and China. There is no evidence that Pyongyang saw the nuclear program as a bargaining chip at its inception, but the record is clear that by the 1990s, it had learned the program's value in relations with the world outside.

North Korea's nuclear debut, in the eyes of outsiders, dated back to April 1982, when an American surveillance satellite whirring unseen in the skies photographed what appeared to be a nuclear reactor vessel under construction in the bend of a river at Yongbyon, sixty miles north of the capital. When the photographs were examined in Washington a few days later, they drew the intense interest of American intelligence analysts, who marked the spot for special attention. In March 1984, as construction proceeded, a satellite pass showed the outline of a cylindrical nuclear smokestack rising from the site. Another set of photographs taken in June 1984 clearly showed the reactor, its cooling tower, and some limited power lines and electrical grid connections for local transmission of the energy to be produced.

Intelligence experts in Washington concluded from the photographs that the reactor utilized two minerals found in abundance in North Korea: natural uranium, to create an atomic reaction, and graphite, to moderate and control it. The layout was startlingly similar to old-model French and British reactors of the late 1950s, built to produce material for atomic weapons.

Taken alone, the North Korean reactor, while highly suspicious, was not conclusive evidence of a weapons program because it could also be the initial element of a civil nuclear power program. However, suspicions were heightened in March 1986, when satellite photographs of the Yongbyon area detected cylindrical craters in the sand of the nearby riverbank. Analysts believed they were the residue of experimental high-explosive detonations in a certain pattern familiar to nuclear weapons experts: the precisely simultaneous explosions that are basic to implosion, one of the standard means of detonating an atomic bomb. After this discovery, restudy of earlier photographs produced evidence of similar craters in the same area since 1983.

With a reactor set to burn uranium and the technique of finely honed explosions appearing to be under development, the principal missing element in a serious atomic weapons program was a reprocessing plant. Using a chemical process, such a plant can separate plutonium, the raw material for a nuclear weapon, from other by-products of spent uranium fuel. Starting in March 1986, satellite photographs detected the outlines of a huge oblong building, nearly the length of two football fields, under construction at Yongbyon. In February 1987 the US cameras looked down into the unroofed plant to see a long series of thick-walled cells in the typical configuration for separation of plutonium. A short time later, when the plant was roofed, US intelligence could only guess at what was going on inside.

The first indigenous reactor at Yongbyon was a relatively modest plant rated by the North Koreans as producing 5 megawatts of electric power. But in June 1988, construction for a much larger reactor, eventually described by the North Koreans as intended to produce 50 megawatts of power, was photographed at Yongbyon. Such a plant, in combination with the huge reprocessing facility under construction, convinced most Washington officials with access to the photography that North Korea was launched headlong on a drive to create its own nuclear weapons, and a highly ambitious drive at that. In what had been the middle of nowhere—a place famous in Korean poetry for its budding azaleas and little more—a stark and imposing industrial works of more than one hundred buildings was rising, surrounded by double fences and antiaircraft weapons and heavily guarded. As these facilities progressed toward completion and North Korea moved closer to being able to produce weapons of immense destructive power, the busy construction site at Yongbyon became increasingly an international problem that could not be ignored.

THE ORIGINS OF THE NUCLEAR PROGRAM

Korea's involvement with nuclear weapons goes back to the dawn of the nuclear age. During World War II, Japan was vigorously pursuing a nuclear weapons program, though it lagged behind the all-out campaigns of the United States, Germany, and the Soviet Union. As US bombing of the home islands increased, Japan moved its secret weapons program to the northern part of its Korean colony to get away from the attacks and take advantage of the area's undamaged electricity-generating capacity and abundance of useful minerals. After the division of Korea in 1945, the Soviet Union mined monazite and other materials in the North for use in its own atomic weapons program.

During the 1950–1953 Korean War, General Douglas MacArthur requested authority to use atomic weapons and submitted a list of targets, for which he would need twenty-six A-bombs. His successor, General Matthew Ridgway, renewed MacArthur's request, but such weapons were never used. In early 1953, the newly inaugurated US president, Dwight Eisenhower, began dropping hints that the United States would use the atom bomb if the deadlock persisted in the negotiations to conclude an armistice ending the war. Eisenhower, Secretary of State John Foster Dulles and Vice President Richard Nixon all claimed later that the nuclear threats had played a major role in bringing about the truce, although revelations from Soviet archives cast doubt on that analysis.

Following the end of the war, the Soviet Union and North Korea signed two agreements on cooperation in nuclear research, and a small number of North Korean scientists began to arrive at the Soviet Union's Dubna Nuclear Research Center near Moscow. The Soviet Union also provided a small experimental nuclear reactor, which was sited at Yongbyon. At Soviet insistence, the reactor was placed under inspection by the International Atomic Energy Agency (IAEA) to ensure that material was not diverted to weapons, even though at that time North Korea was not a party to the Nuclear Non-Proliferation Treaty (NPT).

In its own quest for nuclear weapons, North Korea had turned to China shortly after its giant neighbor detonated its first atomic blast in 1964. Kim Il Sung sent a delegation to Beijing, asking for assistance to mount a parallel program and, in a letter to Mao Tse-tung, declared that as brother countries who shared fighting and dying on the battlefield, China and North Korea should also share the atomic secret. Two former Chinese officials and a Japanese expert familiar with Chinese affairs told me that Mao turned down the North Korean request. "Chinese leaders thought this was a very expensive project," said an official who was in the Korea section of the Chinese Foreign Ministry at the time. "North Korea is a very small country. [Chinese leaders thought] it wasn't needed." Kim Il Sung is reported to have made another request for Chinese aid in 1974, when the South Korean nuclear weapons program was under way, a fact that may have influenced his thinking. Like the earlier appeal, this one was also unsuccessful.

When and why North Korea secretly launched its own program as a major enterprise is still the subject of speculation, in the absence of hard information. American experts believe site preparation for the first North Korean indigenous reactor began around 1979. In the late 1970s, according to an official of the Russian Foreign Intelligence Service, Kim Il Sung authorized the North Korean Academy of Sciences, the army, and the Ministry of Public Security to begin implementation of a nuclear weapons program, including rapid expansion of existing facilities at Yongbyon. As early as February 1976, a Hungarian Embassy cable from Pyongyang reported that the North "wants to construct nuclear reactors, and is holding talks about this issue in order to become capable of producing atomic weapons in the future." This was perhaps a gentle reply from the embassy to a message from Budapest a few days earlier, reporting that North Korean diplomats had claimed the North already had such weapons.

After a high-level delegation from the international department of the East German Communist Party visited Pyongyang in May 1981, it reported in a memorandum to its Politburo, "The DPRK is strongly interested in the importation of nuclear power stations. Here it is estimated that they do not by any means exclude the military use of the nuclear technology." A former East German official said the cautiously worded report, which was written after extensive informal talks with North Korean officials, seriously understated Pyongyang's ardor. "They said very frankly, 'We need the atom bomb,'" according to this source.

North Korea's nuclear weapons program from the first was very self-reliant. Its "godfather" was Dr. Lee Sung Ki, a Korean born in the South who had earned his PhD in engineering from Kyoto Imperial University in prewar Japan and served as dean of Seoul National University's college of engineering before crossing to the northern side during the Korean War. Lee, who became Kim Il Sung's intimate friend and closest scientific adviser, had won worldwide fame by developing vinalon, a synthetic fiber made from coal.

The indigenous nature of the program facilitated the extreme secretiveness in which it proceeded. Not even officials of the North Koreans'

close allies, the Soviet Union and China—both nuclear weapons powers—
were permitted to visit the key facilities at Yongbyon once the nuclear
program was under way.

In the 1980s, in addition to its clandestine program, North Korea
sought to obtain civil nuclear power stations from the Soviet Union to
alleviate its growing power shortages. Kim Il Sung took up the subject
with Soviet leader Konstantin Chernenko in his May 1984 visit to Moscow and won agreement to additional talks on the subject. The United
States, which was watching the developments in Yongbyon with growing
apprehension, urged Moscow to persuade North Korea to sign the Nuclear Non-Proliferation Treaty, hoping this would lead to international
inspection and control of Pyongyang's nuclear facilities.

In December 1985, Moscow agreed to supply four light-water nuclear power reactors but only if North Korea would join the NPT. North
Korea joined the treaty on December 12, and two weeks later the Soviet
and North Korean prime ministers agreed in principle on the power-
reactor deal.

It is unclear what significance North Korean leaders placed on joining
the NPT, or what they expected its obligations would be, but it is unlikely
that they understood the pressures that would eventually be brought to
bear. Under provisions of the treaty, North Korea was allowed eighteen
months to negotiate and sign a safeguards (inspection) agreement with
the International Atomic Energy Agency, which conducts the inspections.
In mid-1987, near the end of the eighteen-month period, the IAEA discovered it had mistakenly sent Pyongyang the wrong kind of agreement
document—one designed for individual sites rather than general inspections. Because of the error, the IAEA gave Pyongyang another eighteen
months, but that deadline passed in December 1988 with no accord and
no movement from Pyongyang. By then North Korea's prospects for ac-
quiring the Soviet-built power reactors—the reason it had joined the NPT
in the first place—had sharply diminished with its declining relations with
Moscow and the dwindling fortunes of the Soviet economy. Yet unless it
was willing to make a big international stir by withdrawing from the pact,
North Korea was stuck with the treaty commitments it had made. There
was little indication then, however, that the IAEA's inspections, even if
North Korea submitted to them, would be very onerous.

NUCLEAR DIPLOMACY:
THE AMERICAN WEAPONS

When the Bush administration took office in Washington in January
1989, information and concern about the North Korean nuclear program
was limited to a small group of American officials with access to the

satellite photographs. Although most intelligence officials had no doubt about the seriousness of the danger, puzzling questions remained. Why, for example, was Yongbyon not better hidden? The flight path for airliners landing at Pyongyang went nearly right over the nuclear complex, making it easily visible to passengers. Such questions were excuses for inaction by a US governmental apparatus that was anything but eager to grapple with this complex and explosive topic. "The real problem was the policymakers' reluctance to face the issue, an avoidance of reality that probably flowed from the realization of the scope and difficulty of the problem," according to a former official who dealt with it in both the Reagan and the Bush administrations.

The first impulse of the Bush administration was to inform others with potential influence about what Washington's space satellites were observing at Yongbyon. If the North Koreans were to be stopped or even slowed, it was clear that the United States would have to gain the cooperation of the other major powers with interests in the Korean peninsula. The chief of the State Department's Korea Desk, Harry Dunlop, briefed Soviet and Chinese officials in February 1989 about the North Korean nuclear program during visits to their capitals. Later Secretary of State James Baker took up the issue repeatedly with senior officials of the two communist giants. According to Baker, "Our diplomatic strategy was designed to build international pressure against North Korea to force them to live up to their agreement to sign a safeguards agreement permitting inspections."

In May a US team of experts traveled to Seoul and Tokyo to provide the first extensive briefing for those governments. By then word of the American findings was trickling out, and the State Department feared that failure to provide information could be a blow to South Korean confidence in the United States. Washington was also eager to put its own spin on the news it was imparting.

Before the briefing, an Arms Control and Disarmament Agency official wrote to her superiors, "I think the South Koreans need to be convinced that their interests would not be served by embarking on a weapons program of their own, or allowing our conclusions to become public." The second of those concerns turned out to be well taken. The highly classified briefing in Seoul, with its gripping conclusion that North Korea might be able to produce atomic bombs by the mid-1990s, leaked almost immediately to the South Korean press, and from there to US and international news media.

After an article that I wrote about the briefing appeared in the *Washington Post*, the North Korea Mission to the United Nations issued a press release, denying any nuclear weapons activity and calling my report "an utterly groundless lie." Despite the denial, the intelligence briefing and the notoriety it attained launched the public and political tumult over the North Korean nuclear program.

The issue was to dominate US policy regarding the divided peninsula for decades to come, at times to the exclusion of almost anything else.

FIRST STEPS

The North Korean response to growing pressure to permit IAEA inspections was to insist it would never agree while being threatened by American nuclear weapons, especially those based in South Korea. The argument had undeniable logic and appeal. As officials in Washington studied the issue, they also realized it would be difficult to organize an international coalition to oppose North Korean nuclear weapons activity as long as American nuclear weapons were in place on the divided peninsula. A Bush administration interagency committee on the North Korean nuclear issue kept coming back to whether the American nuclear deployments should be removed but was unable to reach a decision.

American nuclear weapons had been stationed on the territory of South Korea for more than three decades, since President Eisenhower authorized the deployment of nuclear warheads on Honest John missiles and 280-millimeter long-range artillery in December 1957. As South Vietnam was faltering in the early 1970s, creating fears about South Korea's future, American deployments became notably more prominent. By 1972, according to US documents obtained by nuclear researcher William Arkin, 763 nuclear warheads were deployed in South Korea, the peak number ever recorded.

In 1974 congressional committees began raising questions in public about the security and usefulness of the atomic weapons. As a correspondent who often visited Korea, I learned and reported at that time that American nuclear weapons were stationed uncomfortably close to the DMZ and that nuclear warheads had been flown by helicopter almost routinely to the edge of the DMZ in training exercises.

Public threats to use nuclear weapons were part of the US response to nervousness in Seoul following the fall of Saigon. Secretary of Defense James Schlesinger, publicly acknowledging the presence of American atomic weapons in Korea, declared in June 1975 that "if circumstances were to require the use of tactical nuclear weapons . . . I think that that would be carefully considered." He added, "I do not think it would be wise to test [American] reactions." A year later, well-publicized temporary deployments of nuclear-capable US warplanes to Korea in February 1976 and the first of the annual US-ROK Team Spirit military maneuvers that June involved large-scale movements of troops and practice for use of nuclear weapons. In August 1976, nuclear-capable air and naval assets were massively deployed to Korea after the killing of the two American officers in the DMZ tree-cutting episode.

Thereafter, the trend reversed. The Carter administration reduced the number of American nuclear weapons deployed in Korea to about 250 warheads, a reduction due in part to Carter's withdrawal policies and part to the replacement of some obsolete nuclear weapons by highly accurate conventional weapons. By the onset of the Bush administration in 1989, the Korean deployments had been reduced to about 100 warheads. The cutbacks had been made without public notice, in keeping with the long-standing US policy to "neither confirm nor deny" deployments of nuclear weapons.

American military commanders saw little practical requirement in Korea for the remaining weapons, which were artillery warheads and gravity bombs stored at Kunsan Air Base on the west coast, south of Seoul. In October 1990, US ambassador Donald Gregg, after consulting General Robert RisCassi, the US military commander in Korea, and also the general's two immediate predecessors, recommended to Washington that the weapons be removed to facilitate the negotiations with the North and to avoid their emergence as a serious political issue in the South. The following spring, Admiral William J. Crowe, former chairman of the Joint Chiefs of Staff and an Asia expert, publicly recommended that the nuclear weapons be withdrawn as part of a deal with North Korea. Crowe spelled out in public what others were saying in private, that due to the mobility of US forces, "the actual presence of any nuclear weapons in South Korea is not necessary to maintain a nuclear umbrella over the R.O.K."

These recommendations, however, ran into deep reservations in Washington. President Bush's national security adviser, retired lieutenant general Brent Scowcroft, was strongly opposed to removing the American weapons as a concession to the North on the grounds that Pyongyang had done nothing to earn this reward. Equally serious was concern that removal of the weapons would be seen by the South, and especially by its military, as weakening both the US deterrent against the North and the US commitment to defense of the South.

In the spring of 1991, the topic of the nuclear weapons was broached, gingerly at first, in a series of intimate meetings in Seoul involving Gregg, RisCassi, and several senior officials of the Blue House and ROK Defense and Foreign Ministries. Under previous US practice, only the South Korean president—with no aides present—had been briefed on the nature and location of American nuclear weapons in the country. Until the highly confidential "inner-circle meetings" began in Seoul, a Korean civilian participant recalled, "it was taboo even to talk about the American tactical nuclear weapons; for us, they were shocking to consider."

The discussions deepened in a two-day meeting of American and South Korean military and civilian officials at US Pacific Command headquarters at Honolulu, Hawaii, in early August. While other issues were mentioned, Washington's real purpose was to be sure that the Koreans would be comfortable with removal of the remaining American nuclear weapons. At the high point of the sessions, the representative of the US Joint Chiefs of Staff announced the Pentagon's conclusion that the nuclear deployments in South Korea were not necessary for the country's defense. Although no strong objections to removal of the weapons were raised by the Koreans, some suggested that they be used as a bargaining chip for concessions from Pyongyang. The meeting concluded without formal agreement.

What finally broke through the inertia in Washington was a dramatic and unexpected development in a different part of the world: the coup attempt in mid-August 1991 by hard-liners against Soviet president Mikhail Gorbachev. Although it failed, the coup marked the transfer of real power from Gorbachev to his rival, Russian president Boris Yeltsin, and the beginning of the rapid move toward dissolution of the Soviet Union. On September 27, in an initiative calculated to bring forth reciprocal steps from Moscow, Bush announced the removal of all ground-based and sea-based tactical nuclear weapons from US forces worldwide. The withdrawal of the nuclear artillery from South Korea would leave in place there only some sixty nuclear warheads for air-delivered gravity bombs.

After consulting his advisers, Bush secretly decided to remove these last American nuclear deployments on the peninsula. He also decided in principle to permit North Koreans to inspect the US base at Kunsan where the nuclear weapons had been stored, to meet another of North Korea's demands. "We were able to hook a ride on a Soviet-related decision," said Richard Solomon, who as assistant secretary for East Asian and Pacific affairs had tried unsuccessfully for many months to deal with the issue of the American nuclear weapons in Korea.

Before making his formal decisions, Bush privately informed South Korean president Roh Tae Woo in a meeting at the United Nations that the United States would continue to provide the nuclear umbrella—that is, nuclear protection against threats to South Korea's security—whether or not American nuclear weapons were in place on the peninsula.

In December, when the last of the nuclear bombs had been removed, Roh was permitted to announce officially that "as I speak, there do not exist any nuclear weapons whatsoever, anywhere in the Republic of Korea." Roh's announcement signaling the withdrawal of the American nuclear weapons had a powerful—seemingly immediate—effect in North Korea, contributing in important fashion to an era of compromise and conciliation.

THE DECEMBER ACCORDS

The winter of 1991 inaugurated a period of unusual progress in North-South relations and in North Korea's relations with the United States. It was one of those rare periods when the policies of the two Koreas were in alignment for conciliation and agreement, with all the major outside powers either neutral or supportive.

Economically and politically, 1991 had been a very bad year for Kim Il Sung. His estrangement from the Soviet Union the previous year had cost him a crucial alliance and left him with a painful energy shortage and worsening economic problems. North Korean leaders were briefly cheered in August 1991 by the coup attempt against Mikhail Gorbachev, and they quickly made it known they hoped it would succeed. However, when the coup failed and Russian president Yeltsin became the de facto leader of the failing Soviet Union, Kim could expect no help or even sympathy from Moscow.

In the spring of 1991, Kim's other major ally, China, had forced him to reverse his long-standing opposition to dual entry with South Korea to the United Nations. Now Beijing was moving toward normalization of relations with Seoul. When Kim visited China in October, he was advised to open up economically as China had done and to undertake a rapid settlement with South Korea in the interest of regional peace and stability. Chinese leaders also urged him to give credence to Bush's announcement that American tactical nuclear weapons were being withdrawn and to resolve the concern over the North Korean nuclear program as soon as possible. Even while Kim was still in China, his Foreign Ministry issued a statement welcoming the US move. After returning from Beijing, Kim convened a Politburo meeting, from which emerged new efforts at reconciliation with the South and the world outside.

Simultaneously, South Korea had been shifting toward a more conciliatory posture regarding the North in preparation for the final year of Roh Tae Woo's presidency. High-level talks led by the two prime ministers visiting each other's capitals had already begun in the fall of 1990. In a private conversation with the visiting North Korean prime minister in September 1990, Roh sent word to Kim Il Sung of his desire for a summit meeting as a step toward improved North-South relations. Kim responded, during the visit to Pyongyang of the South Korean prime minister the following month, that he was willing to meet if there was something important to be achieved, but not under other circumstances. After a year's hiatus, which in the view of a senior South Korean participant, Lim Dong Won, was caused by the South's tactical miscalculations, the talks resumed.

Starting with the October 22–25, 1991, prime ministerial meeting in Pyongyang, there was rapid progress. Before the southerners went home, the two Koreas had agreed in principle to work out and adopt at their next meeting a single document setting the terms for broad-ranging accord. When the northern team came to Seoul on December 10, it was prepared to compromise and, as southern delegates saw it, ready to sign an agreement. "This time we brought the seal with us," said a visitor from Pyongyang, referring to the official stamp used to authenticate documents in Asia. This was an astonishing change from the months and years of sterile negotiations in which both sides had refused to budge from fixed positions.

The result of three days of intense bargaining was by far the most important document adopted by the two sides since the North-South joint statement of July 4, 1972. In the "Agreement on Reconciliation, Nonaggression and Exchanges and Cooperation Between the South and the North," adopted and initialed on December 13, 1991, the two Koreas came closer than ever before to accepting each other's regime as a legitimate government with a right to exist. The document portrayed the two Koreas as "recognizing that their relations, not being a relationship between states, constitute a special interim relationship stemming from the process toward unification." The guidelines of the "special interim relationship," if implemented, would have meant a nearly complete cessation of the conflict on the peninsula and a reversal of decades of policy on both sides:

- mutual recognition of each other's systems and an end to interference, vilification, and subversion of each other
- mutual efforts "to transform the present state of armistice into a solid state of peace," with continued observance of the armistice until this was accomplished
- nonuse of force against each other and implementation of confidence-building measures and large-scale arms reductions
- economic, cultural, and scientific exchanges; free correspondence between divided families; and the reopening of roads and railroads that had been severed at the North-South dividing line

Three separate subcommittees on political and military activities and on exchanges were authorized in the agreement, to work out the many details for implementing the accord.

North Korea refused to deal with the issue of its nuclear program in the reconciliation agreement but promised to work on a separate North-South nuclear accord before the end of the year. This was facilitated on

December 18, when Roh announced publicly that the American nuclear weapons had been withdrawn.

On December 24, at a North Korean Workers Party Central Committee plenum, Kim Il Sung praised the recent North-South nonaggression pact as "the first epochal event" since the start of inter-Korean diplomacy in 1972. The meeting, the first party plenum centered on North-South issues in nine years, ended with a public report that contained no criticism of South Korea or the United States.

The party meeting was significant for two other reasons, which may have been connected. Kim Jong Il, the son and designated successor to the Great Leader, was named supreme commander of the DPRK armed forces. And in parallel moves that could not have been made without approval of Kim Jong Il and at least acquiescence by the armed forces commanders he now headed, the plenum apparently gave party clearance for international inspection of the country's nuclear program and for a bilateral nuclear accord to be worked out with the South. Selig Harrison of the Carnegie Endowment for International Peace was later told by a variety of North Korean and foreign observers that the plenum marked a conditional victory for pragmatists who argued for making a deal—compromising the nuclear issues in return for economic benefits and normalization of relations with the United States and Japan. Hard-line elements, according to Harrison, agreed to suspend the weapons program, but not to terminate it—being confident that US and Japanese help would not be forthcoming.

The promised nuclear negotiations between the two Koreas convened at Panmunjom on December 26. As with nonaggression accords, the North's negotiators had instructions to make a deal. On the second day of the talks, they appeared with a written proposal incorporating most of the sweeping South Korean language and dropping several earlier propositions that were unacceptable to the South. At one point, the usually stand-offish North Korean negotiators woke up their South Korean counterparts late at night for a series of one-on-one talks that made important progress. Some sensitive negotiations took place in whispered conversations in the corners of the meeting room, away from the formal conference table, with its microphones hooked up to offices in the two capitals.

A complicated issue for both Koreas was nuclear reprocessing. They were acutely conscious that nearby Japan operated reprocessing facilities for its civil nuclear program under arrangements with the United States that predate the time when Washington had focused on reprocessing as a proliferation risk. Some in the South were eager not to foreclose the option of a future reprocessing plant on economic grounds and, some Americans suspected, as a potential source of weapons material. However, Roh agreed under heavy US pressure to an unqualified commitment to forgo nuclear reprocessing, on the grounds that it would better position the South to bargain against the North's then-suspected reprocessing capability. As for the North, the giant structure being built to house its reprocessing plant at Yongbyon was nearing completion—the most recent US intelligence estimate was that it could be producing plutonium by mid-1992—but this did not seem to faze Pyongyang's negotiators when agreeing to ban reprocessing. When Representative Stephen Solarz (D-NY) met Kim Il Sung on December 18 in Pyongyang, the Great Leader declared, pounding the table at the end of a long and contentious meeting, "We have no nuclear reprocessing facilities!"

Under the bilateral deal as negotiated, the South agreed to cancel the 1992 US-ROK Team Spirit military exercise in return for North Korean willingness to permit outside inspection of its nuclear facilities at Yongbyon. In retrospect, cancellation of Team Spirit was an ROK concession of crucial importance to the North's powerful military, which had consistently resisted compromises affecting the nuclear weapons program.

In the final agreement signed on December 31, both North and South pledged not to "test, manufacture, produce, receive, possess, store, deploy or use nuclear weapons" and not to "possess nuclear reprocessing and uranium enrichment facilities." Moreover, they agreed to reciprocal inspections of facilities of the other side, to be arranged and implemented by a Joint Nuclear Control Commission.

To achieve the agreement, North Korean negotiators were uncharacteristically willing to compromise, suggesting high-level instructions to do so. While the South was exultant at the results, some of its officials felt in retrospect they had pushed the North too hard. Riding together in a car from Pyongyang to Kaesong nine months later, after signing protocols flowing from the December accords, DPRK major general Kim Yong Chul (who remained one of the North's key military negotiators into the mid-2000s, before being given an action-oriented assignment as head of the Reconnaissance General Bureau, charged with anti-ROK operations) complained to his counterpart, ROK major general Park Yong Ok, that 90 percent of the language originated on the southern side, and therefore "this is your agreement, *not* our agreement." At that moment, the South Korean officer began to doubt whether the concessions that had been made could be actually implemented.

At the time of the signing of the agreement on New Year's Eve, however, Kim Il Sung portrayed the North-South nuclear pact as a great victory. In a display of his enthusiasm, he dispatched a helicopter to bring his negotiators home from Panmunjom to Pyongyang in triumphant style. At the dawn of 1992, the *Economist*, the British weekly on international affairs, proclaimed that "the Korean peninsula looked a little safer this week."

MEETING IN NEW YORK

Three weeks into 1992, the United States rolled out its biggest contribution to the positive trend: a bilateral American–North Korean meeting at the political level. Pyongyang had long sought direct discussions with senior levels in Washington, seeing the United States as the heart and head of the West, the superpower overlord of South Korea and Japan. Pyongyang also saw relations with the United States as an important victory in its zero-sum game with the South. And most important, Kim Il Sung sought a relationship with Washington, hoping the United States would act as a balancer and protector against what he feared were potential threats to North Korean security from either China or Russia.

In the fall of 1991, while exploring the range of incentives and disincentives that the United States could wield with the North, Washington officials had begun to discuss the possibility of a high-level meeting. The idea was highly contentious within the administration, but its advocates won approval to discuss it with the South Koreans, who approved it on the explicit condition that it would be only a onetime session that would not lead to further talks. Kim Chong Whi, Roh's national security adviser, as well as State Department experts suggested that the meeting be with Kim Yong Sun, the relatively freewheeling Workers Party secretary for international affairs, who was close to Kim Jong Il.

In December American officials informed the North Koreans, through the US-DPRK political counselor channel in Beijing, that a high-level meeting might be held if Pyongyang agreed to meet its nuclear inspection obligations. In the opinion of several US officials, the promise that such a meeting represented was an important factor in the North's decision to conclude the nuclear accord with the South and in its preparations to sign a nuclear safeguards agreement with the IAEA.

Shortly after 10:00 on January 21, 1992, Kim Yong Sun and several aides arrived at the US Mission to the United Nations to meet an American delegation headed by Arnold Kanter, the undersecretary of state for political affairs (and the third-ranking official in the State Department). Due to the intense antagonism to North Korea and the unprecedented nature of the meeting, there had been fierce debates within the administration not only about whether to have the meeting but also about what Kanter could say, and even whether he could host a lunch.* The bureaucratic compromise, according to Kanter, was that "the meeting would happen, but I would take a tough line."

---

* The tussle over a meal was eventually resolved in favor of those who thought eating with the enemy would do no harm, and Kanter broke bread with the visitor at the now defunct Pen and Pencil Restaurant just off Fifth Avenue. The issue of meals and toasts would come up again a decade later.

Kanter's "talking points"—normally stripped-down notes of the main lines of presentation—were reviewed and approved in advance by an interagency committee and then by the South Korean and Japanese governments. They became virtually a script he had to read, though he did so in the most conciliatory and inoffensive way possible. While urging North Korea to permit IAEA inspections and to give up the nuclear weapons option, Kanter was forbidden to spell out what North Korea could expect in return. He was specifically not permitted even to mention the word *normalization* of American–North Korean relations. Although he referred vaguely to future meetings between the two countries as the principal incentive for Pyongyang, Kanter was required by the arrangement with Seoul to rule out follow-up meetings of this group, making clear that the session itself was not the start of a negotiating process.

The well-tailored Kim Yong Sun, who was wearing a more expensive suit than any of the Americans, impressed Kanter as shrewd and worldly, although he had never been in the United States before. Although North Korea might be a hermit kingdom, Kanter concluded, his interlocutor was no hermit. Referring repeatedly to his intimacy with the Dear Leader, Kim Yong Sun said Kim Jong Il was now in charge of North Korea's foreign relations as well as the military. In the meeting and in a lengthy private talk with Kanter, Kim Yong Sun pushed hard for an agreement in principle to another meeting, or at least a joint statement at the conclusion of this one. When both were refused, he seemed disappointed but not angry. Later in the year, as tension mounted between Pyongyang and Washington, Kim sent a personal message to Kanter through the Beijing channel, appealing for another meeting—but in the midst of an election campaign, this was rejected by the administration.

On January 30, eight days after the Kanter-Kim meeting, North Korea kept the promises it had made by signing the safeguards agreement with the IAEA in Vienna. The agreement was then ratified on April 9, in an unusual special meeting of the Supreme People's Assembly. The following day, the accord was presented to IAEA director general Hans Blix at the agency's headquarters in Vienna to bring it into force.

THE COMING OF THE INSPECTORS

This progress was not to be sustained, and after a few months of grace the situation rapidly headed downhill. Given later developments in the North's nuclear weapons program, the story of the first North Korean nuclear crisis seems almost quaint by comparison. That is not to say that the intense focus on evidence of North Korean "cheating" was misplaced, only that it appears now like a Greek tragedy, with few actors realizing at the time where events were leading despite continuous warning signs and, true to form, with innocence, ignorance, and moral posturing playing equal parts in the drama.

From its headquarters in the towers of the UN complex in Vienna, the International Atomic Energy Agency, created in 1957, runs the world's early-warning system against the spread of nuclear weapons. Since the establishment of the Nuclear Non-Proliferation Treaty in 1968, the most important task of the IAEA has been to send its multinational teams of inspectors to verify that nonnuclear weapon states are keeping their commitments not to manufacture or possess nuclear weapons.

Until 1991 the IAEA limited itself to checking civilian nuclear facilities and materials that NPT signatories reported in voluntary declarations to the agency. The aftermath of the US-led Operation Desert Storm, however, disclosed that Iraq, an NPT signatory, had carried on a sophisticated nuclear weapons program at secret sites adjacent to those being inspected by the agency. The impact on the IAEA was profound.

In the face of withering criticism for ineffectiveness and timidity, the IAEA under Hans Blix underwent an upheaval in personnel and a sea change in attitudes, from complacency to alertness about suspicious nuclear activities. Despite the misgivings of some third-world members of the IAEA board, Blix, a former Swedish foreign minister, established the right to accept intelligence information supplied by the United States and other member states in its investigations and the right to demand access to suspicious facilities through mandatory "special inspections."

Starting in September 1991, in the wake of the Gulf War, the United States began supplying intelligence information to Blix and senior aides at his Vienna headquarters, eventually including the services of its incomparably sophisticated national laboratories and supplied photos from US spy satellites that were rarely shown to outsiders. Armed for the first time with extensive independent information about the nuclear programs that they were checking, the IAEA's leaders and its corps of international inspectors were determined not to be hoodwinked or embarrassed again. North Korea became the first test case of their new capabilities and attitudes. In this first blush of newfound resolve, the IAEA appeared not to realize that North Korea was not prepared to stand and salute.

FIRST INSPECTIONS

For six days in mid-May 1992, Blix led a team to North Korea to establish relations with the country's leaders and prepare for full-scale IAEA inspections. After preliminary discussions in Pyongyang, Blix and his party were taken to the nuclear facilities at Yongbyon. There, as far as is known, Blix and his three technically expert companions were the first outsiders ever to see, from ground level, what the American surveillance cameras had been peering down on for nearly a decade.

Taking no chances that the IAEA chief would miss something of importance, US officials had provided intelligence briefings for Blix and his top aides in September 1991, March 1992, and on May 7, immediately before his departure. On the final occasion, Blix was given a "virtual reality" tour of Yongbyon, complete with ominous background music, using advanced computer modeling based on aerial photographs. Blix and his party were encouraged to memorize the shapes and relationships of the main facilities. The highlight of the intelligence tour was the reprocessing building. North Korea, after consistently denying that it had such a facility, listed the plant as a "radiochemical laboratory" in the declaration of its nuclear facilities provided a few days before Blix's visit.

When they were actually walking through this facility, Blix and his team had two surprises: first, that the six-story-high building was even more imposing than they had expected from the CIA briefings and, second, that the building was only about 80 percent complete, with the equipment inside only about 40 percent ready for full-scale production. An IAEA official described the works inside the giant building as "extremely primitive" and far from ready to produce the quantities of plutonium needed for a stockpile of atomic weapons. This conclusion contradicted worst-case US assessments, such as that by CIA director Robert Gates on March 27 that "we believe Pyongyang is close, perhaps very close, to having a nuclear weapon capability."

North Korea had reported to the IAEA in its initial declaration that in 1990, it had already produced about ninety grams of plutonium, roughly three ounces, on an experimental basis in the "radiochemical lab." In a third surprise, the seemingly obliging North Koreans shocked Blix by proudly presenting him with a vial of the plutonium in powdered form, which is deadly when inhaled. This small amount was far short of the eight to sixteen pounds needed to produce a weapon. Nevertheless, if plutonium had been manufactured at all, it would be difficult to ascertain scientifically how much had been produced, raising the possibility that North Korea had squirreled some away.

While very small quantities of plutonium could be separated using test methods in a laboratory, IAEA officials found it illogical that North Korea would have erected a huge and expensive facility without first building a pilot plant to test its procedures. North Korea denied that such a pilot plant existed, but doubts persisted.

In late May, after Blix and his team returned to Vienna, the agency sent its first set of regular inspectors to Yongbyon. "The first inspection was just to get the picture," said Olli Heinonen, a sandy-haired IAEA veteran who eventually became chief inspector of the North Korean program.

"The second inspection [in July] saw something that didn't fit the picture, the first signals that something was wrong." More discrepancies appeared in September, with the third inspection.

North Korea had reported that it had separated the three ounces of plutonium in an experimental procedure in 1990, when a small number of faulty fuel rods had been taken from its 5-megawatt indigenous reactor. To confirm what had been done, IAEA inspectors swabbed the inside of the steel tanks used to process the plutonium. The inspectors assumed that the North Koreans had previously scrubbed down the equipment, but the IAEA teams employed gamma-ray detectors and other gear capable of finding minute particles clinging to grooved surfaces. The IAEA also convinced the North Koreans to cut into a waste-storage pipe to obtain some of the highly radioactive waste that is a by-product of the plutonium production process.

Tests on some of this material were run at the IAEA's laboratory. Far more sophisticated tests were conducted for the IAEA in supporting laboratories run out of the US Air Force Technology Applications Center at Patrick Air Force Base, Florida. Much of the work of this laboratory, which had pioneered the analysis of Soviet nuclear tests, had been secret during the Cold War.

Precise measurements of the samples indicated that three different episodes of plutonium separation could have taken place in 1989, 1990, and 1991—rather than the single operation in 1990 that North Korea had claimed. In another sophisticated set of tests, the isotopic signatures in the plutonium sample presented to Blix did not match those of the waste products that supposedly had been produced from the same operation. "It was like finding a left-hand glove of plutonium that is missing its right-hand glove, [and finding] a right-hand glove of nuclear waste that is missing its plutonium," Blix said in an interview for this book. There had to be more plutonium, Blix and his experts reasoned, but "whether it is grams or kilograms, we don't know."

Pyongyang's expectations about the capabilities of the inspections probably had been shaped by the limited experiences of a North Korean who had worked as an IAEA inspector before the Gulf War and who in 1992 emerged as director of the safeguards liaison office of Pyongyang's Ministry of Atomic Energy. "It's hard to believe he had seen anything like this," said Heinonen, speaking of the greatly enhanced scientific prowess that provided detailed test results from tiny samples of radioactive material. Said Willi Theis, initially the chief of the IAEA inspection team in North Korea, "North Korea grossly underestimated the agency's measurement capability. . . . They never expected us to be able to perform isotopic analyses. They could not understand this or explain the [test result] differences. The more they learned, the more they provided manufactured responses. We had to approach them harder and harder as they realized we were going to discover their wrongdoings."

FROM ACCOMMODATION TO CRISIS

In the last half of 1992 and early 1993, the euphoria that had resulted from opening North Korea's nuclear program to international inspection gave way to suspicion, antagonism, and, eventually, crisis. The rewards Pyongyang had expected from agreeing to nuclear inspections had not developed; instead, the presence of the inspectors provided the focal point for accusations of cheating and new international pressures. Contributing to the setback was a worsening political climate between the North and the South, brought about in part by preparations for ROK presidential elections in December 1992 as well as bitter personal rivalries within the South Korean bureaucracy over how to deal with the North. The United States, distracted and largely immobilized by its own November presidential balloting, did nothing to forestall the approaching storm.

Since the signing of the unprecedented series of accords between North and South the previous December, negotiations over their implementation had gone slowly. In the North-South Joint Nuclear Control Commission meetings that were charged with preparing the bilateral nuclear inspections called for under the accords, Pyongyang resisted Seoul's demands for short-notice "inspections with teeth" by South Koreans. This deadlock became more worrisome as the discrepancies in the IAEA data accumulated, and conflict grew between North Korea and the international inspectors, providing new ammunition for those who had believed all along that North Korea would never reveal crucial elements of its nuclear weapons activity.

With a record of foreign-policy accomplishments behind him, President Roh Tae Woo was relatively relaxed, telling the *New York Times* in September that he believed North Korea's "determination to develop nuclear weapons has become weaker." Roh still hoped for a meeting with Kim Il Sung, although in April 1992 he had been forced to reject an unexpected and secret invitation to travel to Pyongyang for the Great Leader's eightieth birthday. To meet his counterpart on this occasion would make him seem to be a celebrant at Kim's party. Nevertheless, Roh secretly sent his intelligence chief to Pyongyang to wish Kim happy birthday and express continuing interest in a meeting.

Kim Young Sam, the former opposition leader who had joined the ruling party in 1990 and who became its presidential candidate in May 1992, was apprehensive about the positive aspects of North-South relations. Kim and his political managers feared that continuation of the North-South euphoria of earlier months would benefit his old political rival, Kim Dae Jung, who was shaping up as once again his principal competitor, this time as opposition presidential candidate. As the political authority of Roh as a lame-duck president began to ebb and that of his chosen successor grew in the late summer of 1992, South Korea slowed down its normalization process with the North, and its officials urged Americans to do the same.

In early October, as a part of a campaign of pressure and linkage, the United States and ROK defense ministers announced in Washington that "in the absence of meaningful improvement in South-North relations, especially on bilateral nuclear inspections," they were preparing to relaunch the US-ROK Team Spirit, canceled in 1992 in the period of mutual accommodation that led to the IAEA inspections of Yongbyon.

The South Korean military took the lead in demanding a renewal of Team Spirit, which was deemed important for readiness as well as a potent pressure point against the North. The US Command, under General Robert RisCassi, was determined to go ahead with the exercise unless countermanded by higher-ups for political reasons. Surprisingly, interagency policy committees in Washington were neither informed nor consulted before this politically explosive decision was made in the defense ministers' annual meeting. To Korea experts in Washington and to Donald Gregg, US ambassador to Seoul, it was an unpleasant bolt from the blue—he later called it "one of the biggest mistakes" of Korea policy on his watch.

For North Korea, the cancellation of the 1992 Team Spirit exercise had been the most tangible evidence of its improved relationship with the United States and the US concession of greatest immediate benefit to the North Korean military establishment. Although Americans tended to scoff at Pyongyang's fears that the annual field exercise was a threat to its national security, the landing of large numbers of additional American troops in South Korea by sea and air, the profusion of flights near the DMZ by American nuclear-capable warplanes, and the movement of heavily armed ROK and US ground troops made a powerful impression on the North—as Team Spirit's planners had hoped from the start, nearly two decades earlier. Moreover, Team Spirit was personally important to Kim Il Sung, who had been complaining bitterly about it publicly and privately for many years.

In a public statement, North Korea described the threat to resume the maneuvers as "a criminal act" designed to "put the brakes on North-South relations and drive the North-South dialogue to a crisis." Within weeks, Pyongyang, citing the Team Spirit issue as the reason, abruptly canceled all North-South contacts in every forum except for those in the Joint Nuclear Control Commission. A short time later, those talks also collapsed. For the first time, North Korea warned that it might refuse to continue the IAEA inspections, declaring that the decision to revive the Team Spirit exercise is "an act of provocation breaking the U.S. promise not to make nuclear threats."

The day before the US-ROK Team Spirit announcement, the Agency for National Security Planning, Seoul's renamed domestic and foreign intelligence agency, trumpeted the arrest of sixty-two people in what it charged was the largest North Korean espionage ring in the history of the republic. More than three hundred others were implicated, the agency claimed, including a female member of the North Korean Workers Party hierarchy who had lived in the South under false identities several times in earlier decades. While there is no doubt that North Korea had long had spies in the South, the timing of the NSP's roundup and its revelations raised eyebrows within other elements of the South Korean government, especially because NSP officials—as well as the presidential campaign managers for ruling-party candidate Kim Young Sam—were unhappy with the rapid improvement of relations with the North.

Before the spy-ring announcement, Roh Tae Woo had authorized an ROK deputy prime minister to visit Pyongyang to pursue joint economic development with the North and ordered the Economic Planning Board to prepare a team to travel to the North on a similar mission. In internal discussions, the intelligence agency opposed the Economic Planning Board mission, according to Kim Hak Joon, who was chief Blue House spokesman at the time and an expert on unification policy. After the news of the spy-ring arrests, which may have been "greatly exaggerated or fabricated," according to the former official, Roh was forced to cancel the missions due to the political and public indignation. "Everything stopped," the former spokesman recalled.

It was in this atmosphere that the IAEA, having received new US satellite photographs indicating dissembling at Yongbyon, stepped up its efforts to force North Korea to reveal the full dimensions of its nuclear activity.

On the eve of a previous IAEA board meeting, Blix had obtained permission for his inspectors to "visit" two sites at Yongbyon that appeared to be nuclear related but that had not been declared by North Korea. One of the sites was a two-story structure camouflaged to appear as a one-story building. American overhead photography had recorded the construction, in the original lower level, of thick-walled vaults made of reinforced concrete—suitable for the storage of nuclear waste. When IAEA inspectors arrived, the lower floor was no longer visible, and the inspectors were told it did not exist. The top floor was filled with heavy weapons, including tanks. North Korea subsequently refused to permit formal inspection of the facility on the grounds that it was a military site and therefore exempt from inspection, not an exemption the IAEA allowed.

On November 12, in a telephone conversation from Vienna with Theis, his chief inspector at Yongbyon, Blix said the agency now possessed indisputable evidence that a trench had been dug and then covered up between the reprocessing plant and the "one-story building." Blix said there was also clear evidence that the North Koreans had sought to camouflage a nearby outdoor nuclear waste facility. Blix instructed his inspector to tell the North Koreans that they must declare these sites as nuclear facilities and permit their inspection.

Realizing that North Korean authorities had probably monitored the conversation and that his demands would be difficult for the North Koreans to swallow, Theis immediately summoned two senior nuclear officials of the Yongbyon facility and sought to work with them on amending their initial declaration to the IAEA with as little admission of error as possible. At first the officials seemed amenable and even grateful. The next day, no doubt after receiving instructions, they reversed course, bitterly accusing Theis of being "an agent of the CIA." They refused to cooperate, widening the breach between North Korea and the IAEA.

The two sides sparred inconclusively over the next three months as the IAEA presented the North Koreans with new data on the chemical "inconsistencies" and referred vaguely to "information" on the true purposes of the two suspect sites. By this point, under Kim Jong Il's instructions, the North was already laying plans to withdraw from the NPT and apparently simply stalling for time. Pyongyang's officials made various explanations and denials, none of them credible to the IAEA. In early January, the agency's experts identified two possible explanations for the chemical inconsistencies: undeclared and undetected diversions from the very small Soviet-supplied research reactor at Yongbyon or diversion from the 5-megawatt indigenous reactor.

In the latter case, US intelligence agencies calculated, it was at least theoretically possible that enough plutonium could have been obtained from a full load of irradiated fuel rods to produce one or two nuclear weapons (although very substantial additional efforts, of which North Korea was not then believed to be capable, would be required to weaponize the plutonium). This, and later discredited CIA calculations on the 5-megawatt reactor's operating history, was the basis for worst-case US intelligence estimates and public statements during the coming nuclear crisis.

Eventually, the focus of contention became the two suspect sites that the IAEA had identified as unacknowledged nuclear waste sites. In late-December 1992, Blix requested "visits" to clarify the nature of the sites and make tests. In January Pyongyang responded that "a visit by officials could not be turned into an inspection" and said that inspections of nonnuclear military facilities "might jeopardize the supreme interests" of the DPRK. This was a clear—and very calculated—reference to the

Non-Proliferation Treaty's escape clause, which permits a nation to withdraw from the treaty to avoid jeopardizing its "supreme national interests,"
and which DPRK Foreign Ministry officials had already pointed out to
Kim Jong Il as a "legal" route to getting out of the NPT.

In response, Blix, meeting a North Korean representative in Vienna,
spoke explicitly for the first time of the possible requirement of a "special
inspection." Except for the case of Iraq, the agency had never made such
a demand inspection before. The UN Security Council, meanwhile, declared itself able to take punitive action if IAEA inspection requests were
ignored. Thus, North Korea was set to become the first test of the more
vigorous international consensus against nuclear proliferation.

In preparation for the IAEA board meeting in February, Blix asked
the United States to approve the display of the satellite photographs at
the heart of the agency's demand for inspection of the two suspect sites. The
remarkable high-resolution pictures had been shown to Blix and his staff,
but the CIA bureaucracy was much less willing to display them to a board
that included officials of countries such as Libya, Syria, and Algeria and
in the presence of North Korean representatives. However, in response to
urgent requests from the State Department, outgoing CIA director Robert
Gates overruled his staff. Gates knew that sensitive intelligence photos
had been displayed for the Security Council on the Chad issue in the early
1980s, on the Iran-Iraq War later in the 1980s, and on Iraq's invasion of
Kuwait in 1991–1992. "For me," Gates recalled, "the notion of sharing
imagery with an international agency was not as new or as radical a step as
it may have been to the bureaucracy."

Close to a dozen satellite photographs of North Korean installations
and attempts at deception at Yongbyon were presented to a closed session of the IAEA board on February 22. The impact was electric. The
initially skeptical board was deeply impressed. At the end of its meeting,
on February 25, the board demanded that North Korea permit the special
inspection of the two disputed sites "without delay." As a concession to
Chinese requests, it provided a one-month grace period for North Korean
compliance, making clear that if Pyongyang did not act, it would take the
issue to the Security Council for international sanctions or other actions.

By this time, the credibility and international standing of both the
IAEA and North Korea were at risk, with the stakes very high for both
sides. If the IAEA could not secure international backing for inspections
when there was evidence of cheating, its newly asserted authority could
be defied with impunity, and the post-Iraq drive against nuclear weapons
proliferation would be set back decisively. For Pyongyang, the danger was
that this would be only the first of increasingly intrusive inspections it
regarded as masterminded by hostile US intelligence.

Entwined around the legal questions was the sensitive issue of respect, what Koreans call *ch'emyon* and Westerners call "face," a matter of tremendous, almost overwhelming, importance to the reclusive North Korean regime. "For us, saving face is as important as life itself," a senior North Korean told Representative Gary Ackerman (D-NY) during his 1993 visit to Pyongyang, and experts on North Korea say that may not be much of an exaggeration. Although the "special inspections" were unlikely to clear up the inconsistencies in Pyongyang's program, they would almost certainly provide overwhelming evidence that North Korea had not told the IAEA the whole truth about its nuclear facilities. In the court of international opinion, North Korea would face demeaning condemnation. As the tension increased, the country's minister of atomic energy, Choi Hak Gun, told IAEA inspectors, "Even if we had done it [cheated], we would never admit it."

As the conflict was coming to a head in November 1992, Governor Bill Clinton won the American presidential election over incumbent George Bush. The outgoing administration was unwilling to contemplate long-range policies for dealing with North Korea and the issues posed by its nuclear noncompliance, and in the early months after its January 20 inauguration, the incoming administration was not organized well enough to do so either. Similarly in Seoul, Kim Young Sam, assisted by last-minute red-baiting against Kim Dae Jung, won the presidential election in mid-December and took office on February 25, far from well equipped to deal with immediate crisis.

The IAEA, however, did not wait for the new governments in Washington and Seoul to get settled before pressing its ultimatum. On February 26, the day after the IAEA Board of Governors formally endorsed the demand for inspection of the suspect sites, Blix sent a telex to the North Korean Foreign Ministry, requesting that IAEA inspectors be permitted to travel to Yongbyon on March 16 to examine the two disputed places. It was a tense time in North Korea. March 9 was the kickoff of the new Team Spirit exercise, downsized but still an impressive seventy thousand South Korean troops and fifty thousand American troops, including the landing of nineteen thousand Americans from outside the country and the deployment of the aircraft carrier USS *Independence* offshore.

The day before the exercise, North Korea announced that Kim Jong Il, who had been supreme military commander for a little over a year, had ordered the entire nation and armed forces to assume a "state of readiness for war," ostensibly in response to the Team Spirit "nuclear war test aimed at a surprise, preemptive strike at the northern half of the country." Senior military officials, told that an attack might be imminent, were ordered to evacuate to underground fortifications. All military leaves were canceled, the heads of all soldiers were shaved, steel helmets were worn, and troops were issued rifle ammunition. In Pyongyang armored cars were drawn up in rows near security headquarters, and armed police checked military passes, while in the countryside the civilian population was mobilized to dig trenches near their homes as protection against air attack. In fact, these preparations were part of the plan for the announcement on March 12 of the North's withdrawal from the Nuclear Non-Proliferation Treaty, citing the treaty's escape clause on "defending supreme national interests." As cover for its NPT withdrawal, Pyongyang gave two reasons: Team Spirit, which it charged had violated the spirit of the NPT and of the North-South denuclearization accord, and the IAEA demand for special inspection of two suspect sites, which it described as "an undisguised strong arm act designed to disarm the DPRK and strangle our socialist system." Pyongyang recognized that under the treaty, its withdrawal would not take effect until after a three-month waiting period. In the meantime, Kim Jong Il was in the field with his troops, expecting a military response from the outside.

Although there had been abundant hints that North Korea might withdraw from the NPT, many officials who had not been monitoring the North Korean nuclear situation were unaware of them. Most governments and publics were blindsided. The announcement of the withdrawal was treated as an incomprehensible act of defiance and an ominous sign that North Korea was hell-bent on the production of nuclear weapons. As the world reacted with shock and dismay, North Korea's nuclear program suddenly leaped to the top of the international agenda.

12

WITHDRAWAL AND ENGAGEMENT

THE FIRST NUCLEAR PROLIFERATION crisis of the post–Cold War era came as an unwelcome surprise to the newly installed governments of Kim Young Sam in Seoul and Bill Clinton in Washington, which were both barely organized to deal with routine business, let alone a complex and dangerous confrontation with North Korea.

The South Korean government was in its fifteenth day in office on March 12, 1993, when the new foreign minister, Han Sung Joo, received word of North Korea's announcement that it intended to withdraw from the Non-Proliferation Treaty. A former professor of international relations with a PhD from the University of California at Berkeley, Han was an expert on regional and global issues but a neophyte in governmental service. After trying in vain to reach the new South Korean president, who was attending a naval graduation ceremony outside Seoul, Han sat down to assess the potential consequences of North Korea's precipitating act.

The major concerns, as Han saw them, lined up in this order: first, the possibility that North Korea would actually produce nuclear weapons, thereby changing the strategic situation on the divided peninsula; second, the possibility that the United States and other nations would react so strongly that war would break out in Korea; and third, the expectable demand inside South Korea to match the North Korean bomb program, touching off an arms race that could spur Japan as well as South Korea to become nuclear weapons powers and destroy the international non-proliferation regime that had retarded the spread of nuclear weapons for two decades. These possibilities would engage the two Koreas, the United States, and the international community over many months to come.

Two weeks after the announcement, Han traveled to Washington with the sketchy outlines of what he called a "stick and carrot" approach to persuading Pyongyang to change its mind during the ninety-day waiting period before its withdrawal would become effective. As Han saw it, the stick would be supplied by potential UN Security Council sanctions. Under chapter 7 of the UN Charter, which had been invoked after the Iraqi invasion of Kuwait, these sanctions could range from downgrading or severance of diplomatic relations to economic embargoes or military action. The carrots could include cancellation of the Team Spirit military exercise, security guarantees, trade, and other inducements to cooperate with the international community. "Pressure alone will not work," Han declared.

Han's approach was in line with the thinking of most officials in the State Department, whose business and tradition is to negotiate, but it was controversial among the more hawkish elements in Seoul and many sectors of the US government. "The [US] Joint Chiefs of Staff said, 'Under no circumstances should you engage [the North Koreans] in negotiations. You should not reward them. You should punish them,'" recalled a State Department official. But the official added, "As soon as you said, 'How do you mean, punish them?' of course the JCS would back away from any military options."

The absence of acceptable military options was also evident in Seoul. A few weeks after the North Korean announcement, when US defense secretary Les Aspin made his first official visit to the ROK capital, Defense Minister Kwon Yong Hae warned that even a "surgical strike" against the Yongbyon reactor would lead to a major escalation of hostilities on the peninsula. The result, Kwon said, could be a general war that would wreak death and destruction on South Korea and immediately involve US military forces. Such an attack, even if completely successful, would probably not destroy any plutonium that might already be hidden away in North Korea.

Negotiations quickly emerged as the consensus solution in Washington, not because they appeared to be promising but because nobody could come up with another feasible plan to head off a crisis in Northeast Asia. However, talks with the North Koreans were highly controversial. With no strong signals coming from Clinton, the administration seemed unable to make a clear-cut decision to offer negotiations.

China, which was widely recognized as a crucial participant in the international maneuvering, was urging direct negotiations between the United States and North Korea, which were ardently desired by Pyongyang. South Korean foreign minister Han, in a meeting with Chinese foreign minister Qian Qichen in Bangkok on April 22, said Seoul would drop its long-standing opposition to Washington-Pyongyang talks if China, in return, would agree not to veto a UN Security Council resolution calling on the North to comply with international nuclear inspections rather than withdraw from the NPT. Qian did not immediately accept the deal, but in fact China did not veto the resolution.

With the precedent of the carefully limited 1992 New York meeting of Arnold Kanter and Kim Yong Sun before them, American officials were moving toward a decision to undertake direct negotiations with the North without the participation of the South, which was a reversal of often-declared US policy. The Washington-Pyongyang talks were "the South Koreans' idea. . . . [T]hey actually came to us and suggested it," according to Raymond Burkhardt, who was acting US ambassador in Seoul at the time. Burkhardt added, however, that it was initially understood on both sides that the talks would be limited to nuclear issues, which were peculiarly the province of the United States as a nuclear power.

With Washington still unable to decide what approach to take, Pyongyang forced the issue. In early May, with about a month to go before the June 12 deadline, a diplomat at North Korea's UN Mission in New York telephoned C. Kenneth Quinones, the DPRK country officer in the State Department, to ask if the Americans wanted to meet and, if so, the sooner the better. Some of Quinones's colleagues were amazed that he had spoken on the telephone to North Koreans, but he pointed out that the North Koreans had placed the call. On further consideration, the State Department took North Korea's initiative as a hopeful sign of eagerness to avoid a confrontation over the nuclear issue. The administration decided to move ahead to talks.

The US official chosen to negotiate with North Korea was Robert L. Gallucci, the breezy, Brooklyn-born assistant secretary of state for politico-military affairs. A man of abundant self-confidence and a good sense of humor, he was an expert on nuclear issues and a veteran of the postwar UN effort to dismantle Iraq's nuclear and chemical weapons programs. As Gallucci said later, he was "blissfully ignorant of profound regional contact," having previously spent only five days in South Korea and none in the North. Gallucci was picked largely because the negotiations were conceived as being narrowly focused on the proliferation question, and Washington did not wish to name a more politically oriented official whose outlook and responsibilities might alarm Seoul. Once he began the negotiations, however, Gallucci's perspective widened rapidly.

On the North Korean side, the negotiator was Kang Sok Ju, the deputy foreign minister whom I had met several times in New York and Pyongyang. Kang had attended the International Relations College in Pyongyang and had served in the international department of the Workers Party, the North Korean Mission in Paris, and as a deputy foreign minister for European affairs. A self-assured and evidently well-connected man (his older brother was head of the Workers Party History Research Institute), he was more direct and willing to engage than other senior North Korean diplomats I had met and less openly ideological. Kang was a personal rival to

Kim Yong Sun, and his Foreign Ministry colleagues would later gently in-
quire why the Americans had signaled a preference for meeting with Kim
in the January 1992 talks instead of, in their view, the more capable Kang.
He had more experience in the West than most North Korean diplomats,
and he told American negotiators at one point that one of his favorite
books was *Gone with the Wind*. To their amazement, he quoted from it to
prove the point—though not the passage ("Frankly, my dear, I don't give a
damn") that many had expected.

After three lower-level exchanges to set it up, the first meeting between Gallucci and Kang took place at the US Mission to the United
Nations on Wednesday, June 2, only ten days before North Korea's withdrawal from the NPT was to become effective. Except for one or two
career officials who had been present at the one-day Kanter-Kim meeting
the previous year, the American negotiators had never even met a North
Korean before, and Kang and most of his team had never had a serious
conversation with a ranking American official. Each side was nervous and
uncertain about what to expect from the other. The members of the Korean
delegation wanted to know, "Who is this Gallucci?" and were somewhat
distressed that the Americans did not seem to understand how important
Kang Sok Ju was. If nothing else, in protocol terms, the first vice minister
far outranked a US assistant secretary. Besides, they noted, Kang spoke
directly to Kim Jong Il. Did Gallucci see the US president?

Kang's remarks opened with a lengthy paean to the glories of Kim
Il Sung and the *juche* system, which depressed the Americans, but they
soon learned this was obligatory for most North Korean presentations, at
least until the two sides got down to serious business. The exchanges that
followed did not get far, with North Koreans adamantly refusing to stay
in the NPT and the Americans demanding that they do so. As the talks
seemed to be getting nowhere, the US team returned to Washington at
the weekend and told the North Koreans essentially, "If you want to meet
again, call us and tell us what you have in mind." What the Americans
did not yet understand was that after observing international reaction in
March to the North's withdrawal announcement, the Foreign Ministry
had persuaded Kim Jong Il that the announcement had opened an unexpected opportunity, that the world wanted the North come back to the
NPT and that the North could use this response to advance its goals, most
of all improving ties with the United States. Kang had come to begin that
process, and the first session had been largely shadow boxing.

On Monday morning, responding to a North Korean call, Quinones
returned to New York and met three Pyongyang officials in a Forty-Second
Street coffee shop. There for the next three days, the American diplomat
carried on a Socratic dialogue with the DPRK diplomats, drinking orange
juice and coffee for hours at a time at a table by the front window of the

coffee shop, where nobody paid any attention to them except (Quinones learned later) the FBI, which photographed the rendezvous. Quinones explained to the visitors how the US government and State Department were organized, what was or was not possible in the American system, and what types of security assurances might be provided to them in return for a decision to remain in the NPT.

After another round of seemingly sterile talks between the full delegations, the Americans had a gloomy dinner, not sure what would salvage the situation. Somebody recalled that a *Rodong Sinmun* editorial had contained language suggesting there were circumstances in which a solution was possible. It was decided to replay the words back to the North Koreans at the session the next morning. Gallucci recited the passage, with his interpreter reading directly—and ostentatiously—from a copy of the newspaper. The reaction was immediate and electric on the part of the North Korean delegation. After that, Kang no longer spoke of withdrawal and the mood became more positive.

During an afternoon break, several members of the US delegation crafted prospective assurances against "the threat and use of force, including nuclear weapons," and against "interference in each other's internal affairs." To defend themselves against potential intra-administration criticism that they had given in to Pyongyang, they took the phrases directly from the UN Charter and previous official US statements in other circumstances.

Meeting in lengthy sessions on June 10 and 11—the very eve of the June 12 withdrawal date—Gallucci and Kang hammered out a six-paragraph joint statement. The key points were the American security assurances, an agreement by the two sides to continue their official dialogue, and, in return, a North Korean decision to "suspend" its withdrawal from the NPT for "as long as it considered necessary."

The joint statement removed the immediate threat of North Korean withdrawal from the Non-Proliferation Treaty and defused the sense of crisis, though it did not actually resolve the central issues. The Americans who had participated in the negotiations were elated, especially because Pyongyang's negotiators proved to be open to argument and logic rather than the extraterrestrials some had expected. "I would make a point to Kang and he would make a point," said Gallucci, which would have been unremarkable in most negotiations but had by no means seemed ensured in the case of North Koreans. After the opening lecture, Gallucci found Kang more open to reason than the Iraqis he had dealt with. Above all, Kang handled the nuclear questions in ways that suggested agreements could be made on many issues, if the two sides could agree on the price.

For the North Koreans, a joint statement with the United States was an achievement of immense importance. A year earlier, at the end of the

Kanter–Kim Yong Sun talk, the Bush administration had refused to issue such a document. That Kang came back with a joint statement where Kim could not must have seemed especially delicious to the Foreign Ministry.

More important, the joint statement was of great symbolic value to the Foreign Ministry and to others in Pyongyang arguing for a serious effort to bargain with the Americans on the nuclear program. Even if it had only described the weather in New York, the statement would have been tangible evidence that the United States had recognized the legitimacy of North Korea and was willing to negotiate. By raising the stakes with its nuclear program, North Korea suddenly had become important to the United States. For the same reasons that Pyongyang was satisfied, the joint statement raised hackles in conservative circles in Seoul, where American relations with North Korea were anathema. This zero-sum pattern was to persist throughout the nuclear crisis.

In what seemed only a minor piece of business at the end of the June 11 session, the American side suggested that follow-up communications take place through the North Korean UN Mission in New York. This move, which the DPRK officials immediately understood and accepted, gave the two countries a direct, authorized, and far more workable conduit for exchanges than the rigidly structured diplomatic talks in Beijing that had taken place periodically since 1988. If North Korea's objective had been to seize the attention of Washington and force it to negotiate seriously on a bilateral basis, its strategy had succeeded brilliantly. Undoubtedly, it enhanced Kang's standing with Kim Jong Il, no small achievement that would be important for the years of negotiations that were to follow.

THE LIGHT-WATER-REACTOR PLAN

On July 1, as Washington officials prepared for the next round of talks with Pyongyang on the nuclear issue, the new South Korean president, Kim Young Sam, voiced harsh criticisms of the negotiations in separate interviews with the British Broadcasting Company (BBC) and the *New York Times*. In the *Times* interview, which drew the most attention in the US capital, Kim charged that the North Koreans were manipulating the negotiations "to buy time to finish their project," and he expressed hope that the United States would "not continue to be led on by North Korea." American officials, who had undertaken the negotiations at the suggestion of the South and had kept the South informed step by step, reacted with shock and anger.

This was only the first in a series of surprises from Kim Young Sam. Like much of the Korean public, whose feelings about the North are a complicated mixture of kinship, disdain, and fear, Kim's views on North Korea were replete with inconsistency.

Kim had had little to do with North Korea issues during most of his career as an opposition political leader. Except for his strong prodemocracy stands, he was considered moderate to conservative on most political issues. As noted in Chapter 6, his mother had been murdered in 1960 by a North Korean agent who had invaded his parents' home. In 1992 his successful campaign for president featured anticommunist attacks on his longtime adversary, Kim Dae Jung, whom he falsely accused of being endorsed by Pyongyang. On the other hand, in his February 1993 inaugural address, Kim Young Sam offered to meet his North Korean counterpart "at any time and any place," and he declared that as members of the same Korean family, "no ally can be more valuable than national kinship." The latter remark, implying a higher priority for reconciliation with the North than alliance with the United States, created something of a sensation on both sides of the DMZ.

What drove Kim Young Sam's northern policies above all were the tides of domestic public opinion. Unlike his military predecessors, Kim was a professional politician with a keen interest in the shifting views of the public. Known for relying more on his feel for the political aspects of issues than any overall strategy, he cited newspaper headlines or television broadcasts more often in internal discussions than official papers, which aides complained he did not read. According to a White House official, Kim constantly referred to polling data, public opinion, and political positioning in discussing his reactions to events, even in meetings and telephone calls with the US president.

In mid-July, just prior to the second round of US–North Korean negotiations, Kim was personally reassured about American policy by President Clinton, who came to Korea for a brief visit following the Group of Seven summit conference in Tokyo. Traveling to the DMZ for the traditional meeting with American troops, the US president, clad in a fatigue jacket and "U.S. Forces Korea" cap, was taken to the very edge of the Bridge of No Return—close to where the two American officers had been beaten to death in 1976 and much closer to the border with North Korea than his predecessors had come during their visits to Korea. Turning to a press pool accompanying him, Clinton held forth on the issue of the day: due to US security commitments, he said, "it is pointless for [North Koreans] to try to develop nuclear weapons because if they ever use them it would be the end of their country."

Clinton's remarks went over well in South Korea and at home, where he was considered suspect among many military-oriented people for evading the draft during the Vietnam War, but they were unwelcome in Pyongyang, where Foreign Ministry officials were preparing for the talks with the Americans. When the negotiations convened on July 14 in Geneva, Kang protested that the United States had promised in June not to

threaten the DPRK, yet Clinton had publicly threatened them with anni-
hilation while standing in military garb on their very border. The Americans responded that when it came to bellicose language, Pyongyang had
few peers. "The President of the United States went to South Korea. What
did you expect him to say there?" Gallucci retorted. It soon became clear
that Kang had been obliged to respond with tough rhetoric but had no
intention of breaking off the negotiations.

The second day of negotiations took place in the North Korean Mission in Geneva, the first time they had been on North Korea's home turf;
all the meetings in New York and the first one in Geneva had been in
American buildings. The DPRK Mission had been polished up for the occasion, complete with gleaming silver trays on which were arrayed delicate
Swiss pastries. This was in startling contrast to the minimal hospitality of
the rich Americans, whose entertainment budget was limited to coffee and
rolls served on paper plates.

With appropriate fanfare, North Korea put forward an initiative that
would change the nature of the negotiations. The DPRK had undertaken
a peaceful nuclear program in good faith, Kang Sok Ju began, using natural uranium, of which the North had an abundance, and gas-graphite
technology, which was widely available. Although it had no intention of
producing nuclear weapons, he insisted, other nations were concerned that
the facilities had a big potential for weapons production. The DPRK, he
announced, was willing to shift its entire nuclear development program
to more up-to-date, less proliferation-prone light-water reactors (LWRs)
to fill its energy needs, if these could be supplied by the international
community.

Light-water reactors are much more complex than the gas-graphite
reactors then in service or under construction in the North. Virtually all
the key LWR components were beyond North Korea's technological or industrial capability and would have to be imported from abroad. The Americans at the conference table with technical expertise were unimpressed
with what one called a "totally hare-brained" scheme, because of the expense and complexity involved. Energy experts realized that North Korea's
electricity requirements could be met much more easily and cheaply with
nonnuclear fuels and that large nuclear reactors would actually be a threat
to the North's fragile electric grid.

But other members of the US team immediately saw Pyongyang's
offer as a face-saving way to resolve the proliferation and inspection questions. It could modernize its nuclear power production without ever admitting it had been seeking to make atomic weapons. As soon as Kang
announced his offer, Robert Carlin, the senior North Korea watcher in
the State Department's Bureau of Intelligence and Research, wrote on his
note pad, "They want out of this issue."

Gallucci was skeptical at first that North Korea was serious about trading in its indigenous nuclear program, but he quickly saw the positive possibilities for international control of the North Korean program. He also saw the immense difficulties, especially the high costs involved. "The last time I looked, such reactors cost about $1 billion per copy," he told the North Koreans.

North Korea's quest for light-water reactors, although new to most of the Americans at the conference table, actually had a long history, including, as noted above, the deal with Moscow. Although that deal fell apart after the collapse of the USSR, the allure of more modern nuclear facilities remained undimmed in leadership circles in Pyongyang, which saw nuclear power as a way out of what it worried was a persistent and worsening energy crisis. When IAEA director general Hans Blix visited North Korea in May 1992, he was asked to help North Korea acquire light-water reactors and to guarantee a secure supply from abroad of the enriched uranium fuel they would require. Blix promised to try to help. Two months later, DPRK deputy premier Kim Dal Hyon, on a visit to Seoul, proposed that the two Koreas cooperate on an LWR plant, to be built in the North close to the DMZ, to provide power to both economies. Under this plan, South Korea would provide most of the capital and technology. The proposal, which was kept secret at the time, was shoved aside during the deterioration of North-South relations later in the year and went nowhere. Kim Dal Hyon was demoted, as were others seen as "pragmatists."

When the LWR proposal was resurrected in the Geneva negotiations with the United States, Gallucci was warned by senior State and Defense Department officials against making any commitment, especially a financial commitment, to the proposal. On July 19, at the end of six days of talks, Gallucci agreed in a formal statement that the United States would "support the introduction of LWRs and . . . explore with the DPRK ways in which LWRs could be obtained," but only as part of a "final resolution" of nuclear issues. Gallucci later said this gauzy statement was "seven times removed from any commitment" to provide LWRs. The July announcement was issued as two "unilateral" but identical statements. After the beating it took from the South in June, Washington was not interested in another "joint" statement with the North.

The negotiations adjourned without progress on the contentious issue of permitting IAEA "special inspections" of the two suspected nuclear waste sites. The sides agreed to continue meeting, but in a separate "explanatory" statement Gallucci underlined that the United States would not begin the third round of negotiations until "serious discussions" were under way on nuclear issues in North-South channels and between North Korea and the IAEA.

KIM YOUNG SAM BLOWS THE WHISTLE

The American–North Korean negotiations in June had had the limited objective of persuading Pyongyang not to withdraw from the Non-Proliferation Treaty, and Washington had offered limited benefits in return. Privately, Gallucci characterized his initial negotiating posture as, "If they do everything we want, we send them a box of oranges." The North Korean offer in July, to give up its entire indigenous nuclear program in favor of the proliferation-resistant light-water reactors, had dramatically changed the bidding. Now the objective in view was much more ambitious—but it was also clear that Pyongyang would demand more extensive benefits in return. While American officials were intrigued and some elated, many in Seoul were unhappy with the shift from limited to virtually unlimited US-DPRK talks.

As it turned out, progress toward meeting the American conditions for convening the third round of US-DPRK talks, in which broader issues were to be discussed, was excruciatingly slow, so slow that the third round almost never happened. Talks between North Korea and the Vienna-based IAEA quickly sank into exasperating arguments over the DPRK's obligations. As the IAEA saw it, North Korea was still required by treaty to comply with all nuclear inspection requirements that had been or would be imposed on it, like any other signatory, as long as it had not officially left the NPT. Pyongyang, however, insisted that in suspending its withdrawal from the treaty, it had entered a "special" and "unique" category in which it alone would determine what inspection requirements to accept. It was ready to accept very few.

To keep check on the North Korean program while the arguments continued, Washington invented an interim concept called "continuity of safeguards," which it insisted was essential. This required that agency inspectors be admitted to the Yongbyon site to replace films and batteries in monitoring equipment and to make other nonintrusive tests to check that no diversion of nuclear materials was taking place. The IAEA was uncomfortable with this ad hoc concept—insisting that North Korea should comply in the fullest with its requirements—but reluctantly went along. With film and batteries running down or even running out from time to time, the IAEA repeatedly threatened to declare that "continuity of safeguards" had been lost. It was clear that such a declaration would trigger an immediate demand for UN Security Council sanctions against North Korea.

IAEA inspectors were permitted to return to Yongbyon in August (as they had been in mid-May) but only to replace the film and batteries in the monitoring equipment. The IAEA protested vigorously that this was not enough and publicly criticized North Korea. Pyongyang reacted with bitter rhetoric. Under pressure, North Korea in September and October offered to accept another visit for film and battery replacement, but the IAEA rejected the conditions, declaring them to be insufficient. And so it went.

Action on the North-South front, the other prerequisite for convening the third round of US–North Korean negotiations, was even less productive. In May South Korea proposed meetings between the two sides to work on the nuclear issues, and North Korea counterproposed an exchange of "special envoys" to deal with unification issues and prepare a North-South summit. Despite a series of exchanges over the summer and fall, the two sides could not even agree to convene working-level meetings at Panmunjom to prepare for more important meetings. Working-level contacts were finally convened for three days in October but without results.

In early-October 1993, with no progress being made on any front, Representative Gary Ackerman, the ebullient and earthy Democratic lawmaker from New York City, traveled to Pyongyang on a get-acquainted mission. Earlier in the year, Ackerman had succeeded Stephen Solarz as chairman of the Asia-Pacific Subcommittee of the House Foreign Affairs Committee, and thus he carried considerable weight in Congress. He bore a message from the administration, which he delivered in person to Kim Il Sung, that the United States wished to resolve its issues with the DPRK through dialogue and negotiations and wished to resume the bilateral engagement at the political level.

Accompanying Ackerman was C. Kenneth Quinones, the Korean-speaking State Department desk officer for North Korea. After lengthy talks with Quinones on outstanding issues, Pyongyang's Foreign Ministry presented him with a paper proposing a series of trade-offs to settle the issues at stake with the United States. In the paper, written in English in longhand, the North Koreans said they were ready to remain in the NPT and submit to regular IAEA inspections and to discuss the contentious issue of the "special inspections" that the IAEA had demanded, in return for an end to US-ROK Team Spirit military exercises, the lifting of American economic sanctions, and the convening of the long-delayed third round of US-DPRK negotiations to tackle broader issues. The proposal for trade-offs, in retrospect, was a fundamental shift in the concept of the negotiations, which until that point had been based on making step-by-step progress toward accords rather than one simultaneous and comprehensive deal, later termed "a package solution." The Foreign Ministry officials said the handwritten proposals had been cleared with the top leadership of their country, meaning Kim Il Sung and Kim Jong Il.

When Quinones returned to Washington, he found a very skeptical group of US policy makers, who insisted that details of potential accords be hammered out before proceeding further at the political level. In New York, Quinones and Gary Samore, Gallucci's top aide, engaged in a series of unannounced meetings with officials of the North Korean UN Mission to try to work out a detailed accord. When this effort ran into trouble, a more senior State Department official, Deputy Assistant Secretary of State Thomas Hubbard, began making frequent trips to New York to see the North Koreans.

With little progress being made, public as well as official frustration with the stalemate was soaring. On November 1, IAEA director general Hans Blix reported to the UN General Assembly in pessimistic terms on the agency's standoff with Pyongyang, though he stopped just short of declaring the "continuity of safeguards" to be lost. The General Assembly reacted with a resounding 140-to-1 vote (with China abstaining and only Pyongyang dissenting), urging North Korea "to cooperate immediately" with the IAEA, a demonstration of how isolated Pyongyang had become.

At a press conference in Seoul, the exasperated South Korean defense minister, Kwon Yong Hae, expressed concern about the North Korean nuclear program and mentioned the possibility of using military action to stop it. In a meeting with visiting Secretary of Defense Les Aspin, Kwon agreed to put off any decision about holding the Team Spirit exercise. Aspin said, "The ball is now in North Korea's court. The world awaits."

On the way home from Seoul, Aspin gave a background briefing to journalists aboard his plane that inadvertently gave rise to alarmist reports that war was on the verge of breaking out. The news agency Reuters, which filed the most breathless dispatch, quoted a senior US defense official as saying, "We may be entering a kind of danger zone," because North Korea had massed 70 percent of its military force near South Korea (which in fact was nothing new) and might launch a desperate conventional attack on the South, sparked by hunger and economic frustration in Pyongyang. In a precursor to concerns that later were to be widely discussed, Aspin told the reporters, "These guys are starving" and may feel that "you can either starve or get killed in a war." The Aspin briefing gave rise to a full-scale journalistic war scare—to the surprise and dismay of most officials who had been following the situation.

On November 5, a passionate column by Charles Krauthammer in the *Washington Post* demanded that Clinton "stop talking to the North Koreans—it is time for an economic blockade—and start talking to the American people" about a military emergency in Asia. The administration was so jarred by Krauthammer's column that a State Department meeting was convened to discuss it. Two days later, President Clinton threw oil on the fire by warning on NBC's *Meet the Press* that "North Korea cannot be allowed to develop a nuclear bomb," implying that the United States would take military action to stop it. Weeks later, after various US officials speculated that Pyongyang already had at least one bomb, the White House said Clinton had misspoken.

Suddenly, North Korea was at the top of the news in the United States. An NBC/*Wall Street Journal* public opinion poll reported that North Korea's development of a nuclear weapon was considered the nation's most serious foreign policy problem by 31 percent of a nationwide sample—a larger proportion than any other single issue they picked.

On November 11, amid the war scare and in the absence of diplomatic movement, the chief DPRK negotiator, Kang Sok Ju, made public the proposed "package solution" in Pyongyang. Without revealing its earlier history, he set out the main elements of the paper that had been given to Quinones a month earlier and discussed inconclusively ever since.

On November 15, after fifteen midlevel meetings in New York and a host of letters back and forth to Pyongyang, the administration finally decided to put its own "package deal" on the table. The essence of the immediate bargain was North Korean resumption of regular IAEA inspections and a renewal of dialogue with the South, in return for cancellation of the 1994 Team Spirit military exercise and the convening of the long-delayed third round of US-DPRK negotiations. Phase two, to be bargained in detail when American and North Korean negotiators finally began their third round, would deal with IAEA inspections of the two disputed Yongbyon waste sites, diplomatic recognition of North Korea, and trade and investment concessions from the United States, South Korea, and Japan.

The new administration proposal immediately leaked to the *Washington Post*'s R. Jeffrey Smith, who was following the maneuvering closely. The publicity was a bombshell in Seoul, which was always extremely sensitive to American concessions to North Korea, and especially to suggestions that South Korea was not the dominant force in policy toward Pyongyang. In addition, the proposal was anathema to President Kim Young Sam for another and highly personal reason: a "package deal" similar in name and concept had been publicly suggested in the spring by his longtime rival in domestic politics, Kim Dae Jung. If *he* was for it, Kim Young Sam was automatically against it.

The South Korean president's views surfaced dramatically and unexpectedly on November 23, at the start of his first official visit to Washington. Ushered into the Oval Office for what had been planned as a brief meeting to put a pro forma stamp of approval on the US proposal, Kim announced that it looked to him and his people as if the United States were accommodating North Korea without even giving Seoul a role in the decision process. His eyes flashing and his gestures emphatic, Kim insisted that he, not the Americans, would have the final say on whether to cancel the Team Spirit exercise and that he would be the one to announce the decision when the time came. He also demanded that the long-discussed "exchange of envoys" between North and South actually take place before the third round of US–North Korean negotiations begin.

Clinton was startled and his senior aides mystified by the nature and the vehemence of Kim's objections, as the various elements of the proposed offer had been discussed for months with officials of Kim's government. As the "brief" Oval Office meeting stretched on to eighty minutes, with senior American and Korean officials waiting with growing apprehension in another room, the Americans realized that Kim's objections had as much to do with appearance as with substance. A change in terminology to describe the proposal to North Korea as "thorough and broad" rather than as "comprehensive" or a "package" seemed to ease Kim's concern substantially. The White House also agreed to permit Kim to announce the final decision on postponement of Team Spirit if it came to that and to make the exchange of North-South "special envoys" a prerequisite for the next round of US-DPRK talks. The latter requirement proved to be an important stumbling block: North Korea bitterly resented being required to give in to the South's demand in order to deal with the Americans.

By the end of the Kim Young Sam visit, the Americans understood, if they hadn't before, the complexity and difficulty of negotiating with North Korea. The parties involved were arrayed in a series of overlapping circles: North Korea–International Atomic Energy Agency, North Korea–South Korea, and North Korea–United States. As in a combination lock, all three had to be in alignment simultaneously for the talks to succeed. Now a fourth circle of problems had been added: Washington-Seoul. As the holiday season approached in 1993, negotiations with the DPRK seemed to portend more problems than progress.

THE SEASON OF CRISIS BEGINS

In Pyongyang in early-December 1993, the Workers Party Central Committee made a surprising admission. At a meeting marking the end of the country's current seven-year economic plan, the party announced publicly that the major targets of the plan had not been met, and it warned that the economic situation was "grave." Battered by the collapse of its allies and trading partners and by economic stagnation at home, the North was in its fourth consecutive year of economic decline. Its GNP, once on a par with that of the South, was estimated at one-sixteenth the size of the booming ROK economy, and the situation was worsening.

Instead of adopting a new seven-year plan with the usual emphasis on heavy industry, the party decreed a three-year period of transition, with top priority to agriculture, light industry, and foreign trade. The meaning of the shift was clear: the North's leaders had lowered their sights and were aiming at mere survival. They were failing to feed their people and to provide enough clothing and other consumer goods to avoid privation, hence the new emphasis on agriculture and light industry. In an attempt to ease the situation without making basic changes in its autarkic command economy, North Korea was looking to exports for salvation—but it had little to sell that the world wanted.

Kim Il Sung endorsed the economic shift in his annual New Year's address to the nation. Gone was the traditional goal, repeated incessantly by Kim for decades, that North Koreans would soon be able to "eat rice and meat soup, wear silk clothes and live in a tile roofed house." Kim conceded that during the seven-year plan, "we came up against considerable difficulty and obstacles in the economic construction owing to the unexpected international events and the acute situation created in the country." He described the situation at home and abroad as "complicated and strained."

This departure from Kim Il Sung's eternal official optimism was like God announcing that things weren't what they should be in heaven. Adding to the impact of Kim's change in direction and tone was evidence that in his eighties, he was emerging from semiretirement to reassert himself in day-to-day administration. Some American experts interpreted this as a sign of dissatisfaction with the work of his eldest son, Kim Jong Il, who had been openly designated as his chosen successor in 1980.

How much Kim Il Sung knew—or wanted to know—about the details of his country's problems in his latter years is a debatable point. According to a variety of North Korean and foreign sources, the younger Kim had increasingly assumed the management of governmental and party affairs. On the eve of his eightieth birthday in 1992, Kim Il Sung had told the *Washington Times* that he continued to carry out "some external work," but that "as far as the internal affairs of our country are concerned, everything is dealt with by [Kim Jong Il]."

Nonetheless, according to a North Korean defector, Kang Myong Do, a son-in-law of North Korean prime minister Kang Song San, the turning point in Kim Il Sung's reengagement in the economy had taken place by the time of the interview. In late 1991 or early 1992, the defector said, his father-in-law, who had been prime minister during two earlier periods and was the son of one of Kim Il Sung's guerrilla comrades, gave the Great Leader an unvarnished account of the desperate economic conditions in the strategic province along the Chinese and Russian borders where he was currently serving as provincial governor. Beginning in March 1992, startled by the contrast with rosier reports that he had been receiving through official channels, Kim Il Sung convened a series of extended Workers Party meetings on the economic situation. By the end of the year, the incumbent prime minister had been fired and Kang had been brought back for his third term in the job. In early 1993, Kim presided over an extended Politburo conference on the economic troubles, which led eventually to the new economic policies that he announced in December.

Toward the end of January, Kim Il Sung received an illustrious visitor. America's most famous evangelist, the Reverend Billy Graham, had often carried his crusades to communist and totalitarian countries, but he had a special interest in North Korea because his wife, Ruth, had spent part of her youth attending the American School in Pyongyang while her parents were missionaries in China. In 1992 the evangelist had visited the North and brought a conciliatory message from President Bush. With tension growing again between Washington and Pyongyang, Graham had requested and received a message from Clinton in connection with his current trip. This message, however, was very blunt, only a few sentences long, with no salutations or good wishes. It said, in essence, cooperate on the nuclear issue; only then can relations improve.

The evangelist and his aides, especially Stephen Linton, a missionary's son who knows the culture and the language from years living in the South, sought to surround the Clinton message with grace notes and explanatory phrases that might make it more polite, less stark, and more acceptable to the eighty-one-year-old Korean leader. Nevertheless, when Graham conveyed the heart of the American president's message with its emphasis on North Korea's nuclear program, Kim became visibly angry, speaking loudly and shaking his fist. He harked back to the foreign-policy pronouncements of his New Year's address, when he charged that the United States had raised "the nonexistent nuclear issue" and was itself to blame for bringing nuclear weapons into the Korean peninsula to threaten the DPRK. "Pressure and threat cannot work on us," Kim had said in his address and repeated to Graham. The two countries needed to communicate with each other, Kim said, not confront each other—but if the United States used the language of threats, he declared, it would drive the situation to catastrophe.

As Graham was en route, a development in the United States had made North Korea's mood much less conciliatory. On January 26, the day before he arrived, the *New York Times* reported preparations for highly visible reinforcement of American forces in the Korean peninsula: deployment of Patriot missiles, the antimissile weapons used by American forces in the Gulf War. When Graham and his party landed in Pyongyang, antiaircraft missiles could be seen moving into place around the airport. Troops could be seen digging trenches in the capital, even in the subzero cold of the depth of winter. "The tension crackled," observed a Graham aide.

Deploying the Patriots had been under consideration since December, when they had been requested by the US military commander in Korea,

General Gary Luck, as a precautionary measure in case war broke out. Luck's December request had been temporarily shelved because of State Department objections that the deployments could affect the negotiations with North Korea over resuming international inspections. But when Michael Gordon, the *Times* Pentagon correspondent, returned from a reporting trip to the South with information about the potential Patriot deployment, "the White House went into a panic," Gordon recalled later. Fearful that the administration would be charged with withholding vital military equipment from American troops—as had been the case when a US unit had been overwhelmed in Somalia the previous October—the White House immediately began briefing members of Congress on the Patriot request, and National Security Adviser Anthony Lake telephoned Gordon to tell him that Luck's request was in the process of being approved—giving rise to an exclusive story in the *Times*.

News stories and commentaries about the likely Patriot deployments were replete with references to their use by US forces in Operation Desert Storm in the Persian Gulf. While North Korea was absorbing this decision, the South Korean Defense Ministry announced that the Team Spirit military exercise, which had been a factor in the breakdown of negotiations the previous year, would be held again in 1994 unless North Korea agreed to pending proposals for resumption of international nuclear inspections.

At this point, the tone of North Korean statements shifted from optimistic about the outcome of US-DPRK talks to bitterly accusatory. American experts believed this reflected a shift in the preponderance of opinion among the North Korean leadership. "United States Must Be Held Totally Responsible for Catastrophic Consequences Arising from Its Perfidy" was the headline on the English-language version of a statement issued January 31 by the North Korean Foreign Ministry. The statement cited the decision on the Patriots and reports of the impending decision on Team Spirit as "new war maneuvers the United States has been pursuing behind the screen of the DPRK-USA talks." North Korea threatened to break off the talks, pull out of the NPT, and accelerate its nuclear program—threats that were repeated in a letter to Gallucci from DPRK chief negotiator Kang Sok Ju, one of a series of missives that had been going back and forth in private between Washington and Pyongyang.

The negotiations had been difficult enough without additional complications. Throughout the fall and winter, the main venue of US-DPRK communications had been a dingy basement room at UN headquarters in New York, where Deputy Assistant Secretary of State Tom Hubbard had been meeting North Korean ambassador Ho Jong, with one or two aides on each side. Each time the Americans felt they had reached an agreement with the North Koreans on resumption of IAEA inspections and North-South negotiations, it collapsed, sometimes because the IAEA or South

Korea refused to compromise its position, sometimes because Pyongyang pulled back from a seemingly agreed position.

After a new round of abortive negotiations, the IAEA established a February 21 deadline for continuing its inspections of the Yongbyon nuclear facilities. Unless an agreement could be reached by then, the international agency said, it would turn the stalemate over to the UN Security Council for action. In advance of the deadline, US diplomats began informal discussions with the four other permanent members of the Security Council about economic and political sanctions to be levied against North Korea, and the Pentagon began preparations to order more than a thousand additional troops to South Korea for the Team Spirit exercise.

At this point in mid-February, the US ambassador to South Korea, James Laney, came to Washington deeply concerned and angry that nobody seemed to be in charge of administration strategy as the situation veered toward conflict with North Korea. Laney, former president of Emory University and, in earlier days, an army enlisted man and later a theology teacher in Korea, made the rounds of senior officials at the White House, the State Department, and the Pentagon, and reported that Seoul was calm, but that the ROK government was worried—more about overheated rhetoric and brinksmanship in Washington than about a potential nuclear threat from North Korea. Laney expressed worry about the potential for "accidental war" on the peninsula as the United States unnecessarily "ratcheted up" the IAEA inspection issues and seemed to be pushing North Korea to violent action rather than relying primarily on deterrence, as in the past. General Luck, he reported, agreed with his view. Above all, he insisted, the matter demanded far greater priority and coordination in Washington. Referring to US military and civilian casualties in a new Korean war, Laney warned the White House, "You could have 50,000 body bags coming home."

The ambassador's pleas were sobering for Vice President Al Gore and others in Washington. Partly as a result, Gallucci eventually was named as overall coordinator of US policy toward North Korea, with the rank of ambassador and a charter to coordinate or at least rationalize the disparate views of the White House, State Department, Defense Department, CIA, and various officials and offices within them. Nonetheless, disagreements continued within the executive branch and also in Congress and in the press.

On February 15, North Korea accepted minimum conditions for resumption of IAEA inspections but then, characteristically, refused to issue visas to the inspectors until a number of preconditions were met. Finally, in a renewed set of Hubbard–Ho Jong talks in New York—the twenty-second in a series that had begun the previous September—the two sides agreed on a broad set of measures to take effect simultaneously. On

March 1, which American negotiators dubbed Super Tuesday, everything was to be settled at once: international inspectors were to return to Yongbyon to ensure "continuity of safeguards," the United States and South Korea were to announce cancellation of the 1994 Team Spirit exercise, working-level North-South contacts were to be launched at Panmunjom in preparation for the exchange of "special envoys," and the United States and North Korea were to announce that they would convene their long-awaited third round of high-level negotiations on March 21.

By this time, however, the US government and public were thoroughly exasperated by North Korean foot-dragging and reversals. Under pressure from Congress and editorial columnists not to reward Pyongyang prematurely, American officials announced that the third round of negotiations would not start until the IAEA inspections and now-contentious exchange of North-South envoys had been successfully accomplished.

Not surprisingly, both proved problematic. North-South working-level meetings began at Panmunjom but quickly deadlocked over a series of North Korean demands and a stiffening of South Korean positions. At Yongbyon, while IAEA inspectors were permitted to carry out their maintenance and inspection activities at six sites, they were barred from taking sophisticated measurements at key points in the seventh and most sensitive site, the plutonium reprocessing plant. While the North Koreans produced legalistic justifications for its refusal to permit the measurements, IAEA officials concluded that its real purpose was to apply pressure in connection with its dispute with the South over the exchange of envoys. Tom Hubbard, the deputy assistant secretary of state who was heavily involved in the issue on the Washington end, noted the negative feedback loop: "The international need of the IAEA was linked to North-South dialogue where the two Koreas play games."

From that point on, it was all down hill. On March 15, the international agency ordered its inspectors home, announcing that because they had failed to complete their work, the agency could not verify that there had been no diversion of nuclear materials to bomb production. In a special meeting, the IAEA board finally voted to turn the matter over to the UN Security Council. "The general mood is that the IAEA has really been jerked around long enough," an administration official told the *Washington Post*.

The US military immediately began consulting Seoul about rescheduling the Team Spirit military exercise. Washington canceled its plans for the third round of US-DPRK negotiations and once again resumed preparations to seek UN sanctions.

On March 19, at a final North-South working-level meeting at Panmunjom to discuss the deadlocked exchange-of-envoys issue, North Korean negotiator Park Yong Su dramatically worsened the explosive atmosphere. After harsh words had flowed back and forth across the table,

Park threatened his southern counterpart, Song Young Dae: "Seoul is not far from here. If a war breaks out, it will be a sea of fire. Mr. Song, it will probably be difficult for you to survive." Shortly after that, the northern team walked out of the meeting.

South Korean officials watched the exchange on closed-circuit television, which was rigged up to allow a select group in each capital to observe the Panmunjom meetings, even meetings such as this one that were not open to the press. In an unprecedented move, the Blue House, with the approval of Kim Young Sam himself, ordered release of the videotape of the closed meeting to television stations, alarming the South Korean public.

After the breakdown of IAEA inspections and the "sea of fire" remark, Kim Young Sam summoned an emergency meeting of his national security cabinet to approve deployment of the US Patriot missiles, which had been in limbo while the nuclear negotiations held promise of results. The South's action, in turn, inflamed leadership and military circles in Pyongyang. Suddenly, the Korean situation was headed into a new downward spiral, with potentially calamitous consequences.

13

SHOWDOWN OVER
NUCLEAR WEAPONS

THE CRISIS OVER NORTH Korea's nuclear program that gripped the peninsula and engaged the major powers in the spring of 1994 had much in common with the confrontation a year earlier over North Korea's threat to withdraw from the Non-Proliferation Treaty. As before, the North-South dialogue had broken down, pressures from all sides were building up against Pyongyang, and the International Atomic Energy Agency touched off the crisis by publicly declaring North Korea to be in violation of its international obligations.

Since the early-1993 encounter, Pyongyang had been using its nuclear program as a bargaining chip to trade for recognition, security assurances, and economic benefits from the United States. A failing and isolated regime with few other cards to play, Pyongyang enhanced its bargaining power whenever its cooperation with the IAEA diminished and the threat increased that it might proceed to manufacture nuclear weapons. At the same time, such troublemaking actions, if they went too far, also increased the risk of being confronted and possibly overwhelmed by external forces. By this time, North Korea had become skilled at brinksmanship, increasing its leverage by playing close to the edge of the precipice; the problem was that it wasn't always clear just where the edge was.

In 1994 the crisis intensified, taking on serious military dimensions and falling into a nearly catastrophic action-reaction cycle. As the United States and its allies pushed for UN Security Council sanctions against Pyongyang, North Korea repeatedly declared that "sanctions are a declaration of war." In response, the Pentagon accelerated a US military buildup in and around Korea that had quietly begun several months earlier. Preparations were being made in Washington for a much more powerful buildup of men and matériel, with great potential for precipitating a military clash on the divided peninsula.

For Robert Gallucci, the spring of 1994 had an eerie and disturbing resemblance to historian Barbara Tuchman's account of "the guns of August," when, in the summer of 1914, World War I began in cross-purposes, misunderstanding, and inadvertence. As he and other policy makers moved toward a confrontation with North Korea, Gallucci was conscious that "this had an escalatory quality that could deteriorate not only into a war but into a big war." Secretary of Defense William Perry, looking back on the events, concluded that the course he was on "had a real risk of war associated with it." Commanders in the field were even more convinced. Lieutenant General Howell Estes, the senior US Air Force officer in Korea, recalled later that although neither he nor other commanders said so out loud, not even in private conversations with one another, "inside we all thought we were going to war."

THE DEFUELING CRISIS

The issue that precipitated this showdown was the unloading of the irradiated fuel rods from the 5-megawatt reactor at Yongbyon. Such rods, each a yard long and about two inches wide, could be dissolved and chemically treated in the reprocessing plant at Yongbyon to obtain plutonium for atomic weapons.

Based on satellite surveillance of vapor coming from the cooling tower of the reactor—a technique that came to be known as "plumeology"—the CIA estimated that the reactor had been shut down for up to 110 days in 1989, during which period it was assumed about half of its eight thousand irradiated fuel rods could have been removed from the reactor core and reprocessed to produce plutonium. North Korea had told the IAEA the reactor had been down only about 60 days and that only a few rods had been removed because they were damaged. Based on the higher figure, the CIA calculated at the end of 1993 that North Korea might have enough plutonium for one or two bombs of about ten kilotons of explosive power each, similar to those exploded by the United States at Hiroshima in 1945. This CIA estimate was the basis for a 1993 National Intelligence Estimate that there was a "better than even" chance that North Korea already had the makings of a bomb. In the words of a November 2002 unclassified CIA report to Congress, "The US has been concerned about North Korea's desire for nuclear weapons and has assessed since the early 1990s that the North has one or possibly two weapons using plutonium it produced prior to 1992."

State Department and US national laboratory analysts hotly dissented from the 1993 estimate. The qualifying phrase "better than an even chance" fell away in the public remarks of several senior officials, leaving in its place the perception that Washington *knew* that the North already possessed sufficient plutonium and might even already have nuclear weapons. Eventually, the CIA concluded that "plumeology" was flawed and that the lower figure cited by North Korea, 60 days, could well have been right. The likelihood of a lower figure for reprocessed plutonium was further reinforced by meticulous work done by one of the Department of Energy national laboratories, which bounded an assessment for plutonium production with more precision than observations about the reactor's operations from satellites could do. In turn, a more accurate assessment of the probable range of plutonium produced supported a more accurate judgment of the North's theoretical weapons potential at the time.

Outside the classified debate, some experts believed that the US intelligence estimate was, in the words of the *Bulletin of the Atomic Scientists,* a "worst-case scare-nario"—that it was highly unlikely that North Korea could have unloaded so many rods so quickly and successfully, or that the rods could have been so well made or fully irradiated, or that the reprocessing operation could have worked so effectively that Pyongyang had the plutonium for one or two bombs. Even in the worst case, skeptics pointed out, possession of the plutonium was several key steps away from having a viable, deliverable nuclear weapon. There was so much disagreement within the administration, Clinton's national security adviser, Anthony Lake, told me, that the president often received diametrically opposite estimates on North Korea from the CIA and the State Department's Bureau of Intelligence on the same day.

Unloading the reactor in 1994 was of great importance for two reasons, one concerning the past and the other the future. Regarding the past, IAEA experts believed that systematic sampling of carefully segregated rods from particular parts of the reactor's core would disclose how long the fuel rods had been burned and at what intensity. In this way, they could compile a record of the operating history of the reactor, confirming how many rods had been previously removed, and therefore identify the outer limit of the plutonium that might have been produced. Such a disclosure would be a major step toward eliminating the ambiguity about the DPRK's past acquisition of fissile material.

Of even greater importance was the future of the eight thousand fuel rods, now about to be unloaded from the reactor. Secretary of Defense Perry estimated that this entire load of rods could be converted into enough plutonium for four or five nuclear weapons. Although the United States was not prepared to go to war to clarify the past, it was determined to do so, if necessary, to prevent North Korea from reprocessing these and future irradiated fuel rods. Nearing completion at Yongbyon was a much larger 50-megawatt reactor that could potentially produce much more plutonium, and an even larger 200-megawatt reactor was under construction nearby. The latter was unlikely to be used as a weapons-grade plutonium producer, but the 50-megawatt would be ideally suited for that purpose.

North Korean negotiator Kang Sok Ju had been warned repeatedly by Gallucci that if the refueling of the 5-megawatt reactor took place without IAEA supervision, negotiations with the United States would be terminated, even though such action would be within North Korea's rights under the Non-Proliferation Treaty. However, a US official familiar with the issue said, "We didn't lay down with great force and clarity that this was a drop-dead issue." Moreover, this official said, most of the US–North Korean discussion before the spring of 1994 had been about the *re*fueling of the reactor, not about *de*fueling, or unloading the current stock of irradiated fuel rods. "If North Korea understood, they chose to ignore it," he added.

In Pyongyang opponents of the unloading fought as hard as they dared to get the decision reversed, knowing it would lead to a major crisis, but in the end they were told that the decision had been made and they must support it. On April 19, Pyongyang notified the IAEA of its intention to defuel the reactor "at an early date," and invited agency inspectors to witness the unloading—but without specifying what procedures would be followed or what the inspectors would be able to see and do. There followed weeks of sparring over the procedures, with Pyongyang offering to permit inspectors to observe and take some measurements but not to segregate or sample the fuel rods in a way that would make it possible to determine their past history. The IAEA refused to send inspectors unless its procedures for sampling were fully accepted. Washington backed the IAEA, though some officials believed the agency was being too rigid.

Removal of the spent fuel rods began on May 8 without international observation or approval. To the shock of the IAEA, the operations proceeded much more rapidly than expected. The North Koreans produced a second defueling machine that nobody knew they had. The two machines worked at top speed in three shifts around the clock.

At the end of May, in a last-ditch effort to preserve the reactor's verifiable operating history, the IAEA sent a high-level team headed by Dimitri Perricos, a twenty-two-year, tough-as-nails veteran of the agency and director of its East Asia division of safeguards operations. Perricos got nowhere. With about half of the rods already unloaded, the North Koreans refused to slow down discharge operations or to accept the IAEA's method of segregating the rods to verify their history.

Instead, North Korea proposed a discharge method that the IAEA team judged would not guarantee preservation of the necessary data. Even worse, Perricos observed that the actual unloading of the rods by the

DPRK reactor operators was "a big mess" that would make it impossible to learn much of anything of the past operations, and he concluded—probably accurately—that this disarray was deliberate. He sensed that a political decision had been made, probably at the very top, not to surrender the North's ace—the outside world's uncertainty about how much plutonium it had. The North did, however, permit two IAEA inspectors to remain at Yongbyon to observe the unloading of the fuel rods and the cooling pond into which they were placed.

At IAEA headquarters in Vienna, Hans Blix, the director general, was indignant at North Korea's refusal to cooperate. All along Blix had been uncomfortable with bending the agency's global rules and requirements to meet the self-proclaimed "unique status" of North Korea—partly in, partly out of the international nuclear inspection regime. So far as Blix was concerned, the DPRK was fully in the regime until its withdrawal was official and complete, and in the meantime it should fully comply with IAEA requirements, even though some of these had never been levied on any other state before. Blix feared that tolerating compromises with IAEA directives could damage the agency's shaky authority and credibility with other nations.

Washington officialdom was privately unhappy with the agency's legalistic mind-set. Gallucci, who had gradually become imbued with the regional and political aspects of the dispute, described the workings of the IAEA in May as "medieval or perhaps Talmudic, depending on what religious metaphor you use." The administration did not know from one day to the next, he said, how Blix would react to North Korea's machinations. Gallucci could not pressure Blix, for fear it would be seen as American interference with nonproliferation objectives that everyone held dear. About the same time, a high-ranking Defense Department official whom I met on a social occasion described Blix as "a fanatic" who was single-mindedly protecting his agency with little thought for the overall consequences. Former ambassador to Korea Donald Gregg described the IAEA inspectors as "a bunch of eager proctologists, making painful inquiries without holding out any benefits to North Korea."

On June 2, when more than 60 percent of the fuel rods had been removed, Blix sent a strong letter to the UN Security Council that was an implicit call for international action. Blix reported that despite an earlier appeal to Pyongyang from the Security Council president to heed the IAEA's proposal, "all important parts of the core" had been unloaded, and the agency's ability to ascertain with confidence whether reactor fuel had been secretly diverted "has been lost." The situation, he declared, is "irreversible." Blix's letter was the opening gun in the long-discussed drive for UN sanctions against the recalcitrant, often-maddening DPRK.

In Pyongyang Kim Il Sung explained the situation as he saw it to his friend Cambodian chief of state Norodom Sihanouk: "Please compare us to a man: They want us to take off our shirt, our coat and now our trousers, and after that we will be nude, absolutely naked. What they want us to be is a man without defense secrets, just a naked man. We cannot accept that. We would rather accept a war. If they decide to make war, we accept the war, the challenge we are prepared for." In case anyone failed to get the point, North Korea issued a formal statement on June 5 announcing that "sanctions mean war, and there is no mercy in war."

Undeterred, Washington proceeded with diplomatic consultations aimed at a sanctions vote in the Security Council and, in parallel, with plans for a stepped-up US military presence in and around Korea, preparing for the possibility of war.

THE MILITARY TRACK

Throughout the four decades since the armistice of 1953, the US military considered the renewal of war in Korea to be one of its most dangerous potential challenges. Since the end of the Vietnam War in 1975, American military planners had consistently identified Korea as the most likely spot for hostilities involving the United States in Asia. Although US troops had been reduced over the years to thirty-seven thousand, the presence of these forces guaranteed that the United States would be instantly involved if the massive North Korean army should attack across the narrow demilitarized zone. With the demise of the Soviet Union and the end of the Cold War, US military forces were restructured as a "base force" whose main job was to be capable of fighting two regional wars at once—one of which was consistently identified as a renewal of war in Korea.

In late 1993 and early 1994, as the international tension over North Korea's nuclear program heightened again, the US Command in Korea began to prepare more seriously for new hostilities. For the first time in decades, the US military war plan—Operations Plan 50-27—took on the flesh-and-blood colors of reality rather than remaining abstract papers in folders and computer programs. Although it kept the same designation number, the plan had been updated several times over the years, and its emphasis had shifted from defensive maneuvers to offensive action north of the DMZ, to take the fighting into North Korea after the start of hostilities. The early-1990s revision of the war plan under the supervision of General Robert RisCassi, who was chief of the US Command at the time, authorized a massive US and ROK counterattack to take Pyongyang and topple the North Korean regime, with an option to proceed farther north toward the Chinese border and essentially reunify the country. It also put heavier emphasis on military steps to be taken by the United States and

South Korea in the "prehostility" phase leading up to a potential outbreak of war.

To the surprise of US commanders, ROK defense minister Lee Pyong Tae publicly outlined the essence of the war plan in testimony to the National Assembly on March 23, just four days after the North Korean "sea of fire" statement inflamed the South. "He did it as a threat to the North Koreans . . . as a deterrent measure," said a senior US officer in Seoul, who was initially startled by the disclosure of the highly secret blueprint. For months, as its US ally was becoming alarmed, the ROK military had been relatively complacent about the possibility of military conflict. Now the South Koreans had suddenly become "nervous as a cat," the senior officer said. "They thought we were going to war too."

As tension continued to rise over the unresolved nuclear inspections and defueling of the North Korean reactor, the US Command and the Pentagon moved ahead with military preparations. The first shipment of Patriot antimissiles arrived in Pusan in mid-April and were deployed before the end of the month. A battalion of US Apache attack helicopters was brought in to replace the older Cobras, with more on the way. Additional heavy tanks, Bradley fighting vehicles (the modern replacement for armored personnel carriers), advanced radar tracking systems to pinpoint North Korean artillery, aircraft spare parts, and new ammunition-loading equipment arrived. About a thousand more troops landed quietly with the additional weapons, bringing US forces up to their full authorized strength of thirty-seven thousand. More heavy combat gear was loaded aboard American ships, to be within easy reach of Korea if additional troops were needed.

I met with the then-CINC (commander in chief) of US forces in Korea, General Gary Luck, for the first time on May 3 at Yongsan, headquarters of the command since the time of the Korean War. In the mid-1980s, Luck, fifty-six, had commanded the Second Infantry Division in Korea and led the Eighteenth Airborne Corps into action against Iraq in Operation Desert Storm. Wearing fatigues with his four stars sewn on the collars and his sleeves rolled up, showing his impressive muscles, the gray-haired, crew-cut general had the physique and disarming country-boy drawl that marked him as a combat leader. Given his appearance and bearing, I was not surprised to learn that he often jogged with his troops and lifted weights, but I would not have guessed, and only learned much later, that Luck had earned a PhD in business administration from George Washington University.

The situation in Korea, Luck told me, is "much more dangerous now than a year or two ago," because of a slow-paced but constant military buildup in the North and especially because of the nuclear maneuvering, which he called "the catalyst for a more tension-filled drama." Luck's intelligence officers had coined the phrase "incremental normalism" to describe the creeping buildup and improvement of Pyongyang's forces, so constant that it was now taken for granted. In 1994 roughly 65 percent of North Korean forces, including eighty-four hundred artillery pieces and twenty-four hundred multiple rocket launchers, were estimated to be stationed within sixty miles of the DMZ, compared with 45 percent a decade earlier. US estimates were that in case of war, North Korea could pound Seoul with five thousand rounds of artillery within the first twelve hours, causing havoc, death, and destruction in the capital despite the fierce counterattack planned by US and ROK forces.

At the same time, Luck was impressed with the fundamental weakness of the North Korean capacity to sustain a long war. Privation was taking a serious toll on its military, despite the fact that Pyongyang was estimated to be spending about 25 percent of its GNP on maintaining its huge force of 1.1 million troops. North Korean military pilots had long been able to fly only a few hours a year because of the desperate shortage of fuel. Food was scarce, even for the military. Luck was particularly struck with the condition of two Korean People's Army soldiers, nineteen and twenty-three years old, who had been captured in the South earlier in the year when their small boat had drifted across the sea border. The North Koreans were barely five feet tall and weighed only about a hundred pounds each, which appeared to be typical of KPA regular troops. They were much smaller than average South Koreans of their age group. As they recuperated in the ROK military hospital before being sent back home at their own request, one of the North Koreans was overheard to say to the other that he could never marry a South Korean woman—"they're too big for us."

While fighting a war was never far from Luck's mind, he told me, "my job is deterrence," to make sure it does not happen. He acknowledged that his was a delicate balancing act, to improve the capabilities of US and ROK forces in a very tense situation without the improvements themselves causing the explosion they were intended to deter. What he wanted to avoid, Luck said, was anything that could "spook" the North Koreans and cause them to react by striking out in a "cornered rat syndrome." For this reason, he said, it was not helpful for them to believe that the military balance on the peninsula was turning against them—as demonstrably it was. As I prepared to leave Luck's office, he paused and said gravely, "I just want you to know I'm comfortable in this job. I can do the job. If things go bad, I'm ready. I can handle it."

As North Korea began defueling its reactor and storm clouds darkened, Luck flew to Washington to join an extraordinary military meeting to prepare to fight in Korea. Secretary of Defense Perry and Joint Chiefs of Staff chairman General John Shalikashvili summoned every active four-star general and admiral in the US military, including several brought from commands across the world, to a Pentagon conference room on May 18. The subject was how the entire US military would support Luck's war plan for Korea, with troops, matériel, and logistics. Among other things, the top military brass went over details of preparatory deployments of troops and transport from other commands, the shifting of US aircraft carriers and land-based warplanes closer to the Korean coast, and plans for massive reinforcement—deployment of roughly half of all US major combat forces—if hostilities actually got under way. Everyone was conscious that this was no paper exercise but "a real meeting of real war fighters to decide how they were going to fight a war," according to US Navy captain Thomas Flanigan, an officer on the Pentagon's Joint Staff who helped to set it up. Flanigan described it as "extremely sobering."

The following day, Perry, Shalikashvili, and Luck took the results of the meeting to the White House and informed President Clinton of the gravity and consequences of the conflict shaping up in Asia. If war broke out in Korea, they estimated it would cost 52,000 US military casualties, killed or wounded, and 490,000 South Korean military casualties in the first ninety days, plus an enormous number of North Korean and civilian lives, at a financial outlay exceeding $61 billion, very little of which could be recouped from US allies. This horrendous tragedy would be by far the gravest crisis of Clinton's sixteen-month-old presidency, overwhelming nearly everything else he had planned or dreamed of doing at home or abroad.

As the enormity of the consequences sank in, Clinton summoned a meeting of his senior foreign-policy advisers the next day, May 20, to discuss the Korean confrontation. To the surprise of most journalists and experts who had been following the crisis—but who did not know about the nature or conclusions of the military meetings—the administration suddenly veered back toward diplomatic efforts, offering to convene its long-postponed third round of high-level negotiations with Pyongyang despite the unloading of the nuclear reactor.

North Korea signaled its interest in the US offer by resuming working-level meetings in New York with State Department officials on May 23 to plan for the third round. But before progress could be made, the IAEA declared on June 2 that its ability to verify the reactor's past history had been "lost" due to the faster-than-expected defueling. After receiving the IAEA assessment, the administration decided to seek UN Security Council sanctions against North Korea. "They have triggered this, not the United States or anyone else," Clinton told reporters. "I just don't think we can walk away from this."

Looking back on the crisis, Perry identified the defueling of the North Korean reactor as the turning point, when it appeared that dialogue and "preventive diplomacy" had failed and when US strategy shifted to "coercive diplomacy," involving sanctions. In the view of American military planners, the unloaded fuel rods represented a tangible and physical threat that the DPRK could move ahead to manufacture nuclear weapons. If not stopped near the beginning, they believed, North Korea could eventually possess an entire arsenal of nuclear weapons, which it could use for threats and blackmail and even to sell to high bidders in the Middle East. That simply could not be permitted to happen. Thus, despite the serious risk of war, "we believed that it was even more dangerous to allow North Korea to proceed with a large-scale nuclear weapons program," according to the secretary of defense.

From the American perspective, the unloaded fuel rods were a potential threat—once reprocessed, the North would possess a lot of plutonium. But it is not clear that the North intended to proceed with reprocessing. Rather, all along it may have intended to stop at unloading. That would have served two purposes: first, the North might have hoped, to destroy the history of the reactor's operations and, second, to be in a better position to move on to reprocessing more quickly when and if the situation warranted. If eight thousand irradiated fuel rods sitting in the reactor were good, having those rods out of the reactor and in a cooling pond was even better.

To prepare for the potential storm, the Pentagon moved full steam ahead on its plans for additional US military deployments. Simultaneously, the State Department launched a new round of talks about the nature and timing of international sanctions in the capitals of major powers and at the United Nations.

THE DEEPENING CONFLICT

The devastating possibilities of the deepening conflict were alarming to many of those most familiar with North Korea. Even administration officials conceded that sanctions were unlikely to force Pyongyang to reverse course: the isolated country was relatively invulnerable to outside pressures, since it had so little international commerce and few important international connections of any sort. Moreover, if it felt backed into a corner, it might actually follow through with its threats and fight rather than capitulate.

A gaping omission in all that had been said and done was the absence of direct communication between the US administration and the one person whose decisions were law in Pyongyang. Early in 1993, Les Aspin, Clinton's original secretary of defense, had proposed bringing the nuclear issue to a head by sending a delegation to make a bold and direct appeal to Kim Il Sung, but this was turned down as too risky. Under Perry, Aspin's successor, the Pentagon continued to urge direct contacts with Kim, but high-level dialogue by then had been identified by the State Department as a principal reward for good behavior, not to be permitted until North Korea earned it with agreements and performance.

However, in late-May 1994, when the defueling crisis worsened and the Pentagon presented its alarming war plan, Clinton, at the urging of Perry and Ambassador Laney, asked Senators Sam Nunn (D-GA) and Richard Lugar (R-IN) to fly to Pyongyang to see Kim Il Sung. North Korea turned down the hastily prepared visit at the last minute, apparently because of a conflict with the Great Leader's schedule.

In early June, as Clinton opted for sanctions, former president Jimmy Carter reentered the Korea saga to play another historic role. Having been defeated for reelection in 1980, the successful broker of the Camp David accords in the Middle East carved out for himself a mission of promoting peaceful resolution of conflicts through his Atlanta-based Carter Center. At sixty-nine years of age, the vigorous former president had already played a postpresidential intermediary role in the Middle East, Ethiopia, the Sudan, Somalia, and the former Yugoslavia.

Carter had received invitations from Kim Il Sung in 1991, 1992, and 1993 to visit Pyongyang, but each time he had been asked by the State Department not to go on the grounds that his trip would complicate the Korean problem rather than help to resolve it. The ROK government, mindful of Carter's abortive efforts as president to withdraw US troops, opposed Carter's return to Korean affairs.

As the sanctions drive got under way, Carter expressed his growing anxiety in a telephone call to Clinton. Briefed on June 5 by Gallucci, who was sent to Plains for that purpose, Carter learned to his dismay that there was no American plan for direct contact with Kim Il Sung. He immediately dispatched a letter to Clinton, telling him he had decided to go to Pyongyang in view of the dangers at hand. Clinton, on the advice of Vice President Gore, interposed no objection to the trip as long as Carter clearly stated that he was acting as a private citizen rather than as an official US envoy. As Carter was launching his initiative and proceeding to Seoul en route to Pyongyang, a series of new developments added to the importance of his mission.

In the diplomatic field, the administration drew up a program of gradually enforced sanctions against North Korea for refusing to cooperate with the IAEA. As prepared for the Security Council, the sanctions resolution would have given North Korea a thirty-day grace period to change its policies, after which such relatively lightweight measures as a ban on arms sales and transfers of nuclear technology to Pyongyang would take effect. This would be followed, if necessary, by a second group of more painful sanctions, including a ban on remittances from abroad, such as those from pro–North Korean groups in Japan, and a cutoff of the vital oil supplies furnished by China and others. A potential third stage, if the others failed, was a blockade of shipping to and from North Korean ports.

Among the other major powers directly involved—Russia, Japan, and China—there was little enthusiasm for even the mildest set of sanctions.

Russia was in the process of attempting to rebuild relations with North Korea, which had nearly been destroyed in the abrupt 1990 Soviet turn toward South Korea. In March, in an effort to find a role for itself in the crisis, the Russian Foreign Ministry had proposed an international conference of the two Koreas, the four major outside powers, the UN, and the IAEA to resolve the nuclear issue. None of the other parties had accepted it, but Russia continued to advocate such a meeting prior to any UN sanctions.

For Japan, the crisis on the Korean peninsula was serious and close to home. Tokyo had been severely criticized in the West for failing to assist the American effort in the 1991 Gulf War, despite its dependence on Gulf oil. To fail to do its part to back up sanctions and assist the US military where its own security was potentially at stake would be far more damaging to its reputation and self-esteem and could have been devastating to the US-Japanese alliance. Yet the difficulties were great.

The Japanese political system was in an especially volatile and vulnerable state. At the time of the crisis, the long-dominant Liberal Democratic Party had splintered and lost power, and the eight-party coalition government of Prime Minister Tsutomu Hata was in danger of collapsing. Its continuation in office depended on the acquiescence of the Japan Socialist Party, which had historically close relations with Pyongyang and was reluctant to take action against it.

If full-scale sanctions were to be voted by the UN Security Council, the Japanese government believed it would have no choice but to enforce a cutoff of the remittances from Koreans in Japan to North Korea, which were estimated at about $600 million annually. After extensive study, however, Japanese officials told their American counterparts it was unlikely they would be able to cut this off completely, since there were many ways beyond its control by which such money could flow, ranging from the transfer of suitcases full of currency to electronic transfers through Switzerland, Hong Kong, and other financial capitals. In a secret report, a government task force expressed concern that in case of such a crackdown, pro-Pyongyang residents of Japan would mount "severe protest activities" against Japanese government and UN offices in Japan and the US Embassy, possibly involving violence and the destruction of property, verging on civil war.

An even more vexing problem was what Japan could or could not do to assist the US military in a blockade or shooting war within the bounds of General Douglas MacArthur's post–World War II "no war" constitution, which sharply limits Japanese military actions outside its home islands. As its military buildup neared, US Forces Japan drew up a planning list of nineteen hundred items of potentially needed assistance, ranging from cutting the grass at US bases to supplying fuel, matériel, and weapons and using Japanese ships and planes for sweeping mines and gathering intelligence. The Japanese government, concerned that it might be unable to meet US requests, set up a special headquarters to define what it would be able to do and was preparing short-term legislation to permit military cooperation. Had this been put to the test, said a Japanese diplomat who was deeply involved, it would have been "a nightmare." As a result of this experience, Japan and the United States began an extensive review of Japanese guidelines for military-crisis cooperation.

China, the main source of North Korea's energy and food imports, was by all estimates the most important Asian participant in the sanctions discussion. Because China had a veto in the UN Security Council, no sanctions resolution could be adopted without its acquiescence. While reluctant to use the veto, China consistently opposed sanctions against North Korea, saying that negotiations provided the only solution.

At the same time, the Chinese were privately irritated by North Korea's actions and apprehensive that its policies could lead to a disaster on China's borders. (This was not the first time Beijing was simultaneously annoyed and worried by North Korean actions. It was also not the last.) A key moment came on May 29, when Clinton, in a reversal of previous administration policy, announced he would grant US most-favored-nation trade status to China without human rights conditions. This made it more attractive and politically acceptable for Chinese leaders to cooperate with the United States on the Korea issue.

In the view of White House national security adviser Anthony Lake, a principal purpose of the sanctions resolution was to press the Chinese to use muscle with the North Koreans in order to head it off. In a similar vein, ROK foreign minister Han told his Chinese counterpart, Qian Qichen, on June 9 in Beijing that there was only one way for China to avoid voting on sanctions in the UN Security Council—and that was to persuade North Korea in advance that it could not count on a Chinese veto, and therefore North Korea would have to defuse the situation on its own.

On June 10, according to accounts conveyed by the Chinese to a variety of American, South Korean, and Japanese diplomats, Chinese diplomats in Pyongyang and Beijing presented the North Koreans with a most unpleasant message: although China continued to oppose sanctions, the strength of international opinion was such that China might not be able to veto them. Therefore, Beijing strongly urged Pyongyang to take action to accommodate international opinion on the nuclear issue in its own interest or face drastic consequences without Chinese protection.

There is some evidence that the North had already decided to move in this direction anyway. Thus, whether Chinese veiled threats caused the North Koreans to change course or merely reinforced their belief that the Chinese—who barely two years before had betrayed them by recognizing South Korea—were not to be trusted is not known.

On the same day as the Chinese intervention, the IAEA board in Vienna sharply criticized North Korea and voted to suspend its technical assistance of about $500,000 yearly to Pyongyang's nuclear program. In practical effect, this was an international sanction. However, the Chinese ambassador in Vienna, rather than vote against it, merely abstained. In response to the vote, North Korea announced it would withdraw from the IAEA, expel the remaining international inspectors, and refuse to cooperate with "continuity of safeguards." If carried out, this would have ended the last vestige of international surveillance from the unloaded fuel rods and the nuclear facilities in Yongbyon. This development set off new alarm bells in Washington, Seoul, Tokyo, and other world capitals, sharply increasing international concern about Pyongyang's nuclear intentions.

Even before these developments took place, the North Korean Foreign Ministry began sketching out areas of conciliation and compromise, possibly part of the overall plan already in place to unload the reactor and then move quickly back to negotiations. On June 3, Pyongyang broadcast an unusual statement in the name of its chief negotiator. Kang Sok Ju announced that North Korea was prepared to dismantle its reprocessing plant for manufacturing plutonium in connection with the replacement of its existing facilities by a light-water-reactor project. This went one step beyond a written statement by Kim Il Sung to the *Washington Times* on his April 15 birthday, when he said the reprocessing plant "may not be needed" if the LWRs were supplied. But by early June, the tide in the United States was already moving swiftly toward collision, and analysis calling attention to Kang's formulation was ignored.

The North Korean concession was further developed by Selig Harrison of the Carnegie Endowment for International Peace, who arrived in Pyongyang the day after Kang's statement. Harrison, the *Washington Post* correspondent for Northeast Asia in the early 1970s, had been one of the first American correspondents to interview Kim Il Sung. As a scholar since the mid-1970s, Harrison had kept a close eye on Korean developments, revisiting the North in 1987 and 1992 and making many visits to the South. Harrison was known in Washington policy circles for having an unusually positive view of Pyongyang's willingness to compromise in return for American relationships and concessions, which he believed its leaders badly wanted. Washington conservatives and many officials scoffed, but because Harrison had had a longer acquaintance with policy makers in Pyongyang than almost anyone else, it was difficult to dismiss him.

In his new trip, Harrison concentrated on finding a way to give operational significance to Pyongyang's willingness to abandon its reprocessing plant. In meetings with Kang and others, he argued that North Korea should freeze further development of the reprocessing plant and all the rest of its nuclear program when binding commitments were received for delivery and financing of the LWRs.

On June 9, when Harrison broached the freeze idea in a meeting with Kim Il Sung, the Great Leader seemed not to have heard of it from his aides, raising the possibility that Kang's June 3 statement had been approved not by the Great Leader but by Kim Jong Il. In a show of confidence in Kang that would be repeated with Carter, Kim turned to his chief negotiator for an explanation and discussed the possibilities with him for about five minutes in Korean. Then he turned to Harrison and said, "This is a good idea. We can definitely accept it if the United States really makes a firm commitment that we can trust."

Kim then repeated his denial that North Korea had nuclear weapons or any intention of producing them. "It gives me a headache when people demand to see something we don't have," said Kim. "It's like dogs barking at the moon. What would be the point of making one or two nuclear weapons when you have ten thousand plus delivery systems that we don't have. We would be a laughingstock. We want nuclear power for electricity, and we have shown this by our offer to convert to light-water reactors." Harrison left Pyongyang on June 11 believing that a freeze on the North Korean program in return for light-water-reactor commitments could produce the breakthrough that was desperately needed. The deafness to those signals was baffling to some analysts in Washington.

In June 13, when Carter arrived in Seoul en route to the North, Harrison's optimism was shared by very few in the South Korean capital. The ROK government, while counseling calm, had announced the largest civil defense exercise in many years to mobilize its citizens in case of war. Reacting to the growing atmosphere of crisis, the Seoul stock market dropped by 25 percent in two days, and jittery South Koreans were jamming stores to stockpile rice, dried noodles, and candles. Carter found most members of the ROK government hostile to his mission. Before his arrival, ROK president Kim Young Sam had pronounced the mission to be "ill-timed" and said it could help the North pursue "stalling tactics" on the nuclear issue.

The sense of inexorable drift toward military conflict that had been felt within the high ranks of the US government since the defueling of the Yongbyon reactor in early May was now spreading to an increasingly aroused American public. In June, 46 percent of a nationwide sample of public opinion sponsored by NBC News and the *Wall Street Journal* said North Korea's nuclear development was the "most serious foreign policy issue facing the United States today," outdistancing the next most serious issue, instability in Russia, by more than three to one. At the same time, a nationwide poll for *Time* and CBS News reported that a majority (51 percent) favored military action to destroy North Korea's nuclear facilities if the DPRK continued to refuse international inspection, and a slimmer majority (48 percent yes, 42 percent no) said it was "worth risking war" to prevent North Korea from manufacturing nuclear weapons.

The predominant opinion of national columnists and commentators was that the United States should take a tough line with Pyongyang. Among the most prestigious voices were those of two former Bush administration officials, former national security adviser Brent Scowcroft and former undersecretary of state Arnold Kanter, the official who had met the North Koreans in New York in early 1992. In the *Washington Post* on June 15, the day Jimmy Carter crossed into North Korea, they advocated a US military strike to destroy the reprocessing plant at Yongbyon unless the DPRK was prepared to permit "continuous, unfettered" international monitoring. "The stakes could hardly be higher. The time for temporizing is over," Scowcroft and Kanter wrote.

At the Pentagon, Secretary Perry had requested and received a detailed contingency plan for bombing the Yongbyon facilities and was told that the US Air Force had the technical ability to take them out quickly and effectively, without spreading radiation far and wide. Perry's fear, as before, was that such an air strike "was highly likely to start a general war" on the peninsula. "We were looking for ways of avoiding a general war, not ways of starting a general war," he explained later.

Nevertheless, the Pentagon argued that if North Korea really meant that sanctions would be an act of war, it was incumbent on the United States to be ready. Consequently, in mid-June Perry and the Joint Chiefs of Staff drew up three options for increasing US forces in and around Korea to heighten readiness further. General Luck estimated, on the basis of the experience in Vietnam and the Persian Gulf, that due to the colossal lethality of modern weapons in the urban environments of Korea, as many as 1 million people would be killed in the resumption of full-scale war on the peninsula, including 80,000 to 100,000 Americans; that the out-of-pocket costs to the United States would exceed $100 billion; and that the destruction of property and interruption of business activity would cost more than $1,000 billion ($1 trillion) to the countries involved and their immediate neighbors. The extent of the death and destruction, in the American calculus, would depend to a great degree on the speed with which a counterattack could be mounted by the US reinforcements called for in the war plan.

Option number one as drawn up at the Pentagon was the immediate dispatch to Korea of around two thousand additional troops of the kind needed for rapid deployment of larger forces later—additional logistics, administrative, and supply elements—and additional counterbattery radars and reconnaissance systems, which had been most urgently requested by General Luck.

Option number two, which Perry and the Joint Chiefs of Staff favored, added squadrons of front-line tactical aircraft, including F-117 Stealth fighter-bombers and long-range bombers, to be based near Korea, available for immediate action; the deployment of several battalions of combat-ready US ground troops, principally to augment artillery forces; and the stationing of a second US aircraft-carrier battle group in the area, to reinforce the powerfully armed carrier group that had already been moved close to Korea. This would involve deployment of more than 10,000 US troops, added to the 37,000 on duty in South Korea. Perry hoped that such a dramatic increase in American forces would combine more serious preparations for war with an element of additional deterrence, highly visible to the North Koreans.

Option number three called for the deployment of additional tens of thousands more army and Marine Corps ground troops and even more combat air power. Even this option did not provide enough US forces to fight a general war on the peninsula—Operations Plan 5027 reportedly called for more than 400,000 reinforcements to do that.

The military concern was that if the flow of additional forces did not start quickly, Pyongyang might block it with an early preemptive strike. On the other hand, once the forces did begin to flow, North Korea might feel compelled to strike quickly to forestall an inexorable American buildup that would frustrate its chances for military success. Such an unstable military situation in an increasingly tense situation with an unpredictable foe was extremely worrisome; however, the US military felt that it had little choice under the circumstances but to begin serious preparations for war.

Perry acknowledged in an interview for this book that it was difficult to calculate how Pyongyang might react. "We saw the deployment on the one hand as being provocative. That was the downside. On the other side, we saw it as demonstrating a seriousness of purpose. . . . We didn't know enough about the Korean mentality to know how to gauge the negative aspects versus the positive aspects of the signal we were sending. Therefore, I chose in my own thinking to set that signal aside, not knowing how to assess it, and recognizing we could have either of those two possibilities."

Some senior officers in the US Command in Seoul were extremely concerned about the North Korean military reaction when they heard about the plans for these deployments. "I always got this feeling that the North Koreans studied the desert [Operation Desert Storm against Iraq] more than we did almost," said a general with access to all the available intelligence. "And they learned one thing: you don't let the United States build up its forces and then let them go to war against you. . . . So I always felt that the North Koreans were never going to let us do a large buildup. They would see their window of opportunity closing, and they would come." Adding to this officer's apprehension was a chilling fact not well known outside the US Command: at Panmunjom in May, a North Korean colonel told a US officer, "We are not going to let you do a buildup." He did not say, nor did anyone know, how much of a buildup of American forces might trigger a North Korean preemptive strike.

General Luck had played an integral role in earlier planning for augmentation of his forces under the existing war plan, but he received only a few hours' notice that the Pentagon would ask Clinton to authorize its execution on June 16. He was startled by the timing, concerned that the North Koreans would interpret the reinforcements as a signal of an American decision to destroy their regime and intensely worried that no serious evacuation plan for 80,000 American dependents and other civilians in Korea had been put in place. Japan, which was the logical place for evacuees to go, had not agreed to receive them. Transportation for the evacuation had not been prepared. Most people had no idea an evacuation was imminent and no information about where to go or what to do. Moreover, an announcement of an evacuation of American civilians, and especially the loading of them onto planes and ships, was likely to panic South Koreans as well as many Americans.

Luck and Ambassador Laney met secretly at the ambassador's residence in Seoul the morning of June 16 (the evening of June 15 in Washington). Both felt there was no choice but to proceed with evacuation planning on an urgent basis. The ambassador did not wait for formal orders. He told his daughter and his three grandchildren, who were visiting at the time, that they should leave Korea by Sunday, three days thence.

CARTER IN PYONGYANG

In the meantime, Carter, accompanied by his wife, Rosalynn, and a small party of aides and security guards, had crossed the DMZ on June 15 on his way to see Kim Il Sung. Carter found walking across the dividing line at Panmunjom, then being handed over by US and ROK military to North Korean military "a bizarre and disturbing experience, evidence of an incredible lack of communication and understanding." He was well aware of the risk to his reputation, believing that "the chances of success were probably minimal because so much momentum had built up on both sides of the sanctions issue."

In his initial meeting in Pyongyang, Carter found North Korean foreign minister Kim Yong Nam so uncompromising and negative that the former president awoke at 3:00 A.M., believing it likely that North Korea would go to war rather than yield to international sanctions. In desperation, he dispatched an aide, former ambassador Marion Creekmore, to the DMZ with a message to be sent through secure US channels in South Korea, appealing to Clinton for authorization to agree to the start of the third round of US-DPRK negotiations to head off a crisis. Carter instructed Creekmore not to send the message until receiving a go-ahead after his meeting with Kim Il Sung on the morning of June 16.

For Kim Il Sung, the meeting with the most prominent American ever to visit the DPRK was the culminating moment of his two-decade effort to make direct contact with American ruling circles and a potential turning point in the escalating international crisis over his nuclear program. The Great Leader greeted his visitor with a booming welcome, a hearty handshake, and a big smile, which was returned by Carter's characteristic toothy grin.

When the talks began, Carter explained that he had come as a private citizen rather than as a representative of the US government, but that he had come with the knowledge and support of his government. The presence of Dick Christenson, the Korean-speaking deputy director of the State Department's Korea Desk, was testimony to the semiofficial nature of the mission. Carter emphasized that the differences in the two governmental systems should not be an obstacle to friendship between the two nations, a point he repeated several times. If the current nuclear issues could be resolved, he said, then high-level negotiations on normalizing relations could move ahead.

Kim, responding on the high plane of generality and mutual recognition that is particularly important in Asia, said that the essential problem between the two nations was lack of trust and that therefore "creating trust is the main task." Kim expressed frustration that, although he had often announced that the DPRK could not make and did not need nuclear weapons, he was not believed. The DPRK's requirement was for nuclear energy, he declared: if the United States helped to supply light-water reactors, North Korea would dismantle its gas-graphite reactors and return to the Non-Proliferation Treaty. As part of a solution to the nuclear issue, Kim also requested US guarantees against nuclear attacks on the DPRK. He expressed irritation that South Korea might interfere with whatever solution could be worked out, saying that whenever the prospect of making progress between Pyongyang and Washington came close, Seoul found a way to block it.

Carter, following talking points that he had cleared with Gallucci by telephone before traveling to Pyongyang, asked two things of Kim: that he temporarily freeze his nuclear program until the completion of the planned third round of US-DPRK nuclear negotiations and that the two remaining IAEA inspectors still at Yongbyon, who were scheduled to be expelled from the country on the next flight to Beijing, be permitted to remain. Even though the expulsions might seem a matter of course because North Korea had announced its withdrawal from the IAEA, they were certain to be taken as a sign that Pyongyang was going full speed ahead with a nuclear weapons program. Carter's request that Kim permit the inspectors to remain produced the most revealing and, as it turned out, the most important exchange of the meeting.

Apparently completely unfamiliar with the issue, Kim turned to his deputy foreign minister and chief DPRK negotiator, Kang Sok Ju, who was among the few aides present, and asked what this request was about. Kang jumped to his feet and stood at attention, as all aides did when addressing the Great Leader. Then, as had been the case with Selig Harrison and the freeze proposal eight days earlier (about which Carter had not been informed), Kang patiently explained the issue. Kim seemed wary of giving something important away, but he asked his aide's opinion. Kang responded that keeping the inspectors on duty would be the right thing to do. Following this discussion, all in Korean, Kim turned to Carter and announced that North Korea would reverse the previous order and leave the inspectors in place.

This exchange, one of the few times when outsiders witnessed policy actually being made in North Korea, suggested that Kim Il Sung remained capable of making on-the-spot decisions of great importance without debate or fear of contradiction. It also suggested that he was willing to solicit and take the advice of aides in whom he had confidence—in this case, Kang. Kim's eldest son and anointed successor, Kim Jong Il, was nowhere in evidence in Carter's meetings, although Carter had asked to see him. The younger Kim rarely appeared in meetings with foreign visitors. Nevertheless, Kim Jong Il was closely involved in the decisions and had originally given Kang the orders to fix the problem unloading the rods had created, something the first vice foreign minister was apparently trying to do when he advised keeping the inspectors in country.

When Kim Il Sung agreed to the temporary freeze and to keep the international inspectors and monitoring equipment in place, a relieved Carter told him he would recommend that the US government "support" North Korea's acquisition of light-water reactors (although he made it clear the United States could not finance or supply them directly) and that the long-awaited third round of US-DPRK negotiations be quickly reconvened. Carter said he could speak with assurance that no American nuclear weapons were in South Korea or tactical nuclear weapons in the waters surrounding the peninsula. He and Kim agreed that the Korean peninsula should continue to be free of nuclear weapons from any source.

Believing that he had made an important breakthrough, Carter met later in the day with Kang to confirm the details. Kang warned against proceeding with the UN sanctions (which Carter had opposed from the beginning), telling him that "all the people in this country and our military are gearing up now to respond to those sanctions. If the sanctions pass, all the work you have done here will go down the drain." From the comments of Kang and his nominal superior, Foreign Minister Kim Yong Nam (Kang worked directly with Kim Jong Il; Kim Yong Nam had little to do with the diplomacy on the nuclear issue), Carter concluded that North Korea actually would have gone to war on a preemptive basis if sanctions had been imposed while the United States was engaging in a major military buildup in the area.

Cable News Network correspondent Mike Chinoy and a CNN film crew, who had been permitted to broadcast a rare series of reports from the North at the time of Kim Il Sung's eighty-second birthday two months earlier, had been allowed to return to cover the Carter visit. The only American journalists on hand, they were a channel for worldwide attention. Carter decided to give CNN an interview to announce the results of his meeting with Kim and to halt the rush toward armed conflict. But first it was necessary to inform the White House.

It was the morning of June 16 in Washington, a half-day behind Korea. President Clinton, Vice President Gore, Secretary of State Christopher, Secretary of Defense Perry, Joint Chiefs of Staff chairman Shalikashvili, CIA director James Woolsey, UN ambassador Madeleine Albright, National Security Adviser Anthony Lake, and other senior foreign policy and defense officials were gathered in the Cabinet Room in the second hour of a climactic decision-making meeting about the Korean nuclear issue. At the outset, Clinton gave final approval to proceed with the drive for the sanctions against North Korea in the UN Security Council, where the American sanctions plan had been circulating in draft form for several days. That decided, General Shalikashvili began outlining the US military buildup in and around Korea, which Perry and the Joint Chiefs had recommended in tandem with the sanctions decision. The president was informed that the dispatch of substantial additional forces, as contemplated in the meeting, would require a limited call-up to active duty of US reservists. This would necessarily alert the country to the seriousness of the looming crisis.

The JCS chairman had explained the first option of modestly augmented forces and was well into his discussion of the Pentagon's preferred choice, the second option involving the dispatch of war planes, another aircraft-carrier battle group, and more than ten thousand additional troops. Suddenly, a White House aide entered the room with the news that Carter was on the telephone line from Pyongyang.

Gallucci, who was designated to take the call in an adjoining room, heard the enthusiastic former president say that Kim Il Sung had agreed to freeze the nuclear program and to allow the IAEA inspectors to remain. Carter said he believed the third round of US-DPRK negotiations should be convened in light of this breakthrough, and he was asking for White House permission to say so. Then he told Gallucci, who was startled but made no comment, that he planned to describe the progress he had made in a live interview shortly with CNN. Gallucci told Carter he would report his news to a meeting on these issues taking place as they spoke, and he promised a response later.

Gallucci's report was a bombshell in the Cabinet Room. Except for leaving the inspectors in place, the substance of Carter's accomplishments sounded to some like nothing new. But there was anger in the room about Carter's imminent CNN interview, which seemed likely to upstage and embarrass the administration just as it was reaching major new decisions on a problem it had been living with for more than a year. One participant viewed Carter's actions as "near traitorous." Another feared it was a stalling action by the North Koreans, just as the United States was about to "pull the trigger" on sanctions and the troop buildup. Whatever their private thoughts, Clinton and Gore decreed that it was essential to shape a substantive response, not indulge in mere Carter bashing.

As Clinton left for another event, the others crowded in front of a television set where they stood or sat, some on the floor, as Carter spoke by satellite from halfway around the world in Pyongyang to CNN White House correspondent Wolf Blitzer, who was on the White House lawn a few steps away, and CNN diplomatic correspondent Ralph Begleiter, who was in a Washington office a few blocks away. Carter repeated Kim Il Sung's statements and declared them to be "a very important and very positive step toward the alleviation of this crisis." While saying that next steps would be up to the Clinton administration, Carter publicly proclaimed his preference: "What is needed now is a very simple decision just to let the already constituted delegations from North Korea and the United States have their third meeting, which has been postponed. That's all that's needed now, and that's all the North Koreans are addressing."

Suddenly, a diplomatic-military crisis took on new political dimensions, as it was played out in public on live television in full view of Clinton's friends and foes at home as well as officials around the world. To the consternation of the White House team, the press saw administration officials as bystanders while a private citizen, former president Carter, appeared in control of US policy.

After the officials filed back into the Cabinet Room, National Security Council aide Stanley Roth, a veteran of Asia policy making on Capitol Hill and at the Pentagon, suggested the course of action that was ultimately accepted: that the administration design its own detailed requirements for a freeze on the North Korean nuclear program and send them back to Pyongyang through Carter. In effect, the United States would say, "We agree and accept if you accept our version of the freeze." As was noted in the meeting, the tactic was similar to a celebrated US ploy at the height of the 1962 US-Soviet Cuban missile crisis, when the Kennedy administration had interpreted communications from Soviet premier Nikita Khrushchev in its own way to fashion an acceptable settlement.

Gallucci and two other aides left the room and drafted US requirements for a North Korean freeze that was to be in effect while talks continued. In their version, North Korea would have to agree specifically not to place new fuel rods in the 5-megawatt reactor and not to reprocess the irradiated fuel rods that had been removed. By the time it ended, the marathon White House meeting had stretched on for more than five hours.

Lake then spoke to Carter in Pyongyang, where it was approaching dawn on June 17, and outlined the conditions, which went beyond what North Korea had offered and well beyond the legal restraints of the Non-Proliferation Treaty. Carter objected vociferously to upping the ante, noting that these new conditions had not been mentioned before his trip and that he had not presented them to Kim Il Sung or others in Pyongyang. It seemed far from certain, perhaps even unlikely, that the North Koreans would accept them. In fact, however, perhaps because of their own urgent desire to end the dangerous confrontation, the North Koreans quickly accepted. To make certain of agreement on the details, Gallucci subsequently sent the conditions in writing to Kang through the North Korean Mission in New York, and Carter sent a parallel letter to Kim Il Sung. Both received back formal acceptance.

To celebrate the easing of the crisis, Kim Il Sung invited Carter and his party to a celebration on the Taedong River aboard the presidential yacht. This cruise produced another informative decision-making episode, this one involving Kim Il Sung's wife, Kim Song Ae, who was rarely seen with her husband in public but who participated in the boat ride due to the presence of former first lady Rosalynn Carter. As the yacht sailed by North Korean villages and farmland, the former US president proposed that joint US-DPRK teams discover and return the remains of US servicemen killed during the Korean War as a goodwill gesture to the American people and to forestall the kind of arguments that had long held up improved US relations with postwar Vietnam. Kim was noncommittal, saying this could be discussed in future negotiations, but Carter persisted. At this point, the North Korean first lady spoke up, telling her husband she thought the joint-recovery teams a good idea. "Okay, it's done, it's done," responded the Great Leader.

During the boat ride, the exhausted Carter mistakenly told Kim while CNN cameras were rolling that the American drive for economic and political sanctions at the UN Security Council had been halted due to their discussions the previous day. This action had not yet been taken. Carter's comment, which was played on American television, seemed to suggest once more that the White House had lost control of its Korea policies. This gaffe turned out to be the most controversial facet of Carter's trip in the US press and dominated much of the immediate commentary.

The boat ride was also the occasion for the most important break-through of the mission from the South Korean standpoint. Sitting across a small table in the main cabin of the yacht, Carter brought up the unre-solved state of North-South relations and the possibility of a North-South summit meeting, which ROK president Kim Young Sam had asked him to propose to his North Korean counterpart. Kim Il Sung recounted for Carter his version of the various attempts at agreement between the two halves of the divided country, and he expressed his frustration that lit-tle had been accomplished. In a remarkable statement coming from him, Kim said that the fault for the lack of progress lay on both sides and that responsibility for the mistakes had to be shared. Kim said he had noted his southern counterpart's statements, in his inaugural address the previ-ous year, about the primacy of national kinship and his offer of a summit meeting "at any time and in any place." He went on to say that he was ready to meet Kim Young Sam and that their meeting should be held without preconditions or extended preliminary talks. He invited Carter to pass along this message to the South Korean president.

How and why Kim Il Sung decided to proceed to a summit with the South Korean president in the last days of his life is a matter of great speculation, because he had only come that close to a meeting once before, when he had issued the invitation for Roh Tae Woo to attend his eightieth birthday observance in 1992. One theory holds that Kim sensed he did not have long to live and was seeking to arrange a smoother path for his son and successor. Another theory suggests he realized that it was necessary to improve relations with the South in order to improve fundamentally his relations with the United States. Still another theory is that the decision was a spur-of-the-moment response to Carter's proposal. Whatever lay behind Kim Il Sung's decision, it is clear that he never backed away from it but proceeded to plan energetically for the summit.

Shortly after Carter left North Korea through Panmunjom, he called on Kim Young Sam at the Blue House. The South Korean president was initially cool to Carter and his mission, believing that once again the fate of the peninsula had been under negotiation at a very high level with-out his participation. When Carter conveyed Kim Il Sung's summit offer, however, the South Korean president became visibly excited. Within the hour, Kim Young Sam announced his acceptance of an early and uncon-ditional summit meeting, thereby turning Carter's mission into a personal initiative to achieve what his predecessors had tried and failed to do. In a sudden and entirely unexpected reversal of fortune, the immense tension and great danger in the Korean peninsula gave way to the greatest hope in years for a historic rapprochement between the leaders of the North and South.

Although delighted at the prospect of a summit meeting, the South Korean president privately rejected Carter's account of his counterpart's state of health, which Carter described as "vigorous" and "alert." The South Korean president's own father, whom he spoke to by telephone every morning, was just a year or two older than Kim Il Sung. From television pictures recorded by his intelligence agency, Kim Young Sam believed that his counterpart in the North wasn't all that well. "Carter is a smart man," Kim Young Sam told aides as the former US president left his office, "but he doesn't know much about old people."

Carter called it "a miracle" that his meetings with Kim Il Sung had transformed a confrontation at the brink of war into new and promising sets of US-DPRK and North-South negotiations. "I personally believe the crisis is over," he announced after briefing officials at the White House, and within a few days it was clear that this was so. The sanctions activity and plans for extensive reinforcement of US troops were dropped. After obtaining written confirmation from Pyongyang of its acceptance of the US-devised freeze on its nuclear program, Washington announced readiness to proceed to the third round of US-DPRK negotiations, which were scheduled to begin on July 8 in Geneva.

Despite the positive results of his unorthodox initiative, Carter initially was the object of more criticism than praise. American politicians, public figures, and the press, emphasizing the contradictions between Carter's efforts and Clinton administration policies, were critical of his intervention. The former president was startled to be privately informed, as he came back across the DMZ, that the White House did not want him to return home through Washington or to even make a telephone report to Clinton. Later the administration relented, and Carter paid a visit to the White House en route to Atlanta, although Clinton remained at Camp David during the meeting with his Democratic predecessor and spoke to him only by telephone.

It will be years, perhaps many years, before it will be possible to know with certainty how close the Korean peninsula came to a devastating new outbreak of war in the spring of 1994. It is instructive that those in the US and ROK governments who were closest to the decisions are among those who, in retrospect, rate the chances for hostilities to have been the highest. The United States responded to what it saw as North Korea's nuclear challenge at the time with a combination of force and diplomacy that, although often improvised and lacking coherence, was equal to the seriousness of the issue. How effective the US response was in influencing

Pyongyang's decisions, however, is a judgment that it is still too soon to make.

Whether by blunder or design, North Korea discovered by early 1993 that its nuclear program, with its potential to destabilize Northeast Asia and affect the prospects for nuclear proliferation in other parts of the world, was its most valuable asset in transactions with the outside world, especially after the loss of its Soviet ally and the devaluing of its relations with China. Pyongyang played its card brilliantly, forcing one of the world's richest and most powerful nations to undertake direct negotiations and to make concessions to one of the world's least-successful nations. The nuclear threat proved, up to a point, to be Pyongyang's great equalizer.

In the spring of 1994, however, the growing power of the forces arrayed against it strongly suggested that the situation was getting out of hand, and not necessarily to North Korea's advantage. By the time Carter arrived, Kim Il Sung was seeking a way to end the crisis without losing face or surrendering his bargaining card, and the former president provided the means. By cooperating with Carter, accepting a US-designed nuclear freeze, and agreeing to a North-South summit meeting, the Great Leader defused the explosive confrontation while leaving the future open for further negotiations, which he planned to direct in the months to come.

Justifying his action on the need for national unity to confront the North in talks, South Korean president Park Chung Hee declares martial law in October 1972 to crush all domestic opposition. PHOTO BY KIM IN KON / JOONG-ANG PHOTO

Presidents Park Chung Hee and Jimmy Carter review troops during Carter's 1979 visit to Seoul. While cordial in public, the two presidents quarreled bitterly in private over the US troop withdrawal policy. JIMMY CARTER LIBRARY

Citizens of Kwangju parade through the streets in a popular uprising in May 1980 after brutal ROK special forces units temporarily withdraw. Many Koreans hold the United States partly to blame. PHOTO BY LEE CHANG SUNG / JOONG-ANG PHOTO

President Ronald Reagan, Vice President George Bush, and their wives welcome President Chun Doo Hwan and his wife to the White House in 1981, despite previous US opposition to Chun's assumption of power by a "coup in all but name." RONALD REAGAN LIBRARY

President Kim Il Sung (center) meets Soviet leader Konstantin Chernenko (on Kim's right) and other leaders in his 1984 visit to Moscow. Politiburo member Mikhail Gorbachev, later to be the Soviet leader, is third from right.

Kim is on outwardly cordial terms with Gorbachev in his 1986 visit to Moscow. Privately, however, they distrust each other.

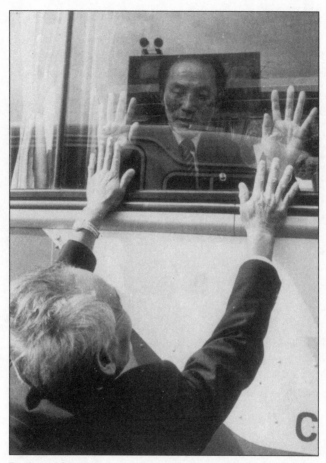

In the mid-1980s thaw, two brothers of a divided family say goodbye after an emotional reunion in Seoul. PHOTO BY KIM JOO MAN / JOONG-ANG PHOTO

Bold protesters battle riot police in 1987 demonstrations demanding direct presidential elections in the South. Faced with widespread protests, the government gave in. PHOTO BY KIM HYUNG SOO / JOONG-ANG PHOTO

Chinese Foreign Minister Qian Qichen and party (foreground) are welcomed in 1991 to Pyongyang by DPRK Foreign Minister Kim Young Nam. Only eight commercial flights a week entered the country of 21 million people. PHOTO BY AUTHOR

Fourth graders in a sword drill in Pyongyang display childhood vigor and regimentation in 1991. In the background, the Pyongyang skyline and the Arch of Triumph, larger than the one in Paris, a tribute to Kim Il Sung. PHOTO BY AUTHOR

The United States feared that North Korea's indigenous 5-megawatt reactor, photographed surreptitiously by a Western visitor, would be the first element of a massive nuclear weapons program.

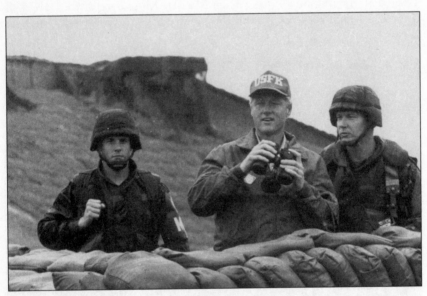

President Clinton, alarmed by the North Korean nuclear program and the confrontation of armies, visits the DMZ in 1993 and calls it "the scariest place on earth." AFP/GETTY IMAGES

Former president Carter meets President Kim Il Sung in June 1994 to head off a military crisis over nuclear issues on the peninsula. THE CARTER CENTER

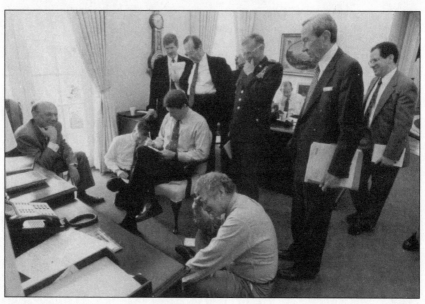

As Carter appears on live CNN television from Pyongyang at the height of White House policymaking on Korea, Vice President Gore and other top US officials are reduced to being amused but powerless onlookers. THE WHITE HOUSE

Kim Jong Il, who inherited power after his father's death, waves to his people but remains mysteriously silent on public occasions.

Secretary of State Albright meets with Kim Jong Il's envoy, DPRK National Defense Commission First Vice Chairman Jo Myong Rok in Washington, October
2000. PHOTO BY MANNY CENETA, AFP/GETTY IMAGES

Japanese Prime Minister Junichiro Koizumi meets with Kim Jong Il during his second visit to Pyongyang in May 2004. AFP/GETTY IMAGES

President Roh Moo-hyun and Kim Jong Il converse at the October 2007 summit. The results of the summit were overturned only a few months later when a new ROK president took office. BLUE HOUSE PRESS CORPS

WPK party secretaries Kim Ki Nam and Kim Yong Gon pay their respects in Seoul in August 2009 during the funeral of former ROK president Kim Dae Jung. The two envoys were sent by Kim Jong Il to explore the possibility of resuming high-level inter-Korean dialogue. AFP/GETTY IMAGES

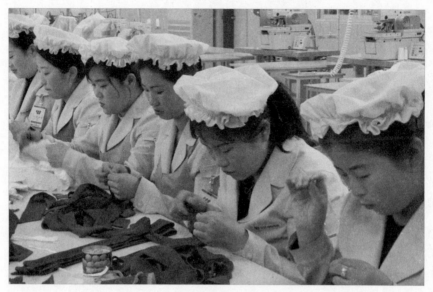

A few of the over 50,000 North Korean workers at a South Korean factory in the Kaesong Industrial Zone. BLUE HOUSE PRESS CORPS

President Park Geun-hye, daughter of Park Choong Hee and South Korea's first woman president, waves to the people at her February 2013 inauguration. HANKOOK ILBO PHOTO

Members of the North Korean military band resting in the heat in Pyongyang before the sixty-fifth anniversary of the end of the Korean War. PHOTO BY ED JONES, AFP/GETTY IMAGES

14

DEATH
AND
ACCORD

O N THE MORNING OF July 6, 1994, less than three weeks after he said
good-bye to Jimmy Carter, Kim Il Sung sat behind the desk in his
office and instructed senior officials on the economic goals for the year
ahead. From all outward signs, the eighty-two-year-old Great Leader was
in good form, wearing a light-blue Western-style suit and wagging his
finger vigorously at two dozen officials arrayed before him.

"Agriculture first. Light industry first. Foreign trade first," declared
Kim, repeating the priorities he had announced in his New Year's address
after conceding that the economy was in trouble. In a rich, husky rumble,
which had been the voice of command in North Korea for nearly a half
century, he set forth specific targets for the year: 850,000 tons of fertilizer,
12 million tons of cement, completion of one hundred ships, and special
priorities for railways and metal industries. In remarks that would take
on important meaning later, Kim gave top priority to the urgent need for
more electric power. Saying that the much-discussed light-water nuclear
reactors would take too long to ease the shortage of energy, he laid down
an immediate requirement for additional power plants burning heavy fuel
oil (HFO).

The meeting with the economic aides was among the last activities of
an aged head of state who had reengaged dramatically in the affairs of his
country, as if somehow he sensed that his time was short. In the month
of June, Kim had taken part in seventeen events and activities, including
on-the-spot inspections at two collective farms and meetings with a variety of visitors from overseas, far more than in previous months.

Following the meeting with Carter, Kim's preoccupation was to
prepare for the unprecedented summit meeting with his South Korean

counterpart, Kim Young Sam, which had emerged from the talks with the former US president and was scheduled to begin in Pyongyang on July 25. After decades of haggling and disagreeing about such a meeting, the North and South this time had smoothly agreed on the overall plan and many of the details. Kim Il Sung personally intervened to facilitate agreement on some of the planning issues.

In Seoul Kim Young Sam was spending days meeting with his ministers, staff, and experts on North Korea in preparation for the momentous conference. The two sides had agreed that the South Korean president would lead a hundred-member delegation to Pyongyang, accompanied by an eighty-member press corps equipped for live television broadcasts to the public back home. The actual meetings, which were to take place over two or three days, would be one-on-one discussions, with only two or three aides and a note taker accompanying each president.

On the crucial subject of national reunification, Kim Young Sam was preparing to contest his counterpart's confederation plan calling for one country with two systems, which South Koreans found biased and unworkable, and to propose instead gradual steps to reconciliation such as the exchange of visits by separated families, exchange of correspondence, and mutual access to television and radio programs of the other side. Kim believed it would take more than one meeting to iron out the historic trouble between the two Korean governments; he therefore planned to propose that this be the first of a series of summits. To ease the way, he was preparing to surprise North Korea by offering to supply 500,000 tons of rice to help feed its people, an amount more than double the 100,000 to 200,000 tons North Korea had been unofficially requesting through ROK businessmen.

Kim Il Sung was also making preparations. On the afternoon of July 6, after meeting his economic ministers in the morning, he traveled to his favorite place of respite from the summertime heat, the beautiful Myohyang Mountains, about a hundred miles north of Pyongyang. Kim's villa there had spectacular mountain views nestled amid a pine forest. It was where he took special visitors whom he was seeking to impress, and he had decided it was just the place to take the South Korean president.

On July 7, Kim made one of his on-the-spot inspections of a nearby collective farm, where he may also have planned to take the South Korean president. The temperature was nearly one hundred degrees Fahrenheit. In the mountains, he personally inspected a guest villa, which was being prepared for his South Korean visitor, checking bedrooms and bathrooms, even making certain that the refrigerators would be stocked with plenty of mineral water.

After these strenuous activities and his dinner, Kim complained of being tired. A short time later, he collapsed with a massive heart attack.

Doctors were summoned, but heavy rains made helicopter flights impossible, and poor dirt roads delayed the arrival of a land convoy.* North Korean officials told Korean American journalist Julie Moon, who obtained details of Kim's death, that doctors opened up his chest, hoping in vain to revive his heart, but it was too late. Kim Il Sung was pronounced dead at 2:00 on the morning of the eighth.

The death of the founding leader of the DPRK came at a time when the outside world was intruding increasingly on the unique dominion Kim had created in his unequaled reign of nearly a half century. In Kim's final months, he was seeking to adjust to the rapid decline of long-standing diplomatic, military, and economic arrangements and to explore new relationships with the United States, South Korea, and the world of his former enemies. Whether he was a leader of great vision or of great folly, he was without question the dominating figure on the stage that he trod. The absence of his controlling hand immensely complicated the problems of North Korea in the second half of the 1990s.

As with other powerful authoritarian leaders, Kim's health had long been a state secret and a matter of intense interest to the outside world. From at least the early 1970s, a large lumpy external tumor had been visible on the back of his neck, but doctors determined it to be benign. German doctors informed Kim it could be removed surgically in two hours; however, because they also said it was not dangerous, he told them to leave it alone. South Korean and US intelligence reports stating that Kim had heart trouble were confirmed by North Korea's official postmortem medical bulletin, which said he had received treatment for arteriosclerosis, or hardening of the arteries.

Personal impressions of Kim's health in his later years varied greatly, which may have reflected good days and bad days. A South Korean official who was among Kim's luncheon guests in February 1992, shortly before his eightieth birthday, found him hardly as fit as had been reported. The official said Kim dribbled food on his clothing, made a half-dozen incomprehensible statements, and left his eyeglasses on the table when he left the room at the end of the meal. On the other hand, Korea expert William Taylor of the US Center for Strategic and International Studies reported after luncheon with Kim just four months later, in June 1992, that "he walks and moves vigorously for age 80. His handshake is firm. When I left,

---

* Within a few months, the road to the Myohyang Mountains was paved in a top-priority operation, reportedly at the personal direction of Kim Jong Il. Kim himself stopped using the Myohyang-san villa, however.

he shook hands and pulled me toward him; his arm muscles are in good tone. His eyes are clear and his eye contact firm and compelling. Most important . . . his mind is quick and crystal clear."

THE END OF AN ERA

Kim Il Sung's death was kept secret for thirty-four hours, evidently to make sure arrangements were in place for the first succession in the country's history. On the morning of July 9, government ministries, offices, schools, and workplaces throughout North Korea were notified to watch television for an important announcement at noon. Many were expecting some good news, perhaps about the forthcoming summit meeting with the South. Instead, they were greeted by an announcer dressed in black, who solemnly intoned a shocking announcement:

> The Central Committee of the Workers' Party, the Central Military Commission of the Party, the National Defense Commission, the Central People's Committee and the Administration Council of the Democratic People's Republic of Korea report to the entire people of the country with the deepest grief that the Great Leader Comrade Kim Il Sung, General Secretary of the Central Committee of the Workers' Party of Korea and President of the Democratic People's Republic of Korea passed away from a sudden attack of illness at 02:00 on July 8, 1994. Our respected fatherly leader who has devoted his whole life to the popular masses' cause of independence and engaged himself in tireless activities for the prosperity of the motherland and happiness of the people, for the reunification of our country and independence of the world, till the last moments of his life, departed from us to our greatest sorrow.

There followed a lengthy obituary in praise of "a great revolutionary . . . genius in leadership . . . the greatest of great men . . . a great military strategist and ever-victorious iron-willed brilliant commander . . . the sun of the nation and lodestar of national reunification." Somber music followed, interspersed with readings from Kim's memoirs.

As the message sank in, officials broke down in front of the television sets and began weeping. Within a short time, residents of Pyongyang began converging on the giant statue of Kim on Mansu Hill near the city center, many of them crying hysterically. Before long, fifteen to twenty thousand people had gathered at the statue and in nearby streets, with lines of others stretching back as far as the eye could see. Ambulances were on duty, with aid workers assisting those who fainted or complained of feeling weak. Within a few hours, Pyongyang hospitals were overrun with heart-attack victims. The areas around the many statues and other monuments to Kim elsewhere in the country were also overflowing with mourners.

In a strange coincidence, American and North Korean delegations headed by US assistant secretary of state Robert Gallucci and DPRK deputy foreign minister Kang Sok Ju finally met to begin the long-awaited third round of nuclear negotiations on July 8, the day Kim died. Oblivious to the momentous but still secret event at home, the Pyongyang delegation reconfirmed the arrangements reached during the Carter mission to freeze its existing nuclear program in return for light-water reactors. From the American standpoint, surprisingly good progress was made. Following the meeting and private talks at a reception that night, US Navy captain Thomas Flanigan, the Joint Chiefs of Staff representative on the US delegation, wrote an e-mail to his superior in the Pentagon, "They're here to deal. We need to understand that. Now it's an issue of what are we willing to negotiate."

At 5:00 local time on the morning of July 9, which was to be the second day of the talks, the news of Kim's death reached Geneva. Later in the morning, the shaken North Koreans, who had not been informed prior to the official announcement, prepared to return to Pyongyang, promising that the negotiations would continue as soon as possible. Before they left, in a gesture that would impress the North Koreans deeply, Gallucci went to their mission in Geneva and signed the condolence book.

In Washington it was shortly after 11:00 P.M. local time when David E. Brown, the country director for Korea, got the news from the State Department Operations Center and began working on an official reaction. Senior officials were scattered around the world: President Clinton, Secretary of State Christopher, and their immediate staffs were in Naples at a Group of Seven summit meeting; Assistant Secretary for East Asian Affairs Winston Lord was en route home from a G-7 meeting between Clinton and Japanese prime minister Tomiichi Murayama; Ambassador Laney was in Ireland to receive an honorary degree; other senior staff members were asleep in their beds in Washington.

In a globe-girdling telephone conference call that lasted most of the night, with various figures joining or leaving as their schedules and state of exhaustion dictated, it was decided to send condolences to "the North Korean people," in hopes of keeping the promising Geneva negotiations on track. A presidential statement was drafted and promptly made public by the traveling White House: "On behalf of the people of the United States, I extend sincere condolences to the people of North Korea on the death of President Kim Il Sung. We appreciate his leadership in resuming the talks between our governments. We hope they will continue as appropriate." There was no consultation about the condolence statement with South Korea, prompting anger in some circles in Seoul. If there had been full consultation, according to a US official involved in the decision, the statement might never have been issued.

Clinton's condolences were sharply condemned by Senate Republican leader Bob Dole, the president's eventual rival in the 1996 election. Dole called the statement "insensitive to the generation of Americans who suffered as a result of the Korean War" and heedless that "Kim Il Sung was a brutal dictator of a government that is neither a friend nor an ally of the United States—a government whose policies and actions have threatened and continue to threaten U.S. security and interests." Clinton responded that his statement was appropriate in view of the ongoing negotiations and that "the veterans of the Korean War and their survivors, as much as any group of Americans, would very much want us to resolve this nuclear issue with North Korea and go forward." What he did not know at the time was that his condolences made a lasting positive impression on Kim Jong Il.

In Seoul, Kim Young Sam placed the ROK armed forces on maximum alert minutes after the news of the North Korean leader's death was broadcast. A National Security Council meeting was convened at the Blue House at 2:00 P.M., followed by an emergency cabinet meeting at 5:00. The only unusual military development in the North was that DPRK forces virtually stopped visible activities, including training, probably both to mourn the Supreme Leader and as an internal security precaution.

As the days wore on, the reaction to Kim's death became the subject of political controversy in the South. When an opposition legislator, Lee Boo Young, suggested that the government express condolences in view of the grief being expressed by North Koreans, he touched off an impassioned debate in which conservatives went on the attack. After a week's delay, the government announced it would crack down on any domestic moves to pay tribute to Kim Il Sung and denounced the expression of condolences as "reckless" and "irresponsible behavior ignoring our history." The government also blocked a plan by leftist students to send a condolence mission to the North, and police warned that any expression of condolence would be met sternly as a violation of the National Security Law.

With old wounds reopened, emotions ran high. The Korean Broadcasting System was forced to terminate its broadcast of a fifty-five-minute Polish documentary about Kim Il Sung after twenty-five minutes due to a flood of complaints from viewers who felt it was too favorable. The same film had run on KBS two years earlier without incident. In a move that fanned the flames, the South Korean government, on the day after Kim's funeral, made public a hundred Soviet documents that had been given to Kim Young Sam during a visit to Moscow in early June, demonstrating that Kim Il Sung had been the moving figure behind the launching of the Korean War. Russian officials complained to Seoul about the inappropriate timing of the documents' release, which was decided without consultation with Moscow.

The actions and statements of Kim Young Sam's government, at a time of intense mourning in the North, generated bitter resentment in Pyongyang. North Korean authorities resumed virulent anti-South propaganda, which had been suspended by agreement in preparation for the summit, and they began refusing to accept official telephone messages from Seoul. Privately, Kim Young Sam was unconcerned, since he was convinced that without its longtime leader, North Korea was on its last legs. The South Korean president's national security assistant, Chung Chong Wook, told his US counterpart, Anthony Lake, in a secure-line telephone conversation that North Korea seemed heading for collapse, a view that was widely held throughout the government. No one in Seoul was operating under the naive assumption that collapse was imminent, but the conviction that the North's time was running out made Kim Young Sam more inclined to undercut than to accommodate the new leaders in Pyongyang.

THE SUCCESSION OF KIM JONG IL

The drawn and haggard man who stood apart and ahead of all others at the state funeral and the memorial service in Kim Il Sung Square was the most important mourner. Despite some expectations to the contrary, however, the eldest son and political heir of the Great Leader said nothing about his father, his loss, or his priorities for the country. Rather, he looked on, distracted and deeply shaken by his father's death, as others spoke in praise of the Great Leader and of the ordained succession process that had been established more than a decade earlier.

In many respects, father and son were a study in contrasts. Kim Il Sung was a guerrilla fighter, the founder of the state, and a charismatic, outgoing, outspoken figure until the day he died. Kim Jong Il grew up in privilege from his teenage years, had never served a day in the military until he was named supreme commander of the People's Army in December 1991, and was notably uncomfortable amid the roar of the crowd. Even when important pronouncements were made in his name, they were read by an announcer while he remained out of sight. Stories circulated outside North Korea that Kim avoided speaking in public because his voice was strange or his thought processes addled. Neither was true. For reasons of his own choosing, the only time the North Korean public heard his voice, however, was in April 1992, when he uttered a single sentence during a ceremony marking the army's sixtieth anniversary: "Glory to the people's heroic military!"

To the outside world, Kim Jong Il's emergence as a leader exemplified the mysterious aura that seemed to surround North Korea. His rise to power and selection as his father's successor were long unacknowledged publicly, and his activities were masked under the vague euphemism "the party center." For many years, he rarely traveled outside the North or met with foreigners, reinforcing the impression that he was "reclusive." In 1965, at the age of twenty-three, he had accompanied his father to Indonesia and then Rangoon, and in 1984 he turned up briefly in his father's entourage in Berlin. East German officials confirmed his presence only later by studying photographs taken aboard Kim Il Sung's special train. Beginning in 2000, however, Kim would meet numerous high-level foreign delegations and travel several times to China and Russia, though by then the adjective "reclusive" was treated by foreign reporters as almost part of his title.

According to North Korean propaganda, Kim Jong Il was born in a log cabin on Mount Paekdu, the legendary birthplace of Tangun, the mythic father of the Korean people. More objective sources say the younger Kim was born on February 16, 1942, in a Russian military camp in the Far East, where his father's guerrilla band had taken refuge from the Japanese. After the Japanese surrender, at age three Kim Jong Il moved to Korea with his father but was evacuated to China at age eight during the Korean War. In his early years, a younger brother accidentally drowned, and his mother died while giving birth to a stillborn child, leaving Jong Il and a younger sister. Kim Il Sung remarried in the early 1960s and had two sons and two daughters by his second wife, Kim Song Ae. As Kim Jong Il took over, he carefully "pruned the branches" of the Kim family tree, making sure there would be no challenge to his position. His half-brother Kim Pyong Il was sent into virtual exile starting in 1988, serving as ambassador in Hungary, Bulgaria, Finland, and then Poland.

Although passage of power from father to eldest son was traditional in Korean dynasties and Confucian families, it was heretical in a nominal "people's democracy." The 1970 edition of the official *Dictionary of Political Terminologies* published in Pyongyang defined hereditary succession as "a reactionary custom of exploitive societies." This entry was dropped in the early 1970s, after Kim Il Sung decided to make his son his closest aide and successor.

Kim Jong Il graduated from Kim Il Sung University in 1964 and went to work in the Central Committee of the Workers Party, with special responsibility for films, theater, and art, which became his lifelong passion. He is credited with the production of six major films and musicals in the early 1970s. Kim became a secretary of the Central Committee of the Workers Party in September 1973 and a member of its Politburo at a rare secret Central Committee plenum the following year. By then songs were being sung about him among party cadres, who carried special note-books to record his instructions.

Despite his prominence in the Workers Party, little was said about him publicly, and nothing at all for foreign audiences, which suggests that his father felt the need to fully prepare the domestic and external public for the first family succession of the communist world. North Korean media re-ferred instead to the "party center," which was given credit for wise guidance and great deeds. The veil was lifted at the Sixth Workers Party Congress in October 1980, when the younger Kim was simultaneously awarded senior posts in the Politburo, the Military Commission, and the Party Secretariat and was openly proclaimed to be Kim Il Sung's designated successor.

For many years, the most extensive glimpses of Kim Jong Il in action came from a prominent South Korean actress, Choi Eun Hee, and her for-mer husband, film director Shin Sang Ok, who were kidnapped separately to North Korea from Hong Kong in 1978 on the younger Kim's orders. Without embarrassment, he baldly told the movie couple in a meeting that they surreptitiously tape-recorded that he had ordered their forcible abduction because "I absolutely needed you" to improve Pyongyang's un-professional film industry. The pair made motion pictures for Kim Jong Il for almost three years. He treated them as important artists and members of his social circle until their escape in Vienna in 1986.

The filmmakers reported that Kim spent money lavishly. He housed Choi and eventually Shin in luxurious surroundings. He gave each of them a new Mercedes 280. He built an expensive new motion picture studio for their productions. An aide told Shin that Kim had use of the proceeds from a gold mine, which provided nearly unlimited funds for his gifts, motion picture hobby, and other activities.

In interviews shortly after their escape, Choi and Shin depicted Kim as confident, bright, temperamental, quirky, and very much in charge of governmental as well as theatrical affairs. To his kidnapped "special guests," he could be privately self-deprecating, as when he said to actress Choi in their first dinner meeting, "What do you think of my physique? Small as a midget's turd, aren't I?"

Although kidnapping Choi and Shin is the best documented of the many violent acts associated with the name of the younger Kim, it is not the only one. The terrorist bombing that killed South Korean cabinet members at Rangoon in 1983 was attributed to a clandestine agency re-porting to him. Kim Hyon Hui, the female agent in the bombing of Ko-rean Air Lines flight 858, in which 115 people were killed in 1987, was told that her orders came directly from Kim Jong Il in his own handwrit-ing, although she did not see them.

At the same time, even in his early years Kim Jong Il may have been more interested in modernizing the country than most others in the ruling circles. In a diplomatic dispatch to Berlin in 1982, the East German Embassy remarked on the younger Kim's "modern" outlook and credited him with a loosening up of popular lifestyles, including the approval of more fashionable women's clothing; the reintroduction of dice, card, and board games; and the increased consumption of alcoholic beverages, especially beer.

In a tape recording brought out by the filmmakers, Kim Jong Il said in 1984, "After having experienced about thirty years of socialism, I feel we need to expand to the Western world to feed the people. The reality is that we are behind the West." At the same meeting, however, he said that North Korea could not open up, as even the Chinese were urging. "We have been stuck strategically" because opening up in his militarily embattled country, even for tourism, "would be naturally tantamount to disarmament." This could only be done after unification, he said. Over the years, Kim vacillated on this point, moving sometimes toward more opening, then retreating.

In July 1994, Korea experts speculated about how quickly Kim Jong Il would assume his father's titles of general secretary of the Workers Party and president of the DPRK. Ignorant of how thorough the preparations had been for the succession or how firmly Kim already held the reins of power when his father died, many observers including the South Korean president predicted Kim would quickly be overthrown. The lengthy (three-year) mourning period that followed, and his failure to assume the top posts right away, stirred speculation—completely mistaken—that Kim Jong Il faced important opposition within the hierarchy.

THE FRAMEWORK NEGOTIATIONS

The long-awaited third round of US-DPRK nuclear negotiations, interrupted by Kim Il Sung's death, resumed in Geneva on August 5. American negotiators were relieved to discover that the death of the Great Leader had not altered the existing DPRK negotiating positions or diminished the desire of its leadership to make a deal. From the outset of the August talks, the North Koreans were impressively businesslike and determined to move ahead.

In a single week of talks ending with a postmidnight press conference on August 12, the two delegations were able to agree on the rough outlines of a settlement of the central issues. Additional progress emerged from tougher bargaining when the negotiations resumed in September after a six-week recess.

As a result of the Carter mission, North Korea had already agreed to freeze its nuclear program while negotiations proceeded. In Geneva the two sides now pursued a permanent solution along the lines they had previously discussed: that Pyongyang would abandon all of its proliferation-prone gas-graphite nuclear facilities in return for modern light-water-reactor nuclear power plants.

Beyond this basic provision, a comprehensive agreement had to take into account a number of lesser items of concern to one side or the other. DPRK negotiator Kang, in a private conversation with Gallucci, referred to several key items as "our chips": the eight thousand irradiated fuel rods that had been unloaded earlier in the year from the 5-megawatt nuclear reactor, the reprocessing facility that could extract from those fuel rods enough plutonium for four or five nuclear weapons, and the mandatory IAEA "special inspections" of the disputed nuclear waste sites, which might cast light on whether North Korea already possessed hidden plutonium. The United States also had some important bargaining chips, especially the possible establishment of political and economic ties that could create a new environment for North Korea and substitute, in some degree, for the loss of the Soviet Union and the shifts in the policies of China.

Early on, the North Koreans asked to be compensated for the energy they would be giving up by shutting down their working reactor and stopping work on the two larger ones long before the promised light-water reactors were on the scene, a period roughly estimated to take at least ten years. They made it clear that they needed something concrete to take home at the end of the negotiations. The Americans explored supplying various energy sources, including surplus Defense Department generators, coal-fired plants, and others. US negotiators were delighted when the North Koreans asked for heavy oil, a little-used sludge-like commodity that is left over from the refining of petroleum. It had previously powered a large electricity plant near the northern border, supplied decades earlier by the East Germans and, unknown to the Americans, had been high on Kim Il Sung's wish list in connection with additional power plants.

How to structure the terms of what was emerging as a comprehensive deal consumed much of the bargaining. North Koreans feared they would be made to give up everything at the beginning and then the Americans would renege in the long run. Americans feared a sweeping agreement in principle that would not be fulfilled by the North Koreans. Gallucci observed that "there wasn't sufficient trust for one to take a very large step assuming the other would take the compensatory counter step. There had to be a series of smaller steps linked with constant checking on compliance." Thus, the core of the agreement was a detailed timetable of reciprocal actions, some of which were spelled out in a "confidential minute" that was not made public due to North Korean sensibilities. In the final stages of the talks, a certain rhythm developed: whenever the two sides became stuck over wording on a sensitive implementation issue, one side or the other would simply say, "Put it in the confidential minute," and the discussions could move on.

The rapid progress toward a far-reaching accord in the first week, as well as continued progress when the negotiations resumed in September after a six-week recess, was surprising to many American officials. US negotiators surmised that, especially after Kim Il Sung's death, the new leadership was under pressure to produce a deal that would enhance Kim Jong Il's stature. Gallucci believed that the tangible threat of UN sanctions in the spring and American willingness to face down North Korea with a major infusion of additional ships, planes, and troops, as worrisome as it had been to all parties, was a crucial reason for his success. He called the events of June "a very good combination of political-military activity" that drove Pyongyang back to the bargaining table with a strong desire to reach a settlement. That view probably underestimated the extent to which the North wanted a settlement in order to get progress on its overarching strategic goal—improving relations with the United States.

One of the thorniest issues was the IAEA's demand, which Washington and the UN Security Council had endorsed, for "special inspections" of the two suspected nuclear waste sites at Yongbyon, which North Korea claimed were military facilities exempt from inspection. Pyongyang maintained that this dispute had caused its startling announcement eighteen months earlier that it was withdrawing from the Nuclear Non-Proliferation Treaty. In the meantime, private declarations of its chief negotiator, Kang Sok Ju, as well as public statements from Pyongyang, warned that North Korea would "never" submit to what it described as a violation of its national sovereignty. Gallucci, on the other hand, came with firm instructions that North Korean acceptance of the "special inspections" must be part of the final agreement. This was clearly a deal breaker—until both sides began showing flexibility.

The State Department's senior North Korea watcher, Robert Carlin, who had spent more than twenty years listening for nuances in North Korean statements, noticed that beginning September 23, Kang had stopped saying "never" about the special inspections. Carlin thought the omission significant. The Pyongyang watcher was even more certain that something was up when, on September 27, Pyongyang radio broadcast a puzzling press statement by "a spokesman for DPRK Ministry of the People's Armed Forces." In blustery language, the statement seemed to attack the ongoing Geneva talks being conducted by the Foreign Ministry, declaring that the army had never expected anything, did not recognize "talks accompanied by pressure," and could "never allow any attempt to open up military facilities through special inspections." CIA experts in Washington, whom I happened to meet that afternoon at a conference on Korea policy, interpreted the statement as presaging even fiercer North

Korean opposition to special inspections and a deadlock in the negotiations. Carlin, however, was convinced that the opposite was true—that the strange military pronouncement had arisen from an outbreak of extremely unusual open bureaucratic warfare between the army and the Foreign Ministry in Pyongyang over making a key concession in Geneva.

Carlin was soon proven right. At the negotiating table on October 6, Kang proposed coolly that North Korea not be required to accept special inspections (he used a euphemism to avoid these words) until 70 to 80 percent of the components of the promised light-water reactors had been shipped. Suddenly, "never" had been transformed into a discussion of the price. Carlin wrote an e-mail to his immediate superior at the State Department: "At 11:50 this morning we won the war. I can pinpoint the time because when Kang said what he said, I knew the game was over, and I looked at my watch." At that point, it was left to Gallucci to nail down the terms and persuade Washington to permit special inspections to be postponed until the delivery of key nuclear components of the promised light-water reactors—at least five years or more away. The postponement became one of the agreement's most controversial features. Gallucci and the US administration defended it as the best they could do.

South Korea had agreed to play the central role and pick up the lion's share of the costs of providing the light-water reactors, but Seoul was absent from the bargaining table at Geneva. Although its diplomats were briefed daily, its absence from direct participation in the US-DPRK negotiations and resulting accords was a bitter pill for South Koreans, who saw themselves as relegated to a marginal role while their sponsor sat down with their peninsular foe. Conversely, a direct, normal relationship with Washington had been the most important objectives for Pyongyang ever since the fall of the USSR.

The anxiety in Seoul emerged dramatically in mid-October, when President Kim Young Sam, in an interview with the *New York Times*, objected to the agreement nearing completion in Geneva on the grounds that "North Korea faces the danger of imminent political and economic collapse" and that "any compromise [at this point] with North Korea will only help prolong its survival." He also declared that the United States, with far less experience than Seoul in negotiations with Pyongyang, was being deceived in Geneva. These comments contradicted the public positions of support for the negotiations that had been taken by Kim's government.

Kim's outburst was shocking to officials in Washington, who feared their ally might torpedo the negotiations at the eleventh hour. Gallucci was furious. When he walked into the meeting room that afternoon, his DPRK interlocutor, Kang Sok Ju, offered a few choice words of commiseration. Kang made his point with a charming smile as if to say, "You see, dealing with the South Koreans is never easy."

Secretary of State Warren Christopher, who was traveling in London, telephoned South Korean foreign minister Han Sung Joo at 2:00 A.M., London time, after receiving a phone call about Kim's interview from an unhappy President Clinton. In the Blue House the following afternoon, Ambassador Laney bearded the South Korean president. "We wouldn't betray you at the DMZ; we wouldn't do it in Geneva," Laney declared. Speaking of the alliance's shared purposes about North Korea, he appealed to Kim to maintain unity when they were finally about to succeed in curbing Pyongyang's nuclear program. In response, Kim said flatly that he could not approve the Geneva accord because of promises he had made to the Korean people. He vehemently objected to postponing the "special inspections" to clear up North Korea's murky nuclear past and to the absence of a North-South aspect of the proposed agreement. Laney countered that early "special inspections" could not be negotiated because Pyongyang would immediately lose all its nuclear leverage and that Gallucci was actively seeking a commitment to North-South dialogue as part of the accord. Laney appealed to Kim as a statesman to rise above popular expectations.

President Kim was not convinced. In conversation with his foreign minister, Han Sung Joo, the following morning, Kim initially resolved to denounce the US-DPRK deal. Such a denunciation would have negated the Geneva negotiations, created a crisis between Seoul and Washington, and potentially led to a renewed confrontation with North Korea. In a series of telephone calls, Han persuaded his president that it was in the ROK's national interest to approve the agreement—but he was able to do so only after harsh words were exchanged. Han told his aide that the intense disagreement would probably cost him his job but that the issue was so important, it was worth the risk. Two months later, Kim dumped Han and named a cautious career diplomat, Gong Ro Myung, in his place.

In view of this situation in Seoul, Gallucci in Geneva was instructed to insist that the US-DPRK agreement include a clause committing North Korea to resume the dormant North-South dialogue. His opposite number, Kang, adamantly refused, on the grounds that North-South relations were inter-Korean business and outside the legitimate concern of the United States. (Inter-Korean matters were also outside the purview of the Foreign Ministry.) North Korean negotiators said flatly that they had instructions to break off the negotiations and return home if the US side insisted on North-South issues as a precondition for the nuclear arrangements. Gallucci insisted that without a North-South commitment, there would be no agreement.

After threats from both sides to leave Geneva in failure, the North Koreans finally agreed to negotiate on the issue. Several days of haggling produced a paragraph declaring, "The DPRK will engage in North-South dialogue, as this Agreed Framework will help create an atmosphere that promotes such dialogue." The United States had argued for including the phrase "at the earliest time." North Korea insisted on the "as" clause, which it later used as an excuse not to perform. Gallucci finally accepted, believing that no language could compel Pyongyang to negotiate with Seoul and that "the exact words were a matter of Talmudic significance to all those who lived on the Korean peninsula."

Although virtually a treaty in form and substance, with binding obligations on both sides, the accord was styled an Agreed Framework because the Clinton administration worried that it might not win approval if submitted to the Senate as a treaty. The North Koreans were gravely concerned that Congress would balk and that Washington would fail to uphold its end of the accord. The day before the signing, as agreed in Geneva, Clinton sent a letter to "His Excellency Kim Jong Il, Supreme Leader of the Democratic People's Republic of Korea," confirming that he would "use the full powers of his office . . . subject to the approval of the U.S. Congress" to arrange for light-water reactors and provide "interim energy alternatives" during the construction period. The North Koreans complained about the less-than-ironclad language, but the Americans explained that under the US separation of powers, even a president cannot act independently of Congress.

The agreement was signed in ceremonies in Geneva on October 21 by Gallucci and Kang for the United States and the DPRK, respectively. According to its main provisions:

> The United States would organize an international consortium to provide two light-water reactors by a "target date" of 2003. Until the reactors were operational, the U.S. would arrange to supply 500,000 tons of heavy fuel oil annually to make up for the energy forgone by the North. In return for the HFO, North Korea would freeze all activity on its existing nuclear reactors and related facilities, and permit them to be continuously monitored by IAEA inspectors. The eight thousand fuel rods unloaded from the 5-megawatt reactor would be securely stored and eventually shipped out of the country.
>
> North Korea would come into full compliance with the IAEA—which meant accepting "special inspections"—before the delivery of key components for the reactors. The DPRK's existing nuclear facilities would be completely dismantled by the time the LWR project was completed.
>
> The two governments would reduce existing barriers to trade and investment and open diplomatic liaison offices in each other's capitals as initial steps toward eventual full normalization of relations.

The United States would provide formal assurances against the threat or use of nuclear weapons against North Korea.

FALLOUT FROM THE AGREED FRAMEWORK

North Korea greeted the accord as a triumph, which was neither surprising nor unjustified in view of the vastly unequal weight of the two countries. DPRK negotiator Kang Sok Ju was greeted with ceremonial honor at the airport in Pyongyang on his return from Geneva. He and his team were feted at a banquet given in the name of (but not in the presence of) Kim Jong Il. The Workers Party newspaper, *Rodong Sinmun,* hailed the agreement as "the biggest diplomatic victory" and boasted, "We held the talks independently with the United States on an independent footing, not relying on someone else's sympathy or advice."

In Seoul public opinion and the views of influential elite groups were extremely negative, even though the ROK government officially endorsed the agreement and pledged to cooperate to make it work. Arriving on one of my periodic visits a month after the signing of the accord, I was startled to run into so many objections expressed in such passionate terms, even by normally pro-American and pragmatic Koreans.

The objections ran the gamut from the failure to consult Seoul adequately to the belief that the US negotiators could have obtained a better deal through tougher bargaining. Moreover, many South Koreans agreed with the sentiments expressed by President Kim Young Sam to the *New York Times* during the last days of the Geneva bargaining: any American deal would help shore up a Pyongyang regime on the verge of collapsing, thus postponing reunification.

However, the most important objection to the Agreed Framework was less specific but much more serious: South Koreans were in anguish that the United States, their great ally and closest friend, would establish any relationship with North Korea, about which nearly everyone had complex feelings and which many regarded as a bitter enemy. All the more infuriating was the fact that the US-DPRK deal had been consummated without the direct involvement of the ROK. Suddenly, Washington was dealing with "the evil twin," as one Seoulite put it to me. The consequences of this shift in relationships with North and South, which were little understood in Washington, made the ROK government and its people immensely more difficult to deal with.

The agreement was greeted coolly by the American public, which had not been prepared for such a broad accord with a pariah nation. The *New York Times* headline was "Clinton Approves a Plan to Give Aid to North Korea." The *Washington Post* announced, "North Korea Pact Contains U.S.

Concessions; Agreement Would Allow Presence of Key Plutonium-Making Facilities for Years."

Seventeen days after the Agreed Framework was signed, its problems in Congress became more serious when Republicans in the 1994 elections unexpectedly won control of both houses for the first time in decades. Foreign policy had been only a minor issue in the political campaigns, but the new Republican Congress was much more conservative and more skeptical of any dealings with North Korea than the outgoing Democratic Congress had been.

THE KIM JONG IL REGIME

On December 17, less than two months after the signing of the Agreed Framework, the new relationship between Washington and Pyongyang was tested in an unexpected way. That morning two US Army warrant officers in an unarmed helicopter lost their way in snow-covered terrain and flew across the DMZ five miles into North Korean airspace before being shot down. Chief Warrant Officer David Hileman was killed, but the copilot, Chief Warrant Officer Bobby Hall, survived. He was immediately surrounded and captured by North Korean troops.

As these events were taking place, Representative Bill Richardson, a New Mexico Democrat, was on his way to Pyongyang via Beijing. When he arrived in the North Korean capital, he tried unsuccessfully to arrange the release of Airman Hall. Foreign Ministry officials told him that the case was in the hands of the less sympathetic Korean People's Army command. When Richardson left on December 22, he took with him the body of Airman Hileman but, despite pleas about the coming of Christmas, only a promise of best efforts to arrange the release of Hall "very soon."

On Christmas Day, Hall, still in captivity, wrote a "confession," accurately setting out the facts of his flight and asking forgiveness for his "grave infringement upon the sovereignty of the DPRK." In line with standard North Korean practice, Hall's confession meant that the way was clear for negotiations over his release to begin. The following day, the North Korean Foreign Ministry asked the State Department to send a senior official to Pyongyang, saying that the release of Hall probably could not be arranged through the military channels at the DMZ that were being used to deal with the issue.

Deputy Assistant Secretary of State Thomas Hubbard, who had participated in the framework negotiations and other exchanges, crossed the DMZ into North Korea on December 28. Immediately, the Foreign Ministry began probing to see what the United States might give up in return for Hall's release. In two days of talks, Hubbard refused to grant the North

Koreans any of the political concessions they sought, such as agreement to begin negotiating a US-DPRK peace treaty, but he did agree to a statement of "sincere regret" for the "legally unjustified intrusion into DPRK air space."

To Hubbard, an illuminating aspect of the negotiations was the difference between the Foreign Ministry, which was eager to protect the just-signed framework accord with the United States, and the military, which was primarily concerned with the defense of borders. Foreign Ministry officials spoke openly of their frictions with military officers; at the DMZ, KPA officers spoke disparagingly to their American military counterparts of the "neckties," as they called the DPRK diplomats.

Such differences, in a less personal vein, had emerged during the course of the Agreed Framework negotiation. To some extent, referring to conflicts with the harder-edged military was a useful bargaining ploy on the part of the North's diplomats, but Gallucci, Hubbard, and other American negotiators became convinced that on another level, the differences were real. In Geneva the diplomats intimated they ultimately won most of the confrontations because, they said, their instructions had been personally signed by the new Supreme Leader, Kim Jong Il. At the climax of the Hall case, the Foreign Ministry's position again won the day, probably because it fitted Kim's own view that advancing relations with the United States was a paramount goal.

On the evening of December 29, Hubbard received final approval from Washington for the public statement of US regret that he proposed to make to accomplish Hall's release. At that point, North Korean deputy foreign minister Kang excused himself from an official dinner, taking a copy of the statement and saying he would submit it to "the Supreme Leader." At 2:00 A.M., another Foreign Ministry official called on Hubbard at the State Guest House to announce that the statement and the release of Hall had been "approved by Kim Jong Il." Hall was released the following morning at Panmunjom, where KPA officers made little effort to hide their displeasure.

Within minutes of Hall's return to South Korea, Clinton telephoned ROK president Kim Young Sam to reassure him that Hubbard's negotiations had not opened a new US channel or line of policy toward North Korea. The telephone call was deemed necessary because South Korean news media and some officials were highly critical of the negotiations, worried that Hubbard had made new deals in the North and finding proof of that in the brief statement Hubbard had made on Washington's authority. "Something strange is going on up there," Kim told Clinton, still trying to keep the United States in check. "We should not move too fast."

VISIT TO PYONGYANG

In mid-January 1995, I was able to take a weeklong look at North Korea in the Kim Jong Il era as part of a four-member academic delegation sponsored by George Washington University's Sigur Center for East Asian Studies. As in my 1991 visit, the small Russian-built airliner that brought us from Beijing was the only one to land in the entire country that day, in stark contrast to Seoul's busy Kimpo International Airport where forty thousand passengers a day were arriving or departing from overseas on an incessant stream of jumbo jets.

Within an hour after landing, however, I was struck by notable changes from my previous trip three and a half years earlier. The first surprise was that our official Mercedes cars—and all other vehicles in sight—were stopped and their occupants examined at a military checkpoint. This had never happened on my previous trip. Moreover, army and internal security police, often armed with automatic weapons, were in much greater evidence in Pyongyang streets than they had been before, and a frequent European visitor said the military was more conspicuous in the countryside than previously. While there was no discernible challenge to the regime (nor would such a challenge have been tolerated), the notably greater military presence seemed intended to convey a message; whether that message was increased vigilance against potential challenge or simply the increased importance of the military in the Kim Jong Il era, I did not know.

As our cars entered the city, we paused en route to our hotel for a new obligatory rite of passage: paying homage to Kim Il Sung at his giant bronze statue on Mansu Hill, overlooking the capital he had built. Beginning with our stop at the statue and continuing throughout our stay, Kim Il Sung seemed as omnipresent in death as in life, dominating the television programs, publications, cultural programs, and even policy presentations of the regime he left behind. With rare exceptions, each official whom we met began his presentation with recognition of the grave historic misfortune suffered by the country and, they claimed, the entire world when the Great Leader died. While mention was made of his son and chosen successor, greater emphasis was placed on the fallen leader.

In all political systems, the death of the leader is a traumatic experience, especially in the case of totalitarian leaders such as Stalin, Mao, and Kim Il Sung, who reigned over their countries for decades. With the choice of his son to be his political heir, Kim sought to avoid the years of confusion and the ultimate repudiation that followed the deaths of his Russian and Chinese contemporaries. Although Kim hoped for a tranquil political succession, he left his son an economy that was on the rocks and

on the edge of a devastating famine. January 1995 marked the beginning
of the sixth consecutive year of negative economic growth, as estimated
by outside experts. Since 1990, the first year of decline, the North Korean
GNP had contracted by about one-fourth, according to these estimates.
Nonetheless, we saw little privation in our one-week visit that was limited
to the capital city, whose specially chosen population obtains the best of
whatever is available. Surprisingly, I noticed more cars, trucks, and buses
on the streets, suggesting that the energy crisis had diminished since my
visit in 1991. That turned out to be a misimpression. By early 1996, as the
famine took hold and the economy plunged ever downward, the streets of
Pyongyang were virtually empty of traffic.

Everywhere we went, it was apparent the North was eager to confirm
and advance its new relationship with the United States. The importance
of the US relationship was explicit in the statements of officials whom we
saw, including Foreign Minister Kim Yong Nam and the more freewheeling Kim Yong Sun, who after further ups and downs had become Workers
Party secretary for North-South affairs. Our visit coincided with that of a
team of experts from US government agencies working with the nuclear
authorities to arrange safe and continuously inspected storage of the fuel
rods that had been unloaded from the now-dormant 5-megawatt reactor
at Yongbyon. The visit also coincided with the arrival of two ships at the
port of Sonbong carrying fifty thousand tons of heavy fuel oil, the first of
the US-supplied energy to be delivered under the Agreed Framework in
compensation for the shutdown of the North Korean nuclear program.
Later I saw the brief cable from the Joint Chiefs of Staff in Washington
to US Commands in the Pacific notifying them that "the Secretary of Defense has directed the [merchant ships] *Da Quing* and *Lark Lake* to deliver
50,000 metric tons of heavy fuel oil to the DPRK." It was hard to believe
that less than a year earlier, the United States and North Korea had been
on the brink of war and that the Joint Chiefs had been contemplating very
different orders to its Pacific commands.

On January 20, the day before we left Pyongyang, the State Department announced the easing of several economic sanctions against North
Korea, as anticipated in the Agreed Framework. However, these were less
than the administration had previously planned because of opposition to
concessions on the part of the Republicans who were now in control of
Congress. For the same reason, the first fuel-oil shipments were paid for
out of Pentagon contingency funds, which did not require new authorization from Capitol Hill. The Agreed Framework, while working as planned
in North Korea, was on thin ice politically in the United States.

The central issue presented to us in nearly every meeting in Pyongyang was the desire to negotiate a US-DPRK "peace insuring system" at
the DMZ to replace the 1953 Armistice Agreement, which North Korea

insisted was obsolete. The demand for a US-DPRK peace treaty was more than twenty years old, but it had been given new impetus starting in April 1994, when North Korea reacted to the US military buildup in technical violation of the armistice. Weeks later, the North withdrew its delegates from the Military Armistice Commission, forced the withdrawal of the Polish participants from the long-standing Neutral Nations Supervisory Commission at the DMZ, and launched a successful diplomatic drive to persuade China to withdraw from the Military Armistice Commission. A senior DPRK foreign ministry official, Kim Byong Hong, told us ominously that if the United States did not respond to the new "peace insuring" proposal, the DPRK would take "unilateral steps."

Due to the opposition to the armistice by then-president Syngman Rhee, South Korea was not a signatory to the armistice; therefore, North Korea insisted that the South not be included in talks about its future. From the American standpoint, it was out of the question to negotiate a bilateral peace treaty or other "peace insuring system" on the divided peninsula without the South Koreans, as our delegation told our hosts in no uncertain terms. Despite this imposing roadblock, the discussion of more permanent arrangements at the heavily fortified DMZ seemed to me a positive development.

The official attitude toward the South was the most troubling aspect of our talks in Pyongyang. DPRK officials adamantly refused to deal with the ROK government, insisting it had irrevocably insulted North Korea by its conduct at the death of Kim Il Sung. The foreign minister and others insisted that the South must formally apologize, which was highly unlikely, before talks could restart.

How much of this was honest anger and how much a tactic to avoid North-South negotiations and bait the South while concentrating on Pyongyang's relationship with the United States was impossible to tell. It was clear enough, though, that the absence of movement toward accommodation or détente between North and South was a serious problem for the United States in moving between a former enemy and a close ally.

THE STRUGGLE OVER THE REACTORS

The most important unresolved problem in implementing the Agreed Framework was the source and description of the light-water reactors to be furnished in exchange for North Korea's existing nuclear facilities. Although the United States had negotiated the deal, Washington did not propose to furnish or pay for the reactors. South Korea had volunteered to provide them, and from the first Washington called on Seoul to underwrite most of their $4–$5 billion cost, with Japan putting up much of the rest. Pyongyang bridled at the idea of giving Seoul a chance to crow about how it was providing this high-tech export to the North, though Gallucci and others insisted there was no alternative to the South as a supplier.

Three rounds of US-DPRK expert talks on the topic in Beijing and Berlin ended in deadlock. Pyongyang was determined to avoid an open acknowledgment that South Korea might be the source of the reactors, insisting that it was up to the United States to provide them under an American label—but also saying that where they actually came from was Washington's business. Seoul was equally determined that North Korea accept its central role in providing the reactors, even more, that this role should be openly acknowledged in the final contract by a reference to "South Korean type reactors."

A face-saving intermediary was the international consortium envisaged in the Agreed Framework. It was established by the United States, South Korea, and Japan in March 1995 as the Korean Peninsula Energy Development Organization (KEDO), with an American executive director, former diplomat Stephen Bosworth, giving overall direction to the project.*

In the Agreed Framework, the United States had pledged to make the "best efforts" to conclude a supply contract for the new reactors by April 21, 1995. As the date approached with negotiations deadlocked on the origin and description of the new reactors, North Korea threatened to abandon the Agreed Framework, ending the freeze on its existing nuclear program by reloading its 5-megawatt reactor. The situation was made more complicated by Seoul's adamant demand that the North clearly acknowledge the origin of its new reactors, on the grounds that this was necessary if the National Assembly was to furnish the billions of dollars required. At the Berlin talks in late March, when the United States proposed to offer the North face-saving language, South Korea refused to approve the talking points. Battered by criticism for ignoring the interests of the South, "we made a very conscious choice between pursuing what we thought was the most likely route to a solution and solidarity [with the South]. We opted for solidarity," according to a White House policy maker. Predictably, the talks ended in failure.

As tensions rose, talk in Seoul and Washington turned again to a show of force to pressure North Korea. This time the adoption of sanctions by the UN Security Council seemed unlikely because the issue boiled down to North Korean pride versus South Korean pride. Moreover, Chinese cooperation was less likely because the United States and China were embroiled in a dispute over a US visit by Taiwan's president.

---

* For KEDO's rise and fall, see Charles Kartman, Robert Carlin, and Joel Wit, *A History of KEDO, 1994–2006* (Center for International Security and Cooperation, Stanford University, 2012).

To exert pressure on the North, ROK foreign minister Gong Ro Myung suggested bringing US aircraft-carrier battle groups into both the seas around the Korean peninsula. Gong's idea was rejected, but officials in Washington began reconsidering the options for major augmentation of US forces in Korea, such as had been on the table at the White House when Jimmy Carter met Kim Il Sung during the June 1994 crisis. According to a military officer who was involved, some senior administration officials, frustrated by the lack of agreement in April 1995 and angered by Pyongyang's threats, were saying, "Here we go again. There's only one way to play with North Korea, and that's very hard. Send in the troops." One option under active consideration at the Pentagon and in interagency discussions would have dispatched seventy-five thousand additional US troops—roughly double the thirty-seven thousand already stationed in Korea.

Once again, Ambassador Laney and the US commander in Seoul, General Gary Luck, were more reluctant than some of their superiors in Washington to risk the beginning of rapid reinforcement, given that the reaction of the North Korean military was unforeseeable. On April 28, they sent an unsolicited joint message to Secretary of State Christopher and Secretary of Defense Perry, strongly arguing that no emergency was at hand that justified a major augmentation of American forces. "Gen. Luck clearly viewed flowing lots of things as a precursor to war and that could lead to a conflict," said a Washington official familiar with his views. Luck's cabled objections arrived while Joint Chiefs of Staff chairman General John Shalikashvili and senior aides were meeting on the subject. It abruptly halted the drift toward large-scale reinforcement.

Unlike the crisis of the year before, this tension was unknown to the public, but it added salience to the diplomatic effort to resolve the LWR identity issue. The principal effort was negotiations held from May 19 to June 12 between US deputy assistant secretary of state Thomas Hubbard and DPRK vice foreign minister Kim Gye Gwan in Kuala Lumpur, Malaysia. Though nominally between the United States and North Korea, in reality much of the bargaining was on the sidelines between the United States and South Korea, which repeatedly rejected proposals that would permit North Korea to save face.

In the end, Washington persuaded Seoul to accept a sleight-of-hand solution. North Korea formally agreed, at Kuala Lumpur, that the project would consist of "two pressurized light-water reactors with two coolant loops and a generating capacity of approximately 1,000 megawatts each . . . the advanced version of U.S.-origin design and technology currently under production." This description perfectly described the South Korean standard reactors and no others in the world. Without explicitly mentioning South Korea, the agreement stipulated that KEDO, the US-led consortium, would finance and supply the reactors. However, as the accord was announced, the KEDO board, in a coordinated action made known to the North in advance, announced simultaneously in Seoul that the state-run Korean Electric Power Corporation would be the prime contractor for the project and that "Korean standard model reactors" would be provided.

"It is not a document of surrender but a product of diplomatic negotiations," said ROK foreign minister Gong, in defending the outcome of the Kuala Lumpur talks. The North Korean Foreign Ministry issued a statement declaring that "what KEDO does is the internal matter of the United States and we do not feel it necessary to interfere and do not care a bit." With the agreement in Kuala Lumpur, the nuclear crisis, while not over, seemed decisively on its way to resolution.

15

NORTH KOREA
IN CRISIS

WITH THE WANING OF the nuclear struggle, North Korea only briefly left the list of pressing concerns of the major powers. Within months it was back, but this time with an abrupt shift in the angle of vision brought on by the regime's inability to feed its people and its unprecedented appeal for outside help. After dealing with the DPRK almost exclusively as a strong and nightmarish threat to peace, policy makers in Washington and other world capitals began to focus on a failing state whose very weakness was a menace, albeit of a different kind. The question being urgently discussed among the experts was, "Is this the beginning of the end for North Korea?" And if so, how would its neighbors and the world deal with a potential economic collapse, the flight of massive numbers of refugees across land and sea boundaries, and civil war that might spread across tense borders?

General John Shalikashvili, chairman of the Joint Chiefs of Staff, expressed the view of many when he said, "We are now in a period where most who watch the area would say it's either going to implode or explode—we're just not quite sure when that is going to happen." Secretary of Defense William Perry, who had been perhaps the most influential policy maker in the nuclear crisis, popularized the metaphor of North Korea as a disabled airliner rapidly losing altitude, as well as the metaphor of seeking a "soft landing," meaning a gradual unification or accommodation with the South, rather than a destructive crash.

The altered optic with which the great powers viewed the northern half of the Korean peninsula was evidence of how much the world had changed in the quarter century since 1972, when the two Koreas had begun to interact peacefully with each other. South Korea had decisively won the economic race, with enormous consequences in the diplomatic and military fields. Although the North retained a formidable armed force, it was no longer a serious competitor to the South in any other field of endeavor, and the disparity of its resources was swiftly eroding its military competitiveness. Following the death of its Great Leader, it was forced to center its attention and energies on sheer survival and little else—and in so doing to ask the assistance of the outside world. Prideful North Korea sought to deal with this reversal of fortunes with a minimum of humiliation, but it was not easy.

For the outside world, realization that North Korea was in deep trouble began with an act of nature. On the sticky midsummer day of July 26, 1995, rains began to pound the earth, rains that were heavy, steady, and unrelenting and that soon turned into a deluge of biblical proportions. The DPRK Bureau of Hydro-Meteorological Service recorded twenty-three inches of rain in ten days; in some towns and villages, according to the United Nations, as much as eighteen inches of rain fell in a single day, bringing floods that were considered the worst in a century.

North Korea traditionally had said little or nothing about domestic disasters. This time, as the rains ended in mid-August, it broke its silence and described the tragedy in expansive terms, even exaggerating the admittedly severe impact of the flooding. In late August, for the first time in its history, the bastion of self-reliance openly appealed to the world for help, asking the United Nations for nearly $500 million in flood relief as well as fuel and medical assistance. Because the UN agencies and other aid givers had no confidence that aid they sent would reach the country's people, they demanded and obtained access to flood-stricken parts of the North Korean countryside as a condition of providing assistance. Whatever the secretive DPRK military and security forces thought of this trailblazing access to some previously inaccessible areas, they had no other choice than to accept it.

Trevor Page, chief of the newly opened UN World Food Program office in Pyongyang, visited the Korean hinterland late in 1995 and found malnutrition rampant and hungry people nearly everywhere. In an area where much of the country's rice was normally harvested, Page observed "people scavenging in the fields looking for roots and wild plants to prepare soup for their families. People were anxious, restless. They are not getting enough to eat." Farther south near the demilitarized zone, in one of the country's prime food-producing areas, Page found "not a cabbage to be seen" after authorities reduced the already-minimal food ration under the Public Distribution System to the bare subsistence level: a bowl or two of rice or corn per person per day. Even that was uncertain due to frequent supply failures.

Based on a visit to farming areas, cities, and DPRK government agencies in early December, a team of experts from the UN's Food and Agricultural Organization and its World Food Program reported that the floods "were extremely serious and caused extensive damage to agriculture and infrastructure." The experts also reported, however, that "the floods made an already and rapidly deteriorating food supply situation much worse, rather than caused the situation in the first place."

The DPRK had been historically able to till only about one-fifth of its mountainous territory and that usually for only one crop annually, since much of the northern land was frost free only six months of the year. In addition, overuse of chemical fertilizers in pursuit of higher yields, failure to rotate crops, and shortsighted denuding of hillsides that accelerated erosion had all severely affected the country's capacity to grow sufficient food. The country had never been self-sufficient in food, and many outside experts considered it crazy to try, given the climate and small amount of land available for cultivation. Better agricultural techniques and inputs could increase harvests, but there would always be a shortfall to make up through imports.

In the past, Pyongyang had coped with dwindling harvests by importing larger amounts of grain under subsidized terms from its communist allies. Such imports were no longer possible when the Soviet Union collapsed and China, whose domestic consumption was rising in a swiftly growing economy, became a grain importer itself and began demanding hard cash for exports to Pyongyang. Despite its need to make up for massive shortfalls of more than 2 million tons of grain in both 1994 and 1995, North Korea lacked the foreign currency or access to credit to do more than very modest buying on international markets.

Long before the floods began, North Korea had been quietly asking selected countries for help in dealing with its food shortage. In the early 1990s, according to the then director of the ROK intelligence agency, Suh Dong Kwon, the North requested 500,000 tons of rice from the South on condition that it be supplied secretly. The idea was dropped after Seoul responded that in its increasingly open society, it would be impossible to hide the rice shipments to the North. After a skimpy harvest in 1992, the regime began to propagandize to the public "Let's Eat Two Meals a Day," a program of austerity. Later, during the 1994 Geneva negotiations with the United States, DPRK officials had spoken with urgency of their severe food problems, but the US team was so fixed on nuclear issues that the comments made little impression.

A more extensive effort began in January 1995, when Pyongyang appealed to Japan and South Korea for emergency food. Japan agreed to supply 500,000 tons. On June 21, after semiofficial North-South talks on the issue were held in Beijing, the ROK government announced it would donate 150,000 tons of rice to the North in unmarked bags "in a spirit of reconciliation and cooperation." Although after Kim Il Sung's death he wavered between wanting to bring the North down and seeking an accommodation, this time President Kim Young Sam enthusiastically declared that the government would purchase the grain on international markets if domestic stocks were insufficient, telling the Blue House press corps that the rice would build trust with the North. In a grand gesture, Kim sent his popular prime minister, Lee Hong Koo, to the port to see off the first rice ships.

Within a few days, events turned this enthusiasm into anger, laying the basis for an abrupt policy reversal. First, a DPRK local official, apparently without central authorization, required a South Korean rice ship to fly a North Korean flag as it entered port on June 27. Although the North promptly apologized, the ROK government demanded a more formal apology and suspended rice shipments until it was received. The incident infuriated the public in the South, as did a later incident in which a sailor on a South Korean rice ship was arrested, also on a local security official's initiative, for taking photographs of a North Korean port. The sailor was quickly released, but the damage had been done.

Another key event was the dramatic losses by Kim Young Sam's ruling party in the June 27 nationwide elections for local offices—the first such elections since the military coup of 1961. It was widely perceived that Kim had been manipulating the rice aid for political gain before the vote and that his strategy had backfired. A political consultant told officials of the ruling party that anger at the aid package and at North Korean ingratitude cost the ruling party a million votes. Although the ROK government eventually provided the undelivered portion of the 150,000 tons, the election results led to a sharp reversal in Kim Young Sam's posture.

As was evident in the nuclear negotiations, Kim had long been ambivalent about the North. A prominent South Korean told me, "I had the feeling from early in his administration, based on several private talks, that [the president] felt it was his destiny to bring about the collapse of North Korea on his watch, and be the man who made history by reunification of the country. He seemed to feel that if he pressed them hard, they'd give way." Ambassador James Laney, who dealt with him frequently, said Kim was a man divided in his own mind: "His more rational side says the collapse of North Korea would be a disaster, and he tells us all the things he's doing or is willing to do to cooperate with North Korea. On the other hand, his emotional side wants North Korea to collapse on his watch, so he can be the first to preside over a united Korea."

Kim's estimate of the situation in the North was repeatedly in flux. In July 1995, according to a State Department official, Kim told President Clinton, "I think [the North Koreans] are going down the tubes, and we should seek a gradual change" north of the thirty-eighth parallel. Four months later, after the flood, Kim told Vice President Gore in a bilateral meeting in Osaka, Japan, "There's no possibility of a soft landing. There's going to be a crash."

In early-January 1996, Kim spoke out publicly against providing additional food aid for the North, declaring in his New Year policy speech that "it is a crime and a betrayal of the Korean people for North Korea to hope to receive aid from the international community while pouring all its natural resources into maintaining its military power." A senior aide to Kim, whom I saw shortly after the policy speech, made little effort to disguise the essentially domestic political nature of the president's turnabout, predicting that he would continue his hard line at least until after the National Assembly elections scheduled for April.

In the meantime, not only was the government unresponsive to UN and humanitarian appeals for food; it also sought to dissuade others from providing aid. In a Honolulu meeting with the United States and Japan in late January, Seoul officials argued disingenuously that North Korea's plight was not so serious, and that in any case Pyongyang should be pressured to resume the formal North-South dialogue as a condition of obtaining more food. A week after the meetings ended, however, Washington announced a $2 million contribution to the UN's emergency appeal without conditions. Whatever Seoul's feelings, it was at that time a tenet of US policy to respond to UN humanitarian appeals, no matter the recipient.

Before the American contribution was announced, North Korean officials had been disheartened by the tepid response to the initial UN appeal. Washington's action, however, opened the way for additional contributions from governments and private groups. On March 29, the DPRK ambassador in Geneva informed UN agencies of North Korea's "urgent need" for additional food and requested a second UN appeal on its behalf.

In this context, it was hard to understand that only a week later, North Korea announced it would no longer accept the duties and limitations of the Korean War armistice and sent 130 soldiers armed with AK-47 automatic rifles, light machine guns, and antitank recoilless rifles into the Joint Security Area at Panmunjom, in deliberate violation of the armistice. Under the agreement that had been generally observed for four decades, each side was limited to thirty enlisted men and five officers armed only with pistols. After two hours, the troops withdrew, but twice as many returned the next night in a further demonstration. After a third night of armistice violations, amid intense international nervousness and widespread condemnation, the demonstrations subsided.

Well before the DMZ incursions, intelligence analysts in Washington and Seoul had been closely watching the growing clout of the KPA in Pyongyang. Since succeeding his father in July 1994, most of Kim Jong Il's public appearances had been visits to military units, in his capacity as supreme commander of the armed forces. Moreover, since Kim Il Sung's death, high-ranking military officers had been elevated in the hierarchy of North Korean officialdom. A large-scale military parade was staged for the anniversary of the founding of the Workers Party, an event that had previously been of a nonmilitary character; the newly appointed defense minister, Choe Kwang, made the keynote address. At the same time, however, Kim Jong Il seemed to have held the military in check on key policy issues involving the United States, overruling military objections in negotiating the Agreed Framework to halt the nuclear activities at Yongbyon and again in releasing American helicopter pilot Bobby Hall.

Equally curious were two unpublicized developments late in 1995. In the early fall, the Korean People's Army Sixth Corps, in the northeastern part of the country, was disbanded, its leadership purged, and its units submerged into others, under circumstances suggesting disarray in the ranks. Moreover, in early December the KPA suddenly halted its annual winter military maneuvers two months before their normal conclusion and embarked on new ideological education instead. This appeared to reflect a scarcity of resources even for top-priority military missions as well as problems of indoctrination and discipline.

During my trip to Pyongyang in early 1995, North Korean officials had spoken repeatedly of their long-standing dissatisfaction with the Korean War armistice and of their proposal to replace it with a US-DPRK "peace insuring system." Our delegation had been warned, as had others, that "unilateral steps" would be taken if there were no movement toward negotiations on the issue—and there had been no movement.

The greatest mystery in April 1995 was not what the KPA forces had done in the DMZ—clearly a demonstration that was intended to call attention to their demands—but how Pyongyang's leaders had calculated or tolerated the strange timing. Coming just as the DPRK government was appealing to the world anew for urgently needed food, the military actions made it more difficult to obtain. In another anomaly of timing, the incursions came less than a week before a new set of nationwide elections in South Korea, this time for seats in the National Assembly. The ruling party, which had been expected to do poorly because of the growing unpopularity of President Kim, did much better than expected, due in part to public alarm over the DMZ incursions, which were heavily covered by South Korean media. Political experts in Seoul said that Kim's party probably won twenty to thirty seats as a result of the DMZ incidents—a crucial margin in assuring Kim legislative control. Twenty-eight percent of those questioned in a postelection poll said the incursions influenced their vote in favor of the ruling party.

The damaging lack of coordination of economic, political, and military objectives in the DMZ incursions was important evidence of Kim Jong Il's governing style. According to a South Korean intelligence official, the reclusive leader was "governing by memorandum," accepting separate reports, and making separate decisions in connection with the various functional groups constituting the North Korean party and governmental apparatus. Unlike his father, Kim Jong Il was reported to have little taste for official meetings at which a more coherent policy could have been thrashed out. With the death of Kim Il Sung, according to Adrian Buzo, an Australian academic and former diplomat, a transfer of power had taken place from an individual to a system. And the system was not working.

POLITICAL EARTHQUAKE IN SEOUL

High school ties are cherished in South Korea, and high school alumni meetings are important celebrations. Such a meeting, in the Crystal Ballroom of the Lotte Hotel, on October 16, 1995, was the occasion for an unplanned encounter that touched off an earthshaking political scandal, uncovering a system of payoffs that had undergirded South Korean politics for decades. The political earthquake made the ROK's democracy more responsive to public opinion and thereby less controllable by the central government, affecting and often complicating the government's dealings with the United States and with the North.

One of the celebrants at the school reunion, a businessman named Ha Chong Uk, was desperately worried about a problem involving money and politics, and he approached a fellow alumnus, Park Kye Dong, with his predicament. Park was a National Assemblyman, and Ha hoped he could get some big shots in government to fix his problem.

The problem dated from February 1993, as President Roh Tae Woo was leaving office. Ha, in a small family business with his father as brokers for shipping companies, received a strange request from the local branch of the Shinhan Bank, where his firm did business. The bank manager asked permission to deposit 11 billion won (about $14 million) of someone else's money in an account using the father's name. Because of favors owed to the bank, Ha agreed. There things remained until, in August 1993, in one of the most important of his domestic reforms, President Kim Young Sam decreed a "real name" bank-deposit system, under which fictitious or borrowed names on bank accounts could no longer be used to hide or launder money for illegal political purposes or other shady dealings. The next step was a new tax system, to begin in January 1996, when taxes would be assessed on interest earned from all bank accounts.

At that point, businessman Ha had a serious problem. He had learned that the money deposited under his father's name actually belonged to former president Roh—yet his father would soon be liable for paying nearly $1 million in taxes on the accumulated interest. He couldn't pay it, and even if the money to pay the taxes magically appeared, Ha feared a tax audit—and the need to explain how a small businessman had obtained so much money. Moreover, he learned that his father's account was one of three borrowed-name accounts at the same bank branch hiding money belonging to the former president.

Assemblyman Park, a member of the opposition Democratic Party, had long opposed the pervasive influence of illegal money in Korean politics. His indignation had been rekindled two months earlier when a government minister had told reporters that a former—unnamed—president had hidden 400 billion won ($500 million) in accounts at city banks, only to be fired for his indiscretion. Park got from Ha a statement of the status of the account, but instead of taking it to be "fixed," he rose on the floor of the National Assembly and delivered a bombshell accusation. Roh, he declared, had deposited the equivalent of $500 million in city banks around the time he left office, with 30 billion won ($37 million) deposited in the bank branch where Ha had his account. He then produced Ha's bank documents as evidence.

The day the furor broke out, Roh Tae Woo's longtime chief bodyguard and his last intelligence agency director, Lee Hyun Woo, hurried to see the former president at his home in Seoul. Lee informed his boss that the money being discussed in the National Assembly indeed belonged to Roh—part of the funds that Lee had been managing since the two men had left government. Roh instructed Lee to report the facts to prosecutors but before doing so to destroy the account books containing the details of the contributors.

Eight days after the revelation in the National Assembly, via television from his home, Roh addressed the nation. The former president announced that while in office he had amassed a "governing fund" of 500 billion won ($625 million), an even more stupefying total than had been rumored, and that he had left office with 170 billion won ($212 million) of the money. (The amount was soon corrected to 185 billion won.)

Saying that raising and using such funds was "an old political practice," Roh declared it to be wrong and said, "I will wholeheartedly accept any kind of punishment you hand out to me." Roh said he hoped that nobody else, including the entrepreneurs who contributed the funds, would be hurt because of his misdeeds. Wiping tears from his eyes, he ended the broadcast by saying, "I have no other words to say as a man who has deeply hurt the pride of the nation. At this moment, I feel deeply ashamed of being a former president. I offer my apology again."

The gigantic size of the funds involved as well as Roh's retention of massive wealth after leaving office shocked the public. His admissions were in startling contrast to his declarations of the late 1980s to create "a great era of ordinary people" after coming into office a hero for submitting to election by popular vote. Korean newspapers recalled that in his first presidential press conference, Roh had pledged to eliminate all forms of corruption and "to be recorded in history as a faithful and honest president."

His declared assets on assuming the presidency had been about 500 million won ($625,000), one-thousandth of the slush fund he admitted to raising in office. Several weeks after his mea culpa statement, a public opinion poll in Seoul identified Roh as "the most loathsome politician" in the country by an overwhelming margin.

The same day as Roh's revelations, opposition leader Kim Dae Jung announced that he had secretly accepted 2 billion won ($2.5 million) from Roh as a gift during the 1992 presidential campaign. This admission tarnished Kim's reformist image, but also raised immediate questions about how much money had gone to incumbent President Kim Young Sam, who had been the candidate of Roh's ruling party in the 1992 race. In making his startling admission, Kim Dae Jung charged that the incumbent president had received much more than he, "hundreds of billions of won," for his well-heeled race. President Kim denied receiving any money personally, but he did not deny that his ruling-party campaign might have received funds from Roh, in amounts that were not established or announced.

Roh was summoned by the prosecutors on November 15 and jailed on corruption charges the following day. Prosecutors soon extended their investigation to his predecessor Chun, who refused to cooperate and, like Roh, destroyed the account books of his contributors. According to prosecutors, Chun collected 950 billion won ($1.8 billion) in slush funds—nearly twice as much as Roh—and left office with 212 billion won ($265 million). Chun later claimed in court that as president, he gave 197 billion won to Roh for his 1987 election campaign. An aide testified he and the wives of both men were present when Chun personally handed over much of the money.

In their investigation, prosecutors discovered hundreds of stacks of 10,000-won notes belonging to Chun, totaling 6.1 billion won, stuffed into twenty-five apple boxes in the cement warehouse of the Ssangyong group, a Seoul conglomerate. Photographs of this mother lode of currency, appearing prominently in Korean media, disgusted the public.

Almost all the funds had come from leaders of Korea's big enterprises. The executives had been called to meetings with Roh on a regular basis and were expected to bring money. They insisted the payments were simply the cost of doing business in Korea, where presidents and their administrations were all-powerful arbiters of tax policy, loan funds, public contracts, and much more.

Furthermore, they all knew what had happened to the Kukje group, which had been one of South Korea's largest conglomerates in the early 1980s. The Kukje chairman recalled how then-president Chun suggested he give $2.6 million to one of the first lady's favorite charities. After the businessman declined, his bank credit was cut off at Blue House orders,

and the finance minister announced that Kukje was being dissolved because of insufficient financial backing—all of which quickly led to the
firm's bankruptcy. Few tycoons were ready to risk such treatment.

In one of the rare specific revelations prior to the 1995 scandal, when
Hyundai group founder Chung Ju Yung visited Washington in September
1992 as a maverick presidential candidate, he told me and other *Washington Post* editors and reporters that Roh was even more corrupt than Chun
Doo Hwan had been. I found this hard to believe at the time and, to my
regret, did not report this remark in my story on the meeting or press the
industrialist for details.

As the furor following Roh's arrest continued, and with his own 1992
campaign suspected of accepting Roh's money, President Kim Young Sam
came under pressure for stronger action. Earlier, Kim had taken the position that the December 12, 1979, military-backed takeover by Chun and
Roh and the May 1980 killing of civilians in Kwangju did not warrant
prosecution but should be left to "the judgment of history." After the scandal broke, Kim abruptly reversed his stand, and a special law authorizing
legal action against those responsible for both incidents sailed through the
National Assembly.

Even before passage of the law, Chun was arrested and jailed when he
defiantly refused a summons from the prosecutors to appear for questioning. Chun's lawyers argued that his arrest was unconstitutional because
the constitution forbade retroactive statutes. Five of the nine members
of the Constitutional Court agreed, but the legal action stood because six
justices were required to overturn a statute.

From March until August 1996, the Korean public watched a regular
spectacle of the two former presidents being taken before the court from
their cells in loose-fitting prison uniforms and rubber shoes to respond to
charges of bribery, insurrection, and treason. Prisoner number 1042, former president Roh, adjusted quickly to prison life, continuing to express
remorse and apologies but shedding little new light on matters. Prisoner
number 3124, former president Chun, was defiant. Shortly after his arrest,
he had protested by going on a hunger strike—an ironic counterpoint to
a hunger strike against Chun by then–opposition leader Kim Young Sam
in 1983—and persistently challenged the court's right to put him on trial
for long-ago events.

On August 26, both former presidents were found guilty by the three-
judge court. Chun was sentenced to death. He flinched on hearing the
judgment before quickly regaining his composure. The court noted Chun's
argument that while president he had contributed to the stabilizing of the
economy and turned over power to his successor by peaceful means, but
it said these acts could not offset his serious crimes. Roh was sentenced
to twenty-two and a half years in prison, rather than life imprisonment as

requested by the prosecutors. The court said it took into account Roh's "achievements in northern diplomacy and the nation's admission into the United Nations," as well as the fact that he had been popularly elected in 1987.

The other defendants—former officials, businessmen, and fourteen retired military officers, eight of whom had left the service with four stars—received lesser sentences. Many of the former generals were taken to jail cells from the courtroom to begin their prison time, but all the business leaders were released pending appeal or given suspended sentences on the grounds that the nation continued to need their best efforts.

As they stood before the court to hear the announcement of their sentences, Chun and Roh, two old friends and military academy classmates who had become estranged after one succeeded the other in the presidency, linked their fingers in a public gesture of solidarity.

On December 16, 1996, the Seoul High Court commuted Chun's sentence to life imprisonment and reduced Roh's to seventeen years. The court also reduced the sentences of all the other military and civilian defendants. It acquitted two of the *chaebol* leaders who had been convicted earlier and suspended the sentences of the other big businessmen. Under the ruling, none of the tycoons who contributed the funds were sent to jail.

A year later, in the Christmas season of 1997, President Kim Young Sam pardoned Chun and Roh, who returned quietly to private life.

SUMMIT DIPLOMACY AND
THE FOUR-PARTY PROPOSAL

As had been the case with the last three South Korean leaders, summit diplomacy with the American president was important to the domestic standing of President Kim Young Sam, a fact that contributed to Washington's leverage in South Korea. In the summer of 1995 and the spring of 1996, the United States sought to use this leverage on North-South issues. Its efforts had mixed success.

President Kim was planning a visit to the US capital in July 1995 to participate in the dedication of a monument on the Washington Mall to American veterans of the Korean War. Although President Clinton had visited Kim for two days in July 1993 and had hosted him in a three-day official visit in November 1993, including the Clintons' first big White House dinner for a foreign guest, Kim was eager to turn the mid-1995 trip into an important visit with even more protocol honors. The US administration told Kim this could be done only if there was a substantive move toward accommodation or peace on the divided peninsula to justify a further allocation of Clinton's time and attention.

In response, the ROK Foreign Ministry devised a "two plus two" formula, whereby the two Koreas would negotiate a permanent peace treaty to replace the Korean War armistice, with the United States and China acting as facilitators and eventual guarantors. The State Department welcomed the proposal as a step in the right direction if it were serious and well prepared, and if Washington were kept informed of what was happening.

The "two plus two" proposal, while still confidential, was enough to obtain the recognition Kim wanted. He was granted a four-day state visit with full honors, including an address to a joint session of Congress. In a conversation at the White House during the visit in late July, Kim looked Clinton in the eye and told him, "We are going to do this on August 15," the fiftieth anniversary of Korea's liberation from Japan and a day for important pronouncements in Seoul. Kim's aides leaked the proposal to the South Korean press, and the ROK president himself said in an interview with CNN that he planned to make "a refreshing and important initiative towards North Korea" on Liberation Day. Based on Kim's assurance, Secretary of State Warren Christopher took up the proposal with Chinese foreign minister Qian Qichen in a bilateral meeting in Brunei.

After returning to Seoul, however, Kim executed another of his sudden reversals in the face of the conservative political tide following North Korea's interference with ROK ships delivering rice to DPRK ports. Without consultation with or notification of the United States, Kim scuttled the initiative he had proposed to Clinton. American diplomats were not pleased.

In the spring of 1996, summit diplomacy reappeared when Clinton planned a state visit to Japan. At this point the US administration was increasingly apprehensive about the reports of privation and instability in North Korea and unhappy with Kim's inconsistent and, lately, unresponsive policies. Although American presidents usually stopped in Korea when visiting Japan, Clinton was not inclined to do so this time. Considering Clinton's earlier visit to Seoul and Kim's two visits to Washington, "we thought we'd done enough" for Kim, said an administration official who was involved in the internal discussions. No stop in Korea was planned.

Kim, however, had different ideas. Clinton's schedule would bring him to Japan on April 16, just five days after the nationwide National Assembly elections in Korea that would have a crucial bearing on Kim's authority in his last two years in office. For it to be known in the campaign period that Clinton would visit Japan but bypass Korea would suggest low regard for Kim; indeed, there were reports in Seoul that the president's longtime rival, opposition leader Kim Dae Jung, was preparing to make the omission an issue. The ROK president was desperate to persuade Clinton to change his mind.

In a repeat of the previous year's discussions, Ambassador Laney, who was gravely concerned about the lack of movement in North-South diplomacy, told the Blue House that Clinton could spare the time for a visit only if a serious peace initiative were to come out of it. Talks between Clinton's national security adviser, Anthony Lake, and his Korean counterpart, Yoo Chong Ha, produced agreement in principle for the two presidents to undertake and announce such an initiative. The details were worked out in person during a trip by Lake to Cheju-do, where he was very well received by Yoo and his deputy, Yu Myung-hwan, and by long distance, in great secrecy, using the telephone instead of cables to bypass the established bureaucracy and other potential sources of leaks.

Kim got his meeting at 5:50 A.M. on April 16, 1996, when Air Force One touched down at Cheju Island, off the southern end of the Korean peninsula. Five days earlier, Kim's party had won a commanding position in the National Assembly elections, due in part to the curiously timed North Korean military incursions in the DMZ. After taking an early-morning walk through a garden of bright-yellow flowers, Clinton and Kim settled down to discussions in the same hotel suite where Presidents Roh Tae Woo and Mikhail Gorbachev had met in April 1991.

In a prearranged declaration that had already been presented informally to North Korea, China, Japan, and Russia, Clinton and Kim proposed a four-party conference of the two Koreas, the United States, and China "to initiate a process aimed at achieving a permanent peace agreement" on the Korean peninsula. In a significant difference from the still-born initiative of the previous year, this was a joint US-ROK proposal rather than an ROK proposal backed by the United States.

Announcing the proposal in a press conference before flying on to Japan, Clinton cautioned against expecting an immediate and positive response from the North: "What is important is to put the offer out there and let it stand and be patient." Clinton and Kim were heartened when Pyongyang did not immediately reject the proposal. Chinese president Jiang Zemin, in a letter to Kim a few days after the Cheju announcement, expressed Chinese support for the four-power talks.

There were only two problems. Pyongyang seemed confused as to why Washington would put a major new initiative on the table when the US-DPRK Agreed Framework was still finding its footing, and the North Koreans did not want Chinese participation in matters they considered to be none of Beijing's business. At the same time, Pyongyang could see that Washington had put some weight behind the proposal—President Clinton had personally announced it—and so rejecting it out of hand was impossible.

Furthermore, the country was on the very edge of famine. The food situation in the winter of 1996 had been extremely bad, and it would only get worse in the summer months before the next harvest. In mid-May the UN World Food Program issued a special alert on North Korea, warning that "the food supply situation has deteriorated more seriously than had been anticipated." The UN agency reported that the DPRK government had reduced rations under its public distribution program to 300 grams (10.5 ounces) of grain per person per day, about 1,000 calories. The UN minimum standard for refugees was 1,900 calories per day.

Diplomatic discussions with the United States, which had revolved around the nuclear issue and political relations in the previous three years, were increasingly dominated in the spring of 1996 by North Korea's urgent need for food. Calling on Deputy Assistant Secretary of State Thomas Hubbard, the State Department's senior point man on Korea following the reassignment of Robert Gallucci to other duties, North Korea's external economic chief, Kim Jong U, offered a frank swap of ballistic missiles exports and food. Kim said the North could either sell missiles to Middle Eastern countries to obtain money and food, as it had formerly done to American disapproval, or it could accept food from the United States to forgo those sales. Another high-ranking DPRK caller on Hubbard that spring, Ri Jong Hyok, pushed hard for additional food aid, warning bluntly that "revolutions are made by hungry people."

Meeting in Jakarta, Indonesia, on July 24, Secretary of State Christopher and his South Korean and Japanese counterparts formally agreed to supply additional food aid and ease some American economic sanctions if North Korea would participate in a joint US-ROK briefing on the four-party peace plan. The same day, the skies over Northeast Asia darkened again, and the heavens opened up with new torrential downpours, three to five times the normal abundant rainfall of that time of year. While the resultant flooding was not as serious as that of the year before, this time it struck more of the country's principal food-producing areas. Once more the forces of nature, compounding the failure of the *juche* system, had dealt North Korea a painful blow.

THE SUBMARINE INCURSION

A few minutes after midnight on the morning of September 18, 1996, a taxi driver speeding along a seaside road near Kangnung, on the east coast of South Korea, noticed a group of men crouched near the highway. Suspicious, the cabbie returned to the area after dropping off his passenger and spotted a large object, which he thought at first to be a giant dolphin, in the water near the beach. On second look, it appeared to be a man-made object. Certain that it wasn't a fishing boat, he reported it to the local police.

Within hours, ROK troops and police identified the object as a thirty-seven-yard-long North Korean submarine of the Shark class that had run aground on the rocky coast and been abandoned. Before dawn that morning, the Defense Ministry was mobilizing forty thousand troops, helicopter gunships, and sniffer dogs in a massive search for an unknown number of intruders from the North.

In midafternoon, on a mountain three miles from the landing site, an army squad reportedly came across a grisly scene: eleven bodies of the North Koreans, all crewmen unequipped for serious infiltration, all executed with bullets to the back of the head. There were no signs of a struggle; one of the dead, an officer on the sub, was armed with a pistol still in its holster. It appeared likely that, in line with standing orders, the eleven had accepted death at the hands of one of their colleagues rather than be captured.

About the same time, local police in a nearby area, acting on a tip from a villager, arrested Lee Kwang Su, a North Korean infiltrator from the sub, in a farmer's field. Lee, who was the only occupant of the submarine to be taken alive, said the personnel of the submarine belonged to the North Korean military's Reconnaissance Bureau, charged with the collection of tactical and strategic intelligence on US and ROK forces. The sub's mission was to test ROK defenses and reconnoiter an ROK air base and radar facility near Kangnung.

Despite the near-hysterical reaction in Seoul, there were probably only three real infiltrators, trained and equipped for the mission. Another three were part of the escort party to get the main group ashore. The rest were crew members who were never supposed to have landed in the South. In the ROK manhunt over the next two weeks, eleven North Koreans, only a few of whom were armed, were killed. Two more, from the original highly-trained three-man infiltration squad, held out for forty-eight days before being pinned down and killed in a final firefight near the eastern end of the DMZ. The organizational discipline and fighting skills of the ROK forces had not been impressive, and the Defense Ministry was relieved to end the search and return to normal operations. The deaths of fourteen South Koreans—four civilians, eight military personnel, and two policemen—were attributed to the infiltrators, although several were actually victims of friendly fire.

South Korea, with dense vegetation close to the peninsula-spanning DMZ and fifteen hundred miles of irregular coastline dotted with offshore islands, is highly vulnerable to infiltration. North Korea has penetrated the South's defenses on many occasions. In the 1970s, as noted in Chapter 4, Kim Il Sung had boasted that his military reconnaissance teams kept American maneuvers in the South under surveillance, and the US Command had concluded that the North could infiltrate and exfiltrate its agents or special warfare units to virtually anywhere in the ROK virtually at will. By the mid-1990s, only modest gains against these operations had been accomplished.

What made the September 1996 incursion different from those of the past was the context. For the first time, Washington found itself positioned between the two Koreas, with important interests on both sides. On the one hand, it was seeking to protect its new relationship with North Korea and especially to keep the freeze of the DPRK nuclear program won through the Agreed Framework. On the other hand, it was still committed to maintaining solidarity with its ally in the South and protecting the security of ROK territory and US troops. The ROK, which had received unqualified US backing in military disputes in the past, was disappointed and angered by the altered American posture, all the more so because policy toward the North—once a taboo subject—had become a central political issue in Seoul.

After alternating for months between taking a hard line against the North, calculated to bring about its early collapse, and backing an accommodation to bring about a "soft landing," Kim Young Sam shifted powerfully to the hard side. He declared on September 20 that "this is an armed provocation, not a simple repeat of infiltration of agents of the past," and began almost daily condemnations of the North, eventually declaring that any further provocation against the South—which he said was likely—would bring a "real possibility of war." Announcing that his government was reconsidering its entire northern policy, Kim suspended inter-Korean economic cooperation and halted ROK activities in KEDO, which was charged with providing the light-water reactors under the 1994 Agreed Framework. In an interview with Kevin Sullivan of the *Washington Post* in early November, Kim said he would not proceed with the four-party peace proposal or provide aid to the DPRK until its leaders apologized for the submarine incursion.

North Korea initially issued a remarkably gauzy statement that "as far as a competent organ of the Ministry of the People's Armed Forces knows," the submarine encountered engine trouble and drifted south, leaving its crew "with no other choice but to get to the enemy side's land, which might cause an armed conflict." As the clash over the incursion deepened, however, the North's rhetoric hardened into threats of retaliation "a hundred or a thousand fold" against the killing of its personnel. When the activities of KEDO were halted by ROK objections, Pyongyang publicly threatened to abandon the Agreed Framework and resume its nuclear program at Yongbyon.

In diplomatic meetings, North Korea notified the United States that it was ready to express regret about the submarine incident and to accept a US-ROK briefing on the proposed four-power peace talks, but it insisted on a package of economic benefits in return. A package deal including the briefing arrangement had been extensively discussed in US-DPRK talks in May and June 1996 and virtually agreed to at the end of August, during a visit to the United States by North Korean diplomat Ri Gun, deputy director of American affairs of the DPRK Foreign Ministry. Representative Bill Richardson, who had taken it on himself to become a political-level emissary to North Korea, was heading to Pyongyang on his third trip, ready to conclude the arrangements, when news of the submarine incursion arrived. His trip was canceled.

Immediately after the incursion, South Koreans were angered by an off-the-cuff comment by Secretary of State Christopher that "all parties" should avoid further provocative steps, a statement that seemed to put the United States equidistant from both the antagonists. The State Department made corrective statements, but the damage had been done. A senior ROK official telephoned Daryl Plunk, a Korea expert at the conservative Heritage Foundation, to say that the highest levels of his government found the Clinton administration's response to the incursion "shameful" and its policies to be "appeasement" of the North.

As hard feelings festered and deepened, American civilian officials in Seoul became alarmed by the gap in thinking between themselves and their allies. In a symbol of the new mood, ROK officers were reluctant to permit a US defense attaché to inspect the North Korean submarine and then, after relenting, subjected him to a body search when leaving the sub. The US Embassy protested. In Washington analysts looked skeptically at Seoul's reports on its findings.

More ominously, the Korean-language *Joong-ang Daily News* reported in mid-October that ROK forces had selected twelve strategic targets in the North for air, naval, and ground retaliation in case of further provocations. The report shocked the US Command, which had theoretical "operational control" of the ROK military in wartime but had heard nothing of these attack plans until publication of the newspaper report. Although ROK defense officials denied that the plans represented serious policy making, the Americans were unable to get what they considered satisfactory assurances that ROK forces would not launch retaliatory military action against the North without US consultation and consent. The issue was quietly taken up in numerous senior-level US-ROK discussions—military, diplomatic, and intelligence—all without clear resolution.

Adding to the American concern, in early November, was Kim Young Sam's abrupt ouster of foreign minister Gong, amid reports that he had expressed reservations about the president's hard line against the North. Gong's resignation was officially attributed to health reasons, but Korean and American officials close to him believed that the precipitating factor was a dossier of remarks reportedly provided to Kim by the NSP, the ROK intelligence agency. In these remarks, believed to have been gathered through telephone taps, Gong expressed personal differences with the president's policy in the aftermath of the submarine incursion. (Another former foreign minister told me he had been cautioned by aides when taking his job that he should assume his telephone conversations were tapped.) Gong was replaced as foreign minister by Yoo Chong Ha, Kim's Blue House assistant for national security, who was considered much more conservative and more independent of US policies than any of his recent predecessors.

In mid-November, with these cross-currents flowing just beneath the surface of the nominally close alliance, *New York Times* correspondent Nicholas Kristof visited Seoul and summarized the consequences of the submarine incursion as "a surge of tension; fears of further military provocations or even war; stalling of the engagement process; a growing number of hungry North Korean peasants who can count on little international help; and a reminder that it is hard to find a place more dangerous and unpredictable than the Korean peninsula." ROK officials did not disagree with that analysis, but they were infuriated by Kristof's further observation that due to a newly created rift between the two allies, "some U.S. officials seem to feel that their biggest headache on the peninsula is the government in the South, not the North." As I learned from conversations in Washington and Seoul, Kristof was on the mark.

North-South relations and US-ROK relations were still tense when President Clinton met President Kim Young Sam on the occasion of the summit of the Asia Pacific Economic Cooperation forum in Manila on November 24. As a result of negotiations before the meeting, the two sides agreed on a three-paragraph statement that avoided the word *apology*, which Kim Young Sam had been demanding, but that called on the North "to take acceptable steps" to resolve the submarine incident, reduce tension, and avoid provocations in the future. Three days after the meeting, however, in the face of criticism that he had given in to Clinton, Kim reverted to his demand for a full-scale apology.

The most important exchange of the meeting took place in a private conversation between Clinton and Kim in a corner away from most of their aides. Clinton bluntly sought to obtain an ironclad commitment that South Korean forces would not initiate military action against the North without American consent. A senior ROK official who participated in the summit told me he believed Clinton had been reassured by Kim's remarks, but an American official said Kim's reaction had still left room for doubt.

Three months later, after Clinton began a new presidential term with a new foreign-policy team, Kim moved preemptively to resolve the issue. During his first meeting with Madeleine Albright in late February, Kim began by volunteering that the new secretary of state could be assured that no South Korean military action would be undertaken without full coordination with the United States. Albright crossed it off her list of issues to discuss. General John Tilelli, the US military commander in South Korea, said later he was completely satisfied there would be no unilateral military action on the part of ROK forces. Nevertheless, the top-level exchanges over the issue demonstrated how strained and mistrustful US relations with South Korea had become.

In the wake of the Manila meeting of Clinton and Kim, the United States renewed its efforts to obtain a settlement of the submarine issue. Mark Minton, the State Department country director for Korea, met North Korea's director general of American affairs, Lee Hyong Chol, in New York on nine separate days in December to hammer out a multifaceted accord, including US insistence that the North issue an authoritative-level statement of regret and transmit it not once but twice via the official Korean Central News Agency (KCNA).

On December 29, North Korea issued a statement of "deep regret" for the submarine incursion and a pledge that "such an incident will not recur." Pyongyang also agreed to attend the long-offered joint US-ROK briefing on the four-power peace talks. As part of a package accord, Washington agreed to resume the supply of heavy fuel oil, and Seoul removed its objections to continued work on the light-water nuclear reactors promised under the 1994 Agreed Framework. North Korea, in turn, permitted work to resume on preserving the fuel rods that had been unloaded from the Yongbyon reactor. In a last-minute accord arranged by the United States, South Korea agreed to return the remains of the North Korean personnel killed in the submarine incursion. When the transfer took place at Panmunjom, DPRK officials were shocked to find that they received only cremated ashes. US officers believed the bodies were too riddled with bullets to be presentable.

Diplomatic delegations from the United States and the two Koreas met in New York in March 1997 for the "joint briefing" on the four-party proposal, the first such meeting about peace on the peninsula ever held among these three parties. That was followed by several preparatory meetings at Columbia University. North Korean officials—who already knew the answer—asked the Americans why the Chinese were there. Once the preparatory work was out of the way, higher-level diplomats from the four nations met in Geneva in December 1997 to officially begin the four-party peace talks. Altogether, there were six four-party meetings held in Geneva, the last in August 1999. Procedurally awkward, and held at a time when inter-Korean relations were at their nadir, when the North Koreans could barely focus on long-term issues because of the pressing problem of the famine, and when the Chinese were still very tentative in their participation in a multiparty setting that included the two Koreas, the talks accomplished nothing. The Swiss were gracious hosts throughout, but in the end one participant observed that the croissants seemed to get smaller as the meetings bogged down.

NORTH KOREA'S STEEP DECLINE

By the winter of 1996, most observers who were following the situation
in North Korea had watched the progressive sinking of the economy for
many months and had become inured to the adverse trends. Portents of
disaster and predictions of impending collapse had become commonplace,
yet the North's ability to absorb external and internal reverses had been
demonstrated time after time as it accepted the loss of its allies, the death
of its founding leader, and the increasingly steep decline in its standard
of living. Thus, it seemed possible to assume, in the face of all logic, that
the country could continue indefinitely on its downward slope without
experiencing a crisis.

Reports from travelers to North Korea, however, suggested this could
hardly be the case. In fact, a principal debate among American government analysts was whether the DPRK economy was collapsing or had
already collapsed. Deteriorating or flooded coal mines and reduced petroleum imports produced insufficient energy for industry, so many factories
had closed or were operating at only a fraction of their previous output.
Fuel was so scarce in some provincial cities that only oxcarts and bicycles
could be seen on the streets. Many office buildings and dwellings, even in
the much-favored capital, were unheated during large portions of a very
cold winter. Electrical blackouts were commonplace. Even the state television station was off the air for long periods of time due to lack of power.
Many trains, some of them coal fired and others powered by electricity,
were idle. An American intelligence official who in the past had been
sanguine about North Korea's prospects compared its plight to that of a
terminally ill patient, whose physical systems were weakening one after
another, with each expiring organ reducing the performance of the others.

A drop in fertilizer production had diminished agricultural yields in
the autumn 1996 harvest, adding to the serious shortages caused by flooding. In many cases, crops that had been harvested could not be moved to
where they were needed due to lack of transport, and more was lost to rain
and rats. The meager public distribution of food in the countryside, which
averaged three hundred grams per day earlier in the year, was cut back
to half or less, barely enough to sustain life, or had stopped completely.
To survive, North Koreans were consuming oak leaves, grasses, roots, tree
bark, and other nonstandard foods, many with little nutritive value, and
buying or bartering food, clothing, and fuel at markets that had sprung up
in many towns in violation of government policy. In some areas, dormant
factories were being dismantled and turned into scrap metal, which was
then bartered across the Chinese border for the cheapest food available.

Although the authorities had no choice but to accept these transgres-
sions and local officials appear to have abetted or even sponsored them,

the remarkable thing was that the authority and cohesion of the regime seemed undiminished, so far as the outside world could see. Song Young Dae, the former ROK vice minister of national unification and longtime negotiator with the North, described the DPRK scene in late 1996 as "stability within instability," with Kim Jong Il at the top of a crisis-management system controlled by the military. Among the greatest unknown factors was how the trauma of the North Korean economy and society would affect the country's political and military systems.

In these dire circumstances, Kim Jong Il paid a visit to Kim Il Sung University on December 7, on the occasion of the fiftieth anniversary of the founding of his alma mater, the nation's foremost institution of higher education. The transcript of his lengthy and rambling remarks, evidently delivered in confidence to several Workers Party secretaries who accompanied him, was brought out of North Korea by Hwang Jang Yop, who was not present but was privy to such materials in his post as a party secretary. The text of the speech was eventually published in *Monthly Chosun* in Seoul. As of the spring of 1997, it was the only record of Kim Jong Il's candid utterances available outside North Korea, except for the tapes surreptitiously made by the kidnapped filmmakers more than a decade earlier.

In his remarks, Kim acknowledged to some extent the difficulties facing the country, saying that "the most urgent issue to be solved at present is the grain problem. . . . [T]he food problem is creating a state of anarchy." Despite the onslaught of "heart-aching occurrences," Kim was highly critical of the street-corner food sellers and peddlers who had spontaneously emerged in response to urgent needs. "This creates egotism among the people, and the base of the party's class may come to collapse. Then, the party will lose popular support and dissolve. This has been well-illustrated by past incidents in Poland and Czechoslovakia."

Kim absolved himself of responsibility for the country's economic problems, maintaining that his father, who had spent much of his time in economic guidance, "repeatedly told me that if I got involved in economic work, I would not be able to handle party and army work properly." He implied that his job was too important to deal with mere economic issues: "If I handle even practical economic work, it will have irreparable consequences on the revolution and construction. . . . The people now unconditionally accept the directives of the Party Central Committee because of my authority, not because party organizations and functionaries carry out their work well. . . . No functionary assists me effectively. I am working alone."

The only institution to win unstinting praise from Kim Jong Il was the army, on which he had become increasingly reliant. Of forty-seven of his activities during 1996 made public in North Korea, thirty were visits to military units or other military-related activities. In contrast to the laggard youth he had observed at Kim Il Sung University, he declared, "all soldiers are politically and ideologically sound and their revolutionary military spirit is lofty." He was satisfied that the soldiers would "protect with their lives the nerve center of the revolution"—himself and other high-level leaders.

Kim's speech confirmed that, as suspected by American and South Korean intelligence, food shortages were affecting even the army. He proclaimed that the people must be told, "If you do not send rice to the army, even if the wretched Americans attack us, we cannot win. Then you will also become slaves, and your sons and daughters and grandsons and granddaughters will too."

In January 1997, despite the catastrophic state of the economy, Kim as commander in chief ordered a return to the full-scale conduct of the winter training exercises, which had been severely truncated the previous year. At great expense in fuel, ammunition, and other resources, a large proportion of North Korea's huge army moved along the roadways and trails to new positions, fired weapons, and practiced for combat operations. In March Kim also ordered highly unusual "total mobilization" exercises in which cars in Pyongyang were covered with camouflage netting and thousands of people took refuge in underground shelters, as they would do in case of war. On April 25, the anniversary of the founding of the army, tens of thousands of troops paraded in mass formations in Pyongyang to mark the occasion.

At his headquarters in Seoul, General Tilelli watched the vigorous military activity in the North with deep concern. He was "intuitively" certain, he told me, that the DPRK military forces had been degraded by shortages and the general deterioration affecting the country. On the other hand, US and South Korean forces had been continuously modernized and improved. Although this had affected the military balance on the peninsula to the detriment of the North, he said, it was impossible to say by how much. The DPRK military continued to be highly capable, making up in mass what it lacked in modernization, the American commander said, and it "might be the only viable instrument of national power the regime has left."

What worried him and his staff was the possibility that the North Korean leadership could become so desperate that the combined power of the US and South Korean forces might no longer deter a massive attack. Tilelli was certain that "the explosion," as such an attack was known among his military planners, would fail after a period of bloody and destructive fighting, which would wreak death and destruction in the South but would also destroy much that North Korea had built in its half century of existence. Given the lack of what Pyongyang's leadership considered its other options, said a member of Tilelli's staff, "I don't think a decision to attack would be irrational—though it might turn out to be wrong."

Beginning in 1997, the supply of food to alleviate the devastating situation at home became increasingly the central focus of North Korean diplomacy and of international concern, eclipsing other issues. This placed the United States and South Korea, and much of the world at large, in a terrible dilemma. North Korea was continuing to feed and supply a huge and menacing army even while many of its people were hungry or even starving. The regime's statist and shortsighted policies, as much or more than the floods, were to blame for its current crisis, but it refused to undertake major changes in economic policy. Few nations wished to aid such a regime. Yet a growing number of reports placed North Korea on the brink of a great humanitarian disaster, making it intolerable to do nothing to help. Moreover, for strategic reasons and considerations of international stability, most of North Korea's neighbors and the US government as well wished to stave off the sudden downfall of that regime, fearing it might bring devastating violence that could affect all of Northeast Asia.

The United States was willing to provide funds to purchase food on a humanitarian basis and proceeded to do so in response to UN appeals. However, Washington rejected attempts by North Korean diplomats to link their attendance at peace talks and agreement to various tension-reducing steps to the supply of food assistance. Washington also ruled out supplying the massive amounts of aid that would be required to end the famine. The US problem was essentially political: Congress would not support "aiding" North Korea, but would permit modest contributions to UN humanitarian efforts intended to feed its people.

South Korea was less hesitant about linking food to its diplomatic and political objectives. Early in 1997, ROK officials sought to use food as a bargaining chip, supplying or permitting private groups to supply only limited amounts in order to maximize diplomatic leverage over North Korea. As reports of starvation multiplied, however, public pain over the suffering of fellow Koreans brought a shift in government policy. Beginning in the spring, Seoul provided 50,000 tons of food—a drop in an ocean of need—through the Red Cross. In 1998, with a new administration in office, the ROK relaxed most restrictions on the nongovernmental supply of food and other aid. In a spectacular consequence of the new policy, Hyundai group founder Chung Ju Yung, who was born in the North, brought 500 head of cattle through the DMZ in June and 501 in October 1998 for starving North Koreans to use in farming. Chung's private diplomacy led to unprecedented visits by South Korean tourists to the North and promises of much bigger North-South economic deals to come.

After initial generosity, Japan, whose warehouses were bursting with surplus grain, was held back by requests for restraint from Seoul and then by new revelations that several Japanese citizens, including a thirteen-year-old girl, had been kidnapped by North Korean agents in the 1970s and never returned. North Korea refused to accept responsibility for the kidnappings, and Japan refused to supply more food.

China, which announced modest contributions of grain to North Korea, was believed to be supplying much greater amounts at cut-rate prices and through private barter deals. Customs data suggested that at least 1.2 million tons of grain crossed the China-DPRK border in 1997. China also supplied more than 1 million tons of oil yearly. These flows of Chinese assistance were essential to the survival of the North Korean regime and maintenance of the status quo on the peninsula, which China strongly favored.

A variety of other nations and charitable organizations also contributed food or funds to purchase food. Yet the emergency continued, compounded by a serious drought in the summer of 1997, followed by tidal waves along the western coast that devastated additional growing areas. It was as if nature had conspired with the unyielding economic policies of their government to bedevil the lives of North Koreans.

The scale of the human tragedy was immense, yet impossible to measure with precision in the secretive country. A team of researchers from the Buddhist Sharing Movement interviewed 1,019 refugees from North Korea just across the Chinese border during eight months in 1997–1998 and reported that a shocking 27 percent of the family members of the refugees had died since mid-1995. The movement's executive director estimated that 2.5 million people or more may die—"a famine that may be among the worst in human history." US intelligence officials who had been accumulating and examining the evidence told me in September 1998 they had no precise data, but that "certainly hundreds of thousands" of North Koreans had died from starvation or starvation-related illnesses and that 1 million deaths up to that time seemed "not impossible." About the same time, a State Department official with direct responsibility for Korean relations said he believed that "easily more than 500,000 people" had died. Besides the toll in human lives, the famine had an enormous impact on the thinking of those who survived. Never again would they completely trust the state to provide for their well-being. The social contract between the regime and the people of North Korea, if not completely broken, had been irrevocably transformed.

THE PASSAGE OF HWANG JANG YOP

On the morning of February 12, 1997, a South Korean businessman in Beijing telephoned the South Korean Consulate in the Chinese capital with a momentous request: that a car and escort be sent to initiate the political asylum and defection of party secretary Hwang Jang Yop, the architect of North Korea's *juche* philosophy. ROK officials, who were expecting the call, declined to send one of their diplomatic vehicles to pick up the seventy-four-year-old North Korean, fearing they would later be accused of kidnapping him. A few minutes later, Hwang, accompanied only by his longtime aide and fellow defector, Kim Duk Hong, arrived by taxi and walked into the consulate, asking for protection and safe transit to Seoul.

The passage of Hwang Jang Yop was the most sensational—and one of the most complex—defections from one side to the other in the half-century history of struggle between the two Koreas. Hwang was the first high-level insider ever to take refuge in the other side. Although Hwang was no longer in the inner leadership circle, and was slowly being pushed aside, his defection was a political blow to North Korea and a potential political bonanza for the South, since he brought to the South a lifetime of experience in rarefied circles in the North. However, what he had to say was complicated by his messianic belief that his mission was to prevent a devastating war on the peninsula, to liberate the North from feudalism, and to pave the way for the reunification of Korea.

Born in 1922, Hwang studied in Japan during World War II and majored in philosophy at Moscow University during the Korean War. After returning home, he was a professor of philosophy at Kim Il Sung University, where he had special responsibility for the education of Kim Jong Il. In 1965, the year after the younger Kim graduated, Hwang was appointed president of the prestigious university. About the same time, he began to assist Kim Il Sung in elaborating the *juche* philosophy, which Kim had mentioned a decade earlier but did not emphasize until the mid-1960s, after the deepening of the Sino-Soviet dispute between his two important sponsors.

Based on his close relationship with the Great Leader, Hwang became an important—and unusual—figure in Pyongyang. From 1972 until 1984, he was speaker of the Supreme People's Assembly, the country's compliant parliament, and after that secretary of the Workers Party for international affairs and chairman of the Foreign Affairs Committee of the parliament. His most important position, however, was that of principal authority on *juche*, which became the official credo of the DPRK in the 1972 constitution. In his dual capacity as a chief philosopher for the regime and an international affairs official, Hwang was freer than others to travel abroad, to have lengthy discussions and close relationships with foreign scholars, and to express opinions that were often less militant than those of others.

When Selig Harrison, the American scholar, was in Pyongyang in 1987, Hwang told him that a communist revolution in the South was "completely out of the question" and that "we must find a way for North and South to co-exist peacefully under different social and economic systems." The same year, Hwang met surreptitiously in Japan with Samuel Lee, a South Korean philosophy professor, who found him "a very reasonable thinker, and quite free from indoctrinated communist and North

Korean ideology." Young C. Kim, of George Washington University in Washington, DC, a political scientist who often visited Pyongyang, found Hwang far more interested in philosophy than in international affairs—and his philosophy abstract and difficult to fathom.

Following the death of Kim Il Sung in July 1994, Hwang helped to establish a trading company in Beijing under the aegis of the International Peace Foundation, to collect foreign currency in support of *juche* teachings and other activities in Pyongyang. The company was headed by Kim Duk Hong, who had been Hwang's senior aide at Kim Il Sung University and later in the Workers Party. Hwang and Kim had many contacts with South Korean businessmen, clergy, and others in appealing for funds or other material support in exchange for access and appreciation in Pyongyang. These activities were authorized and encouraged, at least in general terms, by North Korean authorities and probably, as well, by the South's intelligence service.

In late 1995 and early 1996, in meetings in China with South Koreans, Hwang expressed grave concern about a dangerous shift of power in Pyongyang to the military. Hwang's views, made known to the US Embassy in Seoul, were reported to Washington via intelligence channels. His heightened apprehensions roughly coincided with the notable rise of military influence in the North under Kim Jong Il and the emergence in January 1996 of "Red Banner philosophy," emphasizing revolutionary and martial spirit, which quickly became more prominent than *juche*.

Hwang's first overt move of opposition, according to sources in Japan, had come in early-February 1996, during an international seminar held in Moscow on "the *juche* idea." In this setting, the high priest of *juche* expressed his determined opposition to war, calling it inhuman and comparing military combatants to animals, and he declared his support for Chinese-style market reforms, which were still anathema in Pyongyang.

On March 10, Hwang's world began to change when an article in *Rodong Sinmun* attacked "careerists and conspirators [who] outwardly pretend to uphold the leader and be faithful to the revolutionary cause while dreaming another dream inwardly and making conspiracies behind the scenes." It warned that "socialism will go to ruin if there are careerists and conspirators seated in the leadership." Although the article was one of a continuing series of such warnings and mentioned no names, Hwang was certain it was aimed at him. Surveillance of his activities was increased, and lectures were organized that criticized his views and weakened his authority, again without specific mention of his name. He noticed that government officials began avoiding him, a timeworn signal of trouble ahead. A few days after the *Rodong Sinmun* article appeared, Hwang's aide dropped hints to a South Korean contact in Beijing that Hwang might defect because of his opposition to military dominance and the growing possibility of war.

On July 3, while transiting Beijing on his way home from leading the official DPRK delegation to a congress of the Vietnamese Communist Party, Hwang met Lee Yon Kil, a sixty-nine-year-old South Korean businessman, born in the North, who had been leading a personal crusade to induce and assist defectors from the communist regime since serving as a commando under US and ROK direction in the Korean War. "War must be prevented at any cost," Hwang told him, and to do so South Korea should provide food to the people of the North, which is "50 years behind the South." Hwang emphasized the need for absolute secrecy, telling Lee that a North Korean agent was situated deep in the "power core" of the Seoul regime.

In the late spring, in an attempt to stabilize his position at home, Hwang had taken the advice of high-ranking party figures to compose a self-criticism, admitting to mistakes. Toward the end of July, however, a speech by Kim Jong Il, published in the Workers Party theoretical journal *Kulloja*, returned to the attack against "social scientists" who erroneously interpreted *juche*. Hwang knew then that his self-criticism had been rejected and that his ouster from the seat of power was inevitable. In Beijing in late July, Hwang's aide spoke explicitly of defection for the first time and reported that Hwang requested cyanide ampules in case suicide was his only option. He also asked for money to approach younger people in Pyongyang who he believed were less sympathetic to the regime.

Hwang now began to move decisively to the dissident camp. On August 21, he penned a lengthy treatise summing up his view that North Korea had become "neither a nationalist nor socialist state, but a full-fledged dictatorship" that "has nothing in common with the genuine *juche* idea." As for Kim Jong Il, Hwang wrote that he

> possesses vigorous energy, as well as unswerving will to protect his own interest. His political and artistic sense is very sharp, and his brain functions fast. Since he has only been worshipped by the people without being controlled by anyone, he has never experienced any hardships. As a result, he got to be impatient and has a violent character. He worshipped Germany's Hitler. . . . He never consults with anyone else. No one can make a direct telephone call to him, no matter how high his or her position is. He considers the party and military as his own and does not care about the national economy.

Regarding the possibility of war, Hwang wrote that "the North is developing nuclear, rocket and chemical weapons" and "believes it will win in a war." Therefore, he wrote, "the South should set up a social atmosphere of respecting the military; beef up military forces in all directions; and make impregnable readiness with proper preparations for war" in order to prevent armed conflict from breaking out. Reversing his previous stand, he wrote that to weaken the North, the South should discourage reforms in the DPRK. He advocated continuation of the economic blockade to isolate the North, with the exception of providing food and medicine for the North Korean people.

On January 28, Hwang left Pyongyang to deliver the main address at a symposium in Japan sponsored by the Cho Chongryon, the pro-Pyongyang residents' association. He was closely guarded in visits to Tokyo, Kyoto, and Nagano, during which he extolled *juche* and paid tribute to Kim Il Sung and Kim Jong Il. He flew to Beijing on February 11 for an overnight stop before his scheduled train trip to Pyongyang the following afternoon. Instead, he left the North Korean Embassy on the morning of February 12, pleading that he needed to go shopping for gifts. A short time later, he took refuge in the South Korean Consulate.

Hwang's defection posed a difficult issue for the Chinese government, which sought to maintain good relations with both Pyongyang and Seoul, until North Korea dropped its initial claim that Hwang had been kidnapped and announced that "a coward may leave" if he really wanted to defect. Still, in order to ease the embarrassment to Pyongyang, China did not permit Hwang to leave the ROK consulate in Beijing for five weeks and then only for a third country, rather than directly to South Korea. Under an arrangement worked out with Seoul, the Philippines provided a temporary refuge for Hwang before he was permitted to travel to Seoul on April 20. As he and Kim Duk Hong stepped out of a chartered Air Philippines jet at a military airport, the two defectors raised their arms in the air three times and shouted *Mansei!*—a Korean expression of triumph and good wishes. The South Korean public, watching raptly on live television, suspended its mixed feelings about Hwang, at least for the moment, and warmly welcomed his arrival.

THE TWO KOREAS IN TIME OF TROUBLE

By 1998, a half century after the creation of separate states following the division of the peninsula, the two Koreas were radically different, but both were facing serious difficulties.

South Korea, although far more advanced economically and politically and awash with riches when compared to the North, was beset by problems that would grow dramatically at the end of 1997. In November the financial and economic crisis that had begun in Southeast Asia spread without warning to Korea. By December 31, South Korea's currency, the won, had lost 40 percent of its value against the US dollar as investors fled the country, and the value of securities on the Seoul stock market had dropped by 42 percent. To avoid defaulting on the international debts of its banks and businesses, the country that in 1996 had joined the Organization of Economic Cooperation and Development (OECD), known as the club of the world's richest nations, was forced to go hat in hand to the International Monetary Fund (IMF) for $57 billion in loans—the largest international bailout on record, up to that point—in return for acceptance of stringent economic requirements. Bankruptcies and unemployment soared, with massive social and political consequences.

Amid this turmoil, Kim Dae Jung, the longtime opposition leader, was elected president in the December 18 national election. "We're just entering a dark IMF tunnel," he told the public in a televised "town hall" meeting. "The real ordeal will begin from now on." As the Republic of Korea celebrated the fiftieth anniversary of its founding on August 15, 1998, its economy was still struggling to find the path to recovery. The economy bounced back dramatically in 1999, but began to slip again in the second half of 2000, as it became clear that underlying problems in the banking and corporate structure were more serious and more damaging than had been anticipated.

Kim Dae Jung's policies toward the North were very different from those of his predecessor and rival, Kim Young Sam. From his first years in national politics in the early 1970s, Kim Dae Jung had outspokenly advocated a policy of easing North-South tension and engaging the North. For many years, he was accused of procommunism by military-dominated governments, but he persisted in his views. Now as president, he set out three principles in his inaugural address: "First, we will never tolerate armed provocation of any kind. Second, we do not have any intention to undermine or absorb North Korea. Third, we will actively push reconciliation and cooperation between the South and North beginning with those areas which can be most easily agreed upon." His administration established a program of engaging the North through positive gestures and lowered barriers to trade and other official and unofficial interactions. Early in his administration, Kim's program, which became known as his "Sunshine Policy," was sorely tested by the absence of progress in official relations with the DPRK and by public dismay over another failed North Korean submarine incursion and the discovery of the body of a North Korean commando off the South Korean coast three weeks later. Nevertheless, Kim persevered in his engagement policies.

When I first saw Kim as president in March 1998, a month after his inauguration, he told me, "We're now waiting for the North Korean attitude. I think there is discussion among the North Korean leadership about how to change their policy toward South Korea." The following month, at Pyongyang's initiative, official bilateral talks were held in Beijing, but they broke up without results because the South insisted on reciprocity, in the form of guarantees of reunions of divided families, in return for two hundred thousand tons of fertilizer it was willing to provide. The North, however, insisted on obtaining the aid without conditions.

An important element in Kim Dae Jung's policy was the separation of politics from economics, which in practice meant permitting ROK businessmen to pursue deals with the North, even though there was little or no progress on intergovernmental relations. This proved to be a key in preparing the way to broader contacts.

North Korea, meanwhile, continued to suffer devastating problems. As a result of failed policies, its economy continued to shrink in 1997 for the eighth consecutive year since the collapse of its alliance with the Soviet Union. An International Monetary Fund mission that visited Pyongyang in September 1997 issued a confidential report, on the basis of data largely provided by DPRK officials, that the economy had suffered "a severe contraction," with total national output in 1996 only half of what it had been five years earlier. Industrial output had fallen by two-thirds, according to the report, and food production by 40 percent. Estimates of starvation varied widely, but US Census Bureau estimates suggested that about 1 million North Koreans may have died as result of famine between 1994 and 1998. This "arduous march," as it came to be called in the North, had long-term consequences for economic and social developments in the country and, most of all, the regime's grip on the people.

Kim Jong Il, after the completion of a three-year mourning period for his father, was elected general secretary of the Workers Party in October 1997, placing him officially at the top of the political hierarchy he had headed since his father's death. All signs, however, suggested that unlike his father, he was relying less on the party for control and governance than on the military from his posts as supreme military commander and chairman of the National Defense Commission.

TURN TOWARD ENGAGEMENT

For most of the half century since the creation of its regime, North Korea's role on the world scene was that of menace to the peace. Its attack across the thirty-eighth parallel that started the Korean War, its massive and forward-deployed postwar military force, its practice of terrorism, and its bristling vocabulary of threats made it a pariah state to be dealt with disapprovingly and as little as possible by most of the nations of the world. Beginning with the death of Kim Il Sung and the evidence of its poverty and deprivation in the middle 1990s, North Korea was seen less as a threat and more as an economic basket case and the object of humanitarian assistance. As Kim Jong Il gathered confidence and came into his own, especially after his June 2000 summit meeting with Kim Dae Jung, North Korea and its leader began to be accepted for the first time in terms befitting a normal state. What had been shrouded in mystery began to be explored; what had been cause for either anxiety or pity began to be engaged diplomatically and examined at high levels by many of the world's democratic governments.

North Korea's shift from self-reliance to engagement began amid very mixed portents. The launching of a long-range DPRK rocket late in 1998 accentuated fears in Japan and redoubled concern in the United States, while charges of nuclear duplicity in clandestine underground activity further marred the atmosphere. At the same time, below the level of most outside awareness, domestic developments in Pyongyang began to set the stage for dramatically different policies that would alter the central relationships on the Korean peninsula.

INTO THE HEAVENS, UNDER THE EARTH

At seven minutes after noon on August 31, 1998, North Korea sent a three-stage rocket roaring into the heavens from a launching site on the

shores of the Sea of Japan, which both North and South Koreans patrioti-
cally call "the East Sea." The first stage fell away from the rocket ninety-five
seconds later and landed in the sea 156 miles away, short of Japan. The
second stage flew over the northern tip of the main Japanese island of
Honshu and landed in the Pacific, 1,022 miles from the launch site. The
third stage, a solid-fueled rocket that North Korea had not previously
demonstrated or been known to possess, sought to place a small satellite
in a global orbit broadcasting the revolutionary hymns "Song of General
Kim Il Sung" and "Song of General Kim Jong Il." So far as US monitors
could determine, the effort to launch a satellite failed. But the range of the
rocket, especially its third stage, was a most unpleasant discovery for those
concerned about North Korea's potential for launching ballistic missiles
with highly lethal and destructive warheads.

The test launch of the rocket, called the Taep'o-dong by Western analysts after the area where a mock-up of the projectile was first spotted,
touched off an intense alarm, bordering on panic, in Japan. A man-made
projectile from an unfriendly country flying over the Japanese islands was
the most tangible physical threat to the country since the end of World
War II and a nightmare to many Japanese. The government of Prime
Minister Keizo Obuchi sought to contain the furor with uncharacteristically quick responses. A Japanese official had been scheduled to sign an
agreement in New York that very day to provide $1 billion toward the
light-water reactors promised to North Korea under the 1994 Agreed
Framework. After the test, Japan announced it would not sign (though it
proceeded with the project under US pressure several weeks later). Japan
also announced that it was halting humanitarian food aid to North Korea
and suspending its offer to continue talks on establishing diplomatic ties,
which would be accompanied by large-scale reparations to Pyongyang.
Most significantly, in the long run, the Taep'o-dong test emboldened the
previously divided Japanese government to override its traditional pacifism
and move into the arena of militarized space, deciding to produce its own
satellite reconnaissance system for early warning and to move toward joining the controversial US antiballistic missile project in the Asian region.

In the United States, the test came exactly two weeks after the *New
York Times* reported a leak of highly classified intelligence that the United
States had detected what appeared to be a secret North Korean underground nuclear weapons complex in violation of the 1994 accord. Taken
together, the possibility that North Korea was secretly continuing its quest
for nuclear bombs, while rapidly improving its potential ability to deliver
them via long-range missiles, sounded alarm bells in Congress, greatly
enhancing the credibility of skeptics who had never accepted the idea of
negotiating with North Korea to buy off its nuclear threat. In addition, the
Taep'o-dong test, coming six weeks after a prestigious commission headed

by former—and future—Secretary of Defense Donald Rumsfeld warned of a sooner-than-expected ballistic missile threat to the United States, was a gift to partisans of the controversial national missile defense plan. A Republican member of Congress gleefully told a White House official after the North Korean test, "That did it—we've got the NMD."

In all likelihood, the timing of the test had nothing to do with these US domestic developments, but was keyed to two significant DPRK milestones in early September: the fiftieth anniversary of the founding of the North Korean state and the formal elevation of Kim Jong Il to the top post in the North Korean government. Pyongyang had last tested a ballistic missile, the two-stage Nodong, in 1993. In October 1996, North Korea was observed to be making physical preparations for a new launch, but halted them after US warnings that such an action would seriously undermine bilateral relations and the Agreed Framework. In August 1998, however, the Agreed Framework seemed at a dead end, and so this time the launch went ahead, despite US warnings.

It would be difficult to exaggerate the damage to the existing US policy inflicted by the twin blows of August 1998. Members of Congress who had reluctantly gone along with the US commitments under the 1994 Agreed Framework were incensed by the developments and prepared to cut off the funds. "I think we ought to stop talking to [North Koreans], stop appeasing them," said the chairman of the House Appropriations Committee, Representative Bob Livingston (R-LA). "I see this as a pretty good excuse just to get out of this [1994 agreement]." A senior Clinton administration official with responsibilities in Asia told me, "The [secret] underground facility pulled the plug on the policy, and the missiles hurt even more." US policy toward North Korea, he said, "is in deep shit." Should the United States abandon its commitments under the Agreed Framework, it was clear, North Korea would be free to resume its production of plutonium at Yongbyon, and it was saying it would do so. This activity had brought the two nations to the brink of a military crisis in 1994 and would almost certainly do so again.

Soon after the story broke regarding the secret underground site, the United States demanded to inspect it, in order to determine whether it was indeed a clandestine nuclear facility. In November a US team led by Ambassador Charles Kartman arrived in Pyongyang for the first negotiations the two sides had ever held in the North Korean capital. After initial confusion about the site in question—North Korea thought the United States was concerned about the site depicted on a map in the *New York Times* article, which had indicated the wrong location—Pyongyang's diplomats were remarkably relaxed, expressing willingness to negotiate a site "visit" (they rejected the word *inspection*) if the Americans would pay for the privilege. Naturally, the initial asking price was ridiculously high, probably as much a result of bureaucratic dynamics in Pyongyang as any expectation that the price would be met. The pace at which the North Korean negotiator moved to his bottom line in the first round of talks suggested to some on the US delegation that he was instructed to reach a deal, though not right away. At that point, the North Koreans knew something the Americans were uncertain about: that the underground cavern in question, at a place called Kumchang-ri, was not a nuclear facility and was unsuitable for such a purpose. They also increasingly understood it was essential for Washington to obtain access, and therefore Pyongyang could explore what might be gained in return for letting the United States take a look.

The visit to Pyongyang almost ended in disaster. Moments after the small US Air Force jet carrying Kartman and five other delegation members took off from Sunan International Airport in Pyongyang, the plane's pressurization gauge stuck. Pressure in the cabin quickly grew to excruciating levels and kept climbing. Several passengers, including a Marine Corps general, writhed in pain as the pilot frantically tried to fix the problem. After he succeeded, the pilot calmly explained to the passengers that he had decided not to deal with the emergency by returning to Pyongyang, which he thought they probably didn't want.

The underground nuclear weapons issue was the creation of the Pentagon's Defense Intelligence Agency, a center of extreme skepticism, if not hostility, toward US rapprochement with Pyongyang. American spy satellites had long been monitoring a variety of North Korean military excavations, which were commonplace in a country under continual fear of air attack. In the case of the dig at Kumchang-ri, into a hard-rock mountain in a heavily militarized area northwest of Pyongyang near the Chinese border, excavation had begun a decade earlier, but had only recently attracted serious attention. Calculating the size of the hole from the mounds of soil and rock being extracted and observing a nearby bridge and dam, the DIA proceeded to produce elaborate theories and assumptions, even creating small-scale models of nuclear reactors and plutonium-reprocessing facilities, which the agency believed could be under construction in the growing cavern beneath the surface of the earth.

Some other US intelligence officials and competing intelligence agencies were dubious, but the DIA was insistent. The agency was permitted to begin briefings for US allies and congressional committees in June 1998. With the acquiescence of the Central Intelligence Agency, an official intelligence "finding" was promulgated in mid-July that the Kumchang-ri cavern was "probably" a suspect nuclear facility, at which an active nuclear weapons program could be planned or under way. One month later, *New York Times* correspondent David Sanger was able to confirm rumors of the developments by interviewing former officials at a think-tank meeting outside Washington, DC, and obtaining confirmation of the basic facts from the Clinton administration. Sanger's August 17 story put the issue on the record in highly visible fashion, making it the subject of political and public debate, just as North Korea was preparing its rocket launch.

After five rounds and more than six months of negotiations between US and DPRK diplomats, the two sides produced an agreement that an American team could make multiple "visits" to Kumchang-ri. The final price was six hundred thousand tons of food, most of it to be supplied through the United Nations, plus a new potato-production program. Critics howled that the United States had used food to "buy" the agreement. Most observers seemed not to realize that the deal had been crafted in a way to let the North Korean negotiator claim a larger victory than he got. Washington had already decided on a large contribution to the UN food appeal for the year, and that amount was folded into the negotiations. The US negotiator was given an additional amount of US food to use as necessary. To close the remaining gap, the American negotiator assigned an arbitrary (and sufficiently large) production value to the potato project to bring the entire amount close to what the North Koreans had said was their bottom line. In any case, the key was not the food, but that the United States had established the precedent of almost unrestricted multiple visits by well-equipped technical experts to a secret North Korean site.

The "visit" by fourteen Americans took place over three days in late-May 1999. The inspectors found six miles of crisscrossing tunnels laid out in a grid pattern, plus one chamber near one of the entrances. Neither the tunnels nor the chamber was suitable to do what US intelligence had suggested. North Korean officials who accompanied the team would not describe the purpose of the big dig except to say it was a "sensitive military facility." Following the on-site inspection, the State Department on June 25 announced that the Kumchang-ri excavation did not, after all, contain a nuclear reactor or reprocessing plant, either completed or under construction, and it had not been designed to do so. No one apologized or was penalized for the intelligence fiasco that had endangered US policy in Korea for most of a year.

TOWARD AN AID-BASED STATE

While the eyes of official Washington were riveted on North Korea's nuclear and missile programs, developments of fundamental importance were gaining momentum in Pyongyang. From the vantage point of hindsight, senior officials in both the United States and South Korea identified the final months of 1998 as the time when important shifts began to gather force in the regime north of the thirty-eighth parallel.

The Supreme People's Assembly, in theory the highest legislative authority in the country, met on September 5 for the first time since the death of Kim Il Sung four years earlier. As expected, it named his son and heir, Kim Jong Il, as the governmental leader of the country, although not as president—that post was reserved for the dead leader in perpetuity— but as head of the National Defense Commission, which was declared to be "the highest post of the state." The meeting enacted two other changes that proved to be of major significance. It amended the constitution to introduce some elements of a Chinese-style socialist market economy, and it brought into office a group of the younger, more pragmatic bureaucrats. The government's cabinet, which was given new powers, was henceforth to be composed of thirty-four officials, of whom twenty-three were new faces, replacing elderly figureheads. There was no doubt that these decisions bore the personal imprimatur of Kim Jong Il.

The greatest questions, though, arose from Kim's decision to rule the country from a military post and the increasing prominence of military leaders in the assembly, which suggested to outsiders a further militarization of the country's policies. Although Kim Jong Il, unlike his father, had no military background, since his father's death he had spent a great deal of time establishing and improving close relations with the armed forces, the only group in the country capable of challenging him. Large numbers of officers had been promoted at his direction. The overwhelming majority of Kim's publicly reported activities in his first five years of supreme power were visits to military units or had military-related connections. An American visitor to Pyongyang in 1997 noticed what seemed to be some of the extraordinary ways in which Kim was garnering military support. General officers, of whom there were now many, were being driven around the capital by uniformed drivers in new Mercedes and BMW limousines. Despite the famine in the countryside, a special floor of the Koryo Hotel, the capital's best, had been set aside for the lavish wining and dining of senior military officers. Outside the capital, Russia-style *dachas,* or recreational residences, were springing up for the use of military leaders. As it turned out, Kim Jong Il's new post and his policies appear to have cemented his grip on the military, setting the stage for greater diplomatic maneuvers.

For South Korea and most of the West, the first crack in the depiction of Kim Jong Il as a withdrawn, eccentric, and threatening ogre came in October 1998, a month after the Supreme People's Assembly meeting, when he met in Pyongyang with Chung Ju Yung, the eighty-two-year-old founder and honorary chairman of the South's giant Hyundai group. In his first meeting with an outsider since his formal elevation as head of government, Kim was described by his guest as polite, courteous, and deferential to an older man. Photographs of Kim welcoming South Korea's most illustrious industrialist, and of the two holding hands for the camera, were splashed on the front pages of Seoul's newspapers. Of more lasting significance were business deals that were sealed or seriously discussed during the Hyundai chairman's visit.

Chung Ju Yung, born in 1915, the son of a poor rice farmer in a village just north of the current DMZ, had long been determined to do what he could to improve the lives of the people of his original homeland. In January 1989, he had been the first prominent South Korean industrialist to be welcomed with honors in Pyongyang. In the early 1990s, his attempts to return were blocked for political reasons by the government of President Kim Young Sam. By 1998 Kim Dae Jung's desire to engage the North and his policy of separating business from politics created an opening for a series of imaginative initiatives by Chung. In June he undertook high-profile "cattle diplomacy" by transporting in big Hyundai trucks 500 head of cattle from his farm through the DMZ as a gift to North Korea and by bringing in 501 more in October, plus twenty Hyundai automobiles, including several luxury models suitable for Kim Jong Il.

During the October trip, North Korea granted Hyundai the right to bring tourists from South Korea to the famed Diamond Mountain (Mount Kumgang), just north of the DMZ, for payments totaling $942 million over six years. The tours in Hyundai-chartered ships began the following month, when the South Korean firm also began paying $25 million a month into a North Korean account at the Bank of China in Macao. The deal proved to be instrumental in opening the door to more North-South economic engagement, but by June 2000 Hyundai had sustained losses of $206 million on the Diamond Mountain tours, which it could ill afford in a time of economic downturn. In early 2001, it was forced to appeal for an ROK government bailout.

The supply of so much cash to North Korea without restriction proved to be controversial in South Korea and among Washington policy makers. According to Lim Dong Won, Hyundai's efforts to push ahead with big deals at a politically sensitive moment in 2000 angered President Kim Dae Jung. Nevertheless, as a general proposition, Kim's strategists believed the payments were crucial in demonstrating that the South would keep its economic promises toward the North consistently and reliably. "North Korea was suspicious whether the government would allow Hyundai to pay cash," particularly in periods of tension between the two governments, a senior official told me. When it did so month after month, he said, "they began to trust us." Looking toward more important things to come, he added, the Hyundai deal was "a bite to catch a fish."

Shorn of trade and aid from its original Soviet Union and East European allies, uncertain of China's stopgap assistance, barred from most commercial loans due to the defaults on its debts in the 1970s, and excluded from international lending agencies due to its closed economic and political systems and the opposition of the United States and other key sponsors, beginning in the 1990s, North Korea attempted to turn virtually all of its diplomacy to extracting assistance, if not cold, hard cash. Pyongyang may well have figured that if Moscow and many Eastern European countries could sell their souls for payoffs from the ROK in the 1980s, it could do so, too, and strike a better bargain. Requests from Pyongyang for payments from South Korea in food, fertilizer, and currency became a constant. In addition, owing to the reports of extreme famine in outlying areas, the international community began supplying large amounts of humanitarian assistance, principally food and medicine, to North Korea in the mid-1990s. Attempts by the North to convince the international community that it would prefer capacity-building assistance instead of outright aid were unsuccessful. The result was that the North's image was transformed into that of an international beggar, always with its hand out or, at worst, prepared to extort whatever it could.

The significance of this change has been great in political as well as economic terms, internally as well as externally. Although the regime continued to express fealty to Kim Il Sung's theory of *juche*, or self-reliance, North Korea by the end of the 1990s had become dependent on others for much of its sustenance. Unlike the assistance from communist countries during the Cold War, most of this flow was not from ideological allies or sponsors, but from those who were not committed to survival of the regime. To keep money flowing and improve his standing abroad, Kim Jong Il was required to take greater account of the world outside than his father had done—or than anyone expected.

PERRY TO THE RESCUE

Having achieved a significant accomplishment with the Agreed Framework in October 1994, the Clinton administration was unable to sustain the level of attention and commitment necessary to keep the process on track. In part that was due to the results of the congressional elections weeks after the Agreed Framework was signed, but it was also due to the all too normal inability of the US government—whatever the political party in power—to devote as much effort to implementing as it does to negotiating agreements. The problem came to a head in the summer of 1998. At that moment of maximum peril to the administration's North Korea policy, it was widely agreed in the US Congress, the executive branch, and among numerous foreign policy professionals that the best chance for preservation was a high-level review and revision headed by a respected outsider. Nearly everyone's number-one choice to undertake this job was William J. Perry, the seventy-one-year-old former secretary of defense, who had led the nation's military establishment during the 1994 nuclear crisis. Perry was a figure of strength, maturity, and experience. More than almost anyone else, he had looked into the abyss of horrific bloodshed and destruction that had been threatened. Unknown to most outsiders, he had been seared by the experience. Having returned to the comfortable life of a Stanford University professor and board member of high-tech companies, he did not welcome the call from President Clinton asking him to become "North Korea policy coordinator" on an urgent basis. Perry saw it as "a difficult job, with a low probability of success . . . but I also remembered the 1994 crisis, which I thought then and still do was the most dangerous crisis we faced in this period. And I saw us moving toward another crisis as bad as that one."

Perry recruited Harvard University professor Ashton Carter, who had been one of his assistants in the Pentagon, and assembled a small team of US government officials headed by Ambassador Wendy Sherman, counselor of the State Department and a close confidant of Secretary of State Madeleine Albright. Perry concluded early that it was essential to present North Korea with an unshakably close alliance of the United States, South Korea, and Japan, rather than risk the possibility that Pyongyang would play one nation off against another as it had done with the Soviet Union and China during most of the Cold War. To cement the alliance, Perry created a three-way Trilateral Coordination and Oversight Group (TCOG) of the United States, the ROK, and Japan to consider North Korean issues. Second, he concluded that US policy could not be at odds with that of the South Korean president, who had made engagement with the North the major thrust of his newly installed administration.

The essence of Perry's plan was to offer North Korea's leaders a proposal with two alternative tracks. Track one was to end their long-range missile programs and reconfirm the stand-down of their nuclear weapons program, in return for full diplomatic relations with the United States, a peace treaty ending the Korean War, and improved relations with South Korea and Japan. Track two was to continue down the road of missile tests and nuclear uncertainty, in which case the United States and its allies would take actions to enhance their own security and containment of the North, increasing the likelihood of confrontations.

It was not simple for Perry to persuade the US administration to accept both the positive and the negative elements of his plan. The positive road would accord a greater degree of legitimacy and acceptance to the North Korean regime than had been the case before. Perry argued that even though North Korea was undergoing extreme economic hardships, it was not likely to collapse, and "therefore we must deal with the DPRK regime as it is, not as we might wish it to be." In successive cabinet-level meetings at the White House, Perry argued convincingly that the status quo was unsustainable and spoke in graphic detail from his 1994 experience of the awesome dangers of the downward track. Madeleine Albright, normally a strong opponent of antidemocratic regimes, was persuaded by Perry's views and a private briefing by General John Tilelli, the US military commander in South Korea, that the downward road was exceedingly dangerous and thus a serious effort to put North Korea on the upper path was essential. Albright, and she believes Clinton as well, was deeply affected by the views of Kim Dae Jung, in whom they had great trust and confidence.

It was clear to Perry from the beginning that he would have to travel to Pyongyang to learn which path the North would choose, if he could get an answer at all. He and his party flew into Pyongyang on May 25, 1999—right after the Kumchang-ri inspection ended—aboard a US Air Force special-mission plane, aircraft that were becoming a common sight at the North Korean airport as more official US delegations showed up. Before embarking, Perry and his team had spent an entire day at Stanford University going over every word of a carefully prepared seventeen-page script, and over the Korean translation, to be used as the crucial presentation. The idea of the script was to layer the message Perry would deliver, giving Kim Jong Il—who would be following the discussions via frequent reports from his aides—a chance every step of the way to absorb the US presentation.

After a lavish welcome banquet the night of his arrival, Perry made his presentation the following day, primarily to Kang Sok Ju, the first deputy foreign minister who had negotiated the 1994 Agreed Framework and was the closest diplomatic aide to Kim Jong Il.

Reading from the script inside a file folder, Perry began with references to the difficult history of Korea and its great-power neighbors over the past one hundred years, which included the Russo-Japanese War of 1904–1905, in which Japan gained dominance over Korea. In those days, he said, "events [that] occurred and decisions made in capitals in Asia decisively and tragically influenced the course of the 20th century." Perry said he was there not to apologize for things the United States had done but to seek to work together to heal the wounds. He explained his own role in the nuclear crisis of 1994, how important his understanding of that crisis had been to him, and how perilously close the United States and the DPRK had come to a clash of arms.

The United States as a Pacific power would remain intimately bound up with Asia in the future as it had been earlier in the twentieth century, Perry told the North Koreans. Advancing a theme that was to recur in later ROK and US conversations with Kim Jong Il, Perry said that a Korea surrounded by powerful states could benefit from a positive relationship with a power across the Pacific. The United States, he said, would be prepared to consider the legitimate defense concerns of the DPRK, but the DPRK in return must consider the defense concerns of others in the region. He observed that the status quo was not sustainable due to US concerns about North Korean missile and nuclear programs.

Perry outlined in some detail the actions that North Korea must take to place itself on the positive track he recommended, leading step-by-step to full diplomatic, political, and economic relations with the United States. To obtain these benefits, North Korea must completely halt all missile exports, including related technology and equipment. Even more significantly, North Korea must cease development, production, testing, and deployment of all missiles above the limit of the international Missile Technology Control Regime, which North Korea had not joined. This would eliminate the new Taep'o-dong as well as the Nodong that had been threatening Japan for most of a decade.

Should North Korea continue missile tests and other actions perceived to be hostile, in effect taking the second track, Perry said the United States, South Korea, and Japan were prepared to reverse positive steps that they had taken and to protect their security by military actions of their own. He did not specify what actions they would take and felt it was unnecessary for him to speak in detail, as North Koreans knew his history as defense secretary during the 1994 crisis.

Before leaving Pyongyang, it was clear to Perry that deep divisions existed within the regime, or at least that North Korea wanted the United States to believe there were, about accepting his ideas. At US requests for a meeting with a senior military figure, General Lee Yong Chol, a high-ranking member of Kim Jong Il's entourage, met the Perry team. "We don't normally meet with our enemies," he began bluntly, and proceeded to say he believed it was a bad idea even to discuss giving up North Korean missiles. Referring to the intensive US bombing of Yugoslavia then taking place, he said this was because the Serbs were unable to fire back at the United States and that North Korea was determined never to be in that position. Moreover, Lee referred to the Foreign Ministry officials as wimpish and said the military would pay little heed to what they thought.

The Americans had decided ahead of time that this was not the occasion for a productive meeting with Kim Jong Il, and Perry made only pro forma requests to see him. On the final day of his visit, Perry summarized his proposals in a brief meeting with Kang. The United States had taken an important step in sending him to Pyongyang as the personal representative of President Clinton, and now it was up to North Korea to take the next step, he said. Not surprisingly, Kang was noncommittal. As their plane took off, Perry told his team that he believed his mission had failed. He doubted that the Foreign Ministry and the Workers Party could win a debate with the armed forces, although he conceded he did not know what the ultimate decision maker, Kim Jong Il, might be thinking. The experienced Korean experts in his party read the tea leaves differently. They thought that Kang and some others were clearly intrigued with Perry's ideas and that they might well succeed in moving in a positive direction. In Washington, State Department analysts saw the North's public treatment of the visit as a very positive signal and sent an urgent message to the delegation to that effect. Perry was persuaded that things were not as glum as he first thought.

Before leaving Pyongyang, Perry suggested that if his proposals were too sweeping to digest all at once, North Korea might consider taking a smaller initial bite, such as placing a moratorium on further flight tests of its missiles. The United States could take its own small step by easing some US economic sanctions. On June 23, less than a month after the Perry visit, North Korea's diplomats asked their US counterparts in a meeting in Beijing for more details of what Perry had in mind, a clear sign that Pyongyang was interested. Serious discussions began in August in Geneva, on the sidelines of four-party talks. A month later in Berlin, in mid-September 1999, North Korea agreed to a moratorium on further missile tests while talks continued. In return, President Clinton announced the lifting of sanctions that banned most US exports to and imports from the DPRK. Pyongyang had initially accepted only a first bite-size portion, but to a US negotiator, "They had bitten; they had taken the hook." From the North's standpoint, of course, it was the United States that was being hooked back into working toward a relationship Pyongyang had been pursuing since the early 1990s. Albright declared publicly that the United States was heading down a new and more hopeful road in its relations with North Korea—but that Washington could reverse course if it became necessary. The missile-test moratorium and the visit to the underground cavern took the edge off the anger in Congress that had erupted a year earlier. The future path of the US-DPRK relationship, however, remained uncertain.

TOWARD THE JUNE SUMMIT

For many summers, North Korean fishermen had ventured south into a rich crab-harvesting area across an invisible line on the map that had been utilized as a sea border between the two Koreas since right after the Korean War—a line the North said had been unilaterally established by the UN Command and that it did not recognize. Usually, the crabbers had scuttled back north when confronted with southern ships; in June 1999, they unaccountably did not do so, but stayed to fish under the protection of northern patrol craft. On June 10, a dozen North Korea crab-fishing boats, escorted by six North Korean patrol boats, were confronted by South Korean patrol boats, which began ramming the invading vessels to force them back across the dividing line. After a few minutes, the North Korean boats, several of which had been damaged, fled north.

On June 13, a renewal of the confrontation escalated into a mini war. The southern side had strict orders not to fire first, but the initial shot—possibly a North Korean sailor firing a rifle—from a northern boat was answered by a hail of fire from more modern and better-armed southern vessels, initiating a fourteen-minute gun battle. A North Korean torpedo boat with an estimated twenty sailors on board was sunk before the rest of the flotilla fled.

The first serious naval clash between the two Koreas in the Yellow Sea since the Korean War put nerves on edge, prompted the dispatch of additional US naval forces to the area, and created grave questions about relations between Seoul and Pyongyang. Yet, somehow, it did not escalate. After the shoot-out, the incursions across a line the North had never officially recognized did not continue. Despite fierce rhetoric, North Korea did not put its forces on alert, build up its forces near the battle zone, or counterattack with its nearby shore battery of 100-mm guns or its Silkworm antiship missiles.

Speculation was intense about why North Korea had sought to contest the sea border at that time. Some declared that the incident reflected an effort by hard-liners among the North Korean military to sabotage moves toward rapprochement with the South. Others suggested it was intended to improve Pyongyang's bargaining position in forthcoming talks with Seoul. Others saw the incident as a grave challenge to President Kim Dae Jung's engagement, or Sunshine, policy toward the North. In retrospect, high-ranking South Korean officials became convinced that the confrontation had been unintentional on the part of Pyongyang and that it arose from a much more mundane cause: the fishing fleet's quota for crabs, which are sold by the North for scarce hard currency, had been raised to double that of the previous year, a new quota almost impossible to meet without tapping the southern waters.

The impact of the sea clash was substantial in all directions. Domestically, it appeared to validate the lesser-noticed "hard" side of Kim Dae Jung's Sunshine declaration, as expressed in his 1998 inaugural address: "We will never tolerate armed provocations of any kind." The military action improved his standing, at least temporarily, with those in South Korea who felt his policies toward the North were too accommodating. In an interview months later, Kim told me that the naval clash had been "a decisive success" that taught North Korea a great lesson, while improving the morale of South Korean armed forces. The embarrassed North, although it avoided any military response, reacted politically. Two weeks after the battle, long-delayed meetings of North and South Korean vice ministerial officials in Beijing broke down in arguments over the sea battle and without a widely anticipated agreement on meetings of divided families in return for ROK economic assistance. Senior South Korean officials who subsequently dealt extensively with the North believe the clash in the Yellow Sea may have delayed Pyongyang's movement toward accommodation with the South by six months or more. If so, the delay proved to be a costly one in the developments on the divided peninsula.

In the summer and fall of 1999, North Korea was reaching out to a variety of key countries. In mid-May, Kim Jong Il summoned the Chinese ambassador, Wan Yongxiang, for the first meeting with a Chinese ambassador since his father's death. Kim applauded China's reform and open-door policies and asked that China receive a mission to reestablish the high-level relations that had been dormant for more than five years; a few weeks later, he dispatched the mission, headed by Kim Yong Nam, the former foreign minister who was now nominally the head of state for protocol purposes. In November Russian foreign minister Igor Ivanov was received in Pyongyang to make preparations for a new bilateral treaty on trade and cooperation, replacing the old Soviet military alliance. In early December the North welcomed a Japanese parliamentary group headed by former prime minister Tomiichi Murayama and including Hiromu Nonaka of the Liberal Democratic Party, which paved the way for resumption of Japan–North Korean normalization talks. Japan then announced the lifting of some economic sanctions.

Relations with the United States, however, appeared to be drifting, if not stalled. In September 1999, North Korea proposed sending a high-level emissary to Washington to confirm officially the missile moratorium and move relations to the next level. Throughout the fall and winter, US diplomats urged their Pyongyang counterparts to send the emissary soon, lest North Korean policy become embroiled in the US presidential debate in 2000. From meeting to meeting, North Korean diplomats were unable to set a date, suggesting to some of the Americans disagreement in Pyongyang over what to do. Among other impediments, North Korean diplomats complained bitterly that the US economic sanctions that President Clinton had publicly promised to lift were still in force. Neither they nor the public was told that the White House had made a private commitment in writing to Republican leaders of the Senate not to lift the sanctions until the high-level visit began to discuss elimination of long-range missiles—and nobody could say when that would be.[*]

---

[*] The sanctions were finally lifted in June 2000 after the North-South summit meeting and after DPRK diplomats furnished their American counterparts at a bilateral meeting in Rome with a restatement of the missile-test moratorium that was used to gain the acquiescence of Senate leaders. The Italian Foreign Ministry made available the sixteenth-century Villa Madama for the talks, a gracious setting for negotiations normally held in more straitened circumstances.

I was in Seoul in early January 2000 and met privately with Kim Dae Jung to discuss North-South relations for the third time since he had become president two years earlier. The previous month, Kim had begun to receive signals from a variety of channels that Pyongyang wished to move again toward official cooperation and economic assistance, but he did not tip his hand. Asked about the lack of a clear-cut response to his overtures, Kim told me, "We told North Korea when they respond to our efforts for peace, we will respond." He expressed the belief that the activities of former secretary of defense Perry and the growing solidarity of the United States, South Korea, and Japan would have a positive influence on North Korea. Citing Pyongyang's efforts to reach out, he said, "They realized if they continue like this without cooperation with the outside, they cannot maintain their system." The day before our meeting, Italy had become the first Western European country to establish diplomatic relations with North Korea. Kim said the Italians had spoken to him ahead of time, and "I told them to go ahead." His objective, he said, was "to liquidate the Cold War structure on the Korean peninsula within three years"—the time remaining in his presidency. He did not predict what would happen next, but I sensed he was more confident than before.

In the early months of 2000, in fact, decisions were jelling in the North. On March 5, in the first observable sign to the outside that something different was happening, Kim Jong Il made a well-publicized visit to the Chinese Embassy in Pyongyang. The nearly five-hour meeting was a farewell gesture to Ambassador Wan, who was soon to leave his post—but it had greater significance than that. Kim Jong Il normally did not receive ambassadors, and a visit by him to an embassy was astonishing in North Korean terms. It appears he used the evening to notify Chinese leaders what was coming and to set the stage to see them in Beijing two months later.

Kim Dae Jung had decided early in the year that his top priority would be a summit meeting with Kim Jong Il, as difficult is that might be to arrange, because he believed the only way to negotiate successfully with a dictatorial government was from the top down. On January 20, he publicly proposed a summit meeting to discuss issues of mutual cooperation, peaceful coexistence, and coprosperity.

At that point, the machinery of secret North-South contacts went into gear. Over the next three months, public comments and behind-the-scenes meetings fed into each other. The secret meetings started with low-level feelers and quickly grew to higher-level exchanges that nailed down an agreement and, always crucial in these matters, worked out the wording for a joint press announcement. It was a good example, once again, of the care and choreography necessary for making progress on the Korean issue. In the first stages, the contacts were conducted even without the knowledge of the head of the National Intelligence Service, the new name for the South's intelligence organ. Once that was remedied, the NIS chief, Lim Dong Won, became personally involved in conveying Kim Dae Jung's views to key North Korean officials and, eventually, to Kim Jong Il himself.

On February 2, a longtime go-between, Yoshida Takeshi, met at the Lotte Hotel in Seoul with ROK minister of culture and tourism Park Ji-won—who had been designated by Kim Dae Jung to deal with the summit issue—to convey a message that Pyongyang was interested in a summit. In a public statement on February 6, Kim said he would not be bogged down by matters of location or format. His aim and flexibility were also made known in low-level channels that had been opened to the North. Perhaps more important, Kim began to speak publicly in startlingly positive terms about his potential opposite number at a North-South summit. A meeting of the top leaders is essential, the South Korean president said in February in an interview with the Tokyo Broadcasting System, and it is practical as well: "I believe [Kim Jong Il] is a man of good judgment, equipped with great knowledge." This surprising statement about a man who had been routinely and roundly condemned as the ultimate enemy brought a storm of protests from conservatives in the South, including those among the United Liberal Democrats, Kim Dae Jung's own coalition partner. No South Korean president had ever said such positive things about a North Korean leader.

At the end of February, the North sent a message that it wanted to meet with Park Ji-won in Singapore for preliminary talks. On March 2, Kim left Seoul for state visits to Italy, France, and Germany. On March 9, the secret meeting in Singapore took place. That same day, at the Free University in Berlin, Kim called for a government-to-government dialogue with the North without delay and announced extensive new proposals for ROK assistance. These included a government role in expanding the North's "social infrastructure, including highways, harbors, railroads and electric and communications facilities." He proposed business-related treaties on investment guarantees and prevention of double taxation. To deal with the underlying causes of the North's famine, he proposed "comprehensive reforms in the delivery of quality fertilizers, agricultural equipment, irrigation systems and other elements of a structural nature," with the assistance of the South. US officials, who were in the midst of negotiating with North Korean diplomats in New York, were taken aback by his ambitious offers, which they heard about only hours before the speech in Berlin. Secretary of State Albright protested the lack of advance notice to the ROK foreign minister, Lee Joung Binn, who apologetically said Kim had been working on the details of his speech right up until the time it was given.

On March 17, Park Jie-won flew to Shanghai. He told reporters and staff members that he was taking a leave of absence to be hospitalized for a checkup. Actually, he began four rounds of talks with Song Ho Gyong, a veteran North Korean diplomat who was vice chairman of the DPRK's Asia-Pacific Peace Committee, an influential Workers Party unit in charge of policy toward the South. According to a high-ranking ROK official, the North sought to explore details of the economic assistance mentioned in the Berlin speech. There was also a question of where to meet and when to announce a meeting. No agreement was reached in the first two days of secret talks, nor in a second round the following week in Beijing. But when Park was summoned back to the Chinese capital by his negotiating partner on April 8, he and Song, "under instruction from the highest authority" of each side, signed an agreement on a North-South summit meeting to take place in Pyongyang on June 12–14. The agreement was announced on April 10, just three days before nationwide parliamentary elections in South Korea, generating skepticism and charges of "obvious politicking" from the political opposition. As it turned out, the announcement had little effect on the elections, in which the president's party failed in its bid to become the number-one party in the National Assembly.

SUMMIT IN PYONGYANG

Following the announcement that the leaders of the two Koreas would meet, midlevel officials of the two governments met at Panmunjom in five sessions of preliminary talks from April 22 to May 18 to hammer out summit details: the agenda, participants, press attendees, travel arrangements, security. The central issue and the greatest unknown, however—the intentions and even the character of the North Korean leader—remained a mystery.

On the afternoon of May 27, Lim Dong Won, the South Korean president's closest adviser on North-South affairs, drove to Panmunjom and from there helicoptered to Pyongyang. The diminutive former general, who had been born in the North but who became an army major general, a professor, and a military and diplomatic strategist in the South, was the most trusted and most powerful foreign-policy official in Kim Dae Jung's presidency. Lim had been deeply involved for many years in policy toward and negotiations with the North, but he had played little role in domestic politics until he joined Kim Dae Jung in 1995 as director general of Kim's Asia-Pacific Peace Foundation. Kim had been outspokenly determined for decades to pursue engagement with the North rather than confrontation; Lim, who agreed, brought expertise and enterprise in making it happen. After serving in two earlier senior posts, Lim in December 1999 became director general of the NIS. In that post, he had a hand on all intelligence concerning the North and could direct and even participate in secret activities.

In Pyongyang Lim held talks with Lim Dong-ok, first vice director of the Workers Party United Front Department, which is in charge of handling inter-Korean relations. In those talks, the North Korean official raised what would become a major sticking point in the summit arrangements— the issue of whether President Kim would visit Kim Il Sung's preserved body at the Kumsusan Palace. Lim said no, the North Korean insisted, and the atmosphere deteriorated. The NIS chief was then informed it would be impossible for him to meet with Kim Jong Il, which was the purpose of his visit in the first place.

On June 3, Kim Dae Jung sent Lim back for a second try. Lim did not know what kind of man he would meet at the top of the North Korean hierarchy. He had collected ten books that had been written about Kim Jong Il, all from the negative side. Most of the intelligence that had been gathered and promulgated by the NIS was also harshly negative. Yet some other people and materials, including the accounts of Russian and Chinese officials who had met Kim Jong Il, were much more positive about his ability, his interests, and his inclinations.

After arriving in Pyongyang, Lim met with party secretary Kim Yong Sun, the most senior party official in charge of inter-Korean matters. Again the question of the ROK president's visit to Kumsusan came up, and again Lim said no, explaining that the negative political ramifications in the South from such a visit would cancel out anything the summit might accomplish. This time the North Koreans did not push back, but said they would report Lim's views. Lim was then flown to Sinuiju to meet with Kim Jong Il, who had recently returned from his trip to China. The conversation covered a wide range of issues, including the question of US troops in South Korea. Lim explained Kim Dae Jung's position that they should remain, even after reunification. The North Korean leader essentially agreed, noting that he had sent Kim Yong Sun to the United States in 1992 to convey their views on the issue, and adding that "if we become too anti-American, it could hurt the interest of our nation." The issue of a visit to Kumsusan came up again, with no change in positions, though Kim did not seem adamant on the point. In four hours of talks, Lim found a North Korean leader very different from most of the advance accounts. On returning to Seoul, he made a six-point report to Kim Dae Jung about his summit partner:

1. He is a strong dictator, stronger than his father, whom Lim had met on two occasions in the early 1990s.
2. He is the only person who is open-minded and pragmatic in the North Korean system.
3. He is a good listener. He took notes on the meeting with Lim, like a student with a professor.

4. When he is persuaded to another's point of view, he is decisive.
5. He is gentle and polite to older people around him, as he was to Hyundai founder Chung Ju Yung.
6. He has a sense of humor.

Lim sought to negotiate a joint statement to be issued at the end of the summit by the two leaders, but Kim Jong Il refused. He said he wished to work out such a statement in person with Kim Dae Jung during their meetings.

After a last-minute one-day postponement, probably due to the concerns of Kim Jong Il's security officials about having their leader appear according to a preannounced schedule, the North-South summit began on the morning of June 13. When the plane from Seoul bearing the ROK president, his wife, ministers, and aides and an accompanying press corps landed at Pyongyang airport, meeting them on a red carpet laid on the tarmac was Kim Jong Il, clad in his characteristic khaki trousers and zippered khaki jacket. The North Korean leader greeted Kim Dae Jung with a warm two-handed handshake and words of welcome. As millions of South Koreans watched with high emotion via a television hookup, their president was accorded full honors, including a military band, an honor guard of North Korean soldiers with rifles and bayonets in salute position, and hundreds of women in traditional billowing gowns waving colorful flowers. The two leaders got in the backseat of Kim Jong Il's limousine for a forty-minute ride through the streets, which were lined with an estimated six hundred thousand cheering people waving pink and red paper flowers. En route to a state guesthouse, the two leaders occasionally held hands in a gesture of friendship as they chatted. To Lim Dong Won's immense relief, there was no surprise stop at the Kumsusan Palace. Later, at the banquet the first night, Kim Jong Il told Lim that no visit to Kumsusan would be necessary.

In three days of talks, accompanied by only a few aides during serious discussions, the leaders covered the many issues between the two Koreas. They discussed the possibilities of South Korean assistance and of North Korean concessions on such issues as reunions of divided families, exchanges of cultural and sporting groups, and meetings of the military and civilian government officials that had long been desired by the South.

After much bargaining, the two Kims worked out, signed, and promulgated a joint declaration:

1. The South and the North have agreed to resolve the question of reunification on their own initiative and through the joint efforts of the Korean people, who are the masters of the country.

2. Acknowledging that there are common elements in the
   South's proposal for a confederation and the North's proposal
   for a federation of lower stage as the formulae for achieving
   reunification, the South and the North agreed to promote
   reunification in that direction.
3. The South and the North have agreed to promptly resolve
   humanitarian issues such as exchange visits by separated
   family members and relatives on the occasion of the August
   15 National Liberation Day and the question of former long-
   term prisoners who had refused to renounce communism.
4. The South and the North have agreed to consolidate mutual
   trust by promoting balanced development of the national
   economy through economic cooperation and by stimulating
   cooperation and exchanges in civic, cultural, sports, public
   health, environmental and all other fields.
5. The South and the North have agreed to hold a dialogue
   between relevant authorities in the near future to implement
   the above agreement expeditiously.
6. President Kim Dae Jung cordially invited National
   Defense Commission chairman Kim Jong Il to visit Seoul,
   and Chairman Kim Jong Il decided to visit Seoul at an
   appropriate time.

Some difficult moments and disagreements took place that, according
to the South Korean president, nearly caused the talks to break off, among
them the question of whether Kim Jong Il should sign the joint statement
rather than Kim Yong Nam, the protocol head of state, and whether Kim
Jong Il would commit himself to a return summit in Seoul. In retrospect, the
South Korean president said the success of the summit meeting "was due
in large measure to [Kim Jong Il's] ability to be receptive to new ideas and
a willingness to change his own views. . . . He didn't appear to be a cold-
minded theoretician, but a very sensitive personality who had a sharp mind."

Some of the discussions went far beyond bilateral questions to international issues. Kim Dae Jung handed his opposite a number of written
statements, urging him to adhere strictly to the 1994 Agreed Framework
with the United States on nuclear issues and to bring the negotiations
with Washington on curbing North Korean missiles to a smooth and
satisfactory conclusion. Without good North Korean relations with the
United States, the South Korean president said, relations between North
and South Korea could not continue to make progress.

In virtually a repeat of the exchange between Kim Jong Il and Lim
Dong Won in late May, the two leaders expressed their views on the presence of American troops on the peninsula. When Kim Dae Jung asked

why, if Pyongyang was not opposed to their remaining, North Korean radio broadcasts continued to attack the presence of US troops, Kim Jong Il responded that this was for internal propaganda purposes—and would continue.

"A new age has dawned for our nation," Kim Dae Jung declared when he returned home on the afternoon of June 15. "We have reached a turning point so that we can put an end to the history of territorial division."

In the aftermath of the June summit, there was worldwide speculation about why Kim Jong Il suddenly emerged from the shadows and appeared to be opening his previously closed society. Was the change real or cosmetic? Had he changed strategy or only tactics? What were his main objectives?

Kim Dae Jung, in a dinner for Korea experts and friends in New York three months later, said he believed the most important reason for the opening was North Korea's desperate economic travail, which made assistance from the outside essential to its survival. "Without improved relations with South Korea, others won't help them," he said. Other reasons he cited were the failure of North Korea to sideline the ROK while responding to the United States; global pressure for détente from China, Russia, and other nations; and Pyongyang's growing trust that the South's policy was actually aimed at assisting the North rather than undermining it. Scholars also noted that a summit with the South had long been under consideration in Pyongyang and that Kim Il Sung had been preparing for a full-scale summit meeting with Kim Young Sam on the very day he died.

After the June summit, South Korea and the world were treated to a rapid, almost dizzying series of developments on the divided peninsula. Before the end of the year, the two Koreas held four rounds of formal ministerial talks to authorize a wide range of cooperative activities, and aides agreed to four North-South pacts to encourage trade and investment. Kim Jong Il invited forty-six top executives of the South Korean media to Pyongyang and opened himself to a wide range of questions. Two sets of emotional meetings temporarily reuniting one hundred families on each side were held, and more were scheduled, along with the first exchanges of mail between separated families. The DPRK defense minister came south to meet his opposite number, authorizing lower-level military working groups from the two opposing armies. The two sides agreed on plans to repair and reconnect the severed North-South railroad that ran through the peninsula until the outbreak of the Korean War, and to build a highway alongside the tracks to facilitate commerce and other exchanges through the heavily fortified DMZ. Harsh propaganda broadcasts against each other were toned down or stopped. In one of the most memorable moments of the 2000 Sydney Olympics, the athletes of North and South Korea marched together under a single peninsular flag, in sharp contrast to their bitter disputes over the 1988 Seoul Olympics. Hyundai and North Korea agreed to begin construction of a massive industrial park and export-processing zone at Kaesong, close to the northern edge of the DMZ, initially to involve hundreds of South Korean companies employing tens of thousands, eventually hundreds of thousands, of North Korean workers. The Hyundai-sponsored tourism to Diamond Mountain continued, although the losses on the tours and the company's overall economic difficulties cast a shadow over its continuing inter-Korean activities.

Many conservatives, who are powerful in the South, were uncomfortable with the sudden warming and rush of developments. After a period of muted criticism, the opposition Grand National Party began finding fault with Kim Dae Jung's policy, largely on the grounds of its lacking reciprocity for the South's concessions. Skeptics pointed out that despite symbolic acts, there had been no reduction in DPRK military forces or their potential threat to the South. As the ROK economy and stock market began to sink anew after the Pyongyang summit, disenchantment and impatience with the northern policy mounted, although specific steps of DPRK cooperation continued to be applauded by the majority of the public. Even the awarding of the highly prized Nobel Peace Prize to President Kim in early December for his painstaking efforts at reconciliation with the North and his lifelong struggle for freedom and democracy provided only a temporary boost in Kim's popularity at home, while plaudits reverberated throughout the rest of the world.

In July, a month after the Pyongyang summit, North Korea joined its first regional security organization, the Asian Regional Forum, sponsored by Southeast Asian nations. A month after that, it renewed its previous application for membership in its first international financial organization, the Asian Development Bank. Meanwhile, Kim Jong Il received Russian president Vladimir Putin and prepared for his second journey in a year to meet Chinese leaders. In September his Foreign Ministry sent letters to the European Union and every European country, proposing the opening of relations. Just prior to the summit, the DPRK established diplomatic relations with Italy and Australia. Between the summit and early 2001, North Korea established diplomatic relations with the Philippines, Great Britain, the Netherlands, Belgium, Canada, Spain, and Germany and moved toward opening relations with several others. The whirlwind of diplomatic activity on the part of previously reclusive North Korea was startling.

ENGAGING THE UNITED STATES

While the remarkable opening to the South was taking place, North Korea's engagement with the United States was marking time. From September 1999 to September 2000, US and North Korean diplomats met in formal bilateral sessions five times in Berlin, Rome, and New York City, with only marginal progress on the issues before them. In an effort to signal to the North where Washington hoped to move relations, at talks in Berlin in January 2000 the US delegation passed a draft of a possible joint communiqué to the North Koreans. Once it became clear, in March, that the action for the moment was in the inter-Korea arena, Washington decided to hang back and not get in the way. Almost as soon as the Pyong-yang summit was over, however, signs of movement on the US-DPRK front appeared.

On September 27, 2000, North Korean vice foreign minister Kim Gye Gwan sat down with Ambassador Charles Kartman, the chief US nego-tiator with Pyongyang, in the twelfth-floor conference room of the US Mission to the United Nations to begin a new round of comprehensive talks on issues between the two governments. Before bargaining could begin, however, Kim announced that Pyongyang at last was ready to send to Washington the special envoy it had long promised to advance the re-lationship. The North may have signaled weeks earlier that it was plan-ning such a move when midlevel State Department officials had traveled to New York to meet their counterparts in the DPRK UN Mission. The purpose was to follow up a US proposal—conveyed to the North Koreans when a US delegation was in Pyongyang for talks on terrorism—for Sec-retary of State Albright to meet with Kim Yong Nam in September when he would be in New York, leading the North's delegation to the annual UN General Assembly meeting.* The State Department officials were told that, regrettably, such a meeting with Kim could not happen, but that they should not be discouraged, as other possibilities would become apparent.

To the surprise of the Americans, Kim Gye Gwan revealed that the visitor would be Vice Marshal Jo Myong Rok, first vice chairman under Kim Jong Il of the ruling National Defense Commission and by most calculations the second most important person in the country; few in the US delegation had ever heard of Jo, much less understood how impor-tant the choice of the NDC first vice chairman as the envoy actually was. Moreover, Pyongyang proposed to send Jo immediately. The dates for his

---

* As it happened, Kim Yong Nam's visit to New York was interrupted in Germany when, while changing planes, he was ordered by airport authorities to undergo a security search. He protested and, when that made no difference, turned around and went home. The United States quickly de-livered a message of apology to the DPRK UN Mission in New York, which obviously mollified the North. The incident caused bemused satisfaction to officials in the Foreign Ministry's American section. They had advised that Kim travel to New York via a well-worn route through Beijing on United Airlines, which was familiar with the drill of screening officials from the DPRK. However, the ministry's International Bureau (which had the lead because Kim was going to a UN meeting) insisted it knew better and that the routing, though unusual, should go through Germany to con-nect with the US "flag carrier," American Airlines.

visit were quickly fixed at October 9–12, less than two weeks away. The selection of such a high-level emissary—and especially a top-level military figure—suggested that Kim Jong Il was prepared to deal with Washington's central concerns, which were security issues.

After an overnight stopover in Northern California, which was hosted by William Perry and included visits to Silicon Valley high-technology firms, Jo and his party, which included the highly trusted First Vice Foreign Minister Kang Sok Ju, arrived in Washington on October 9. As a young man, Jo had been a minor aide to Kim Il Sung at the end of World War II and had cradled the toddler Kim Jong Il in his arms. A military pilot, he became commander of the DPRK Air Force around 1980. After the death of Kim Il Sung in 1994, he began a meteoric rise from 89th on the 273-man funeral committee to 11th among leaders of the party, the government, and the military in 1996, and second only to Kim Jong Il as first vice chairman of the ruling National Defense Commission in 1998. Although a military professional with a soldier's bearing who displayed little interest in politics, Jo was also chief of the General Political Department of the Korean People's Army and was therefore in a position as the senior political commissar of the armed forces to protect the interests of Kim Jong Il.

Jo appeared that morning in a conservative dark-blue suit at the State Department to meet Secretary Albright, but changed to his marshal's uniform, replete with row after row of campaign ribbons and decorations, for his meeting with President Clinton. In the Oval Office, he handed Clinton a letter from Kim Jong Il and then verbally stated his breathtaking objective: to invite Clinton to visit Pyongyang to iron out differences between the two governments in personal conversation with the North Korean leader. Tipped off by Albright, Clinton explained it would be impossible for him to undertake such a visit without thorough preparations and preliminary agreements. He proposed to send Albright first to accomplish these aims, with the hope he would be able to follow before he left office on January 20, only three months away.

While Jo toured the Air and Space Museum and other sights of Washington, Kang Sok Ju provided Ambassador Wendy Sherman and several other officials with advance indications of the extraordinary compromises Kim Jong Il had in mind. Without firmly committing his leader, Kang suggested that North Korea was ready to contemplate steps down a positive path along the lines proposed by Perry in Pyongyang seventeen months earlier: an end to exports of ballistic missiles, technology, and equipment on negotiable terms of compensation, which might be food or other necessities rather than cash; termination of development, testing, production, and deployment of long-range ballistic missiles; potential stationing of US military forces on the Korean peninsula on a long-term basis; and establishment of full diplomatic relations between the United States and the DPRK.

Under pressure of time to follow up, Secretary Albright flew into Pyongyang on October 23, only eleven days after Jo and Kang had left Washington. For the North, the timing of the visit was exquisite. It meant Albright would be in Pyongyang on October 25, the fiftieth anniversary of the entry of the Chinese People's Volunteers into the Korean War. As a result, the PRC defense minister who was leading a celebratory delegation to the North to mark the anniversary would symbolically have to cool his heels at the gates of Pyongyang while Kim Jong Il entertained the American secretary of state.

Hosting Albright at a small dinner the first night of her visit, Kim Jong Il kept the conversation relaxed. When Albright raised what might have been a difficult subject, he paused for the blink of an eye and then reached for his wineglass to propose a toast, neatly sidestepping the problem. During the dinner, the subject of the Korean War Memorial in Washington, DC, came up. Albright noted that it was not an anti-DPRK memorial but was meant to honor those who sacrificed themselves in the war. Kim replied that he did not think that later generations should be prisoners of the mistakes made by an older generation—a remarkable comment about the Korean War, but one that was never followed up. After dinner Kim sprang a surprise invitation on the Americans to a mass display of choreography and chorus by one hundred thousand people in a Pyongyang sports stadium—a repeat of a spectacle previously staged to celebrate the fifty-fifth anniversary of the founding of the Workers Party. With Albright sitting beside him, a potent image signaling to his people that relations with the United States might be changing, Kim pointed to the depiction on a giant screen of the Taep'o-dong launch of August 1998, which had so unnerved Japan and worried the United States. He quipped to the US visitor that this had been the first North Korean satellite launch—and that it would be the last.

Born in Czechoslovakia, the daughter of a diplomat, Madeleine Albright had spent much of her life studying communism and had been in nearly every other communist country. She found Pyongyang "not an unattractive place" given the heroic architecture, but was surprised by the lack of interest shown by the population in her entourage. Her greatest surprise was Kim Jong Il himself, with whom she had lengthy conversations. Despite his reputation as a strange and reclusive person, she found him striving to be an affable, normal leader, even though it was clear that the adulation for him was extreme and that he was in complete control.

In their initial business session, Kim volunteered that he was prepared to give up further production and deployment of his long-range missiles. He also began to define what a ban on missile sales abroad might mean, including contracts not yet fulfilled, and made it clear that North Korea would accept such items as food, clothing, and energy instead of money to compensate for the sales it would lose.

In their next session, Albright presented to Kim, who was accompanied only by Kang and an interpreter, a list of missile-related questions the US team had given to North Korean experts several hours earlier. After she commented that some of the questions were technical and might require study, Kim picked up the list and began immediately to provide answers one by one without advice or further study, in what Albright later called a "quite stunning" feat, which could be performed only by a leader with absolute authority. He agreed to ban future production and deployment of all ballistic missies with a range exceeding 500 kilometers (310 miles), although he did not specify a payload weight limit or what would be done with missiles already produced. Such a range limit would preclude the Taep'o-dong I, which had been test-launched in 1998, as well as its reported intercontinental successor, Taep'o-dong II, which was believed to be capable of reaching the US mainland and was among the principal motivations for the proposed US national missile defense plan. A 500-kilometer limit would also encompass the Nodong missiles, with a range of about 1,300 kilometers (807 miles), which had been a principal threat to Japan for several years. Under questioning by Albright, Kim accepted the need for verification of compliance with the missile agreements, but he also said that he could not accept "intrusive verification" because North Korea was neither an outlaw state nor a defendant on trial. Extensive progress had been made, but many details remained to be negotiated.

As partial compensation for the limits on his domestic missile programs, Kim proposed to Albright that other nations launch three or four North Korean scientific satellites per year into outer space, as the DPRK would no longer possess the rockets to do so itself. Such a possibility had been raised in general terms by US negotiator Robert Einhorn in the bilateral missile talks a month after the August 1998 test and also by Perry in his Pyongyang visit the following year. Kim Jong Il had first expressed interest in the idea during the visit of Russian president Vladimir Putin in July 2000, in a remark that Putin was quick to pass on to Clinton and other world leaders and quickly became the subject of public speculation.

The most important compensation, it was clear, would be the visit to North Korea of the president of the United States, which in Pyongyang's view would end its pariah status and be tangible acceptance of its legitimacy and sovereignty for all the world to see. Even more than economic or other benefits, this had been the central objective of North Korea since the collapse of the Soviet Union. The 1993 Joint Declaration with the United States, including its "assurances against the threat and use of force" and its "mutual respect for each other's sovereignty, and non-interference in each other's internal affairs," had been an important initial step. The Agreed Framework of 1994, which specifically endorsed the earlier declaration, created the first nonhostile relationship between the two countries and was instrumental in ending the nuclear crisis. William Perry's statements of US acceptance of North Korea had been among the most important aspects of his proposals. Most recently, the US-DPRK joint communiqué issued on the conclusion of Vice Marshal Jo's visit to Washington declared that "neither government would have hostile intent toward the other" and "reaffirmed that their relations should be based on the principles of respect for each other's sovereignty and non-interference in each other's internal affairs." That language, especially the latter formulation, was largely boilerplate, but coming from the United States was especially important to Pyongyang. From Kim Jong Il's standpoint, the presence of a US president on its soil would demonstrate not only that the words had meaning but also that the diplomatic-security landscape in Korea had undergone a profound and historic change.

Until the events of October, virtually no progress had been made in six years of talks about curbing North Korea's missiles, perhaps not least because Washington never seriously committed itself to those talks, which were held only about once a year. Suddenly, the prospect of nearly limitless agreement had opened up at the eleventh hour of the Clinton administration, with only two weeks to go before the election of a new president and less than three months before Clinton would leave office. Although many concessions and compromises had been outlined by Kim Jong Il, most details remained to be worked out. As Albright knew from watching decades of US-Soviet arms control negotiations, the devil is in the details, especially in such matters as limitations on weapons and the verification thereof. Among the "details" to be ironed out were the terms of compensation by the United States and other nations, precisely which weapons would be covered, what would happen to missiles already produced or deployed, and the whole issue of verification.

It was clear that Clinton could neither sign nor endorse with his presence any vague or loosely worded agreement on such weighty matters; the signing of any agreement in North Korea, particularly in the final days of his presidency, would carry an additional political burden. Time was of the essence if a deal was to be struck. The Americans suggested Kim send missile negotiators to Kuala Lumpur seven days later to discuss the details, with no expectation they would be able to settle the outstanding issues. In the rush of events, Kang Sok Ju was apparently not fully consulted. When told by the Americans at a dinner that night of the plan, he threw up his hands. "I don't have enough people for that," he said. In Seoul Kim Dae Jung strongly endorsed the idea of a Clinton trip to Pyongyang, but many experts in Washington told Albright the time was too short and the gamble too great.

It was not to be. Instead of learning the identity of the new president a few hours after the polls closed on November 7, the disputed election dragged on for five weeks in the state of Florida. The president-elect, Governor George W. Bush, indicated to the White House that he was not in favor of further negotiations with North Korea, though he was not similarly negative on Clinton's continuing efforts on the Mideast, where serious violence had erupted between Israelis and Palestinians. On the final weekend before the New Year of 2001, the State Department notified North Korea that it was now impossible for the outgoing US president to travel to Pyongyang. Clinton telephoned Kim Dae Jung in Seoul to break the news, and the State Department notified all the other countries that had participated in the effort to capitalize on the dramatic opening in North Korea.

North Korean diplomats in New York expressed disappointment at the news and said a great opportunity had been missed. Shortly before turning over her office to a new administration, Wendy Sherman received a New Year's card postmarked Pyongyang from Kang Sok Ju. It was the first such missive she had ever received from North Korea, and she took it as a positive sign.

On January 20, as Bill Clinton was turning over the US presidency to George W. Bush, Kim Jong Il was ending a six-day visit to China, his second in less than a year, during which he visited the Shanghai stock market and a General Motors joint-venture plant making Buicks in China's largest city. The bustling Shanghai Kim experienced, with its towering skyscrapers and torrid industrial pace, was a far cry from the city he had seen during his only previous visit there in 1983, near the start of China's market-oriented reforms. Beijing's Foreign Ministry spokesman said the North Korean leader praised what had been accomplished by policies of economic reform and opening up. At the dawn of 2001, there was widespread hope that Kim Jong Il would steer his country in the same direction.

17

THE END OF THE
AGREED FRAMEWORK

WHEN THE ADMINISTRATION OF George W. Bush came to office in January 2001, it inherited a better situation than any US administration in the past fifty years in regard both to Washington's sometimes troublesome ally in the South of Korea and to its long-term adversary in the North. By 2000 Seoul felt that the United States, even while it moved ahead in relations with Pyongyang, had wisely given the overall lead to the South—a sentiment that seemed to guarantee an increasingly harmonious partnership. There were no more issues with the Republic of Korea on human rights, and any problems about the status of US troops were on a low simmer. Above the thirty-eighth parallel, the North's nuclear center at Yongbyon was frozen and under continuous monitoring by inspectors from the International Atomic Energy Agency. An initial proposal for limiting North Korea's ballistic-missile program was on the table. North-South tensions were low, interchange between the two sides was growing, and prospects for the future looked promising. The Korean Peninsula Energy Development Organization was functioning well as a multilateral organization and making progress at the construction site for the light-water reactors on North Korea's east coast. The Kim-Albright exchange combined with the October 2000 joint communiqué had provided a plateau from which Washington and Pyongyang could negotiate new, more stable arrangements. If the Agreed Framework, now almost seven years old, needed updating and improving, the way seemed open for doing so.

As Bill Clinton left office, the one cloud on the horizon as far as Washington was concerned was hardly minor, but neither was it seen as unmanageable. The US government was fairly sure that the North was working on uranium enrichment, probably with help from A. Q. Khan, the Pakistani nuclear scientist whose network was clandestinely supplying nuclear know-how and material to a number of countries. Midlevel officials in the State Department were already devising a strategy to address that problem with the North once the intelligence community gave the okay to raise the issue in the diplomatic arena. That assumed US policy would stay on course, slowly improving relations with Pyongyang as North Korea addressed issues of priority concern to Washington and Seoul.

Things began to veer off track, however, as soon as the new president took office. Intense, poisonous disagreement within the administration hobbled policy discussions about Korea at every turn. Several top-level officials came to office thoroughly opposed to the Agreed Framework, determined to do away with it. Even those prepared to live with the agreement thought it failed to get at the nuclear problem decisively enough and avoided forcing the North Koreans to make a strategic choice to give up the program soon enough, leaving Pyongyang with a dangerous nuclear capability while supplying the regime with aid that prolonged its life.

This idea of forcing the North to make a "strategic choice" was pervasive in the administration and one of the few points of agreement between the warring parties in Washington. Without pressure on the North Koreans, the thinking went, they would never be forced to choose between nuclear weapons or regime collapse, and if they were not forced to choose, then they would never give up their nuclear program. In a sense, pressure was the easy choice, negotiations the more difficult one. The latter required understanding Pyongyang's perspective. The South Koreans wrestled with that challenge constantly, but it was not the sort of contemplation the Americans, who tended to think of North Korea as a "black box," did very well or, indeed, cared to do at all. Moreover, many of the US government's officials with the longest experience dealing with the North fled to posts overseas to escape the fetid atmosphere in Washington or left the government altogether. Whether intentional or not, beginning in 2001, a climate of intimidation descended over the policy process that closed off the possibilities for calm discussion or dispassionate consideration of options. Anyone connected with the Clinton administration was suspect by the new administration's appointees; anyone attempting to discuss policy options toward North Korea that resembled those of the Clinton years was told in no uncertain terms that this was "not the president's view." The suspicions and ill feelings were reciprocated, with the result that the administration was soon, and virtually for its entire term in office, at war with itself over North Korea policy.

In October 2002, less than two years after they took office, those who thought the Agreed Framework had been a bad idea could congratulate themselves for having swept it away. Only a few more months passed before it became obvious that there was no serious plan for what to do next. Moreover, the ad hoc steps that Washington did take—over the strenuous objections of Seoul and Tokyo—ended up, in short order, precipitating exactly what the United States said it did not want to see, that is, the restart of the North's plutonium production facilities at Yongbyon. From that point, the progress from 1994 to 2000 on limiting the nuclear program unraveled at a breathtaking pace.

Overall, in regard to Korea, the Bush administration's eight years in office fall roughly into three phases: pre-9/11/2001, when after internal battles (largely between those focused on global nonproliferation objectives and those focused on regional East Asia concerns) the policy toward North Korea appeared to be settling on a somewhat rocky and constricted diplomatic path; from 9/11 through 2005, when there was a rigid, almost theological cast to the administration's approach; and from 2005 to 2008, when, in his second term, President Bush became convinced that a more normal diplomatic track was necessary in order to present the North with a "strategic choice."

To review the record of the Bush administration's first-term approach toward North Korea is to summon up eerie reminders of President Jimmy Carter's ill-fated stance on US troop withdrawals, only this time with more serious consequences. Once again, an American president entered office with an almost messianic belief in the rightness of his position, prepared to roll over South Korean sensibilities, and deaf to the advice of his experienced Asia hands. The major difference is that in the Carter administration, persistent efforts by senior officials managed to blunt and eventually reverse the president's single-minded impulse. In Bush's case, his senior staff was engaged in open internecine warfare, with those counseling caution usually outmaneuvered and overwhelmed by those advocating hardline policies. Even when the president made the "right" policy decision from the standpoint of the experienced Asia hands, the hard-liners found ways to hammer it into a different shape at the operational level.

Personally, George Bush was not nearly as extreme on North Korea as the administration's rhetoric often was. As John Bolton, then undersecretary of state and one of the hardest of the hard-liners, says in his memoirs, "Ironically, Bush is blamed for following confrontational policies he didn't follow." Fundamentally, the president grasped the dangers of a war in Korea, an understanding sharpened by the downward course of US fortunes in Iraq after the 2003 invasion. While intensely opposed to US–North Korea talks, and genuinely repelled at the thought of doing anything that might help perpetuate the North Korean regime, Bush was willing to put his money on the efficacy of multilateral negotiations. When those bogged down, he was finally convinced to fall back to where he had insisted he would never go, bilateral diplomacy with Pyongyang.

Where the administration's first term was dysfunctional in dealing with North Korea, the second term saw major efforts to correct the distortions in policy. Yet these efforts, too, were riven with contradictions and suffered from a fundamental lack of understanding of what worked with the North Koreans and what did not. In any case, by January 2005 the damage from earlier decisions had been done, and once Pyongyang tested a nuclear device in October 2006, America's Korean problem became significantly more difficult to solve.

A ROCKY START

Weeks before George W. Bush's inauguration, South Korean president Kim Dae Jung was anxious to get to Washington to talk to the new US president as soon as possible. Based on reports he received of early conversations between ROK and US officials, Kim was concerned that his policies toward the North—policies he was convinced had led to considerable progress on both the North-South and the US-DPRK fronts—were not getting the right reception from his ally. In an interview with the *Washington Post* on January 8, Kim noted with utmost understatement the existence of "different voices" in the new administration.

In his usual fashion, Kim thought it would be little problem personally for him to convince the president that Seoul was on the right track and that the United States only had to stay the course. Even an early, sobering report from South Korean intelligence chief Lim Dong Won, who went to Washington in February to see the situation for himself, did not change Kim's mind. The Americans who met Lim immediately sensed his concern that the momentum of the past several years in engaging the North needed to be maintained. The first question he asked, according to one US official, was when would George Bush go to Pyongyang? Lim says that in his meetings, he encouraged the new administration to follow through on the progress made to date with North Korea, singling out the missile issue. He portrays Secretary of State Colin Powell's response as encouraging, though he admits Powell also warned that the administration was suspicious of the North Koreans and "not in a hurry" to reengage Pyongyang. Other administration officials were decidedly more negative, so much so that in his memoirs, Lim says he was "shocked" by their attitude toward the North. He quotes National Security Adviser Condoleezza Rice as telling him, "We should seek North Korean change not through the leader's change of belief but through a collapse of the failed system."

Lim's findings, and warnings from the State Department that it was too early for Kim Dae Jung to show up in Washington, that the ground had not been prepared, and that the atmosphere was still too unsettled, clearly did not faze the South Korean president. Kim had not survived the many challenges in his long career by turning back in the face of adversity. If anything, the negative reports probably spurred him on.

The South Koreans were not the only ones concerned about what was brewing in Washington. The North Koreans were also nervous. Back in November 2000, an article in the North Korean party daily timed to appear on the day of the US presidential election had laid out in unusually positive terms the North's position—that the October 2000 joint US-DPRK communiqué was a "historic document," that Pyongyang was committed to honoring it, and the United States should do so too. In January 2001, as the change of administrations was under way, Pyongyang sent its UN ambassador, Li Hyong Chol, to Washington to ask where things stood and underline to the Americans that Kim Jong Il hoped to continue the process of improving relations. Ambassador Li had long experience working with the United States. He had taken part in the Agreed Framework negotiations in Geneva and had been through the ups and downs of talks in the intervening years. It was Li who led the North Korean delegation to the December 1996 talks in New York over the submarine incident. If anyone knew how to read the Americans and communicate with them effectively, Pyongyang surely thought, it would be him.

Thomas Hubbard, the acting assistant secretary for East Asia, invited the North Korean diplomat to his office in the State Department, where he and Charles Kartman, the four-party negotiator, gave Li a diplomatic answer: things in Washington were not yet clear, there was going to be a policy review, but as this process was under way the two sides should maintain communications. Kartman had been part of the briefings for the incoming administration and had sensed the Bush team's coolness toward the Clinton-era policies, but neither of the American diplomats had any idea of the drastic change of course in US policy waiting in the wings. For a ranking State Department official to have a diplomat from the Democratic People's Republic of Korea in his office to discuss bilateral relations was in itself a reflection of how far things had progressed since 1994. Few could have guessed that after this meeting, no North Korean diplomat would be allowed in Washington for similar discussions for at least the next twelve years.

By the time Kim Dae Jung arrived in Washington in early March, it was clearly no longer possible to say US and ROK policies were moving in tandem. Cracks had become crevices and were widening into canyons. As if things were not bad enough, in talks with Russian president Vladimir Putin in Seoul at the end of February, Kim had agreed to a joint statement that seemed to put the South Korean leader on record as siding with the Russians on the issue of preserving the Anti-Ballistic Missile Treaty. This was read in Washington as implicitly opposing US plans to build a national missile defense system, a centerpiece of the Bush administration's security policy. Kim's subordinates scrambled to repair the damage, but the antiballistic-missile issue was an exposed nerve in Washington, and Kim had managed to step on it in the worst way at the worst time.

Kim's visit to Washington was a disaster, worse even than those fretting about it ahead of time had imagined. US presidents had been through

rough meetings with ROK leaders before, but this was one for the record books. Neither side had been ready for this meeting, though the new Bush administration in Washington—barely six weeks in office—was especially unprepared for a top-level discussion on the North Korea issue.

As the visit began, the *Washington Post* carried a story headlined "Bush to Pick Up Clinton Talks on N. Korean Missiles." It quoted Secretary of State Colin Powell as saying that the administration would pick up where President Clinton and his administration had left off. In his memoirs, Bush notes that he was not pleased when he saw the *Post* article and immediately reached for the phone to tell his national security adviser, Condoleezza Rice, to fix the problem or he would do it himself. Rice says she had a collegial conversation with Powell about the quote; other sources close to the secretary have said it was not all that friendly and that it marked the beginning of a frosty relationship between the two senior officials.

Friendly or not, Rice's message was effective. During the Bush-Kim meeting later that day (a meeting Powell attended), the secretary of state came out of the room to issue the sort of retraction to waiting reporters that only a veteran of Washington could muster, masking it as an interim report on the state of the two presidents' conversation. President Bush, Powell said, had emphasized to Kim that the United States was "undertaking a full review of our relationship with North Korea, coming up with policies that build on the past, coming up with policies unique to the administration, the other things we want to see put on the table." When the review was finished, "We'll determine at what pace and when we will engage with the North Koreans." Any suggestion that "imminent negotiations are about to begin" was "not the case." In the context of the South Korean leader's visit, this dance at the very top of the administration was widely—and correctly—interpreted as a sign that the Clinton approach was dead. Some White House officials considered Powell's remarks to the *Post* a bad misstep, putting him and the State Department further outside the president's trusted inner policy circle.

On the morning before his mea culpa, Powell had met President Kim for breakfast in Blair House, across Pennsylvania Avenue from the White House. The South Korean leader was at his best, drawing from his deep experience to discuss trends in Asia and US-Korean relations. Powell was impressed and pleased, convinced things might actually be on track. A few hours later, however, at the meeting between the two leaders in the White House, it became clear that things were not on track at all. To the Koreans, Bush was insultingly informal, almost dismissive of Kim. To the Americans, the South Korean leader was stiff and didactic. Afterward, Kim said nothing publicly to indicate his displeasure, but his aides got the word out. South Korean media were filled with expressions of outrage at what was portrayed as Bush's disrespectful treatment of their aged leader. Even Koreans who did not otherwise support Kim were dismayed and angered. Among Washington's Asia hands, there was a sense that the breach would take considerable work to repair, and they set about quickly to do so.

Early in 2001, soon after the Kim visit, the administration launched its review of North Korea policy. A few months before the work was finished, one of the State Department's North Korea experts met a DPRK official traveling in Europe. The Korean expressed serious concern about the tone of statements coming out of Washington and worry that the agreements reached with the Clinton administration were unraveling. Those in Pyongyang who had never favored the Agreed Framework, he said, were starting to suggest it was time to reevaluate the policy. When the American offered his own views of developments, the North Korean stopped him. "We know what you people think," he said, meaning those with whom the North had negotiated previously. "We need to meet the new people." Not long afterward, an authoritative article signed "Commentator" appeared in the North Korean party newspaper. It voiced similar concerns, warning that Washington seemed to be changing the basis for US-DPRK engagement and reopening issues, such as reductions in North Korean conventional forces, that both sides had already tacitly agreed to put lower on the bilateral agenda.

Unlike the review headed by former secretary of defense William J. Perry only a few years earlier, the Bush administration's policy review had a predetermined outcome. Whatever was decided, the conclusions and recommendations had to be different from the Clinton approach. An early indication of the problem was when Deputy National Security Adviser Stephen Hadley ordered that the review be divided into two subgroups, with the National Security Council in charge of the functional (i.e., nonproliferation) issues, whereas State would chair on the regional questions. This step essentially gave those opposed to negotiating with North Korea the upper hand in shaping the review. At an early meeting, Tom Hubbard offered a suggestion that he thought would be approved with little comment—that the State Department maintain contacts with the North Korean UN Mission in New York during the review. The idea instantly ran into a buzz saw of opposition, however. Senior administration officials at the meeting made clear that they thought continuing contact meant perpetuating the Clinton policy. The result was that US contacts with the North would be all but cut off during four crucial months.

The review was not actually finished when ROK foreign minister Han Song Soo arrived in the United States in early June 2001. The administration's plan had been to discuss the review with Han before releasing it in order to give the appearance of bilateral consultations with its South Korean ally. Instead, as so often happens in Washington, there was a leak.

To get out in front of the story, the White House decided it had to release the conclusions before the ROK visitor had a chance to see them.

The conclusions were couched in stock Washington verbiage, and most looked innocuous enough on paper. Those in favor of continuing the negotiating track—primarily at the State Department—took solace from the fact that the review did not explicitly rule out dialogue with the North. A few of the conclusions, however, were flatly inconsistent with what several senior administration officials—including Vice President Dick Cheney, Secretary of Defense Donald Rumsfeld, and Undersecretary of State John Bolton—believed the policy should be. The White House press release on June 6 said that future discussions with North Korea would cover a broad agenda to include "improved implementation of the Agreed Framework relating to North Korea's nuclear activities," as well as "verifiable constraints on North Korea's missile programs and a ban on its missile exports." In fact, Cheney and the others had no intention of improving the Agreed Framework; they meant to toss it overboard. Furthermore, focused on getting congressional approval for its national missile defense program, the administration had no plans to discuss missiles with North Korea, which it held up as one of the primary reasons for needing missile defense.

Through the spring, the North Koreans waited anxiously for the results of the policy review. When the news came out in June, they reacted negatively, focusing on what seemed to many in Washington a fussy technicality. The North complained that it should have received advance notice of the review's conclusions rather than learn them from a White House press release. For Pyongyang, not receiving word made the new US policy "unilateral," something it believed was hardly acceptable after all of the progress and the high-level meetings barely eight months before. Even more, the North Koreans were concerned that Washington was pulling back from the October 2000 joint communiqué—and, implicitly, on Vice Marshal Jo Myong Rok's visit—on which they placed so much importance. If the joint communiqué that had seemed to open the door to a new relationship between the two countries was no longer part of US policy, they wondered, where were things headed?

The State Department accentuated the positive aspects of the policy review, and Secretary of State Powell adopted the public position, often repeated, that the United States would meet the North "anytime, anyplace." That was largely an empty offer, since the vice president was determined not to let serious talks with the North get under way. To most people in Washington, though, Powell's offer demonstrated flexibility that the North simply ignored. As far as the North Koreans were concerned, the formulation was just rhetoric; worse, to them it was an annoying mantra designed to cover up the fact that the United States had retreated from the October

2000 joint communiqué. At one point, a DPRK diplomat told his American interlocutor that the United States should stop repeating the phrase because it was getting under Pyongyang's skin, and rather than a genuine offer to meet for serious discussions, it was viewed as Washington's way of needling the North.

The continuing importance, in DPRK eyes, of the October 2000 joint communiqué was highlighted when a small Stanford University delegation arrived in Pyongyang in late June. A midlevel US State Department officer in the delegation was along in an unofficial capacity in order to hear out the North Koreans and transmit their views back to Washington. The North understood this sort of kabuki, but the exercise nearly came unglued when, out of an abundance of concern caused by the ugly state of affairs in Washington, the State Department went out of its way to tell the North Korean UN Mission that its own officer had no "official" standing on the visit. As the delegation alighted from the plane, a Foreign Ministry representative there to meet it expressed surprise and dismay at the US message that had just been received. The ministry had arranged for some important meetings for the delegation, he said, but now, based on the State Department's communication, they did not see the point.

On further reflection, the North Koreans decided to go ahead with the planned schedule, and the next day the delegation met with the deputy head of the Foreign Ministry's American Affairs Bureau, Jong Chong Chol, an official sometimes referred to by American negotiators as Mr. No because he was so difficult to deal with.* Reading from a piece of paper, an indication this was an official position prepared in advance, Jong began his presentation by saying that the North and the United States did not have to be eternal enemies—a key formulation from a Kim Jong Il work of the late 1990s and a signal that Pyongyang obviously wanted transmitted back to Washington. The presentation then went on to note the importance of the October 2000 joint communiqué.

Later in the visit, the North Koreans and the "unofficial" US official explored an approach to dealing with the communiqué issue—that is, finding a way to script an encounter in New York at which DPRK and US diplomats could utter the right phrases, enough so the North could satisfy itself that the United States had reaffirmed the document, but not so much as to cause heartburn in Washington. After the Stanford delegation's visit ended, the idea was brought back to the State Department, where it died. Even a nod in the direction of the October 2000 document was impossible.

---

* His superiors apparently did not see this trait as a black mark; Jong later became DPRK ambassador to Indonesia.

THE IMPACT OF 9/11

On the morning of September 11, 2001, America's sense of security in
the post-Soviet world vanished. As the first of three hijacked jetliners
exploded into the World Trade Center in Lower Manhattan, the Bush administration found itself confronted with what seemed to be an existential
challenge, launched from half a world away and symbolic of a new world
order in which America and its allies faced off against enemies great and
small, seen and unseen, in an ideologically charged battle of proportions
not witnessed since the Cold War.

The world expressed horror at the attack and loss of life in New York
and Washington, DC, but few at home or abroad understood right away
how profoundly events of that late-summer morning had shaken the people of the United States and their government. The attacks transformed
US calculations about the type and magnitude of the threats it faced as
well as the actions necessary to defend itself in a world now seen as sharply
divided between good and evil. A primary concern of Washington became
the frightening possibility that terrorists would gain possession of weapons
of mass destruction. Of all the places terrorists might obtain such awful
tools, North Korea was considered by most to be at the top of the list.

Given the North's checkered history in carrying out or supporting terrorism, it seemed only prudent to fashion a policy anticipating such a danger and to deal with it proactively. Thus, the North Korean nuclear program
became seen as not only a threat to East Asia, but potentially the source of a
horrific terrorist attack on the United States as well. There was no evidence
that Pyongyang was considering such a course, but there was absolutely
no inclination to take the chance. Pyongyang quickly sent two condolence
messages to Washington after the 9/11 attack, and sometime later North
Korean UN ambassador Li Hyong Chol, clearly shaken personally by what
he had seen in New York, expressed his shock to American officials.

If Pyongyang saw 9/11 as an opportunity to signal the United States
that the two governments could find common ground on the issue of
countering terrorism, Washington clearly did not. The North had previously (in October 2000) issued a joint statement with the United States
on terrorism that might have been activated at this crucial moment, but
a suggestion along those lines by Ambassador Jack Pritchard, the US negotiator with the North, was ignored. In remarks at the Foreign Press
Center on November 19, Assistant Secretary of State James Kelly noted
that the North's response to 9/11 had "not been bad" and acknowledged
that the North had sent condolences and even had signed UN antiterror-
ism conventions. Curiously, he made no mention of the joint statement on
terrorism. In any case, by then the question was already moot. NSC Asia
director Michael Green called it "flagrantly ridiculous" to think that the

United States might work with the North on counterterrorism after 9/11. Given the tenor of the times, that was undoubtedly true.

The wounds of the 9/11 attacks were still fresh and the general mood in the country still very tough when the president gave his annual State of the Union address to Congress in January 2002. In the address, Bush used the phrase *Axis of Evil* to describe Iran, Iraq, and North Korea. It was a rhetorical flourish, a speechwriter's meat and potatoes, but it stuck in the public's mind and for years afterward came to define policy, or at least the general perception of policy, toward Pyongyang. The Asian experts in the State Department saw the phrase as troubling, unnecessarily complicating efforts to reengage Pyongyang, confusing to US allies in the region, and raising concerns in several key capitals about the possibility of US military action against North Korea. (Unsurprisingly, both Seoul and Pyongyang, each for its own reasons, reacted negatively to the phrase.) In the eyes of the hard-liners in Washington, these consequences were of secondary concern. More important was that the questioning of the president's words by the State Department was a sign of disloyalty.

At the time of the president's speech, tensions between the United States and North Korea had already ticked upward. Shortly before the State of the Union, the Department of Defense released an unclassified executive summary of the Nuclear Posture Review; classified excerpts were leaked and appeared in the *New York Times* and the *Los Angeles Times* in March. The NPR was a congressionally mandated review meant to provide guidance on a number of very broad, strategically important questions concerning the numbers, disposition, and targeting of US nuclear weapons. For Pyongyang, these broader issues in US policy were not germane. What were germane were the references to North Korea. According to the leaked portions, North Korea and Iraq were described as "particular problems," and, in addition to Russia, the North was on a list with six other countries as potential nuclear targets: North Korea, Iran, Iraq, Syria, Libya, and China.

The targeting list itself may not have been new, and in the context of the entire document the references to North Korea were minor. Fundamentally, it was hardly news to the North Koreans that they were an object of US military contingency planning, but the press reports about the NPR presented two problems. First, they excited a long-standing North Korean aversion to public, overt expressions of US military pressure. As one North Korean official had put it during offline discussions in Geneva in the autumn of 1994 in response to a US naval demonstration and remarks by a US admiral, "We know you have aircraft carriers, we know they are off our coast, but why do you have to talk about it?"

The second problem had to do with this public statement of intent. Given Washington's commitments to the North in various agreements during the Clinton years not to threaten the DPRK with nuclear weapons, the North took the reports about the NPR as yet another sign of serious US backsliding. It is not clear that everyone in Washington understood how mentioning the North in the NPR contradicted previous policy. When a North Korean diplomat complained about it in a meeting in New York in the spring, one US official taking part scratched his head and asked what the complaint was all about.

The South Koreans, for their part, were alarmed by what they perceived as US policy going in the wrong direction and creating a drag on their own efforts to engage Pyongyang. They fretted constantly about President Bush's negative public statements about the North and considered his colorful rhetoric about Kim Jong Il particularly neuralgic. Washington might have thought the president's candid remarks were leavened by frequent official protestations that he favored diplomacy and that the United States had no intention of using military force against the North. Seoul did not see it that way.*

Given the evolving plans for the invasion of Iraq, ensuring that the Korean issue did not boil over was crucial to the president. In a trip to South Korea in early-February 2002, soon after his "Axis of Evil" remarks, Bush demonstrated that he understood the need to repair the damage with the South, and especially to restore personal ties between the two leaders. This time his meeting with President Kim Dae Jung went well, in stark contrast to the March 2001 conversations. The centerpiece of the February trip was a joint visit by the two leaders to the final train station on the South Korean side of the demilitarized zone, restored in anticipation of concrete progress on an inter-Korean agreement to reconnect the long-severed railroad lines. The symbolism was clear—the United States supported Kim in his efforts to restore the railroad as part of the South Korean leader's larger effort to knit the two Koreas together.

Yet even here, the administration had problems pulling in one direction. The Defense Department was strongly against the sort of breach in the DMZ that reconnecting the railway would create. The US military in South Korea had been dragging its feet, and in some cases actively opposing, the South's efforts to open transportation corridors through the DMZ to the North. Where the US Embassy was doing its best to keep US-ROK ties intact, the US military in Korea, through its own channels, was portraying Blue House policy as anathema to the alliance. According to one observer on the scene, as soon as the Bush administration had come into office, the US military in Korea felt free to begin more open criticism of the ROK approach.

---

* The president repeated his candid assessment of Kim Jong Il very clearly in his memoirs, *Decision Points.*

Things almost came unglued when Bush arrived in Seoul. The president's statement at Dorasan Station would be watched closely as a signal of the state of the US-ROK alliance. On landing, Secretary of State Rice had a copy of the president's proposed remarks and flashed it in front of Tom Hubbard, who by this time had become US ambassador to Seoul, and his deputy. Looking quickly at the text, the two diplomats saw it contained a reference to the Axis of Evil. "It stays in," said Rice curtly. She did not specify what she meant, but both men understood perfectly. When the Blue House somehow obtained a copy of the remarks, it created problems the next day. Rice was furious that the South Koreans had seen a copy of the remarks—which surprisingly were not supposed to be passed to the host government—and blamed the US Embassy. The South Koreans, in turn, were furious that the president planned to include "Axis of Evil" on such an occasion and in a location picked to represent Kim Dae Jung's policy of engagement and reconciliation. The discussions between the two sides were heated, but over the course of a long meeting, Kim and Bush found a basis for understanding. When the president made his remarks at the train station, the phrase had disappeared.

THREADS COME TOGETHER:
JAPAN–NORTH KOREA TALKS

In January 2001, at about the same time Kim Jong Il was visiting China, DPRK first vice foreign minister Kang Sok Ju had flown to Singapore for a secret meeting with Hidenao Nakagawa, a former top aide to then Japanese prime minister Yoshiro Mori. At that point, Kim Jong Il was probably still proceeding on the assumption that the progress with the United States achieved in late 2000 was secure and would help him promote relations with Japan as part of a broader strategy to improve the North's external security environment. Perhaps more important, a breakthrough in relations with Japan would feed into Kim's evolving ideas for major domestic economic policy initiatives. These plans for significant changes in the North's economy—normally, they would be called "reforms," but the North Koreans did not like the word—required money, money the North Korean treasury did not have. Normalizing relations with Tokyo would open the door for Japanese reparations for its occupation of Korea earlier in the century, similar to the 1965 Japan-ROK settlement—though, with the passage of a quarter century, this sum could potentially be considerably larger than the $800 million in grants and loans Japan had paid to Seoul. But reparation could not be discussed unless Tokyo and Pyongyang reached some sort of understanding about how to deal with the question of Japanese abducted by the North Koreans over the past thirty years.

The January meeting in Singapore got nowhere, but on coming into office in April 2001, the new Japanese prime minister, Junichiro Koizumi, decided to continue the contacts. In a series of secret meetings that stretched from the summer of 2001 until August 2002, sometimes in Kuala Lumpur, sometimes in northern China, Japan and the DPRK maneuvered, probed, parried, and tested each other's intentions at both the personal and the official levels. In September 2001, Kim Jong Il replaced his representative in the talks with a mysterious figure whose identity was never revealed to the Japanese but who may have been a ranking official in the Ministry of State Security named Ryu Kwang.* In response, in November, Koizumi replaced his own representative with Hitoshi Tanaka, director general of the Foreign Ministry's Asia Bureau. In March 2002, the Japanese said they wanted Kang Sok Ju to attend, and at the next meeting, in April in Kuala Lumpur, Kang appeared. Rather than explore broader questions of Japan–North Korea relations, Kang wasted much of the time talking about a Japanese payment to the DPRK, something Tanaka had already clearly indicated in previous meetings that he could not touch.

To keep the threads aligned, in early April, and after urging from South Korean intelligence chief Lim Dong Won during a meeting with Kim Jong Il, Pyongyang tendered an invitation for a US delegation to visit the North. Unexpectedly, Washington held back because it was now moving into another policy review sparked by George Bush's "gut instinct" that the United States should not get bogged down in a long series of messy negotiations with the North. What was needed, the White House decided, was something clean, clear, and, as it came to be called, "bold." According to the US negotiator with North Korea, Ambassador Jack Pritchard, there wasn't much guidance from the White House on what "bold" meant, nor was there much time to flesh out the idea. The basic idea was that the United States would provide assistance to the North, if and when Pyongyang addressed US concerns in the area of weapons of mass destruction— nuclear, chemical, and biological weapons and missiles—terrorism, and human rights.

All the while, Kim Jong Il was working on his own bold approach, an elaborate choreography involving a number of players and moves. As far as the North Koreans were concerned (and they were the only ones who knew about all of the moving pieces), by late spring the DPRK's agenda for the remainder of 2002 apparently looked like this: promulgation of

---

* According to some accounts, Ryu Kwang, who served in the sensitive post of vice minister of the Ministry of State Security, was close to Kim Jong Il. In addition to the talks with Japan, Kim used Ryu for special assignments, most notably in secret contacts between the North and South Korean intelligence services during Lee Myung-bak's administration. In January 2011, however, there were reports of his execution, attended by senior North Korean cadres.

new economic measures, a visit by a high-level US official to put talks back on track, a summit meeting with Japan, a spurt of forward movement in inter-Korean relations (including North Korean participation in the Asian Games in Pusan), and, always concerned to have his back covered, a visit by Kim Jong Il to Russia, for his third meeting with Putin in as many years.

By early July, only days after Kim Jong Il's new economic measures went into effect, the DPRK's secret talks with Japan had reached the point that Kim could well have felt that the plan for a summit meeting was falling into place. By the time he left for Russia on August 20, the North Korean leader probably knew the deal with Japan was a sure thing. What he likely did not realize was the delicate situation that now existed in Tokyo, where the few in the government who knew about the secret talks with North Korea faced the painful task of briefing their very senior colleagues who were still in the dark. Kim was on the train returning from his meeting with Putin when he received a message from Prime Minister Koizumi, effectively sealing the deal. Kim replied immediately, and Kang Sok Ju relayed the message to Director General Tanaka, who was in Pyongyang to finish off details for a "Pyongyang Declaration" that was to be the capstone of a Koizumi-Kim meeting planned for mid-September.

For the Japanese, besides the delicate task of briefing others in the Koizumi government who had been unaware of the secret talks with Pyongyang, there also remained the business of letting the Americans in on the momentous news that Koizumi would soon visit the North Korean capital to meet directly with Kim Jong Il. US deputy secretary of state Richard Armitage was in Tokyo in late August, intending to give Koizumi an early—if not very detailed—warning about a new US intelligence community estimate on the North's uranium enrichment program. Instead, the Americans were invited to a meeting where they were told that in about seventy-two hours, Tokyo would publicly announce plans for Koizumi's upcoming trip to Pyongyang. Several American officials had been kept informed in general over the course of Tanaka's meetings and had encouraged the Japanese to move ahead with their talks with the North Koreans, so the news was not a total surprise. In the Tokyo meeting, the Japanese went over with the Americans the draft of the Pyongyang Declaration, word by word, according to one of the participants. Armitage went back to the US Embassy to contact Secretary of State Powell, who replied a short time later that President Bush was comfortable with Koizumi's plans, though once the word spread, others in Washington were not so relaxed about the prospect of a Japan-DPRK summit. In early September, just before Koizumi's trip, Bush and the Japanese leader met in New York at the annual UN General Assembly meeting. Bush embellished on the warning about the North's uranium enrichment program, and Koizumi indicated he would be careful.

For their part, the Japanese were not completely taken aback by the news of the North's enrichment program. They had received an early warning about it from American officials during an Asia-Pacific Economic Cooperation (APEC) summit held in Brunei that July. Moreover, they had suspected something ever since the Clinton administration a few years before had asked them to stop exports to North Korea of material that could be used for uranium enrichment. In fact, what did surprise Tokyo was that the Bush administration had not raised the issue for two years, and then suddenly, seemingly out of nowhere, it had zoomed to the top of Washington's list of problems with Pyongyang.

SLOUCHING TOWARD THE CLIFF

Washington's focus on the North Korean nuclear threat sharpened suddenly in the early summer of 2002. While the State Department was working on a new version of the "bold approach" toward Pyongyang, the administration's hard-liners were encouraging the intelligence community to develop a convincing case that the North had for the past half decade been pursuing a uranium enrichment program. In midspring there had been intelligence briefings on the program, but these did not receive much notice, except by those hawks like Undersecretary of State John Bolton who saw the new findings as ammunition to use in the ongoing bureaucratic struggle against starting talks with the North. If there had been more attention to the possibility of serious US-DPRK negotiations, the enrichment issue might have received closer scrutiny by policy makers. Diplomacy was still considered nothing more than necessary theater with little likelihood of success, however, and so for most officials enrichment remained wrapped in the gauzy impression that it was a minor laboratory-type experimental program.

In June Blue House national security adviser Yim Sung Joon visited Washington to take soundings on the administration's thinking. He returned to Seoul with discouraging news that the hard-liners were in the saddle, but apparently with no inkling about the intelligence assessment under way on the issue of North Korea's highly enriched uranium (HEU) program. Ambassador Jack Pritchard, who had been one of those receiving the briefing on the DPRK's enrichment efforts, proposed to the North Koreans that a visit by a high-level US envoy be scheduled for July 10—a date that probably suited Pyongyang well enough. Earlier might have been better from Kim Jong Il's standpoint, as it would have been provided a useful drumroll to his plans to unveil new economic measures on July 1. But July 10 was still tolerably close.

Even with what it saw as accumulating and nearly overwhelming evidence that decisions in Washington were moving in the wrong direction,

Pyongyang seemed determined to resume talks with the United States. For its part, Washington did not understand, nor would it have cared even if it had noticed, that Kim Jong Il was in the final stages of a major diplomatic effort to create the peaceful security environment he thought was required for his economic initiative to succeed. That meant securing ties with his great-power neighbors Russia and China, improving relations with the European Community, breaking the logjam with Japan, moving ahead on the inter-Korean front, and, above all else, getting relations with the United States back on track. If there were new possibilities for US diplomacy created by Kim's economic plans, Washington did not grasp them.

On June 29, barely forty-eight hours before Kim's new economic policies were to be rolled out, the waters of the West Sea were again the scene of a clash between the two Korean navies. Two North Korean navy ships crossed the Northern Limit Line and opened fire on several smaller South Korean patrol boats, killing and wounding several sailors and sinking an ROK speedboat. In an unprecedentedly quick move, Pyongyang sent a message via the inter-Korean hot line to Seoul, expressing regret over the incident and informing the South that "lower ranks" were responsible for the "unintended clash." Given that Kim Jong Il's economic measures were set to go into effect only two days later, it is hard to believe that the naval incident had Kim's blessing ahead of time. Nevertheless, the clash was a symptom of a festering problem in the West Sea, one that would grow worse and more deadly over time. Eventually, there would be an escalating series of naval incidents accompanied by a military buildup by both sides in the area near the disputed sea border. The situation in the waters off the west coast would become as dangerous as anything that existed along the well-marked and formally accepted military demarcation line on land.

The naval clash gave Washington a perfect excuse to postpone the planned July 10 meeting in Pyongyang. The real reason for the postponement was the new intelligence assessment that suggested the need for a reinterpretation of the North's enrichment program. The analysis was not based on any direct knowledge of how far the program had actually developed; rather, it was a synthesis of information about material and machinery the North had procured—or sought to procure—over the past several years. The procurement effort suggested to analysts a major effort to move beyond small-scale experimentation and launch a production-scale program, though as the CIA was at pains to make clear, it was impossible to say if all the pieces had already been assembled and were actually operating.

The new assessment, which sent shockwaves through Washington, left the hard-liners feeling vindicated and exuberant. Bolton called the intelligence community analysis "the hammer I had been looking for to shatter the Agreed Framework." He says in his memoirs that he told representatives of the intelligence community that he intended to use their analysis "to go straight for the Agreed Framework's jugular." Even those in favor of negotiations instantly concluded that the North Koreans had been caught "cheating" on the Agreed Framework.

To the Americans, the idea that the North had been "cheating" was almost as important, maybe even more so, than the possibility that the DPRK uranium enrichment program had shifted into high gear. The North's conduct, real and supposed, was taken collectively as something akin to a moral affront. To the Americans, "cheating" meant that the North Koreans had to be punished. It meant that a US delegation, when it finally got to Pyongyang, would not negotiate, would not host a dinner, and would not engage in any of the normal practices of diplomacy that might begin the process of dealing with the problem. The US delegation would, in effect, give the North Koreans an ultimatum—although no one would have used that word—and then leave.

This tactic suited the hard-liners. Neither the vice president nor Secretary of Defense Rumsfeld believed that negotiations with the North Koreans would ever accomplish anything significant anyway. They were willing to let a senior official go to Pyongyang, but only on a leash so short that it would make a North Korean diplomat look like a free spirit.[*] The leash on the American negotiator stayed attached well into the multilateral talks that eventually began in 2003.

KIM JONG IL'S PROGRESS

Unaware of the storm in Washington over enrichment, Kim Jong Il went ahead with the rollout of his new economic policies. These were never publicly announced in a single official document, nor were they ever identified as "reforms," but rather were presented as improvements to "socialist economic management." Later that summer, the North Korean press was filled with an unusual number of articles praising the party's economic policies, but there was nothing explicit in the media about what changes were taking place. It did not take long, however, for foreign reporters to get wind of developments. As early as July 11, the Japanese news agency Kyodo published a lengthy and fairly detailed report on the new measures. Sometime later, a busload of KEDO employees traveling on the country's east coast saw marked improvements in a hotel where they often stopped on the way to or from the reactor construction site. The changes ranged from simple things, like an aquarium in the hotel's entrance hall no longer filled with lifeless, scummy water, to considerably more important matters,

---

[*] In her memoirs, Condi Rice says she realized that Assistant Secretary of State James Kelly, who would eventually be sent to Pyongyang, and the State Department more generally were on a "short leash." Apparently, she did nothing at the time to remedy the situation.

like a bathroom cleaned and renovated so that it that no longer required risking one's health to use it.

Kim's new measures were not meant to be applied in a single big bang. Rather, they appear to have been planned in phases, involving gradually widening circles of adjustments. A group of North Koreans traveling to a meeting in Europe, for example, showed a set of slides portraying the various planned phases. At this point, they said, they were looking for practical advice on how to operate markets. They indicated they were under pressure to make the early phases of the new policies show results in order to win over the skeptics in the leadership. The skeptics apparently were making their views known publicly. Signs in North Korean media of an extended debate over how far, and how fast, to move suggested that although Kim Jong Il had made the decision to implement new economic policies, much remained unsettled, open to interpretation, and with enough room left for those opposed to full-scaled reforms to push back.

The intellectual underpinnings for the new policies went back several years, at least to early 2000, not long before Kim Jong Il's first visit to China in seventeen years. After another visit to China in January 2001, during which Kim toured Shanghai with a large group of military and economic officials, planning apparently continued. In the autumn, Kim gave instructions on key issues that would form the basis of the measures to follow: economic management, profits, results, and expertise.

In the initial phase of the North's new economic policy, the measures included increasing salaries as well as reducing subsidies for such things as bus and train fares and the cost of housing. The purpose, in part, was to get at the population's psychology of dependence, to wean people away from feeling the state would provide everything and bring them to a stage where they had to make choices on how to spend their money. Subsequent phases included establishment of large central state-sanctioned markets, permission for selected industries to engage in autonomous economic activity, and changes to the structure of cooperative farms.

Parallel with and apparently intended to work in support of these new measures, Kim approved the establishment of a Special Administrative Region (SAR) in Sinuiju, the gateway city across the Yalu River from the Chinese city of Dandong. The two cities were connected by a relatively narrow bridge consisting of a single rail line and a single vehicular lane, each permitting traffic in only one direction at a time. Built by the Japanese in the 1930s, this bridge and another older one a few yards away had been destroyed by US bombs during the Korean War. The "new" bridge was repaired while the older one was left in its ruined state, eventually to become a popular tourist attraction.

The law governing the Sinuiju SAR was announced on September 12, less than a week before Japanese prime minister Koizumi was to arrive in

Pyongyang. It provided for an unprecedented amount of autonomy for the area, similar to the liberties granted to Chinese special economic zones in the 1980s. In addition to a variety of industries, the zone would also, it was rumored, host gambling casinos.

The Chinese, who might have been expected to support this development in the North's economy, did just the opposite. Virtually as soon as the North Koreans announced the SAR, media reports appeared citing Beijing's opposition to it. The Chinese crushed the SAR as quickly as they could, charging that the area's newly appointed "governor"—a shadowy Dutch Chinese figure named Yang Bin whom Kim had somehow been persuaded to pick—was a big-time crook who owed millions in taxes and that a fleshpot and magnet for money laundering on their border was more than they could tolerate. Yang was arrested in short order and sentenced to eighteen years in jail.

The explanations the Chinese advanced may have had some merit, but neither seems convincing as a reason to act so decisively to undercut Kim Jong Il as he was inching down the economic path the Chinese had long hoped he would take. Perhaps just as likely, as rumors had it at the time, the biggest problem was that Kim had gone ahead with plans for the Sinuiju SAR without consulting the Chinese, something for which Beijing has very little tolerance.

The Sinuiju SAR never got off the ground, but the rest of Kim Jong Il's plans were moving ahead. In late August, Tokyo and Pyongyang announced the DPRK-Japan summit; through the summer and fall, the two Koreas also pushed ahead with plans for a long list of inter-Korean talks and exchanges. In July, in a virtually unnoticed but major breakthrough for the KEDO project, Pyongyang had agreed to a direct air route between North and South Korea, connecting Yangyang International Airport in South Korea with Sondok Airport near the North Korean city of Hamhung, both on the east coast. By October, when a small KEDO delegation boarded the first flight, the sight of a North Korean airliner at the airport in Yangyang was considered so routine that South Koreans took no notice of an Air Koryo Tupelov sitting on the tarmac. Instead, waiting passengers crowded around the televisions in the lounge, mesmerized by pictures of a North Korean cheering squad—a group of several hundred beautiful young women—seated in the stands at the Asian Games in the South Korean city of Pusan, a city where UN troops had long ago made their final stand against the invading North Korean army.

THE UNQUIET AMERICANS

The story of the mission to Pyongyang by US assistant secretary of state James Kelly in October 2002 and of North Korea's undisguised and unrestrained drive for a nuclear arsenal that followed is a cautionary tale of action and reaction between unfriendly nations with intersecting national interests. The developments in the final months of 2002 set the stage and launched a clash over the North's development of nuclear weapons that in the intervening years has waxed and waned, appeared to approach resolution, and then fell back into confrontation. Some of the interactions between Washington and Pyongyang during this period were and remain highly controversial.

In late-August 2002, when the news broke of the planned Koizumi visit to Pyongyang, Undersecretary of State John Bolton was in Seoul to warn the ROK about the US analysis concerning the North's HEU program. Like Deputy Secretary Richard Armitage, who was in Tokyo on a similar mission, he could provide no details to the ally to back up the US claim. Bolton also gave a speech while in Seoul, a typically hard-line address about North Korea. As usual, in his negative remarks about the DPRK, he was in front of where policy actually was at the moment, but also as usual he wasn't wrong about where it was headed.

The North Korean response to Bolton's speech showed up in a relatively restrained statement from the Foreign Ministry, slamming Bolton personally, but more important ending on a note meant to signal where Pyongyang hoped to lead the upcoming talks with the Americans: "The DPRK has clarified more than once that if the U.S. has a will to drop its hostile policy toward the DPRK it will have dialogue with the U.S. to clear the U.S. of its worries over its security." In view of what occurred a little over a month later, when James Kelly led a delegation to Pyongyang for talks on October 3–5, the formulation in the North's statement takes on added significance. It suggests not only what the North had in mind when the Americans finally showed up, but also how thoroughly it was prepared to put the negotiations on a new footing. It also raises important questions as to what Pyongyang might have been expecting the United States to put on the table once those talks began.

In his talks with Kim Jong Il in September 2002, Japanese prime minister Koizumi obliquely raised the enrichment issue. Kim, who was emotional about what he saw as Washington's pullback from the Agreed Framework and the bilateral engagement that had developed in its wake, did not respond, but it would be hard to suppose the point was missed when North Korean officials pored over the transcripts of the meeting.

Koizumi's reference would have fit with other evidence that Pyongyang had no doubt been collecting about Washington's concerns with the enrichment program. The North Korean Foreign Ministry has a good clipping service, allowing it to track closely important American statements on the Korean issue. Just how closely had been demonstrated in November 1998, at the talks in Pyongyang on the issue of the underground cavern at

Kumchang-ri. When the head of the US delegation, Ambassador Charles Kartman, pointed out on a large map unfolded on the conference room table where the Americans believed the secret facility was, the North Koreans were flummoxed. They had thought the United States would point to a site that had previously been pinpointed in a graphic on the front page of the *New York Times*, as part of the story that had initially put the issue into the public realm. The North Korean negotiator looked at where his US counterpart was pointing and said, "Are you sure?"

With such close attention to US media, it is unlikely Pyongyang would have missed two high-profile American references earlier in 2002 to the issue of a "covert" North Korean nuclear weapons program. In early May, John Bolton made the charge in a speech at the Heritage Foundation. A month later, the same charge was gingerly picked up and discussed at some length by former US negotiator Robert Gallucci in a presentation to the Council on Foreign Relations. As if that weren't enough, in July, at a meeting with the North Korean foreign minister during an Asia-Pacific Economic Cooperation session in Brunei, Secretary of State Powell warned his North Korean counterpart that when Kelly made his scheduled visit to Pyongyang in early October, he would raise some tough issues.

At a meeting in mid-August with North Korean UN diplomats in New York, Leon Sigal of the Social Science Research Council, who often met with the North Koreans, raised Bolton's charges. The diplomats didn't push back. Later, when the *Los Angeles Times* carried an op-ed by Sigal that specifically cited Bolton's accusation, Pyongyang took note of that article in its party daily, *Rodong Sinmun*. In other words, there was at some level in the North Korean apparatus knowledge of the American accusation of a "covert" nuclear program. Given that the plutonium program at Yongbyon was fully monitored by the IAEA, a "covert program" could refer to only one thing—enrichment. Exactly how much detail officials in the Foreign Ministry knew about the program is an open question, but they certainly knew that the Americans had it high on their list of issues.

Despite evidence that North Korea anticipated that the subject of the HEU program would come up, the impression of those on the Kelly delegation on the first afternoon of the talks was that the North Koreans were caught off balance by the US accusation and that the head of the North Korean delegation, Vice Foreign Minister Kim Gye Gwan, was unprepared with an answer until he checked with someone higher up during a break in the discussions. There is another scenario to consider, however, and that is what Kim was unprepared for was not the accusation itself. Rather, he may have been caught off balance by what he perceived—and in fact what Kelly's presentation as written by the hard-liners meant to impart—was the imperious tone of the US presentation, especially the nonnegotiable position that dialogue was impossible until the North's enrichment program was halted. After the fact, some in the US delegation have said they thought that the main point of Kelly's presentation was to make clear that if the enrichment program was stopped, the United States would pursue the "bold approach." That, however, does not appear to be the central message the North Koreans heard.

Putting diplomacy with the United States back on track at this point was absolutely essential for Kim Jong Il's new economic policies. For the United States to come in with an ultimatum that no talks were possible until the enrichment program was addressed was exactly what the North Korean diplomats had told Sigal was the fundamental problem—that the Americans were not leaving room for discussion. In Pyongyang's view, the United States wanted the North to disarm first, before talks, whereas the North thought it had signaled (certainly in its response to John Bolton's speech in Seoul) that US security concerns could be addressed during, but not before resuming, dialogue. Moreover, in a comment that obviously needled the North Koreans terribly because it was pointed directly at Kim Jong Il's personal initiatives toward Tokyo and Seoul, Kelly's presentation warned that if the enrichment program were left untouched, that would negatively affect Pyongyang's initiatives toward Japan and South Korea.

After a break, Vice Minister Kim parried Kelly's accusation in standard North Korean fashion—he said the charge was false and represented an effort by those opposed to improving US-DPRK relations, a response that left open the possibility that there were others in the United States not so opposed and thus with whom the North could do business. Having dispatched the issue, the North Korean negotiator moved on to his prepared presentation, which was no doubt precisely where Kim Jong Il wanted the discussion to be in the first place. The vice foreign minister's presentation, totally ignored after the fact in Washington, included initiatives on the timing of special IAEA inspections (a point John Bolton had been pressing for months), missile exports (a serious US proliferation concern, though the administration hadn't made an effort to discuss it with the North since coming to office), conventional power plants versus light-water reactors (at that point KEDO had just poured "first concrete," the symbolic start of construction), and the status of US troops in South Korea (for more than a decade the North had been hinting, signaling, and explicitly explaining that it was not opposed to the presence of US troops on the peninsula as long as they weren't a "threat"). The North Koreans were almost certainly expecting Kelly to pick up on one or all of those ideas. Instead, he stuck to his instructions—no negotiating.

At dinner that night, Vice Minister Kim made an effort—disguised as a joke—to see if there was any way to get Kelly off to the side where the two might go beyond their talking points and engage in a more constructive discussion. Kelly's instructions wouldn't allow it, nor would those in his delegation who were determined to see that he didn't slip his leash.

The next morning, the two delegations met again for another sterile exchange of accusations and counteraccusations. The real fireworks started that afternoon when the Americans met with Kang Sok Ju. Anyone who had dealt with Kang—and almost no one on the Kelly delegation had much experience in negotiations with him before that session—knew that the first vice foreign minister could get prickly, bombastic, and sarcastic, especially when he was tired. In the 1994 Geneva talks, in fact, there had been an unspoken agreement between the lower-ranking members of the delegations to avoid afternoon meetings as much as possible because any progress made in the morning between Kang and his American counter-part tended to get frayed, if not actually undone, as the day wore on.

Kang told Kelly he had been up all night in important meetings, dis-cussing the US position with very senior officials.* Even if Kang had had a good night's sleep, what followed probably would have been, as in fact it turned out to be, an unmitigated diplomatic disaster, one that was in-evitable given the circumstances, the background preparations, and espe-cially Kelly's rigid instructions not to negotiate or even engage in normal diplomatic courtesies. Prior to the delegation's arrival in Seoul on its way to Pyongyang, the US Embassy had been told to stand by for important, high-level last-minute instructions to pass on to Kelly. The instructions, it turned out, were that the US negotiator was not to toast the North Ko-reans and not to host a dinner for them. It was hard to see how the leash could have been any shorter.**

In many respects, the Kang-Kelly meeting was similar to what hap-pened in January 1992, when Undersecretary of State Arnold Kanter met with North Korean party secretary Kim Yong Sun in New York: the same concern on the US side with something so trivial as whether to host a meal, the same insistence that the US delegation was not there to negotiate, and the same take-it-or-leave-it approach the US negotiator was instructed to bring to the table. There was a crucial difference this time, however. This time the North Koreans had considerably more leverage—eight thousand spent fuel rods sitting in cans in the cooling pond at Yongbyon, fuel rods

---

* When I was in Pyongyang weeks later with Ambassador Donald Gregg, Kang told us that the reason for the all-night meeting among the "agencies concerned" was a heated discussion of whether he should say the DPRK was "entitled to have nuclear weapons." From the vantage point of 2013, that might seem like a minor quibble, but in 2002, with the Agreed Framework still in effect, it would be a major step.

** Actually, some in Washington thought any dinner would be one too many. In a note to Nation-al Security Adviser Condoleezza Rice while the Kelly delegation was still in Pyongyang, Secretary of Defense Donald Rumsfeld observed, "I thought you told the President in my meeting that there weren't going to be any meals at the North Korean event. I notice they had one or two dinners." See http://papers.rumsfeld.com/library/2002-10-04 to Honorable Condoleezza Rice re North Korea.

that when reprocessed would yield around twenty-five kilograms of plutonium, enough for at least three or four nuclear weapons.

These were extremely high stakes, but they were not what the Americans at the table had been told to consider. Their sole purpose was to let
the North Koreans know that they had been caught "cheating" and that
until this problem was fixed, there would be no further discussions. Consequently, when Kang Sok Ju began to talk about the nuclear issue, they could
hardly believe their ears. In fact, that stunned reaction turned out to be the
problem. Sitting at the table in the Foreign Ministry conference room,
the delegation members each interpreted what they heard as an admission
by Kang that the North had an enrichment program. After the meeting,
they reinforced each other's impressions, filling in the blanks of each other's uncertainties. Looking back years later, several of the delegation members saw what had gone wrong in their first reaction. When Kang referred
to Kelly's charges, they took that as an implicit admission of enrichment.
When Kang said the North had a "right" to nuclear weapons, they took
that as an implicit admission of enrichment. When Kang said the North
had something "even more powerful than nuclear weapons," they took that
as a threat of biological, or chemical, or who knows what kind of weapons.

What was probably the most fateful meeting the two countries ever
had lasted less than an hour. There was no discussion of Kang's position that as part of any resolution of Washington's concerns, the United
States should recognize the North's political system, conclude a peace
agreement with a nonaggression commitment, and refrain from interfering with the North's economic development. Kelly asked no questions,
probed nothing. The American diplomat knew exactly what his instructions were—deliver the message on enrichment. Period. He had done
that. The only thing left for him was to close his notebook and leave.
From then on, it was all down hill.

After the meeting, the delegation went to the British Embassy to send
a quick initial message on Kang's remarks back to Washington, using the
UK's secure communications equipment.* Under considerable time pressure and less than optimal physical conditions in the cramped space, the
Korean speakers in the group did what they could to reconstruct a transcript based on what Kang had said in Korean, as opposed to what his interpreter had rendered into English. The North's interpreters at high-level
talks are usually good at either translating directly or capturing in English
the proper meaning of what the DPRK negotiator has said. On occasion,

---

* At the time, the British Embassy's communications facilities were better than what the traveling US delegation had available (e.g., the fax at the hotel), but not by much. The embassy equipment
was not rated for classified communications, but something much less, "Limited Official Use."

though, the translation is vague. If the point seems important, the best thing is to stop and seek clarification. In this case, the American Korean speakers had to compare notes among themselves as there was no opportunity to go back and ask the North what it meant. There was no second meeting with Kang to clarify what had been unclear.

The delegates' first message was titled "North Koreans Defiantly Admit HEU Program," and once it went out there was never any chance that its first impressions—impressions that should have been questioned and carefully analyzed on arrival in Washington—would get judicious treatment. Those six words were in essence all that anyone who looked at the message in Washington remembered, and they sealed the fate of the Agreed Framework. US policy on the North Korean issue went into a free fall from which it never recovered. Almost every senior official who saw the message jumped to the conclusion that the North Koreans had "admitted" to uranium enrichment, even though a closer reading of both the summary and the reconstructed transcript revealed no such thing. In a Principals Committee meeting that followed Kelly's return to Washington, it was already set in concrete that the North Koreans had admitted to the program and that this "admission" had somehow altered the entire policy landscape.

What difference it should have made whether the North admitted to anything was never really clear, then or later. If the United States thought it had conclusive evidence of a clandestine HEU program, the central question was not whether the North Koreans admitted it, but what to do about it. Yet in the highly charged atmosphere in Washington, the issue of the admission became like high-octane fuel for the hard-liners. There was no question that the meeting with Kang had been negative. The first vice foreign minister had jumped directly into bristling mode, but whether that was because of the US accusation itself or because of the tone of the US presentation—which the North later complained was haughty, rude, and arrogant—wasn't considered.

From North Korea's viewpoint, Kelly—however soft-spoken and gentlemanly his actual delivery—had presented a brusque ultimatum and left no opportunity for discussion. In fact, that was the only way to read the core of Kelly's instructions. In an odd way, for the first time in two years the North Koreans and the Americans were finally on the same page.

THE MORNING AFTER

The US delegation flew to Seoul the next morning. Once there, tired but revved up by what they had convinced themselves they had heard, they briefed the ROK. They did not, however, offer detailed notes of Kang's remarks, an omission that irked the South Koreans. After the briefing,

ROK officials were shaken and more than a little doubtful. It did not seem, based on their own extensive contacts with Kim Jong Il over the past few years, that the North Koreans would have wanted to see such a crucial meeting with the Americans go so badly.

And there was no need for the Americans to tell them things had gone badly. Only a few hours after the Kelly delegation had departed, the North Korean Foreign Ministry had released a statement complaining that the US envoy had come with a "high handed and arrogant attitude" in claiming that North-South Korean and DPRK-Japanese relations could not move ahead unless the North first met the US "unilateral" demands on "nuclear, missile, and conventional armed forces and human rights issues." Kelly's remarks on the North's initiatives toward Japan and South Korea, as much or maybe even more than the enrichment accusation, had obviously struck home. The North's statement had also dryly noted, without elaboration, that the DPRK side had "clarified its principled position" to Kelly.

On October 10, the South's National Security Council met and, with an eye to the looming storm clouds, laid out steps it hoped would keep the situation from worsening. Noting that abrogation of the Agreed Framework would be dangerous (a position very much at odds with the Bush administration's viewpoint at this juncture), the group decided that, in addition to keeping in touch with allies on the enrichment issue, the South should attempt to arrange a visit by First Vice Foreign Minister Kang Sok Ju to Washington. The latter idea was an indication of how out of touch America and its South Korean ally had become on the North Korea question; such a visit might have seemed to make good sense in a policy paper in Seoul, but it would have been laughed out of the room in Washington.

The South's ongoing contacts with Pyongyang provided a channel for Seoul to air its concerns with the North Koreans at the highest level. ROK unification minister Chung Se-hyon was to be in Pyongyang for previously scheduled talks on October 19–23. President Kim Dae Jung instructed him to deliver to Kim Jong Il a message with the following points: the North should send Kang Sok Ju to Washington to keep the dialogue going, it should not take any steps that would hasten the demise of the Agreed Framework, and it should make its position clear prior to a US-ROK-Japan summit in Mexico scheduled to take place on the margins of an Asia-Pacific Economic Cooperation meeting.

To reinforce his message to the North Koreans, and also to make things clear to Washington, on October 23 President Kim publicly warned against scrapping the Agreed Framework. "Military action can result in great tragedy," Kim's spokesman quoted the president as saying. "Nobody wants that." Economic sanctions, he added, would give North Korea "the freedom for nuclear responses."

Kim Jong Il was paying attention. On October 25, his Foreign Ministry released a statement repeating the complaints about the Kelly delegation's high-handed attitude and reiterating the points Kang had made to Kelly about what the United States should do to resolve the problem, but ending on a conciliatory note about the need for negotiations to continue. It made a special point of referring to Kim Jong Il's recent economic measures, noting, "The DPRK has taken a series of new steps in economic management and adopted one measure after another to reenergize the economy, including the establishment of a special economic region, in conformity with the changed situation and specific conditions of the country."

If the statement was meant to turn the tide, it didn't. What the South Koreans, and probably the North Koreans as well, didn't fully realize was that in Washington, the Agreed Framework, a crucial underpinning for Seoul's Sunshine Policy, was doomed. In the initial shock of Kelly's report on his meeting, the Bush administration was as close to having a unified view as it would ever achieve on the North Korean issue. The hard-liners considered this the final nail in the Agreed Framework's coffin, and even those who had backed negotiations reluctantly agreed.

The more fundamental problem at this point was the same one facing the dog who chases the bus and one day catches it: what next? Given the administration's planning for an attack on Iraq—a Senate measure on the use of force in Iraq was up for a vote that very week—the administration did not want or need a distracting bombshell about North Korea, although it quickly offered classified briefings on the Kelly trip to select members of Congress. (Not all took up the offer—and then those who didn't complained later that they had not been briefed.) Besides the tactical question of what to do with the news of the Pyongyang meeting, there was a larger strategic one: if the Agreed Framework was dead, "shredded" in the words of some officials, what would take its place to keep the North's plutonium production frozen? According to John Bolton, there was "no need to replace it [the Agreed Framework] with anything." Astonishingly, nothing was decided on the overall approach until December 2002, two months after the Kelly visit and just as the situation was starting its rapid slide over the cliff.

Information about the Kang "admission" leaked before the White House had decided how to handle the news. The administration needed to put out its own account and did so through a restrained statement by the State Department's press spokesman on October 16, noting that because the North Koreans had "acknowledged" to Kelly that they had an enrichment program, the United States was "unable" to pursue the president's bold approach to improving relations with the North. A KEDO delegation was in previously scheduled talks in Pyongyang exactly at that time, and one of the delegation members, unsure of how the North Koreans would react to what was liable to be a very negative story once it became public, had asked acquaintances in Washington to give him a heads-up if the news broke while he was in North Korea. "Just call me and say the weather in Washington has turned bad." In the early hours of October 17 (late on the sixteenth in Washington), the phone rang and the weather report came through. It was bad.

The next day, the North Koreans carried on with the KEDO talks as if nothing had happened, though one member of their delegation flashed a particularly sour look across the room. At dinner, after the talks, the same North Korean vented. Washington had released a story that the North had acknowledged an enrichment program to the Kelly delegation, he said. The North Korean, who had been at the Kelly meetings, insisted Kang had done no such thing. The real problem, he said, was that the DPRK side had been astonished and offended at the US delegation's demeanor. "They were diplomats, but they wouldn't even discuss things," he complained. "They just repeated the same thing over and over."

The first shock of the report from the Kelly delegation that the North had "admitted" to an enrichment program had brought the warring camps in Washington into a temporary consensus, but like a soap bubble it vanished in short order. The hard-liners wanted to jettison the Agreed Framework immediately. Others didn't want to go quite so far, but were not sure of the way ahead. At an APEC meeting in Mexico, October 21–27, open, no-holds-barred warfare broke out within the US government. The *New York Times* and the *Washington Post* were wheeled into position for the opposing camps to fire broadsides at each other. The Agreed Framework was "dead," one unidentified US senior official was quoted as saying. A few days later, Secretary of State Colin Powell responded, saying no such decision had been made and that if the North Koreans called, "We'll listen, and I hope vice versa." The next day, the unidentified senior official was quoted as making the eye-popping statement that Powell's remarks might represent the State Department position, but it didn't represent the administration view.

In the middle of that open debate, on October 26, President George Bush, Japanese prime minister Junichiro Koizumi, and South Korean president Kim Dae Jung issued a joint statement asserting that North Korea's uranium enrichment program violated the country's nuclear agreements. The statement called upon Pyongyang to "dismantle" the program "in a prompt and verifiable manner and to come into full compliance with all its international commitments." Stressing the three countries' desire for a peaceful resolution to the nuclear issue, the declaration made clear that both Japan and South Korea intended to continue their bilateral engagement efforts with Pyongyang. At this point, Seoul and to a lesser degree Tokyo were seeking to control and contain Washington, thinking the joint statement preserved their room for maneuver. It is not at all clear they understood how little control they would have over events to come.

The North Koreans had been watching, probably in consternation, the way the story was developing. As reflected in their statements from the moment Kelly left Pyongyang, they were especially concerned about US interference with inter-Korean relations. (DPRK-Japan relations had by then already hit a major obstacle in terms of negative Japanese public opinion sparked by Pyongyang's assertion that several of the Japanese abductees had died while in the North.) Both the message from the ROK leader and his public comments may have given them reason to hope something could yet be salvaged. If not, they would try to make clear, certainly to the South Koreans, that it was the Americans who had failed to make the extra effort.

On October 27, the day after the tripartite statement in Mexico, an eighteen-member North Korean delegation flew into the South for a nine-day tour of South Korean industry, part of the inter-Korean exchanges that had been launched by the June 2000 summit. The nominal leader of the group was Pak Nam-ki, head of the Workers Party Finance and Planning Department.* The real leader was Kim Jong Il's brother-in-law, Chang Song Taek. South Koreans who accompanied the group on the tour found Chang intelligent, attentive, and, though he wasn't an economist, interested in ways to enhance inter-Korean economic cooperation.

On November 2, former ambassador Donald Gregg and I, along with Korea Society vice president Fred Carriere, arrived in Pyongyang.** We had hoped to drive to the North Korean capital, transiting the DMZ, but US military officials in Korea blocked the move, requiring us to fly via Beijing. We saw the same people US assistant secretary James Kelly and his party had seen. The Foreign Ministry officials were obviously perturbed at the course of events, a little defensive, and more than a little apprehensive. Although as in Kelly's case there was no clear or explicit admission, there was also not a word of denial that they were actively pursuing a highly enriched uranium program. We told them flatly that their enrichment program was an extremely serious breach of the relationship between the United States and North Korea and that any future agreement would require the most rigorous verification because of this violation of nuclear accords. They said that they would "clear the concerns" of the United States in return for three things: first, recognition of their sovereignty, in a statement that would imply their acceptance as a legitimate state that is not to be attacked or overthrown; second, no interference with their economic development—that is, no economic sanctions or embargoes against

---

* In 2010 Pak was blamed for the failure of a badly conceived plan for currency revaluation and, according to some accounts, executed.

** This account of the visit is largely taken from Don Oberdorfer's earlier writings.

them, a request that was not accompanied by any solicitations of economic assistance; and third, negotiation of a nonaggression treaty by which the United States would legally assure North Korea that it would not attack with nuclear weapons or other means.

These were broadly consistent with what Kang had told Kelly and the conditions the Foreign Ministry had included in its October 25 statement. My own belief was that this was their opening bid for negotiations, not necessarily what a negotiation would produce if and when one got under way. Don Gregg several times urged that Kim Jong Il send a message to President Bush in order to calm the situation. On the last day, almost at the last hour, Kang Sok Ju came into the meeting room with a piece of paper. He explained it was an "oral message" from Kim for the president.

The message was simple and, as these things go, relatively positive. It gave nothing away, but did suggest the door was open to finding a way to address US concerns if the Americans would deal with the North's. Kim noted "the nuclear issue that has emerged recently"—seemingly a careful reference to the enrichment question—and suggested, "If the US were willing to recognize our sovereignty and to offer firm assurances of non-aggression, I believe there would be a way to resolve the nuclear issue in a manner befitting the demands of the new century." Kim went on to acknowledge "President Bush's statement that the U.S. has no intention to invade our country," adding that "the critical issue now is the provision of legally binding assurance of nonaggression by the U.S." The message ended on a positive note: "If the U.S. takes a resolute decision in this regard, you can be assured that we will respond accordingly."[*]

We left with some hope but also with Kang's sober warning that the Agreed Framework was "hanging by a thread." Ambassador Gregg and I brought the message to the White House on our return from the North and discussed it with Deputy National Security Council Adviser Steve Hadley. Hadley's response was quick, negative, and definitive: "We don't reward bad behavior." He asked no questions about our discussions or impressions of Pyongyang.

There may have been something beside concern with "bad behavior" at work in Hadley's brusque dismissal. Around the same time, through a variety of channels, Washington had received several other messages from Pyongyang about a desire to meet. After considerable internal discussion, the administration had decided to move ahead on one of the channels, but it never got under way. The oral message from Kim Jong Il was apparently put in the same category with the others—distracting and unwelcome

---

[*] Kim's message was similar to what Kang had told Kelly and what the North Koreans had reiterated several times after that, including to Don Gregg and me. The crucial difference was that Kim was personally taking note of the US president's statement, while himself carefully using language that left room for negotiations.

noise designed to pull the United States off base after the Kelly meeting in Pyongyang.

There was no reply to Kim. Few people in Washington even knew the message existed until Don Gregg and I revealed it in a *Washington Post* article in June 2005. Only a few high-ranking officials in the State Department saw what Kim had sent. They decided that although the message held some promise and might be worth pursuing, given the mind-set at the White House, it would be a hopeless quest. The rest of the government's Asia hands never saw the message. Considering the mood in Washington at the moment, it probably would not have made any difference even if they had.

Given the context of events and the decidedly negative turn matters had taken over the preceding month, the message was as important for the symbolism of the gesture as for the content of the message—and the administration's rejection of it was equally symbolic. To the North Koreans, for the White House to ignore a message from Kim Jong Il was probably chalked up as an insult, but even more as a sign that Washington was not interested in doing anything to reverse the deteriorating situation. If that was their conclusion, then once again the North Koreans were reading US signals loud and clear.

The South Koreans made one more effort to head the Americans off from the dangerous course their policy was taking. At a meeting of the Trilateral Coordination and Oversight Group, or TCOG, in early November, ROK Deputy Foreign Minister Li Tae-sik, who had been a deputy director of KEDO a few years earlier, tried to dissuade the Americans from immediately cutting off the heavy fuel oil that KEDO was scheduled to deliver, warning it would lead to serious consequences, including the North restarting its nuclear program. A compromise was finally reached, allowing the November shipment, already on a ship headed for a North Korean port, to proceed but halting subsequent shipments.

The view in Seoul was that it was a mistake to cut off the HFO shipments, but there was no way to fight the decision because the Americans were so adamant about it. Soon after, on November 14, and under extreme US pressure, the KEDO Executive Board, composed of the four member countries, agreed to a statement halting HFO shipments, with key wording dictated by the NSC over the phone to the American representative, Ambassador Jack Pritchard. The Japanese and South Korean delegates were ashen faced when they arrived at KEDO headquarters in New York that morning. When the meeting ended, the atmosphere was funereal. Another confrontational session followed upstairs between lower-ranking KEDO staff and members of the US delegation, a meeting intended not to try to change what had already been decided, but simply to vent frustration and to warn of consequences. The Americans shrugged—they themselves did not agree with the decision, they made clear, but they had been ordered to push the position, and that was what they had done.

On November 16, the North Korean delegation that had toured South Korea and had then gone on to Indonesia, Malaysia, and Singapore returned home. The situation had been getting bad when they left Pyongyang. Now, on their return, it was unsalvageable.

Pyongyang waited a week before directly responding to the KEDO statement. On November 21—a day before the oil tanker *Sun River* docked in Nampo with a final 42,886 tons of heavy oil—the North Korean Foreign Ministry raised the stakes, pointing to a passage in the Agreed Framework that linked KEDO's supply of HFO to the North's obligation to freeze its reactor and "related facilities." It did not press this point, however, and—suggesting that the North might be leaving the way open for a reply from Bush to Kim Jong Il's message—characterized the president in neutral terms. Nevertheless, the essential message was clear: cutting off the HFO would have dire consequences; no HFO, no freeze on operations of the reactor at Yongbyon.

A question about the HFO had come up during a background briefing by two "senior State Department officials" in October at the time of the APEC meeting in Mexico. A reporter had observed that "it seems you can't cut off the fuel supplies because that would provoke an even deeper crisis." The answer from one of the officials was revealing: "I think it would be a mistake to suggest . . . X follows and then Y and Z, and A and B follow after that." In other words, there was no necessary sequence to, or connection between, events. Cutting off the HFO would not inevitably provoke a deeper crisis. As it worked out, however, there were consequences to stopping the HFO, and they were severe. A and B did follow.

Due to problems at the port, the last drops of HFO from the tanker were not unloaded until December 10. Two days later, exactly four weeks after the KEDO statement, and about five weeks after Kim Jong Il's message to Bush arrived at the White House, the North Koreans pulled the trigger. The pace at which they moved suggested both that they had put together an action plan during the time they had been waiting and that they had decided to pause for brief periods to see how the Americans would react.

Pyongyang's first step was to restart the facilities at Yongbyon. On December 12, the Foreign Ministry announced the North would "immediately resume operation and construction of facilities [in Yongbyon] to generate electricity." Even then it signaled the action was not irreversible, asserting that whether the facilities were refrozen depended on the United States. The North also sent two letters to Vienna, on the twelfth and fourteenth, asking the IAEA to remove seals and monitoring equipment from the main nuclear facilities at Yongbyon: the reactor, the spent-fuel pond, the reprocessing plant, and the fuel-fabrication facility. The letters warned that if the IAEA did not do so "expeditiously," the North would act unilaterally. After waiting more than a week, on December 22, the North did just that. The two remaining IAEA inspectors were summoned to the nuclear reactor building to witness the cutting of the seals and disabling the surveillance cameras that had guaranteed the reactor would remain shut down. The deed was done with ceremony. About a hundred North Koreans and technicians gathered for the occasion, which was celebrated with patriotic songs and the tossing of flower petals. Consuming beer brought into the reactor building for the occasion, they drank toasts to the country's nuclear future. Curiously, the North Koreans only covered the surveillance cameras and pointed them toward the wall, almost as if to say that they expected the IAEA to be back eventually.

On the twenty-sixth, the IAEA inspectors reported that the North had started moving fresh fuel to the 5-megawatt reactor, which had sat unfueled since being unloaded in June 1994. Refueling the reactor was a sure sign that the North intended to resume making plutonium. The following day, the North informed the IAEA that because there was no reason for the inspectors to be in North Korea, they should leave. The IAEA asked if their people could have a little extra time to make a more graceful exit. The North Koreans refused. The next plane to Beijing was on December 31, and the inspectors were on it.

In the middle of this crisis over the nuclear question, on December 19, 2002, South Korea held a presidential election. A little-known, politically inexperienced human rights advocate and lawyer, Roh Moo-hyun, won the election, after furious anti-US demonstrations sparked by a tragic accident in which two young South Korean schoolgirls were run over by a US Army armored vehicle. Roh would spend his term in office walking a tightrope, trying to maintain good relations with the United States while building on what seemed to be important gains in inter-Korean relations.

At the end of the Bush administration's second year, the United States was left with the tattered remains of the Agreed Framework. That agreement had, for eight years, halted the production of fissile material at Yongbyon, created from scratch a multilateral organization (KEDO) that successfully forged working relations with the North Koreans, and provided an opening for the United States to address its concerns about the proliferation of North Korean missiles. Now, this crucial agreement was dead—and there was no way to know what would take its place. On the verge of launching a war against Iraq, the administration knew it could not afford a major confrontation in Korea, but without anything to fill the vacuum created by the destruction of the Agreed Framework, it was ill-prepared to manage the new crisis that was emerging in Northeast Asia. There was no mistaking that things were bad. The real question was, how bad would they get?

18

TROUBLE IN THE US-ROK ALLIANCE

ONCE THE TWO KOREAS began to develop ties that went beyond rhetoric, differences between Washington and Seoul were inevitable. In the late 1980s, these differences remained relatively minor, but when the North Korean nuclear issue took center stage in the 1990s, and North-South dialogue shifted to a more active phase, the US-ROK policy divide grew. American nonproliferation concerns collided again and again with different priorities in South Korea. From then on, finding the right balance between the goals of the two alliance partners became problematic, no matter who sat in the Blue House. Conservative and liberal ROK leaders each saw Washington as sacrificing South Korean interests in favor of US concerns over the North's nuclear program.

The nuclear threat looked less serious from Seoul than it did from Washington. For many years, most of the ROK political spectrum had remained unconvinced that North Korea's nuclear program posed a real, physical danger to the South. Even conservatives thought there was little chance the North would use nuclear weapons on the peninsula. Rather, the worry was that the mere existence of the North's program made the ultimate goal of reunification more difficult, perhaps impossible, to attain.

In the first years of Kim Dae Jung's presidency (1998–2003), Washington and Seoul smoothed over their differences on how to deal with North Korea, but in 2001 with the historical mismatch of Kim's Sunshine Policy and the Bush administration's skepticism about the worth of talking with North Korea, relations hit a series of bumps. These grew into mountains in 2003 when a new South Korean president, Roh Moo-hyun, assumed office. US-ROK ties had been strained many times in the previous half century, but the period 2001–2007 was surely among the worst. The consequences would reverberate in both domestic South Korean politics and alliance relations for the next decade.

By January 2003, with the United States moving toward full-scale invasion of Iraq, an undercurrent of worry existed in Seoul (and apparently Pyongyang as well) that after a swift victory in the Middle East, Washington would turn to North Korea as next on its list for a military solution. It was in that atmosphere that a documentary airing on South Korean television caught the attention of President-elect Roh Moo-hyun. The television show included the recollections of former president Kim Young Sam, who recounted that in the spring of 1994 the United States was on the verge of attacking North Korea and would have done so but for his strong intervention. This account—while historically inaccurate—evoked familiar fears of a big power trampling on Korean interests, and it struck a chord with Roh. Convinced that the South Korean Foreign Ministry was too pro-American and unwilling to stand up to Washington, after taking office in February the new president ordered his diplomats to watch the documentary. In a curious way, Roh's concerns mirrored those in Washington, where administration hard-liners thought elements of the State Department too flabby in dealing with North Korea. In his memoirs, John Bolton calls the State Department section handling the Korean issue—the Bureau of East Asia and Pacific Affairs—the "EAPeasers."

This concern about the balance of the US-ROK relationship became a cause for increasing tension within the South Korean government. A year after Roh took office, in early 2004, the Foreign Ministry was again the focus of Blue House attention when an intraministry feud broke out between two sections—the Treaties Division, which advocated that the United States should pay for whatever changes it wanted in the disposition of American troops in South Korea (the so-called pro-independence school) and the North America Division, which considered maintaining the US-ROK alliance as paramount and was less willing to make an issue of the expenses (hence its label as the pro-alliance school). In January 2004, chafing at the policies of the Blue House, which was leaning toward the "independence school," some Foreign Ministry officials criticized President Roh during an internal staff meeting. Word reached the Blue House, and there quickly followed what some considered a purge. The term *Taliban* was used to describe the inquisitors, and in the uproar Foreign Minister Yoon Young-kwan was forced to retire, after less than a year in office. It was the sort of episode that reinforced Washington's concerns that the alliance had entered stormy waters and that Roh Moo-hyun was an unreliable partner.

PROBLEMS FOR DIPLOMACY

In January 2003, as members of the incoming Roh administration had been preparing to move into their new offices, North Korean technicians were bringing the decadelong frozen nuclear facilities at Yongbyon back on line. During the 1994–2002 Agreed Framework freeze, portions of the nuclear center—notably the fuel-fabrication facility and the still-unfinished 50-megawatt reactor—had collapsed into unsalvageable disrepair. But the North had performed limited maintenance on the smaller 5-megawatt reactor and the reprocessing plant. Firing these up again, even in the middle of the cold of Korea's winter, did not take long.

While the technicians at Yongbyon set the dials on their 1950s-technology control panels, diplomats in Washington and the capitals of Northeast Asia scrambled to catch up. With considerable arm-twisting, Beijing got the North Koreans to agree to enter talks—first among three parties (US, China, DPRK) and soon after that with six (US, China, ROK, DPRK, Japan, Russia). Negotiations in these various configurations ground on for the next five years, producing countless official briefing papers and endless newspaper-column inches but few results. Public expectations for the talks exceeded anything they could possibly produce. As negotiations stalled again and again, bogged down by stubbornness in Pyongyang matched by that in Washington, for the first time since the end of the Korean War American influence on the peninsula waned relative to that of China, whose diplomatic rise was boosted by the remarkable performance of its economy.

Despite agreement among the various capitals that diplomacy was the preferred option for dealing with the nuclear issue, significant differences persisted over ends and means. One senior Chinese diplomat noted that although all the parties agreed on the end point, no one could agree how to get there. To some extent, the problem was compounded because rather than building on an existing foundation, diplomatic efforts had to start from zero. The Americans did not want to be seen as signing on to anything that even looked like the Agreed Framework, with the result that terminology had to be reinvented and practical solutions discarded or bent into unworkable shapes.

Most damaging, the US ability to deal with Pyongyang was constricted by President Bush's personal, oft-stated loathing for Kim Jong Il. When it came to North Korea, frustration and distaste were nothing new in Washington. What was unusual was the public airing of these feelings at the highest levels. The personal animus toward the North ended up interfering with consideration of policies that, in the long run, might have produced better results. Over and over, Tokyo, Seoul, and especially Beijing advised Washington at least to tone down its rhetoric to create a more productive atmosphere for diplomacy, but to no avail. Each time the president or a high-level US official made a negative comment about Kim Jong Il, Pyongyang responded with a furious rhetorical broadside of its own. There was no way diplomacy could establish a foothold, however much Washington insisted that was its chosen path.

At the same time, in misreading the history of the previous eight years of engagement with Pyongyang, the administration failed to take seriously that what the North wanted above all else was improved relations with the United States. This was probably Washington's most effective leverage with the North, but it was never utilized because, notwithstanding the rhetoric, from 2001 to 2005 the administration was not effectively committed to a diplomatic process. Instead, barely hiding its aversion to the chore of dealing with Pyongyang, Washington seemed mesmerized by a preference—sometimes explicitly expressed but always clearly implied—for regime change.

That option never reached the point of established or approved American policy, but Pyongyang could read between the lines.* No matter how often Washington stated for the record that it had no intention of invading, from Pyongyang's vantage point the overall message was clear—Washington wanted North Korea to disappear. In his memoirs, Defense Secretary Rumsfeld notes that in 2006 he advocated a course that he hoped might encourage a military coup in the North. Other officials kept hoping for something along those lines that might solve the problem without their having to act. In late 2002, according to some accounts, Washington picked up indications of serious opposition to Kim Jong Il within North Korea, suggesting the likelihood of his overthrow had increased. In an atmosphere where such a development was the administration's fervent wish, there was a temptation to believe what in the end turned out to be bad information.

A widely held belief, from the president on down, was that by conducting bilateral talks with the North from 1993 to 2000, the United States had allowed Pyongyang to pit Seoul, Tokyo, and Beijing against Washington. According to the common wisdom, the North had "immediately" breached with impunity the Agreed Framework that had resulted from the bilateral approach. A less ideologically tainted examination might have yielded different conclusions. In his memoirs, Vice President Cheney emphasized that "effective diplomacy requires our diplomats study and learn from our history." His point was right on the mark; it was his history that was off target.

There is no question that during Kim Young Sam's administration, the bilateral approach had caused strains in US-ROK relations. Overall, though, the years of the Agreed Framework witnessed a high-water mark

---

* In her memoirs, former NSC adviser Condoleezza Rice says that regime change was prepared as one of three option papers advanced for the president's consideration in late 2002. She calls it an "interesting idea" but dismisses it because "it would have had no support internationally and would have scared our already nervous allies even more." Rice, *No Higher Honor: A Memoir of My Years in Washington* (Crown, 2011), 163.

in coordination among Seoul, Tokyo, and Washington on the North Korea issue, especially through the TCOG mechanism developed in 1999 as part of the Perry process. Similarly, through KEDO the three capitals overcame obstacles and presented a common front toward North Korea. Perhaps most important, under the Agreed Framework the North's plutonium production program at Yongbyon was completely frozen and subjected to constant IAEA monitoring for eight years, from 1994 to 2002.

These were not lessons the White House wanted to study. Rather than admit that the bilateral approach had yielded results, the administration defined it as a failure and declared it out of bounds. In a few instances, this led to absurd orders that United States negotiators could not even be alone in the same room with North Koreans, especially not if the room had sofas where people might sit and talk. Unconcerned with furniture arrangements, all this time the North's nuclear technicians at Yongbyon were operating without constraints, making more plutonium.

SUNSHINE, BARELY

It would be hard to imagine less propitious circumstances for a new South Korean president entering office than those that confronted Roh Moo-hyun in February 2003. Things were bad on every front. Relations between Seoul and Washington were in decline, the North Koreans were restarting their nuclear program, and a major US military campaign halfway around the world was only days away. Stepping into this unhappy scene, the fifty-six-year-old human rights lawyer–turned–politician Roh was completely unprepared either by previous experience or by personal temperament.

Born in August 1946 in Kimhae, South Kyongsong Province, Roh was the first ROK president to grow up after the end of Japanese colonial rule and the first to suffer the trauma of the Korean War as a child. Too poor to attend university, he did not take part in the student protests and street battles against the Park Chung Hee regime in the 1970s. Rather, with great determination, Roh spent several years teaching himself the law and in 1981 became a pro-democracy activist and human rights lawyer, a commitment that during the Chun Doo Hwan years took considerable courage and sacrifice. Eventually turning to politics in the late 1980s, Roh ran for the National Assembly several times, losing more elections than he won. In 2000 he served briefly as minister of maritime affairs and fisheries under Kim Dae Jung.

Without the torrent of anti-American outrage that swept South Korea in the weeks before the country's 2002 presidential elections, Roh might not have ended up in the Blue House. In late November, two US Army enlisted men were acquitted by a US court-martial in the deaths earlier that year of two teenage Korean schoolgirls, crushed by an armored vehicle on maneuvers. Gruesome photographs of the girls' bodies on the roadside inflamed emotions, and clumsy handling of the incident by the US military in South Korea compounded the problem. Even the conservative party presidential candidate, Lee Hoi-chang, who would normally have been expected to show support for the United States during such a difficult period, backed calls for changes to the US-ROK Status of Forces Agreement to give South Korea more jurisdiction over such incidents. Lee's position infuriated the US Embassy in Seoul, which noted that although Roh Moo-hyun's campaign might be helping to fan the flames of the anti-American movement, at least Roh—unlike Lee—was not personally and visibly taking part in the demonstrations.

Although they did not stem from deep-rooted anti-Americanism, the protests reflected a historical ambivalence toward the United States lying just beneath the surface in South Korea, a mix of emotions in the smaller country toward the larger patron and protector. Opinion polls cannot quite capture this pool of combustible nationalism, frustration, and resentment that from time to time ignites almost without warning, but has always burned out just as quickly. The situation in 2002 may have been especially volatile because of the coming of age of the so-called 386 generation—a phrase coined in the 1990s to describe thirty-year-olds, born in the 1960s, many of whom had gone to school in the turbulent years of the 1980s when the United States was seen as supporting the dictatorship of Chon Doo Hwan. Even before the death of the schoolgirls, Ambassador Thomas Hubbard experienced what he sensed was a dangerous upsurge in nationalist, anti-US sentiment during the World Cup soccer tournament held in Seoul in June 2002.

To some extent, Roh himself reflected this deep-seated ambivalence. He accepted the importance of the US-ROK alliance—at least as he understood it—yet he also believed strongly that Washington did not fully comprehend Korea's interests and could not be expected always to take them into consideration. Roh was brilliant, moral, folksy, and probably ill-suited to high office at any time, especially at a moment when South Korea faced such serious challenges. With neither extensive military nor long political experience, he lacked the seasoning of his predecessors in the Blue House, but also their pretensions. His was not the typical Korean imperial presidency, even if he sometimes succumbed to the temptation to use the considerable power of his office against those he considered not the "real" voices of the public. He engaged in a running battle against the country's hostile press, and at one point even brought a lawsuit against South Korea's major newspapers for printing what he said were false accusations against him.

Roh had no familiarity with foreign policy—indeed, he had never been to the United States before becoming president—and he was burdened with terrible political instincts that left him poorly equipped to deal with many domestic issues. None of that was helped by the fact that he was the target of a South Korean press that relentlessly painted him as a radical anti-American working to undermine US-ROK security relations. Roh's approach to North Korea was seen by many American officials and South Korean conservatives as Sunshine II, a continuation of Kim Dae Jung's policies toward Pyongyang. Yet as one close observer put it, Roh "did not give a damn" about North Korea, and he certainly did not have Kim Dae Jung's ideological outlook.

According to Moon Jae-in, Roh's closest adviser and an unsuccessful candidate in the 2012 ROK presidential race, Roh's main focus when he entered office was to rid South Korea of the remnants of its authoritarian past and to firmly establish democratic habits in the government and the economy. What he cared about was changing South Korea's political culture, with its embedded traditional approach to nearly unfettered authority. In the end, Roh was a tragic figure, a leader deeply offended by the injustices committed during the years of dictatorship, yet one who—in his efforts to right the wrongs and correct the historical record—ended up adding fuel to the political passions that had kept his country's politics bitterly divided for decades. That legacy, and the lingering conviction among many both inside and outside Korea that Roh's leadership was simply "weird," largely obscured the role he played in encouraging institutions that would help the still young democracy in South Korea deepen its roots and develop a civil society. His suicide in 2009, after he appeared tainted by the very sort of corruption that he had pledged to banish from Korean politics, shocked the nation and only reinforced the impression of the tragedy of his era.

Despite the adjectives tossed around in South Korean media, Roh was not a radical in any sense of the word. Above all, to those who observed him closely, Roh was a lawyer, with a lawyerly approach to problems. Too often, this technical approach left him seeming unmoored from the hard realities of South Korean politics. While conservatives attacked him from the right, his former allies complained from the left. In August 2005, at the midpoint in his term, the *Hangyore Sinmun*, a voice for liberal-leaning politics, sighed that Roh had been "trapped in the fortress called power and has lost his feeling for the real world."[*]

Where Kim Dae Jung, a politician of long experience, knew how to maneuver and cajole, Roh's approach was to go at issues head-on. Roh told his advisers that he had a good relationship with President Bush, and even

---

[*] To some extent, Roh's problems stemmed from style rather than substance. In the words of one US official, Roh was like Mark Twain's characterization of Wagner's music—better than he sounded.

those American officials who observed the two leaders together agree that the personal chemistry was better than outsiders might imagine. The two were "straight shooters," and in their own minds that was a major plus. On their first meeting in Washington, in May 2003, President Bush took Roh—who was a Lincoln fan—to see the Lincoln bedroom in the White House. The gesture got relations off to a good start. At another meeting, when he was working from briefing notes apparently prepared by aides who were skeptical of the United States, Roh would raise a point and Bush would answer it to the ROK president's satisfaction. Finally, after several such volleys, Roh put the notes aside, saying, "Well, these are worthless." Not every meeting went so well. On a few occasions, in public and in private, Roh pressed Bush to the limit. At a meeting in 2005, Roh would not let up in challenging Bush. After the South Korean leader had left the room, the president turned to his aides and said, "He's pissing me off." ROK officials who heard the remark hurried over to calm things down, and the atmosphere at the lunch that followed was fine.

Whatever their differences and occasional scrapes, Bush seemed to understand that Roh "delivered" on issues important to the United States, sometimes breaking with his own supporters to do so. In 2004, despite considerable popular resistance, Roh sent three thousand ROK troops to join the US-led coalition in Iraq.* He even went ahead after a South Korean hostage was beheaded in Iraq by a group demanding that Seoul cancel the deployment decision. Roh also went against his party in pushing for the Korea-US Free Trade Agreement, which was finally passed by the legislatures of both countries in 2011. Bush was in the minority in his views of Roh. Many in the upper ranks of the administration were utterly dismissive of the South Korean leader and his policies, reinforcing the general perception in both Seoul and Washington that the two governments were increasingly at odds.

As different as he was in most respects from his predecessors, Roh shared with them the stubborn conviction that Korean interests could not be advanced by always bowing to the priorities of a larger power. In 2004 and 2005, this conviction led him and his government into troubling internal debates over what, from Washington's perspective, was a false and destructive dichotomy—the value of the ROK-US alliance versus the imperative of national sovereignty. In this case, "sovereignty" was seen as the need to weigh the alliance against the impulse for progress with North Korea—a balancing act that made absolutely no sense to Washington,

---

* US ambassador to the ROK Alexander Vershbow, among others, criticizes Roh for making the right decision for the wrong reason, that is, wanting to use the offer of troops in order to obtain more American support for his efforts to engage North Korea. Roh later publicly characterized his decision to send the troops to Iraq as a "historical error."

which believed without question that the alliance was essential to the security of the South as well as the bedrock for its economic and political progress over the years. As a result, there came a point in the minds of US defense planners, not unlike that often reached during difficult periods in earlier decades, when they felt they had to look past the storms swirling around an incumbent ROK administration and craft policies that would eventually bring the alliance intact to a more stable future. Even those in Seoul who were largely sympathetic to US views, however, considered the tactical approach Washington took in pursuit of this goal to be flawed, seeming to ignore Koreans' sense of vulnerability and exciting concerns about the country's defense when, in their minds, the United States should have been calming them.

The result was that concerns about US intentions and misperceptions on both sides about the future of US-ROK security relations became the basis of deep and persistent problems throughout the Roh years. During this stormy period, the habits of alliance and personal ties between Americans and Koreans built up over the decades proved crucial in keeping matters from getting worse than they did. That Roh himself did not fundamentally oppose the alliance but, in fact, saw it as crucial to ROK security may have been the biggest—if largely invisible—source of overall stability. On taking office, Roh told his advisers, and always seemed to believe, that his first priority had to be maintaining close relations with the United States. Although often accused of causing strains in the relationship, given the circumstances he faced he did a better job keeping ties intact than his critics were willing to acknowledge. The list of accomplishments in support of US-ROK relations in his years as president is reasonably long, even though the lasting impression of problems is stronger still.

Blunt and sometimes seemingly undisciplined, Roh in his public remarks often fed the fires of doubt about the future of the alliance with his own words. On a visit to Turkey in April 2005, he created controversy at home when he spoke out against "working-level" South Korean officials who, he said, did not grasp the "big picture" about the "gradually changing" ROK-US alliance. Unclear about the trends of the times, these people, Roh said, made "sullen" or "outlandish" remarks. That would have been enough to set off a firestorm in Seoul, but Roh, in typical fashion, proceeded to make things worse: "What I am most concerned about are the ROK people. Some considerably highly educated ROK people appear to have a more pro-American way of thinking than Americans themselves. . . . The ROK people should think and make judgments the way most ROK people do. What is important in guiding the ROK-US alliance is to effectively coordinate the American people's perception of Asian order and the ROK people's perception of Asian order and make a good judgment."

The criticism of Koreans who seemed "more pro-American" than the Americans themselves naturally sparked outrage in South Korean media. The Blue House presidential secretary for public information did not help matters when, faced with criticism of Roh's remarks, she responded, "It has been [the] ROK presidential offices' mission to keep the alliance with the U.S. while preserving national interest." That just further inflamed the situation, not only reinforcing the image that the government saw the two—the alliance with the United States and the "national interest"—as separate things, but worse, seeming to accuse those who were "more pro-American" than the Americans of favoring US over ROK interests.

Only a few months later, US-ROK relations faced what might have become a truly major storm. At a reception in the upscale Silla Hotel in Seoul just before the annual Security Consultative Meeting between top defense officials of the two countries, the ROK Foreign Ministry representative, Kim Sook, under instructions from Blue House National Security Council deputy Lee Jong-seok, informed the Americans that Seoul did not want to include a reference to the US "nuclear umbrella" in the traditional SCM statement. (The NSC had previously discussed the question and decided that dropping the term would help provide a positive environment for diplomatic efforts on the North Korean nuclear issue.) The US officials were dumbfounded. SCM statements had for decades contained a reference to the "nuclear umbrella." Dropping it suddenly would be a major, inexplicable change and could mislead the North Koreans into thinking the United States had reduced its commitment to South Korea. After long, difficult discussion in the hotel's bar, the Americans told Kim in so many words, "No reference to the nuclear umbrella, no communiqué." Kim called that information in to Lee Jong-seok, who was attending a dinner with his NSC colleagues. Lee expressed surprise that the United States was so firm on the issue, even though he had been forewarned by the Foreign Ministry that dropping the reference would cause big problems. He told Kim to wait while he did some checking. A few minutes later, he called back: the reference to the nuclear umbrella could stay.

This sort of internal discord within the establishment in the South, added to the differences between Seoul and Washington, became corrosive, continuous drops of acid on the alliance. From the standpoint of some in Washington, Roh's closest Blue House advisers—especially Lee Jong-seok—did not understand the nuances of military-security issues. When the ROK military complained to its US counterparts that it was being shut out of the Blue House decision-making process, Washington's suspicions fed on themselves. American NSC staffers did their best to form good personal relations with their Blue House counterparts, and in their view succeeded in building bridges. The problem was that the gulf in perceptions had become too wide and personal impressions in some quarters on both sides had hardened.

The ROK military was particularly unhappy with policy and had been since the days of Kim Dae Jung. The army viewed many of the steps the Kim administration had taken to advance inter-Korean relations, such as opening transportation corridors through the DMZ, as having undermined South Korean security and set bad precedents. To those charged with protecting the country's security, holes poked through the DMZ were not knitting the two Koreas together, but rather opening dangerous routes for a North Korean armored attack. These concerns would grow throughout the Roh administration.

As intense as this criticism became, however, it never got beyond grumbling. The idea of a military coup against the civilian government, even when fears about the country's security were involved, now seemed unthinkable. Military officials, instead, looked ahead to the possibility that the next ROK government would be a conservative one, and thus present an opportunity to reverse what many of them believed were terrible mistakes. In effect, members of the once politically decisive ROK army found themselves using guerrilla tactics against their own government, ceding bureaucratic space for time.

Concerns about the breaches in the DMZ were not confined to the US or ROK side, either. The DPRK army apparently had its own problems with the idea of opening up corridors that would permit high-speed access to the North by American and ROK troops. During one meeting with Kim Jong Il, South Korean officials saw what they interpreted as the supreme North Korean leader working to rope his own military into approving the construction. Rather than simply order his generals, Kim co-opted them, pushing them to take an active part in planning and building the transportation corridors—a rail line and two roads, one in the eastern part of the country and one in the west.

One of the most vexing problems that arose in the US-ROK bilateral security area had to do with OPCON, the proposed transfer of wartime operational control of ROK forces from US to South Korean hands. That would be a big step psychologically, reflecting Korea's sense that it had entered the ranks of the middle powers and was no longer a dependent of the United States. But OPCON transfer would also involve changes to key aspects of long-established bilateral security structures. Theoretically, it could weaken deterrence by suggesting to Pyongyang that there were now gaps in the alliance, most specifically in the ability to coordinate a ROK-US military response to a North Korean attack. South Korean conservatives, prepared to battle Roh on every front they could find, charged that OPCON transfer was part of the president's effort to weaken the alliance. Retired ROK army generals considered it a terrible idea, and they opposed it in droves.

Over the decades, the issue of wartime operational control had been raised several times by ROK leaders, who felt the United States used it to tie the South's hands in dealing with North Korea during crisis situations. This time, however, was different. This time it was the Americans who proposed the OPCON transfer. Washington's hope was to deal preemptively with what appeared to be signs that the Roh administration would eventually try to recast the alliance in ways that could weaken it. By jumping out in front on the issue, the Americans gambled they could shape the enormously complex process of the transfer of wartime operational command and keep the alliance effective. Once the South Korean military recovered from the shock that it was actually the Americans who were proposing such a big step, the two sides spent several years bouncing proposals back and forth over when the transfer should occur. The ROK military offered a date of 2012, which would be partway through the next South Korean administration. The Americans proposed the transfer take place much earlier—2009—setting off an uproar in Seoul and reigniting fears in some quarters that US secretary of defense Donald Rumsfeld was punishing South Korea for its perceived anti-American tendencies.

Although Rumsfeld was certainly not happy with some of what he saw in ROK policies, there were broader problems he was trying to deal with in terms of US forces worldwide. As early as July 2001, in a brief note to his special assistant, Larry Di Rita, he had raised the problem of getting the "allies to do more—transfer responsibility i.e., Japan, Korea." Rumsfeld also thought it was past time to reduce the US military "footprint" in Korea and move its forces' Yongsan headquarters, which sat in the middle of the South Korean capital, farther south.

Reconfiguring the US-ROK alliance, making it more flexible and less expensive, required changes that ROK conservatives found difficult to comprehend or accept. It wasn't until early 2007, after Rumsfeld had left office, that the allies announced that they had finally settled on April 2012 for OPCON transfer. When the new ROK administration of Lee Myung-bak took office in 2009, it wanted that date put off, and so in June 2010, citing recent examples of North Korean aggression, the allies selected a new date—December 2015.

TENSIONS RISE

At the same time it was reevaluating the military arrangements on the Korean peninsula and gathering its forces to attack Iraq in early 2003, the United States found itself faced with a growing nuclear problem. North Korea was rapidly restarting its nuclear program and beginning to reprocess those eight thousand irradiated fuel rods that contained approximately twenty-five kilograms of plutonium ideally suited to the production of nuclear weapons. For Washington, the need to concentrate on the final diplomatic and military preparations for Iraq was all consuming, meaning it could not afford to have the situation on the Korean peninsula boil over. Moreover, despite the official position that the United States could fight two wars at the same time, military planners knew they could not do much more than "hold" the North if fighting broke out on the peninsula while the US military was involved halfway around the world in Iraq.

Notwithstanding rumors that the Pentagon was working on plans for military action against the North, or public bluster from hard-liners seeming to support that option, a military solution in Korea was not widely seen in the administration as a viable course. The president himself was firmly convinced it was not the path he wanted to follow. The administration's immediate concern was that the North might take advantage of US military involvement in the Middle East, provoking a military confrontation to test the American commitment to South Korea. To forestall such a contingency, Washington relied on an escalating series of high-level public warnings backed up by well-publicized movement of potent military equipment, primarily aircraft, to the Pacific. If deterrence failed, the Pentagon hoped at least to have additional forces in position to use against a DPRK foray.

Although the Americans had no plans to take military action in Korea, the North Koreans may not have been so sure. Taking note of US statements and reinforcements, Pyongyang responded in an unusual, and to the US military completely unexpected, fashion. On the morning of March 2, 2003, in an audacious gambit, four North Korean Air Force MiG fighters intercepted a US RC-135S reconnaissance aircraft over the Sea of Japan. North Korean pilots usually stayed close to land; for a formation of fighters to fly some 150 miles over the ocean was extraordinary. This surprise move could not have been the result of a sudden scrambling of aircraft in response to that particular US reconnaissance flight on that particular day, either. Rather, it had to have come about after planning and preparation. Aircraft had to be transferred from airbases elsewhere in the country to be in position to launch the operation. Though the preparations went undetected, there had been indications in the preceding weeks that something might be coming. Beginning in late February, North Korean public complaints about US military activity in the Pacific and around Korea began singling out RC-135S flights.

The North Korean fighters flew close to the unarmed US reconnaissance plane, but did nothing reckless. Reportedly, one of the pilots asked for permission from his central authorities to fire, but whether this was bravado or a serious step, permission was denied. After twenty hair-raising minutes, the US aircraft turned back to its base on Okinawa. For the North Koreans, simply putting its fighters up and out to meet the American plane was enough of a gesture, a warning to Washington to keep back. Although the military leadership was doubtless pleased to declare the mission a success to Kim Jong Il, Pyongyang did not publicly crow over the episode. No mention of it appeared in North Korean media for more than a week, and then it was buried in a longer article in the party daily arguing that the "incident" would "never have taken place" if the Americans had not ratcheted up tensions in the area.

The episode at the beginning of March with the MiGs occurred as developments at Yongbyon were moving into a critical phase. On January 10, the North had announced that its final withdrawal from the Non-Proliferation Treaty would be effective the following day, on the grounds that there had been only twenty-four hours left on the clock when its initial thirty-day withdrawal notification had been "suspended" in June 1993.* At the end of January, American media reported that US satellites spotted trucks apparently moving the thousands of spent fuel rods from the cooling pond, where they had been stored and monitored since 1994 by the IAEA, across the river to the reprocessing plant a few kilometers away. There was some debate in the US intelligence community about whether those trucks were actually moving the fuel rods or, indeed, whether the rods had been moved at all. Only later did it become clear that the rods had, in fact, been transported to the reprocessing plant, probably sometime in January. The North Koreans subsequently told a visiting American delegation that they had reprocessed all of the spent fuel in one continuous campaign, starting in January and finishing by the end of June 2003.

Early in 2003, a North Korean official quietly told a foreign contact that the people who had all along wanted the country to develop nuclear weapons had moved into a position of influence on the policy, and they would not stop until they had succeeded. On March 12, the North Korean UN Mission passed a message to former US ambassador Donald Gregg, who had remained in contact with the North over the years. The message was that in the face of what Pyongyang saw as a growing, almost imminent, threat from the United States, if Washington failed to do something very soon to start a direct bilateral dialogue, the North would take a number of steps, including launching a multistage missile and accelerating the pace of reprocessing—which, according to the North Korean message, "had already started."

Coming in the middle of concerted efforts to restart their nuclear program, it seems unlikely that Pyongyang was offering to step back. The

---

* This attention to detail showed Pyongyang at its most punctilious. When it serves their interests, the North Koreans can be legalistic to a fault. As one observer has opined, whether they wear military uniforms or not, they are all lawyers and they "live in the loopholes."

North may have calculated, however, that the message would encourage the United States to explore the possibility of resuming talks, to reduce a potential threat in Korea in order to concentrate on Iraq. If so, Pyongyang totally misjudged the Bush administration's single-minded opposition to bilateral talks, or even, at that point, to pursuing serious diplomacy with the North at all.

THE SIX-PARTY MIRAGE

The multilateral diplomacy that was to be the focus of so much attention over the next several years, and would ultimately prove to be a dead end, began in March 2003. At that point, the Chinese became increasingly worried by what they saw and heard from Washington, namely, warnings that if Beijing did not rein in the North Koreans, the United States would form of "coalition of the willing" to do so—a phrase implying that the United States might solicit similar international support for action against the DPRK as it had for its unfolding invasion of Iraq. Former secretary of state Condoleezza Rice says in her memoirs that this was deliberate theater on the part of the White House to scare the Chinese into action. If so, it only partly succeeded. The US warnings did not push the Chinese into applying pressure on Pyongyang, but they did help feed a debate in Beijing about the dangers of the North's nuclear program—not in terms of the physical threat but rather the action-reaction cycle it could set off, leading to instability in the region and threatening the core Chinese interest in its own economic development.

In an effort to keep the situation within bounds, the Chinese eventually chose a backdoor solution. After highly contentious talks between Kim Jong Il and senior Chinese diplomat Qian Qichen (the same PRC official who had tried to soothe the North's anger after Beijing's decision to recognize the ROK in 1992), the Chinese squeezed out of Pyongyang an agreement to trilateral—US-China-DPRK—talks. They intended for these to evolve quickly into a US-DPRK bilateral meeting, the only outcome with which they could convince the North Koreans to attend talks at that point. Washington, however, refused to play along. The Americans said they would attend only one such meeting, and on this they held firm; the single three-way meeting, convened in Beijing on April 24–25, accomplished nothing.

The meeting did give the chief North Korean delegate, Ri Gun, a chance to make ambiguous and ominous remarks in a side conversation to Assistant Secretary of State James Kelly. Kelly and Ri had sat next to each other during dinner, conversing in English. As dinner ended, Ri called his interpreter over and began a presentation to Kelly in Korean. The North had warned the United States that it had nuclear weapons in

1994, Ri claimed, and asked rhetorically, why hadn't Washington taken it seriously?* Ri went on to warn that the North might have to "demonstrate" its capability and might "transfer" nuclear material, though to whom Ri did not specify.

Ri's remarks—leaked to the American press virtually as soon as Kelly's reporting cable reached Washington—were widely seen as a threat by the North to proliferate its nuclear technology or weapons and move on to conducting a nuclear test. President Bush called it "blackmail." But given that the presentation was just weeks after pictures of Saddam Hussein's statue being toppled in Baghdad, with an accompanying sense internationally that the American military was unstoppable and the American president a master of strategy, Ri's presentation was probably meant less a serious threat than as an effort by the smaller, weaker country to brush back the Americans along lines similar to the MiG intercept of the US reconnaissance aircraft a month earlier. It also fit with an apparent North Korean decision, in the middle of the spent fuel reprocessing campaign at Yongbyon, to speak more openly about its nuclear weapons program. In early April, for the first time, Pyongyang spoke of the need for "a physical deterrent force, tremendous military deterrent force," to protect the country.

Although the North did not publicize Ri Gun's remarks, in May it responded to the charge that it was engaged in "blackmail," arguing that it had merely "clarified" its stance in the Beijing talks and that its position constituted "neither a threat nor blackmail but a legitimate self-defensive measure." Within a few months, Pyongyang edged back from the position Ri had conveyed to Kelly. It went on the record several times emphatically denying it would transfer nuclear material. It also, on June 9, announced it would build a "nuclear deterrent" unless it saw significant change in US policy. That position cut both ways. It implicitly denied Ri Gun's assertion to Kelly that the North already had the bomb, but it also went another rung up the ladder to state clearly in public that Pyongyang had a nuclear weapons program.

Regardless of the North's official posture, however, the dinner episode helped establish for Ri Gun a reputation with some Americans as tough and irascible, an image that probably did him no harm in Pyongyang after his several years mixing with the enemy while stationed in New York at the DPRK's UN Mission.

With three-party talks at a dead end from the moment they began, the United States resurrected a proposal for a larger multiparty meeting, something Tokyo had also been pushing for some time. The Japanese had

---

* In fact, the North never told the United States any such thing during the Geneva talks in 1994 or at any other point that year.

wanted to include a reference to multiparty talks in the September 2002 Pyongyang declaration when Prime Minister Junichiro Koizumi met Kim Jong Il, but at that point the North Koreans said they were not ready.* Six-party talks convened in Beijing in August 2003 and staggered through their first two years. They would probably have died but for Chinese persistence in producing "chairman's statements" at the end of each session declaring that there had been agreement over what, on closer examination, was essentially meaningless rhetoric. It was fiction, but it worked. The chairman's statements painted a picture of at least minimum consensus, enough to keep the talks alive.

At this point, one of Washington's strongest beliefs was that six-party talks would, through the sheer arithmetic of the setting (optimistically assumed to be five against one), apply new and effective pressure on Pyongyang. Furthermore, it was argued, these talks would result in agreements more difficult for the North to break precisely because they were multilateral. Finally, and this notion gained adherents over time, the talks were seen as a way to get the Chinese "invested" in the process and encourage them to put effective pressure on the North Koreans, leverage that the United States was thought to lack.

The prospect of Chinese pressure on the North was an enticing but ever-fading goal. In late-October 2002, not long after the Kelly mission to Pyongyang, President Bush met PRC president Jiang Zemin at the Bush ranch in Crawford, Texas. The Americans were pleased that the Chinese leader publicly expressed support for the goal of a nuclear-free Korean peninsula, but privately, according to Bush, Jiang said that North Korea was not his problem. Jiang may have been worried at that point that the United States was preparing to take action against the North and hoped to calm the situation. Nevertheless, as much as Beijing was annoyed with Pyongyang—which it frequently was, and which it continues to be—the Chinese certainly had no interest then or later in putting sustained pressure on the North. As far as Beijing was concerned, the North Korean issue was something to be managed so that it did not interfere with a number of other higher-priority Chinese concerns. The best crisis management, in the Chinese view, was crisis avoidance.

From the beginning, six-party talks faced several serious obstacles. The theory behind them contained a major flaw. Multiparty negotiations were conceived by Washington as a way to avoid US-DPRK bilateral talks, out of the mistaken belief that direct negotiations had worked to North Korea's advantage. Yet, in practice, as long as Washington stuck

---

* The six-party talks had many fathers. The United States claims it came up with the idea, as do the Japanese, the Chinese, and possibly even the Russians. The North Koreans take no credit; they often complain that the forum was nothing but a gabfest.

to its resistance to bilateral talks, the six-party arrangement never worked. The North Koreans controlled the pace of the multilateral forum, and they would not relent until they regained serious bilateral contact with the United States. Moreover, the first three years (2003–2005) of six-party talks were mostly wasted as the American side fought endless internal bureaucratic battles to ensure that the US position did not in any way resemble the approach of the Clinton administration. Any description of meetings with the North as "negotiations" set off frenzied denials. The word *freeze* was considered poisonous, even though, as the North pointed out, a freeze of the facilities at Yongbyon was logically the first step in any new deal. Perhaps the most deadly taboo for the Americans was any hint that the North had a right to civilian nuclear power. That position put the United States at odds with Beijing, Moscow, and even Seoul, helping ensure that the hoped-for phalanx of five-against-one never materialized.

All the while, the North's nuclear weapons program moved ahead without hindrance. In early-October 2003, barely a month after the first round of six-party talks ended, Pyongyang announced that it was changing the purpose of reprocessing the spent fuel rods from civilian needs to building a "nuclear deterrent," terminology the North had introduced a few months earlier as part of the slow buildup to explicitly acknowledging its weapons program. Later that month, Pyongyang announced that at "the appropriate time," it would display its nuclear deterrence to the skeptics. It turned out to be not too long of a wait.

NUCLEAR PEEK-A-BOO

In January 2004, in a calculated gesture of "transparency" to demonstrate how far its nuclear program had progressed while the diplomatic front was stalled, Pyongyang opened the nuclear center at Yongbyon to a visiting American delegation led by Stanford professor John Lewis. North Korean technicians handed to one of the Americans—Dr. Siegfried Hecker, a plutonium specialist who was formerly the director of the Los Alamos National Laboratory—two sealed glass jars, one containing a greenish plutonium compound and the other a thin-walled metal funnel. The North Koreans claimed these were the products of the previous year's reprocessing campaign. From their appearance, Hecker concluded that both jars might well contain forms of processed plutonium. If so, it would mean the North was indeed on its way to producing a bomb.

Once back in the United States, in order to provide a factual basis for evaluating progress in the North's nuclear program, Hecker presented his observations as widely but as carefully as possible, without creating undue alarm. It made no difference to US policy. The Bush administration was determined not to give the North Koreans what it thought they were after—a flustered reaction from the United States and its allies. Secretary Colin Powell made sure to appear unflappable in public when questioned about the North's nuclear capabilities. Early in the crisis, he emphasized that the North Koreans needed to concentrate on their economy. They couldn't, Powell said, eat plutonium.

The North would invite American delegations back to Yongbyon several more times over the next six years, on each occasion attempting to demonstrate that what it was claiming in public about its nuclear program reflected reality on the ground. As of this writing, the last visit took place in mid-November 2010, when Lewis, Hecker, and Robert Carlin were given a quick tour of a new modern uranium enrichment facility (the North Koreans referred to it as a uranium enrichment "workshop") at Yongbyon containing around two thousand centrifuges.* Why the North chose that moment to show this critical development in its program was as unclear then as it is now. The day after the tour, one of the group's Foreign Ministry escorts said to Carlin, "You weren't happy with what you saw, were you?" Asked why he thought so, the official knitted his brows into a mask of unhappy concern and said, "Because you looked like this afterwards."

Through both official and unofficial channels, and at almost every step of the way, Pyongyang privately advised the United States ahead of time what it planned to do next, or what it had just done, in the nuclear program. In 2004, explaining the rationale for bringing the Americans to Yongbyon, a North Korean Foreign Ministry statement argued that "transparency serves as a basis of realistic thinking and, at the same time, a basis for solving the issue." The statement went on to say, "We never employ a sleight of hand. Whenever an opportunity presented itself, we opened to the public our fair and aboveboard nuclear activities as they were and informed the U.S. side of them through a diplomatic channel."

Some observers viewed these notifications of what was widely considered provocative actions not as transparency but as "blackmail," an effort to strengthen the North's bargaining position and extract maximum concessions from Washington. A few saw it as a sign that Kim Jong Il continued to seek ways to put back on track the process of improving ties with the United States, something that he had come tantalizingly close to achieving in October 2000. There is no way of knowing, however, if Kim

---

* For a full account, see Hecker, "A Return Trip to North Korea's Yongbyon Nuclear Complex" (Center for International Security and Cooperation, Stanford University, November 20, 2010). Hecker notes that the North Koreans hustled the group through the facility. They said they had not wanted to show it to the visitors, but had been ordered to. Although the North Koreans would not explicitly say so, from their explanation of the design and components it seemed possible that the centrifuges were what are known as P-2s, a more advanced design capable of higher production rates.

would really have slowed his nuclear program, much less reversed it, once he put Yongbyon into operation again in 2003. It was four years before Washington made a serious effort to find out.

A YEAR OF ZIGZAGS

The failure of the negotiations to move off dead center, and the persistent evidence that open warfare in the US administration over North Korea policy was blocking effective diplomacy, helped convince Seoul and Tokyo of the need to redouble their own efforts to engage Pyongyang. The North Koreans probably would have been happy to oblige, but the unexpected, as often happens, interfered.

Although inter-Korean relations appeared to be on track for noticeable progress through the first part of 2004, the process was suddenly interrupted in March by the ROK National Assembly's impeachment of President Roh for a minor election-law violation. Pyongyang characterized the development as reflecting "chaos" in the South, but rather than take advantage of the situation, the worst the North did was to propose that the next round of inter-Korean talks, scheduled to take place in the South, be moved to the North. When Seoul protested that the North was interfering in its internal affairs, Pyongyang reacted with barely concealed contempt, noting that the South's chief executive was, in effect, the North's interlocutor in the talks, and if his removal from office did not constitute an issue that affected the North Koreans, they didn't know what did.

The South Korean Constitutional Court ruled in Roh's favor in May, putting him back in charge of the country's affairs—but then inter-Korean relations hit another bump, this time a big one. In July 2004, a group of more than four hundred North Korean refugees, who had made their way across China to Ho Chi Minh City in Vietnam, arrived at an airfield south of Seoul. China was an inhospitable place for North Korean refugees, and so those who could undertook the difficult journey across China to relatively safer havens in Southeast Asia and Mongolia, where they could apply for entry into South Korea. In early 2004, the numbers in Ho Chi Minh City had swelled to such an extent that emergency measures were necessary to move them to South Korea.

The Roh government had been trying to maintain a low profile for its refugee program, and now it was in a bind. Not to accept the refugees would be inhumane, as well as a sure way to generate bad publicity, but to bring in such a large number would risk a negative reaction from Pyongyang. Seoul wanted to keep the transfer low-key, but that proved unrealistic in South Korea's hothouse media environment. Once the news leaked, it attracted considerable attention in the South Korean and international press. The North Koreans reacted even more negatively than had been feared, somewhat surprising given how much progress there had otherwise been in North-South engagement. One explanation for that unusually tough response is that it reflected an effort by the Workers Party section tasked with dealing with South Korea, the United Front Department, to shield itself against criticism from Kim Jong Il for not doing a better job with Seoul. In any case, inter-Korean relations went into the tank for nearly a year, a delay with serious consequences down the line.

While progress slowed the inter-Korean front, Pyongyang made yet another try at improving relations with Tokyo. Kim Jong Il had a second summit meeting with Japanese prime minister Koizumi on May 22. This second Japan–North Korea summit, lasting ninety minutes, was largely consumed in discussing the still-festering problem of the North Korean abductions, an issue that the first summit in 2002 had not resolved, despite Kim Jong Il's admission and quasi apology. When Koizumi, reiterating a favorite line in Washington, suggested that the North follow Libya's example in giving up its nuclear weapons program, Kim reportedly replied, "We are no Libya," a position Pyongyang was subsequently to reemphasize many times, most especially after March 2011, when the UN Security Council approved the use of force against Libyan leader Muammar Gaddafi's regime.* Kim went on to tell Koizumi, according to one account, that he wanted improved relations with the United States and hoped to "sing and dance with Bush until I lose my voice."

Unhappy that Washington, by refusing contact with the North, was creating an atmosphere that undercut their own efforts, both the South Korean and the Japanese leaders urged Washington to modify its opposition to bilateral talks with North Korea. At a Group of 8 meeting in the United States in July, Koizumi made the case to Bush once again. The president liked Koizumi and he listened, but listening and dancing were separate things, and US opposition to bilateral talks with the North remained firm.

In more ways than one, 2004 was an explosive year. In April a powerful blast at the Ryongchong rail station in North Pyongan, not far from the border with China, leveled buildings and tore through a nearby schoolyard filled with students. There was no way to hide the event from the outside world, and the North did not seem inclined to try. It quickly invited foreign aid workers to view the damage and arrange for relief supplies and construction materials for a major rebuilding effort. North Korean television showed scenes of wounded children and their parents being helicoptered to hospitals. Rumors made the rounds that the explosion had been

---

* Pictures of Gaddafi's bloodied corpse in October 2011 no doubt further convinced Kim that he had made the right choice in not taking the Libyan route. Subsequently, Washington switched to suggesting that the North emulate Burma.

a bomb meant for Kim Jong Il, whose train returning from China had passed through the station a few hours earlier, but this theory appears to have no basis. Soon after the explosion, the authorities banned cell phones, which had started appearing in the North not long before. Although the connection between the ban and the explosion at Ryongchong was never clear, the move helped feed speculation about an assassination plot. Other rumors pinned the explosion on a shipment of fuel bound for the Syrian missile program. These rumors, too, apparently had no basis.

The North's official version was that the disaster was the result of "electrical contact caused by carelessness during the shunting of wagons loaded with ammonium nitrate fertilizer and tank wagons." According to a report from the UN Office for the Coordination of Humanitarian Affairs, the explosion came from the "contact of two train wagons carrying ammonium nitrate with a wagon containing fuel oil. Each wagon contained 40 MT [metric tons] of ammonium nitrate enroute to a construction site for the Pakma-cheol san irrigation project. This resulted in a massive explosion creating a large crater and leveling everything in a 500 m [meter] radius."

A few months later, South Korean sensors picked up another explosion in the North, this one fairly large. Immediately, South Korean and Western media were filled with stories that it might be a nuclear test. Pyongyang announced the explosion was connected with blasting for a large hydroelectric project in Ryanggang Province and invited diplomats to take a look. The real test site, as became clear a few years later when the North exploded its first nuclear device, was about a hundred kilometers away to the southeast, in the rugged mountains of North Hamgyong Province.

As the US presidential campaign swung into gear in the summer of 2004, the North Koreans observed it with great interest. Much as they might have hoped for a victory by the Democratic nominee, Senator John Kerry, the America specialists in the Foreign Ministry understood that an incumbent, even one facing an uphill battle as President Bush seemed to be, had numerous advantages in an election. In late September, in remarks that do not appear to have been made with the US elections in mind, a DPRK Foreign Ministry official attending the annual UN General Assembly session in New York told reporters that the North had "made clear that we have already reprocessed 8,000 fuel rods and transformed them into arms." Pyongyang did not report the remarks in its own media, and South Korean officials nervously dismissed them as similar to what the North had said before. In fact, this was a new North Korean position, one that flew in the face of the guarded optimism in some quarters that the fourth session of the six-party talks, held in June 2004, had made progress. The remarks implied that a decision had been made in Pyongyang to cross the nuclear threshold publicly, and soon. There would be no turning back.

Once the US election was over, with George Bush returned to office for a second term, the North Koreans apparently saw no reason to suppose the administration's next four years would be any different from the first four, and so they moved to put on the record a new, tougher public position on their nuclear program. On February 10, Pyongyang made clear in a high-level Foreign Ministry statement that North Korea had manufactured nuclear weapons. For good measure, the statement added that the North was "indefinitely" suspending participation in the six-party talks. A month later, the Foreign Ministry released a lengthy memorandum providing detailed justification for the new position. The memorandum also included the news that the North's 1999 unilateral missile moratorium was no longer valid.

Pyongyang's threat to leave the talks proved to be tactical, but developments on the nuclear front were real. In mid-May the North announced that it had unloaded its 5-megawatt reactor, "taking necessary measures to bolster its nuclear arsenal," meaning it had an entirely new load of eight thousand spent fuel rods waiting to be reprocessed, a step that would add to its stock of weapons-grade plutonium. The North was back in six-party talks by July, but by now the talks could no longer hope to stop the DPRK from "going nuclear." Instead, the negotiators faced the vastly more difficult task of dealing with a declared nuclear-armed state.

ROK president Roh, who at this point had no illusions about how difficult the North could be to work with, was jarred and angry at Pyongyang's February announcement that it had developed a nuclear weapon. He was also more concerned than ever that the situation was lurching dangerously off track and that the long hiatus in North-South dialogue had gone on for too long. In June he sent his minister of unification, Chung Dong-young, to Pyongyang with a new proposal, offering the North 2,000 megawatts of electricity if it would return to the six-party talks. Chung also stressed to Kim the importance of a second inter-Korean summit. Not long after, the North did return to the six-party talks, but a summit would have to wait another two years. The delay in achieving the latter frustrated Roh, who rightly believed that he could not move toward summit talks in the absence of significant progress on the denuclearization issue. The South Korean president needed to nudge the North not only back to the table but also into a six-party agreement.

The 2,000 megawatts of electricity in the South Korean offer was, not coincidentally, exactly the figure the North had been promised from the KEDO reactors. By now, it was clear from the cessation of work at the Kumho construction site and the pullout of most of the workers that the reactor project would never be completed. Proffering the same amount of electricity from the ROK grid was an unmistakable signal that Seoul had finally given up on KEDO, having concluded that continuing to fight with the Americans on that front was unwinnable. The North Koreans, who at some level are essentially pragmatists, probably did not expect to be receiving electricity from the South anytime soon. But allowing Seoul to be seen as spearheading a breakthrough in talks that it could claim were deadlocked because of American intransigence was always a game Pyongyang enjoyed playing. Crucially, however, by accepting the South's offer, the North did not mean to signal that it had softened its insistence on the "right" to civilian nuclear power. That became clear a few weeks later as the six parties reconvened in Beijing.

Like the South Koreans, the Chinese were unhappy with Pyongyang's February 2005 statement on nuclear weapons, and DPRK first vice foreign minister Kang Sok-ju made an unusual trip to Beijing in April for what turned out be rough discussions. Almost certainly, Kang also heard strenuous Chinese arguments that the North had to get back to the six-party talks. Once the multiparty talks resumed in July in Beijing, the rest of the summer was consumed in Chinese efforts to produce, after much pulling and hauling with the United States and North Korea, a declaration of principles to serve as a foundation for what was supposed to be the next step—discussion of concrete implementation measures to halt the North's nuclear weapons program.

During the summer's negotiations, the core North Korean goal—and one Pyongyang made abundantly clear—was to ensure that a reference to light-water reactors made its way into the final document. A prime goal of the hard-liners in Washington, on the other hand, was to make sure that no such reference appeared. The US delegation came to the July talks with strict instructions not to concede an inch on this issue. The South Koreans did their best to work alongside the Chinese to get agreement on the wording of the statement, and if a deal meant a formula that would satisfy the North on the issue of a light-water reactor, then Seoul wanted to find it. Other delegations thought the South Koreans were making an effort not to be seen as lining up with the United States, although whether they were doing so to please their superiors in Seoul or keep on the good side of the North Koreans was not clear.

As talks bogged down in disagreements over how to deal with the issue of the reactors, the Chinese worked through several formulations. The Chinese diplomats were especially taken by the utility of an old and largely forgotten North-South agreement—the 1992 Joint Declaration of the Denuclearization of the Korean Peninsula, in which the North and South agreed not to possess reprocessing or enrichment facilities but which, implicitly, granted both the right to civilian nuclear energy. In a deft use of the dead document, the Chinese massaged it into a loosely worded, and in some respects admirably ambiguous, sentence. But in the end, it didn't solve the basic problem: Washington was unwilling to even consider, however vaguely, North Korea's right to civilian nuclear power.

The negotiations went down to the wire, with the Chinese finally telling the Americans that if they didn't bend and agree to the formulation implicitly acknowledging the North's right to civilian nuclear energy, there would be no deal. The chief ROK delegate, Song Min-soon, blew up while talking to South Korean reporters outside his hotel, warning emotionally that if Washington scuttled the deal by refusing to accept the Chinese compromise wording about LWRs, it could negatively affect US-ROK ties. Finally, the US delegation decided that the best way to break the deadlock was to accept the proposed Chinese language but then have the US, Chinese, Russian, ROK, and Japanese delegations in their final statements lay out the conditions under which the discussions on the LWRs could take place, i.e., the need for the North to become an NPT member in good standing before the others could legally provide assistance to its civilian nuclear program. Ambassador Christopher Hill, who had replaced James Kelly as assistant secretary of state earlier in 2005,[*] convinced Secretary of State Condoleezza Rice of the wisdom of that position, and she, in turn, had no trouble convincing the Deputies Committee that if the United States was to accept the joint statement's language on LWRs, the United States should state publicly and unequivocally how Washington interpreted that language.

After the fact, the American participants of the talks in Beijing remember their role as working to find a solution during this fifth session. The other parties remember mainly Washington's intransigence on a number of issues. There is, however, also a general sense by the participants that, in the end, all six of the delegations (including the North Koreans) worked together, creating a momentum toward a final resolution that no one who was not sitting in the room at the time could quite understand.

Although the joint statement that finally emerged was only meant as an initial declaration of principles, in the public mind, and in the minds of many officials in Washington, it quickly morphed into a hybrid of principles and concrete commitments, the most important of which was the commitment of the North to get completely out of the business of producing nuclear weapons. For the Americans, the various parties' commitments in the joint statement were set forth in order of importance, and to some extent in the sequence the United States wanted them to occur as well—with the North Korean pledge on denuclearization listed first and foremost. The North Koreans insisted the list was simply that, a list, with no implementation sequence agreed or implied. As far as Pyongyang was concerned, the mention of the light-water reactor in the joint statement's first article was the key to the deal, a sine qua non if ever one existed.

---

[*] Hill also served briefly as US ambassador to the ROK in 2004.

The first article of the September 19 joint statement included the following points:

> The DPRK committed to abandoning all nuclear weapons and existing nuclear programs and returning, at an early date, to the Treaty on the Non-Proliferation of Nuclear Weapons and to IAEA safeguards.
>
> The United States affirmed it had no intention to attack or invade the DPRK with nuclear or conventional weapons.
>
> The ROK reaffirmed its commitment not to receive or deploy nuclear weapons in accordance with the 1992 Joint Declaration of the Denuclearization of the Korean peninsula, while affirming that there exist no nuclear weapons within its territory.
>
> The 1992 Joint Declaration of the Denuclearization of the Korean Peninsula should be observed and implemented.
>
> The DPRK stated that it had the right to peaceful uses of nuclear energy. The other parties expressed their respect and agreed to discuss, at an appropriate time, the subject of the provision of light water reactor to the DPRK.

On September 19, the final day of the session, Assistant Secretary Hill read a closing US statement sent to him overnight from Washington. The delegation had sent off to Washington for clearance a proposed closing statement. What came back, with Hadley's and Rice's approval, was very different, so different that on its receipt the normally soft-spoken US legal adviser was, in the words of one member of the delegation, "apoplectic." The new text, which spelled out the US interpretation of what the term *appropriate time* meant, had been drafted by the NSC—split, as always, between the hard-line nonproliferation section and the less hard-line regionalists. After the work was done and one of the drafters, Michael Green, had left town, he received a call informing him that the statement had been rewritten. He was given an opportunity to review the revised message, but working out the new language proved difficult because the classified phone connection was bad and time was short. The end result, what Hill finally read, fulfilled the marching orders from the Deputies for an explicit US closing statement but was wrapped in the tone and rhetoric chosen by the hard-liners. It asserted that the "appropriate time" for discussion of LWRs would not come until the North had "eliminated all nuclear weapons and all nuclear programs, and this has been verified to the satisfaction of all parties by credible international means, including the IAEA; and when the DPRK has come into full compliance with the NPT and IAEA safeguards, and has demonstrated a sustained commitment to cooperation and transparency and has ceased proliferating nuclear technology." The formulation had a "when pigs fly" ring to it, unmistakable to the North Koreans and to everyone else in the room.

To drive home the point of how dead the prospects were for light-water reactors, the drafters in Washington had added that "the United States supports a decision to terminate KEDO by the end of the year." The news earlier that summer of Seoul's offer to supply the North with electricity had been met with gloom in KEDO as a sign that the organization's days were numbered. That was nothing, however, compared to the thunderbolt of the first press reports of Hill's statement, revealing that the United States was publicly advocating the termination of the organization by the end of the year. KEDO officials at first thought it must have been the result of misreporting and that there would soon be some sort of clarification. KEDO still had a great deal of equipment, not to mention more than a hundred workers in North Korea, workers whose safety would now be at risk if the reports were accurate. Like KEDO headquarters in New York, none of the other three governments involved—all of which had spent considerable political capital and funds on the project—had been informed in advance.

Ambassador Hill realized the statement might provoke the North Koreans and risked derailing what he had accomplished; it made him uncomfortable, yet he did not attempt to get it amended or revised. Several others in the US delegation hoped the North Koreans would shrug off Hill's remarks as "simply words." At least one of the other delegations, noting the American's sharp tone, felt that the momentum of the talks, with the cooperation that had emerged among the six delegations to produce the final joint statement, would carry the process over this hump.

But after two years of fruitless negotiations, and particularly after the difficult six-party sessions over the summer to find the exact words to express a series of principles around which future diplomacy might be organized, the statement Hill read was not the sort of thing that would smooth the way forward. Putting on the record different shadings of meaning after reaching agreements is not unusual, and in the past US and North Korean negotiators had often come out of meetings to give briefings highlighting their own interpretation of the results. Often, the chief negotiators discussed with each other ahead of time what they planned to say in order to avoid unpleasant surprises. These unilateral interpretations, it was generally understood, were modulated in nuance and tone for the audience back home, but were not meant to undermine the core of whatever agreement had been reached.

There was nothing nuanced in this American presentation. It was aimed squarely at the issue of light-water reactors for North Korea and, by design, blew away the carefully ambiguous formulation the joint statement had employed to deal with the issue. Not surprisingly, as far as North Korea was concerned, Washington's "words" virtually nullified the joint statement. The North Korean delegation sitting across the room said nothing directly in response to what the American negotiator read. Kim Gye Gwan, the chief DPRK delegate, had no instructions on how to reply to anything so unexpected from Washington. His only observation, bitterly poetic, was that he had thought they had climbed the mountain, but now he saw that there were still more mountains ahead. There was no poetry the next day, the twentieth, when the DPRK Foreign Ministry issued its own statement warning that if the United States was pulling back on the LWRs, then it should not expect the North to move forward on any of the items of interest to the United States.

The North's statement was widely interpreted in the Western press as Pyongyang retreating from what it had agreed to in the joint statement. Few people saw it for what it was—a reaction, and a very predictable one, to the provocative message that Hill had read. In Washington the State Department's press spokesman tried to thread his way around the problem, saying that different interpretations were normal in the process of negotiations. Indeed, some differences are normal, but these were not, nor was the US action that followed.

Part of Ambassador Hill's closing statement had noted "for the record that the United States will take concrete actions necessary to protect ourselves and our allies against any illicit and proliferation activities on the part of the DPRK." This pointed directly to a time bomb that had already been announced by Washington, but one that so far had been overshadowed by the six-party talks and was still waiting to explode—a US Treasury Department notification on September 15 signaling that Washington had set in motion steps that would amount to international banking sanctions against North Korea.

The same day as the North's statement, the *Federal Register* published a notice that the secretary of the Treasury "finds that reasonable grounds exist for concluding that Banco Delta Asia SARL (Banco Delta Asia) is a financial institution of primary money laundering concern." This small Macau bank was not really the issue. The real target of the Treasury action was North Korea. Underlining that point, the notice stated that "government agencies and front companies of the Democratic People's Republic of Korea (DPRK or North Korea) that are engaged in illicit activities use Macau as a base of operations for money laundering and other illegal activities. The involvement of North Korean government agencies and front companies in a wide variety of illegal activities, including drug trafficking and counterfeiting of goods and currency, has been widely reported. Earnings from criminal activity, by their clandestine nature, are difficult to quantify, but studies estimate that proceeds from these activities amount to roughly $500 million annually."

The finding meant that any bank dealing with Banco Delta Asia, or in fact with North Korea itself, was now possibly subject to Section 311 of the USA PATRIOT Act, which had been passed by Congress within weeks after the attacks on 9/11. Under this section of the act, US financial institutions were required to take steps that would, in effect, stop their dealing with any foreign institution that itself had links with an entity named in the relevant Treasury finding. The Treasury Department's press release on section 311 says simply that "taken as a whole, Section 311 of the USA PATRIOT Act provides the Secretary with a range of options that can be adapted to target specific money laundering and terrorist financing risks. These options provide the Treasury Department with a powerful and flexible regulatory tool to take actions to protect the U.S. financial system from specific threats."

It turned out to be a classic case of a tool meant for one purpose being used for something entirely different, with correspondingly unforeseen results. Washington tried to pass off this blow to the six-party talks as a simple legal action by the Treasury, divorced from the diplomacy and, most especially, not linked to the September 19 statement. The full explanation for the Treasury Department's decision to institute the financial sanctions at this very moment—as nearly as can be determined—is tangled, even as the results were painfully clear. The two policies—new financial measures against the North and the six-party agreement—put on the same track at the same time and heading toward each other could have only one result: a train wreck.

For more than a year, US law enforcement agencies had been working on leads about various North Korean illegal activities, of which there were many. President Bush made it clear that measures to protect the United States against these activities were not to be compromised or diluted in order to make way for diplomatic progress. The issue of what to do, and when, came to a head in the summer of 2005, around the same time as the wrangling in Beijing over the statement of principles for the six-party talks. US officials from several law enforcement and foreign-policy agencies had to decide whether to approve the Treasury action before or after the diplomatic efforts in Beijing moved off dead center (and at that point, it was not clear they would actually succeed). The decision was made—one participant says it was unanimous—to keep strictly with the president's orders and push ahead on what was conceived as the defensive-legal front. No one at that point thought the Treasury action would end up being the tsunami in the international financial community it turned out to be.

The explanation that the Treasury action was necessary to protect the United States was hardly credible to the other countries involved in the six-party talks. The South Koreans were distressed; the Chinese could hardly believe what Washington had done. To them, it was as clear as

could be that at a minimum, the US action put at serious risk the progress made only a few days before. In their darkest moments, many even
wondered if the Treasury action was a deliberate US attempt to make sure
that the September 19 joint statement never got off the ground. In fact,
the move made it hard to convince either Beijing or Pyongyang that the
United States was serious about the joint statement or that the principles
set out in that statement had any meaning. Another six-party meeting
was held in Beijing in November, but it could not possibly put Humpty-
Dumpty together again. The joint statement, though it continued to exist
on paper, had been shattered. The talks were blown completely off track for
fifteen months, and inter-Korean relations fell onto a path from which, as
of this writing, they have still not recovered.

As valid as the accusations of North Korean criminal activity that
sparked the Treasury action might have been, the central question was
whether *this* action at *this* time made sense in terms of broader US goals.
It clearly did to those in Washington who thought that the exercise of
leverage in the international financial system would be an effective way
of finally "punishing" the North. There was no serious thinking in the
Treasury Department, and little elsewhere in the administration either,
about how this move might fit with the overall diplomacy. Worse, no
consideration was given to how Washington might turn off the effects
of the Treasury action when that became necessary. After the fact, it became obvious that there were no plans to handle the possibility that the
North might eventually come back to six-party talks and agree to concrete steps to implement the September 19 joint statement. Clearly, the
North would insist the US financial measures be rolled back as part of
such a deal, but no one understood how Treasury would do that. Asked
about an "exit ramp," a Treasury official directly involved admitted there
wasn't one.

In Seoul President Roh received the news of the Treasury action with
consternation. In November 2005, several weeks after the measure had
been announced, the South Korean leader met President Bush in Kyongju,
the capital of one of Korea's ancient kingdoms, where he pressed Bush over
and over on the issue, insinuating numerous times that the "coincidence"
of the Banco Delta Asia action and the September 19 joint statement was
actually something darker. Each time the president explained his views on
the need for this legal action to protect the United States, and each time
Roh went back to his barely disguised accusations. It was one of the worst
meetings the two ever had.

To the North Koreans, the Treasury action—coming right on the
heels of the September joint statement—may have been reconfirmation
that Washington was not really interested in anything but bringing the

regime to its knees. Those in the DPRK Foreign Ministry who had been arguing in favor of diplomacy with the United States might at that point have regretted their choice of profession.

Given the way US officials and others focused for so many years afterward on the September 19 joint statement, it is a fair question as to whether the document represented a moment when the North Korean nuclear problem and all of the attendant issues might have started to move in a positive direction. Unfortunately, there is no way to tell, because if there was such a moment, it disappeared immediately and the path led elsewhere. The statement turned out to be too vague to cope with the lack of trust on all sides. As one keen observer describes it, the statement was "sitting on air," with no bilateral US-DPRK diplomacy to support it and no political will in Washington, either. The United States had immediately distanced itself from a key formulation of the declaration, while Tokyo quickly ducked its obligations by refusing to take part in the supply of "energy assistance" to North Korea promised by the other five parties. Determined, as they always are, never to allow themselves to be seen as weak or yielding to pressure, the North Koreans seized the opening presented by what became known in shorthand as "BDA" (Banco Delta Asia) to advance their nuclear weapons program to a new and more dangerous phase.

THE END OF KEDO

On September 19, 2005, when the United States announced that it supported a decision to disband the organization by the end of the year, KEDO was already on its last legs. In practical terms, the announcement made little difference, apart from the burden it suddenly put on the organization to work out the final extrication of its workers and the settlement of claims by its contractors under less than ideal circumstances.

On another level, however, both the fate of KEDO and the way it was dispatched reflected Washington's determined effort to purge itself of the remnants of the Clinton administration's approach to North Korea. Since its formation in 1995, KEDO had functioned as a multilateral organization able to maintain relations with North Korea, whatever the state of bilateral ties between any of the individual governments and the DPRK. KEDO was not autonomous but under the control of the governments involved; its separate organizational persona was obviously a fiction, yet all sides, including the North Koreans, found it a useful one. Most important, the extended commitment by the United States to KEDO demonstrated to Pyongyang that whatever temporary problems might arise—and there were many—Washington was sticking with the process of engagement.

Whether Washington had deluded itself into thinking the North would collapse before the United States had to go through with all of its obligations under the Agreed Framework was, for Pyongyang, beside the point.

Washington's commitment to KEDO had also helped convince Seoul and Tokyo that the United States was serious about a long-term diplomatic settlement of the North Korean nuclear problem. However, neither of them fully grasped the extent to which the American contingent in KEDO was separated from the US government, very different from the organization's South Korean or Japanese employees, most of whom were closely tied to their respective government bureaucracies. In some respects, it turned out KEDO was more effective than the six-party talks in dealing with the North on a multilateral basis. The KEDO office at the LWR construction site was in constant contact with its North Korean counterparts, allowing the two sides to develop working relations that often proved invaluable when problems arose. And in the days before North-South industrial or commercial projects got under way, through its use of numerous South Korean subcontractors, KEDO gave South Korean companies their first experience working in the North.

The organization had faced numerous challenges along the way. In 1996 when a North Korean submarine ran aground off the coast of South Korea, and in 1998 when the North launched a rocket that passed over Japan, first Seoul and then Tokyo balked at continuing to fully participate in KEDO, but in both cases the governments worked to overcome the challenges. What could not be overcome was when the United States essentially pulled the plug on its participation in KEDO in 2002, continuing to fund its portion of the administrative expenses but otherwise backing away from the organization's major purpose, building two light-water reactors in the North. At that point, the organization began to fall apart. For reasons of personal pique and policy exhaustion, the possibilities for utilizing KEDO in the broader diplomacy sphere were not seriously considered by the Bush administration, even though KEDO managed to sustain working relations and access to the North when communications largely broke down between Washington and Pyongyang in late 2002 and 2003. In different political circumstances in Washington, it might have been possible to keep the organization intact, or at least build on it to devise a new diplomatic tool for dealing with North Korea. But no one in the Bush administration had the time or inclination to suggest such a course against what was certain to be bitter opposition.

Besides, there was the not-so-minor matter of funding. In a nonpartisan way, the US Congress had never been happy providing money for KEDO, and after the uranium enrichment issued surfaced lawmakers would not have given a dime. Even if it had wanted to (which it clearly did not), the administration could not have certified, as required by Congress as a prerequisite for funding, that the North was in compliance with the Agreed Framework. At that point, had the president used the provision of a waiver to get around the need for certification, it would have provoked a fight with Congress no White House would want.*

What finally stripped away the last vestiges of the leading American role in the organization turned out to be not serious policy considerations but petty animosities between the State Department and the KEDO front office, leaving the organization leaderless. And without American leadership in the organization, old tensions between Seoul and Tokyo reemerged, eventually showing up in bad blood between individual KEDO employees.

When on a freezing morning in early-January 2006 the last ship carrying the remaining KEDO workers and officials slipped away from the dock at the LWR construction site and headed out to sea, the folly of the pullout was obvious to everyone who stood on the stern of the MSS *Hangyore* and watched as nearly a decade of effort and more than a billion dollars spent disappeared from view. Subsequent meetings of the KEDO Executive Board, where the representatives discussed how to divide up the organization's remaining assets and debts, were bitter and often ugly. It was hard to imagine that either Seoul or Tokyo would again trust an American commitment to a negotiated settlement with North Korea, especially one that called on governments in South Korea or Japan to spend their own taxpayers' money.

TRACTION, AT LAST

With personnel changes in the Bush administration's second term, and especially after the midterm elections in November 2006 in which the Republicans lost majorities in both the House and the Senate, US policy toward North Korea was refined. The State Department regained some of its footing under Condoleezza Rice, the Department of Defense under Robert Gates ceased to be an obstacle, and the vice president's office lost much of its ability to influence the policy. Even so, fully half the second term was wasted in trying to recover diplomatic ground squandered in the first four years and in digging out from under the unexpected consequences of the Treasury's action against the North. What the administration eventually saw as the high-water mark of its policy—agreement and partial implementation by the North of concrete steps toward disabling its nuclear program in 2007—in the end did not lead to sustained progress.

---

* The Clinton White House had repeatedly used waivers for North Korea, not because it wanted to, but to keep its North Korean policy intact. The point was moot for the Bush White House because John Bolton had already made clear in late 2001—a year before the Kelly visit to Pyongyang—that the administration would not ask for any more money for KEDO.

In late-May 2006, the first signs appeared of possible preparations for a North Korean missile test at the launch site near the coast in South Hamgyong Province. The preparations had to have been the result of careful, long-term planning by Pyongyang. Decisions to conduct missile launches are made months in advance of activity that eventually becomes visible to reconnaissance satellites; in this case, Kim Jong Il may have given approval to proceed with the test sometime in the early winter, in response to Washington's applying Section 311 and derailing the September 19 joint statement. In fact, if the message the North Koreans passed to Donald Gregg in March 2003 was serious, plans had existed even then for eventually launching a "multistage" rocket.

Almost immediately after its preparations for a missile test were detected, in a Foreign Ministry spokesman's statement on June 1 "reclarifying" the North's position on the six-party talks, Pyongyang "kindly" invited Ambassador Christopher Hill to visit. The purpose, the statement said, was for the United States to explain directly that it had "true political intention" to implement the September 19 joint statement. The invitation, released just after the DPRK foreign minister held talks in Beijing with his Chinese counterpart, was a typical move on the North's part, possibly as much to appease the Chinese as a genuine offer. Even so, if Hill had been allowed to go, it might well have broken the North's momentum toward launching a missile. At this point, North Korea was under growing international pressure not to proceed with the test. Having Hill in Pyongyang could have provided a graceful excuse to delay the launch. Washington did not even pause to consider. The same day the North announced its invitation, the White House press spokesman rejected it. A few weeks later, the North finished the preparations, and in the early-morning darkness of July 5 (July 4 in the United States), it launched the first of seven missiles fired off that day.

Because this would be the maiden launch of the missile that was the focus of so much attention—an intermediate-range Taep'o-dong II—no one (including the North Koreans) knew how far it could fly. Some estimates were that it could hit Alaska or Hawaii, and US officials at first braced themselves for the possibility that they would have to use the country's still developing antimissile defenses. In his memoirs, Secretary of Defense Rumsfeld describes the missile interceptors as being on "high alert" and preparations for him to give the order to launch them if it was determined the Taep'o-dong was heading toward the United States. As it turned out, the North Korean missile failed less than a minute into flight, allowing Rumsfeld to enjoy the rest of the July 4 weekend and NORTHCOM—in charge of missile defense for the United States—to use the opportunity for a real-life dry run of its operational readiness. It seems unlikely that the North meant for the missile to go anywhere near the continental United States. Most probably, the plans were for this first attempt to end up in the mid-Pacific.

Even so, it appears the North wanted this Taep'o-dong launch to be seen as menacing. Unlike a previous missile launch in August 1998, and subsequent ones (once in 2009, twice in 2012), the North did not claim the July launch as part of its space program. In fact, a statement released after the tests portrayed the activity as "missile launches by the Korean People's Army." The six other missiles—a combination of short- and medium-range missiles—had more success, splashing down in the Sea of Japan off the Russian coast.

In response to the missile launches, Washington and Tokyo pushed for a tough UN Security Council sanctions resolution that included reference to Chapter Seven, authorizing the use of force. China and Russia, not surprisingly, balked. The final Security Council resolution (1695) called for member states to prevent "missile and missile-related items, materials, goods and technology" from being transferred to or from the DPRK. The resolution also demanded that the North "re-establish its pre-existing commitment to a moratorium on missile launching."

In Pyongyang the idea that the international community thought that the 1999 launch moratorium had any validity in the current circumstances, or that the UN had any standing to tell the DPRK when it should or should not implement its own unilaterally declared moratorium, must have seemed astounding. In a Foreign Ministry statement on July 6, the North went to considerable lengths to make the point that its launch moratorium had been conditional, that the relevant conditions no longer existed, and that, in fact, Pyongyang had already announced in March 2005 that the 1999 moratorium was no longer valid.

At the time, no one realized that perhaps the most important result of the UN resolution was to lock Washington into an escalating series of responses. Each time the North launched another ballistic missile, which it proceeded to do three more times over the next seven years, the United States felt obliged to ratchet up the pressure in the form of new sanctions resolutions, which in turn sparked new North Korean countermoves. Whether there was anything to Pyongyang's persistent claims that what it was really after was establishing its right to the peaceful use of outer space—comparable to that of South Korea and Japan—no one could tell because no one probed. It was not even possible to determine if there was any negotiated basis at all for dealing with the North Korean missile issue because the only arrow in the international community's quiver was sanctions.

Immediately after the July missile launches, Ambassador Hill was sent to Asia to discuss a coordinated response to the North's move. Before Hill's departure, President Bush told him, "You tell the Chinese I can't solve this—they need to solve this." By this time, Kim Jong Il's October 2000 offer to negotiate with the United States on the missile issue had been long forgotten by Washington; the North Koreans apparently did not think it worth raising again, either. As Washington would soon discover, Pyongyang had already decided to follow up its missile salvo with action on the nuclear front, crossing the nuclear threshold in a way that would complicate US efforts to achieve the denuclearization of North Korea and would rattle capitals around the region.

RUMBLE IN PUNGGYE

The first signs that the North would test a nuclear device appeared in August, only a month after the missile barrage. The evidence of preparations set off increasingly shrill—and to some extent bombastic—warnings in the press from officials in the various concerned capitals, making the remainder of the summer and the early fall a repeat, in many respects, of what had occurred prior to the July missile launches. At times it was hard be sure which were stronger, the pressures on the North not to test or those on Washington to talk to Pyongyang. Washington was at its worst, blustering about what would happen to the North if it went through with the test. The North Koreans either did not believe the threats or did not care.

On October 3, the DPRK Foreign Ministry ended the uncertainty with a statement announcing that Pyongyang had decided it had no choice but to conduct a test. Six days later, on the morning of October 9, it did exactly that. The North Koreans informed the Chinese a few hours ahead of the time, location, and expected yield—around four kilotons. Such prenotification of a first nuclear test was an unusual move—no other country is known to have done so. Presumably, the North Koreans wanted to be able counter what they knew would be complaints from Beijing by saying they had given advance warning. In terms of actual yield, this first test was judged by outside experts to be only partially successful and not very impressive, in the neighborhood of one kiloton. When a small group of Americans—including former US negotiator Jack Pritchard, Sig Hecker, John Lewis, and Robert Carlin were in Pyongyang at the end of October, they asked a North Korean military official, Colonel General Ri Chan Bok, about the reports of the small yield.* General Ri did not miss a beat. "You should know," he said, "that it is easier to test a larger device than a smaller one." After discussions with officials from the Foreign Ministry and the Yongbyon nuclear center, the Americans came away with the

---

* For many years until his retirement in 2009, General Ri was the North Korean military figure whom visiting American delegations usually met. He was the compleat America handler, able to switch from courtesy to sarcasm to angry threats as the occasion demanded.

strong impression that the test had marked a turning point, that the North Koreans were heartened by what they had accomplished, whether it was fully successfully or not, and that Pyongyang would be less likely than ever before to give up its nuclear weapons program.

Whatever the failure in physics, the test's political ramifications were significant. Even a small yield demonstrated that what the North had announced in February 2005—that it had developed a nuclear weapon— was a fact. The second thing it demonstrated, most of all to Washington, was that the US policy of the past four years on North Korea had failed.

Nevertheless, according to Secretary of State Rice, there was actually a silver lining. In her view, the test finally gave Washington the opportunity to put into practice important decisions, reached in April 2006, that would significantly alter the US approach to North Korea.

In her memoirs, Rice portrays this new approach as a "strategic leap" in the president's thinking on North Korea and says it had been communicated to Chinese leader Hu Jintao during his April 2006 visit to Washington. Others in the NSC at the time explain the change in US policy somewhat differently. They suggest that the North's test created the opportunity not to uncork decisions already in place but finally to make the argument to the president that previous US policy had not worked and that it was time to remove the restraints on diplomatic engagement with the North that the administration had imposed since coming to office in 2001.

Either way, the test triggered a response from Washington that one can only imagine was greeted by the North Korean Foreign Ministry with grim satisfaction. Three weeks after the test, Ambassador Hill was in Beijing for what turned out to be bilateral discussions with his DPRK counterpart, Kim Gye Gwan. This was not exactly the script that Washington had approved for Hill, who was supposed to engage in tripartite sessions that included the Chinese. Hill's action caused a mini storm in Washington, but one that blew over in only a few weeks. The administration—minus the vice president—was now too interested in engaging the North Koreans to let an ambassador's sidestepping his instructions get in the way.

A six-party meeting convened in December in Beijing, and in January 2007 Hill again met Kim Gye Gwan, this time in Berlin for an approved bilateral discussion—approved, anyway, by Secretary Rice, who had not consulted the US interagency, thereby obviating the chance that contrary instructions might get in the way of Hill's talks with the North Koreans. The two negotiators quickly agreed on concrete steps for implementing the September 2005 joint statement. The North Koreans apparently also came away from the meeting with the impression that Washington would move to release the twenty-five million dollars that was frozen in its BDA accounts. Finally undoing the consequences of the Treasury action turned out to be more difficult than Washington had imagined, however. It would probably have seemed to suspicious minds in Pyongyang that the delay was one more example of bad faith on the part of the Americans, all too similar to the constantly late HFO deliveries in the 1990s.

Rice says the United States wanted to get the North back to six-party talks and used the political fallout from the nuclear test as an opportunity to pressure Pyongyang. Others contend that the financial and banking squeeze was having an effect on the North Korean leadership. The NSC director for Asian affairs at the time, Victor Cha, says that a tipsy DPRK official admitted at a dinner in Beijing in November 2005 that the Americans had finally found a way to hurt North Korea. Neither of those explanations seems adequate to explain Pyongyang's willingness to return to the talks.

In retrospect, the year following the October 2006 nuclear test bore the hallmarks of considered North Korean strategy rather than a sudden shift in direction by a leadership caught off balance. Rice's interpretation that Pyongyang worried it had gone too far by carrying out the first test underestimated the North's commitment to its nuclear program. The contention that the Treasury's financial measures had really begun to "bite," and that the North Korean leadership was desperate to end them, appears similarly off the mark. More likely, the North Koreans were surprised by the Bush administration's decision, in the wake of the test, not to increase pressure but to quickly agree to ease off and move even further into bilateral talks.[*]

Later in 2007, Pyongyang may have concluded that its estimates of US policy were confirmed when, after the Israeli Air Force destroyed a nuclear reactor in Syria (a reactor widely reported to have been under construction with North Korean assistance), Washington barely broke stride in pushing ahead its own agenda with the North. In fact, the low-key US reaction to the discovery that the North was proliferating its nuclear technology may, in the long run, have strengthened Pyongyang in its calculations that there was almost nothing it might do on the nuclear front that would trigger a forceful response from Washington. To the contrary, to the North it may well have seemed that its demonstrated nuclear capability was providing a degree of diplomatic leverage and, more than that, a modicum of respect that it had long sought.

---

[*] This was also the vice president's interpretation, and on this, at least, he may have been right.

19

THE EMPEROR'S
NEW CLOTHES

JUST PAST SIX IN the evening of February 26, 2008, North Korean state television broadcast images of an orchestra playing the country's national anthem. The scene might have been unremarkable were it not for the fact that the orchestra was the New York Philharmonic and the performance was coming live from the newly renovated East Pyongyang Grand Theater. What followed minutes later was even more stunning: the strains of "The Star-Spangled Banner" filled the hall and the international airwaves. Viewers in both parts of Korea watched as the camera panned across the audience, focused tightly on the American flag onstage and then, as the music reached its climax, pulled back dramatically for the anthem's final notes.

The New York Philharmonic's program that night—Wagner, Dvorak, Gershwin, Bizet, and Bernstein, and ending with a beautiful arrangement of the Korean folk song "Arirang"—lasted for an hour and a half. When it was over, there was polite applause, swelling into an ovation that went on for six long minutes. Near the end of the ovation, cheers broke out, with the audience waving at the orchestra, and orchestra members waving back. The smiles onstage were radiant, in marked contrast to the musicians' reserved demeanor when they first took their places. The orchestra members, some with tears in their eyes, said later they were amazed; many avowed that the response to their performance was nothing like anything they had ever seen. In this of all places, it seemed, music had built a bridge.

North Korean television viewers may have missed the final cheers from the audience. The program schedule for that night called for coverage of the concert to last until 7:43 P.M., at which point another program was to run—*Treasure House in Praise of Great Men: Visiting the International Friendship Exhibition Hall*, lasting until the regular news began at 8:00 P.M. For a network, even in North Korea, a schedule is a schedule.

The path to Pyongyang had begun a half year earlier, in the summer of 2007, when the Philharmonic received a message that North Korea was interested in having the orchestra perform in its capital. That message had been preceded by a long series of hints, dropped at meetings on the nuclear issue with Ambassador Christopher Hill earlier in the year, that the North wanted cultural exchanges with the United States, including a visit by the New York Philharmonic. The first invitation arrived in August 2007; it did not come directly from Pyongyang, but rather from a businessman in Northern California, acting as an "authorized agent" of the North's Ministry of Culture. That approach was quickly followed by a fax to the orchestra from the ministry itself.

The orchestra's president, Zarin Mehta, and its director of communications, Eric Latzky, were intrigued both by an unsolicited fax from Pyongyang and by the prospect of a trip to North Korea. They quickly decided the idea was worth pursuing. The New York Philharmonic had performed all over the world, including in the Soviet Union in the coldest days of the Cold War, but there had been no opportunity recently for this sort of overseas trip to a politically hostile country. Not all the orchestra's members were so convinced, however. Some of the musicians balked at "serenading a dictator," and it took a long, spirited meeting with Mehta and Ambassador Hill to convince the doubters that this was a worthy enterprise.

As it turned out, the summer of 2007 was a good moment to launch such a venture. Six-party talks were making visible progress on the nuclear front. In July the North had shut down the Yongbyon complex again, and the IAEA had gone back to monitor the facility. By early August, the two Koreas had agreed on summit talks to be held later that month.[*] The State Department was quietly supportive of the proposal for the concert, and Ambassador Hill's assistant, Yuri Kim, was assigned to ensure that things proceeded smoothly on the official level. Secretary of State Condoleezza Rice, an accomplished musician herself, saw the value of the enterprise, and may even have contemplated attending.[**]

At what point North Korea's Supreme Leader, Kim Jong Il, became aware of the proposal for the orchestra's visit is not known, but if it had not already crossed his desk by August, it did not take long for word to reach him—and he clearly liked the idea. At an initial meeting with diplomats from the North's UN Mission in New York to discuss the invitation, Zarin

---

[*] Due to torrential rains and flooding in Pyongyang, the summit was rescheduled for October.

[**] Negative views within the administration about dealing with North Korea made such an idea impossible to consider for very long. Besides, there was an enduring fear of "doing an Albright"—being perceived as somehow endorsing the Kim regime. That fear lasted into the next US administration as well.

Mehta noted that when performing abroad, the orchestra, in addition to the national anthem of the host country, always played "The Star-Spangled Banner." The DPRK officials did not blink an eye—that would be fine, they said. From that point on, it was clear that Kim had given not only his blessing, but, more important, his full support. In the following months, the degree of cooperation the orchestra's planning teams received on their visits leading up to the concert underlined that the event served a greater purpose for the regime than simply satisfying Kim's well-known interest in the arts. In October the first advance team arrived in Pyongyang. Leaving the airport, the delegation assumed it was being driven to the same hotel where the orchestra would stay. Instead, the caravan—one aged black Mercedes followed by three white Volkswagen Rabbits—pulled up to an elaborate guesthouse on a hill overlooking the Taedong River, a place reserved for very important visitors.

In the days that followed, it seemed there was nothing the North Koreans would not do to make the orchestra's visit a success. Whatever the orchestra wanted—and it had high standards for both its musicians and their instruments—the North Koreans were willing to supply. The venue initially offered for the concert was too small; the Koreans found a bigger one. The hall that was finally selected lacked an orchestra shell; the North Koreans built one. The food was not right for the orchestra members; the North Koreans asked what the musicians would prefer and were handed a picture of a buffet in a Paris hotel. The orchestra wanted the performance open to the public; the North Koreans agreed. The orchestra felt that it was important that students attend the performance; the North arranged to open the full dress rehearsal to students.

What must have looked to Pyongyang like a relatively simple affair quickly ballooned into something much more complicated. International media clamored to be included in the orchestra's entourage. A German production company wanted the international rights to the broadcast of the performance. South Korean media wanted to take part in covering the event, as did American broadcasters and print media. They all demanded high-speed Internet and international phone connections from Pyongyang. The orchestra's instruments also had demands. Because there were no heated facilities in the North Korean capital, special vans would have to be driven up across the DMZ from South Korea to store the instruments overnight. The North Koreans agreed to all of it. The last time anyone had seen such cooperation for an American delegation was in October 2000, when US secretary of state Madeleine Albright flew to Pyongyang.

The reason for this level of accommodation became clearer at a lunch with Vice Foreign Minister Kim Gye Gwan in October, during the first advance team's stay in Pyongyang. When Zarin Mehta asked why the North Koreans wanted the orchestra to visit, Kim replied that they hoped to improve relations with the United States in order to open up possibilities for developing their economy. "We'd like to supply Walmart," he said.[*]

The seemingly unlimited reservoir of cooperation dried up on one issue, however. Zarin Mehta told the North Koreans that the performance had to be broadcast live in order to reach as wide an audience as possible. This was not a request, he made clear; it was a requirement. The North Koreans demurred.

Communications have always been a sensitive issue with Pyongyang, and decisions about communications links with the outside world are not in the Ministry of Culture's purview. Having the international media as part of the orchestra's entourage was one thing; giving foreign newsmen access to real-time, uncensored broadcasting from the country was something else. Live broadcast was rare even for North Korean television, and to allow foreign television that right was not something the regime's security organs could accept. When there was still no answer from Pyongyang about the broadcast issue in February as the orchestra began a tour of China prior to going to North Korea, Mehta told Eric Latzky, "Tell them if they don't agree, we won't come." It was a monumental bluff. Canceling the Pyongyang concert would have been a disaster for the orchestra, but it would have been even worse for the North Korean officials, who knew they were under the gun to make this visit a success, no matter what. The answer came back: yes, a live transmission is approved.

Other logistical details, especially given the compressed time to work matters out, were also complex: obtaining a plane (South Korean carrier Asiana Airlines had one of the few special 747s in the world that could transport a group of three hundred people and the full load of the orchestra's equipment), arranging passage across the DMZ for the special vans needed for the instruments, and getting approval for expedited immigration procedures for the orchestra members on their arrival at the North Korean airport. It was almost a miracle that everything came together.

Yet while Pyongyang pulled out all the stops to make the orchestra's visit a success, Washington steadily distanced itself from the affair. Initial support in Washington for the visit, never widespread, dried up abruptly. The personal involvement of Assistant Secretary Hill, who looked to be leaning forward on the visit, ended unexpectedly and without explanation when he pulled out of a December press conference at which the orchestra

---

[*] The theme was strikingly similar to what a North Korean negotiator had said several years before during US-DPRK missile talks in New York. The North had looked around stores in Manhattan, he noted. "We don't need to sell missiles if we can use our light industry to earn money selling goods to the United States." Even during the Kumchang-ri negotiations in 1999, the North Koreans had suggested that the empty cavern might be utilized by American companies interested in a place for a light industry factory.

planned to make its official public announcement of the trip. The *Washington Post*'s Glenn Kessler later reported that Vice President Cheney's office had applied the brakes after learning that Hill would stand on the stage with the North Korean UN ambassador at the event. According to Kessler's account, Secretary of State Rice was "furious" with Hill and told him to back away from the orchestra's arrangements. Hill's staff assistant continued what the orchestra's officials characterized as invaluable help, but the assistant secretary was thereafter nowhere to be seen in connection with the visit.

In an earlier meeting in 2007, Kim Gye Gwan had told Ambassador Hill that the North Koreans hoped Secretary of State Rice would attend the concert and suggested that if she did, Kim Jong Il would be there as well. In February, as the orchestra was making its final preparations, it heard rumors that an official US party—possibly including the secretary of state—would be in the audience in Pyongyang. The rumors, it turned out, were just that. The orchestra's performance took place a day after the inauguration of the new ROK president, Lee Myung-bak, a high-profile event Rice had flown to Seoul to attend. Briefly meeting a former American official during the festivities, she waved away the upcoming performance in the North as unimportant. "It's only a concert," she said.

That was the secretary's public line, and she was going to stick to it. "The North Korean regime is still the North Korean regime," she had said earlier in a briefing in Washington, "and so I don't think we should get carried away with what listening to Dvorak is going to do in North Korea." In Washington on the day of the concert, the State Department's spokesman noted US support for private cultural events such as the one in North Korea, but—referring to public remarks on the subject by Secretary of State Rice—went on to say, "You have to be realistic about what kind of impact such things would have on the leadership of the country and its policies."

This dismissive treatment was wide of the mark and may even have gone against Rice's better instincts. The US government might publicly portray the concert only as a private cultural event, but those involved in the State Department—including the secretary of state—knew Pyongyang had freighted it with considerable significance and lavished on it top-level attention. Days in advance of the orchestra's arrival, North Korean media announced to the population news of the planned concert and, in an unusual step, even provided background on the orchestra.

The real issue was not what impact the performance might have on the North Korean leadership, but rather what impact the North's leadership intended the orchestra's Pyongyang trip to have on Washington, and what signal the regime might be sending to its own people as well. Pyongyang's handling of the visit had all the signs of a major effort by Kim Jong Il to put things back on track with Washington. In February 2007, with the

Bush administration suddenly open to dealing with the US Treasury financial measures, and then in the summer with movement toward inter-Korean summit talks, Kim may have felt he was making the sort of multifront progress that had not been possible for many years.

There was a confluence of events in October 2007—exactly a year after the North's first nuclear test—that was uncanny, marking one of those moments when the streams of history flow into each other in weirdly improbable ways. On October 3, a new six-party implementation agreement emerged; on the fourth, ROK president Roh left Pyongyang after the two-day North-South summit; and on the sixth, the first planning team for the New York Philharmonic arrived in North Korea.

The streams did not flow together for very long. The foundation for the six-party implementation process was shaky from the start and started to crumble within months, South Korean presidential elections in December essentially negated the results of the October North-South summit, and the unexpected opening provided by the concert in Pyongyang quickly vanished when Washington proved unsupportive of the Philharmonic's visit. As propitious as the diplomatic environment was for the North's initial invitation to the orchestra in August 2007, by the end of that year storm clouds were beginning to gather. To those few in Washington who—like Rice—favored the diplomatic track for dealing with North Korea, signs of trouble on the negotiating front dictated a need to protect one's bureaucratic flanks and be seen as aloof toward Pyongyang. Hence Rice's public line: a concert, after all, is just a concert.

After the concert, the North pressed for a reciprocal visit by its State Symphony to the United States. The persistence with which it made the case suggested either that the idea was Kim Jong Il's or at least that it was one he very much supported. There was little appetite in Washington for proceeding down this path, however, and even less when the six-party process started coming apart in earnest later in 2008. Despite private efforts in the following years to bring the North Korean orchestra to the United States, it was impossible for them to get visas.

SIGNS OF SUCCESSION

If Kim Jong Il watched the Philharmonic concert on television,[*] his third son and eventual successor, Kim Jong Un, could well have been sitting beside him. By February 2008, the political succession may already have been in its initial stages. According to a North Korean defector with ties

---

[*] To avoid a potentially embarrassing situation of orchestra members having to decide whether to stand if Kim Jong Il walked into the hall, the musicians had waited to go onstage until the audience filled the hall and the lights went down.

to the country's police, as early as February 2007 Kim Jong Il had told his security services that they were to support Kim Jong Un. Whether this meant the elder Kim had by then decided on his youngest son as successor, or was just starting the grooming and testing process, is not known. But looking back, there is tantalizing evidence that several years earlier, the younger Kim's fortunes had already begun to rise.

In 2004, after a long battle with cancer, Kim Jong Il's consort and Kim Jong Un's mother, Ko Yong-hui, died. Ko had been with Kim Jong Il since at least the mid-1970s, and sources with knowledge of the North Korean leader described the two as very close. Born in Japan, Ko came to North Korea with her parents in the 1960s as part of the large migration of Koreans in Japan back to the North. She became a leading dancer in the Mansudae art troupe, which was under Kim Jong Il's personal direction. The couple had two sons and a daughter, all of whom were briefly educated in Switzerland in the 1990s, where they were looked after by the North Korean ambassador to the UN organizations in Geneva, Ri Chol.* In the later years, Ko apparently traveled abroad frequently, sometimes with her children, seeking medical help.

Ko was reportedly popular with the North Korean military leadership, and in 2012 the regime released for internal use a film showing her accompanying Kim Jong Il on inspections of army units. Already by 2001, there were signs that she was working to ensure that one of her sons be named successor. Perhaps not coincidentally, in May 2001 Kim Jong Il's oldest son, Kim Jong Nam, was stopped at Japan's Narita Airport, traveling under a false passport. Despite a widespread belief outside North Korea that Kim Jong Nam was being groomed as the successor and that after the airport incident he was discarded, Kim had probably never been tapped by his father to be next in line. For sure, no one actively being groomed as the North Korean successor would have been traveling in mufti to Japan.

According to some sources, in 2005, the year after Ko Yong-hui's death, several senior generals approached Kim Jong Il to suggest he consider the youngest son, Kim Jong Un, as his successor. The elder Kim is said to have waved them away, protesting that the boy was still too young. Only a few years later, however, the grooming and testing phase for Jong-un appears to have begun.

Sometime in mid-August 2008 (his last public appearance was a visit to a military unit, publicized on August 15), Kim Jong Il suffered a severe stroke. Foreign doctors were urgently summoned, chief among them a French brain specialist, Dr. François-Xavier Roux, whom the North Koreans

* After decades in Geneva, Ri Chol returned to Pyongyang in early 2010 to become an important figure among Kim Jong Un's advisers.

had consulted years earlier after Kim fell from a horse. According to Dr. Roux, Kim's own doctors were too nervous about treating their Supreme Leader in a life-or-death situation, and Kim was very close to death. In a 2011 media interview, Roux said that Kim had been "in intensive care, in a coma, in a bad way. . . . He was in a life-threatening situation."

Kim's condition was kept a tight secret within the country, though it did not take long for American and South Korean intelligence to realize that a major medical emergency had occurred in the North. Key individuals in the North's elite Guard Command, the military unit charged with Kim's personal security, certainly knew what had happened, as did his immediate family—most important, Kim Jong Un, who Dr. Roux says often came into the room at the Red Cross Hospital where his father lay.

Kim Jong Il's sister, Kim Kyong Hui, also knew of her brother's stroke and according to some sources played a key role bolstering the regime while Kim was incapacitated. Brother and sister had always been close, and Kim Jong Il often made an effort to praise her in front of other officials, even though it was well known that, for health reasons, Kim Kyong Hui had not been active in fulfilling her formal duties for some time. After the stroke, as Kim regained his strength and gathered those he thought he could trust close around him, he made sure to raise his sister's profile. Beginning with a visit to one of the country's model farms on the east coast in June 2009, Kim Kyong Hui would begin to appear more frequently in public with her brother. In September 2010, he would elevate her to the party's ruling Political Bureau and appoint her—somewhat improbably—a four-star general.

The long-term prognosis for someone with a stroke of the magnitude Kim suffered, especially for someone with his other ailments (rumored to be diabetes, hypertension, and possibly heart disease), was not good. How well Kim grasped that danger is not known, though Dr. Roux said that once Kim could talk, he asked questions that suggested he understood the gravity of his condition.

Gravely ill or not, Kim's recovery period would, of necessity, be abbreviated. No country, especially one so focused on the top as North Korea, can afford to have the Supreme Leader out of sight for an extended period. Kim's absence from the celebration of the country's sixtieth National Day, on September 9, was glaringly obvious both in North Korea and to foreign observers. It was imperative to get him into view again. The first North Korean mentions of Kim appearing in public came in early-October 2008, less than eight weeks after his stroke, when he was reported to be at a university soccer game. The first pictures of Kim appeared in North Korean media a few weeks later at a military unit, but at the time South Korean analysts suggested that, judging from the background foliage, these were actually taken earlier in the year. More pictures, apparently genuine, waited until early November, when Kim showed up at another soccer match, this time between army teams. For many months after he reappeared in public, Kim looked gaunt and alarmingly frail. The explanation presented to the population was that he had gone on a diet and that the diet medication had been too extreme. Given the North Korean rumor mill, however, it would not have taken long for people to hear that something more serious had happened. In Pyongyang wives frequently learned through their own channels what their husbands were supposed to keep as closely guarded secrets.

Watching soccer matches was not Kim's normal activity, and over the next three years, once he had recovered more fully, the Supreme Leader threw himself into his work to a degree that suggested he realized his time on earth was rapidly coming to a close. From late 2008 until his death in December 2011, Kim would make well over three hundred public appearances, including on-site visits throughout North Korea and four long train trips out of the country—three to China and one to Russia. The stroke appears to have affected Kim's motor functions but not his cognitive abilities. Despite rumors in South Korean media, fed by official sources, that Kim's mental faculties had seriously deteriorated, foreigners who met him over the several years between his stroke and his death seemed to think he was still capable of clear thought and effective verbal interaction. He was also in better physical shape than they had expected. There were stories of bouts of depression and crying jags. If so, these could have been the side effects of medication prescribed for his other ailments.

Yet even with the special care Kim undoubtedly received from a brigade of doctors, nutritionists, therapists, and others, it was an exhausting schedule and not one recommended for a man in his condition. Besides his busy schedule, he drank, smoked, and regained weight—risky behavior for someone who had suffered such a massive stroke. Although Kim had rebounded for the moment, no one close to him in the DPRK, certainly no one who had seen him in the hospital room in August 2008, could have any illusions that his days were anything but numbered.

DIPLOMATIC DOWNTURN

As Kim Jong Il slowly recuperated, the situation on the diplomatic front took a major turn for the worse. Through much of 2007, there had been sustained, almost giddy, progress on implementation of the six-party joint statement, giving rise to hopes that after four rough years, the process of negotiations was at last on solid ground. In July 2007, the North had shut down Yongbyon; in September representatives from the other five parties visited the nuclear center, and work started on "disabling" key facilities. In a development that probably surprised Pyongyang, the early-September bombing by the Israeli Air Force of a nuclear reactor in Syria built with North Korean assistance did not slow activity on the six-party front. On October 3, in the midst of the second inter-Korean summit, the six-party representatives released an agreement on the next stage of implementations calling for completion by year's end of the disablement of Yongbyon's reactor, reprocessing plant, and fuel fabrication facility and a "complete and correct" declaration by the DPRK of "all its nuclear programs." In return, the United States reaffirmed, in vague language, its willingness to remove the DPRK from Washington's list of state sponsors of terrorism (a goal of the North since it signed a joint statement on terrorism with the United States in October 2000) and to "advance the process terminating the application of the Trading with the Enemy Act with respect to the DPRK." Also, the North would be provided with "economic, energy and humanitarian assistance up to the equivalent of one million tons of HFO." The parties put off what might have been a key step—holding a six-party ministerial meeting—until an "appropriate time."

Then, abruptly, the situation became confused again. Despite Washington's efforts to keep the six-party structure intact, it was too frayed and in some sense cobbled together to withstand the various pressures placed on it. Deadlines for implementation (both by the North and by the other five parties) were pressing, while the issue of verification, always a sensitive point in dealing with the North, again blocked the way forward.[*] Secretary Rice and Ambassador Hill moved as fast as they could to secure enough progress to keep the process ahead of the critics—in and out of the administration—who continuously snapped at it from behind.

Ironically, a serious blow to the diplomacy began with an attempt by the North Koreans to assuage American fears that they had a hidden enrichment program. In 2002 Washington had charged that the North Koreans had imported large numbers of aluminum tubes that, some analysts argued, were perfectly suited as parts for centrifuges needed in a uranium enrichment facility. In November 2007, the North Koreans took a US diplomat to a facility outside of Pyongyang and handed over what they said was aluminum from the imported tubes, which they claimed were not for enrichment but for another purpose. Testing of the aluminum in US laboratories, however, revealed a few minute particles of highly enriched uranium. The results leaked to the press in December, setting off accusations that the North had been lying all along about its HEU program and had still not stopped. Even if the tubes themselves had nothing to do with HEU, the particles had to come from somewhere. Speculation ranged

---

[*] The Verification Bureau in the State Department, as verification specialists naturally do, devised what would be an ideal program. North Korea, however, tended to see as espionage what the United States considered verification.

from the obvious possibility that the HEU was on the tubes because they really had been used in an enrichment program to the chance that it had migrated from other sources in the North to hypotheses that the amount of the particles was so minuscule as to be inconclusive.

Meanwhile, the North had slowed one of the agreed-to disablement measures—the discharge of fuel rods from the 5-megawatt reactor—probably partly in response to the fact that the Japanese were not delivering their portion of the promised HFO.* In a statement to the Senate Foreign Relations Committee on February 6, 2008, Ambassador Hill put the best face on the situation, but not everyone—including the North Koreans—shared his sunniness. A few weeks later, at the time of the Philharmonic's concert in Pyongyang, Vice Foreign Minister Kim Gye Gwan told an American attending the performance that the six-party process had run into serious problems and that the situation was "bad."

In May 2008, the North turned over to the Americans around nineteen thousand pages of documents related to its plutonium program—and minute traces of HEU were reportedly detected on the paper. Paper is clearly not a dual-use or proscribed item, but again the argument was that the HEU had to come from somewhere.

The skies cleared momentarily in late June, when on the twenty-sixth the North Koreans delivered (six months late) to the Chinese a "declaration" of their past nuclear activities, as required by the February and October 2007 implementation agreements. Playing its part, Washington responded the same day. The president announced that the United States was lifting provisions of the Trading with the Enemy Act applied to North Korea and that he was starting the forty-five-day notification clock required to remove the North from the terrorism list. The following day, with CNN cameras and Ambassador Hill's deputy, Sung Kim, looking on, the North took another step toward disablement and blew up the cooling tower for the 5-megawatt reactor at Yongbyon.

An airplane gathering speed on the runway usually lifts off. This one did not. The situation deteriorated again on August 11, when Washington informed the North Koreans that they would not be removed from the terrorism list until, in the words of the State Department spokesman, there was a "strong verification regime" in place to ensure Pyongyang would fulfill its commitment to give up nuclear weapons and all of its nuclear programs. North Korean diplomats complained that the United States had "moved the goal posts" and that the two issues had not previously been linked. Some American negotiators privately agreed.

---

* By January 2008, the United States was looking for other countries outside of the six-party talks who might supply the Japanese portion.

A few days later, the disablement at Yongbyon stopped, though a public announcement would wait until August 26, when the North Korean Foreign Ministry issued a statement accusing Washington of violating the six-party implementation agreements. As a result, the statement said, the North had decided "to immediately suspend the work of neutralizing our nuclear facilities," a measure that, it revealed, had come into effect on August 14—three days after Washington announced it was not taking the North off the terrorism list, and very possibly the same day as Kim Jong Il's stroke.[*] The statement said the North would "consider soon the measure of restoring the Yongbyon nuclear facilities to their original state, per our relevant agencies' strong demand."

In September 2008, the North announced it was "restoring" the facilities at Yongbyon—that is, reversing the disabling measures. Pyongyang told the IAEA to remove its seals and surveillance from the reprocessing plant and informed the inspectors that they would no longer have access to the facility. Although Washington did not sense it at the time, this move signaled a North Korean decision to undertake a major reversal in approach toward the United States, one that would last for the next nine months.

Events had already started drifting in a negative direction in July, and assuming Kim was healthy on August 12 (when word was flashed to Pyongyang from the North's UN Mission in New York that the United States was linking the terrorism list to verification), Kim may have quickly decided to counter what would have been seen as Washington's perfidy. After Kim's stroke, no one in North Korea, at whatever level, was going to fiddle with that decision. Certainly until Kim recovered, no official would have advocated a course that might be seen as betrayal of a policy formulated when the Supreme Leader was still fully in charge.

At the beginning of October, Ambassador Christopher Hill drove across the DMZ to Pyongyang to see if it would be possible to put the six-party process back on track. In the weeks since Kim's stroke, Washington had put together a clearer picture of the North Korean leader's condition, but the Americans had no idea whether there was anyone in Pyongyang who could reverse the August decision to abandon the disablement measures at Yongbyon. Although Kim was slowly recovering, decision making in Pyongyang was likely still paralyzed.

Vice Foreign Minister Kim Gye Gwan's opening statements to Hill were blunt. "Mutual cooperation has collapsed," he said. The deal they had previously reached was "over." The die, Kim said, "has been cast." Pyongyang had been testing US intentions, Kim warned, watching how

[*] August 14 was either the very day of, or a day or two after, Kim Jong Il's stroke.

Washington followed through on the question of removing the North from the terrorism list. Because the US had backed away, it was clear that Washington was not serious and that the only thing left for the North was to "strengthen our deterrent." By the end of the visit, after several more meetings, Hill thought he had worked the North Koreans out of the corner, but the question of who was leading whom at that point seems open to debate.

At the time of Hill's trip, no one in Washington or Pyongyang had to look at a calendar to know that the US elections were only four weeks away and that the Bush administration was running out of time. A month later, Barack Obama was elected president. The change of administrations would make no difference to Pyongyang's plans, however, which were already in motion. In an early warning of what was to come, one ranking North Korean official told an American in a private conversation soon after the US elections that the situation was already out of the hands of the diplomats. Similar warnings would come from other North Korean officials a few months later—all to the effect that decisions sure to cause serious problems with the United States had been reached at the top levels in Pyongyang, and there was nothing that could be done about it.

When the Obama administration took office, the six-party talks were as good as dead, though no one in Washington seemed to notice. Kim Jong Il's stroke and the succession already had a significant influence on decision making in Pyongyang, but again Washington did not seem to notice or to understand how to factor that into its approach. The Obama administration was new and needed to set its image. Through its early actions, the North challenged the new president, and the administration never found its balance after that.

A TERRIBLE START

One of President Obama's signature lines in his January 20, 2009, inaugural address was aimed at America's enemies: "We will extend a hand if you are willing to unclench your fist." Soon after the inauguration, it became clear that North Korea was not prepared to take up the offer.

In February, according to press reports, US intelligence saw unmistakable signs that North Korea was planning a long-range ballistic missile test. Several nonofficial American delegations were in Pyongyang that month, and they all received the same message—nothing would stop Pyongyang from conducting another launch. In fact, one of the delegations was told by a Foreign Ministry official, "You have no idea how bad things are about to get." Arguments that the North needed to give the new administration some breathing room were rebuffed out of hand. In late February, the North formally announced plans to launch a satellite; in

March, as a defensive maneuver, it signed the international Outer Space Treaty and gave the requisite notice to mariners and airmen of the impending launch.*

Newly appointed US negotiator Stephen Bosworth, who had been in Pyongyang with a private group in February, was sent out to the region in early March, prepared to go to Pyongyang for talks if the North Koreans guaranteed there would be no missile launch around the time of the visit. The North was not interested in even the appearance of compromise, and after hearing all of the threats and blandishments from the United States, the international community, and most of all China, Pyongyang went ahead with the launch on April 5, 2009.

The first and second stages of the U'nha-2 rocket performed successfully, but as happened in the 1998 attempt, the third stage malfunctioned and the satellite plunged back into the Pacific. Pyongyang television aired pictures of Kim watching the launch and celebrating with the technicians at the control center not far from Pyongyang; yet unless the large screen at the front of the control center depicting the flight's progress was preprogrammed to show success, Kim would have known within minutes that the attempt had failed. Nevertheless, he posed for a picture with the control center's personnel, and North Korean media announced that the satellite had entered orbit. Years later more pictures of the event were released that showed Kim's son Kim Jong Un had been present as well.

A few days before the launch, a statement issued in the name of the KPA General Staff warned that if Japanese or US Navy ships in the sea off the launch area "show even the slightest move for interception regarding our peaceful satellite, our revolutionary armed force will unhesitatingly deal a retaliatory strike of justice." At the time, that seemed like routine North Korean bluster, but when the subject came up later that year, a KPA general told a visiting group of Americans that KPA air force fighters had been standing by with orders to attack enemy vessels if they interfered with the launch.

The missile launch was followed a week later by a UN Security Council statement of condemnation. The North responded the next day (April 14) with a statement announcing it was withdrawing from the six-party talks and restarting the nuclear facilities at Yongbyon. (This was a step beyond Pyongyang's September 2008 announcement that it was "restoring" the nuclear center.) Once again, the IAEA inspectors were told to pack their bags, and two days later, on April 16, they were on a plane out of the country.

---

* One of the charges in the 2006 UN Security Council resolution had been that by failing to give such notice, the North had endangered ships and aircraft. That charge, at least, the North Koreans were preemptively swatting away.

In rapid-fire succession, the UN announced details of new sanctions measures, and the North released another statement, warning that if the Security Council did not issue an apology (which Pyongyang knew would never happen), it would take further, even more provocative, action. "Firstly," it warned,

> the DPRK will be compelled to take additional self-defensive measures in order to defend its supreme interests. The measures will include nuclear tests and test-firings of intercontinental ballistic missiles.
>
> Secondly, the DPRK will make a decision to build a light water reactor power plant and start the technological development for ensuring self-production of nuclear fuel as its first process without delay.

The reference to an "intercontinental ballistic missile" deliberately took the North's missile program out of the "space launch" box into the military sphere, while the reference to producing fuel for an LWR was a blatant signal about development of a uranium enrichment program.[*]

The warning of measures to defend the country's "supreme interests" was followed by the North's second nuclear test, on May 25. This explosion, unlike the first, was large enough (estimates ranged from two to six kilotons) to convince skeptics that the North could make a nuclear weapon. The science of estimating yield from afar is not exact, and much depends on knowing where the actual explosion takes place in order to refine the calculations. After reexamining the data, some experts concluded that the yield for the second test was at the upper end of the calculations and might even have exceeded six kilotons. Unlike the first test, no particles from the nuclear explosion vented into the air, making it impossible to determine certain characteristics of the device. That ability to seal the underground test tunnel became of crucial importance after the third test, in February 2013.

After the North tested a nuclear device early in Obama's presidency, there was little chance of getting the White House to take seriously the possibility of negotiations with Pyongyang. The Obama administration took the missile and nuclear tests almost as a personal affront, and certainly as confirmation that the most important US goal should be to alter North Korea's "behavior," as administration spokesmen constantly repeated, or, in another favorite phrase, to break a cycle of "provocation and reward." Some members of the administration said they were prepared to

---

[*] The North sent a similar message to the administration via the New York channel shortly before releasing its formal public statement, though as is often the case, the private message was tougher than the public one.

pick up where the Bush administration's North Korea policy had left off if Pyongyang had kept the six-party talks on track. But those talks were already moribund when the Obama administration took office, and there was not much left in terms of policy to pick up.

Facing a collapsing US financial system, the new president had more than enough to do without chasing what was, in the view of his advisers, an unreliable negotiating partner in pursuit of will-o'-the-wisp outcomes. The "bandwidth" of attention could accommodate only so many issues, and these had to be ones that either the president absolutely could not avoid or he had a fair chance of winning. North Korea did not fall in either category. Those who looked at the experience of the past eight years quickly came to the conclusion that there was no basis for a deal with Pyongyang, and thus no reason to expend high-level time or effort trying to achieve one.

The irony is that during Obama's first term, there were more high-level policy meetings (the so-called Deputies Committee and the highly secret "small group" meetings) on North Korea than any other Asian problem, sometimes at critical moments, on a few occasions with heated debate, but often on mundane issues that lower-level officials could just as easily have handled. By late 2009, the administration had adopted a strategy dubbed "strategic patience," refusing, it said, to become exercised over North Korean actions or to rush back to negotiations after every new "provocation" from Pyongyang. Critics would charge that strategic patience was turning into "strategic passivity," but as usual it wasn't the critics who made the difference—it was reality. Once again, events would prove that the stakes in Korea are always too high, and the confrontations too volatile, for Washington to hope that it could simply wait out the North Koreans.

For the first four years of the Obama administration, the center of gravity of Washington's approach toward North Korea was negative, rather than proactive. In the words of Secretary of Defense Robert Gates, the United States was not going to "buy the same horse twice." That turned out to be more or less the totality of US policy. Unlike the first Bush administration, Obama's advisers were not opposed to sitting down with the North Koreans, but their deep skepticism that anything useful could be achieved, that there could ever be a "deal," meant that they were not inclined to look for or to exploit possible openings.

The question is often asked why the North went ahead with such provocative actions when it had a new US administration offering a better path.[*] The evidence suggests that Pyongyang's decisions about backing away from the six-party agreements and conducting the nuclear and mis-

---

[*] How much better was never clear. Seoul would probably have balked at too forward leaning a US policy, and, as previously noted, there was deep skepticism in the White House that engagement with Pyongyang was worth trying.

sile tests had already been made before the elections and that there was never any hope that the North would back off, no matter who came to office. The six-party process, never favored by the North Koreans anyway, had run its course, and the hothouse atmosphere building around the political succession in Pyongyang ensured that timelines, perspectives, advice, and decisions would all take on a different color in the North Korean leadership than in the past.

If Washington wanted to see old patterns broken, it would soon get its wish, though not in the way it hoped. Following the North's second nuclear test, the UN Security Council on June 17, 2009, passed a new resolution (1874)—once again with the Chinese and Russians agreeing to a condemnation of the North Korean missile and nuclear tests. Beijing, however, made sure to include in its own name a proviso:

> The sovereignty, territorial integrity and legitimate security concerns and development interests of the Democratic People's Republic of Korea should be respected. After its return to the Nuclear Non-Proliferation Treaty, that country would enjoy the right to the peaceful use of nuclear energy as a State party. The Council's actions, meanwhile, should not adversely impact the country's development, or humanitarian assistance to it. . . . The issue of inspections was complex and sensitive, and countries must act prudently and under the precondition of reasonable grounds and sufficient evidence, and refrain from any words or deeds that might exacerbate conflict. Under no circumstances should there be the use of force or threat of the use of force.

This careful language carving out space for continued Chinese economic and political interaction with Pyongyang turned out to be more than rhetoric. Over the next several years, Sino-DPRK trade would grow (from under $3 billion in 2008 to almost $6 billion in 2012), official visitors would travel back and forth in increasing numbers, infrastructure projects in the North funded by the Chinese would rapidly proceed, and overall Chinese economic involvement in North Korea would increase significantly. And all of this support flowed to North Korea from China no matter how irksome Beijing found its neighbor to be.

CLINTON'S VISIT

Following the passage of UNSC resolution 1874, North Korea made a classic turn from tough to mellow. In this case, however, it did so with added urgency because of the growing need to establish external and internal conditions that would support the political succession under way in Pyongyang.

In March 2009, before the missile and nuclear tests, two young American journalists had gone to the North Korean border with China to research a story on defectors. The two women recklessly followed their guide across the ice-covered Tumen River into North Korea, were taken prisoner and roughed up by border guards, and then transferred quickly to Pyongyang, where they were interrogated and scared out of their wits, but not badly mistreated. After an "investigation" lasting a month, in late April the North announced that the two would go to "trial," an event that took place in early June. The sentence was twelve years of "reform through labor" for both women, "with no chance of appeal."

The sentence was shocking, but the chance of the two Americans ever having to serve time was practically nil. It was by now common practice for an American of rather high-level, or at least high-profile, stature to come to Pyongyang to take home US citizens who crossed illegally into the North. Several well-known figures offered to go, but all were rejected by Pyongyang. At last the Obama administration offered up former vice president Al Gore, whose network the journalists had worked for, but the North Koreans told Washington that it had to be Bill Clinton or the prisoners weren't going anywhere.

Several ranking officials in the administration were firmly opposed to using Clinton for such a mission, worried that doing so would send the wrong message not only to Pyongyang but also to Seoul and Tokyo. Those arguing against sending Clinton were forceful, and the matter seemed resolved until Secretary of State Hillary Clinton pointed out that the administration faced a public relations nightmare if word got out that the journalists could have been released but weren't because the White House refused to send the former president.

Even after the administration resolved to send Bill Clinton to extricate the two Americans, there was considerable nervousness in the White House that the North Koreans might lure him to Pyongyang and then not produce the journalists. That was never actually likely, however, because the North—and especially Kim Jong Il—wanted any visit by Clinton to go well. Kim had hoped to receive Clinton in Pyongyang in the last months of 2000, when US–North Korean relations seemed to be on an upward path. By meeting Clinton now, he could let Washington know that he had still not entirely given up hope of returning to it. Equally, Clinton's presence in Pyongyang gave Kim the chance to show his son and successor how it was possible to command conciliation and contrition from the United States.

Before he left, Clinton received a briefing held at his wife's house in Washington, DC, where he was given strict marching orders—essentially: go, come back with the journalists, and do not under any circumstances smile. Standing around the snack table that evening, the former president asked one of the briefing's participants, "Do you think I really have to be so careful?" As it turned out, he did.

Much of the one-day schedule for Clinton's early August visit was worked out ahead of time in secret contacts between US and DPRK officials. In the end, the North Koreans stuck exactly to the agreed-upon arrangements. During a brief meeting before dinner, Kim gave Clinton an overview of North Korean policy, and Clinton weighed in with his own views of the value of denuclearization to the North. Kim agreed, but the conversation went no further. One of the participants thought Kim was trying to make clear to Clinton that he had tried a path of engaging the United States, but it had been blocked.

At the lavish banquet that followed, Kim might have noticed how closely the small American delegation (which included an American physician) was watching and calibrating his every gesture for evidence of his health. Undoubtedly, he saw how nervous they were. When during the meal Kim offered to take Clinton to a showing of the famous North Korean mass games, with tickets he playfully suggested he had purchased for the occasion, the Americans threw up their shields. Clinton pretended not to hear Kim's invitation. There was no way he was going to be photographed, like Madeleine Albright was in October 2000, sitting next to Kim at one of those displays. After several attempts by Kim's aides to convince the Americans that they could not refuse such an offer by their leader, the North Korean leader waved them off. It was all right, he said lightly; he had already "returned" the tickets. The delegation's plane took off the next morning, with the two journalists aboard.

The Clinton visit might have provided an early opening for a thaw with North Korea, a chance to convince Kim to "unclench" his fist, but Washington was not in a frame of mind to probe. By the time the administration was ready, in late 2009, the situation had already taken another bad turn.

TURNING TO THE SOUTH

On May 23, 2009, a little more than a year after leaving office, former South Korean president Roh Moo-hyun committed suicide. News of his death came in the midst of the run up to the North's second nuclear test. Even if he had been so inclined, Kim Jong Il could do little more at that moment than offer condolences.

But Kim had another chance to reach out to the South in August when, a few weeks after the Clinton visit, Roh's predecessor Kim Dae Jung died. The North Korean leader quickly decided (possibly with prodding from pro-dialogue figures in the South) to use the opportunity to send a small delegation to Seoul carrying an important message for the then

South Korean president, Lee Myung-bak. The delegation consisted of two high-ranking party figures—Kim Ki Nam, the senior party secretary in charge of ideology, and Kim Yong-gon, director of the Central Committee's United Front Department, handling engagement with (and intelligence operations against) South Korea.

In typical fashion, President Lee's conservative advisers, including his unification minister, Hyun In-taek, did what they could to irritate and humiliate the visitors before letting them get to the Blue House. Both North Korean officials had been to Seoul before, but never with the burden of a sick and possibly dying leader on their shoulders, and they knew they had to endure these insults in order to get the message to the South Korean president. They met with Lee early in the morning on August 24. The South Korean press line was that the president had been firm and agreed to nothing. One South Korean newspaper wrote that the North Koreans' message "conveyed the North Korean leader's willingness to improve inter-Korean relations, but had nothing on an inter-Korean summit." But that was hardly true. The essence of Kim's message was simple and clear: let's talk.

A former highly successful and well-respected businessman, Lee Myung-bak had been a popular mayor of Seoul (2002–2006) and a one-term member of the National Assembly (1996–1998), in an odd twist of fate having defeated in the 1996 election none other than Roh Moo-hyun, who would later precede him in the Blue House. Lee took over the presidency in February 2008, unwilling to follow the previous two administrations' line of engagement with North Korea. The new president was not so much a hard-liner as a deeply religious man, not so much a statesman or a politician as a businessman capable of understanding world events in terms of broad trends. Lee's perspective and insights were impressive to Americans who met him. President Obama and his senior foreign-policy advisers, in particular, found Lee's grasp of developments in Northeast Asia and his insights into North Korea refreshing.* Translating those views and that broader perspective into an effective policy, however, proved to be another matter—especially given the difficult situation presented by a North Korean regime undergoing a political succession.

In the presidential election of December 2007, the South Korean public, concerned as usual with domestic economic issues but also disillusioned with the pro-engagement policies toward the North the previous two administrations had followed, voted for Lee over the somewhat flamboyant Chung Dong-young by fairly large margins among all age

---

* They were also moved by Lee's telling of his impoverished childhood and how his experience, multiplied many times over by the generation growing up after the Korean War, meant that Koreans were truly pro-American in their hearts.

groups. It was different enough from the normal pattern—older voters going for the conservative candidate, younger voters tending toward the progressive one—that it caused many analysts to wonder if there had been a major shift in the fundamental outlook of the Korean electorate. South Korean conservatives, after ten years in the policy wilderness, were straining to get back into power and to undo the damage they thought a decade of pandering to the North had produced. Among those involved in setting the administration's initial policy course were figures from the nation's old-line anticommunist wing, a group that held fast to the belief that a sizable minority of the population remained under the sway of North Korea and that the communists continued to have dangerous influence in such areas as labor, the arts, and education. In some respects, Lee's administration brought South Korean policy toward the North back a quarter century, to the era of Chun Doo Hwan, when there was virtually no contact between the two Koreas and the rhetoric within the South was often harsh and ugly. It might be a new century, but the old battles were not over.

A SECOND NORTH-SOUTH SUMMIT, BUT NOT A THIRD

A high-water mark in inter-Korean relations had been reached under Lee Myung-bak's predecessor, Roh Moo-hyun, though not without difficulty and certainly not without fiery criticism from the conservatives. Through most of his administration, Roh had pressed the North for a summit, but it was not until the early summer of 2007, Roh's final full year in office, that the idea gained traction. In August, prodded by Seoul's warning that the opposition party would soon have its presidential candidate in place and after that happened moving to a summit would be much more difficult, the North had finally indicated it was ready to go ahead. This was much the same problem Washington had experienced in 2000, trying to get Kim Jong Il to agree to a high-level meeting earlier rather than later in a crucial election year in order to avoid problems set in motion by domestic political developments.

The summit was scheduled for late-August 2007, but heavy rains in the North caused a postponement until the autumn. Finally, on the morning of October 2, President Roh Moo-hyun walked across the military demarcation line at Panmunjom and drove the ninety-odd miles to Pyongyang, leading several busloads of officials, journalists, and businessmen. South Korean media scrutinized and commented on every detail of Kim Jong Il's reception of the ROK president, comparing it unfavorably with the meeting between the North Korean leader and Kim Dae Jung seven years earlier. Kim Jong Il appeared to the media less effusive, not as deferential, and, to some observers, even a little stiff. The photographs suggested his health was not good, and there was considerable speculation that rumors earlier in the year of heart problems might be true.

The summit visit ended on October 4 with the release of a joint statement. Statements emerging from summits are often largely verbiage. This one contained its share of airy phrases, but it also identified a large number of concrete steps that Seoul and Pyongyang agreed to take to improve relations. The list demonstrated, at least on paper, how far the two Koreas might go in cooperation. The steps included:

- convening a meeting between the two side's defense ministers by November 2007 to discuss building military trust, including a plan for "designating a joint fishing area to prevent accidental clashes in the West Sea, the turning of this area into a peace zone, and the issue of military guarantee measures for various cooperation projects"
- establishing a West Sea "special peace and cooperation zone comprised of the Haeju District (in North Korea) and its neighboring areas" and "pushing ahead with the establishment of a joint fishing area and peaceful waters, the construction of a special economic zone, the practical use of Haeju Port, the direct passage of civilian vessels to Haeju, and joint use of the estuary of the Han River"
- completing the first-phase construction of the Kaesong Industrial Complex as early as possible, launching the second-phase development, and starting the railway freight transport between Munsan (in the South) and Pongdong (in the North)
- reconstructing and repairing the railways between Kaesong and Sinuiju (on the Amnok River) and the motorway between Kaesong and Pyongyang for joint use
- constructing a zone for cooperative shipbuilding in Anbyon and Nampo (on North Korea's east and west coasts) and conducting cooperative undertakings in various fields, including agriculture, health care, and environmental protection
- conducting tours of Mount Paektu and opening a direct flight between Mount Paektu and Seoul
- having the "cheering squads" of the two sides travel to the 2008 Beijing Olympics on the train running on the Seoul-Sinuiju railroad
- holding the first meeting of premier talks to implement this declaration "sometime this November [2007], in Seoul"

This was an enormously ambitious agenda, and virtually none of it would survive beyond Lee Myung-bak's inauguration in February 2008.

Many commentators called the steps completely unrealistic given Roh's low ratings in the polls and the upcoming presidential elections. The US Embassy in Seoul had been worried that the outcome of the talks would undercut the six-party efforts on denuclearization and had sought reassurances beforehand that Roh would take a strong stance on the nuclear issue. It ended up making no difference whether he pressed the denuclearization issue or soft-pedaled it; the six-party process was about to run into problems that had nothing to do with Roh.

South Korean officials involved in the planning of the meeting say that, from their perspective, one of the main goals of the summit was to create a framework for easing tensions in the West Sea. (The importance of that issue comes through in the emphasis it received in the October 4 joint statement.) They shake their heads ruefully and say they knew the timing for the summit was not good, but that was not by South Korea's choice. If there is to be another summit, they say, it should come early in a president's term, to give whatever agreements emerge time to take root and become part of an established strategic landscape before a new administration comes to office.

The provisions on the West Sea in the October summit agreement may have been among the most important; they were certainly the most controversial, in public and within the administration itself. The two Koreas had spent considerable time in military talks in 2006 and 2007 discussing the Northern Limit Line, the de facto boundary separating the two sides in the West Sea. For the South Korean military, the NLL was a core issue for national security. Holding the islands and the waters around them was considered crucial to denying North Korean forces an advance position for attacking the ROK via the west coast near Seoul. For South Korean conservatives, the NLL was not just militarily but also psychologically important. To cede any territory at all to the North would, in their view, signal fatal weakness on the South's part, weakness that Pyongyang would exploit to the maximum. Whereas some in Roh's administration saw a potential for turning these dangerous waters into something less volatile, opponents saw the step as naive in the extreme and surrendering to North Korean extortion.

Once in office in late-February 2008, Lee Myung-bak made clear that his administration would almost entirely dismiss the Kim-Roh summit agreement. The argument often heard from his supporters was that the previous two presidencies—of Kim Dae Jung and Roh Moo-hyun—had resulted in a "lost decade" in terms of inter-Korean relations and that Seoul had given away too much while asking too little of the North Koreans. Lee was not opposed to dealing with the North, and his advisers as a whole were not blindly ideological. They had convinced themselves, however, that the long-term trends within North Korea were working in their favor and that the best way to encourage those trends was to turn off the aid and cash spigot and deal with Kim Jong Il from a position of strength. By the end of Lee's term, however, the general sentiment in South Korea was that this approach, though it had offered a correction to the Sunshine Policies of the earlier decade, had not in the end left the situation in better shape.

In July 2008, Lee was at the National Assembly, scheduled to give what his aides say was meant to be his most positive speech to date on inter-Korean relations, when terrible news came in. A South Korean tourist at the Hyundai-run Mount Kumgang resort in North Korea had been shot and killed by a North Korean soldier during a predawn stroll into an off-limits area. The circumstances were not clear, but the public response to the killing of the tourist—a middle-aged housewife and mother—was one of outrage. This public anger, whipped up further by inflammatory media coverage, caused a quick decision by the administration to close down the tours to Mount Kumgang even before all the facts could be determined. The North apologized immediately but blamed the South for the incident; for its part, Seoul said the North rejected its demands for an investigation.

In August, when there was still no resolution of the incident in sight, Pyongyang released an unusual "special statement" in the name of "a spokesman for the unit of the Korean People's Army stationed in the area of Mt. Kumgang." It noted that the North had already "expressed regrets" for the "unpleasant incident," but it pushed the blame for the incident onto the victim, whom it argued had not paid attention to the regulations in the area. The statement went on to declare that, because Seoul was making such an issue of the incident, the North would expel "unnecessary personnel from the tourist area," tighten control of passage of vehicles across the military demarcation line to enter Mount Kumgang, and "take strong military counteractions against even the slightest hostile actions in the tourist resort in the area of Mt. Kumgang and the area under the military control from now on."

Under other circumstances, Seoul might have found a way to accept the North's expression of regret, but the conservatives in the government were determined not to let the tours—which they considered to be a money pot for Pyongyang—reopen. Over the next few years, they came up with a variety of reasons that the enterprise had to remain closed. Eventually, the North argued that South Korea could not forbid the North to use its own territory to earn tourist dollars. Even after the chairwoman of Hyundai Group, Hyon Jong Un, met with Kim Jong Il on August 16, 2009, and received his assurances for security for the tours, Seoul would not relent. Among the North Korean officials at the meeting with Hyon was Kim Yang-gon, who a week later would be in Seoul carrying the message from Kim Jong Il.

After Lee Myung-bak heard the North Korean supreme leader's proposal to meet, and over the grumbling of some of his advisers, he instructed Labor Minister Im Tae-hee, formerly his chief of staff, to arrange for secret talks with Kim Yang-gon. Seoul did not convey its answer to the North right away, however, and after waiting a few weeks, Pyongyang inquired why there was no word. Finally, Lee sent a response, telling Kim Jong Il that he basically agreed with the idea of improving relations. At this point, it was barely two months after the UN Security Council resolution calling for increased international sanctions on the North. To have Seoul peel away from the solid phalanx supposedly confronting Pyongyang would not be helpful to Washington's strategy. Aware of the talks but largely in the dark about the details, the White House watched somewhat nervously, but held out hope that the initiative would, in the end, go nowhere. It turned out to be a good bet.

SECRET TALKS, PUBLIC CLASHES

Throughout 2008 and into 2009, as inter-Korean relations deteriorated, the threats from the North became more strident. A particular area of concern was the West Sea, where several smaller naval clashes between the two sides had already taken place. Increasingly, it looked possible that a major incident could occur at any time. Within a year, there would be such serious developments, but with Kim Jong Il's push in the summer of 2009 for improved ties with the United States and South Korea, the path detoured first to Singapore, where representatives of the two Koreas met in October 2009 to discuss the possibility of a third inter-Korean summit.*

From sources who were very well placed to observe the events directly, there are significantly different versions of what happened in the talks. In later accounts, the South Korean delegate, Im Tae-hee, has publicly claimed that over their two days of discussions, he and his interlocutor, Kim Yang-gon, came extremely close to agreeing on the basic framework for a summit, including a venue in the North, taking into account Kim Jong Il's health. A contrary account holds that Im exceeded

---

* The Singapore meeting almost never happened. In early September, the North Koreans, without warning to the South, released a large amount of water from one of their dams near the demilitarized zone. Six campers downstream in South Korea were swept away in the ensuing flood. The ROK government quickly sent a message to Pyongyang calling for an explanation. The North, literally within hours (and probably under Kim Jong Il's direct, urgent orders), replied that it had been forced to release the water because levels behind the dam had risen unexpectedly and that it would give advance notice of future discharges. The reaction by the South Korea public to the episode was ugly enough that a different or laggard response from Pyongyang would probably have made it impossible for the Blue House to proceed with Kim's August initiative for talks.

his instructions from President Lee and that the two sides were not really close when the Singapore meeting ended.

Im says the North was amenable to talking about the return of abducted South Koreans and ROK prisoners of war held in the North since 1953; in return, the North was looking for compensation—primarily food. According to Im, this sort of exchange was in line with the West German policy of "Frei Kauf," in which the Bonn government had supplied money to the communist government in Berlin in return for the ability of East Germans to move west. Even South Korean unification minister Hyun In-taek, hardly a pushover when it came to dealing with North Korea, acknowledged that the government was considering a similar but noncash approach. According to an account of the meeting that appeared in public a few months before the 2012 presidential elections (and was probably an inspired leak meant as ammunition against the progressive candidate, Moon Jae-in), the deal foundered because the North Koreans asked for too much compensation. Im Tae-hee firmly denies this.

Not long after the Singapore meeting, the secret talks continued in Beijing, but these did not close the deal, either. By then, Lee Myung-bak had decided he did not really want a summit, at least not yet. He especially did not want to be seen as following in the footsteps of Roh Moo-hyun or Kim Dae Jung. By contrast, whether through self-delusion or misreading signals, the North Koreans apparently still thought they were close to a deal. Word was already swirling around the South Korean press about the "possibility of a summit," and after first denying everything the Blue House admitted there had been contacts, but nothing else.

In November lower-level representatives of the two sides met in the border town of Kaesong. The South Koreans indicated there was a considerable gap and much left to settle before there could be a summit. Not least, the South Koreans now said they wanted the summit to be held in the South, not in Pyongyang. The North Koreans were outraged at what they saw as a reversal in Seoul's approach to the idea of a summit. A few days later, during a break in the talks, South Korean naval vessels attacked a North Korean patrol boat that had crossed the Northern Limit Line in the West Sea. The South Korean guns poured fire into the North Korean ship, which retreated badly damaged, likely with serious casualties. The South Korean warships were virtually unscathed. It was the sort of victory—near total and annihilating—the South Korean navy loved, but ROK officials were cautious about what had happened. The normal public accusations about North Korean "aggressive behavior" were tempered by speculation that the northern ship had crossed the line by mistake. For its part, Pyongyang appeared particularly incensed by the incident, accusing the South Korean ships of firing "thousands of bullets" aimed at not simply warning the smaller North Korean patrol ship but destroying it.

Neither event by itself, the clash in the West Sea or the breakdown in the talks, might have been enough to tip the scales in Pyongyang, but the two together appear to have combined to convince Kim Jong Il that it was time to teach the Blue House a lesson.

The "lesson" was delivered on the night of March 26, 2010, when the *Cheonan,* a South Korean naval corvette on routine patrol, was blown in half and sank within minutes, with the loss of forty-six sailors. The aftermath was badly handled by the South Korean military, logs were altered to show defense officials were somewhere other than they actually were, and details of the event in reports were changed or inaccurate. The mood of the South Korean public was shock and sadness mixed with considerable skepticism about the government's handling of the affair. The US Embassy suggested that the ROK government organize an international group to review the evidence. After investigation, the five-country team released a report concluding that strong circumstantial evidence, including a torpedo motor recovered from the waters around the explosion, indicated that the sinking had been caused by the shock wave and so-called bubble effect resulting from a North Korean torpedo that had exploded directly beneath the *Cheonan's* hull. Even the presentation of these findings was bobbled, however, when the wrong picture of a North Korean torpedo was displayed at the public briefing.

After the findings were released, a Russian naval delegation went to Seoul to review the records, but did not publicize its own conclusions. The Chinese, who did not take part in the review, generally took the position that there was not enough evidence to say what had happened, though some in Beijing thought it more than likely that the North had been responsible. Critics of the findings argued that for the North to explode a torpedo so expertly under the South Korean vessel would take inordinate skill or luck beyond measure. Not surprisingly, the North Koreans denied any part in the incident, though their denials were not especially convincing. Their protestations were not helped when, shortly afterward, Kim Jong Il insouciantly reviewed a unit of the KPA Reconnaissance Bureau, which in all likelihood was the organizational element that would have carried out the sort of operation that sank the *Cheonan.*

Throughout the remainder of the Lee administration, there was a series of secret North-South talks, but never anything with enough commitment or vision from either side to begin and sustain a serious process of engagement. On Seoul's part, there was often a feeling that the North was near the end of its rope, that Kim Jong Il was in decline, and that the resulting political succession would be more than the North Korean system could handle. It was, in essence, a waiting game, keeping the North occupied with one hand, while squeezing it with the other. Once again, waiting for the end of North Korea proved not to be a good strategy. Once again, as secret North-South talks went on, Washington did not know what its ROK ally was doing, what the contacts between the North and South meant, or where they were leading. When they asked for clarification, the Americans received routine assurances that they would be kept fully informed when and if any developments occurred.

THE RISE OF CHINESE INFLUENCE

When Chinese premier Wen Jiabao's airplane landed under the high blue autumn sky at Pyongyang's airport on October 4, 2009, there was an unusually important guest on hand to meet him. Workers Party General Secretary, Chairman of the National Defense Commission, and Supreme Commander of the Korean People's Army Kim Jong Il did not normally come out to the airport to meet people below his station.* He did for Wen, and as the premier's special Air China 747 taxied to a stop in front of the terminal, Kim was at the bottom of the stairs, waiting to give the Chinese guest a welcoming hug.

On August 17, about two months before he landed in North Korea, Premier Wen had chaired a meeting of the PRC State Council Leading Group for Revitalizing the Northeast Region and Other Old Industrial Bases. The meeting passed an "implementing strategy" for development of the country's rust belt—the northeastern region that had formerly contained many of the nation's important heavy industry factories but was now, in the country's improved economic circumstances, lagging far behind. Among the many recommendations was to "raise the level of opening up the Northeast Region to the outside world, organize the proper implementation of the 'Liaoning Coastal Economic Belt Development Program,' and firmly seize the formulation of the Tumen River Regional Development and Opening Up Program."

For provincial and local officials in China, the high-level attention signaled by this State Council group with the overly long name meant they might finally find support (and, equally important, funds) for plans they had been dreaming about for many years to bring economic development to their region. A key part of the plans for Jilin Province was access to the North Korean port of Rajin. Provincial officials had long complained that the Chinese port of Dalian in neighboring Liaoning Province was always backed up and that Jilin could not get goods to market or raw materials delivered in a timely fashion through that route. Rajin, however, was another story. It was nearby (only about twenty-five miles as the crow flies from the nearest bridge across the Tumen River), it faced the Sea of Japan

---

* The exception to this iron rule had been the arrival of ROK president Kim Dae Jung in 2002, but that was an extraordinary event, and no one could doubt it.

and the Pacific, and—to put it mildly—it was underutilized. That the port was in North Korea presented challenges, and opportunities, of its own.

Before Wen finished his visit to North Korea, he and his delegation had signed a number of agreements aimed at facilitating economic activity between China and North Korea. Among the deals was one to build a new bridge across the Yalu River downstream from the present smaller bridge between Dandong on the Chinese side of the river and Sinuiju on the North Korean side. The older bridge had one rail line and a single lane for automobile traffic. It served well enough for the relatively small volumes of trade the region had grown accustomed to, but the flow was expanding and plans were for it to grow even more. If there were to be significant increases in the amount of goods and numbers of people going between the two countries, the existing bridge would be a choke point. The new bridge would be larger, stronger, and positioned to fit into a still-notional transportation network designed with an eye to even more ambitious plans—eventually to move people and cargo all the way from South Korea into China, and possibly beyond.

For nearly a decade, PRC-DPRK relations had been caught in the backlash of North Korean anger at China's great betrayal—the recognition of the ROK in August 1992. In the latter half of the 1990s, the North was focused on improving relations with the United States, at China's expense if possible. In a particularly rough incident, in 1997, for example, North Korea reached a deal with Taiwan to store the country's nuclear waste. Pyongyang had partially wanted the fee for the service—well over $100 million—but also, during a low point in North Korea–PRC relations, it no doubt wanted to twist the tiger's tail. For reasons of its own, Washington worked on Taipei to stop the deal from going forward, but that was nothing compared to the pressure Beijing put on Pyongyang not to consummate such a major tie-up with Taiwan. Eventually, Taipei "discovered" a problem with the necessary permits, and the deal fell apart.

Kim Jong Il's visit to China in May 2000 had signaled that Sino–North Korean relations were at least back to normal. After that the frequency and level of visits began building again, as did Chinese business activity. By 2009 the two sides had already signed new agreements to facilitate increasing numbers of Chinese tourists arriving by air, rail, and even automobile, and North Korean delegations—educational, economic, and artistic—regularly moved back and forth across the border. On the Chinese side of the rivers separating the two countries, local officials drew up plans for strengthening transportation links, reinforcing existing bridges, or contemplating new ones. Chinese companies made major investments in large North Korean mines, such as the Musan iron-ore mine and the Hyesan Youth copper mine, both directly across the Tumen River. Already in June 2008, satellite pictures showed scores of Chinese trucks crossing into the North to pick up loads of iron ore from the Musan mine.

Over the several years after Wen's visit, Chinese economic penetration of North Korea developed to an unusual degree, beyond anything the two sides had ever experienced. In October 2010, a delegation consisting of the party heads of every North Korean province went to Beijing, almost certainly an effort by Kim Jong Il to impress on provincial-level officials that they had to be ready for major interaction with Chinese businesses moving into their areas. In July 2011, groundbreaking ceremonies were held for new joint economic zones with the Chinese on several North Korean islands in the Yalu River, and the North signed new agreements with the Chinese for developing Rajin.

To this extent, Lee Myung-bak's observations were exactly right: the North was not static, and the outside world was becoming a regular part of the existence of more and more North Koreans. Unwittingly, Lee himself may have encouraged this when he reversed field on inter-Korean cooperation. During the Roh Moo-hyun years, Seoul had encouraged South Korean firms to explore what sort of joint activity might be possible with the North. South Korean companies had looked at mining ventures as well as ways to use cheap, easily trained North Korean labor. The Kaesong Industrial Zone (KIZ), which opened in 2004, was to be only the first of several such areas Seoul hoped to develop in the North.

After the South Koreans pulled back, Chinese saw an opportunity to move aggressively into the North, not to make money so much as to position themselves for a time when they could. North Korea was a frontier, and the rule of law—business or otherwise—was not what dictated winners or losers. Who was there when the situation finally shifted to a more business-friendly environment would, it was hoped, reap the rewards. The situation that existed in North Korea—teetering on the edge or well short of legal guarantees—was not completely unfamiliar to Chinese businessmen, who nevertheless complained of sharp practices on the part of their Korean business partners. The North Koreans, in turn, considered the Chinese totally unscrupulous. North Korean consumers, and there were a growing number of them, complained of Chinese companies unloading shoddy, and in some cases dangerous, goods into the North Korean market. Westerners who brought presents for their North Korean contacts were told not to bring Chinese manufactured items but rather to carry ones from West Europe.

After the long period of frostiness in relations through most of the 1990s, from 2000 to 2011 Kim Jong Il made seven publicized visits to China.* There are a number of good explanations for Kim Jong Il's

---

* May 29–31, 2000; June 15–20, 2001; April 19–21, 2004; June 10–18, 2006; May 3–7, 2010; August 26–30, 2010; and May 20–26, 2011. Top-level Chinese leaders visited North Korea less frequently—Jiang Zemin, September 3–5, 2001; Hu Jintao, October 28–30, 2005, but there is a long list of exchanges just below the top level, especially from 2009 to 2011.

willingness—evident beginning in 2009 with Wen Jiabao's trip—to accept what he had so long worked to avoid, falling under China's shadow. One explanation is that he had no other potential partner to turn to, though at the time he entertained Wen Jiabao, Kim was also toying with the notion of improving relations with Seoul. A second explanation is that after the Clinton visit in August 2009, Kim realized that the goal of a breakthrough with the United States was unattainable. Finally, and maybe the best explanation, is that as part of the preparations for succession, Kim felt that, as a priority matter, he needed to secure ties with China on both the strategic and the economic fronts.

Kim may also have hoped to capitalize on a downturn in Beijing's political ties with South Korea. Although China had spectacular success engaging South Korea economically (China has been South Korea's largest trading partner since 2003), it stumbled badly on the political front in 2004 and again in 2006. South Koreans reacted negatively to Chinese academics' claims that the ancient Korean state of Koguryo (37 BC until AD mid-seventh century) was a Chinese vassal and not, as the Koreans see it, a brave battling kingdom that extended its domain into what is now Northeast China and for years held off invading Chinese armies. Centuries later, low-level irritation, such as regular scenes of Chinese fishermen caught in South Korean waters violently resisting arrest by the ROK coast guard, have kept popular prejudices against China simmering. There is lingering suspicion, as well, among some South Koreans that in an emergency situation (such as the collapse of North Korea), the Chinese army would move to a preestablished line in North Korea and not go home, either to ensure a rump North Korean state or to provide a buffer between the Sino-Korean border and ROK or US troops that might move north.

RARE BACKLASH

Only a month after Wen's visit, Kim Jong Il took a major and, as it turned out, nearly disastrous step: he ordered the revaluation of the North Korean currency. This was not the first time Pyongyang had undertaken revaluation, but the four previous episodes that had occurred since the country's founding had not caused much trouble. This time was different—and it might have been even worse if the regime had not relatively quickly recognized its mistake and pulled back by early 2010 in the face of what many foreign press reports portrayed as serious discontent and even individual protests by North Korean citizens. For Kim, the problem may have appeared especially acute because of loud complaints from a key segment of the population—the emerging consumer class. This sort of widespread, manifestly negative response was unnerving to the regime and may have driven home to Kim and others in the leadership that significant numbers of the people, having survived the famine years of the late 1990s, considered the social contract between the general population and regime broken. When Pyongyang moved to confiscate their savings, which is what the revaluation amounted to, it crossed a line that had not even existed in earlier years.

It is still not known why the regime attempted the revaluation in the first place. One well-accepted theory is that Kim Jong Il simply wanted to crush the markets. The motivations may have been more complicated. Kim could have wanted to make a second try at moving to new economic policies, as he had done in 2002, but was again stymied by a lack of funds. Reforms, even simple ones, would take money, and there was a lot of money sloshing around in the markets, among merchants and budding entrepreneurs. The currency revaluation would transfer the money to the treasury and also be a useful reminder to the emerging middle class that, whatever benefits the new policies might bring, in the end it was the regime that held the reins.

The currency revaluation is usually viewed in isolation, but it may have been part of a larger plan to smooth the way for Kim Jong Un's succession, which at that point was moving into a new phase. By introducing new elements into the economy, Kim Jong Il may have hoped to provide better economic conditions later in 2010, when he planned to hold a major party conclave at which Kim Jong Un would step into public view. Seen in that context, the failure was not only a bad surprise; it risked completely upending the succession planning.

A scapegoat was necessary, and one appeared in the guise of Pak Nam-ki, a longtime party functionary then serving as the chief of the party's finance department. Pak had regularly accompanied Kim Jong Il in 2009 on the leader's public inspection visits, but disappeared after appearing with Kim one more time, in early January 2010, as public opposition to the revaluation was growing. He was reportedly executed in March, possibly on the same day that Kim Jong Il, along with a few party veterans who no doubt had known Pak well, traveled to a cooperative farm in North Hwanghae Province. Looking at their faces in the photographs from that visit, one wonders what they were thinking.

In mid-December 2009, just as the effects of the currency reevaluation were taking hold, Kim Jong Il made a rare visit to Rason, on the country's northeast coast.* Two weeks later, Pyongyang declared Rason a "special city," conferring upon it an administrative status that would give it more freedom to host foreign business activity. Port facilities were improved, the

---

*"Rason" is the administrative area that was created by combining Rajin city and nearby Sonbong county.

Chinese paid to improve the road from the crossing point over the Tumen River all the way to the port, and the Russians moved ahead to upgrade the rail line from their own crossing point at Khasan down the east coast to Rajin port. At the same time, Kim and other officials made numerous visits to inspect developments elsewhere on the east coast: tourist facilities, factories, mines, and especially Tanchon, a port some 140 miles south of Rason and designed to handle the output of the North's rich but still underdeveloped magnesite mines.

YEONPYEONG ISLAND

Months after the *Cheonan* sinking, the West Sea witnessed one more violent clash. On the afternoon of November 23, 2010, North Korean artillery on the mainland and a small island off the coast shelled one of the five South Korean–held islands, Yeonpyeong-do. Several days before, North Korean artillery units in the vicinity had moved to new positions. That morning the North passed a message to the South Korean military, warning of a "resolute physical counterstrike" if the South did not cancel an artillery exercise on Yeonpyeong-do planned for later in the day.* The warning did not seem serious to the South Koreans, so the exercise went ahead on schedule. Around 2:45 P.M., not long after it ended, North Korean shells began to fall on and around the island—eventually around 170 over the next hour. Rattled and caught by surprise, South Korean Marines asked for guidance up the chain of command, then returned fire as best they could given failures in their equipment. Two Marines and two civilians who had been working on one of the island's military posts at the time were killed. Several more Marines and a few civilians were listed as wounded. The North Korean shells caused several fires, and scenes of the smoke rising from the island were quickly available on the cell phones of the South Korean population on the mainland.

The South Koreans, stung by their losses and seeming inability to respond quickly and forcefully to an attack on their soil, announced they would hold another exercise in December. The North Koreans issued a warning that such a move would result in its army carrying out "a second and third unpredictable self-defensive blow." Washington, worried that another clash would escalate out of control, attempted to persuade the South not to proceed. Amid thunderous warnings from the North, US

---

* The warning was the latest in an escalating series from the North since early in the year about the South "firing shells into the territorial waters of the DPRK side." In parallel, the North also began to conduct its own artillery exercises that came closer and closer to challenging NLL and asserting DPRK claims. Whether these steps were originally designed to lead to an eventual attack is not known.

officials held tense meetings in Washington to decide what to do, and the JCS chairman, Admiral Mike Mullen, was sent to Seoul to lay out the case for restraint before President Lee. South Korea went ahead with a slightly altered exercise. The North Koreans did nothing, beyond noting that "the revolutionary armed forces of the DPRK did not feel any need to retaliate against every despicable military provocation," dismissing the South's move as "child's play" and claiming that for fear of additional retaliation, the South had changed the direction in which its artillery had fired.

The attack on Yeonpyeong-do is usually lumped together with the sinking of the corvette *Cheonan* earlier in the year, but the two events were fundamentally different. Sinking the *Cheonan* was almost certainly a retaliatory move by North Korea for an earlier naval defeat in the West Sea. Yeonpyeong-do was not. The *Cheonan was* attacked by stealth, a particularly deadly part of a long game of black operations by the two sides. The Yeonpyeong-do shelling was openly prepared and executed by the North Korean People's Army Fourth Corps and set off an artillery duel, the first such large-scale exchange of fire between the two armies in decades. What we do not know is why, at a time when there was every indication that Kim Jong Il wanted a stable environment externally to help secure the succession, he would have approved such a blatant large-scale attack so much out of character with past North Korean practice.

KIM JONG IL'S DEATH AND BEYOND

Kim Jong Il did not pay taxes, but he could not avoid the second of the inevitable fates. When he died in December 2011, his plans for the political succession of his son Kim Jong Un were under way but incomplete. In August 2010, Kim had visited China, perhaps to inform the Chinese of his intention to proceed in September with a Workers Party conference (only the third such meeting since the party's founding in 1945) at which he would publicly debut his son. Some sources contend that he brought Kim Jong Un on the trip, especially to show him those parts of northeast China where his grandfather Kim Il Sung had conducted anti-Japanese guerrilla operations.

After a slight unexplained delay, the party conference was held in September, and as part of the succession scenario, in addition to Kim Jong Un's emergence, a number of personnel changes were announced, bringing in or elevating figures to support the succession. The very fact the conference was held reinforced earlier signs that Kim Jong Il was moving to put the party back in place as the regime's leading political force, after years of emphasis on "military first." Over the next year, Kim Jong Un appeared regularly with his father on inspection visits, with the media using photographs to make clear what was not expressly stated in public, that he was the designated number two and preparing to step into the post of top leader. In May 2011, as a test, it appears Kim Jong Un was left in charge of the country when his father traveled to China. When the senior Kim's train returned, the son greeted it at the station, and North Korean television showed high-level cadre bowing low to the younger man as they emerged from the train.

The elder Kim would not survive to see these rituals reach their logical conclusion. According to an official North Korean announcement on December 19, 2011, Kim died of a heart attack—brought on by "physical and mental exhaustion"—on the morning of the seventeenth while on his train traveling to yet another on-site inspection. The delay in announcing the death was not unusual for the North—the announcement of Kim Il Sung's death in July 1994 had been similarly held up for nearly two days. One of Kim Jong Il's last public appearances, reported two days before his death, was to the Hana Electronic Joint Venture Company—a joint venture with a European group—only a few hundred yards from the Tongil Market, one of the markets that his July 2002 economic measures had helped establish.

From time to time, North Korean television has carried a program for children called *World's Classic Fairy Tales*. In the past, the selections had included "The Snow Queen," "The Little Match Girl," and even "Fine Dog Lassie." In October 2012, the choice was "The Emperor's New Clothes." For many foreign observers—and perhaps for a few North Koreans in positions of authority as well—there were questions when Kim Jong Un, the relatively untested successor, was suddenly thrown into the role of Supreme Leader in December 2011. Was he really ready to assume power? Like the emperor in the children's tale, would he walk essentially naked, clothed in imaginary trappings of power until someone in the leadership, perhaps a disgruntled army general brandishing a revolver, pointed out that a twenty-eight-year-old had no business ruling a nuclear-armed country of 24 million people? On December 30, the day after the memorial service for Kim Jong Il, North Korean media announced that Kim Jong Un had "assumed the supreme commandership of the KPA at the bequest of leader Kim Jong Il on October 8, 2011." That put the new leader in control of the army explicitly at the direction of the former Supreme Leader—a bequest no one would dare (or so it was hoped) contradict.

It did not take long for Kim Jong Un to make clear that, unlike his father who had seemed emotionally paralyzed after Kim Il Song's death in 1994, he was going to move quickly to assert himself. North Korean media over and over conveyed the message to the population that as bad as it was to lose their Great Leader, Kim Jong Il, no one should stop work, but rather turn their "grief" into increased production. After the funeral was over, the younger Kim immediately began appearing in public, showing off his new, youthful, hands-on style of leadership. On the first day of the new year, he appeared at one of the army's premier tank units. North

Korean television showed Kim meticulously inspecting the base, exactly as his father had in the past, and then appearing with the soldiers who deliriously chanted his name.

Besides attending to the business of consolidating power internally, the new leader had a pressing foreign-policy matter. One of the main pillars for the succession, putting relations with the United States back on track, was still in process when Kim Jong Il died. US and North Korean negotiators were in Beijing on the day of his death, waiting to put final touches on the first agreement Washington and Pyongyang had reached since the Obama administration took office in 2009.

Pyongyang had laid the groundwork for the negotiations in March 2011, when, following discussions with Russian deputy foreign minister Aleksei Borodavkin, the North announced it was "not opposed to" discussion of "a moratorium on nuclear test and ballistic missile launches, access of IAEA experts to uranium enrichment facilities in the Yongbyon area, and discussion of the issue of uranium enrichment." In July US-DPRK talks began, focusing on these points. The talks continued in October and were prepared to wrap up in Beijing in December after nailing down details, under the overall deal, of US provision of 240,000 tons of food assistance. Kim's death put off the final agreement until February 29, 2012, when it was announced in parallel but not completely identical press releases from the two capitals. This was not a case of postmeeting press statements with different nuances, but actually different versions of what had been agreed on—and the differences were not minor.

For the Americans, the most important result of the talks was the North Korean agreement to "implement a moratorium on long-range missile launches, nuclear tests and nuclear activities at Yongbyon, including uranium enrichment activities. The DPRK has also agreed to the return of IAEA inspectors to verify and monitor the moratorium on uranium enrichment activities at Yongbyon and confirm the disablement of the 5-MW reactor and associated facilities."

The North Korean version of this key section was different in important respects, adding the proviso that the moratorium would last "while productive [US-DPRK] dialogue continues" and limiting the description of the IAEA's activities to monitoring "the moratorium on uranium enrichment." In addition, the North Korean version of the overall results was much fuller than Washington's. Pyongyang presented the outcome in the form of a joint agreement, noting at a few points that "both" sides had agreed to particular provisions: for example, "Both the DPRK and the U.S. agreed to make a number of simultaneous moves aimed at building confidence as part of the efforts to improve the relations between the DPRK and the U.S." The American version avoided any sense that there had been common agreement and went out of its way to downplay the results, pointing out that they were "limited" and underlining that the "United States still has profound concerns regarding North Korean behavior across a wide range of areas."

If the so-called Leap Day Agreement had lasted, these differences might have become serious points of contention. As it happened, the deal turned out to be not even a first "limited" step; it fell apart quickly and acrimoniously. In early March, a high-level DPRK Foreign Ministry official was in New York at an academic conference also attended by US and ROK officials. The North Korean told participants that the DPRK's new leader wanted a new, peaceful relationship with the United States. That olive branch was soon swept away when on March 16, barely two weeks after the talks in Beijing had concluded, Pyongyang announced that in April it planned to launch into polar orbit a "working satellite" from its newly completed launch center on the country's west coast.[*]

For all the differences in the two sides' announcements of the results of the Leap Day Agreement, the sticking point turned out to be North Korea's claims to a space program, for which it would need ballistic missiles as launch vehicles—forbidden to the North by a series of UN Security Council resolutions. In late March, a DPRK diplomat told Americans at a conference in Europe that at the talks leading up to the Leap Day Agreement, the North several times had rejected US formulations on the missile issue on the grounds that these precluded the North's "right" to a space program. The chief US negotiator, Ambassador Glyn Davies (who had replaced Stephen Bosworth at the end of 2011), has said that at the final session of the talks, in February 2012, he impressed on the North Koreans that a space launch would completely scuttle the deal and that they indicated they understood.

Mindful of previous complaints, the North's announcement about the planned launch noted that "a safe flight orbit has been chosen so that carrier rocket debris to be generated during the flight would not have any impact on neighboring countries." In this case, given the flight path from the new launch center, it was Filipinos rather than Japanese who might be concerned.

In a completely unprecedented development—seemingly in line with Kim Jong Un's new leadership style—a few days before the launch Pyongyang invited the foreign press into the country to visit the new launch facility as well as the launch control center near Pyongyang. The rocket blasted off in the early morning on April 13, but veered off course and exploded about a minute into flight. Several hours later, in another unprecedented move of openness, DPRK television interrupted normal programming to announce the satellite had "failed to enter its preset orbit."[**]

---

[*] A good question is if Kim Jong Il had lived and the deal had been closed according to schedule in December, would the extra couple of months to get it under way have made a difference when the North announced its plans for the space launch? Or, indeed, would Kim Jong Il have postponed the launch?

[**] The admission of failure to the domestic audience was so unusual that it was probably cleared, if not actually instituted, by Kim Jong Un himself.

Washington declared the Leap Day deal no longer valid. Administration officials portrayed the deal as a "test" of North Korea, a test that, in their eyes, North Korea had failed. Whether something could have been salvaged from the deal—assuming the political flak in Washington from going back to the table was survivable—is impossible to know. Getting IAEA inspectors to Yongbyon and into the enrichment facility might have yielded valuable insights, but IAEA director general Yukiya Amano was not prepared to take the initiative.

Speculation that the launch failure was a serious embarrassment to Kim Jong Un, possibly undermining his position, proved baseless. Two days before the launch attempt, Kim had assumed the title of "first secretary" of the Workers Party, and his formal grasp of the levers of power was now complete.

THE NEW LOOK

A few days after the launch, Kim gave his maiden address in public, on the centennial of his grandfather's birth. In tone and substance, it was not the speech of a young ruler shaken by recent failure. Kim laid out (as he had to party cadres a few days earlier) what seemed to be a new approach on several levels. Though paying homage to his father's rule, he strongly implied that his was the start of a new era, that North Koreans could look to the future with confidence, "without tightening their belts any longer and fully enjoy wealth and prosperity under socialism." He left the door open to dealing with Seoul, and, by implication, with Washington as well.

For the rest of 2012, Kim Jong Un set about establishing an image for himself vastly different from his father's. Where Kim Jong Il had seemed aloof, Kim Jong Un was publicly warm. He hugged babies, sat on the floor with new apartment dwellers, and brought his wife along with him into the public eye. He posed patiently as women soldiers, one by one, stood beside him for their pictures to be taken.

The regime encouraged stories in the international media of major economic reform efforts, especially in the agricultural area, but then pulled back. The theme of "belt tightening" became a focus of disagreement, much as Kim Jong Il's new economic measures in 2002 had been debated in the media. Yet it seems unlikely that such disagreement—then or now—would emerge if change were not in the wind. How much change, how far it might be developed, and how long it could be sustained remained an open question at the end of Kim Jong Un's first year in power.

AFTERWORD

WHEN DON OBERDORFER ENDED the second edition of this book, in December 2000, there was reason to be optimistic about the future of the Korean peninsula. Then, diplomatic and security trends between the two Koreas and between each of them and the larger powers finally appeared to be moving in a positive direction. That is not the case today. From almost every angle, the past dozen years has been unrelievedly negative. As of this writing, not quite halfway through 2013, the way ahead for Korea appears not simply hazy but also unusually perilous.

Two landmark developments seem to offer an indication of what the future has in store for the two Koreas. On December 12, 2012, after a calculated (and highly successful) effort to make the outside world believe it had postponed a planned rocket launch due to technical difficulties, North Korea put a satellite into orbit from its west coast launch center. A week later, in South Korea, sixty-year-old Park Geun-hye, the daughter of former dictator Park Chung Hee, was elected president of the Republic of Korea. Though unrelated on the surface, each of these events has set in motion a train of policies and actions that are already shaping Korea's future course.

THE GREAT LEADERSHIP DIVIDE

It was a remarkable sign of the changes in South Korea: in what was once (and to some extent still is) an intensely conservative, male-dominated society, a woman was elected president. And it was an impressive victory. Park Geun-hye won with a majority rather than just a plurality of the vote, the first of Korea's democratically elected presidents to do so. Having won the election, however, Park's celebration could be only short-lived. She was propelled into a welter of domestic social, political, and economic problems every bit as serious as those her father confronted more than fifty years before. Yet Park cannot stay in office nearly as long as her father did to deal with the challenges, nor does she have anything like the powers he had.

Park Geun-hye has inherited a South Korea many times more prosperous than it was in 1961, its position vis-à-vis the North is much stronger, and its role as an important international actor (a role that seemed light-years away at the time of Park Chung Hee's 1961 coup) is firmly established. Yet the foundations of almost everything South

Koreans have believed about themselves for the past several decades look to be in jeopardy. Self-congratulations about the "miracle" of the country's economic growth and its remarkably peaceful transition a generation ago from dictatorship to democracy have grown stale.

There is a constant urge by politicians and commentators, inside and outside the ROK alike, to compare South Korea with the North, a comparison that for the past thirty years has been less and less revealing of anything other than the fact that the South always comes out ahead. It is hardly news that there is a gap between the two parts of Korea, and everyone (including the leadership in Pyongyang) knows that the gap is growing. Focusing on the gap, however, has become a distraction, a veil covering the reality that all is not well in South Korea. To take only one tragic example, South Korea's suicide rate is far above that of all other OECD countries. There are many explanations for such a grim statistic, but in a deeper sense, the figure speaks for itself.

Park Geun-hye will hold office until early 2018, her five-year term prescribed under the ROK Constitution. In other words, on taking office she had only sixty months to address urgent and growing problems of enormous long-term consequence, ranging from South Korea's low birthrate and the rapid decline of the traditional family to a lack of a strong safety net for the aging population and growing disparities in wealth. None of these problems is unique to South Korea, but they have hit the South all at once and picked up speed so quickly that there is hardly any time to deal with them before their impact will be felt with full fury.

As if this basket of problems were not enough, there is the ever-present shadow of the country's division hanging over the scene. At this juncture, the core question of how to deal with the other half of the Korean nation, the 24 million people north of the demilitarized zone, appears intractable. South Koreans have gone through a succession of phases in thinking about the North—hatred, contempt, pity, frustration, and now a sort of ennui— but it is more clear than ever that nothing they try will work without a sustained national policy combining vision, commitment, persistence, and, of course, money—a lot of it. Whether the South Korean body politic and its leaders can devise and sustain such a course remains to be seen.

In contrast to Park Geun-hye's relatively small window of opportunity, Kim Jong Un could sit in power for the next three or even four decades. Even if his life span is more like his father's (sixty-nine years) than his grandfather's (eighty-two years), he will still be making policy and influencing events in 2050. At this point, of course, it is early in Kim's rule and not wise to try to predict his career arc from the outside. For now, however, well into his second year as the North's supreme leader, he appears to be securely in power. So far, he has shown himself capable of the same sort of agility, in political and diplomatic terms, that has marked North Korea's performance ever since the end of the Korean War. And if he dies at a ripe old age, as his forebears did, the younger Kim will watch a succession of four, five, maybe six South Korean presidents come and go.

Like Park Geun-hye, Kim has inherited a country stronger than it was even twenty years ago, when his father assumed power. Despite years of predictions from outside analysts that pressure for change is growing within North Korean society, and even taking fully into account all of the economic and political problems Pyongyang faces, North Korea continues to demonstrate an ability to survive as a coherent, functioning entity. However lamentable the regime's policies and treatment of its own people, North Korea is not a "failed state." The introduction of technology may ultimately play a critical role in undermining the regime's grip on power. But for now, the North has been able to absorb and adapt to fairly widespread use in the population of computers and cell phones, digital cameras and electronic libraries. The regime is using the image of technological prowess as a way to demonstrate that, despite its obvious challenges, the country is modern, forward looking, and revitalized. It remains to be seen whether the population's widespread access to the Internet, still severely limited in the North, will turn out to be the straw that breaks the camel's back.

NEW HEIGHTS

After a string of failures going back to 1998, North Korea's successful launch of a satellite into orbit in December 2012 demonstrated that Pyongyang is technologically able—and has the industrial wherewithal—to achieve some of its most ambitious goals, contrary to what many observers had thought. At the same time, the launch was a source of considerable pride within North Korea and very likely gave a boost to its young leader's self-confidence.

Yet the missile launch also set in motion a new crisis between Pyongyang and Washington. On January 22, 2013, the UN Security Council passed yet another resolution (2087) condemning the launch. Not long after, on February 12, the North responded with its third nuclear test, the largest and apparently most successful to date in the test program that began in October 2006. The subsequent action-reaction cycle was unusually fraught. It was quite different from what has often—and erroneously—been described by Washington as "the cycle" of North Korean provocation and negotiations. This time, events snowballed into something that appeared more dangerous.

A day after the UN's public condemnation of the launch, Pyongyang released a Foreign Ministry statement proclaiming, in addition to the obvious point that the North would continue to launch satellites, that the DPRK government had drawn the "final conclusion that the denuclearization of the Korean Peninsula is impossible unless the denuclearization of the world is realized as it has become clear now that the U.S. policy hostile to the DPRK remains unchanged." In other words, the North Korean nuclear issue was no longer to be considered in isolation but rather as part of efforts by the nuclear weapons states to reduce and abolish nuclear weapons worldwide. If there was any doubt as to their meaning, the Foreign Ministry emphasized that the September 19, 2005, six-party joint statement was "defunct" and that talks for the North's denuclearization were no longer possible.* Finally, the statement warned that North Korea would "take steps for physical counteraction to bolster the military capabilities for self defense, including the nuclear deterrence, both qualitatively and quantitatively." Put plainly, the DPRK planned to produce more and better nuclear weapons.

To underline the point that a new, far-reaching policy was in the works, over the next few weeks Kim Jong Un took part in three unusual, high-profile meetings—a small group session with his security and foreign-policy advisers (January 26), an enlarged meeting of the party's Central Military Commission (February 3), and a Politburo meeting (February 11) involving the top-ranked members of the Workers Party of Korea. Judging from the brief North Korean media reports that accompanied each, Kim spoke at the meetings about the main components of what, at the end of March, he would announce as a new two-line strategy. On February 12, the day after the Politburo meeting, the North moved ahead on one part of the strategy by conducting its third nuclear test.

Thereafter, almost every day for the next month and a half, Washington and Seoul on one side and Pyongyang on the other took steps or made statements that added to the sense of an open-ended escalation. By the time the storm had passed, the United States had flown strategic bombers over South Korea on at least three separate occasions, the North Koreans had announced that the Armistice Agreement had been nullified, and Kim Jong Un had convened an "urgent operation meeting" to consider new operational status for the KPA Strategic Rocket Force (SRF). To add spice to the drama, North Korean media even noted the time of the meeting—00:30.** At the meeting, according to KCNA, Kim "examined and finally ratified the plan of the Strategic Rocket Forces,"

---

* From Pyongyang's viewpoint, it had warned of this course in July 2012, when several Foreign Ministry officials met a delegation of Americans in Singapore. In a formal presentation, the North Koreans said Pyongyang had conducted a policy review and had concluded that if there was no change in Washington's approach, the North would no longer deal with it on the question of denuclearization. Soon after that meeting, in an unconnected move, the US government sent a secret mission to Pyongyang. According to South Korean reports, this was the second such US mission of the year. What the purpose of these missions was, who took part, whom they met, and what was accomplished are still not known. For a review of the information and speculation about the missions, see the *Los Angeles Times,* http://articles.latimes.com/2013/feb/23/world/la-fg-us-north-korea-20130224.

** North Korean reports rarely mention the date of an appearance by the Supreme Leader, much less the time.

ordering standby status so that in case the United States launched a "huge provocation," the SRF could "strike any time the U.S. mainland, its military bases in the operational theaters in the Pacific, including Hawaii and Guam, and those in south Korea."

The warning of that wildly improbably scenario was followed the next day by something even more extreme: a "special statement" in the name of the "government, political parties, and organizations" of the DPRK, announcing that "from this moment, North-South relations will be put in a state of war and all issues arousing between north and south will be dealt with according to wartime regulations." Taking the bait (for that is apparently what this statement was), the English-language *Japan Times* on March 31 carried an article headlined "North Korea Tensions Near Boiling Point."

In fact, rather than increase tensions, Pyongyang pivoted and headed in the opposite direction. At a Korean Workers Party Central Committee plenum on the last day of March, the North began lowering the temperature on both the domestic and the international fronts.* The major signal came in Kim Jong Un's address to the plenum, laying out in detail the new two-line policy he had apparently been contemplating and discussing internally for the previous two months.**

That policy took the North into new territory on both the economic and the nuclear fronts. Justifying a retreat from the economic theme he had introduced a year earlier (in April 2012) about no longer forcing the people to "tighten their belts," Kim said that events had demonstrated that an end to economic belt tightening was not possible as long as the North was under external military threat. As a result, improvements in the economy would have to be accompanied by continuing efforts to develop the North's nuclear weapons program. Kim charged that the United States was creating obstacles to the North's economic development by "dragging us into an arms race." His response was that the new strategic line would make it possible to reinforce the country's defense capabilities "with a small outlay without increasing national defense spending, while directing great efforts to economic construction and improvement of the people's living standards."

Further indicating that he did not want to be seen as having given up on new economic policies, Kim underlined the need to improve economic "management," terminology the North has long employed to avoid having

---

* About the same time, *DailyNK*, a Seoul-based online "newspaper" utilizing sources inside the North, reported that the internal mobilization of the North Korean population was easing.

** Foreign commentators suggested that this two-line strategy was a copy of the (failed) strategy adopted by Kim Il Sung in 1962, of building the economy and the defense sector simultaneously. As if in anticipation of such comparisons, the younger Kim in his plenum speech noted the earlier approach, but called his own "a succession to and in-depth development of" the earlier line.

to use the term *reform*. Looking beyond the current crisis, Kim exhorted officials to "organize tourism areas in various parts of the country, including Wonsan and Mt Chilbo areas [on the country's east coast], briskly promote tourism, and set up economic development zones in *all* provinces in line with their actual circumstances" (emphasis added).

The sense of renewed focus on the economy was reinforced by a symbolically potent promotion at the March 31 plenum. Pak Pong Ju, who had served as prime minister during the years of Kim Jong Il's new economic measures a decade earlier before being relieved of his duties and demoted, was named a full Politburo member. The next day, at the annual spring Supreme People's Assembly meeting, Pak was appointed prime minister, replacing the eighty-three-year-old Choe Yong-rim.

In parallel developments over the next few days, Pyongyang also pressed ahead on the nuclear front. The SPA meeting promulgated a new "Law on Consolidating the Position of Nuclear Weapons State for Self-Defense," setting forth provisions for the use and safekeeping of nuclear weapons, as well as cooperation in "international efforts for nuclear non-proliferation and safe management of nuclear substance." The next day, Pyongyang announced that it would "restart and readjust" its nuclear facilities at Yongbyon, specifically naming the "uranium enrichment plant and 5[-megawatt] graphite moderated reactor, which had been mothballed and disabled under an agreement reached at the six-party talks in October, 2007."* On April 12, the Atomic Energy Bureau was upgraded to a full cabinet ministry to develop the country's "independent nuclear energy industry." That, presumably, meant increased resources would be devoted to completing the experimental light-water reactor under construction at Yongbyon. (Indeed, commercial satellite photography from the spring showed that construction of the reactor was making progress.) The upgrading of the DPRK's Atomic Energy Bureau could also indicate that plans for new, larger power reactors would be drawn up.

As the military situation on the Korean peninsula eased, another more familiar confrontation between North and South began in early April. This tension centered on the Kaesong Industrial Zone. From its beginnings in 2003, the KIZ had slowly and somewhat fitfully grown to be home to around 120 small South Korean firms employing more than fifty thousand North Korean workers. For reasons that remain unclear, in the spring of 2013 Pyongyang decided to bring operations at Kaesong to a sudden halt.

---

* In November 2010, technicians at Yongbyon had told the Stanford delegation that the 5-megawatt reactor was "in stand-by status with regular maintenance." See Siegfried S. Hecker, *A Return Trip to North Korea's Yongbyon Nuclear Complex* (Center for International Security and Cooperation, Stanford University, November 20, 2010), http://iis-db.stanford.edu/pubs/23035/HeckerYongbyon.pdf, 5.

The North announced that as of April 3, it would no longer allow passage of personnel or material from the South through the DMZ into Kaesong. In short order, the North withdrew its workers, essentially shutting the zone down. With no supplies or personnel replacements for managers and technicians arriving from the ROK, South Korean operators reluctantly closed up shop and went home. The last seven South Korean staff left on the evening of May 3, after two armored vehicles arrived from the South with final payment (reportedly more than $13 million) for taxes, some of the back salaries of North Korean workers, and other expenses. How closing down the KIZ squared with Kim Jong Un's plenum speech—which urged North Korean provincial authorities to set up "economic development zones," presumably with the participation of foreign investors—is hard to fathom.

THE CHINESE SHADOW

The first months of 2013 witnessed public expressions by both Beijing and Pyongyang of anger and frustration with the other. A debate in China over what to do about its troublesome ally has gone on for years. Similarly, North Korean distrust of the Chinese is long-standing and, in Pyongyang's view, completely justified. Rifts in relations between the two have occurred frequently.

Westerners often talk about the Chinese–North Korean "lips and teeth" relationship, but neither Pyongyang nor Beijing has thought of their ties in those close terms for at least thirty years. The private characterizations are less polite and more graphic. A ranking North Korean diplomat complained in the late 1990s that the Chinese treat the North like "dirt between their toes."

Kim Jong Il's shift to a much closer and more active economic and political relationship with China from 2009 until his death was driven by necessity, not by any love on his part for the North's overbearing neighbor. After Kim's death, relations drifted back to something more familiar—coldhearted smiles in public and expressions of thinly disguised contempt behind the scenes.

Many Western observers believe that since the North's most recent missile and nuclear tests, Chinese–North Korean relations have truly entered a new phase and that Beijing's overall approach to the Korean issue is undergoing a fundamental shift. But history suggests that we are equally likely to be watching the development of another period of frosty ties between Beijing and Pyongyang, of uncertain depth and duration but with the likelihood of reconciliation (of sorts) sooner or later. Either scenario will create new dangers and opportunities not just for North Korea but also for the South. With the continued growth of Chinese power and influence, the dynamics on the peninsula are changing in ways that no one can yet predict.

AN UNEASY PEACE

By May 2013, the situation on the Korean peninsula had calmed, for the moment. But history suggests that until and unless new, predictable patterns emerge, the two Koreas may find themselves living closer to the brink of conflict than ever before, with the surrounding big powers pulled into frequent storms.

The storm of early 2013, and the unusually long sense of crisis it produced, was fed almost daily over two months by a sharp escalation of North Korean rhetoric, breathless Western media reporting, and apprehension in Washington over the leadership situation in Pyongyang, especially how to judge Kim Jong Un's reactions and decision-making style. Curiously, throughout this period, the public mood in the South was remarkably calm. The situation clearly would not have benefited if South Koreans had started panic-buying instant noodles, as happened in the crisis of June 1994. Nevertheless, the calm this time around may be masking a deeper problem: South Koreans have lived with the northern threat for so long and are so tired of worrying about it (or have convinced themselves it is all a bluff) that the ROK government faces an ever more difficult task convincing its people that they cannot simply shrug off the longer-term issue of how to deal with North Korea.

The complex story of the Korean peninsula in the first dozen or so years of the twenty-first century is one of considerable, even momentous, changes. But none of these changes has altered the basic fact that nearly seventy years after division, there remain two Koreas. Perhaps nothing so clearly illustrates the problem as the sheer persistence of the formal structures left over from the Korean War. The summer of 2013 witnessed the sixtieth anniversary of the July 27, 1953, Korean Armistice Agreement. The anniversary was to celebrate not an armistice document long ago replaced, but one that, at least nominally, has remained in force for six decades. That longevity is testament not to the agreement's vitality or utility—it has enjoyed neither trait for decades—but rather to the stasis, almost paralysis, that has become tacitly accepted as the norm by all the players on and around the peninsula. Sadly, nowhere are there any signs of movement toward ensuring that this state of affairs does not last as a festering national wound far into the twenty-first century. Should two hostile regimes continue to exist on the peninsula, it will be a tragedy not only for the Korean nation but for all of Northeast Asia, warping policies and hobbling developments for decades to come.

PRINCIPAL KOREAN
FIGURES IN THE TEXT

DEMOCRATIC PEOPLE'S REPUBLIC OF KOREA (NORTH KOREA)

Han Se Hae, Workers Party official and secret emissary to the ROK

Ho Dam, foreign minister and secret emissary to the ROK

Hwang Jang Yop, Workers Party secretary for international affairs and juche theoretician; defected to the ROK in 1997

Jo Myong Rok, vice marshal and first vice chairman of the National Defense Commission

Kang Sok Ju, deputy foreign minister and chief nuclear negotiator with the United States

Kim Gye Gwan, vice foreign minister and deputy negotiator with the United States

Kim Hyon Hui, DPRK agent; bomber of Korean Air Lines flight 858; incarcerated and pardoned in the ROK

Kim Il Sung, leader of the Workers Party; prime minister, later president of the DPRK

Kim Jong Il, eldest son of Kim Il Sung; leader of the DPRK following his father's death

Kim Jong Un, third son of Kim Jong Il; became leader of the DPRK after his father's death

Kim Yong Nam, deputy prime minister and foreign minister of the DPRK, later chairman of Supreme People's Assembly and nominal head of state

Kim Yong Sun, Workers Party secretary and head of the DPRK delegation in 1992 talks with the United States

Yun Ki Bok, Workers Party official; political adviser to the DPRK delegation to the Red Cross talks; secret emissary to the ROK

REPUBLIC OF KOREA (SOUTH KOREA)

Choi Kyu Ha, prime minister of the ROK; briefly president after death of Park Chung Hee

Chun Doo Hwan, leader of the 1979 military takeover; president of the ROK

Chung Ju Yung, chairman of the Hyundai conglomerate; chairman of the campaign committee to win the Seoul Olympic Games; presidential candidate in 1992

Gong Ro Myung, foreign minister of the ROK

Han Sung Joo, foreign minister of the ROK

Kim Chong Whi, national security assistant to President Roh Tae Woo

Kim Dae Jung, opposition political leader and presidential candidate in 1971, 1987, 1992, 1997; popularly elected president, 1997

Kim Jae Kyu, director of KCIA; assassin of President Park Chung Hee

Kim Jong Pil, prime minister of the ROK; presidential candidate in 1987

Kim Woo Choong, chairman of the Daewoo conglomerate; unofficial envoy abroad and to the DPRK

Kim Young Sam, opposition political leader, later government party leader; popularly elected president in 1992

Lee Hu Rak, director of the KCIA

Lee Myung-bak, president from 2008 to 2013

Lee Yon Kil, businessman and anticommunist activist who arranged the defection of Hwang Jang Yop from North Korea

Lim Dong Won, senior adviser to President Kim Dae Jong on North-South affairs; secret emissary to DPRK in May 2000

Park Chul Un, presidential staff and intelligence official; ROK secret emissary to the DPRK

Park Chung Hee, leader of the 1961 military coup; later president of the ROK

Park Geun-hye, daughter of Park Chung Hee; elected ROK president in 2012

Roh Moo-hyun, elected president of the ROK in 2002

Roh Tae Woo, division commander in 1979 military takeover; popularly elected president in 1987

Sohn Jang Nae, KCIA minister in the ROK embassy, Washington; deputy director of the KCIA in Seoul

Yoo Chong Ha, national security assistant to President Kim Young Sam; later ROK foreign minister

Koreans in Japan

Mun Se Kwang, attempted assassin of ROK president Park; killer of Yook Young Soo (Mrs. Park)

ACKNOWLEDGMENTS

DON OBERDORFER

A great many people and institutions of many nationalities and points of view contributed to the research and writing of this book. I conducted more than 450 interviews in South and North Korea, the United States, China, Japan, Russia, Germany, and Austria in the course of the four years I was working on it. I was also aided immeasurably by documentary material from American, Russian, and East German archives, as well as journalistic and scholarly articles and books. All those who contributed, in large ways and small, have my thanks.

I am particularly grateful to Johns Hopkins University's Paul H. Nitze School of Advanced International Studies (SAIS), which accorded me a convenient and prestigious scholarly perch after my retirement from the *Washington Post* and sponsored the book. I am also very grateful to the Rockefeller Brothers Fund, New York, and the Korea Foundation, Seoul, for grants that supported my extensive travel and research. I wish to thank SAIS students Narushige Michishita and Choo Yong Shik, who were my research assistants.

It was my good fortune that Carter Eckert, director of the Korean studies program at Harvard University, was on a fellowship in Washington during the final stages of my writing. He gave generously of his time and suggestions. A number of present and former officials of the United States and the ROK governments and personal friends also offered valuable comments on various parts of the manuscript.

I wish to thank the National Security Archive, Washington, for assisting my Freedom of Information Act requests and providing materials obtained by other researchers; the FOIA staff of the Department of State for processing my requests; the Gerald Ford Presidential Library, particularly archivist Karen Holzhausen, and the Jimmy Carter Presidential Library, particularly assistant director Martin Elzy and archivist James Yancey, for identifying and helping to declassify valuable documentation; the FOIA staff of the Eighth Army, Korea, for declassifying the intelligence portions of its command histories for 1972–1987; Jim Mann of the *Los Angeles Times* for providing materials on US-China diplomacy affecting Korea; and Tim Shorrock of the Journal of Commerce for sharing the extensive material he has obtained under FOIA.

Joong-ang Ilbo, one of South Korea's leading newspapers and the publisher of the Korean edition of this book, graciously provided many of the photographs.

I am very grateful to Mark Â. M. Suh of the Free University of Berlin for obtaining important documents from the archives of the former East German Communist Party, the Socialist Unity Party, including transcripts of meetings of East German leader Erich Honecker with Kim Il Sung and diplomatic dispatches from the East German Embassy in Pyongyang.

In Seoul former ambassador to the United States Kim Kyung Won accepted me as a guest scholar at the Institute of Social Sciences, which greatly facilitated my interviews there. I am grateful to him and his efficient secretary, Mrs. Park Soon Rye. I also appreciate the work of the Korean Overseas Information Service, Seoul, especially Suh Sang Myun, in arranging interviews with government officials.

My South Korean journalist friends, especially Kim Yong Hie and Kim Kun Jin of Joong-ang Ilbo, Cho Kap Che and Kim Dae Joong of *Chosun Ilbo*, Shim Jae Hoon of the *Far Eastern Economic Review*, and Lee Keum Hyun, special correspondent of the *Washington Post*, were especially helpful. Sam Jameson, the longtime Tokyo correspondent of the *Los Angeles Times*, now an independent journalist and scholar in Japan, provided information and suggestions.

My 1991 visit to North Korea was as a *Washington Post* diplomatic correspondent. My return visit in 1995 was under the sponsorship of George Washington University's Sigur Center for East Asian Studies, then headed by Young C. Kim, to whom I am grateful. I also wish to express appreciation to officials of the DPRK Mission to the United Nations for many courtesies, including providing me with copies of the works of President Kim Il Sung from 1965 to 1983.

In Beijing my 1993 research trip was sponsored by the Chinese Academy of Social Sciences, which also provided introductions and translating assistance, for which I am grateful.

My research and interviewing in Moscow was facilitated by the Moscow Bureau of the *Washington Post*, which generously treated me as a colleague even though I had retired. Anatoly Chernyayev and Pavel Palazchenko, who continue as aides to Mikhail Gorbachev, helped in obtaining materials from the Gorbachev archive.

David Kyd, the public information officer of the International Atomic Energy Agency, Vienna, provided information and arranged interviews for me there.

I wish to thank former president Jimmy Carter for his written responses to my questions about Korea policy in his administration, and especially for assistance in dealing with his 1994 mission to Pyongyang. Marion Creekmore and Dick Christenson, who accompanied him to North Korea, also helped me.

In Japan, Izumi Hajime of Shizuoka University was particularly helpful in providing insights and materials about the DPRK, on which he is a leading expert.

Among the many persons who agreed to interviews, I wish especially to thank the following:

In the United States

Former secretaries of state Cyrus Vance and George Shultz; former undersecretaries of state Michael Armacost, Robert Zoellick, Arnold Kanter, and Frank Wisner; former assistant secretaries of state for East Asian and Pacific affairs Marshall Green, Richard Holbrooke, Paul Wolfowitz, the late Gaston Sigur, Richard Solomon, and William Clark, as well as Winston Lord, who was assistant secretary during my research; former deputy assistant secretaries of state Robert Oakley and Thomas Hubbard and the current holder of the post, Charles Kartman; former chief US Korea coordinator and negotiator Robert Gallucci and his senior deputy, Gary Samore; and former Korea country directors Robert Rich, Harry Dunlop, Spence Richardson, David E. Brown, and David G. Brown, and the current country director, Mark Minton.

At the Pentagon, former secretaries of defense James Schlesinger, Donald Rumsfeld, and Harold Brown, as well as William Perry, who held the post during my research; Morton Abramowitz; Admiral William Pendley; Captain Thomas Flanigan; and Wally Knowles.

At the White House, former national security advisers Zbigniew Brzezinski, Richard Allen, and Brent Scowcroft, as well as Anthony Lake, who held the post during my research; and former National Security Council staff members William Hyland, Nick

Piatt, Jim Kelly, Doug Paal, Torkel Patterson, Kent Wiedemann, Stanley Roth, and Daniel Poneman.

In the intelligence community, former CIA director Robert Gates; the expert North Korea watchers in the State Department's Bureau of Intelligence and Research Robert Carlin, Kenneth Quinones, and John Merrill, as well as nuclear expert Steve Fleischmann; former national intelligence officers Evelyn Colbert, John Despres, Nathanial Thayer, Carl Ford, and Ezra Vogel; Morgan Clippinger and other Korea experts of the Central Intelligence Agency; and former US intelligence officials John Armstrong and the late Jim Hausman.

Former congressman Stephen Solarz.

From the US Embassy, Seoul, former US ambassadors to the ROK William Gleysteen, Richard Walker, James Lilley, and Donald Gregg, as well as James Laney, who was US ambassador during the period of my research; former deputy chiefs of mission Francis Underhill, Richard Ericson, Raymond Burkhardt, and Dick Christenson; former US Embassy political counselors Paul Cleveland and Daniel Russel; and former military attaché Jim Young.

In the US Command, Korea, former commanders in chief Generals John Wickham, Robert Sennewald, Robert RisCassi, Gary Luck, and current CINC General John Tilelli; Lieutenant General Howell Estes; retired lieutenant generals James Hollingsworth and John Cushman; special assistant to the USFK commander Stephen Bradner; USFK historian Major Thomas Ryan; former US representative to the Military Armistice Commission (MAC) Jimmy Lee; former MAC secretary Colonel Forrest Chilton; and public information officer Jim Coles and his predecessor Billy Fullerton.

Among Korea experts in the United States, Peter Hayes of the Nautilus Institute; nuclear weapons expert Bill Arkin; Bruce Cumings of Northwestern University; Joseph Ha of Lewis and Clark College; Dae-Sook Suh of the University of Hawaii; Charles Armstrong, then of Princeton University; Han S. Park of the University of Georgia; Edward Olsen of the Naval Postgraduate School; Manwoo Lee of Millersville University; and Sanghyun Yoon of George Washington University.

Also Larry Niksch and Rinn Sup Shinn of the Congressional Research Service; Tony Namkung of the Atlantic Council; Selig Harrison and Leonard Spector of the Carnegie Endowment for International Peace; Ralph Clough of SAIS; Daryl Plunk of the Heritage Foundation; Michael O'Hanlon of the Brookings Institution; Scott Snyder of the US Institute of Peace; William Taylor of the Center for Strategic and International Studies; Chen You Wei; Norm Levin and Kongdan (Katy) Oh of the Rand Corporation; David Albright; and Steve Linton and Robert Manning of the Progressive Policy Institute.

Also, *New York Times* correspondent Michael Gordon and managing editor Josette Shiner of the *Washington Times*.

IN SOUTH KOREA

President Kim Young Sam and former presidents Choi Kyu Ha and Roh Tae Woo; Blue House national security advisers Chung Jung Uk and Ban Ki Mun; former presidential press secretaries Kim Seong Jin and Kim Sung Ik; former Blue House economic advisers Oh Won Choi, Kim Ki Whan, and Kim Jong In; and former spokesman Kim Hak Joon.

Former prime ministers Lho Shin Yang, Roh Jae Bong, and Lee Hong Koo; Deputy Prime Minister Kwon O-Kie; and former deputy prime ministers Choi Yong Choi and Han Wan Sang.

Former ministers of foreign affairs Choi Kwang Su, Choi Ho Joong, Lee Sang Ok, Han Sung Joo, Gong Ro Myung; Foreign Minister Yoo Chong Ha; former deputy foreign minister Park Soo Kil; former minister of home affairs Chung Ho Young; former minister of culture and information Lee Kyu Hyun; former minister of science and technology Kim Jin Hyon; and former chief of protocol Lee Byung Gi.

Former ROK ambassadors to the United States Kim Kyong Won, Hyun Hong Choo, and Han Seung Soo and the current ambassador, Park Kun Woo; ROK ambassador to the United Nations (and currently foreign minister) Yoo Chong Ha; ROK ambassadors to China Roh Jae Won and Whang Byong Tae; unofficial negotiator with China Lee Soon Sok; and ROK ambassador to Russia Kim Suk Kyu.

Former minister of defense Choo Yong Bok; Lieutenant General Park Young Ok, assistant minister of defense; retired general Kim Choi Chang; and Han Yong Sup of the National Defense University.

Former directors of the Agency for National Security Planning Suh Dong Kwon and Kim Deok; deputy NSP director Rhee Byong Ho and former deputy director Sohn Jang Nae; former NSP special assistant (now National Assembly member) Lee Dong Bok; and former KCIA officials Kang In Duk and Chung Hong Jin.

Former North-South negotiator Lim Dong Won; former delegate to the North-South talks Chung Hee Kyung and former North-South spokesman Chung Choo Hyun; Kim Dal Sul, of the North-South dialogue office; Kil Jeong Woo and Ahn Inhay of the Research Institute on National Reunification; Yu Suk Ryul and Kim Choong Nam of the Institute of Foreign Affairs and National Security; and former vice minister of unification Song Yong Dae.

Chung Ju Yung, founder and honorary chairman of the Hyundai group, and Kim Woo Choong, founder and chairman of the Daewoo group.

Kim Dae Jung, opposition political leader; members of the National Assembly Chung Jey Moon, Hur Hwa Pyung, Kang Sin Ok, Kim Yoon Hwan, Lee Boo Young, Park Kye Dong, and Park Se Jik.

North Korean defectors Koh Young Hwan, Kim Hyun Hui, Kang Myung Do, and Colonel Choi Ju Hwal.

Ahn Byung Joon of Yonsei University and Rhee Sang Woo of Sogang University.

Kim Jin, reporter of *Joong-ang Ilbo*, Kim Yong Sam of *Monthly Chosun*, and Songhee Stella Kim of *Time*.

I also wish to thank Russian diplomats in Seoul, Ambassador Georgi Kunaidze and Minister Georgi Toloraya; Siegfried Scheibe, former East German economic minister in the DPRK, now in the German Chamber of Commerce, Seoul; and David Steinberg, the representative in Seoul of the Asia Foundation.

In North Korea

I met Deputy Prime Minister and Foreign Minister Kim Yong Nam, Workers Party secretary Kim Yong Sun, Vice Minister of External Economic Affairs Kim Jong U, and other officials during my January 1995 trip. I wish to acknowledge the assistance of the Institute of Disarmament and Peace, Pyongyang, which made the arrangements and was the host of this visit.

In China

Wu Dawei, deputy director of Asian Affairs; Li Bing of the Ministry of Foreign Affairs; and former Foreign Ministry official Li Xiang Wei.

Tao Bing Wei, a leading Chinese expert on Korea, now a senior fellow at the China Institute of International Studies; Pu Shan of the Chinese Academy of Social Sciences; Jin Zhen Ji of the Institute of Contemporary International Relations; Xu Man Zhang, former Chinese military attaché; and Colonel Shi Jin Kun of the Institute of International Strategic Studies.

At the Russian Embassy, Beijing, Ambassador Igor Rogachev and Minister Sergei Goncharov.

Mike Chinoy, CNN correspondent, Beijing.

IN RUSSIA

Former president Mikhail Gorbachev; former national security adviser Anatoly Chernyayev; former foreign minister Alexander Bessmertnykh; former ambassador Anatoly Dobrynin; Sergei Tarasenko, former Foreign Ministry official; Vadim Tkachenko, former director of Korean affairs of the Central Committee of the CPSU; Igor Rakhmanin, former Asian affairs director of the Central Committee of the CPSU; and Gorbachev aides Karen Brutents, Georgi Ostraumov, and Pavel Palazchenko.

Yevgeni Primakov, then chief of the Russian Foreign Intelligence Agency, now foreign minister; Deputy Foreign Minister Alexander Panov; and Yevgeni Afanasyev, Valery Denisov, and Vladimir Rakhmanin of the Russian Foreign Ministry.

Mikhail Titerenko, director of the Institute of Far Eastern Studies, and Roald Seleviev of the institute.

Vitaly Ignatenko, general director of ITAR-Tass news agency; Tass correspondent Vladimir Nadashkevich; journalists Yuri Sigov and Alexander Blatkovsky.

IN JAPAN

Kawashima Yutaka, director general of Asian Affairs, Ministry of Foreign Affairs; Okazaki Hisahiko, former Foreign Ministry official; Ambassador Endo Tetsuya, negotiator with North Korea; and Takeuchi Yukio, deputy chief of mission, Washington.

Takemura Masayoshi, member of Japanese Diet.

Okonogi Masao of Keio University and Major General Tsukamoto Katsuichi of the Research Institute for Peace and Security.

IN VIENNA

Director General Hans Blix of the International Atomic Energy Agency; Dmitri Perricos, director of East Asian safeguards operations; Olli Heinonen, chief inspector for North Korea; and Willy Theis, former chief inspector for North Korea.

John Ritch, US ambassador to international organizations; and Mike Lawrence and Marvin Peterson, US mission officials.

IN GERMANY

Hans Maretzki, former ambassador of the GDR to North Korea; Gunter Unterbeck, former GDR diplomat; and Ann-Katrin Becker, former correspondent of the GDR news agency in Beijing.

I also am grateful to several people whose insights were important but who asked that their names not be used, even in acknowledgment, and quite a few people who took the trouble to read and correct major chunks of the manuscript. You know who you are, and you have my thanks.

Finally, I would like to thank those whose work was essential to the writing and editing of this book: Tong Kim, for translations from Korean; Mary Drake, for transcription of interviews; Zhaojin Ji, the secretary of the SAIS Asia program; Joy Harris, my literary agent; Bill Patrick, formerly of Addison-Wesley, who saw the merit in the book, and his colleague Sharon Broil, a wonderful editor who found ways to make it better; and my wife, Laura, my own best editor and inspiration.

ROBERT CARLIN

There are countless reasons to thank people for their help in the writing of a book. I am grateful to those mentioned below for their support in all forms, their insights, and their encouragement. In some cases, where it would be impolitic to name individuals, I hope my gratitude is clear.

Dr. Gregory Albers, Bradley Babson, Jeffrey Bader, Jeffrey Baron, Stephen Bosworth, Robert Boynton, Hyesuk Brown, Kurt Campbell, Major General Edward C. Cardon, Frederick Carriere, Victor Cha, Mike Chinoy, Sang-hun Choe, Sherrie Chung, Peter Davis, Dr. Kenneth Dekleva, John Delury, Joseph DeTrani, Edward Dong, Thomas Fingar, Michael Finnegan, Carl Ford, Robert Gallucci, Christopher Green, Michael Green, Donald Gregg, Siegfried Hecker, Olli Heinonen, Christopher Hill, James Hoare, Allison Hooker, Thomas Hubbard, Eric John, Charles Kartman, Glenn Kessler, James Kelly, Duyeon Kim, Ambassador Sung Kim, Yuri Kim, Eric Latzky, Jean Lee, Ambassador Miklos Lengyel, John W. Lewis, Ambassador Eamonn McKee, Zarin Mehta, Niko Milonopoulos, James Person, John Podesta, Evan Ramstad, Samantha Ravich, Evans Revere, Daniel Russel, Gary Samore, Michael Schiffer, Gi-wook Shin, Leon Sigal, Kathleen Stephens, David Straub, Robert Suettinger, Sidney Syler, Jenny Town, Ezra Vogel, Lawrence Wilkerson, Jay Yim, Katharina Zellweger.

Choi Jinwook, Choi Young-jin, Chung Chong-Wook, Chun Yung-woo, Dong Yongsueng, Han Sung-Joo, Hong Yang-ho, Hyun In-Taek, Im Tae Hee, Colonel (Retired) Jang Sam Yeol, Kim Hyunjin, Kim Sook, Kim Tae-hyo, Kim Young-mok, Kim Young-sik, Lee Hawon, Lim Dong-won, Lim Sungnam, Min Ji Kwon, Moon Chung-in, Moon Jae-in, General Moon Sung-mok, Park Jeong Eun, Rhee Bong-jo, Ryoo Kihl-jae, Shin Eun-seo, Song Min Soon, Suh Hoon, Wang Son-taek, Yang Chang Seok, Yoon Young-kwan, Yoo Sun, Yu Myong Hwan, Yun Byung-Se.

Izumi Hajime, Sakamoto Takashi, Ambassador, Sasae Kenichiro, Tanaka Hitoshi.

NOTES AND SOURCES

According to an entry in the spiral-bound notebooks I kept as a journal, I first began thinking about a book on Korea in 1988, about the same time I began work on *The Turn*, my history of US-Soviet relations at the end of the Cold War. I realized even in that early note that this book would have to be a postretirement project, as it would take much time and travel that would be incompatible with full-time work for the *Washington Post*. Although there were a few interviews earlier, work began seriously after my retirement in May 1993. Over the next four years, I conducted more than 450 interviews in a variety of countries, consulted books and archives, and obtained new information under the Freedom of Information Act. With a few confidential exceptions, the principal interviewees and sources of materials are mentioned in the Acknowledgments.

As in my earlier books, I am providing here information on the sources for *The Two Koreas*, except for those that were confidential or are well known to people in the field. In order to facilitate scholarly research, I deposited within the first half of 1998 copies of US documents used in this book that were obtained under the Freedom of Information Act in the National Security Archive, an independent nongovernmental research institute in Washington, where they will be available to any researcher.

The following abbreviations are used in the notes:

CWIHP—*Cold War International History Project Bulletin* (Woodrow Wilson International Center for Scholars)

DOS cable: Cable from the Department of State in Washington to the US Embassy in Seoul; date and subject are given if available

Emb. cable: Cable to the Department of State in Washington from the US embassy in Seoul; date and subject are given if available

FBIS: Foreign Broadcast Information Service, published by the US government

KH: Korea Herald, an English-language newspaper in Seoul

KIS Works: Kim Il Sung Works (Foreign Languages Publishing House), in English

KT: Korea Times, an English-language newspaper in Seoul

NYT: New York Times

SED Archives: Archives of the Socialist (Communist) Unity Party of the former East Germany, obtained in Berlin (in German)

USFK Hist.: US Forces Korea /Eighth US Army Annual Historical Reports, the intelligence sections of which were declassified for me under the Freedom of Information Act; the year of the report quoted is given

US-PRC Chronology: Richard H. Solomon, *US-PRC Political Negotiations, 1967–1984: An Annotated Chronology* (Rand, 1985), Secret (declassified 1994)

WP: Washington Post

CHAPTER 1: WHERE THE WILD BIRDS SING

DMZ setting, see Fran Kaliher of Two Harbors, MN, research associate of the International Crane Foundation; Yoon Moo Boo, "DMZ: Paradise for Migratory Birds," *Koreana* (Winter 1995); and Jimmy Lee, interview, July 8, 1995.

The Emergence of Two Koreas: Historical details from Carter J. Eckert et al., *Korea Old and New: A History* (Ilchokak Publishers, for the Korea Institute, Harvard University, 1990), and interviews with Eckert. For invasions and occupations, Donald S. Macdonald, *The Koreans* (Westview, 1988), 1–2. Stertinius's ignorance from Louis J. Halle, *The Cold War as History* (London: Chatto & Windus, 1967), 202n. The Whelan quote is from Richard Whelan, *Drawing the Line* (Little, Brown, 1990), 27. The Rusk quote is from Dean Rusk, *As I Saw It* (Penguin Books, 1990), 124. The Summers quote is from Summers telephone interview, February 11, 1997. The Henderson quote is from Gregory Henderson's chapter in *Divided Nations in a Divided World* (David McKay, 1974), 43.

War and Its Aftermath: Kim Il Sung on not sleeping, ciphered telegram from Shtykov to Vyshinsky, January 19, 1950, in "Korea, 1949–50," *Cold War International History Project Bulletin* (Woodrow Wilson International Center for Scholars) (Spring 1995): 8. For origins of the Korean War, see especially Kathryn Weathersby's work for the Cold War International History Project. The casualty figures are from Whelan, *Drawing the Line,* 373. Kim Il Sung's secret emissary was Hwang Tae Sung; his mission was described by Chinese and Russian sources as well as by Lee Dong Bok, interview, July 15, 1993.

The Origins of Negotiation: For Kim Il Sung's presence in Beijing, see Henry Kissinger, *White House Years* (Little, Brown, 1979), 751. For new insights into Chinese efforts to deal with Pyongyang immediately after the Kissinger visit, see Bernd Schaefer, "Overconfidence Shattered: North Korean Unification Policy, 1971–1975," North Korea International Documentation Project (Woodrow Wilson International Center for Scholars), Working Paper 2, December 2010, 6. For Chinese military supply, see *USFK Hist. 1974,* Secret (declassified 1994). Kim Seong Jin quote, Kim interview, October 15, 1993. For Park remarks to correspondents, Son U Ryun, "Voice Testimony of Park Chung Hee," *Monthly Chosun* (March 1993), in Korean.

For Park letter to Nixon, Theodore Eliot, "Reply to President Park Chung Hee's Letter on East Asian Problems," Department of State Memorandum, November 4, 1971, Secret (declassified 1978); "For Ambassador," Department of State Telegram (December 13, 1971), Secret (declassified 1996); and "Seoul Receives Assurances from Nixon on China Talks," *NYT,* December 26, 1971. The Park quote on unprecedented peril is from Park Chung Hee, *Korea Reborn* (Prentice Hall, 1979), 48.

For the secret plenum of the Workers Party, conversation of Hermann Axen (member of GDR Politburo) with DPRK ambassador Lee Chang Su (July 31, 1972), *SED Archives.* Henderson quote on KCIA is from Mark Clifford, *Troubled Tiger* (M. E. Sharpe, 1994), 85. Lee Hu Rak quotes are from Michael Keon, *Korean Phoenix* (Prentice Hall International, 1977), 129–130. This controversial book contains one of the few interviews with Lee on his Pyongyang mission. Lee was among a mere handful of Korean figures who declined to be interviewed for this book. On Lee Hu Rak's harrowing ride, see Kim Chung Shik, *Directors of KCIA,* vol. 1 (Dong-Á Ilbo, 1992), in Korean.

Kim Il Sung: Separating fact from fiction about Kim's early life is a formidable task. I have relied primarily on the most authoritative biography in the West, Dae-Sook Suh's *Kim Il Sung: The North Korean Leader* (Columbia University Press, 1988). For Kim's Christian background, see Yong-ho Ch'oe, "Christian Background in the Early Life of Kim Il-Song," *Asian Survey* (October 1986). For Kim's own account, see Kim Il Sung, *With the Century* (Foreign Languages Publishing House, 1992), 1:105–107. Kim in Soviet uniform, Suh, *Kim Il Sung,* 60.

The Stalin quote on "young country, young leader" comes from US expert John Merrill, who heard it from a Russian with extensive experience in Pyongyang. Medvedev on Kim as a "normal person" is from Vadim Medvedev, *Collapse* (International Relations, 1994), in Russian. For Kim's mansions and isolation from the people, see the memoir of Hans Maretzki (former East German ambassador to North Korea), *Kimism in North Korea* (Anita Tykve Verlag, 1991), in German. The 1984 train procedure was told to me by a Soviet official who took part.

Special health arrangements for Kim in Germany, former East German diplomat, interview, June 10, 1994. The Rakhmanin quote is from Rakhmanin interview, April 8, 1994. The Talleyrand quote is from Roald Seveliev (of the Institute of Far Eastern Studies, Moscow), interview, April 8, 1994. On the early history of *juche*, see Michael Robinson, "National Identity and the Thought of Sin Ch'aeho: *Sadaejuui* and *Chuche* in History and Politics," *Journal of Korean Studies* (1984).

The Kim quote on "special emphasis" is from *KIS Works*, 27:19–20. Han Park on *juche* is from his book *North Korea: Ideology, Politics, Economy* (Prentice Hall, 1996), 10. On the thirty-four thousand monuments, see Maretzki, *Kimism in North Korea*. The "cult of personality" quote is from Rakhmanin interview, April 8, 1994. The Suh quote is from Suh, *Kim Il Sung*, 314–315. South Korean visitor quotes, interview, November 22, 1994.

Kim on the "situation at my fingertips," *KIS Works*, 31:87–88. Kim to Solarz, transcript of Kim Il Sung–Solarz conversation, from the Jimmy Carter Library. On the ouster of high officials for new ideas, "Number One Taboo in Pyongyang: Challenging Kim's Authority," *Vantage Point* (Seoul) (May 1995). Kim's words "said forever," former communist diplomat, interview, June 10, 1994. On Kim's statue, Suh, *Kim Il Sung*, 316. Kim description from Harrison Salisbury, "North Korean Leader Bids U.S. Leave the South as Step to Peace," *NYT*, May 31, 1972.

Conversations with the South: For the Kim-Lee meeting, see the transcript published in *Monthly Joong-ang* (March 1989), in Korean. Chong Hong Jin, who was present with Lee, told me in an interview (May 27, 1993) that it is essentially accurate. A North Korean version can be found in *KIS Works*, 26:134ff. Additional documents on the inter-Korean meetings in 1972 are in "New Evidence on Inter-Korean Relations, 1971–1972," North Korea International Documentation Project (Woodrow Wilson International Center for Scholars), September 2009. The story of twenty-one-year-old Poco Underhill is from his father in a telephone interview, August 26, 1996. Ambassador Lee's presentation to the GDR, from conversation of Hermann Axen with Lee Chang Su (July 31, 1972), *SED Archives*. Kim Seong Jin's quotes on Park are from Kim interview, May 24, 1993.

CHAPTER 2: THE END OF THE BEGINNING

On the Red Cross exchange, the Chung quote is from Chung Hee Kyung interview, July 19, 1993. "Bringing all the tall buildings": This is one of the most oft-repeated anecdotes about the visit of the North Korean Red Cross delegation to Seoul and has been attributed to several different South Korean hosts. The Yun speech at the opening ceremony is from "Public 'Disappointed' in Propaganda" (September 14, 1972), 14; and National Unification Board, ROK, *A White Paper on South-North Dialogue in Korea* (Seoul, 1982), 119. On the South Korean decision to televise the opening ceremony, Kim Seong Jin interview, November 15, 1992. On intelligence management of South Korean protest, Chung Hee Kyung interview, July 19, 1993.

On the talks and meaningless agreement, National Unification Board, *White Paper on South-North Dialogue,* especially 119. On Park's views, Kim Seong Jin discussion, November 15, 1992.

Park Chung Hee: For my interview with Park, see Don Oberdorfer, "Korea: Progress and Danger," *WP,* June 29, 1975. The story of Park's office safe is from a senior Korean diplomat who learned of it from a close aide to Park. On Park and the Yosu rebellion, James Hausman telephone interviews, April 26 and September 23, 1995. See also Allan R. Millett, "Captain James H. Hausman and the Formation of the Korean Army, 1945–50," unpublished paper from the Mershon Center, Ohio State University, 30. The embassy cable about Park is published in "Investigation of Korean-American Relations," *Appendices of the Report of the House Committee on International Relations,* Subcommittee on International Organizations (October 31, 1978), 1:64.

Military assessment of Park, *USFK Hist. 1975,* 47, Confidential (declassified 1994). On Park's intelligence countermeasures, see No Chae Hyon, *Office of the Secretary of the Blue House,* vol. 2, *Joong-ang Ilbo* (1993), in Korean, 254. For the poll on Park's greatness, *Chosun Ilbo,* March 5, 1995, in Korean. Park quote on "pilfered household," Frank Gibney, *Koreas Quiet Revolution* (Walker, 1992), 50. On Park's plans and operations in the economic field, see the excellent book by Mark Clifford, *Troubled Tiger* (M. E. Sharpe, 1994), from which the quote from the first economic plan is taken. The same source is used for the ROK's Vietnam earnings (57) and the Pohang steel mill (67–75). Park as "orchestra conductor" quote, Michael Keon, *Korean Phoenix* (Prentice Hall International, 1977), 79. The Kim quote on Park's economic choices is from Chung-yum Kim, *Policymaking on the Front Lines* (World Bank, 1994), 30.

On Park's honesty and modesty, Kim, *Policymaking on the Front Lines,* 117–118, and an interview with Jim Kim, political writer for *Joong-ang Ilbo* and author of a book on Park, May 18, 1996. The Cho Soon quote is from his book *The Dynamics of Korean Economic Development* (Institute for International Economics, 1994), 180. The growth data are from Kihwan Kim and Danny M. Leipzinger, *Korea: A Case of Government-Led Development* (World Bank, 1993), 1. The income distribution data are from D. M. Leipziger et al., *The Distribution of Income and Wealth in Korea* (World Bank, 1992), 7.

Washington Blinks at Park's Coup: On Habib and the *yushin* plan, *Emb. cable,* "ROKG Declaration of Martial Law and Plans for Fundamental Government Reform," October 16, 1972, Confidential (declassified 1996). On Habib's anger at lack of forewarning, Francis Underhill, telephone interview, July 29, 1996. Marshall Green quote, Green telephone interview, August 13, 1996.

Habib's hands-off recommendation, *Emb. cable,* "Comment on Martial Law and Government Change in Korea," October 16, 1972, Secret (declassified 1996). Washington's reaction, *DOS cable,* October 16, 1972, Secret (declassified 1996). Habib's policy of disassociation, *Emb. cable,* "U.S. Response to Korean Constitutional Revision," October 23, 1972, Secret (declassified 1996). Washington's endorsement, *DOS cable,* "Ref Seoul 6119," October 26, 1972, Secret (declassified 1996). Nixon to Kim Jong Pil, Don Oberdorfer, "South Korean Abuses Tolerated," *WP,* May 19, 1976. The quote was supplied by Donald Ranard, then Korea country director, who obtained it from a White House participant.

The Impact of Yushin: On the harassment of Chang Chun Ha, see Don Oberdorfer, "Korea: The Silencing of Dissenters," *WP,* December 31, 1972. Chang was the man referred to as "Mr. Lee." For his death, "Controversy over Dissident's Death

Rekindled," *Newsreview,* April 13, 1993. On the silencing of Korean press, see Don Oberdorfer, "The Korean Press," *WP,* December 28, 1973.

On differences in Pyongyang over policy toward South Korea, see *Cold War International History Project* (Wilson Center), "North Korea's Efforts to Acquire Nuclear Technology and Nuclear Weapons: Evidence from Russian and Hungarian Archives," Working Paper 53, Hungarian Embassy report, November 22, 1973, Document no. 25, 51.

On Donald Gregg's opposition to Lee Hu Rak, Gregg interview, March 12, 1995. For country recognition data, see Samuel S. Kim, "North Korea and the United Nations," paper prepared for the 1996 Annual Conference of the International Council on Korean Studies, 31.

CHAPTER 3: THE TROUBLE DEEPENS

This account of the assassination attempt on Park is based on my eyewitness recollection and several published accounts. The number of bullets fired and the issue of whose bullet killed the first lady were extensively investigated by two of my colleagues who were also on the scene, Sam Jameson of the *Los Angeles Times* and Bruce Dunning of CBS News. They found many inconsistencies between the government's official account and their reporting but were unable to reach conclusive judgments. The Kim Seong Jin quote is from Kim interview, May 24, 1993. On the shoes and handbag (which I did not notice at the time), see Michael Keon, *Korean Phoenix* (Prentice Hall, 1977), 199.

On students and Christians, see Koon Woo Nam, *South Korean Politics* (University Press of America, 1989), esp. chap. 4. On the Niedecker incident, Richard Ericson interview, February 16, 1994, and Gregg interview, June 21, 1993. For Niedecker's account, memorandum from John E. Niedecker to General A. M. Haig Jr., July 29, 1974, Confidential (declassified 1997). It was also widely reported after the fact. For the intelligence assessment about student radicalism, *USFK Hist. 1974,* 37, Confidential (declassified 1995).

The Struggle with Japan: Mun as a "jackal," interview with former Korean prosecutor, October 23, 1992. On the plight of Koreans in Japan, see Don Oberdorfer, "An Assassin Comes 'Home' to Korea," *WP,* September 3, 1974, my investigation of Mun Se Kwang's life and background in Osaka. The Chung Il Kwon quote is from Ericson interview, February 16, 1994. Park's diary quotes from "Blue House Diary," *Minju Ilbo,* November 24, 1989, in Korean, translation by Carter Eckert.

The Underground War: Material on the tunnels is based primarily on the tunnels sections of *USFK Hist. 1972–87,* which were declassified and released to me in 1995 under the Freedom of Information Act. See also Don Oberdorfer, "Korea's DMZ-Security Undermined?," *WP,* May 27, 1975. The "needle in haystack" quote is from *USFK Hist. 1979,* 44, Secret (declassified 1995). For the psychics, see "US Spy Agencies Field Psychics to Pinpoint North Korean Tunnels Under DMZ," *KT,* December 2, 1995. Nathanial Thayer quote, Thayer interview, August 1, 1995.

Challenge from the North: Retrospective US military analysis, *USFK Hist. 1982,* 30, Secret (declassified 1995). Chinese officer quote, Xu Xian Zhang interview, July 8, 1993. Gates on "black hole," interview, May 16, 1994. Gregg on intelligence failure, Gregg interview, March 12, 1995. On JCS reduction of resources, see *USFK Hist. 1972,* 14, Secret (declassified 1995).

Kim Il Sung on preparations for war, "Excerpts from Interview with North Korean Premier on Policy Toward the U.S.," *NYT,* May 31, 1972; 1974 US intelligence estimate, *USFK Hist. 1974,* Secret (declassified 1995). Hollingsworth section is based on a telephone interview with Hollingsworth, August 26, 1995, as well as an interview with Gregg, June 21, 1993. See also John Saar, "The Army's Defiant Anachronism," *WP,* February 15, 1976. NSC objections, Thomas J. Barnes, "Secretary Schlesinger's Discussions in Seoul," National Security Council Memorandum, September 29, 1975, Secret (declassified 1995).

For the US Command's estimate of Soviet/Chinese intentions, *USFK Hist. 1974,* 21, Secret (declassified 1995). For Kim Il Sung's speech, *FBIS,* PRC International Affairs, April 21, 1975, A17. Kim had also used the formulation that there was nothing to lose but the DMZ on the eve of his Beijing journey, in a talk to the secretary of the Panama-Korea Association of Friendship and Culture. See *KIS Works,* 30:2. For the internal leadership situation in Beijing at the time, see Ezra F. Vogel, *Deng Xiaoping* (Harvard University Press, 2011), 116. Kim Il Sung's views on Vietnam are in CWIHP, Working Paper 53, 13. Chinese reaction, interview, former Chinese official, July 5, 1993. According to South Korean data, Chinese military assistance to North Korea diminished sharply following Kim's 1975 trip. On the Soviet reaction, Russian Foreign Ministry official, interview, April 15, 1994. For Kim's roundabout flight avoiding Soviet airspace, see Don Oberdorfer, "Korea: Progress and Danger," *WP,* June 29, 1975.

Echoes of Saigon: For Sneider on the review, *Emb. cable,* "Review of U.S. Policies Toward Korea," April 22, 1975, Secret (declassified 1996). His more considered judgment, *Emb. cable,* "U.S. Policy Towards Korea," June 24, 1975, Secret (declassified 1996). On the NSC interpretation of Ford's promise and objections to Schlesinger's statements, see Thomas J. Barnes, "Secretary Schlesinger's Discussions in Seoul," National Security Council Memorandum, November 29, 1975, Secret (declassified 1995). For Schlesinger comments to Park, Memorandum of Conversation Between President Park Chung Hee and Secretary of Defense James Schlesinger, August 27, 1975, Secret (declassified 1996).

For Park's actions in 1975, *USFK Hist. 1975,* 45, Confidential (declassified 1995). For defense budget impact, *The Military Balance* (International Institute of Strategic Studies, 1975–1976 through 1979–1980). The South Korean military buildup data are from the Institute of International Strategic Studies' *Military Balance,* 1975–1980.

The South Korean Nuclear Weapons Program: Oh Won Choi's comments, interview, June 24, 1996. See also his article "Blood Battle Between Park Chung Hee and Carter on Nuclear Development," *Shin Dong-A* (November 1994), in Korean. See also Robert Gillette, "U.S. Squelched Apparent S. Korean A-Bomb Drive," *Los Angeles Times,* November 4, 1978. For many years, this well-researched article, based in part on congressional testimony, has been a key source on the South Korean nuclear program. On the South Korean reprocessing effort, the best source is Cho Kap Che, "Nuclear Game on the Korean Peninsula," *Monthly Chosun* (June 1993), from which these details were taken. For the quote on "snapped into place," see Gillette, *Los Angeles Times,* November 4, 1978 (as above). Cleveland quote from Cleveland interview, March 8, 1994.

Embassy intelligence and Washington instructions, *DOS cable,* "ROK Plans to Develop Nuclear Weapons and Missiles," March 4, 1975, Secret/Nodis (declassified 1997).

The French ambassador's quote is from Steve Weissman and Herbert Krosney, *The Islamic Bomb* (Times Books, 1981), 252. Park's quote on nuclear capability is from Rowland Evans and Robert Novak, "Korea: Park's Inflexibility . . . ," *WP,* June 12, 1975. The National Security Council Memorandum on persuading Seoul, Memorandum for Secretary Kissinger from Jan M. Lodal and Dave Elliott, July 24, 1975, Secret (declassified 1995).

Schlesinger's meeting with Park, Schlesinger interview, July 6, 1995. For Sneider's "real consideration" statement, *Emb. cable,* December 16, 1975, Nodis (declassified 1996). On the Rumsfeld threat against the ROK, Cho Kap Che, "Interview with Jae Nae Sohn," *Monthly Chosun* (August 1995). For Sneider's postcrisis views, Memorandum of Conversation of Brent Scowcroft, Richard Sneider, William Gleysteen, September 15, 1976, Secret/Sensitive (declassified 1995). On Carter-Giscard diplomacy, see Zbigniew Brzezinski, *Power and Principle* (Farrar, Straus, and Giroux, 1983), 134.

On Park's plan to unveil the A-bomb, Son U Ryun, "Voice Testimony of Park Chung Hee," *Monthly Chosun* (March 1993), in Korean. For continuing development, "95 Percent Development of Nuclear Weapons as of 1978," *Joong-ang Ilbo,* October 2, 1993, in Korean; "Korea Close to N-bomb Development in Late 1970s," *KH,* October 6, 1995.

Murder in the Demilitarized Zone: For this section, I relied heavily on materials obtained under mandatory declassification review from the Gerald Ford Presidential Library and from the Department of State under the Freedom of Information Act, as well as interviews with a number of former officials who were on the scene in Korea or Washington. Three books were also of great value: Richard G. Head, Frisco W. Short, and Robert C. McFarlane (the last a future White House national security adviser), *Crisis Resolution: Presidential Decision Making in the Mayaguez and Korean Confrontations* (Westview Press, 1978), which covers Washington policy making; Colonel Conrad DeLateur, *Murder at Panmunjom: The Role of the Theater Commander in Crisis Resolution,* research paper for the Senior Seminar, Foreign Service Institute, 1987, dealing primarily with General Stilwell's role; and Major Wayne A. Kirkbride, *DMZ: A Story of the Panmunjom Axe Murder* (Holly, 1984), which deals with the episode as seen by US officers and men at the DMZ.

The CIA report, titled *DMZ Incident,* was dated August 18, 1976, Top Secret (declassified 1996). The discussion at the WASAG meeting was taken from the minutes of the meeting obtained through the Ford Presidential Library, Secret (declassified 1995). For the historical buildup cable, ComUSKorea to AIG Washington, August 18, 1976, Confidential (declassified 1996). For the warning effort by intelligence analysts, see Head, Short, and McFarlane, *Crisis Resolution,* 155. For Hyland's recommendation and discussion of punitive measures, see Memorandum for Brent Scowcroft from W. G. Hyland, August 18, 1976, Top Secret/Exclusively Eyes Only (declassified 1994).

On military views of punitive actions, see JCS Assessment and Addendum, Top Secret (declassified 1994). Scowcroft's "wimpish" quote is from Scowcroft interview, March 29, 1995. For military "handwringing," William Hyland interview, May 15, 1995. Ford's summary quote is from Head, Short, and McFarlane, *Crisis Resolution,* 193.

For the Pyongyang radio programming and blackout, US Liaison Office Beijing to SecState Washington, "Panmunjom Incident and Situation in Pyongyang," August 21, 1976, Confidential (declassified 1994). See also *South-North Dialogue in Korea* (International Cultural Society, November 1976), 64. On the military precautions in the DPRK, Colonel Choi Ju Hwal, a high-ranking DPRK defector, interview, June 24, 1996. For Ho Dam quote, AmEmbassy Colombo to SecState Washington, August 20, 1976, Unclassified.

Stilwell's reaction, cable from Stilwell to JCS, August 19, 1976, Secret (declassified 1995). Park's quotes are from Park Chung Hee, "Blue House Diary," *Minju Ilbo,* November 24, 1989, in Korean. Stilwell quote on Park, cable from CINCUNC Korea (Stilwell) to JCS, August 19, 1976, Secret (declassified 1995). On the arms of the tae kwon do group, Lieutenant General John Cushman telephone interview, May 4, 1995. Park quote on retaliation, *Emb. cable,* August 20, 1976, Secret (declassified 1994).

Stilwell's battle plan is set out in his cable to the JCS, August 19, 1976, Secret (declassified 1995). On North Korean notification, see DeLateur, *Murder at Panmunjom,* 20. Peter Hayes, *Pacific Powderkeg* (Lexington Books, 1991), 60, on "blew their minds."

Kim quote about North Korea not resisting, "Talk to a Professor of SOKA University in Japan," November 13, 1976, in *KIS Works,* 31:401. Scowcroft quote on the impact on US election, Scowcroft interview, March 29, 1995. Lee's comments on North Koreans, Jimmy Lee interview, July 8, 1995.

CHAPTER 4: THE CARTER CHILL

For Carter on the origin of his position, letter from Carter to me, March 12, 1994. Brzezinski quote from "President Carter's Troop Withdrawal from Korea," Harvard University case study by Major Joseph Wood, 1990.

Carter's Withdrawal: Origins and Implementation: For Ford review, National Security Study Memorandum 226, "Review of U.S. Policy Toward the Korean Peninsula," May 27, 1975, Secret/Nodis (declassified 1994). A notation in the Ford Presidential Library file says that Scowcroft approved suspension of work on the study on May 29, with no reason given. For Powell quote and other details of my 1977 research on the origins of Carter's ideas, Don Oberdorfer, "Carter's Decision on Korea Traced to Early 1975," *WP,* June 12, 1977. For Carter's views on stationing troops and his recollection of poll data, Carter letter to me, March 12, 1994. For priority given Korea, see Zbigniew Brzezinski, *Power and Principle* (Farrar, Straus, and Giroux, 1983), 51. Quotes from PRM-13 from "Presidential Review Memorandum/NSC 13," February 26, 1977, Secret (declassified 1991).

Abramowitz quote from interview, April 22, 1995. For Sneider and Vessey meeting with Park, *Emb. cable,* "Meeting with President Park," March 1, 1977, Secret (declassified 1996). Carter's informal instructions are on a handwritten memo from "J. C." to "Zbig and Cy," March 5, 1977, in the Carter Presidential Library, Secret (declassified 1996).

Talking points from "Meeting with South Korean Foreign Minister Pak Tong-Chin," Memo from Brzezinski to Carter, March 8, 1977, Secret (declassified 1996). Foreign Minister Park's version is from his memoir, *One Will on a Long Road* (Seoul Dong-A Publishing, 1992), in Korean. Failure to approach Soviets and Chinese, "Approach to Soviets and Chinese on Our Troop Withdrawals from Korea," Department of State Action Memorandum, June 10, 1977, Confidential (declassified 1996).

Quote on "missing dimension," "Talks Between South Korea and North Korea With or Without PRC Participation," Memorandum for the President (believed to be from Vance, about July 25, 1977), Secret (declassified 1996). For Carter's response, see Zbigniew Brzezinski, "Talks Between North Korea and South Korea," Memorandum for the Secretary of State, August 5, 1977, Secret (declassified 1996).

For Vance efforts in China, David Anderson for Peter Tarnoff, "Efforts to Promote a Dialogue Between South and North," Memorandum for Dr. Zbigniew Brzezinski,

September 2, 1977, Top Secret (declassified 1996). This was amplified by a telephone interview with William Gleysteen, who accompanied Vance to China, November 19, 1996. Carter atomic weapons quote, *WP,* March 21, 1976. For numbers of weapons at the time, William Arkin telephone interview, March 4, 1995. For Harold Brown's view on nuclear weapons, Brown interview, July 12, 1995.

"Rebellion" against the president, Richard Holbrooke interview, August 10, 1993. Harold Brown on limits of loyalty, interview, July 12, 1995. Cyrus Vance view, Vance interview, February 4, 1994. Zbigniew Brzezinski on Carter's beliefs, Brzezinski interview, March 1, 1994. Carter's withdrawal order, Presidential Directive/NSC-12, May 5, 1977, Top Secret/Sensitive/Eyes Only (declassified 1991). The nuclear aspects of the decision remain classified.

For Park's comment to reporters, Sunwoo Ryun, "Voice Testimony of Park Chung Hee," *Monthly Chosun* (March 1993), in Korean. For Park's position on withdrawal, former Korean official, interview, July 20, 1993. Brzezinski comments on "uphill battle" in Congress, Memorandum for the President from Zbigniew Brzezinski, "Congressional Reactions to Our Korean Policy," July 21, 1977, Confidential (declassified 1996).

Carter on cooperation with corruption probes, Memorandum from Robert Lipshutz and Zbigniew Brzezinski, "White House Role in Congressional Investigation of Korean Misdoings," June 23, 1977, Confidential (declassified 1997).

The Rich quote is from Robert G. Rich Jr., *U.S. Ground Force Withdrawal from Korea: A Case Study in National Security Decision Making,* Executive Seminar, Foreign Service Institute, June 1982. Carter comment to Brzezinski, Brzezinski interview, March 1, 1994; telephone conversation, March 3, 1994. For Harold Brown on aide's dilemma, letter to me, July 23, 1996.

For senior aides' meeting on withdrawal, Zbigniew Brzezinski Memorandum to the President, "Summary of April 11, 1978, Meeting on Korea and China," Secret (declassified 1996). Carter irritation with Brown, Brown interview, July 12, 1995, and Brzezinski interviews.

The View from Pyongyang: North Korea on nepotism, cited in Jae Kyu Park, "North Korean Policy Toward the United States," *Asian Perspectives* 5 (Fall–Winter 1981): 144. The history of North Korean efforts to negotiate with Washington is recounted in Michael Armacost Memorandum for Zbigniew Brzezinski, "Contacts and Communications with North Korea," February 28, 1977, Secret (declassified 1996); Douglas J. Bennett Jr., Draft Letter to Rep. Lester Wolff, April 28, 1978, Secret (declassified 1996); and Don Oberdorfer, "North Korea Rebuffs Carter's Bid to Open 3-Country Negotiations," *WP,* July 15, 1979.

For Kim's quotes on Carter, *KIS Works,* "Talk to the Delegation of the International Liaison Committee" (June 15, 1978), 33:257; and "Talk with the Chief Editor of the Japanese Political Magazine *Sekai,*" (October 21, 1978), 33:493.

For Kim's discussion with Honecker, "Transcript of Official Talks Between the Party and State Delegation of the GDR and North Korea in Pyongyang, 12/9–10/77," *SED Archive.* For CIA economic analysis, *Korea: The Economic Race Between the North and the South* (CIA, National Foreign Assessment Center, January 1978), i. On South Korean military spending, *The Military Balance* (International Institute of Strategic Studies, 1976 and 1977). Chinese troops near DPRK border, "Conversation Between Honecker and Kim, 5/31/84," *SED Archives.* US Command on North Korean infiltration, *USFK Hist. 1977,* 5455, Secret/Noforn (declassified 1995).

End of the Carter Withdrawal: The section on Armstrong's work is based on interviews with Armstrong, July 7 and 20, 1974, Evelyn Colbert, February 14, 1994, and Nathanial Thayer, August 1, 1995, former CIA national intelligence officers for

East Asia; Alan MacDougall, former DIA senior analyst for Korea, August 2, 1995; and an excellent case study, "President Carter's Troop Withdrawal from Korea," written for Harvard University in 1990 by Major Joseph Wood. For Vessey's intelligence request, *USFK Hist. 1978*, 57, Secret (declassified 1995). New North Korean estimate, *USFK Hist. 1980*, 17, Secret (declassified 1995). The Thayer quote is from Thayer interview, August 1, 1995.

On Carter's suspicion of intelligence, letter to me, March 12, 1994. Quote from new review, Presidential Review Memorandum/NSC-15, November 22, 1979, Secret (declassified 1991).

Carter's plan for meeting of Park and Kim, Nicholas Piatt interview, February 10, 1994; William Gleysteen interview, September 29, 1993. Carter-Deng talks, Jimmy Carter, *Keeping Faith* (Bantam Books, 1982), 205–206. See also *U.S.-PRC Chronology*, 75. Carter on three-way talks, Gleysteen interview.

For Carter-Park bilateral talks, interviews with Piatt, February 10, 1994, and Holbrooke, August 10, 1993. Also White House Memorandum of Conversation, Secret (declassified 1997). For argument in car, interviews with Gleysteen, Vance, Brown, Brzezinski, Holbrooke, Piatt, and Rich as well as Vance, *Hard Choices* (Simon and Schuster, 1993). For Carter proselytizing Park, "Private Meeting with President Park, Seoul, Korea," 7/1/79, notes by Carter, from Carter Library. Final strength figures from USFK, November 25, 1996. On nuclear weapons, Arkin telephone interview, March 24, 1995.

CHAPTER 5: ASSASSINATION AND AFTERMATH

On the postassassination situation, see Gleysteen's first dispatch, *Emb. cable*, "Initial Reflections on Post–Park Chung Hee Situation in Korea," October 28, 1979, Secret (declassified 1993). Gleysteen's postmidnight actions, interview, October 12, 1993. On details of the White House meeting, see Chung Chin Suk, "Power Vacuum in Korea," *Hankook Ilbo*, December 13, 1996, in Korean. On the last days of Park and other late-1970s developments in Korea, I have relied on Koon Woo Nam's useful book, *South Korean Politics: The Search for Political Consensus and Stability* (University Press of America, 1989).

Embassy on Pusan protests, *Emb. cable*, "Embassy Thoughts on Current Mood Following Declaration of Martial Law in Pusan," October 20, 1979, Confidential (declassified 1993). US warnings about Kim Young Sam's expulsion, NSC Memorandum from Piatt to Brzezinski, "Opposition Leader Ousted," October 4, 1979, Confidential (declassified 1997). Brown-Gleysteen meeting with Park, *Emb. cable*, "Meeting with President Park Regarding Domestic Political Crisis," October 18, 1979, Confidential (declassified 1993).

"Pervasive worry" quote, *Emb. cable*, "Initial Reflections on Post–Park Chung Hee Situation in Korea," October 28, 1979, Secret (declassified 1993). Extraordinary security measures, William Chapman, "Park's Legacy: Prosperity and Fear," *WP*, November 3, 1979. On the absence of grief, *Emb. cable*, "Surprisingly Few Mourn Park Chung Hee," November 14, 1979, Confidential (declassified 1993). Holbrooke's quote, Holbrooke interview, August 10, 1993.

Kang Sin Ok quote, interview, November 25, 1994. Gleysteen on noncomplicity, *Emb. cable*, "Charges of Complicity in President Park's Death," November 19, 1979, Secret (declassified 1993). Young's search, James V. Young, manuscript for *Monthly Chosun* (1994). Gleysteen on Kim Jae Kyu, Gleysteen interview, September 9, 1993. Kim Il Sung's reaction, *KIS Works*, "Let Us Strengthen the People's Army," 34:419. On US advice to Choi, *Emb. cable*, "Korea Focus: Meeting with Acting President, November 29," November 29, 1979, Secret (declassified 1993).

The Coming of Chun Doo Hwan: For a report on the events of 12/12 as they emerged from the 1996 trial of Chun and Roh, see "Arrest of Two Ex-Presidents and May 18 Special Law," *Korea Annual 1996* (Yonhap News Agency, 1996), 46–55. My account of 12/12 is based on interviews with Gleysteen and Wickham and on the written account by James V. Young, who was deputy US military attaché at the time. Gleysteen's "bad news" cable is *Emb. cable,* "Younger ROK Officers Grab Power Positions," December 13, 1979, Secret (declassified 1993).

For Chun's family background, Sanghyun Yoon (Chun's son-in-law), "South Korea's *Nordpolitik* with Special Reference to Its Relationship with China," PhD diss. (George Washington University, 1994), 281. Chun's stoplight anecdote, Chun Doo Hwan interview, July 22, 1980. For Hana-hoe, see "Army Reforms Sweep Hana-hoe into History," *Newsreview,* March 9, 1996. Gleysteen on Chun, Gleysteen interview, October 12, 1993. Walker on Chun, Walker interview, February 18, 1995. Gleysteen exchange with academic, *Emb. cable,* "Telegram from Professor Choi and Response," December 19, 1979.

Gleysteen quote on not reversing coup, *Emb. cable,* "Discussions with the New Army Leadership Group," January 26, 1979, Secret (declassified 1993). On Gleysteen-Chun initial meeting, *Emb. cable,* "Korea Focus: Discussion with MG Chon Tu Hwan," December 15, 1979, Secret (declassified 1993). Carter letter and other details from *U.S. Government Statement on the Events in Kwangju, ROK, in May 1980,* June 19, 1989, supplemented by James V. Young's memoir written for *Monthly Chosun* in 1994. Gleysteen on US dilemma, *Emb. cable,* "Korea—Ambassador's Policy Assessment," January 29, 1980, Secret (declassified 1993).

The Kwangju Uprising: Embassy reaction to KCIA appointment, Gleysteen interview, February 10, 1997. Gleysteen on ROK contingency plans, *Emb. cable,* "Korea Focus: Building Tensions and Concern over Student Issue," May 8, 1980, Secret (declassified 1993). State response, *DOS cable,* "Korea Focus: Tensions in the ROK," May 8, 1980, Secret (declassified 1993). Chun's statement, meeting with Wickham, *U.S. Government Statement,* 10.

Intelligence officer's revelation, Park Hee Chung, "Chun Exaggerates North Korean Threat," *Hankuk Ilbo,* December 13, 1995, in Korean. The flash cable, *Emb. cable,* "Crackdown in Seoul," May 17, 1980, Secret (declassified 1993). Contradiction of Chun and Kim Dae Jung, *Emb. cable,* "Yet Another Assessment of ROK Stability and Political Development," March 12, 1980, Secret (declassified 1993).

Gleysteen on "incendiary arrest," *Emb. cable,* "May 17 Meeting with Blue House SYG Choi Kwang Soo," May 17, 1980, Secret (declassified 1993). Warnberg and Huntley eyewitness account from Kwangju from Tim Warnberg, "The Kwangju Uprising: An Inside View," *Korean Studies* 11 (1987). Gleysteen on "massive insurrection," *Emb. cable,* "The Kwangju Crisis," May 21, 1980, Secret (declassified 1993). NSC meeting on Kwangju, "Summary of Conclusions," National Security Council Memorandum, Secret (declassified 1994).

Regarding operational control and the US role, see *U.S. Government Statement.* The troop-movement cable, Defense Intelligence Agency, "ROKG Shifts SF Units," May 8, 1980, Classified (declassified 1993). Tape recording of Wickham interview courtesy Sam Jameson. See also Sam Jameson, "U.S. Support Claimed for S. Korea's Chon," *Los Angeles Times,* August 8, 1980. Choi's regrets, "Choi Terms Kwangju Incident 'Mistake,'" *KT,* August 20, 1996.

On US "cool and aloof" policy, Gleysteen interview, October 12, 1993. For US intelligence, Gregg and Aaron comments, Gregg to Brzezinski memo, July 1, 1979, Secret (declassified 1997).

The Fight to Save Kim Dae Jung: Lilley on Kim Dae Jung, Lilley interview, June 8, 1993. Gregg on Chun's "terrific pressure," Gregg interview, March 12, 1995.

ROK contemporaneous notes of the discussions were published in Kwan Young Ki, "Behind the Scenes: Chun Doo Hwan–Reagan Relationship," *Monthly Chosun* (August 1992). Chung Ho Young on Kim "card," Chung interview, April 20, 1994. On Allen's discussions regarding Kim Dae Jung, Allen interviews, December 27, 1993, and January 14, 1994, plus interviews with Sohn Jang Nae on April 21 and 29, 1994, and with Chung Ho Young, April 20, 1994.

Gleysteen on Chun's visit to Washington, *Emb. cable*, "Agenda Suggestions for Reagan-Chun Meeting," January 22, 1981, Secret (declassified 1996). Haig views, Memorandum for the President from Alexander Haig, January 29, 1981, Secret (declassified 1993). The US buildup data are from *USFK Hist.*, "Personnel Strength in Korea," November 25, 1996. F-16 offer, *DOS cable*, "President Chun's Meeting with President Reagan, February 2, 1981," February 12, 1981, Secret (declassified 1996). For Carter's refusal to approve F-16 sale, Memorandum for the President, "Harold Brown's November Asian Trip: Decision to Proceed with F-16 Sale to Korea," November 1, 1978, Top Secret (declassified 1997). Reagan's quote on dissenters, Zbigniew Brzezinski interview, March 1, 1994. See also Jimmy Carter, *Keeping Faith* (Bantam Books, 1982), 578.

CHAPTER 6: TERROR AND TALK

An authoritative account of the fate of KAL 007 is Murray Sayle, "Closing the File on Flight 007," *New Yorker*, December 12, 1993. On Soviet decisions about trading, Georgi Toloraya interview, May 4, 1994. Details on the Rangoon bombers and the bomb are taken from the official account of the Burmese government, as published in the *Guardian* newspaper, Rangoon; and from the Burmese government report to the UN General Assembly, reprinted in *KH*, October 4, 1984. Koh on the African assassination plot, Koh Yong Hwan interview, October 25, 1993.

On Chun's amended schedule in Rangoon, Lho Shin Yong interview, May 27, 1993; and Richard L. Walker interview, February 18, 1995. On North Korean plans after Chun's assassination, see Don Oberdorfer, "N. Korea Reportedly Set Coordinated Offensives After Rangoon Blast," *WP*, December 2, 1983.

Proposal to bomb North Korea in retaliation, Kang Kyong Shik (who had been minister of finance before Rangoon and was later Blue House chief of staff), conversation in Washington, March 22, 1995. Chun on his talk to ROK commanders, Kim Sung Ik, *Voice Testimony of Chun Doo Hwan* (*Chosun Ilbo*, 1992), in Korean. Chun statements to Walker, Walker interview, March 30, 1995; also Harry Dunlop (former US political counselor, Seoul), interview, January 12, 1994. Reagan's quotes, "Presidential Visit Meetings in Seoul," Memorandum from Assistant Secretary Paul Wolfowitz to Secretary Shultz, November 19, 1993, Secret/Nodis (declassified 1995). The censure offer was in Shultz's bilateral talks with Korean foreign minister Lee Won Kyong.

The Negotiating Track: The Kissinger proposal was authorized by President Nixon in National Security Decision Memorandum 25-1, March 29, 1974, Top Secret/Sensitive (declassified 1996), which also involved substitution of a US-ROK Command for the UN Command and negotiation of a nonaggression pact between the two Koreas. It evidently was discussed by Kissinger with the Chinese in March 1974, October 1974, and October 1975. See *US-PRC Chronology*, 40, 45, 54.

For the Deng-Weinberger talks, *US-PRC Chronology*, 110. For Deng's reaction to the Rangoon bombing, Ralph Clough, *Embattled Korea* (Westview, 1987), 269. For Deng's reaction to the bombing, see Jonathan D. Pollack, *No Exit: North Korea, Nuclear Weapons, and International Security* (Routledge, 2011), 90.

For the early history of the three-way talks proposal, see Kim Hak Joon, *Unification Policies of North and South Korea, 1945–1991* (Seoul National University Press, 1992), esp. 380–385. On the continued promotion of the three-way plan, William Gleysteen interview, September 13, 1995. On US backing for three-way talks, Don Oberdorfer, "North Korea Says U.S. Proposals Merit Discussion," *WP,* October 8, 1984. Wolfowitz on "boilerplate," Wolfowitz interview, July 19, 1994. Ho Dam's comments were in his report to the opening session of the Supreme People's Assembly on January 25, 1985. Kim Il Sung on "exposing" the United States, transcript of conversation between Kim Il Sung and Erich Honecker, May 30, 1984, *SED Archives.*

Floods and Face-to-Face Talks: Haberman dispatch, "North Korea Delivers Flood Aid Supplies to South," *NYT,* September 30, 1984. On Liem's trip, Yang Chin Young, "Kim Il Sung Whom I Met," *Joong-ang Monthly* (April 1989), in Korean; also Sohn Jang Nae interview, April 29, 1994. On contention in Pyongyang, see "Kim Endorses Dialogue Amid Signs of Contention on Issue," *FBIS Trends* (CIA, Foreign Broadcast Information Service, January 3, 1985), Confidential (declassified 1995). For details of the Ho Dam–Chang Se Dong trips, see Park Bo Kyon, "Chang Se Dong–Ho Dam, Each Visited Pyongyang-Seoul," *Joong-ang Ilbo,* January 7, 1994, and following days, in Korean. A transcript of the talks in the South was published as "Secret Talks Between Chun Doo Hwan and Ho Dam," *Monthly Chosun* (November 1996), in Korean.

On Chun shutting down the nuclear weapons program, Kim Jin Hyun (former ROK minister of science and technology), interview, July 23, 1993. Sohn quote on talks, Sohn interview, April 29, 1994. US intelligence official on talks, interview, May 14, 1994. Kim Il Sung on "great losses" from Team Spirit, stenographic transcript of "Official Friendship Visit of North Korean Party and State Delegation to the GDR," May 30, 1984, *SED Archives.*

Kim Il Sung and the Soviet Connection: For Stalin's role in the armistice, Kathryn Weathersby, "Stalin and a Negotiated Settlement in Korea, 1950–53," paper prepared for the conference "New Evidence on the Cold War in Asia," Hong Kong, January 1996. For Kim's situation in the Sino-Soviet split, see Dae-Sook Suh, *Kim Il Sung* (Columbia University Press, 1988), 176–210. Tkachenko quote, Tkachenko interviews, October 24, 1993, and April 12, 1994.

For Central Committee quote on DPRK, Eugene Bazhanov, "Soviet Policy Toward North Korea," *Russia and Korea Toward the 21st Century* (Sejong Institute, 1992), 65. Hu Yaobang to Reagan, *US-PRC Chronology,* 111. Rakhmanin on Kim in Moscow, Rakhmanin interview, April 8, 1994. Gorbachev on Kim's "socialist monarchy," *Erinnerungen* [Memories] (Siedler Verlag, 1995), the German-language version of his memoirs.

Kim's comments in Moscow 1984, "On the Visit of North Korea's Party and State Delegation Led by Kim Il Sung to the USSR," May 29, 1984, *SED Archives,* in German and Russian. Kim's worry about China, from transcript of "Official Friendship Visit of North Korean Party and State Delegation to the GDR," March 31, 1984, in German. Soviet official's quote from "On the Visit of North Korea's Party and State Delegation." Soviet agreement to build light-water reactors is in Pollack, *No Exit,* 94, citing Georgiy Kaurov in *The North Korean Nuclear Program,* edited by Clay Moltz and Alexandre Mansurov, 18–19. The North Koreans had been badgering the Soviets to supply them with a nuclear power plant since at least 1967. See *CWIHP,* Working Paper 53, 42.

The USSR-DPRK economic data are from an excellent analysis by Nicholas Eberstadt, Marc Rubin, and Albina Tretyakova, "The Collapse of Soviet and Russian Trade with the DPRK, 1989–1993," *Korean Journal of National Unification* 4 (1995). Details of Soviet military aid agreements in 1984 and 1986 from Joseph M. Ha, Ha interview, February 21, 1995. Record of overflights, *USFK Hist. 1985*, 25, Secret (declassified 1995). Satellite avoidance, *USFK Hist.*, with chapter headings on SATRAN, esp. 1979 report, 51.

For the protests by North Korea in Moscow, see the outstanding scholarship of Eugene Bazhanov and his wife, Natalia Bazhanova (a Russian expert on Korean affairs who had access to Central Committee archives), esp. her chapter, "North Korea and Seoul-Moscow Relations," in *Korea and Russia Toward the 21st Century* (Sejong Institute, 1992). The Georgi Kim quote is from Eugene Bazhanov, "Soviet Policy Towards South Korea Under Gorbachev," *Korea and Russia Toward the 21st Century*, 65. On Kim Il Sung on flying, Vadim Tkachenko interview, October 24, 1993. For Kim's quote and attitude in Gorbachev meetings, Vadim Medvedev, *Collapse* (International Relations, 1994), in Russian. For the May 1986 Politburo document, Bazhanov, "Soviet Policy," 95. For Gorbachev's surprising declaration, Tkachenko interview, October 24, 1993.

For the Gorbachev quote on the situation in 1986, Mikhail Gorbachev interview, April 13, 1994. On North Korea as a privileged ally, Gorbachev, *Erinnerungen*. USSR weapons promises, Ha interview, February 15, 1995. For aid levels, see Han Yong Sup, "China's Security Cooperation with North Korea: Retrospects and Prospects," paper prepared for conference "Sino-Korean Relations and Their Policy Implications," American Enterprise Institute and George Washington University, December 2–3, 1993, and additional details provided to me by Han. On Kim's view of Gorbachev as a revisionist, Koh Young Whan interview, October 25, 1993.

CHAPTER 7: THE BATTLE FOR DEMOCRACY IN SEOUL

For excellent descriptions of the 1987 events, see Manwoo Lee, *The Odyssey of Korean Democracy* (Praeger, 1990); and Sang Joon Kim, "Characteristic Features of Korean Democratization," *Asian Perspective* (Fall–Winter 1994).

Chun's Succession Struggle: Chun to Walker, Walker interview, February 18, 1995. Lee Soon Ja views, from my journal, February 1981, based on a conversation with the first lady while sitting next to her at the luncheon for Chun at the National Press Club. Regarding the Ilhae Foundation, see Don Oberdorfer, "Korean Conundrum," *WP*, May 25, 1986. On the forced contributions, see Donald Kirk, *Korean Dynasty* (M. E. Sharpe, 1994), 273. The Shultz quote is from his memoir, *Turmoil and Triumph* (Scribner's, 1993), 977–998. Shultz's concerns were expressed to me in an interview, March 16, 1995.

Chun pledge to Reagan, "Presidential Visit Meetings in Seoul," Memorandum from Assistant Secretary of State Paul Wolfowitz to Secretary Shultz, November 19, 1983, Secret/Nodis (declassified 1995). Chun quote to Blue House reporters, *KH*, January 9, 1988. For the Seoul National University poll, Se Hee Yoo, "The International Context of U.S.-Korean Relations: Special Focus on the 'Critical Views of the United States' in Korea Since 1980," in *United States–Korea Relations* (Institute of East Asian Studies, 1986).

Shultz on Sigur speech, Gaston Sigur interview, September 16, 1993. On dominance of Korea story in the American press, Don Oberdorfer, "U.S. Policy Toward Korea in the 1987 Crisis Compared with Other Allies," in *Korea-US. Relations* (Institute of East Asian Studies, 1988). US warning to Pyongyang, Michael Armacost telephone interview, August 9, 1993. Pyongyang reaction, "Pyongyang Maintains Cautious Posture Toward Situation in South," *FBIS Analysis Note* (CIA, Foreign Broadcast Information Service, June 29, 1984).

Reagan's letter to Chun, dated June 17, 1989, in author's possession. Dunlop on "stone-walling," Dunlop interview, January 12, 1994. Riot details are from John Burgess, "Seoul Says Crackdown 'Inevitable,'" *WP,* June 19, 1987. On June 19 meeting and Chun's previous statements to aides, Kim Sung Ik, *Voice Testimony of Chun Doo Hwan* (*Chosun Ilbo,* 1992), in Korean. Lilley's presentation to Chun, Lilley interviews, June 8, 1993, and February 17, 1997. Chun on suspending the mobilization order, Kim Sung Ik, *Voice Testimony.* Chung Ho Yong on the military views, Chung interview, April 20, 1994.

Roh Tae Woo's recollection, Roh interview, October 21, 1993. Chun quote to Sigur, Sigur interview, September 16, 1993. Roh's near apology for Kwangju, Hyun Hong Choo interview, October 17, 1995. Chun camp's version of June 29 origins: "The Truth of the 6/29 Declaration," *Monthly Chosun* (January 1992), in Korean. Lee Soon Ja's declaration, "Wife Says Chun Is Real Architect of the June 29, 1987, Declaration," *KT,* December 19, 1996.

The Election of 1987: Chun's doubts about Roh, Kim Yoon Hwan interview, October 18, 1993. Kim Young Sam's age has been a source of consistent confusion. He told Blue House reporters his birth date was misregistered at his birthplace and was actually December 4 (on the lunar calendar), 1927. "Kim's Birthday," *KT,* January 24, 1996.

Kim Young Sam's mother's death, Kim interview, April 14, 1995. Cholla's disadvantages, Manwoo Lee, *The Odyssey of Korean Democracy* (Praeger, 1990), 49–51. Lee quote on electoral territoriality from Lee, *Odyssey,* 47.

CHAPTER 8: THE GREAT OLYMPIC COMING-OUT PARTY

The Coming of the Olympics: On Park Chung Hee's instructions, Park Seh Jik, *The Seoul Olympics* (Bellew, 1991), 5. On Korea's and Chung Ju Yung's efforts, Mark Clifford, *Troubled Tiger* (M. E. Sharpe, 1994), 289. For a full account of Chung's remarkable career, see Donald Kirk, *Korean Dynasty* (M. E. Sharpe, 1994). *Rodong Sinmun* quote, Park, *Seoul Olympics,* 8. Hwang Jang Yop on political significance, his letter to Hermann Axen (secretary of SED Central Committee), June 19, 1985, *SED Archives,* in German. Shevardnadze quote from "About the Visits of Soviet Foreign Minister Eduard Shevardnadze to North Korea and the Mongolian People's Republic," January 28, 1986, *SED Archives,* Confidential, in Russian and German. Maretzki quotes from his cable to Berlin, May 11, 1987, *SED Archives.* North Korea "cornered" quote from Parks, *Seoul Olympics,* 20.

The Bombing of KAL Flight 858: My account is based on Kim Hyun Hui interview, October 25, 1993; her memoir, *The Tears of My Soul* (William Morrow, 1993); a chapter in Eileen MacDonald's *Shoot the Women First* (Random House, 1993); and *Investigation Findings: Explosion of Korean Air Flight 858* (KOIS, January 1988). Kim's "military order" quote, Kim interview, October 25, 1993. The Shevardnadze quote is from Shultz, *Turmoil and Triumph,* 981.

The Rise of Nordpolitik: For Roh's interview, Don Oberdorfer and Fred Hiatt, "S. Korean President Urges End to Isolation of North," *WP,* July 2, 1988. On the early *Nordpolitik* policy making, see Park Chul Un, "Northern Policy Makes Progress Toward Unification," *KH,* March 13, 1991. Kim's July 1988 reaction, "Visit of an Official Military Delegation of the GDR to North Korea, Between July 19 and 13, 1988," *SED Archives.*

Kim Woo Choong in Hungary, from an unpublished manuscript furnished me by Daewoo in December 1994, "The Civilian Ambassador Kim Woo Choong"; Chong Bong Uk, "Ties with Budapest Result from Spadework," *KH,* January 29, 1988; and interviews with several former Korean officials. Data on ROK-Hungarian economic deals from a confidential source. Bazhanova report from "North Korea and Seoul-Moscow Relations," in *Korea and Russia Toward the 21st Century* (Sejong Institute, 1992), 334. On Soviet-ROK connections at the Olympics, see James F. Larson and Heung-Soo Park, *Global Television and the Politics of the Seoul Olympics* (Westview Press, 1993). For the booty the Russians took home, see the unpublished Daewoo manuscript, "The Civilian Ambassador Kim Woo Choong."

Washington Launches a Modest Initiative: State Department view, *DOS cable,* "ROK President Roh's Visit: US Policy Re N. Korea," October 25, 1988, Secret (declassified 1995). Sigur quote, Sigur interview, September 16, 1993. Clark quote, Clark interview, June 23, 1993. State cable on "staying in step," *DOS cable,* "ROK President Roh's Visit: U.S. Policy Re N. Korea," October 25, 1988, Secret (declassified 1995).

State Department instructions, *DOS cable,* "Policy/Regulation Changes Regarding North Korea: Informing Seoul, Tokyo, Moscow, and Beijing," October 28, 1988, Confidential (declassified 1995). Burkhardt meetings, Burkhardt interview, September 28, 1993. See also B. C. Koh, "North Korea's Policy Toward the United States," in *Foreign Relations of North Korea* (Sejong Institute, 1994), a particularly helpful account of US–North Korean diplomacy prior to 1994.

CHAPTER 9: MOSCOW SWITCHES SIDES

My account of the Politburo meeting on November 10, 1988, including quotes, is from notes by Gorbachev aide Anatoly Chernyayev. Minister's quote on the ROK as "most promising partner," Eugene Bazhanov, "Soviet Policy Towards South Korea Under Gorbachev," *Korea and Russia Toward the 21st Century* (Sejong Institute, 1992), 94n.

The Roots of Change: Soviet news reports and journalists' quotes from Yassen N. Zassoursky, "The XXIV Olympic Games in Seoul and Their Effect on the Soviet Media and the Soviet Public," in *Seoul Olympics and the Global Community* (Seoul Olympics Memorial Association, 1992). Pravda quote from Park Seh Jik, *The Seoul Olympics* (Bellew, 1991), 175. Muscovites survey, Park, *Seoul Olympics,* 175. The "Welcoming Soviets" quote is from Bazhanov, "Soviet Policy," 96.

The North-South economic comparisons are from Kwang Eui Gak's monumental study, *The Korean Economies* (Clarendon Press, 1993). Soviet aid figures are found on 204. The subsidized trade figures are from an excellent account by Nicholas Eberstadt, Marc Rubin, and Albina Tretyakova, "The Collapse of Soviet and Russian Trade with the DPRK, 1989–1993," *Korean Journal of National Unification* 4 (1995). The Soviet memorandum to the DPRK is quoted in Natalia Bazhanova, "North Korea and Seoul-Moscow Relations," in *Korea and Russia Toward the 21st Century,* 332. For the ROK proposed loans, Kyungsoo Lho, "Seoul-Moscow Relations," *Asian Survey* (December 1989): 1153.

Shevardnadze's visit to Pyongyang, personal impressions of Pyongyang from Pavel Palazchenko, *My Years with Gorbachev and Shevardnadze* (Pennsylvania State University Press, 1997), 111. For Shevardnadze's report, "The Main Results of Eduard Shevardnadze's Visit to Japan, the Philippines, and North Korea," memorandum of February 2, 1989, *SED Archives.* Shevardnadze's "I am a communist" quote, Bazhanova, "North Korea and Seoul-Moscow Relations," 332–333.

Gorbachev Meets Roh: The Gorbachev memoirs quote is from the German version, *Erinnerungen* (Siedler Verlag, 1995). Gorbachev on the process of change, Gorbachev interview, April 13, 1994. Roh on "smelling their intention," Roh interview, July 22, 1993. Lifting of Soviet restrictions, Bazhanov, "Soviet Policy Towards South

Korea Under Gorbachev," 97. ROK industrialists in Moscow, Kim Hak Joon, "South Korea–Soviet Union Normalization Revisited," prepared for the Conference on Northeast Asia and Russia, Sigur Center for East Asian Studies, March 17–18, 1994, 11. "Inventing new reasons" quote, Georgi Ostroumov interview, April 12, 1994.

Chernyayev quote from Chernyayev interview, April 12, 1994. Gorbachev–Li Peng exchange, Bazhanov, "Soviet Policy Towards South Korea Under Gorbachev," 92–93. Impact of Moscow trip on Kim Young Sam's political fortunes, Yoon Sang Hyun, "South Korea's *Nordpolitik* with Special Reference to Its Relationship with China," PhD diss. (George Washington University, 1994), 255. Tkachenko quote from Tkachenko interview, October 24, 1993. On the appeal to Germany, see Philip Zelikow and Condoleezza Rice, *Germany Unified and Europe Transformed* (Harvard University Press, 1995), 256ff.

Dobrynin quote and activities, Dobrynin interviews, June 22, 1993, and February 23, 1994. Roh Tae Woo on Soviet desperation, Roh interview, July 26, 1993. Gregg on "stake through the heart," *Emb. cable,* "Roh Tae Woo on the Eve of Meetings with Soviet and U.S. Leaders," June 1, 1990, Confidential (declassified 1995). Sensitivity about Soviet consulate, Kim Hak Joon, "South Korea–Soviet Union Normalization Reconsidered," 13. Gorbachev on "radical change," Bazhanov, "Soviet Policy Towards South Korea Under Gorbachev," 103. Kim Jong In quote, Kim interview, April 26, 1994.

Soviet meeting notes, "M. S. Gorbachev's Conversation with Roh Tae Woo in San Francisco," obtained by author from the Gorbachev archive, Moscow, in Russian. For Roh's requests to Gorbachev, "M. S. Gorbachev's Conversation." See also *Emb. cable,* "MOFA Readout on Roh-Gorbachev Meeting," June 12, 1990, Secret (declassified 1995). Pyongyang's reaction, Bazhanova, "North Korea and Seoul-Moscow Relations," 336. Dobrynin quote on photograph, Dobrynin interview, June 22, 1993. Roh on the road to Pyongyang, "Opening Remarks by President Roh," *Yonhap Annual* (1990), 410.

The Shevardnadze Mission: My account of Shevardnadze's September 1990 trip to Pyongyang comes from interviews with three members of the Soviet delegation who were present. Shevardnadze on the "most difficult, most unpleasant" mission from former Soviet diplomat, interview, July 7, 1993. Bessmertnykh quote, Bessmertnykh interview, April 14, 1994. Chernyayev quotes from Chernyayev interview, April 12, 1994.

Choi's argument to Gorbachev, Choi interview, April 25, 1995. Shevardnadze on "our friends," Sergei Tarasenko interview, April 10, 1994. *Rodong Sinmun* on Soviet perfidy, "Commentary Denounces USSR Diplomatic Ties," *FBIS-EAS,* October 5, 1990, 8. Economic data from Nicholas Eberstadt et al., "The Collapse of Soviet and Russian Trade with the DPRK, 1989–93," *Korean Journal of National Unification* 4 (1995); Young Namkoong, "An Assessment of North Korean Economic Capability," in *Economic Problems of National Unification* (1993); *North Korea: Insights into Economy and Living* (Korean-German Chamber of Commerce and Industry, 1991), in German.

"How Long Will the Red Flag Fly?": On the Korea desk reaction, "North Korean Reaction to Roh-Gorbachev Meeting," Department of State Briefing Paper, June 1, 1990, Confidential (declassified 1995). For the INR report, Douglas P. Mulholland, "Soviet Initiative in Asia," Information Memorandum, May 30, 1990, Confidential (declassified 1995). On State's view, "Talking Points for the President's Use in His June 6 Meeting with President Roh," Memorandum for the White House from the Department of State, June 2, 1990, Secret (declassified 1995).

The account of the Chinese meeting with Kim is from a former Chinese diplomat, interviews, January 23 and October 4, 1993. For Kanemaru's trip, my account is based on interviews with a senior parliamentarian and a Foreign Ministry official who accompanied Kanemaru; interviews and writings of Hajimi Izumi and Masao Okonogi, leading Japanese experts on Korea; and an excellent reconstruction by Ushio Shioda, "What Was Discussed by the 'Kanemaru North Korean Mission'?," *Bungei Shunju* (August 1994). On the shift in Japanese policy, see B. C. Koh, "North Korea's Approaches to the United States and Japan," draft paper for a conference, "The Two Koreas in World Affairs," November 1996. On "yellow skins" and "white skins," Japanese official, interview, May 21, 1993. On Kanemaru's apology to the United States, Michael H. Armacost, *Friends or Rivals?* (Columbia University Press, 1996), 147.

An account of the secret 1990 meetings can be found in "Secret Meeting Between Suh Dong Won and Kim Il Sung and Kim Jong Il," *Monthly Chosun* (August 1994), in Korean. This account was verified for me by a former high-ranking ROK official. For Kim's conciliatory speech, see *FBIS–East Asia*, May 24, 1990. On the disarmament proposal, William Taylor, "Shifting Korean Breezes," *Washington Times*, June 6, 1990.

Soviet–South Korean Economic Negotiations: On Medvedev's mission, see his *Collapse* (International Relations, 1994), in Russian. Roh on "exerting influence" from "M. S. Gorbachev with the President of ROK (Roh Tae Woo)," December 14, 1990, notes of conversation, from the Gorbachev archive, Moscow, in Russian. Roh's "don't worry" quote is from Georgi Toloraya interview, October 19, 1993. On the Saudi loan, see James A. Baker, *The Politics of Diplomacy* (G. P. Putnam's Sons, 1995), 294–295. For Roh's "out of the question" quote, Kang Sung-chul, "'Foundation Laid for Ending Cold War': Roh," *KH*, December 18, 1990.

The Maslyukov exchange is from a confidential source. For military supply data, Nicholas Eberstadt et al., "The Collapse of Soviet and Russian Trade with the DPRK, 1989–1993," *Korean Journal of National Unification* 1 (1995). Han Yong Sup of the National Defense University, Seoul, has produced some different numbers that show the most precipitous drop in Soviet military assistance to North Korea in 1990 and a further drop in 1991. Roh money to Gorbachev, discussion with former Roh aide, June 1996. On Boldin's comment, see his book *Ten Years That Shook the World* (Basic Books, 1994), 283.

CHAPTER 10: CHINA SHIFTS ITS GROUND

On Chinese casualties in the Korean War, see Richard Whelan, *Drawing the Line* (Little, Brown, 1990), 373. The quotes from Chou and Kim are from Ilpyong J. Kim, "China in North Korean Foreign Policy," paper for the East Asian Institute, Columbia University, May 31–June 1, 1996. The disparity between DPRK and ROK trade with China, Tai Ming Cheung, "More Advice than Aid," *Far Eastern Economic Review* (June 6, 1991): 15.

A Visit to North Korea: My impressions of Pyongyang were recorded in my notebooks and in a *Washington Post Magazine* article, "Communism Lives," September 22, 1991.

On the cutback on USSR-DPRK trade, see Nicholas Eberstadt, Marc Rubin, and Albina Tretyakova, "The Collapse of Soviet and Russian Trade with the DPRK, 1989–1993," *Korean Journal of National Unification* 4 (1995). On the cutback in DPRK energy consumption, see Chung Sik Lee, "Prospects for North Korea," in *Democracy and Communism* (Korean Association of International Studies, 1995). For the history of "own style" socialism, "North Korean Brand of Socialism," *Vantage*

Point (Seoul, February 1996), 42. The Pyongyang bombing quote is from Daewoo Lee, "Economic Consequences of the Korean War and the Vietnam War," *Korea Observer* (Autumn 1996): 413n.

My first interview with Kim Yong Nam was published on October 8, 1984, in *WP* under the headline "North Korea Says U.S. Proposals Merit Discussion." Koh quote on Kim Yong Nam, Koh interview, October 25, 1993.

China Changes Course: Deng quote to Carter, *US-PRC Chronology*, 75. Sino-ROK trade figures, Kim Sung Yoon, "Prospects for Seoul's Entering Relations with Beijing and the Effects on Inter-Korean Relations," *East Asia Review* 4, no. 2 (1992). Sino-DPRK trade, Nicholas Eberstadt (unattributed author), "China's Trade with the DPRK, 1990–1994: Pyongyang's Thrifty New Patron," North Korea Trade Project Memorandum, US Bureau of the Census, May 1995. On the workings of China economic committee, former South Korean official, interview, October 27, 1995.

On the North Korean protests about the hijacking negotiation, "Chinese Hijackers Sentenced," *Facts on File* (1983): 632. Torpedo boat crisis, Richard L. Walker interview, March 30, 1995. Deng's refusal of massive military aid, former Chinese official, interview, October 4, 1993. Roh's medical doctor emissary, Kim Hak Joon interview, December 20, 1993. The "no filter" quote, former Roh Tae Woo aide, interview, March 14, 1995.

On Roh's lobbying after Tiananmen, Kim Hak Joon, "The Establishment of South Korean–Chinese Diplomatic Relations," paper for American Enterprise Institute and George Washington University conference, December 2–3, 1993. On unofficial Sunkyung contacts, Lee Sun Sok interview, November 24, 1994. Trade offices, Roh Jae Won interview, December 3, 1993.

On the new Chinese policy on DPRK trade, Ilpyong Kim, "North Korea's Relations with China," in *Foreign Relations of North Korea* (Sejong Institute, 1994), 265. Lee Sang Ok–Qian Qichen meeting, Lee interview, October 26, 1993. Roh-Qian meeting, from memorandum of conversation, "Dialogue with Foreign Minister Qian Qichen—11/12/91," in Korean. Roh Tae Woo on Qian's "kowtow," Kim Hak Joon interview, December 20, 1993.

China's 1992 normalization priority, former Chinese official, interview, December 2, 1993. On the April 13, 1992, meeting, interviews with Lee Sang Ok, October 26, 1993; Roh Jae Won, December 3, 1993. On Taiwan envoy's arguments, Lee Sang Ok interview. On the Taiwan threat to expand trade with the DPRK, Kim Hak Joon, "The Establishment of South Korean–Chinese Diplomatic Relations," 11. The source is Kim's diary, which he kept while he was an official of the Blue House. On China's face-saving statements to the DPRK, Japanese diplomat, interview, November 8, 1993. Kim Yong Nam's quote on PRC-ROK normalization, Don Oberdorfer, "N. Korea Says U.S. Blocks Progress on Nuclear Inspection," *WP*, September 29, 1992.

Chapter 11: Joining the Nuclear Issue

Kim Chong Whi quote from my personal journal, November 15, 1991.

The Origins of the Nuclear Program: On Japanese and Soviet early activities, Joseph Bermudez interview, 1992. See also Bruce Cumings, "Spring Thaw for Korea's Cold War?," *Bulletin of the Atomic Scientists* (April 1992): 17. MacArthur-Ridgway requests, Cumings, "Spring Thaw," 18–19. For Eisenhower's claims, see Michael J. Mazarr, *North Korea and the Bomb* (St. Martin's Press, 1995), 15–16. Nixon also made this claim on several occasions, including one I covered in 1968. Dubna activities, Alexandre Y. Mansourov, "The Origins, Evolution, and Current Politics of the North Korean Nuclear Program," *Nonproliferation Review* (Spring–Summer 1995): 25–26.

On the exchange of Hungarian Embassy cables, see *CWIHP*, Working Paper 53, Documents 28 and 29, 55–56.

On refusing the DPRK request for nuclear weapons, the quote is from a former Chinese Foreign Ministry official, interview, July 6, 1993. The Japanese expert is Major General (retired) Katsuichi Tsukamoto (executive director of the Research Institute for Peace and Security, Tokyo), interview, July 30, 1993. On Kim's 1974 request, Bermudez interview. Russian intelligence information from Mansourov, "Origins, Evolution," 26.

On the East German nuclear report, "Information for the Politburo," June 12, 1981, *SED Archives*. For key figures in the DPRK nuclear program, Tai Sung An, "The Rise and Decline of North Korea's Nuclear Weapons Program," *Korea and World Affairs* (Winter 1992): 674–675. On Kim's requests to Chernenko, "On the Visit of DPRK's Party and State Delegation Led by Kim Il Sung to the USSR," memorandum dated May 29, 1984, *SED Archives*, Confidential, in Russian and German. Also see Pollack, *No Exit*, 93–94.

For US urging to the Soviets on the NPT, Paul Wolfowitz interview, July 14, 1994. On NPT and the power reactor deal, Mansourov, "Origins, Evolution," 37.

Nuclear Diplomacy: The American Weapons: Baker on the diplomatic strategy in Baker's memoir, *The Politics of Diplomacy* (Putnam, 1995), 595. The Arms Control and Disarmament Agency concerns quote, Kathleen C. Bailey, Memorandum to Solomon on Intelligence Briefings Concerning North Korea, June 23, 1989, Secret (declassified 1994). My report and the DPRK reaction, Don Oberdorfer, "North Koreans Pursue Nuclear Arms," *WP,* July 29, 1989; "Preposterous Fabrication by *Washington Post*," Press Release of DPRK Permanent Observer Mission to the UN, August 9, 1989. On Eisenhower's nuclear deployments, "U.S. Nuclear Warheads First Deployed to Korea in 1957," *Dong-A Ilbo* (April 29, 1993).

William Arkin data, Arkin interview, March 24, 1995, citing National Security Decision Memorandum 178 of July 18, 1972. My report on DMZ vicinity weapons, Don Oberdorfer, "U.S. Weighs Risk of Keeping A-Arms in Korea," *WP,* September 20, 1974. Schlesinger quote is from AP, "Schlesinger Warns N. Korea U.S. May Use Nuclear Arms," *St. Louis Post-Dispatch,* June 22, 1975. On reduced deployments, Arkin interview. Gregg recommendation, Gregg interview, June 21, 1993. Crowe's views, Crowe and Alan D. Romberg, "Rethinking Security in the Pacific," *Foreign Affairs* (Spring 1991): 34. Scowcroft's objections, Scowcroft interview, March 29, 1995. Solomon's "hook a ride" quote, Solomon interview, March 22, 1996.

The December Accords: Chinese advice to Kim Il Sung, Lim Dong Won interview, May 2, 1994. Roh's 1991 exchange with Kim Il Sung, Roh Tae Woo luncheon conversation, July 22, 1993. The seal quote from "Two Koreas Celebrate New Era of Rapprochement," *Korea Annual, 1992* (Yonhap News Agency, 1992), 88. For North Korean reaction to accords, Don Oberdorfer, "U.S. Welcomes Koreas' Nuclear Accord," *WP,* January 1, 1992. Harrison on "conditional victory," Selig Harrison, "North Korea and Nuclear Weapons: Next Steps in American Policy," testimony to the Senate Foreign Relations Subcommittee on East Asian and Pacific Affairs, May 26, 1993.

Kim Il Sung's denial of reprocessing, Stephen Solarz, "Interview with DPRK President Kim Il Sung," December 18, 1991, transcript in my possession. Kim Yong Chul quote from Park Yong Ok interview, November 29, 1996. Kim's enthusiasm about

accord, Han Yong Sup interview, November 29, 1995. *Economist* quote from "The
Koreas: Look, No Bomb," *Economist,* January 4, 1992.
Meeting in New York: This section is based on my reporting at the time and a subsequent
interview with Kanter, February 25, 1994.
The Coming of the Inspectors: Gates quote, Don Oberdorfer, "N. Korea Is Far from
A-bomb, Video Indicates," *WP,* June 4, 1992. Olli Heinonen quote on early in-
spections, Heinonen interview, June 21, 1994. An excellent description of the
IAEA's sleuthing and the US role, from which some of these details are taken,
is R. Jeffrey Smith's "N. Korea and the Bomb: High-Tech Hide-and-Seek," *WP,*
April 27, 1993. Blix quote from Blix interview, June 22, 1994. Theis quote from
Theis interview, June 21, 1994.
From Accommodation to Crisis: Gregg on Team Spirit "mistake," Gregg interview, March 12,
1995. Kim anger in Ackerman meeting, State Department official, interview, May 15,
1995. Kim Hak Joon on spy case, Kim interview, January 5, 1994. Gates on imagery,
Gates interview, May 16, 1994. Choi quote to IAEA, Heinonen interview, June 22,
1994. DPRK war alert, Lee Chung Kuk, *The Nuclear Weapons and Army of Kim Jong
Il* (Kodansha, 1994), in Japanese. Also Colonel Chjoi Ju Hwal (a high-ranking North
Korean defector who experienced the alert), interview, June 24, 1996.

CHAPTER 12: WITHDRAWAL AND ENGAGEMENT

Han Sung Joo on repercussions of withdrawal, Han interview, April 12, 1995. Han's
"stick and carrot" approach was outlined in a meeting with *Washington Post* editors and reporters, which was so close to all that he was saying privately that he
was admonished to be less candid by some State Department officials. See Don
Oberdorfer, "South Korean: U.S. Agrees to Plan to Pressure North," *WP,* March
30, 1993. JCS on "punishing" North Korea, State Department official, interview,
May 15, 1995. Burkhardt on ROK "suggestion," Burkhardt interview, September
29, 1993.
Gallucci's initial impressions of Kang, Gallucci interviews, June 21, 1993, and August
10, 1995.
The Light-Water-Reactor Plan: On Kim Young Sam's objections to negotiations, Da-
vid Sanger, "Seoul's Leader Says North Is Manipulating U.S. on Nuclear Issues,"
NYT, July 1, 1993. White House official on Kim's references to politics and polls,
interview, May 3, 1995. Gallucci retort to Clinton threat, Gallucci interview, September 1, 1993.
Contrast between US and DPRK hospitality, Daniel Russel interview, November 7,
1996. Carlin quote on "they want out" from an excellent case study by Susan
Rosegrant, for the Kennedy School, Harvard University, "Carrots, Sticks, and
Question Marks: Negotiating the North Korean Nuclear Crisis," 30. Gallucci's
reaction to the LWR offer, Gallucci interview, August 10, 1995. Request to Blix
for LWRs, "IAEA Director General Completes Official Visit to the Democratic
People's Republic of Korea," *IAEA Press Release,* May 15, 1992. See also R. Jeffrey
Smith, "N. Korea May Consider Reducing Atom Program," *WP,* June 20, 1992.
DPRK plan for reactors in DMZ, Lim Dong Won interview, June 25, 1996. Warning to
Gallucci, Gallucci interview, August 10, 1995.
Kim Young Sam Blows the Whistle: Gallucci "seven times removed" and "box of oranges"
quotes, Rosegrant, Harvard study, 30, 27. Aspin quote on "ball in their court,"
Michael J. Mazarr, *North Korea and the Bomb* (St. Martin's Press, 1995), 133. Smith
report on package deal, R. Jeffrey Smith, "U.S. Weighs N. Korean Incentives: New
Approach Taken on Nuclear Inspection," *WP,* November 17, 1993.

On Kim Young Sam in Oval Office, senior Clinton administration official, interview, January 13, 1994.

The Season of Crisis Begins: North-South economic disparity, "N. Korea's Per-Capita GNP at $904, Eight Times Lower than South's $7,466," *KH,* June 11, 1994. The US interpretation of Kim Il Sung's reemergence, State Department official, interview, April 14, 1995. Kim Il Sung on Kim Jong Il activity, "Q&A: 'We Don't Need Nuclear Weapons,'" *Washington Times,* April 15, 1992. Kang Myung Do on Kang Song San's role in reemergence, Kang Myung Do interview, April 11, 1995.

The report on the Graham mission is based on interviews with Graham's aide Stephen Linton, March 30, 1994, and (by telephone) August 10, 1996, and several published reports including that in Mazarr, *North Korea and the Bomb,* 123–125. On Michael Gordon and the Pershings, Gordon interview, November 20, 1995. Laney quote on body bags, Laney interview, November 22, 1994. IAEA on purpose of DPRK refusal to permit full inspections, David Kyd (IAEA spokesman) interview, April 6, 1994. Hubbard quote, Hubbard interview, March 31, 1994.

CHAPTER 13: SHOWDOWN OVER NUCLEAR WEAPONS

Gallucci on "guns of August," Gallucci interview, March 11, 1995. Perry quote on "risk of war," Perry address to World Affairs Council, Philadelphia, November 3, 1994. Estes quote, Estes interview, April 4, 1995. CIA reevaluation of reactor downtime, US intelligence officials, interview, November 1, 1996. "Scare-nario" quote, David Albright, "North Korea and the 'Worst-Case' Scare-nario," *Bulletin of the Atomic Scientists* (January–February 1994). Lake on disparate intelligence findings, Lake interview, April 5, 1994.

The Defueling Crisis: For the unclassified CIA report, see www.fas.org/nuke/guide/dprk/nuke/cia111902.html. "Not a drop dead issue," senior US official, interview, November 14, 1994. Perricos on the DPRK "poker game," Perricos interview, June 16, 1995. Gallucci on the "medieval" IAEA, Gallucci interview, May 19, 1994. Gregg "proctologists" quote, Gregg interview, March 12, 1995. Kim Il Sung "naked man" quote to Sihanouk, *Far East Economic Review* (June 23, 1994).

The Military Track: O'Hanlon estimates, O'Hanlon telephone interview, February 20, 1997. On the war plan, "U.S.-Seoul 'Strategic Concept' on DPRK Noted," *Joong-ang Ilbo,* March 24, 1994, in *FBIS-EAS,* March 24, 1994. See also the war-plan description by Michael Gordon with David Sanger in "North Korea's Huge Military Spurs New Strategy in South," *NYT,* February 6, 1994. ROK "nervous as a cat" quote, senior US military officer, interview, April 4, 1995. US military preparations from various news reports and Perry's testimony before the Senate Foreign Relations Committee, January 24, 1995. Luck comments, Luck interview, May 3, 1994. Flanigan on Pentagon preparatory meeting, Flanigan interview, August 11, 1995. Flanigan "extremely sobering" quote from Rosegrant, Harvard study, 51.

Estimates given to Clinton, Captain Thomas Flanigan, letter to author, September 20, 1995. Perry "even more dangerous" quote, Perry speech before the World Affairs Council, Philadelphia, November 3, 1994.

The Deepening Conflict: On the Aspin appeal for direct negotiations with Kim Il Sung, Mazarr, *North Korea and the Bomb,* 102–103. Estimates of remittances to the DPRK by Koreans in Japan are very uncertain, but $600 million was the figure used in governmental circles. A serious study by Nicholas Eberstadt of the American Enterprise Institute concluded from financial data that the transfers to North Korea from private groups in Japan have not exceeded $100 million yearly since 1990. On Japan's difficulty in cutting off remittances, former White

House official, interview, October 28, 1996. Secret Japanese report on effect of sanctions, Asao Iku, "North Korea Will Act This Way," *Bungei Shunju*, July 1994, in Japanese. Japanese preparations for assistance to United States, "Government Was Preparing Limited Legislation in 1994," *Asahi Shimbun*, September 16, 1996, in Japanese. "Nightmare" quote from Japanese diplomat, interview, November 6, 1996.

Selig Harrison's trip to Pyongyang, from interview with Harrison, July 14, 1994; a Carnegie Endowment press release with details of the Harrison trip published June 16, 1994; and Harrison's "The North Korean Nuclear Crisis: From Stalemate to Breakthrough," in *Arms Control Today* (November 1994). Kim Young Sam's criticism of Carter mission, "Seoul Denounces Carter Trip as 'Ill-Timed,'" DPA (German Press Agency), June 11, 1994. Poll data on opinion toward North Korea, *American Enterprise* (July 8, 1994): 83. Scowcroft and Kanter views, "Korea: Time for Action," *WP*, June 15, 1994.

The section on US military preparations is based largely on an interview with William Perry, April 25, 1995, as well as his testimony before the Senate Foreign Relations Committee, January 24, 1995, and the Senate Armed Services Committee, January 26, 1995, and on news reports and a variety of other sources. For Luck on casualties and the costs of war, testimony of Luck before Senate Armed Services Committee, January 26, 1995. DPRK lessons from Gulf War, senior US officer, interview, April 4, 1995.

Carter in Pyongyang: Jimmy Carter, "Report of Our Trip to Korea, June 1994," unpublished manuscript from the Carter Center. The account of the Carter mission is also based on Marion Creekmore interview, August 1, 1994; input from Carter to the author via his aides; and a variety of other published and unpublished sources. Carter's "chances are minimal" quote, Elizabeth Kurylo, "Revisiting a Mission to Korea," *Atlanta Journal-Constitution*, July 3, 1994.

My report of the crucial White House meeting is based on interviews with four of the participants. Carter clarified for me in October 1996 that it was he who brought up the topic of a potential summit in the conversation with Kim Il Sung.

CHAPTER 14: DEATH AND ACCORD

A video of Kim's last year taken from official footage, containing good coverage of the final economic meeting, was broadcast on North Korean television and shown to me at my request during my January 1995 visit to Pyongyang. I also spoke about the meeting with Kim Jong U, one of the senior officials who were present. Other details, including Kim's intervention in summit planning, are from the North Korean official version of his final meetings in *KIS Work* (the Korean-language edition), vol. 44, published June 21, 1996. For Kim's recent appearances, "Seoul Speculates Kim's Death May Be Result of Power Struggle," *KH*, July 10, 1994. Kim Young Sam discussed his plans for his summit meeting with Kim Il Sung with me in an interview in the Blue House, April 14, 1995. Other than the official autopsy report, the details and circumstances of Kim Il Sung's death have never been made public by North Korea. My account relies on the reporting of Julie Moon, who was given special access to senior North Korean officials at the time of Kim's funeral. A senior North Korean official confirmed the authenticity of her account in a conversation with me in Pyongyang in January 1995.

German doctors on the growth on Kim's neck, former East German diplomat, interview, September 10, 1994. Kim's 1992 luncheon troubles, former ROK official, October 1994. Taylor's assessment of Kim's health, "Report on Bill Taylor's Third Trip to North Korea, 23–29 June 1992," unpublished manuscript supplied by Taylor. Kim's "good for another ten years" quote, Cho Kap Che, "The Information War with North Korea," *Monthly Chosun* (September 1990), in Korean. Kim to Carter on living another ten years, David Sanger, "Kim Il Sung Dead at 82," *NYT,* July 9, 1994.

Reactions to Kim's death, conversation with a senior North Korean official in Pyongyang in January 1995; see also "'Enormous Crowds' at Monument" from the Kyodo News Agency and "'Mass Hysteria' in Pyongyang" from the Polish Press Agency, published in *FBIS-EAS,* July 11, 1994. Flanigan's e-mail on North Koreans "here to deal," Flanigan interview, August 31, 1995. On KBS film incident, Sohn Tae Soo, "Some TV Programs on Kim Il Sung Draw Fire," *KH,* July 13, 1994.

On the inappropriateness of the release of the documents, Russian diplomat, interview, March 27, 1995. On the DPRK reaction to the Seoul postdeath events, Steve Glain, "Turmoil Marks Relations Between Pyongyang, Seoul," *Asian Wall Street Journal,* August 15, 1994. Chung quote to Lake on the DPRK collapse, US official, interview, December 11, 1996.

The Succession of Kim Jong Il: Kim Jong Il in Berlin on his father's train, former East German official, interview, June 10, 1994. On Kim Jong Il's birth date, Aiden Foster-Carter has written that Kim Jong Il was actually born a year earlier than acknowledged, in 1941, but his age was adjusted to make him exactly thirty years younger than his father. Aiden Foster-Carter, "Birth of a Legend," *Far Eastern Economic Review* (February 21, 1991).

Cumings "corporate and family state" quote, Bruce Cumings, "The Corporate State in North Korea," in *State and Society in Contemporary Korea,* edited by Hagen Koo (Cornell University Press, 1993). DPRK dictionary on hereditary succession, Kong Dan Oh, *Leadership Change in North Korean Politics* (Rand, October 1998), 10.

About the filmmakers, some in South Korea and elsewhere have raised doubts about the credibility of Choi and Shin, but they returned with photographs and tape recordings of themselves with Kim Il Sung and Kim Jong Il that have been accepted by US and ROK intelligence as authentic. I had three meetings with them, the first shortly after their escape through Vienna, and I believe they are credible. My report here is based in part on my three interviews with the couple for the *Washington Post* in the mid-1980s. The quotes are from Choi Eun Hee and Shin Sang Ok, "Kidnapped to the North Korean Paradise," unpublished manuscript (English translation of their Korean book), 246.

On Kim Jong Il's connection to the Rangoon bombing, Joseph Bermudez, *Terrorism: The North Korean Connection* (Crane Russak, 1990), 9. The East German report on Kim Jong Il's "modem" tendencies, "Information About Current Features in Some of North Korea's Cultural Areas," Embassy of the GDR, June 9, 1982, *SED Archives.* The Kim Jong Il quotes are from the filmmakers' tape recording published by *Monthly Chosun* (October 1995), in Korean.

The Framework Negotiations: This section is primarily based on interviews with Gallucci and several other members of the US negotiating team. Carlin on Kang's failure to say "never," Carlin interview, November 7, 1994. Carlin "game was over" quote, Carlin interview, November 26, 1995. Gallucci on "Talmudic significance," Gallucci interview, October 8, 1996.

The Kim Jong Il Regime: Hubbard discussions in Pyongyang, Hubbard interview, January 6, 1995. DOD cable on heavy oil, Joint Staff, Washington, DC, cable, "Subject: Delivery of Heavy Residual Fuel Oil to the Democratic People's Republic of Korea," January 14, 1995, unclassified.

The Struggle over the Reactors: "We opted for solidarity," White House official, interview, October 21, 1996. Luck's cable to Perry, Pentagon official, interview, August 31, 1995.

CHAPTER 15: NORTH KOREA IN CRISIS

Shalikashvili quote on "implode or explode," Mary Jordan, "Speculation Grows on Demise of N. Korea," *WP,* April 6, 1996. For the North Korean rainfall figures, "Pyongyang Media Report on Flood to Get Aid," *Vantage Point* (Seoul, September 1995). Also, "FAO/WFP Crop and Food Supply Assessment Mission to DPRK," FAO, Rome, December 1995. Trevor Page quotes, Pierre Antoine Donnet, "Widespread Signs of Famine in North Korea: U.N. Official," *KH,* December 6, 1996. Floods "made situation worse," "FAO/WFP Crop and Food Supply Assessment Mission to DPRK."

The DPRK request to supply grain secretly, Suh Dong Kwan interview, October 28, 1993. Quotes on Kim Young Sam as the man to bring down the DPRK, a prominent South Korean, interview, November 25, 1996. Laney quote on Kim Young Sam, interview, June 27, 1996. For details of DMZ incursions, Oh Young Jin, "Heavily Armed NK Troops Enter JSA in Panmunjom," *KT,* April 7, 1996.

Disbanding of Sixth KPA corps, curtailment of winter exercises, US intelligence officials, interview, November 1, 1996. On impact of DMZ incursions on election, Sun Phil Kwon, "Policy Issues in the 1996 General Election," *Korea Observer* (Spring 1997). Adrian Buzo quote from his article "The DPRK and Late De-Stalinization," *Korean Journal of National Unification* 4 (1995).

Political Earthquake in Seoul: The account of the inception of the scandal is from an interview with Park Kye Dong, June 25, 1996. On Roh's postscandal unpopularity, "Roh Named as Most Hated Politician: Poll," *KH,* November 19, 1995. Kukje episode, Sam Jameson, "Fall of Kukje Corporation Illustrates South Korea's Corruption," *KT* reprint of *Los Angeles Times,* November 19, 1995.

Chung Ju Yung's revelation and Roh's response are reported in Park Byeong Seog, "Political Corruption in South Korea: Concentrating on the Dynamics of Party Politics," *Asian Perspective* (Spring–Summer 1995): 172.

Summit Diplomacy and the Four-Party Proposal: My account of the 1995 and 1996 diplomacy is based on interviews with four US officials who were involved. For Kim Young Sam quote to Clinton about August 15, US official, interview, August 14, 1996. "We thought we'd done enough," US official, interview, May 8, 1996.

Chinese response to four-way-talks proposal, "Jiang Sends Letter to Kim to Support 4-Way Peace Talks," *KT,* May 22, 1996. On the Kissinger proposal of peace talks and others along this line, see Kim Hak Joon, *Unification Policies of South and North Korea, 1945–1991* (Seoul National University Press, 1992), 371ff. The UN special alert, "WFP Warns North Korea Food Situation Deteriorating Sharply," press release and report of World Food Program, United Nations, May 13, 1996. Contrast in South Korea, "One in Four Koreans Is on Diet: Survey," *KH,* April 9, 1996.

The Submarine Incursion: For details on the submarine incident, see "Chronology of Events Surrounding Incursion on the Territory of the ROK by North Koreans," information office of the ROK Embassy, Washington, October 4, 1996, and reporting in *KH* and *KT.* The 1976 quote on infiltration, *USFK Hist. 1976,* 53, Secret (declassified 1995).

On DPRK submarines, "PRC Magazine on DPRK's Submarine Strength," *FBIS-EAS,* February 21, 1995, 36. Kim Young Sam quotes on submarine incident, Shim Jae Hoon, "Submarine Shocker," *Far Eastern Economic Review* (October 3, 1996);

Chon Shi Yong, "Kim Sees 'Possibility of War,'" *KH*, October 8, 1996. Kevin Sullivan's interview with Kim Young Sam, "S. Korea Demands Apology from North; Kim Suspends Nuclear Deal After Sub Incident," *WP*, November 9, 1996. Initial DPRK announcement, "Statement by a Spokesman for North Korea's Armed Forces Ministry," September 23, 1996, *Korea and World Affairs* (Fall 1996): 516.

Plunk quotes from senior ROK official, "No Way to Deal with North Korea," *WP*, September 29, 1996; and Plunk telephone interview, February 6, 1997. Revelation about unilateral attack plans, "ROK Ready to Hit 12 DPRK Targets in Event of Attack," *FBIS-EAS*, October 16, 1996. Kristof's article in the wake of the submarine incursion, "How a Stalled Submarine Sank North Korea's Hopes," *NYT*, November 19, 1996.

US-ROK discussions on unilateral military action, from confidential interviews in Seoul and Washington with officials involved. Tilelli on "complete" satisfaction, Tilelli interview, April 22, 1997.

North Korea's Steep Decline: Song Young Dae on "stability within instability," his article "Changes in North Korea and How to Respond," *Korea Focus* (January–February 1997). I also interviewed Song in Seoul, April 22, 1997. The Kim Jong Il speech of December 7, 1996, was published by *Monthly Chosun* in March 1997. My English translation was from the BBC, March 21, 1997. I learned that Hwang Jang Yop was the source of the speech from Kim Yong Sam, the *Monthly Chosun* reporter who obtained it, and whom I interviewed April 16, 1997.

Tilelli quotes from Tilelli interview, April 22, 1997. China customs data for food, fuel from US Institute of Peace, Special Report on Korea, June 1998.

Kim Jong Il's military and nonmilitary activities in 1996 are listed in *Vantage Point* (Seoul, December 1996 and January 1997). The Tilelli quotes are from the Tilelli interview, April 22, 1997.

The Passage of Hwang Jang Yop: This section is based largely on Hwang's letters and other documents provided to *Monthly Chosun* reporter Kim Yong Sam by intermediary Lee Yon Kil and published after Hwang's defection. It is also based on interviews with Kim Yong Sam on April 16, 1997; with Hajime Izumi on March 8, 1997; and with Songhee Stella Kim on April 23, 1997; and on Kim Yong Sam's retrospective article in *Monthly Chosun* in June 1997.

The phone call to set up the defection from interview with a senior ROK official, April 21, 1997. Hwang's letter written in the South Korean Consulate was released by the ROK Foreign Ministry, February 13, 1997.

On "Red Banner philosophy," see "Red Banner Philosophy as Kim Jong Il's Ruling Tool," *Vantage Point* (Seoul, March 1997). Hwang's views as expressed in the Moscow meeting of February 1996 are from the Izumi interview, March 8, 1997.

The Two Koreas in Time of Trouble: South Korean economic data from Korea Economic Institute of America. North Korea in eighth year of economic decline, *Vantage Point* (Seoul, July 1998), quoting the Bank of Korea (Seoul). IMF report on North Korea, confidential, prepared by Asia and Pacific Department, IMF, November 12, 1997. US Census estimates from Nicholas Eberstadt.

CHAPTER 16: TURN TOWARD ENGAGEMENT

Into the Heavens, Under the Earth: Satellite launch data from KCNA, September 4, 1998. Sanger's article "North Korea Site an A-bomb Plant, U.S. Agencies Say," *NYT*, August 17, 1998. Livingston quotes from the *WP*, September 1, 1998.

Toward an Aid-Based State: The new DPRK cabinet, from Yoo Young-ku, *Vantage Point* (Seoul, March 1999).

Perry to the Rescue and *Engaging the United States:* These sections are based in part on interviews with William J. Perry, Madeleine Albright, Wendy Sherman, Charles Kartman, Robert Einhorn, and other US officials. Vice Marshal Jo's bio is from *Vantage Point* (Seoul, March 1999) and ROK press reports.

Summit in Pyongyang: Translated text of Joint Declaration from ROK Embassy, Washington, March 23, 2001. Kim Dae Jung quote on one people, *Financial Times,* July 16, 2000.

CHAPTER 17: THE END OF THE AGREED FRAMEWORK

The observations on George Bush are in John Bolton, *Surrender Is Not an Option* (Threshold Editions, 2008), 99.

A Rocky Start: For Lim's trip to Washington in February 2001, see Lim Dong-won, *Peacemaker* (Walter H. Shorenstein Asia-Pacific Research Center, 2012), 266–268.

The *Rodong Sinmun* article was carried by the Korean Central News Agency, "Our Principle Position Regarding Issue of DPRK-US Relations," November 7, 2000.

A version of Secretary of State Powell's misstep is in Karen DeYoung, *Soldier: The Life of Colin Powell* (Vintage Books, 2007), 324–326. For an account of the Bush-Kim meeting, see "At White House, Kim Hears U.S. Hard Line on Pyongyang: Bush Tells Korean He Distrusts North," www.nytimes.com/2001/03/08/news/08iht-kim.2.t.html.

The Impact of 9/11: North Korea's terrorist acts include assassination attempts against the ROK president, blowing up a South Korean airliner, and support for groups the United States considered terrorists (others considered them "freedom fighters"). By the late 1990s, North Korea had pulled back from supporting (funding or training) such groups and was no longer seen as active on the terrorist front. Discussions started between the State Department's Counterterrorism Office and the North Koreans to deal with lingering US concerns.

The October 6, 2000, US-DPRK joint statement on terrorism says: "As a demonstration of their cooperation in the fight against international terrorism, the US and the DPRK intend to exchange information regarding international terrorism and to resolve outstanding issues in this regard between the two sides." The statement also states: "On the basis of their common concerns about the threat of terrorism to international peace and stability, the two sides underscored their commitment to support the international legal regime combating international terrorism and to cooperate with each other in taking effective measures to fight against terrorism. The sides shared the view that such measures included not providing material support or resources, including safehaven, to terrorists and terrorist groups, bringing terrorist s to justice, and fighting terrorist acts against the safety of civil aviation and maritime navigation." Any one of these points might have been laid before the North Koreans as a way they could demonstrate their seriousness in cooperating on an issue that had suddenly leaped to the very top of Washington's priorities. Whether the North actually had any useful information about those responsible for the 9/11 attacks is another question.

Threads Come Together: Japan–North Korea Talks: For a detailed account of the secret Japan-DPRK talks and the resulting September 2002 summit, see Yoichi Funabashi, *The Peninsula Question* (Brookings Institution Press, 2007), 1–49. The operative sections of the Japan-DPRK Pyongyang Declaration issued after the summit read:

    1. Both sides determined that, pursuant to the spirit and basic principles laid out in this Declaration, they would make every possible effort for an

early normalization of the relations, and decided that they would re-sume the Japan DPRK normalization talks in October 2002.

Both sides expressed their strong determination that they would sincerely tackle outstanding problems between Japan and the DPRK based upon their mutual trust in the course of achieving the normalization.

2. The Japanese side regards, in a spirit of humility, the facts of history that Japan caused tremendous damage and suffering to the people of Korea through its colonial rule in the past, and expressed deep remorse and heartfelt apology.

Both sides shared the recognition that, providing economic co-operation after the normalization by the Japanese side to the DPRK side, including grant aids, long-term loans with low interest rates and such assistances as humanitarian assistance through international organizations, over a period of time deemed appropriate by both sides, and providing other loans and credits by such financial institutions as the Japan Bank for International Co-operation with a view to supporting private economic activities, would be consistent with the spirit of this Declaration, and decided that they would sincerely discuss the specific scales and con-tents of the economic cooperation in the normalization talks.

Both sides, pursuant to the basic principle that when the bilateral relationship is normalized both Japan and the DPRK would mutually waive all their property and claims and those of their nationals that had arisen from causes which occurred before August 15, 1945, decided that they would discuss this issue of property and claims concretely in the normalization talks.

Both sides decided that they would sincerely discuss the issue of the status of Korean residents in Japan and the issue of cultural property.

3. Both sides confirmed that they would comply with international law and would not commit conducts threatening the security of the other side. With respect to the outstanding issues of concern related to the lives and security of Japanese nationals, the DPRK side confirmed that it would take appropriate measures so that these regrettable incidents, that took place under the abnormal bilateral relationship, would never hap-pen in the future.

4. Both sides confirmed that they would co-operate with each other in or-der to maintain and strengthen the peace and stability of North East Asia. Both sides confirmed the importance of establishing co-operative relationships based upon mutual trust among countries concerned in this region, and shared the recognition that it is important to have a framework in place in order for these regional countries to promote confidence-building, as the relationships among these countries are normalized.

Both sides confirmed that, for an overall resolution of the nuclear issues on the Korean Peninsula, they would comply with all related international agreements. Both sides also confirmed the necessity of resolving security problems including nuclear and missile issues by promoting dialogues among countries concerned. The DPRK side expressed its intention that, pursuant to the spirit of this Declaration, it would further maintain the moratorium on missile launching in and after 2003.

Both sides decided that they would discuss issues relating to security.

An official text of the document is found on www.mofa.go.jp/region/asia-paci/n_korea/pmv0209/pyongyang.html.

Slouching Toward the Cliff: The North's unusually fast apology is described in Lim, *Peacemaker*, 320.

The colorful expressions of the potential for ending the Agreed Framework are in Bolton, *Surrender Is Not an Option*, 106–107.

Cheating is a loaded word, and the State Department lawyers who helped draft the Agreed Framework laugh at the thought that by developing an enrichment capability, the North was "cheating." The 1994 agreement was silent on enrichment, except for the thin reed of a reference to the 1992 North-South joint statement, which was already at a dead end. For practical reasons, Ambassador Gallucci wanted to include only those activities in the Agreed Framework that the United States could monitor, and enrichment was not one of them. Going down the enrichment path may have been a monumental miscalculation by Kim Jong Il. It was very typical of the North Korean propensity to hedge and exploit the seams. To call it "cheating" put the situation into a legal and moral box where it became more difficult to resolve—and where the administration's hard-liners were happy to have it.

Kim Jong Il's Progress: A discussion of Kim Jong Il's July 2002 measures and the debate they set off in North Korea is in Robert L. Carlin and Joel S. Wit, "North Korean Reform: Politics, Economics, and Security," *Adelphi Paper* 382 (July 2006): 35–52.

An account of Chinese reaction to the Sinuiju SAR is in "Does Beijing Back North Korea SAR?," *South China Morning Post*, www.scmp.com/article/392912/does-beijing-back-north-korea-sar.

The Unquiet Americans: For a discussion of the "bold approach," see Charles L. Pritchard, *Failed Diplomacy* (Brookings Institution Press, 2007), 25.

For a description of the Kelly-Kang meeting, see Pritchard, *Failed Diplomacy*, 37–39. Also see Mike Chinoy, *Meltdown: The Inside Story of the North Korean Nuclear Crisis* (St. Martin's Press, 2008), 120–124.

The Morning After: Seoul's advice to Pyongyang after the Kelly visit is in Lim, *Peacemaker*, 341.

Bolton's view on what to do if the Agreed Framework collapses is in Bolton, *Surrender Is Not an Option*, 115.

CHAPTER 18: TROUBLE IN THE US-ROK ALLIANCE

Problems for Diplomacy: For Rumsfeld's description of his thinking on a coup, see Donald Rumsfeld, *Known and Unknown: A Memoir* (Sentinel, 2011), 642.

The vice president's thoughts on history are in Richard Cheney, *In My Time* (Threshold Editions, 2011), 493.

Sunshine, Barely: The upsurge in anti-US demonstrations and threats to individual American soldiers was a serious concern, especially so because Washington felt the ROK government was not doing enough to tamp down the emotions. For Hubbard's views, see chapter 9 in *Ambassadors' Memoirs: U.S.-Korea Relations Through the Eyes of the Ambassadors* (Korea Economic Institute, 2009).

Moon Jae-in granted a long interview for this book in March 2012, contributing to a more balanced view of Roh Moo-hyun.

The episode about the "nuclear umbrella" was clarified through interviews with several participants from both sides.

Tensions Rise: The North's first mention of the incident with the US reconnaissance plane was in a *Rodong Sinmun* commentary entitled "Whom Are You Daring to

Challenge?" on March 10, 2003.

The Six-Party Mirage: Rice's recollection of her advice is in Condoleezza Rice, *No Higher Honor: A Memoir of My Years in Washington* (Crown, 2011), 248. An informed view of the early debate in China is in John W. Lewis and Robert L. Carlin, *Negotiating with North Korea, 1992–2007* (Center for International Security and Cooperation, Stanford University, January 2008).

An account of the talks with Jiang is in George Bush, *Decision Points* (Broadway Paperbacks, 2010), 424. Beijing has at various times over the years told Washington that North Korea was not a Chinese but a US problem to solve. Since 2002 the Americans have put most of their eggs in China's basket. So far, nothing has hatched. It might be well to remember that the Chinese have a dish called thousand-year-old eggs.

Nuclear Peek-a-Boo: See the DPRK Foreign Ministry spokesman's statement of January 10, 2004. For whatever reason, the Foreign Ministry is very concerned with consistency and, to a certain extent, credibility. One thing North Korean diplomats do not like is to be told that they have reversed their position without warning, or that they are contradicting themselves. They prefer being able to say they gave warning of where Pyongyang was thinking of moving—and much of the time, that is so. In 2010, asked why they had shown their enrichment facility at Yongbyon to a group of visiting Americans, the answer was, "No one believed us when we said in 2009 that we were going to do it, so we had to make clear we meant what we said." See Siegfried S. Hecker, *A Return Trip to North Korea's Yongbyon Nuclear Complex* (Center for International Security and Cooperation, Stanford University, November 20, 2010), http://iis-db.stanford.edu/pubs/23035/Hecker Yongbyon.pdf.

A Year of Zigzags: For an account of Prime Minister Koizumi's discussions in Pyongyang in 2004, see Funabashi, *The Peninsula Question*, 53.

Various high-level North-South discussions in Pyongyang in June 2005 are covered in Lim, *Peacemaker*, 368.

The instructions to the US delegation not to give an inch on the LWR issue at the six-party talks in the summer of 2005 were explained in interviews with participants from several of the parties to the talks.

The North Korean delegation's reaction to the final American statement is described in Victor Cha, *The Impossible State* (Ecco, 2012), 263–264. Pyongyang's official response the following day came in the form of a Foreign Ministry spokesman's "press statement" whose full text was carried in English by the North's press agency, KCNA.

The Treasury Department's press release on Section 311 of the PATRIOT Act can be found at www.treasury.gov/press-center/press-releases/Pages/tg1591.aspx.

In interviews, explanations of why and how the decision was made in July 2005 to move ahead with the Treasury action are all over the map. All of them seem to agree, at least implicitly, on one key point—that whether this action would jeopardize the chances for positive developments on the diplomatic track ended up being of secondary consideration.

The End of KEDO: A detailed oral history of KEDO can be found in Charles Kartman, Robert Carlin, and Joel Wit, *A History of KEDO* (Center for International Cooperation and Security, Stanford University, 2012).

Traction, at Last: Pyongyang's decision to cancel its unilateral moratorium on missile launches was included in a lengthy DPRK Foreign Ministry memorandum dated March 2, 2005, carried in full by KCNA the next day. On the issue of the missile moratorium, it said, "We are also not bound to any international treaty or law as far as the missile issue is concerned. Some forces claim that the DPRK's moratorium on the missile launch still remains valid. In September 1999, the period of the previous U.S. administration, we announced the moratorium on the missile launch while dialogue was under way but the DPRK-U.S. dialogue was totally suspended when the Bush administration took office in 2001. Accordingly, we are not bound to the moratorium on the missile launch at present."

The UN Security Council resolution adopted after the launch, Security Council Condemns Democratic People's Republic of Korea's Missile Launches, Unanimously Adopting Resolution 1695 (2006), is found on www.un.org/News/Press/docs/2006/sc8778.doc.

Rumble in Punggye: The president's instructions to Hill are noted in Chinoy, *Meltdown,* 283.

See Cha, *The Impossible State,* 266, for the quote from the Beijing dinner.

Chapter 19: The Emperor's New Clothes

Rice's instruction to Assistant Secretary Hill to keep away from the Philharmonic's press conference is noted in Glenn Kessler's article in the *Washington Post,* May 26, 2008, "Mid-level Official Steered U.S. Shift on North Korea."

Signs of Succession: For an account of Japanese consternation at discovering they had detained Kim Jong Nam, see Funabashi, *The Peninsula Question,* 61–63.

On Kim Jong Il's stroke, see www.huffingtonpost.com/2011/12/19/kim-jong-il-stroke_n_1157688.html.

Diplomatic Downturn: On Washington's decision to lift trade sanctions, see www.npr.org/templates/story/story.php?storyId=91934883.

Ambassador Hill's testimony can be found on http://foreign.senate.gov/imo/media/doc/HillTestimony080206a.pdf.

For the verification issue, see www.armscontrol.org/act/2008_09/NKnuclear.

A useful timeline of IAEA activity in North Korea is on www.iaea.org/newscenter/focus/iaeadprk/fact_sheet_may2003.shtml.

A Terrible Start: The North's warning on its next steps after the Security Council action is in "UNSC Urged to Retract Anti-DPRK Steps," KCNA, in English, April 29, 2009.

A careful study of the North's third test appears in Siegfried Hecker and Frank Pabian in www.thebulletin.org/web-edition/features/contemplating-third-nuclear-test-north-korea.

On strategic patience, see www.washingtonpost.com/wp-dyn/content/article/2010/05/26/AR2010052605047.html. See also www.donaldgross.net/2010/12/strategic-patience-has-become-strategic-passivity/.

The PRC proviso in the UN Security Council resolution can be found on www.un.org/News/Press/docs/2009/sc9679.doc.htm.

Turning to the South: For the official ROK press line on what happened in President Lee's meeting with the North Korean visitors, see *Dong-A Ilbo,* August 24, 2009, in English.

Secret Talks, Public Clashes: The story of the flood is covered in several items carried by the Yonhap news agency. See, for instance, http://english.yonhapnews.co.kr/news/2009/09/07/0200000000AEN20090907006600315.HTML.

The official ROK findings on the *Cheonan*'s sinking can be found on www.securitycouncilreport.org/atf/cf/%7B65BFCF9B-6D27-4E9C-8CD3-CF6E4FF96FF9%7D/DPRK%20S%202010%20281%20SKorea%20Letter%20and%20Cheonan%20Report.pdf.

The Rise of Chinese Influence: For the North Korean television coverage of Wen's arrival, see www.youtube.com/watch?v=1pj4iGY8nQE.

A Rare Backlash: For an initial account of the currency revaluation, see Evan Ramstad's report in the *Wall Street Journal,* http://online.wsj.com/article/SB125975276400572645.html.

One example of foreign interest in the North's magnesite deposits is found on www.nkeconwatch.com/nk-uploads/quintermina3.pdf.

Kim Jong Il's Death and Beyond: The announcement by a spokesman for the Korean Committee for Space Technology of the plans for a space launch was carried by the official North Korean news agency, "DPRK to Launch Application Satellite," KCNA, March 16, 2012.

AFTERWORD

The observations about an apparent easing of the alert situation in the North are found on www.dailynk.com/english/read.php?cataId=nk01500&num=10452.

For an analysis of the commercial satellite photographs showing progress on construction of the LWR at Yongbyon, see http://38north.org/2013/05/yongbyon050113/.

INDEX